ENCYCLOPEDIA OF ESPIONAGE

BOOKS BY RONALD SETH

A Spy Has No Friends
Spies at Work
The Art of Spying
A New Prose Translation of Ovid's *Art of Love*
Lion with Blue Wings: The Story of the Glider Pilot Regiment
Two Fleets Surprised: The Battle of Cape Matapan
The Undaunted: The Story of Resistance in Western Europe
For My Name's Sake: Roman Catholic Resistance to the
      Nazis and Communists
The Specials: The Story of the Special Constabulary
The Fiercest Battle: The Story of Convoy ONS 5
Petiot—Victim of Chance
Stalingrad—Point of Return
Operation Barbarossa: The Defence of Moscow
Anatomy of Spying
Caporetto—The Scapegoat Battle
Forty Years of Soviet Spying (American title: Unmasked)
Witches and Their Craft
The First Time It Happened
The Day War Broke Out
The Russian Terrorists
The Executioners: The Story of SMERSH
Great English Witchcraft Trials
The Sleeping Truth: The Hiss-Chambers Affair
The Spy in Silk Breeches
The Truthbenders: The Story of Psychological Warfare
Children Against Witches
In the Name of the Devil: Great Scottish Witch Cases
Secret Servants: The Story of Japanese Espionage
The Spy Who Wasn't Caught
Russell Pasha: A Biography
Jackals of the Reich

FICTION:

The Patriot
Spy in the Nude

ENCYCLOPEDIA OF ESPIONAGE

BY RONALD SETH

DOUBLEDAY & COMPANY, INC.,
GARDEN CITY, NEW YORK

For
BARBARA
with all my love, devotion,
admiration and gratitude.

FIRST PUBLISHED IN GREAT BRITAIN BY
NEW ENGLISH LIBRARY, 1972
AN NEL ORIGINAL

COPYRIGHT © 1972 BY RONALD SETH

FIRST NEL HARDBACK EDITION 1972

LIBRARY OF CONGRESS CATALOG CARD NUMBER: 76-131105

ISBN 0-385-01609-3

PRINTED IN THE UNITED STATES OF AMERICA

ENCYCLOPEDIA OF ESPIONAGE

AUTHOR'S INTRODUCTION

My object in writing **An Encyclopedia of Espionage** has been two-fold: I want to make available to espiomanes, in a handy form for reference purposes, the facts about this subject which has been of perennial interest since the beginning of recorded history; and at the same time to present the information in such a way that it will interest the general reader.

My **modus operandi** has been to cover as wide a spectrum of espionage history as I can. For this reason besides the well-known spies, I have included also many practically unknown ones from all periods of history.

At the end of each entry I have attached a bibliography for the guidance of readers who wish to study the subject of the entry in greater detail. Where no such bibliography is provided, in most cases the information has come only from my note-books. I have been collecting espionage material for the past twenty years and have culled it from sources of every description. A careful reading of newspapers and periodicals has been a lucrative source, while in some cases the information has reached me by word of mouth. It is these two categories of information which is the matter of entries-with-bibliography.

I must record here my most grateful thanks to my friend and neighbour Mrs Patricia Nunneley, who has spent many hours checking much of my information by independent research. (I must stress, however, that no responsibility rests with her for my final version.) Mrs Nunneley and my wife have also devoted long hours in putting my typescripts in order, and correcting my typographical errors. Without the help of both my task would have been almost overwhelming.

R.S.

ABEL, Colonel Rudolf. Russian spy. Operated in the United States.

In Great Britain and America the activity of Soviet espionage since the Second World War has been much less diffuse in the effort carried out by agents of the very top flight, though there have been weak links in some of the networks which have eventually brought about disaster. Nevertheless, the penetration of Allied secrets of the highest calibre has been effected, as one outstanding case in the United States and three in Great Britain have made all too obvious.

The chief objectives in the military field have been under-water detection devices, nuclear armaments and rocket techniques, but the political fields and any other subject of strategical importance in any sphere has not been neglected. Many mistakes have been made by counter-espionage agencies on both sides of the Atlantic, but where the master-spies have been trapped they have dealt a blow at Soviet espionage from which it took some time to recover.

For some time in the middle 1950s the FBI and other US counter-espionage agencies had been aware that many American top secrets in the fields mentioned above had been finding their way to Moscow. This indicated that networks were operating particularly in the eastern regions of the United States. But the fact that search as diligently as they might they could not pick up the trail of any Soviet agents who could be responsible for acquiring the rocket, submarine and under-water detection secrets indicated that the quality of espionage performance was of a kind never before met by the counter-espionage agencies. In 1957, however, the FBI was given a break. It came to them not from their own efforts, but from the defection of a Soviet agent whose choice for the work still makes one wonder what is really in the minds of the Soviet Union's spy masters when they select their agents.

Rudolf Ivanovich Abel had

been an agent for many years, and because he had a genuine appreciation of the value of Security, though he had served with distinction in Germany and elsewhere before the war, he had not come to the notice of any of the counter-espionage agencies. This fact when he was chosen to operate in the US after World War II, gave him a very considerable advantage.

For two years after the war he had lived in East Germany, under an assumed name. In 1947 he entered Canada on a German passport in this name, and from Canada made his way to the US on a forged Canadian passport. For a time after his arrival he travelled about the country, noting all he saw and heard, and by degrees built up a useful knowledge which would in ordinary conditions allow him to pass for an American.

When he felt that he had sufficient background knowledge, he was provided by the section of the US Communist Party responsible for arranging cover-identities, with the birth certificate of a child who had died in New

York at the age of two months, by name Emil R. Goldfus. (This was standard practice at this time.) From now on he adopted the name of Goldfus, and with the birth certificate was able to procure genuine American papers.

The cover he adopted was that of a photographer, in which he had sufficient skill to pass as a professional of some ability. He also let it be known that he liked to be considered an artist, and he had enough talent in this respect to allow him to be accepted as a painter in the not too discriminating circles in Brooklyn in which he moved. The few friends he permitted himself to make knew him as a man of several accomplishments, for besides his photography and painting, he was fluent in a number of languages, proved himself a reasonable musician, a craftsman in metal work and a first-class radio mechanic.

This last skill made his usefulness to the Soviet networks in the US invaluable, for he maintained the radio sets of other agents, was an expert in the production of microfilms and microdots, and with his other accomplishments could provide secret containers for the passing of reports e.g. hollowed-out screws, cufflinks and coins.

He was a mild, insignificant man to all outward appearances. He was not very interested in sartorial smartness. He rarely betrayed his wide reading in highly esoteric subjects. In fact, he set out to be, what every good spy should aim to be, an inconspicuous individual, pleasant to know, but not so striking that one remembered him without conscious effort.

His instructions from his Soviet Intelligence superiors were that he was to have no contact with the Soviet embassy in Washington or with any of the consulates in America, or with any other clandestine agency working there. He was to control a network of agents which had already been chosen by Moscow and were at their posts by the time he arrived. Working through only one cut-out (see under **Cut-out**) he drew up instructions as an expert in Finnish Intelligence

matters, and from that year, until summoned to Moscow in 1950, he was active in Finland, searching out anti-Soviet elements among the local population.

Arrived in Moscow, he was told that he had a new assignment. There he was trained in codes and photography, given a false identity and then sent to Finland to establish a background.

He later went to Turku, the Finnish west-coast port. There he worked as a plumber, and there, although he had a wife in Russia, he married a Finnish girl, Hanna Kurikha.

In 1951, he went to the American embassy in Helsinki, and produced a birth certificate which showed that he had been born in Enaville, Idaho and asked for a permit to return to the US. A passport was issued to him some months later, and he set off for New York in 1952, sailing from Southampton in the **Queen Mary.** His Finnish "wife" followed him a few months later.

Not until 1954 did he meet his chief, Abel/Goldfus, and the latter had a shock at their very first encounter. The

11

security-minded Resident Director found to his horror that not only had his new assistant forgotten most of his training in codes, but that his ideas about security were so rudimentary — indeed, they seemed to be lacking altogether — that he constituted a danger to himself and to the network.

In the circumstances in which he was placed, however, Abel had to make the best of the situation. He set Hayhanen up in a shop and gave him instructions on how to operate. But all the time he was apprehensive about the safety of the network.

By 1955 Abel had been working in the field at considerable pressure for six years, and when the Centre instructed him to return to Moscow for six months' leave, he gratefully accepted, though with considerable misgivings.

When he returned early in 1956, he discovered to his horror that Hayhanen had committed every crime which a spy can commit. He had operated a transmitter from one site during all that time instead of seeking out new sites in the suburbs; he had not bothered to collect all the

information from "letterboxes"; and he had closed his shop, while retaining the tenancy of the premises.

This was too much, and Abel complained to Moscow.

The Centre's wheels grind with the slowness of the proverbial legal mill, and it was not until some months later that Hayhanen was recalled to Moscow.

To remove suspicion of the cause of recall from his mind, the Centre promoted him to the rank of Major, and when he arrived at Le Havre he was handed 300 dollars as expenses for his onward journey. But he had not been deceived, and now that he was back on European soil, he decided that he would not return to Moscow. So he made his way to Paris and there approached the American authorities with an appeal for asylum, in return for which he would supply information about Abel's work.

Before accepting his offer, the FBI checked all Hayhanen's information carefully, and had him examined by psychiatrists. The latter found him to be unstable and an alcoholic. Nevertheless some of his information did prove that he was not playing a game with them.

As far as the members of the network were concerned, he could not help them at all, except in one case. He identified a US Army sergeant who had been posted for a time to the American embassy in Moscow, where he had been recruited into Soviet espionage, and who, since his return home had supplied important information. The sergeant was arrested — and eventually sentenced to five years' hard labour — but he could not help with other members of the network; he could only point out some of the "letter-boxes" he had used, and identify Hayhanen as the go-between he had sometimes met.

In all his dealings with Hayhanen, Colonel Abel had observed the strictest security precautions — except on one occasion. For some reason he had had to examine some material Hayhanen had brought to him in the latter's presence so that he might question him if need be. For this reason he had taken him to a store-room which he had rented away from his studio for his photographic material.

Presently Hayhanen recalled this occasion, but as he did not know his superior's cover name, he could tell the FBI only that the storeroom was somewhere near Clark and Fulton Streets in Brooklyn. A somewhat lengthy search at last revealed that there was such a storeroom rented to a man called Emil Goldfus, and gave the address of his studio. (This was Abel's only other lapse from one hundred per cent security; he ought to have rented the store-room in another name and given a false address.) When FBI agents called at the studio they found that Emil Goldfus was out of town for a few months.

When Hayhanen had not arrived in Moscow on schedule, the Centre had at once realized what had happened, and they had warned Abel. They had also instructed him to leave New York and lie low to see what would happen, and he had paid two months' rent for the studio in advance and gone down to Florida, from where, if the FBI pressure became too intense, he could escape across the American border.

As nothing had happened at

the end of two months, and as Abel was invaluable to the Centre, they ordered him to return to New York to take up his work again. On his arrival, he was arrested by the FBI on charges of illegal entry into the country.

He was brought before the court on 14th October 1957, on charges of conspiring to obtain secrets of military importance and of illegal entry into the United States, the first charges carrying the death penalty. He was provided with the best defence attorney that the Brooklyn Bar Society could provide — the distinguished Irish-American lawyer James Donovan.

But the evidence found in the studio — transmitter, microfilm and other espionage paraphernalia — was too strong, and Abel was found guilty of conspiracy as charged. Sentence was to be pronounced a few weeks later.

During this period Donovan addressed to the judge an appeal for clemency, in which he said, "Who knows but that at some later date an American might not fall into Russian hands charged with similar offences. If Colonel Abel is then still alive, maybe

it will be possible to effect an exchange of prisoners."

The judge took note of this argument and sentenced Abel to thirty years' imprisonment.

Though Mr Donovan could not have known it, Gary Powers was to fly his U-2 aircraft over Russia three years later, be shot down and captured, and brought to trial as a spy. When Powers had served twenty months of his ten year sentence, what Abel's defence attorney had foreseen happened. The two men were exchanged in East Berlin on 10th February, 1962. Certainly the Russian got the best of the bargain, for Abel was a spy of the first calibre. During his questioning by the American authorities he betrayed not the slightest hint which placed his network in jeopardy.

On his return to Moscow, Abel was promoted to general in recognition of his services, and was appointed head of the Anglo-American "desk" in the Centre.

In 1968 he published his memoirs, but like most of the "revelations" authorised by the Centre, they are distinguished for their non-adherence to the facts.

Abel died early in 1972.

BIBLIOGRAPHY :

Forty Years of Soviet Spying —Seth.

The Great Spy Ring—Lucas.

ABWEHR, the German Army Intelligence Service.

Under the Nazis, this traditional German secret service was maintained, though it was to have several rivals — the SS Sicherheitsdienst, Himmler's Gestapo and so on — as the Nazi machine developed; secret organisations which, more than anything else, were designed to enhance and to a degree protect the position of their leaders.

When, on 1st January, 1921, the Allies agreed, under the terms of the Versailles Treaty, to permit the Germans to establish an army of 100,000 men, the Abwehr came into being in its modern form, as a small intelligence section within the Ministry of Defence. Its first director was Colonel Gempp, who had been a colleague of the outstanding Colonel Walter Nicolai (q.v.), head of the Abwehr under the Kaiser.

Shortly after the Nazis came to power in January 1933, Gempp was replaced by a Navy captain, Patzig. Patzig did not last long, however, for he quickly fell foul of Himmler over the question of "spheres of interest" between the Abwehr and the recently created Gestapo. In 1934 Patzig was replaced by another naval captain, Canaris (q.v.) who was promptly promoted to admiral.

Once Hitler had with impunity flouted the military clauses of the Versailles Treaty, and embarked on his policy of rearmament, the financial restrictions which had been imposed on the Abwehr were lifted. From then on, under Canaris's direction, it developed into a powerful, though not proportionately successful, secret organisation, with its headquarters at the Tirpitzufer, in Berlin.

It was organised into four large divisions.

Division I, commanded by Colonel Piekenbrock, was concerned with "operational reconnaissance" (spying) and secret mobilisation.

Division II, commanded by Lieutenant-Colonel Lahousen, was responsible for contacts with discontented minority groups in foreign countries, and with the planning of sabotage activities and other special tasks.

Division III, under Lieutenant-Colonel Bentivegni, was the counter-espionage organisation, responsible for protecting the State against foreign spies and saboteurs.

The Central Division, commanded by Colonel Oster, was responsible for the administration of the Abwehr as a whole.

Personnel of the Abwehr were recruited from all the Services, so that, in effect, it represented **the** German Secret Service, analogous with the so-called British Secret Service.

ADAMS, Arthur see under **Soviet American Network.**

ADAMS, Eric see under **Soviet Canadian Network.**

AIR MALI

One of the few links between Africa and Eastern Europe, Air Mali flies communist agents and arms into Africa. During the Simba War in the Congo, it infiltrated adviser teams and arms into Brazzaville, in the Congo

Republic, from Leopoldville. These flights started from Prague, which accounted for the many Czech weapons found in Simba hands. In Bamako, Air Mali has established a communist strongpoint in West Africa.

AKAGI, Roy see under **Furusawa, Dr Takashi.**

AKASHI, Colonel Motojiro.

In the autumn of 1900 the Japanese War Office appointed Colonel Motojiro Akashi to be military attaché in France, Switzerland, Sweden and Russia. His appointment, which had been resisted by the War Office at first, had been made at the insistence of Ryohei Uchida, a prominent member of the powerful secret society, the Black Dragon Society, who had threatened that unless Akashi were appointed the society might find it necessary to withhold the reports of its agents from the military.

A short time before he left Japan for Europe, Akashi was summoned to a meeting with Uchida and another leading executive of the Black Dragon, Sugiyama, who had once been director of the

16

Hall of Pleasurable Delights (q.v.) in Hankow. From these two members of the Black Dragon Akashi received his orders.

He was to visit France, Switzerland and Sweden just for long enough to make himself acquainted with the situation there. He was then to go to St Petersburg, which he was to make his headquarters. Japan, he was told, would soon find herself striking a blow against her enemies in Siberia — Russia. European Russia was a long way from Japan, but it was there that policies were made and instructions given concerning Asiatic Russia. Black Dragon believed that Japan could acquire important information if she had agents there.

Akashi agreed, but suggested that there might be difficulties. Sugiyama replied that this was understood, "But," he went on, "we believe there is a way in which we could not only acquire information but cause difficulties for the Russian government at the same time. As you are probably aware, there is much dissatisfaction with the regime in Russia. For many years now revolutionary societies have been formed and have operated in secret to bring about the overthrow of the Tsar. If we made contact with some of these revolutionaries, I think that, in return for offers of money and materials which would help them to carry on their activities, we could obtain from them information regarding policies and military strength in east and central Asia, for these revolutionaries have their agents in high places."

There were two leading revolutionaries, Akashi was told. One was a priest of the Russian Orthodox Church, a Father Gapon (q.v.); the other an electrical engineer called Eugene Azeff (q.v.). If contact could be made with either or both of these men, it was certain that a high measure of success could be achieved.

The three men then discussed details of what Akashi could offer the revolutionaries in Russia, how he should transmit to the Black Dragon the information he acquired, and what he could do to encourage the revolutionaries to intensify their pressure on the Russian government.

The following day Akashi set out for Europe, and some months later arrived in St Petersburg. There he lost no time in making contact with Gapon and Azeff, and in a few weeks could regard himself as their friend. His efforts met with approval in Tokyo, where the Black Dragon soon looked upon him as one of their outstanding agents.

The Colonel achieved the peak of his success on 4th February, 1904. On this day, two days before their formal declaration of war, the Japanese attacked the Russian fleet at Port Arthur.

At the moment of the attack Akashi was addressing the Russian Socialist Revolutionary C o n g r e s s, which was being held secretly in Stockholm, and to which he had been invited through the good offices of Azeff.

As the guns of both fleets fired salvoes at one another, Akashi was telling the Congress : "I am authorised by my superiors to inform you that Japan is prepared to supply arms for revolutionary uprising in St Petersburg, Odessa and Kiev."

It has not been possible to discover whether the Social Revolutionary Party received either money or materials from Japan, though there can be no doubt that both Gapon and Azeff both benefited personally.

Another friend of Akashi's in St Petersburg at this time was a noted Tartar Muslim, Abdur Rashid Ibraham, who, besides publishing a Tartar newspaper called **Ulfet,** was adviser to the Russian government on Muslim affairs. He and Akashi understood one another very well, and when the Russo-Japanese war eventually broke out, they worked together in organising Muslim resistance in the Russian rear. As a recompense for the aid Ibrahim had given him, when he returned to Tokyo Akashi arranged for Ibrahim's son to be educated in Tokyo at the Black Dragon's expense. In 1906 and 1909 Ibrahim himself visited Tokyo, and entered into even closer collaboration with the Japanese.

In World War I Akashi was appointed Assistant Chief of the General Staff. With the collaboration of General Sadao Araki he encouraged

Baron Ungern von Sternberg's project for establishing an autonomous Mongol empire. As a part of this plan, Akashi, together with Araki, was to organise and direct the Japanese occupation of Siberia.

Akashi died in 1919, however, before the full fruits of all his schemes could be gathered in.

ALBANI, Alessandro.

Born at Urbino, Italy, on 15th October, 1692, the youngest son of Orazio Albani, brother of Pope Clement XI, on whose election to the Tiara, Orazio moved his family to Rome to take advantage of the privileges accruing to the relatives of a pope.

Clement XI was a notable collector and a patron of the arts, and he devoted some time to developing similar tastes in Alessandro, and his brother Annibale. Of the two brothers, it was Alessandro who most repaid his august uncle's efforts, and very early in his teens he acquired a passion for classical antiquities which was eventually to make him one of the outstanding figures in this field.

In 1718 Albani became domestic chaplain to his uncle, Clement XI, and after a brief period was appointed Secretary of the Memorials. He clearly had the confidence of the Pope, who had ambitions for him. Quite early on, when Clement wished to deal with certain matters which he did not wish to be handled by his Nuncio at the court of the Holy Roman Emperor, he proposed sending Alessandro as his confidential agent. Though the British disapproved strongly of this proposal, because they feared that Clement would use his nephew in intrigues with the Hapsburgs against the Bourbons, Alessandro went to Vienna. British fears proved groundless, for the young delegate's mission was designed to reassure them.

The British were also apprehensive about Clement's intentions on another count. The Pope had always been a champion of the Jacobite cause, and Whitehall feared that he might be tempted to make some desperate move which would draw the Imperial troops out of Italy and at the same time give prominence to the Pretender's cause. The Pretender had made Rome his base, and many of his supporters were in attendance on him there.

While in Vienna, Alessandro gained admission to the Congress of Cambrai, which had been called to resolve the differences between the Pope and the Emperor over certain Italian territories. Whatever Clement had hoped he would be able to do, he completely failed. This, however, did not prevent the bestowal of the Red Hat by his uncle.

Clement died on 19th March, 1721, and Alessandro returned to Rome a few days later with his negotiations at the Congress uncompleted. The death of his uncle, despite the fact that his brother was an influential cardinal, checked the young man's career, and he disappeared from the political scene for a few years.

Clement was succeeded by Innocent XIII, who, on his death in 1724, was, in his turn, succeeded by Benedict XIII. With the accession of Benedict, Alessandro Albani's fortunes took an upward turn. He had already begun to acquire a reputation as a connoisseur and collector of

antiquities, and it was through this interest that he made the acquaintance of Philip von Stosch (q.v.), the chief British agent in Rome, whose mission was to report to the British Government everything that went on at the Pretender's Court.

The death of Innocent XIII had deprived Stosch of his contact at the Papal Court as the result of intrigues. Stosch, himself, was a notable collector of antiquities and it was this common interest with Albani which, together with certain other factors, drew the two men together. One of these other factors was the enmity towards Alessandro of a powerful group at the Papal Court, which intervened with the Pope when Alessandro applied for the post of Prefect of the Signature, with the result that despite the fact that Benedict owed his election to the Albanis, he rejected Alessandro's application.

Albani agreed to supply Stosch with the information he required, and he proved a source of outstanding importance throughout the remaining years of Stosch's stay in Rome. This was terminated in

1731 when powerful supporters of the Pretender, having discovered what his role was, were able to prevail on the Roman authorities to have the secret agent deported from the city.

Though Stosch's activities had been uncovered, it would appear that his connection with Alessandro Albani was not, for after Stosch's departure, the Cardinal continued to supply important information about Jacobite activities in Rome and elsewhere on the continent, until a short time before his death, which took place on 11th December, 1779. Without Cardinal Albani's assumption of the role of informer, the British Government would not have been able to counter the rebellious activities of the Jacobites so successfully as they did.

BIBLIOGRAPHY :

Connoisseurs and Secret Agents — Lesley Lewis (London 1961).

ALEXANDER THE GREAT, inventor of Postal Censorship.

In 334 BC, Alexander the Great was besieging the Persians under their general Memnon at Halicarnassus, the city in Asia Minor with the famous Mausoleum, the tomb which his sister-wife built to honour King Mausolus.

Stories began to seep through to Alexander of disaffection and discontent among his soldiers. Since he intended these men to be his army of occupation in Persia after he had conquered it, it was essential that they should be thoroughly reliable.

While Alexander was actively campaigning, he forbade his soldiers to communicate with their families for security reasons. In order to discover the truth of the situation he now announced that he was raising this ban, and scarcely a man did not avail himself of the opportunity of writing home.

Two or three days later the couriers carrying these letters set out, but they had not gone far when, on the instructions of Alexander, they turned aside and handed over the contents of their pouches. Alexander went through all the letters very carefully, and from these he learned the true situation. For the men, never imagining that the privacy of their correspondence would be violated, had written exactly how they thought and felt, and what their grievances were. The result was that all legitimate grievances were redressed, while the chronically disaffected and the unreliable were sent home.

ALFRED THE GREAT,
King of Wessex, 849-901 AD.

The departure of the Roman legions from Britain in 407 AD left the country without any controlling government, and during the next two hundred years a series of invaders from Europe landed, some of them making permanent settlements in various regions. In the second half of the ninth century, a desperate struggle was waged between the English and the latest of these invaders, the Danes, who established their mastery over half the island, until pushed back by Alfred the Great, King of Wessex. In his campaign against the Danes, King Alfred acted as his own secret agent.

The climax of the struggle came in the spring of 878. In the previous year Guthrum, the Danish king of Mercia

and Denmark, had pushed the Saxons far to the west. Alfred, with a tiny handful of his followers, when winter put a stop to fighting, had taken refuge on a little islet at the confluence of the rivers Parret and Tone in Somerset, called Athelney. Not far away, Guthrum pitched his winter quarters.

Here one day about the turn of the year, Guthrum called to him his generals and captains, and began to speak to them again of his plans for overcoming the Wessex king once and for all; for while Alfred lived he was sure that he could hope for no quiet occupation of his conquests in Britain. The experience of the last year, however, had been so satisfying that a creeping sloth had settled about the Danish armies. Only a score or two of Wessex warriors, they said, were skulking on an island with their chief. What harm could they do to the glorious arms of Denmark?

Guthrum, their king, they said, was obsessed with the military skill of the King of Wessex; though they could not imagine why. The enemy had shown no skill at all, except in allowing himself to be defeated in battle after battle. Besides, they had earned a respite, and the fair-haired, blue-eyed Saxon women, reminiscent of the women left at home, encouraged a return to humanity. Guthrum must be made to see that. Day after day he had called them to council; day after day they had discussed plans. But always they had reached no conclusion. Today there must be a decision.

Yet it was difficult to concentrate on organisation and strategy when the little Saxon harpist sat under his nearby tree strumming his melodies softly to the quiet accompaniment of his deep, rich voice. He had been in the camp with them now for so long that only when there was no music did they become aware of him.

He had just been absent for two days, and that was why ears were more readily tuned to his harp than to the rough gutterals of their king's voice. He was a quiet, likeable man, who played for his food. He spoke little, for what he knew of their tongue and they of his did not make

communication easy. He kept a wallet, they knew, into which he collected crusts and scraps of meat left over by replete soldiers. No doubt he took them home to his family. He had not said that this was what he did, but why else should he go away from the camp periodically?

"This and this shall be done," the king was saying. "This and this shall be prepared, and as soon as the spring sun has hardened the winter mud, we will march against Alfred the King and his fifty warriors, and destroy him once and for all."

The strings of the harp under the caress of the rough man's fingers sang the encouraging accompaniment to the King's commands. The player leaned back against the trunk of the tree, his eyes closed, his lips drawn open in a smile, smiling perhaps at visions inspired by the words of the song which fell in infrequent snatches from his lips.

"So it is understood?" Guthrum asked his captains.

"It is understood," his captains answered, and the remembrance of the swirling flesh-pots drew them away

23

from the council.

As they ate they talked of what the King had said; they made the first tentative details of plans; and the harpist moved among them with his bowl, smiling still.

Then came the day when the harpist went away and did not return. For the first week they missed his music, but already the sun was drying out the mud and the day for the final expedition against Alfred of Wessex came nearer.

But as Guthrum drew up his armies to march on Athelney, news was brought to him that his quarry was in his realm not with a few score men but with a sizeable army. Perplexed, though not dismayed, the Danish King turned his men about and went to meet these Saxon fools who never knew when they were defeated. This time they should be left in no doubt at all.

And yet, when the battle was joined at Ethandun, they countered his every move as skilfully as if they knew his strategy and tactics beforehand; and when the night came down, Guthrum realised that it was he who must

24

surrender, and, perplexed still, he laid down his arms.

When the King of the Danes and his generals and captains came to the King of Wessex to sue for terms, perplexity changed to amazement, and the riddle of their defeat was answered.

For the victor greeted them in their own tongue, as though he were one of them, and with a smile they recognised at once; and in his left hand he held a harp.

BIBLIOGRAPHY :

Life and Times of Alfred the Great — C. Plummer (London, 1900).

Political History of England — T. Hodgkin Vol. 1 (London, 1906).

Alfred the Great — F. H. Hayward (London, 1936).

AMANA, Yoshitaro (Japanese agent in Panama, mid-30s).

In 1934 the Japanese increased their efforts to obtain a base near the Pacific entrance of the Panama canal. Permission was sought to set up a refrigeration plant on Taboga, a small island facing Panama, not to be confused with the British-owned island of Tobago, in the Lesser Antilles. Taboga would have been an excellent vantage point from which to observe the canal's Pacific defences.

When permission was refused, and a rumour became current that the authorities were considering banning all foreign fishing in Panamanian waters, a Japanese store-owner in Panama, Yoshitaro Amana, was so undismayed that he formed a new company called Amano Fisheries Ltd. The flag-ship of Amano Fisheries was the **Amano Maru.** Built in Japan in July 1937 it was the largest and most luxuriously appointed fishing-boat in the world at that time. When in September 1937 it became known that the United States was considering excavating another canal through Nicaragua, and that some unusual fortifications were being built in the military zone at Managua, Amano lost no time in going to investigate.

He arrived in the area at 8 a.m. on 7th October, 1937. At 8.30 a.m. he was under arrest, charged with suspected sabotage and taking photographs in a prohibited area. He was acquitted.

Within a week or two, he had a similar experience in Costa Rica from which he had to be rescued by a direct appeal to the President of the Republic. Recalled to Japan he was heard of no more.

BIBLIOGRAPHY :

Honourable Spy — J. L. Spivak (New York, 1939).

Betrayal from the East —Alan Hynd (New York, 1943).

AMERASIA CASE, The (1945).

During the Second World War, Soviet Intelligence had been very active in the United States. The American Administration, however, for various reasons had turned a blind eye on this activity, even to the extent of forbidding the FBI to make any move against suspected spies and traitors. (Consult article on Soviet Spying in the US.) In February, 1945, a case broke which compelled the Administration to change its attitude, for it brought to light facts which startled not only the American people but people throughout the world.

In this month a magazine called **Amerasia**, published, with only a few minor changes, the text of a report on British policy in Thailand. This report could only have come from the files of the Office of Strategic Services (see under OSS), which had been provided with a copy by the British Government. Objecting strongly to the publication of its secret diplomacy, the British Government complained to Washington, and since the complaint was an official one, Washington had to take action.

Amerasia had come into being in 1936, and its **raison d'etre** seems to have been the formation of the United Front in China, under which the Chinese Communists and the Kuomintang of Chiang Kai-shek agreed to take common action against Japanese aggression. The magazine was owned by Philip J. Jaffe, a Russian-born American and successful businessman, and by Frederic Vanderbilt Field. Its policy was to support the United Front, and it was read with close attention in the State Department.

Among its regular contributors was Andrew Roth, who had been appointed to Naval Intelligence against the advice of the security services,

26

and who had access to many secret documents; Emmanuel Larsen, of the Office of Far Eastern Affairs of the State Department, who had also worked in Naval Intelligence; Mark Gayn, a Manchurian-born freelance journalist. Larsen, for example, supplied Jaffe with documents from the State Department, Naval and Military Intelligence, the OSS and the Office of War Information.

Among the secret papers passed to **Amerasia** was a report of the disposition of Chinese Nationalist troops, secret reports on the private life of Chiang Kai-shek, a report on the decline of Chiang's prestige and on criticism of and opposition to his leadership, together with an order of battle report showing the disposition of the Japanese fleet before the Battle of Leyte.

When the British complained of the publication of their secret report on Thailand, the OSS began an investigation and eventually decided to raid the offices of the magazine. This raid was carried out on the night of 11th March, 1945. In four drawers were found photostats or originals of 267 documents from the State Department, 50 from the OSS, 58 from the Office of War Information, 34 from Military Intelligence and 19 from Naval Intelligence.

This was as far as the OSS could go, so they handed over their haul to the FBI. The latter watched Jaffe and his staff for three months.

Despite the fact that all these Government documents had been found where they should not have been, the first reactions of the Administration were exactly those which it had exhibited on all previous occasions when the FBI had asked permission to move against spies. A prime mover in this embargo on FBI action was Secretary of the Navy James Forrestal, though Naval Intelligence documents were among those seized. Forrestal even went so far as to appeal to the Department of Justice to issue instructions to J. Edgar Hoover, head of the FBI, enjoining him to refrain from action. The Department of Justice complied with Forrestal's request, but only for the time being until the first meeting of the United Nations at San Francisco should have been completed.

President Truman, however, reversed this decision and on 6th June, the FBI arrested Jaffe, Roth, Gayn, Larsen and one other. In the **Amerasia** offices they found another 1700 Government documents which the OSS had overlooked. However, there was no evidence that the documents had been "passed to a foreign power", and the charges laid — against Jaffe, Roth and Larsen — were that they had removed confidential documents from Government offices. Jaffe pleaded guilty and was fined 2,500 dollars; Larsen entered a **nolo contendere** and was fined 500 dollars, which Jaffe paid. The charge against Roth was later dismissed.

The case itself, which took on the nature of a **cause célèbre,** and the comments of the Press and leading members of the community, made it impossible thereafter to curb the probing of the FBI, even if the Administration had wanted to, which the new President, Harry S. Truman, had so clearly shown that he did not. In any case, public opinion was fully roused, and began to demand, in an ever-increasing crescendo, for every step to be taken to discover exactly how deep Soviet penetration of the US Administration had gone. This led to the emergence of McCarthyism eventually, and all its inherent evils.

ANDRE, Major John (1751-1780).

The case of Major John André is one of the most significant cases in the history of espionage, for it raises a vital issue — when is a military scout a spy or a spy a scout? In other words, is there any justification in the difference of treatment meted out to a scout who operates in uniform, and a spy who operates in ordinary civilian clothes?

The American General, Benedict Arnold, was a man who believed that he had been wrongly accused of immorality early in his career, and that as a consequence had been passed over for promotion. Even when he was reinstated and made Commander of West Point, the most important junction in the whole American supply

system during the War of Independence, he was still determined to have his revenge. In fact, he had manoeuvred the command purely for this reason.

As the War progressed he entered into communication with the British secretly, and partly because André already knew him, but chiefly because the British Commander-in-Chief had complete faith in his ability, he was appointed to parley with the traitor.

André was the son of a Swiss couple who had settled in London. He had been educated in Geneva, and it was intended that he should follow his father as a merchant. But on his return from Switzerland he fell in love with a Miss Honoria Sneyd, who unhappily did not return his love. Thereupon he gave up all idea of being a merchant and joined the British Army.

He was a natural soldier, and his abilities were soon noted. He was just twenty when he received his commission in March, 1771. Early in the American war he was captured at St John's, but being quickly exchanged, he was appointed aide-de-camp to General Grey, and when Grey was succeeded as Commander-in-Chief by General Sir Harry Clinton, remained in his post. Clinton was so impressed by his abilities that he quickly made him Adjutant-General of the British Forces in North America. André was then twenty-seven.

By September 1780, he and Arnold had reached the point in their negotiations when only a final meeting was necessary to arrange the last details for the betrayal of West Point to the British, and on the 20th of the month, André boarded the British sloop **Vulture** and sailed up the Hudson River to a secluded place about six miles below Stoney Point where Arnold was to wait for him. He met the American shortly after midnight on the 21st.

The conference should have taken two hours at the most, and André could have been back on board the **Vulture** and away before dawn. But Arnold, who was a loquacious individual, drew out the discussions and first light was actually breaking when they were concluded. Arnold then insisted that André should have breakfast with him be-

fore returning to the sloop. Much against his judgment, Andreé agreed, and the two men crossed to the nearby farmhouse of one Joshua Smith.

While they were at breakfast, they were suddenly startled by gunfire. The Americans had discovered the presence of the **Vulture,** opened fire, and the sloop weighed anchor without waiting for André.

Stoney Point was some forty miles from the British lines, and getting back was now the most difficult problem facing the Englishman. Arnold made light of the situation, and said that Smith would guide him through the American lines. Smith refused to do so unless André changed into civilian clothes.

After some initial resistance to this suggestion. André gave way on the point, and Arnold gave him a safe-conduct in the name of John Anderson. Smith brought him safely to within three miles of the British lines and then would go no further. Using what cover there was, André went forward alone.

As he was passing through a small wood he was suddenly accosted by three men wearing British Army greatcoats, and taking them to be British soldiers he said to them: "Good morning. I hope you belong to our party."

"What party?" asked the leader.

"Why, the lower party," André replied, waving a hand in the direction of the British lines.

There was a short pause as the leader looked in silence at his companions, then turning back to André he said: "We do."

With considerable relief, André replied: "Good. I am Major John André of his Majesty's Army. I have been conducting some secret and important business in American territory. I shall be glad to have your protection as far as the lines."

"How can you prove yourself?" one of the men asked.

"I have a pass signed by the American General Arnold, made out in the name of John Anderson, but my own name is engraved in my watch."

He flicked open the back of his watch, and the men crowded round to see. The next moment, to André's great surprise, he was seized and told that he was a prisoner. The three men were actually farmers of the neighbourhood, and were wearing greatcoats which had been left behind by the retreating British soldiers at their leader's farm.

Recovering quickly from his surprise, André laughed and exclaimed that he was an American, and had been testing the men's gullibility. The watch, he explained, he had taken from the corpse of a dead British soldier. But the men were not so naive as to believe him and insisted that he should submit to a search.

Hidden in André's boots they found incriminating documents, and realising that their prisoner was a spy, they refused all the Major's bribes, and took him to their commanding officer, Lieutenant-Colonel Jameson.

Jameson immediately sent the papers to General Washington, who by a strange coincidence was in the neighbourhood of Arnold's headquarters with General Lafayette, and had arranged to have breakfast with Mrs Arnold, a celebrated beauty.

By the time they sat down

to breakfast, Arnold had arrived. They had been at table only a few minutes when a messenger arrived with a letter for Arnold telling him of André's arrest. With great presence of mind, Arnold excused himself and left the room. A moment or two later he called his wife to him, told her what had happened, and when she fell at his feet in a swoon, left her there, took to his horse and was away to safety before anyone realised what had happened. He reached the British lines, and eventually he was granted a considerable sum in compensation for the loss of his American property, and the rank of General in the British Army.

On 26th September, André, in the charge of a Major Tallmadge (q.v.) arrived at Washington's headquarters. Washington refused to see him. The following day he was brought before a court-martial of high-ranking officers, found guilty of espionage and condemned to death.

General Clinton appealed to Washington to reprieve "my scout" and surprisingly sent a letter written by Arnold explaining how it had been necessary for André to wear civilian clothes, and taking full responsibility. Washington ignored this fantastic letter, and though he received a deputation of British officers under a white flag to plead for André, he would not vary the sentence.

André was hanged on 2nd October, meeting his death with the quiet courage of the really brave man. The British Army went into mourning for him, and George III ordered a memorial to be erected in his honour in Westminster Abbey. In 1821, when all the bitterness had dispersed, his body was brought to England and buried with full military honours in the Abbey.

The question, however, remains — was André a spy or a scout? International Law lays it down that a soldier caught spying in uniform is to be treated as an ordinary prisoner of war. André entered American-held territory in uniform, and but for Arnold's dilatoriness would have returned in uniform. Had he been able to do this, he would have done no more damage to the American cause than if he had succeeded in getting through in civilian clothes.

Many authorities, including some Americans, suggest that Andre's execution was motivated by revenge for the British hanging of Nathan Hale (q.v.), the American spy who had been caught in New York by the British. But this seems to charge Washington with pettiness and he was too great a man for that.

Nevertheless, the law regarding spies and scouts has remained unchanged to this day.

BIBLIOGRAPHY :

Narrative of the Causes which led to the Death of Major John André — J. H. Smith 1808).

The Two Spies — Morton Pennypacker.

Life and Career of Major John André — R. Sargent.

ANDRINGEN (Dutch agent, World War II) see under **Giskes, Col H. J.**

ARCOS AFFAIRE, The.

Whenever the Soviet Union established diplomatic relations with a country in the early years of its existence, more important than the setting up of an embassy was the establishment of a permanent trade organisation. The most important of these organisations were the Handelsvertretung in Berlin, Amtorg in the United States, and Arcos in London. In its legal role the trade delegation was highly important to the Soviet Union; and according to the enthusiasm of the political leaders of the host country, of varying degrees of importance to the industries of that country as well. In Great Britain in the middle twenties, enthusiasm was not very great, and Arcos was not, therefore, a very significant organism in the relations between the two countries.

Arcos Ltd was established in London, in two sizeable office blocks in Moorgate, in the City, within a very short time of the opening of diplomatic relations between Britain and Russia in 1924. From its London offices it engaged in both legal trading activities and, it was soon to be discovered, in illegal activities as well. For while the Soviet Union was fairly anxious to trade with the West, the trade delegations were in fact a cover for extensive espionage operations.

In England, Soviet espionage stood at a disadvantage. In this early period of spying activity, the Soviet organisation relied on the national Communist Party to such an extent that its effort was entirely influenced by the size of that Party. The British Communist Party, when compared with the French or German, represented only a very small splinter of the International. The British Socialists had made such headway since the end of World War I, and their views, in a Conservative Britain, were so left-wing, that they seemed to satisfy the political aspirations of the majority of the workers. From the beginning, therefore, Britain was protected from any really intensive Soviet espionage effort, though she was not to escape entirely.

For a couple of years, Arcos operated both legally and illegally quite undisturbed by any opposition which it could reasonably have expected from the British authorities, when what was happening in France at the same time was taken into account. In fact, it would appear that the simple-minded, trusting British had no suspicion that Arcos was not all it purported to be, and this state of affairs might have continued had not the Soviet government, or rather the Russian Communist Party, made a serious blunder in 1926.

During the General Strike of this year, the Russian Party sent more than a quarter of a million pounds to the English miners to support their strike effort. This caused fierce resentment in the Government of the day who felt that it was an unwarranted intrusion in the internal affairs of the country. The Trades Union Congress reacted in much the same way, and returned the money; but Mr Winston Churchill, Chancellor of the Exchequer, and chief strike breaker, threatened to break off all trade relations with Russia.

The incident served to focus interest on Arcos, and it began to occur to people that the small amount of trade which was being done with the Soviet Union surely did not warrant the maintenance of the staff of more than three hundred in the Moorgate offices of Arcos.

It was also discovered by British counter-espionage (MI5) that at least one of the leaders of the trade delegation, N. K. Jilinsky, was a member of the Russian espionage organisation, and that the Commercial Counsellor at the Embassy, Igor Khopliakin, was a colleague in the same organisation.

The effect of this was to make the British government withhold from Khopliakin's successor, L. B. Khinchuk, the diplomatic immunity which his predecessors had enjoyed, and this seems to have disturbed the Soviet agency's chiefs in England, for a dispatch, which later came into the possession of MI5, from the chargé d'affaires in London to the Soviet Deputy Commissar for Foreign Affairs, Litvinov, asked the latter to agree to the temporary suspension of the forwarding to Moscow of all documents relating to espionage.

There had been another incident which, besides the investigation of MI5 into the workings of Arcos, had prompted this demand. A young Royal Air Force technician had been caught stealing secret drawings and calculations, and it was revealed that he had been intending to send them, as he had sent others previously, to Arcos.

Not long after this disquieting incident, yet another occurred, again involving British aircraft and weapons, particularly a new monoplane still on the secret list, and machine-guns manufactured by Vickers. The man involved was an Englishman who had apparently become a professional mercenary spy, willing to sell his information to the highest bidder, until taken into the ranks of the Soviet organisation in Germany.

This happened in 1926. Early in 1927 a secret government document dealing with strategic plans for aerial bombardment, was found to be missing. The Special Branch of Scotland Yard and MI5 informed the government that they were convinced that this document had also found its way to Arcos, and recommended that the Moorgate offices should be raided. After much consideration had been given to the political implications of such an act, Prime Minister Stanley Baldwin eventually gave instructions for the raid to be carried out.

At dawn on 12th May, City of London and Metropolitan Police surrounded the Moorgate offices and their officers demanded entrance under warrant. They made their way to the basement of the building where, after forcing a door, they found two men and a woman burning papers. One of the men was the chief cipher clerk at the Soviet embassy, the other was an Arcos man.

One man fought to evade arrest, but was overpowered, and on his being searched, a list of the cover addresses of agents and of "letter-boxes" not only relating to Europe, but to North and South America and a number of Commonwealth countries, were found as well. The paper seemed to justify the Special Branch and counter-espionage authorities in seizing all the papers found in Soviet House, and a haul was taken away for examination.

These documents proved beyond any doubt that Arcos had been used as cover for espionage activities, for among them were found copies of several vital British government documents and a list of some of the Russian agents who had been active in Britain. The document, however, which had precipitated the raid was not found. It was believed that a member of the organisation had escaped with it by means of a secret shaft which had been built by Arcos, and which was not discovered until some time later.

The British government was coldly furious, especially when it was revealed that "all our military and naval centres, Aldershot and Plymouth in particular", had been penetrated by Soviet agents. Diplomatic relations with the Soviet Union were broken off, and the trade delegation sent about its business. For two years no Russian was allowed to enter the country.

The three-year period of Arcos activity represents the only serious attempt by the Russians to spy in England in the pre-Second World War era.

Amtorg, Arcos's counterpart in the US, which also functioned in a dual role, remained undetected until the beginning of World War II.

BIBLIOGRAPHY :
Soviet Espionage

35

— David Dallin
(New York, 1955).
Soviet Spy Net
— E. H. Cookridge
(London, undated).

ARMAND, Major le Comte
(First World War).

Count Armand was the son of a former French ambassador to the Vatican, and an influential member of the board of the great armaments combine, Schneider-Creusot. One of the richest men in France, (before the First World War his fortune was estimated at £4 million), his great ambition was to follow in his father's footsteps as an ambassador. This is thought to be the reason which motivated him to accept a personal secret mission from his prime minister, Painlevé, in 1917.

In the spring of 1917, the Austro-Hungarians were already beginning to regret having become involved in the war, and the new emperor Karl decided to conduct secret negotiations with France — secret, because the Austrians were completely dominated by their German allies — with a view to making a separate peace. Karl sent as his envoy to these negotiations Prince Sixte de Bourbon-Parma, and the plan might well have succeeded but for Karl's flat refusal to abandon Trieste to the Italians, and the Italian's refusal to accept anything less.

Already the first mutinies had broken out in the French army; the Germans were preparing a new great offensive; and Painlevé was afraid that neither the armed services nor the civilians would be able to withstand another colossal assault. With Lloyd George's concurrence, therefore, he decided to make an attempt to reopen negotiations with the Austrians.

Looking round for an agent to conduct the new talks, his choice fell upon Armand, partly because of his connections and partly because, after a distinguished combatant career, Armand had been posted to the Deuxième Bureau — French Military Intelligence — and had therefore experience of clandestine activities. He was also a close personal friend of Count Nicolas Rovertera, one of the most influential advisers of the Austrian government.

Painlevé, therefore, instructed Armand to put out feelers, and to this end the Count invited Rovertera to visit him at his magnificent country house at Fribourg, in Switzerland. There the two friends met on 7th August, 1917. Despite their close friendship, both men were determined to secure the best terms for their respective countries, and though their parleys gave every appearance of gentlemanly ease, their bargaining was sharp.

After a few days of talks, each returned home to report progress and to receive fresh instructions. While Armand was in Paris he was received by Marshal Foch, who had just returned from an inspection of the Italian front, which he saw was dangerously weakening.

The Count returned to Fribourg on 22nd August, and Rovertera arrived the following day. The Austrian brought news that his government was as intransigent as ever about Trieste.

The French government fell on 24th August, and Painlevé was succeeded by "Tiger" Clemenceau, who approved Armand's mission and or-dered him to persevere. But nothing could budge the Austrians from the stand they had taken, and no headway was made throughout the autumn of 1917.

In the hope of encouraging Armand to make greater efforts, Clemenceau promised that if he brought the talks to a successful conclusion, he would appoint him to an embassy, and on 2nd February, 1918, the Count returned to Fribourg to make a final attempt. But he could not prevail upon the Austrians to move from their position one inch. Clemenceau set Easter as the deadline for concluding the negotiations, but on 3rd April, the Austrian prime minister, Count Czernin, afraid that the Germans might have got wind of the negotiations, put an end to them in melodramatic fashion.

In a speech to the municipal council of Vienna, he declared "Monsieur Clemenceau, some time before the beginning of the offensive on the western front, asked me if I were ready to enter into negotiations and upon what terms. At my orders the counsellor of legation Nicolas

Rovertera has had several interviews in Switzerland with Commandant Armand, who is attached to the French Ministry of War and is in Monsieur Clemenceau's confidence.

"During the course of a conversation at Fribourg, Switzerland, on 2nd February of this year, these two gentlemen discussed the question whether and upon what basis a conversation intended to lead to general peace would be possible between the Austro-Hungarian and French Ministers of Foreign Affairs, or their official representatives.

"Count Rovertera, following my instructions, and according to my order, told Commandant Armand, and requested him to inform M. Clemenceau, that the Austrian Minister of Foreign Affairs was ready to confer with a representative of France and that he considered such an interview might be successful as soon as France renounced her intentions with regard to Alsace-Lorraine.

"Count Rovertera was then informed, in M. Clemenceau's name, that the latter was not in a position to accept the proposed renunciation on France's part, with the result that an interview between the delegates would, in the opinion of both parties, be useless at present."

When this speech was reported to Clemenceau, he declared succinctly, "Count Czernin has lied!"

In fact, of course, Czernin had not lied. His motive for dropping his bombshell was his hope that by bringing the negotiations out into the open he would appease the Germans. Clemenceau had played deftly into his hands, which was extraordinary for one so experienced in politics to do, and why he should try to deny the actuality of the negotiations still remains a mystery.

The talks, however, were effectively brought to an end by the incident, and Armand, who could so simply have proved the Tiger a liar had he chosen to open his mouth, was recalled. Clemenceau clearly thought that he constituted a danger, for he had him transferred from the Deuxième Bureau to the staff of the general commanding an army corps at Orleans.

But this was not sufficient

for the Tiger's peace of mind. One morning Armand returned from his customary ride to find officers of the Sûreté searching his rooms. When he asked what was happening, he was struck and threatened, and then forcibly stripped — for documents which would "prove" his treason and which he was obviously concealing. He reported what had happened to his commanding officer and asked for immediate leave to go to Paris, where he intended to demand an explanation from the Minister of War.

In Paris the Minister refused to see him, but after several applications he was eventually sent for by the Deuxième Bureau. There one of his former chiefs gave him no chance to defend himself against the charge that he had had traitorous intercourse with the enemy. Armand was unable to believe his ears, and he seems to have lost all courage, for when the officer left the room suggesting that there was only one course which the count could honourably follow, Armand shot himself with a revolver which was lying on the desk. It was officially announced to

the count's family that he had died of a virulent attack of influenza.

BIBLIOGRAPHY :
The Secret Services of Europe
— Robert Boucard,
trs. R. Leslie-Melville.

ARNOULD, Rita see under **Trepper, Leopold.**

AZEFF, Eugene (Russian double-agent, 1869-1919).

Eugene Phillipovitch Azeff was born in 1869 in the Russian town of Lyskovo, to a poor tailor. The Azeffs were Jews and at this time, the Jews in Russia suffered many restrictions, the result of which was to bind them to an almost perpetual state of poverty.

In order to escape from the direct consequences of this state, Fischel Azeff moved his family in 1874 to the new and rapidly developing industrial town of Rostov-on-Don, where he opened a grocery and drapery store. He seems to have lacked the acumen usual in the members of his race, for he failed to improve his fortunes though the place and the time were favourable.

Eugene Azeff, despite the poverty of the family, was

sent to Rostov high school, from which he passed in 1890, aged 21. Here he had already begun to exhibit those qualities which were to make him notorious later. He incited a number of his fellow pupils to acts of disobedience, and then denounced them to their teachers.

On leaving high school, he wandered from job to job, until finally he became a commercial traveller. In 1892 he fell under suspicion of being involved in the dissemination of a treasonable manifesto. Rightly believing that his arrest was imminent, he decided that his safety lay in flight. But he had no money — of his own.

It so happened, however, that he had just received a consignment of goods from his employers. Rapidly disposing of them to his customers, he pocketed the proceeds and removed himself from Russia with the aid of £85 of his employers' money. Making his way to Germany he came to Karlsruhe, where in May 1892 he enrolled as a student at the Polytechnic for a course in electrostatics. He was not the only Russian at Karlsruhe Polytechnic; he found there a number of contemporaries from the Rostov high school, who had formed themselves into a small Social Democratic society which he was invited to join.

The money which he had embezzled had to come to an end sometime, no matter how carefully he eked it out. He was living only just above the starvation level, and was in a constant state of hunger and cold. When only a few roubles remained, and seeing no possible way in which he could raise money, he came to a decision.

Not quite a year after arriving at Karlsruhe he wrote to the Ochrana (the Soviet Secret Police, q.v.) in which he offered to report upon his Russian fellow-students' activities. With caution he signed the letter with a false name. It seems that he feared that it might in some way, fall into the hands of the revolutionary students. At least that was the excuse he gave.

At the same time, however, he sent a second letter in almost identical terms to the Rostov Gendarmerie. The number of Rostov students in Karlsruhe was not so great that it was a comparatively easy task to identify the handwriting of this letter.

The Ochrana replied at the end of the month that they knew about this Karlsruhe group, and that it had so little importance that they were not interested. (As a matter of fact, they knew nothing about it.) They were nevertheless prepared to pay him for any information he cared to send, on condition that he would reveal his true name, "for we have strict principles and will have no dealings with certain people." Azeff replied at once that he would be willing to work for the pittance of 50 roubles a month, the equivalent of £5.

He still hesitated to sign his name, but before his acceptance reached the Ochrana, they had received a note of his identity from the Rostov police, who reported that he was an intelligent and clever intriguer who was in close touch with Jewish students living abroad, and that he could be of real use as an agent.

The report also added that the covetous characteristics of his nature and his present state of penury would combine to make him "zealous in his duty." Having received such a glowing account of the volunteer the Ochrana was eager to employ him and in June 1893 Azeff received his first payment of 50 roubles.

To overcome his difficulty in appearing to support himself without an income, he had the idea of writing beggin letters to Jewish charitable organisations which he showed to his companions, but did not post. Thus he was able to alleviate his standards of living without raising the suspicions of those upon whom he was being paid to spy.

On his arrival in Karlsruhe he had been moderate in his political views, but now he swung to the extreme left. He was not a great talker or theoretician, and very cleverly set himself up as a man of action. He also volunteered to carry out a number of tasks which took him travelling about Germany and Switzerland. This also, naturally, enlarged the circle of his revolutionary acquaintances, and added to the importance of his work for the secret police.

In 1894 he met in Berne the founders of the Union of Russian Social Revolutionaries Abroad, the Zhitlovskys, husband and wife, by whom he was invited to join the movement. He was able to make such an impression on the Zhitlovskys that when it was decided to send a representative to make contact with the leaders of the movement elsewhere in Europe and in Russia itself, Azeff was chosen, and was received everywhere on the glowing recommendation of the Zhitlovskys. The information which he was able to pass to the Ochrana as a result of these visits, brought him to the notice of Zubatov, the notorious chief of the secret police.

Zubatov was something similar in characteristics and in background to Azeff, and he recognised in Azeff the exact qualities needed for the work of a secret agent, and throughout their association did everything to protect this man after his own heart. It was Zubatov's idea to use Azeff as an **agent provocateur.**

Up to this time there had been a certain chivalry even among the secret services, and provocation had been looked upon as contrary to the special code defining the activities of secret agents. The spread of the revolutionary movement in Russia and out-

side Russia but directed towards her, had reached such proportions, however, that every method could be justified when it came to combating it to secure the preservation of autocracy.

In order to be able to call upon his pet spy — his pet though he was now unaware of his true motives; "Azeff," he wrote once, "looked at everything from the point of view of personal gain, and worked for the government out of no conviction but for the sake of personal profit" — he moved him to Moscow, obtaining a good position for him as an engineer with the General Electric Company. This brought him to the very centre of the revolutionary movement.

Still maintaining his initial insistence on terrorist acts as the only way of effectively furthering the cause of revolution, Azeff soon found himself an outstanding figure in a movement the majority of whose members were composed of the intelligentsia and theorists, who were more inclined to the dissemination of propaganda printed on secret presses. Over and over again he preached that terror was

42

the only way, and in so doing he gained the approval and support of the tiny minority whose inclinations also tended that way.

He supplied information for the arrest of revolutionaries with great skill, and when this was supplemented by Zubatov's determination to protect his master-spy, no suspicion could ever fall on him. So successful was he in avoiding suspicion, in fact, that when Gershuni, the leader of the militant Battle Organisation of the Revolution, was denounced by Azeff and arrested at Kiev, Azeff was promoted by the revolutionaries to the post. In this position he organised more killings than all his predecessors together and than any of his successors until the revolution flared into the open.

Not all of his revolutionary confederates regarded him with the boundless confidence which the majority of their comrades gave him, and from time to time he was 'investigated', emerging on each occasion with enhanced reputation.

In 1904 a small band of revolutionaries unconnected with the Battle Organisation plotted the assassination of Plehve, the Minister of Police, the most feared and hated man in all Russia. Azeff knew of the plot and the identification of the plotters. He denounced them and they were arrested before they could act, and executed.

It was not long, however, before Azeff himself was busy with a similar scheme for the elimination of the same victim. Working out the smallest details of the plot personally, and distributing tasks, even to selecting the bomb-throwers and reserve of bomb-throwers should the first fail, he proved himself a master.

The day chosen for the attempt was 21st July, 1904. With great discretion Azeff arranged to be out of St Petersburg that day on a visit to Vilna, where he waited for the news. Something went wrong with Plehve's arrangements and his carriage was held up, and rather than kill innocent people the attempt was abandoned by the actual assassins. It was then agreed that another attempt should be made in the following week, on 28th July. This time Azeff went off on a visit to Warsaw. This attempt was a success, Plehve was killed, and only the actual bomb-throwers were caught and executed.

A short time later Azeff plotted the assassination of the Grand Duke Serge, the Tsar's uncle. Again he planned all the details of the plot, and even supplied the dynamite for the bomb. The Grand Duke, who was Governor-General of Moscow and leader of the reactionary party, was saved by the presence of his wife in his carriage with him on the first occasion, but a second attempt was successful.

As a representative of the revolutionaries Azeff took part in a conference in Paris later in 1904, and sent a copy of the report of the proceedings, which was given him for distribution among the revolutionaries in Russia, to the chief of police, Lopukhin. He followed this with other plots against a number of high-ranking officials, most of which failed. These failures led to the demand by Azeff for bigger and better bombs.

In the middle of 1905 one of the members of the committee of the St Petersburg branch of the movement received an anonymous letter, denouncing Azeff as a police

agent. He was brought to trial by a secret tribunal of the Revolutionary Party, but the judges refused to be convinced by such evidence as there was. How could the man who had been responsible for the deaths of such tyrants as Grand Duke Serge and Plehve be a secret agent?

Then came the case of Father Gapon. Gapon was the open leader of the people in their struggle to alleviate their plight, and on a Sunday in 1905 marched to the Winter Palace at the head of a great crowd to present a petition to the tsar. Troops opened fire on them and thousands were killed, but Gapon escaped abroad and lived for a time in London. Unfortunately he became a victim to comfortable living and the revolutionaries lost confidence in him.

Gapon then returned to Russia, but on finding that he was distrusted by the movement, began to work with the police. On 28th March, 1906 he was hanged by the Party in an empty house.

Azeff had planned the "execution", because he feared that Gapon would discover his own connection with the police and betray him to the Party. As a matter of fact, the chief of police had told him that Gapon had offered to betray him to the police for a large sum of money. Azeff had originally proposed to the Party that the chief of police should be removed at the same time as the priest, but he warned Lopukhin of the plot and he failed to keep the appointment arranged by Gapon ostensibly for a conference with Azeff, but at which he intended to denounce him to Lopukhin, who was to come there secretly.

During the period which followed, Azeff consolidated his position with the police by wholesale betrayals of his confederates in the Party. But never once did any suspicion fall on him. At the same time he felt that it would be wise to make himself supreme in the movement, and to this end put forward a plan to assassinate the tsar. Though he had previously opposed such plots, he now took an active part in discussions for the elimination of Nicholas II. Several attempts were planned, and the last one only failed because the assassin lost his nerve at the crucial moment.

This seemed to mark the beginning of Azeff's end, which was eventually accomplished by the editor of an historical review.

Vladimir Burtzeff was an ardent admirer of the Revolutionary Movement, and for long had had his suspicions of Azeff. For many months he had been busy gathering evidence of Azeff's connection with the police. By the end of 1908 he needed only one more piece of evidence to make his case complete.

It so happened that one day he shared a railway compartment with the former chief of police (now retired) Lopukhin, from whom he was anxious to obtain confirmation that Azeff had been employed by the police under Plehve and himself. To induce Lopukhin to give him this information, Burtzeff told him that Azeff had planned the murder of Plehve and the Grand Duke Serge. Perhaps it was the shock of this information that made Lopukhin give Burtzeff the evidence he required. He did, however, obtain from Burtzeff a promise that his name should not be mentioned, and that Azeff should not be liquidated on the strength of his denouncement alone.

Some time later Azeff went to Lopukhin and implored him to deny that he had told anyone that he had ever had any connection with the police. Lopukhin replied that he would not give any evidence before a revolutionary tribunal, but he also forbade Azeff to use his name in any denial he might make otherwise he (Lopukhin) would have to speak the truth.

In December 1908 a revolutionary tribunal sat in Paris to try Azeff. He tried to prove an alibi with a forged hotel bill, but when he was asked to describe in detail the room he had engaged, he could not do so. Thereupon he disappeared.

Lopukhin was brought to trial by the Ministry of Justice on the indictment of betraying Azeff to the revolutionaries. The indictment set forth a complete account of Azeff's fifteen years' service with the police. Lopukhin tried to prove that he had denounced Azeff because he feared that the activities of the double-spy would constitute a menace to the life of the tsar himself, were he allowed to continue.

The repercussions which Lopukhin's trial had on the Ochrana were nothing short of a catastrophe, for, it was asked, if a police agent could plot and carry out the assassination of the supreme police chief and of a Grand Duke, where did the protection of the secret police begin?

For the next ten years Azeff wandered about Europe in obscurity, for some years accompanied by a mistress, identified only as Madame N, and still something of a mystery. In 1912 he met Burtzeff in Frankfurt-am-Main and told him with wistful reproach that if he had not exposed him he would have killed the tsar. He was arrested by the Germans in 1915 and interned. He died in Berlin on 24th April 1918. Madame N was his only mourner when he was buried in the Wilmersdorf cemetery two days later.

BIBLIOGRAPHY:

Azeff: the Russian Judas— B. Nikolaevsky (London, 1934).

The Ochrana—A. T. Vassilyev (London, 1930).

BADEN-POWELL, Lord Robert (1857 - 1941).

On leaving school in 1876, Robert Baden-Powell entered the British army. He passed the preliminary examination so well that he was excused all early training and was commissioned at once in the 13th Hussars, who were about to leave for India. After seven years' service there, the regiment was posted to Natal, in South Africa, and it was while on duty there that Baden-Powell carried out his first intelligence assignment, a secret reconnaissance of the six-hundred-mile frontier of the province.

In 1887, after two years in England, he was back again in South Africa, and in the following year took part in the Zululand c a m p a i g n against Dinizulu, during which he acted as intelligence officer of the famous Flying Column.

In 1890 he became Military Secretary to his uncle, Sir H. A. Smyth, Governor of Malta, and the following year was appointed intelligence officer for the Mediterranean, when he worked for the first time in civilian clothes as a spy.

He was very well fitted for his work in this capacity by his earlier self-training in tracking and observation, and his ability in amateur dramatics, which proved of great service to him in the matter of disguise.

During his duty as intelligence officer in the Mediterranean he reconnoitred fortifications in Herzgovina (a province of what is now Yugoslavia, but then part of the Austro-Hungarian Empire). Posing as a bespectacled short-sighted naturalist armed with a large butterfly-net, he was able to approach near to the defences without rousing suspicions. An expert artist he was able to draw exact plans, doing so on the spot, incorporating the lay out in the designs of butterflies' wings in his nature sketch-book.

Later he investigated a rumour that a large new dry-dock was being constructed in Hamburg. He successfully completed the mission, confirming the rumour.

His activities, one is led to

infer from his own account (see below) took him over a large area of potential enemy territory. Unfortunately his book was published early in 1915, which may be the reason for its somewhat nebulous nature. We are told nothing of the actual missions, except in terms of narrow escapes, risks and techniques. No places are named, which greatly detracts from the value of the record. Nevertheless there emerges from it the indisputable fact that the founder of the Boy Scout Movement was an expert agent, endowed with all the successful agent's qualities.

BIBLIOGRAPHY:

My Adventures as a Spy— Robert Baden-Powell (London, 1915).

Some of My Favourite Spies —Ronald Seth (Philadelphia, 1968).

BAKER, Lafayette, General. (Northern spy and later US director of intelligence.)

One day in 1862 the veteran Federal general, Winfield Scott—he was seventy-six— was in his tent studying the map of the Confederate territory and wondering what "President" Davis and his commander-in-chief General Beauregard might have in mind. He was working under much disability, for sometime earlier the North had lost its outstanding network of secret agents — "Stuttering Dan Graham, John Scobell, Miss Carrie Lawton and the brilliant Timothy Webster — and as a consequence intelligence from the South was sparse.

As the old general bent over his maps, his ADC came into the tent and asked if he might speak. Permission granted, he told General Scott that there was a young man in the camp, a civilian, who had been making something of a nuisance of himself for three or four days. He would not go away, he declared, until he had spoken personally and privately with the general, nor would he say what he wished to see the general about. What were the general's wishes in the matter? Nothing was known about the young man except that his name was a somewhat fanciful one — L a f a y e t t e Baker, named he declared, after the famous French general who had fought with

Washington in the War of Independence. He did not appear to be a crank, and that was what made his persistence all the more puzzling.

General Scott said that he would see the importunate young man, and when Baker was brought in, he refused to speak until the ADC had left the tent. The general who had been expecting that his visitor might be a fanatic, was surprised to find him quite calm and self-possessed, and dismissed his assistant. When they were alone, Baker said that he had come to offer his services to General Scott as a spy in the South and went on to explain that he had lived for a few years in Richmond and knew a number of people there who would vouch for his being a Southern sympathiser if he told them he was.

Scott pointed out that that was scarcely a sufficient recommendation; what he would need from a spy was the strength of the Confederate forces, their dispositions, their defensive lines, the strength and nature of their defences, and so on, and such information could not be acquired merely by sitting in Richmond, even if Richmond were the hub of all Confederate affairs. This kind of information could only be obtained by an agent who could travel about the territory freely and see things for himself, and this would not be possible, for quite wisely General Beauregard allowed no civilian whose background was not fully attested near any military installation.

Baker replied that he appreciated all that, but he thought he had the means of overcoming the difficulty. As he spoke he was busily erecting a tripod, on which he eventually set a black box.

"What's that you've got there?" the general asked. "It looks like one of those newfangled photographic cameras."

That was precisely what it was, Baker told him, and suggested that if he posed as a photographer, wandering about from place to place, he was sure he could get permission to visit Southern milita posts to take photographs of the men to send home to their families as souvenirs. After a moment or two's thought, General Scott agreed that the plan had possibilities, but warned Baker that there was very little money in spying. Baker replied that all he asked for was a little cash for running expenses, and, if he succeeded, a commission in the army. If he failed he wanted nothing.

So the bargain was struck, and the next twenty-four hours the general and his volunteer spy spent in close discussion of the army's requirements. Then, with only the two of them sharing the secret, Lafayette Baker, his camera slung across his back, set off for the South.

The boundary line between the Southern and Northern territory was the frontier of Maryland and Virginia. It was not clearly defined, though both sides had established a kind of frontier guard with posts and pickets at intervals. In theory it should have been a simple matter for an alert young man to be able to cross the line undetected, but the fact that the guard was constantly on the move introduced a certain hazard into the operation, especially as both sets of guards had to be evaded.

At this first attempt,

Baker's luck was out. He knew that he was in the frontier zone, but he could not tell whether he had passed out of Maryland into Virginia, and he was still going forward with extreme caution when he walked into the arms of a lone armed picket. Within a very short time he found himself before a court of Northern officers who were convinced that he was a Confederate agent and were proposing to hang him. Not until he saw that his life was actually in danger did Baker demand to be taken before General Scott, and he had the greatest difficulty in persuading his captors to communicate his request to the commander.

Scott fully expected this experience to change Baker's mind about wanting to be a spy, but the young man was now more determined than ever. At his second attempt he was successful in getting through both lines, but he was not more than a mile or two inside Virginia when he was accosted by a Confederate mounted patrol, who also arrested him as a spy.

Initially, Baker believed his mission was finished almost

before it had begun, but his camera was an object of much interest and he soon found that though they would not grant him his freedom, the officers of the Confederacy were eager to pose for him, and as higher echelons heard about him, so he was passed up the chain of command, until eventually he was brought to Richmond and lodged in the jail there.

From his cell he made a determined effort to regain his freedom. He petitioned General Beauregard, who was also interested in the comparatively novel photographic camera, though he pretended to be more interested in the "information" brought by the young man, for as part of the cover story which General Scott and he had devised, he was posing as a Southern itinerant photographer who had been caught in the North by the outbreak of the war, and on his way south had "worked his passage" by photographing F e d e r a l officers and men, to do which he had visited military headquarters and camps and garrisons, and was only too willing to tell what he had seen. When they asked him,

he planted on them the cunning false intelligence which the veteran general had concocted just for this purpose.

General Beauregard was interested enough to order the young man to be brought to him, and at the interview the Confederacy's President Davis and Vice-President Alexander H. Stephens were also present. All three w e r e sufficiently impressed by his protestations of innocence of spying that they were prepared to consider favourably his plea to be allowed to earn his living by his camera. He was released from prison and given permission to approach the military wherever he found them, and to start him off General Beauregard and his staff were the first to pose for him.

At the beginning he was accompanied always by a guard, but this did not worry Baker. He could see as much with a guard at his side as he could unaccompanied. Wherever he heard there were soldiers, he asked to be taken, and singly or in groups, officers and men posed for him. What they did not know, however, was that the little black box before which they solemnly, self-consciously stood contained no photographic plates, and that since the camera was itself broken and let in the light, could not have taken likenesses of them even if it had contained plates. However, the camera was still such a rarity that very few outside the ranks of professional photographers had any idea of the principles on which the apparatus worked.

Little by little, Baker gained the confidence of the army men in Virginia, and the check on his movements was relaxed. Taking advantage of this freedom, Baker allowed himself more latitude in his espionage, until having covered all that part of Virginia which he judged to be important, he began slowly to work his way northward toward the frontier.

So one day he came to Fredericksburg.

To guard against awkward questions about when the photographs he was supposed to have taken would be forthcoming, he had carefully avoided visiting twice any place where he had operated his camera. Now, quite by chance, a group of soldiers who had sat for him in Richmond had been transferred to Fredericksburg, and some of them, seeing him in the street, recognized him and accosted him, demanding their portraits. Baker tried to explain that he had been overwhelmed with business and had had no time to develop all the photographs he had taken. The soldiers, however, were not satisfied, and with that rapidity which, in retrospect always surprises, a scene developed, a crowd gathered, and almost before he realised it, Baker found himself under military arrest charged with spying for the North.

Fredericksburg jail was full and to accommodate him a cell on the ground floor, normally used as a store, had to be cleared. Whether the authorities who had arrested him were not experienced or too harassed to attend to him properly, they did not search him, and so he was allowed to take into the cell with him a sturdy pocketknife which he always carried with him.

It was quite clear to him that if he were to be brought before judges, he would have little hope of hoodwinking them now, so he decided that, if possible, he would avoid such a meeting. An inspection of the bars of the window quickly revealed why the cell had for some time in the past been designated as a store. They were so loose that only a little superficial chipping at stone and cement with the point of his pocketknife was sufficient to allow them to be removed altogether.

By good fortune this part of the prison backed immediately on to a narrow, little-used side street. After dark, Baker removed the bars, climbed through the window, and headed north out of the town. By dawn, when he was able to orient himself, he discovered that he had covered part of his route twice and was still ten miles from the border. So he lay up until nightfall, and then went forward once more.

The technique of crossing a frontier undetected seemed to be beyond him, for once more he walked into a picket and narrowly escaped with his life, when, believing the man to be a Confederate soldier, he ran. But when others came up at the sound of the shot, he was cornered, and only then discovered to his relief that they were General Scott's men.

Once more he demanded to be taken to the general, and once more it required all his powers of persuasion to save himself from the firing squad. However, the general and his spy did meet, and despite the fact that General McClellan, by halting his army when it was on the point of victory, later nullified his efforts, the intelligence Baker brought with him was of such an order that General Scott at once acquired a commission for him and placed him on his way to rapid promotion.

Baker's rise in the army was, in fact, phenomenal even under the conditions of the day. Within a fantastically short time he was appointed to the rank of brigadier general, and when Allan Pinkerton, head of the world-renowned detective agency and organiser of the Union's first espionage system, proved, by the failure of that system, that the detective of crime is far removed from the practice of spying, and resigned, Baker was chosen by President Lincoln to succeed him.

Baker, without doubt, had

been born with that special brand of instinct for espionage which stamps the great chiefs of intelligence. The Union's secret services under his direction became an extremely potent weapon in Lincoln's armoury, and it is ironic that its subsequent failure should have been in a measure directly responsible for that great President's death.

When the war was over, Baker remained in charge of the intelligence operations, which were now devoted entirely to counter-espionage activities. Unhappily as he grew older, certain undesirable traits in Baker's character began to be revealed. He became greedy for wealth, and in his efforts to acquire it, he became involved with shady characters in their more than shady transactions. So keen did his avarice become that he neglected his duties in order to devote time to satisfying it, with the result that his service rapidly ran downhill and became so ineffectual that despite John Wilkes Booth's arrant exhibitionism no one, and certainly not Baker, was aware of the mad actor's conspiracy to assassinate Lincoln.

After the President's death an inquiry was held into this failure and not only was Baker dismissed, but Congress withheld appropriations for an intelligence agency. Thereafter, although the United States Secret Service was established under the Treasury Department in 1865 to combat counterfeiting, the United States maintained no centralised intelligence organisation, until the delegation to the Federal Bureau of Investigation of certain counter-espionage and sabotage activities of the three independently operating agencies — the FBI, the Military Intelligence Division and the Office of Naval Intelligence — that anything like a national service such as is found in other countries was established.

BIBLIOGRAPHY:
History of the United States Secret Service — Lafayette Baker.

BANCROFT, Dr Edward, Fellow of the Royal Society (late 18th century).

When the American War of Independence broke out, so fierce was the hatred of

54

the French for England that the ruling classes were not long in openly declaring their sympathy for the colonists in their revolt. Hoping to profit materially by this sympathy, George Washington sent to Paris as his ambassador the famous scientist and diplomat, Benjamin Franklin, with plenipotentiary powers to negotiate a treaty with France; to accompany him, Franklin took his friend Dr Edward Bancroft, MD, internationally known as a chemist, who had invented various dyeing processes, and who had attached himself to Franklin.

Franklin had been in Paris little more than a year when information was laid before him that his friend and disciple, Bancroft, was a spy in the pay of England. Franklin would have none of it. Admittedly Bancroft made frequent visits to England, but he was doing so to spy on the English, and not for them. Whenever he returned to Paris, the doctor brought back always a portfolio full of the most useful intelligence concerning British troop and fleet movements and ministerial plans. It was fantastic to

suggest that his friend was spying for the English.

But despite Franklin's loyalty, that is exactly what Bancroft was doing. His frequent trips to London, made possible by the curious conventions of the times which laid down that war did not involve civilians, who might travel in the enemy's country, even while a state of open war existed, were for the express purpose of taking to the English all American and French secrets entrusted to Franklin. The English, in fact, thought so highly of the doctor that they were paying him the handsome salary of £1,000 a year for his services.

How he managed to dupe Franklin so successfully for so long is one of the mysteries of this aspect of history. But while he was receiving his £1,000 a year from the British, he was also receiving a considerable sum for his "dangerous espionage exploits" on behalf of America. Once, when his American pay was delayed a little, he sat down and wrote a sharp letter of reproof, which made certain that the instalments arrived when due.

Bancroft even undertook to

spy for France. His mission was to Ireland where he was to investigate ways and means for the French to assist an Irish rebellion. He demonstrated a curious kind of loyalty to the English, however, for the report he made on his return to Paris was so discouraging that the French abandoned the plan forthwith. How he was ever able to square his conscience is to pose a question that it would be a waste of time to try to answer, for basically he was a scoundrel.

Source material : The Auckland Manuscripts, known in America as the Stevens Facsimiles.

BARCZA, Margarete see under **Trepper, Leopold.**

BEAUMARCHAIS, Caron de (1732-1799, French dramatist and secret agent).

Pierre Augustin Caron was the son of a watchmaker born in 1732. Owing to his skill in making time-pieces, he presently found himself watchmaker to King Louis XV. He also discovered in himself other talents — those of the skilled dramatist. By marrying a wealthy widow and by

successful speculation, he was able in 1761, to buy himself a patent of nobility and style himself thereafter de Beaumarchais. It is by this name that he has achieved world-wide fame, chiefly on account of two of his plays, **The Marriage of Figaro** and **The Barber of Seville,** set to music respectively by Mozart and Rossini.

His official place at Court was as Comptroller of the Royal Pantry. Later he became teacher of music to the King's daughters. His introduction to secret service came after he had been found guilty of forgery, and disgraced by loss of citizenship and civil rights.

The lieutenant-general of police was de Sartines, who was the confidant of the current royal mistress, Du Barry. When it came to his knowledge that the exiled Morande was threatening to publish a little volume entitled **Memoires secrètes d'une fille publique** — the account of his own amorous adventures with the Du Barry — de Sartines believed that if anyone could buy Morande off, it was de Beaumarchais.

De Beaumarchais, realising

that if he could please the royal favourite he would be a long way back on the road to the restoration of his respectability, accepted the mission. He succeeded so well that unfortunately there is no record of this part of Du Barry's career.

De Beaumarchais' reward was the restoration of his civil rights, and he was planning a glamorous future when unluckily the king died.

Before long, the Chevalier d'Eon (q.v.) was threatening the new king, Louis XVI, with the publication of his correspondence with Louis XV dealing with the latter king's proposed invasion of England. Negotiations were in train for the return of these letters — for a consideration — when Louis XV died, but their publication could be just as dangerous for the new king. In view of his success with Morande, de Sartines proposed to de Beaumarchais that he should personally open negotiations with the Chevalier.

To everyone's surprise, he enchanted d'Eon and was able to come to terms.

Later, still, de Beaumarchais was engaged by the French government to supply the Americans with arms and other essential equipment for their struggle against the British for independence. This he achieved by setting up a "cover" firm called Roderique Hortalez et Cie, and was so successful that he rendered vital aid to Washington and his forces.

In 1792 he was in trouble with the authorities again, and this time imprisoned. When he was released, he lived abroad, for a time in Holland, and later in England. He eventually returned to Paris where he died on 19th May, 1799.

BIBLIOGRAPHY :

Beaumarchais and his Times —L. le Lomenie (Eng. trs. H. S. Edwards : London, 1856).

Beaumarchais : An Adventurer in a Century of Women — P. Frischauer (London, 1936).

BENNING, James see under **Soviet Canadian Network.**

BERIA, Lavrenti Pavlovich (1899-1953) Soviet Russian Director of Intelligence.

Lavrenti Pavlovich Beria was born in 1899 in Merkheuli, Georgia, a seaside resort on the Black Sea coast, the son of peasants. Before he left school he had attracted attention on account of his Marxist views, and at college he joined a group of the Social Democratic Revolutionary Party, of which he soon became the leader.

In 1917 he was conscripted into the Imperial army, but he had not been serving long, when the Revolution established Soviet power in Russia. On demobilisation, he returned home, and tried to resume his studies at Baku university, intent upon equipping himself for a career as an architect. But the development of political events attracted him too strongly and before long he had acquired a post in the Caucasian Tscheka, the secret police set up to protect the state from counter-revolutionaries. Shortly after joining the Tscheka, he was transferred to Georgia, then still an anti-Bolshevik stronghold, to carry out intelligence work. This marked his entry into the field of espionage.

Within a short time he had proved himself an outstanding agent, and was to exhibit the

first signs of the ruthlessness which was later to make him the most hated and feared man in Soviet Russia. Chief of the Transcaucasian Tscheka was a brother-in-law of his fellow Georgian, Josef Stalin, a man called Redens. Beria, who had his sights set upon Redens' post, made a close study of the private life of its holder, and discovered that he was extremely susceptible to pretty women. He decided to use this weakness to accomplish Redens' downfall.

Taking into his confidence a striking, dark-haired, young married woman, he engineered her introduction to Redens at a cocktail party. Redens fell a victim to the young woman's charms, and presently was caught with her in a situation so compromising that he had no defence, by the woman's husband, who had been warned by Beria of what was happening. As a result of the ensuing "scandal" Redens was recalled to Moscow, and Beria was given his post.

Within a year of his appointment, the Tscheka was nationalised and became the **Gosudarstvennove Politiches-**

kove **Upravlenve** (GPU- State Political Administration). The GPU, in turn, was reorganised in November 1923, as the **Obevdeinnove Gosudarstvennov** (the OGPU), under the direction of F. E. Dzershinsky. Beria was appointed to one of the senior posts in the OGPU, and quickly became notorious for the methods he used to liquidate numerous opponents of Stalin, which brought him the gratitude of the dictator who gave expression of his gratitude by awarding him the Order of the Red Banner of Georgia Armenia and Azerbaijan.

The post of chief of the OGPU was no bed of roses despite the power it carried, and its holders, at least in the early days, invariably met with mysterious deaths. The first victim was the veteran Dzershinsky, who is believed to have been poisoned by his successor Vyacheslav Menzhinsky in 1926, who in turn was removed in May 1934 by his deputy, Genrikh Yagoda, who took over the post.

Shortly after Yagoda's appointment, the OGPU was reorganised again, and became the NKVD — **Narodny Komisariat Vnutrennikh Dvel** (the People's Commissariat for Internal Affairs. In 1936, Stalin claimed Yagoda as a victim, and he was succeeded by Nicolai Yezhov, a fanatic with an oriental potentate's blood-lust. He was uniquely suited for the post, for Stalin had begun the first of his Great Purges, and could have found no better agent for carrying his orders out. Yezhov responded to his master's commands with such zeal that the mass arrests, purges and mass executions he organised have become known in Soviet history as the **Yezhovshchina.** He went too far, however, and Stalin was compelled to liquidate his liquidator-in-chief. In December 1938, Yezhov disappeared and was replaced by Lavrenti Pavlovich Beria.

Beria had earned this promotion, for he had been one of Yezhov's most loyal lieutenants. Stalin ordered him to put an end to the purges. To project himself to the terror-ridden Russian people as their saviour, his first act was to order the execution of five officials in the Ukraine on the charge that they had carried out unnecessary exterminations.

His appointment as Commissar for Interior and State Security was not Beria's only promotion. At the same time he was made a Candidate-Member of the Politburo, the most important department of the Central Committee of the Communist Party, which not only decided internal policy but foreign policy as well. (At least, this was its role in theory, but during Stalin's dictatorship it had little real power. Its members, however, were, in fact, the most powerful men in Russia after Stalin.)

As Commissar for Interior and State Security, Beria was in reality responsible for both the counter-espionage, espionage (abroad) and secret police organisations of Russia. Operating from The Centre, (q.v.) in Moscow, he set about producing an organisation which was to make Russian espionage the most feared spying organisation in the world after the British Secret Service. He introduced innovations of his own devising, such as The Index (q.v.) he established training schools for agents which aimed at making his espionage service no longer dependent on the

co-operation of foreign Communist Parties, and he vastly widened the spying activities of Russian intelligence abroad. He also brought SMERSH, the department for Terror and Diversion responsible for tracking down and liquidating enemies of the state abroad, to a pitch of performance it had never before achieved.

Internally, he gradually tightened his grip on the Soviet people with a secret police force whose activities made the imperial Ochrana's, the Tscheka's, the OGPU's pale into insignificance. Ever since his early days with the Caucasian Tscheka he had gathered every scrap of information about the private lives of potential obstacles to the policies of the Soviet government, and later of his hero Stalin. At the same time, he kept similar files on all the leading members of the Party and government, and thus acquired a position of power, which, secret though it was, made him a threat to practically everyone of any influence in the Soviet Union.

It is small wonder, therefore, that when his friend and

protector died, the new rulers should waste little time in ridding themselves of the presence of this threat, not only to their peace of mind, but to their very lives. In his rise to power, Beria had overlooked only one thing — the opposition of the Army commanders to him; and he made a very serious underestimate of the cunning of his closest rival Malenkov. Long before Stalin died, Malenkov, who had been Stalin's closest friend and blue-eyed boy, made a pact with the military men in return for their s u p p o r t when the time came.

For a month or two after Stalin's death nothing happened, then suddenly Malenkov pounced. Beria was arrested, accused of conspiracy to overthrow the new regime, tried secretly and executed, and nothing was said until he was dead. Arrested and executed with him were Merkulov, chief of State Security throughout World War II, and Minister of State Security and Control until 1953; Dekanosov, chief of the Foreign Department of the First Directorate of State Security; Mesnik, chief of

SMERSH — all of whom had been his creatures — and every other who had received his appointment from Beria.

This latest purge (December 1953) reached out far and wide. In effect, it removed all the old leadership of the secret services to quite a low echelon, and consequently set back the operation of Russian intelligence quite a way. But the new leaders obviously believed that even such a sacrifice was justified by the removal from the Russian scene of the man who had kept the whole nation in a state of terror for more than a dozen years.

BIBLIOGRAPHY :

Forty Years of Soviet Spying
— Ronald Seth (London, 1965).

The Great Spy Ring
—Norman Lucas (London, 1966).

BERNARD, Paul (British agent of World War I).

A member of the net-work in Belgium and Northern France led by Louise de Bettignies, alias Alice Dubois. (q.v.) Bernard was a brilliant cartographer, who, by using a peculiar short-hand code, and his calligraphic skill, could write reports of a thousand to fifteen hundred words in the space covered by a postage stamp on a postcard.

BIBLIOGRAPHY :
Louise de Bettignies
　—Antoine Redier (Brussels, 1928).

BERRYER,
Lieutenant-General of police under Louis XV of France.

The mistress of a king who desires to dabble in politics and retain her position, particularly if she has middle class antecedents, automatically has enemies who equally automatically contrive to ruin her by exposing all the scandal about her that is possible, and of inventing it if none exists. In her early days the Marquise de Pompadour, before she came to love Louis XV with the genuine and loyal love which raises her above many of her kind, realised that she must protect herself from such attacks by knowing what the scandal was before it reached the King.

Her first step in achieving this was to acquire for an acquaintance of hers called Berryer, the post of lieutenant-general of police. Immediately on appointment, Berryer concentrated the activities of his police and spies on the protection of his patronness. Between them they devised what came to be known as the **Cabinet Noir.**

The **Cabinet Noir** was the headquarters of a secret postal censorship which was the first to operate on a nation-wide scale. Every single letter sent by the French postal system was routed through the **Cabinet,** where a large staff of clerks was kept busy reading and making notes of all letters which contained matters of interest to the police and the Marquise.

Letters in those days were sealed with the seals of their senders. In order that the recipient — and through him the writer of the letter — should remain ignorant of the censorship, an impression of the seal was first taken, the wax was then steamed off, and when the letter had been read, a fresh seal was made by the impression and fixed to it before it was sent on its way.

BIBLIOGRAPHY :
Princesses, Ladies and Salonnières of the Reign of Louis XV—Thérèse Louis Latour.

BEST, Captain S. P. (British agent, World War II).

For several years before the outbreak of World War II, on the evidence of Reinhard Heydrich, chief of the Nazi SD (Security Service) as quoted by General Walter Schellenberg in his **Memoirs,** the SD had been in contact with the British Secret Service through a German agent known only as F 479. F 479 had been feeding the British with prepared information supplied by the SD, which, on the face of it, indicated that there was a resistance group within Germany anxious to bring about the overthrow of the Nazi regime. The information was skilfully prepared, and the British responded favourably.

When war broke out, contact with this (mythical) group obviously assumed an even greater significance for the British. Heydrich, on the other hand, could not make up his mind whether to put an end to the "game", or to go on with it. In order to help him to come to a decision he detailed Schellenberg, then one of his assistants to explore the possibilities that might accrue from continuing the contact.

After a preliminary survey of the material available, Schellenberg came to the conclusion that continued contact with the British would be valuable. He decided that he would go to Holland and meet the British agents himself. When he put his proposal to the British, they welcomed the idea and agreed to meet him at Zutphen on 21st October, 1939.

For the operation Schellenberg adopted the cover of a transport officer, a certain Hauptmann (Captain) Schaemmel. Accompanied by another agent, who knew the details of the "game" since he had at one time been in charge of agent F 479, Schellenberg set out for Zutphen early on the morning of 21st October.

On arrival at Zutphen, a large Buick was waiting for the Germans, and the man at the wheel introduced himself as Captain Best of British Intelligence. Schellenberg joined Best, and the other agent followed in their car. Schellenberg and Best very quickly established friendly relations, but he refused to discuss the operation until they reached Arnhem,

63

where they were to be joined by a Major Stevens and a Lieutenant Coppins. Stevens and Coppins were waiting for them in Arnhem, and when they, too, had entered the car, Best drove on, and as they drove round the Dutch countryside they talked.

The British government, said Best and Stevens, were definitely interested in the removal of Hitler and his pack, and would render the group all the assistance they could. However, it would be most helpful if the leader of the group, or any other German general could be present at the next meeting, because then they would more easily get a definite declaration from London. When they parted it was arranged that they should meet again on 30th October at the Central Office of British Intelligence in The Hague.

When Schellenberg reported to his superiors, he was given the go-ahead and permission to operate as he thought best. He persuaded his best friend, Dr. Max de Crinis, director of the Psychiatric Department of the Charité Hospital in Berlin, to impersonate the general's right-hand man. Together

they set out for Dusseldorf, where Schellenberg had set up an operational headquarters for himself, on 29th October, and on the following morning crossed into Holland.

At Arnhem they waited at the agreed rendezvous for half an hour but Best and Stevens did not arrive. Their presence attracted the attention of the Dutch police who insisted on taking them in for questioning. While they were being interrogated, Lieutenant Coppins came in, and vouched for them. Best and Stevens were extremely apologetic, but Schellenberg believes that the British had arranged the incident with the Dutch police in order to check on the identity of the Germans.

Subsequently at The Hague, they had a thorough discussion, and finally agreed that the overthrow of Hitler would be followed at once by peace; Austria, Czechoslovakia and Poland were to be restored to their former status; all Nazi economic policies would be renounced; and there would be a possibility of the former German colonies being restored to her. At the end of the talks, an **aide mémoire** was drawn up, and Stevens informed London by telephone of the results of the discussions.

The German party stayed in Holland overnight at the house of a friend of Best, and after breakfast next morning they held a final meeting at which it was arranged that they should be provided with a radio transmitter-receiver and a special code, which would enable them to keep in touch with British Secret Service HQ in The Hague. It was agreed that the time and place for the next meeting should be arranged by radio, and Best then accompanied them back to the Dutch-German frontier.

During the next week they maintained daily contact by radio with the British, who asked repeatedly for the next meeting to be arranged. Schellenberg was waiting instructions on the next move from Berlin, but when these did not arrive by 6th November, he decided to go ahead on his own initiative, and agreed to a meeting in a café at the little town of Venlo on the frontier next day. At this meeting, Schellenberg told Best and Stevens that he would try to bring the leader of the resistance group to Holland the next day so that they might fly to London for discussions with high-ranking representatives of the British government. The British agents promised to have a courier plane ready to fly them to London from Schipol airport.

On his return to Dusseldorf, Schellenberg found that his instructions still had not arrived, but nevertheless he contacted the British in The Hague and told them that all was arranged for the general and him to go to London next day. He had selected an industrialist, who held high honorary rank in the Army and was a leader in the SS, to impersonate the general, and having had a talk with him, that he decided to go to the rendezvous next day alone was due to the fact that the group wished to see how Hitler would react to new offers to negotiate a peace just put forward by the King of the Belgians and the Queen of Holland, but that the general would probably arrive next day. There was nothing the British could do but accept this explanation, but they

65

urged that as little time as possible should be wasted in making the trip to London.

That night, after he had gone to bed, Schellenberg was awakened by the telephone, and found Himmler, the Reichsführer SS, on the line. On 8th November every year, that is, on the anniversary of Hitler's Munich **putsch** in 1923, the Führer made a speech in the Munich beer-cellar where he had been in the habit of meeting his cronies in the early days of the Nazi movement. Schellenberg realised that today was 8th November and that Hitler would have made his speech a few hours earlier. His presentment that something had happened was confirmed when Himmler told him that an attempt had been made to assassinate the Fuhrer in the beer cellar, but that the bomb had not gone off until Hitler had left. Hitler was convinced that the British Secret Service was behind the attempt, and he had given orders that when Schellenberg met Best and Stevens at Venlo next day, he was to seize them and abduct them across the Dutch-German frontier. Though this would be a violation of the

Dutch frontier, Schellenberg was not to let this deter him. When Schellenberg was about to protest, Himmler cut him short.

Heydrich had been worried that the British might discover the "game" and seize Schellenberg, and had ordered a detachment of SS to guard the frontier around Venlo to protect him. Schellenberg went at once to the leader of this detachment and explained Hitler's order to him. The leader pointed out that the operation of seizing Best and Stevens would be difficult for several reasons, and not likely to be accomplished without some shooting. However, since it was Hitler's order he would have to make the attempt whatever the consequences might be. So they laid their plans.

Next day Schellenberg crossed the frontier at the appointed time. At the café he ordered a drink and awaited the arrival of Best's Buick. At twenty-past three in the afternoon, the Buick was seen approaching at speed, and Schellenberg and his companion went out into the street to meet it.

Best drove the car into the

car park behind the café, and Schellenberg sauntered towards it. He was about ten yards from the car, he heard the SS car approaching, and almost immediately the sounds of shots and a good deal of shouting. The SS car had been parked behind the German Customs office, and had smashed its way through the Dutch frontier barrier when the Buick had come in sight. The Dutch frontier guards had opened fire.

Best had Coppins sitting beside him in the Buick, and on hearing the shots Coppins jumped out and levelled a service revolver at Schellenberg. At that moment the SS car came skidding round the corner into the car park, and Coppins opened fire on it. The SS Leader dismounted and began to return Coppin's fire, and almost at once wounded him.

While this duel was in progress, the remainder of the SS men seized Best and Stevens, dragged them to their car and drove back into Germany. The British Secret Service had had no hand in the beer cellar attempt, which was the work of a German called Elser, an anti-Nazi.

Best and Stevens, however, were kept prisoner for the remainder of the war, and eventually liberated in 1945.

The Venlo Incident, as it became known, made a world-wide impression that did the Nazi cause no good, though this impression was to be mitigated somewhat when Hitler embarked on his conquest of the West in the following spring.

BIBLIOGRAPHY :

The Venlo Incident—Captain S. P. Best (London,   ).

The Schellenberg Memoirs, chapters 7 and 8 (London, 1956).

BETTIGNIES, Louise de see **Dubois, Alice.**

BfV (Bundesamt für Verfassungsschutz West German Federal Office for the Protection of the Constitution.)

The West German counterespionage service, it has headquarters in Cologne and branches in each of the ten states of the Federation. It was set up to collect information relating to attempts — should there be any — to undermine the constitution of West Germany.

The BfV has five main

directorates. The first deals with administrative and legal matters; the second deals with Right-wing extremism; the third with Communist political activities; the forth with counter-espionage; and the fifth with security matters.

The headquarters staff numbers in excess of two thousand. Its agents are largely drawn from the same strata from which the police draw their informers.

On an average the BfV arrest 3,000 enemy agents a year, only three per cent of whom are found to be operating from political conviction. Ninety per cent of all cases involve Communists.

Its first chief was Dr. Otto John (q.v.).

BLACK CHAMBER, The American see under **H. O. Yardley.**

BLAKE, Al see under **Kono, Torchichi.**

BLAKE, George (British traitor and double-agent, post WWII).

George Blake was born on 11th November, 1922, to Albert and Catherine Behar in Rotterdam, Holland. His father came of ancient and aristocratic Jewish stock, his mother of equally distinguished Dutch lineage. After a period at a Dutch school, following his father's death in 1936, in accordance with Blake senior's dying wish, the boy was sent to live with relatives in Egypt where he attended the English School in Cairo.

After two years there, he returned to Holland, and became a pupil at Rotterdam High School, which he was still attending when the Nazis overran Holland in May 1940. On the first day of the invasion, Mrs. Behar and her two daughters escaped to England. They had discussed this possibility beforehand, and George had pleaded to be allowed to stay behind so that he might finish his course at the school, and this had been agreed when an uncle had undertaken to look after him.

When George had finished school he became one of the first members of Dutch resistance. In this he gained a reputation for courage and cunning, but eventually the Gestapo got on his trail and he escaped to England, going via France and Spain.

Arrived in England he

68

changed his name to Blake, and volunteered for the Royal Navy. His ambition, however, was to join Intelligence, and his efforts to achieve this eventually bore fruit. He was seconded to SOE (Special Operations Executive, q.v.), trained by them, and then, to his disgust given a desk job.

Then in the spring of 1944 he was posted as an interpreter to the newly-formed SHAEF headquarters, commissioned as a sub-lieutenant RNVR, where his duties consisted mostly in translating and interpreting German documents that were constantly falling into Allied hands.

Shortly after the war finished, Blake was posted to Hamburg in charge of a small Intelligence unit, with instructions to seize and interrogate all the U-boat commanders he could find. He carried out this work with a ruthless efficiency. When it came to an end, he was recalled to England, and on the advice of the Foreign Office obtained his demobilisation from the RNVR, and went to Cambridge University, where he learned Russian for a post ostensibly in the Foreign Service, though he would in fact be a secret agent in the employ of MI6.

This course successfully completed, he was posted to Seoul, in Korea, as vice-consul to the chargé d'affaires, Captain (later Sir) Vyvyan Holt.

When the Korean war broke out, and the Communist troops entered the city, Blake, with Captain Holt and other members of the British colony there, was taken prisoner. Throughout his imprisonment, his fellow prisoners have declared, Blake set the highest example of courage and fortitude.

The arrest and imprisonment of diplomatic and consular officials was contrary to all usages of war, and the British government at once began negotiations for the release of Captain Holt and his companions. But the Communists were loath to let them go, and while the negotiations dragged out, attempts were made to brain-wash certain of their prisoners. Again according to his friends of this time, Blake resisted all such attempts, but it is now known that this experience was the turning point of his life.

Once he tried to escape, was caught and stood before a firing squad on the charge of being a spy. As the order to fire was about to be given, he shouted out in Russian, "I am not a spy. I am a civilian internee, a British diplomat. I went out of the camp at Man-po and lost my way."

By a stroke of good fortune, the North Korean officer in charge had been trained in Russia and could speak the language. He dismissed the firing squad and taking Blake on one side, held a long conversation with him in Russian on the rights and wrongs of the war. He then returned him to the camp, with the advice not to try to escape again.

Not until the cease-fire had been arranged in the spring of 1953 were the survivors of the British party set free. Arrived home, Blake was regarded by the Foreign Office as one who had upheld the highest traditions of foreign service. Whether it was as a reward for this service has never been revealed, but his one ambition to be a secret agent was now fulfilled. He was transferred to MI6.

This appointment was an extremely odd one, for the rules stipulated that all officers of MI6 must be of entirely British parentage. How it came about that the rule could be waived in Blake's case has never been explained; that it was fatal is known.

For a time Blake worked at the Foreign Office, where he met and fell in love with a young colleague. They were married in October 1954, and shortly afterwards Blake was posted to Berlin where he was attached to the Commandant of the British sector in Berlin.

He took up this appointment in April 1955. In Berlin the Blakes kept themselves rather aloof from the social life that went on around them, and Blake's irregular hours, which he explained to his wife, were necessitated by his job, soon began to have an effect on their marriage.

In fact, he had not been long in Berlin when he became involved with a double-agent who while working ostensibly for the Russians was also in British pay. Blake himself made trips into East

Berlin to contact this man. It was a dangerous job, made all the more so by instructions to make contact with yet another supposed informer, a man called Horst Eitner. However, Eitner and Blake quickly became close friends, and it was not long before Blake, who had undergone a sudden conversion to Communism while in Korea in 1951, and had planned to become an agent for the Soviet Union if and when the circumstances permitted, was actually a double-agent himself.

The information which he passed to the Russians was of sufficient importance at this time for them to allow him to retain the confidence of his superiors by giving him information about a number of their petty spies to hand over to the British. Indeed, the British were becoming worried by the indications that their own and their Allies' innermost counsels were obviously known to the Russians, but no suspicion fell on Blake.

For three years Blake continued his double role in Berlin. Then he made the discovery that Horst Eitner was also a Russian agent. From that moment he made every effort to get posted from Berlin, but was unsuccessful for some time, because his superiors were loath to let him go. However, he was eventually able to convince them that the Russians suspected he was a hostile double agent, and for security reasons they let him go.

The Blakes returned to England and settled near Bromley in Kent, from where Blake commuted each day to Whitehall. Presently he was told that if he wished he might have a posting to the Middle East. He accepted eagerly, and in September 1960, he and his family arrived in Beirut in the Lebanon. Here, before going to his posting he was to study at the Middle East College for Arabic Studies, run by the British Foreign Office for the special training of its candidates for posts in the Middle and Near East.

Shortly before the Blakes arrived in Beirut, Eitner had at last been uncovered as the Russian agent he was, and was arrested. The Blakes did

71

not know this. During his interrogations, Eitner disclosed that he knew Blake to be an agent working for the Russians, and produced convincing evidence to support his claim.

Blake was instructed to return to London immediately. He had no idea why he was being recalled, but he went willingly enough. On arrival in London he heard for the first time of Eitner's arrest and accusations, and faced with this he immediately wrote out a full confession.

On 22nd April, 1961, the Chief Metropolitan Magistrate issued a notice to the Press stating briefly that George Blake, a government official, had been sent for trial at the Old Bailey on three charges under the Official Secrets Act. The seriousness of the case became apparent immediately. D-notices — the security ban on the publication gathered from whatever source disclosure of which might constitute a national danger — were issued. This secrecy which was maintained until Blake was sentenced and after, gave rise to many rumours and many conjec-

tures, which by not being answered by the authorities shook the confidence of the public more than they need have done.

Though no indication of the material handed to the Russians by Blake has been given other than that it was in the political field, it is not difficult to surmise what some of it must have been. The period which Blake spent in Berlin was a period of great diplomatic activity the object of which was a Summit meeting. During the preparations for this meeting, which lasted for many months, the British Secret Service in Berlin was bombarded with a constant stream of questions dealing with every aspect of the Berlin problem. Blake saw most of these questions and prepared, or helped to prepare many answers. Ergo . . .

The only part of the High Court proceedings that was made public were the judge's comments to Blake before he sentenced him. "Your full written confession," the Lord Chief Justice told him, "reveals that for some years you have been working continuously as an agent and spy for a foreign power. Moreover, the information communicated, though not scientific in nature, was clearly of the utmost importance to that power and has rendered much of this country's efforts completely useless.

"Indeed, you yourself have said in your confession that there was not an official document of any importance to which you had access which was not passed to your Soviet contact.

"When one realises that you are a British subject, albeit not by birth, and that throughout this period you were employed by this country — your country — in responsible positions of trust, it is clear that your case is akin to treason. Indeed, it is one of the worst that can be envisaged other than in time of war.

"It would clearly be contrary to the public interest for me to refer in sentencing you to the full contents of your confession. I can, however, say without hesitation, that no one who has read it could possibly fail to take that view.

"I have listened to all that has been so ably said on your behalf and I fully recognise that it is unfortunate for you that many matters urged in mitigation cannot be divulged, but I can say this, that I am perfectly prepared to accept that it was not for money that you did this, but because of your conversion to a genuine belief in the communist system. Everyone is entitled to their own views, but the gravamen of the case against you is that you never resigned, that you retained your employment in positions of trust in order to betray your country.

"You are not yet thirty-nine years of age. You must know and appreciate the gravity of the offences to which you have pleaded guilty. Your conduct in many other countries would undoubtedly carry the death sentence. In our law, however, I have no option but to sentence you to imprisonment and for your traitorous conduct extending over so many years there must be a very heavy sentence.

"For a single offence of this kind the highest penalty laid down is fourteen years' imprisonment and the Court cannot, therefore, even if so minded, give you a sentence of life imprisonment."

73

Then followed one of the most severe sentences ever imposed by an English Court in peace-time, one which, in the view of many, and the present writer included, was completely unjustified by any action which Blake may have committed, however serious.

Lord Parker went on, "There are, however, five counts to which you have pleaded guilty, each dealing with separate periods in your life during which you were betraying your country. The Court will impose upon you a sentence of fourteen years' imprisonment on each of the five counts. Those in respect of counts one, two and three will be consecutive, and those in respect of counts four and five will be concurrent, making a total of forty-two years' imprisonment."

With a slight bow towards the bench, the wretched, misguided man turned slowly and went down the steps leading from the dock to the cells below to begin a sentence which, if he were to complete it, would restore him to the outside world an old man of eighty-one.

But he was not destined to complete it. In October 1967, with the help of a former prison inmate, Seamus Bourke, an Irishman, he escaped and got completely away. After hiding up for some weeks with Bourke, he was smuggled out of the country by the Russians and taken to Moscow. Bourke also went to Moscow, but got homesick for Eire and returned there. The escape of Blake from Wormwood Scrubs ranks with the greatest escapes of history.

BIBLIOGRAPHY :
Traitor Betrayed
—E. H. Cooridge
(London, 1962).
The Great Spy Ring
—Norman Lucas
(London, 1966).

BLOCH, David (French secret agent, World War I).

It is a widespread belief that spies were first dropped by parachute in the Second World War. In fact, on several occasions during the 1914-18 conflict, agents were infiltrated behind the enemy lines by this means. One such agent was David Bloch, of Gübwiller, in Haute-Alsace, who had joined the 152nd Infantry Regiment and had subsequently volunteered for secret work in his native Alsace, which was under German occupation.

On the night of 22nd June, 1916, Bloch was warned to stand by for an operation. He was handed papers in the name of Karl Sprecher, representative of a silk firm in Mulhouse, and told that he was to be dropped about twelve miles from his home town of Gübwiller. He was not to go to Gübwiller on any account, and he was to drop in uniform, but change afterwards. This precaution was taken because the risk of capture was always greatest immediately after landing, and if he were caught in uniform, he would be treated as an ordinary prisoner of war.

"The password this time," he was told, "is **Wagram,** and the signal for the aeroplane which will pick you up at 3 a.m. exactly a week from today, is three green flashes on your signal lantern; the spot for the pick-up, near Merxheim, at the place marked X on this map."

With Bloch went a basket of carrier-pigeons, which were to carry back his reports.

Bloch landed safely, and for the next six days he gathered much useful information which his pigeons carried back to his headquarters. On the sixth day, however, he was overcome by a desire to visit Gübwiller. Disguised as a commercial traveller, and with a tuft of beard, he felt that there would be little risk of his being recognised.

He had not been long in the town, however, when he realised how foolish he had been to pander to his sentimental desire to get a glimpse of his home, and perhaps, from a distance, of his parents. He decided that he must get out of the place as quickly as possible, and strode out along the road leading to Colmar. He had not gone far when he was stopped by a German patrol, who demanded to see his papers.

The man did not appear to be satisfied with the identity-card Bloch proffered him, and took him to the Kommandantur, where he was interrogated by an officer. Bloch maintained that he had never been in Gübwiller before, and denied that he had any relatives in the town. Unfortunately, he had been denounced by someone who recognised him, and when he was confronted by his elderly father, he realised there was no hope of escape.

Taken to the Ile Napoleon, near Mulhouse, Bloch fell before the bullets of a firing-squad on 1st August, 1916.

The most tragic aspect of this story is the terrible risks these agents were required to run from the very outset of their missions. They were given no training in espionage techniques but thrust into the midst of enemy territory carrying equipment which was almost guaranteed to betray them. Pigeons, unlike radio-transmitters, cannot be buried or hidden and forgotten until needed. They require to be fed twice a day which means either that the agent must carry their basket with him wherever he goes, or operate only within a very small area, restricted by the necessity of visiting the birds daily.

The practice of the authorities in this respect seems to be all of a piece with the general disregard for human life which distinguished field marshals and generals on both sides throughout hostilities.

BIBLIOGRAPHY :

The Secret Services of Europe —Robert Boucard (Eng. trs. Ronald Leslie-Melville, London, 1940).

BLOWITZ, Henri de (British journalist-spy, 1825-1903).

Henri Georges Stephane Adolphe Opper de Blowitz was born at the Château Blowsky in Pilsen, Bohemia, three days after Christmas in 1825. He lived in France as a young man and was later a professor at Tours and then at Marseilles.

His first venture into journalism appeared in a Lyons newspaper, and de Lesseps, builder of the Suez Canal, owed his defeat in the elections of 1869 entirely to de Blowitz's articles attacking him. This incident gave rise to a demand for the journalist's deportation from France, which he countered by successfully applying for naturalisation in the following year. He first joined the staff of the London **Times** in 1871, as a temporary correspondent; and in 1875 was appointed chief Paris correspondent of the same paper, a post which he held until his death in 1903.

When the Congress of Berlin was convened in 1878 to counter the political situation which would undoubtedly arise if the Treaty of San Stefano, which had ended the Russo-Turkish War, were allowed to go unchallenged, the **Times** temporarily transferred de Blowitz to Berlin in the certain knowledge that if any correspondent could break through the security curtain which had been drawn round the conference by the Prussian authorities, it was he.

De Blowitz's very first move was to secure for a friend the position of an attaché at the Congress. It seems so simple that one wonders why other correspondents did not attempt the same move. But a little deeper consideration elicits certain dangers in this arrangement, the chief of which was the relationship between correspondent and attaché during the conference, dangers which others might not care to risk.

De Blowitz recognised these difficulties, and it was in this that he showed his appreciation — conscious, perhaps — of the agent's craft. He never met his informant, and if they happened to be in the same room they ignored one another completely. They never used go-betweens or made rendezvous. The plan was much simpler than that; and it was the simplicity of it which exhibited the touch of the brilliant agent.

The two men dined at the same restaurant every evening, at the same time. They wore hats of the same colour and pattern, which were fortunately much the same size. When de Blowitz had dined and left the restaurant he took his friend's hat from the peg on which it was hanging, and back in the privacy of his hotel room he extracted from the hat-band notes of the day's proceedings, and the following day an accurate report appeared in **The Times.**

When the first report appeared everyone attending the Congress was shaken. When the second and third appeared Stieber, the outstanding Prussian spy-master, was in despair, and Chancellor Bismarck apoplectic. De Blowitz was known to be the correspondent, but Stieber surrounded him with counter-agents who followed his every movement, and still the solution came no nearer. Five years afterwards Bismarck was still puzzled by de Blowitz's success and when the Chancellor and correspondent met, he inquired how it was done. But de Blowitz refused to reveal his method, and, in fact, did not do so until he published his **Memoirs** shortly before his death.

The Congress of Berlin followed a pattern which is so familiar to us in the mid-twentieth century. In spite of the pre-arranged secret agreement between Disraeli and Russia, an **impasse** was reached on the Bulgarian question. It seemed that the conference would be wrecked on that one issue; and the wily English statesman, as unwilling for this to happen as he was to give way, resorted to a ruse. He ordered a special train to be ready to take him home at any moment. In the end it was the Russians who capitulated, and within twelve hours the people of England and Europe knew of it from de Blowitz's report in **The Times.**

The greatest triumph that could be achieved by any correspondent would naturally be the ability to publish the terms of the Treaty which was the **raison d'être** of the Congress, before it was actually signed. Bismarck's insistence on secrecy, however, was designed to prevent such an event from taking place. Because of this opposition de Blowitz was all the more determined that he would "scoop" the Treaty.

His attaché friend could not help him, but he found a delegate willing to do so. He met this delegate towards the end of the Congress, and during conversation let fall the remark that if he were asked to choose between all the decorations and orders in the world and the Treaty, he would choose the Treaty. He went on to say that he believed Bismarck would give him an advance copy as a reward for his reporting of an interview with the Chancellor, with which Bismarck had been exceptionally pleased.

The delegate did not think that Bismarck would make an exception of de Blowitz, and suggested that the correspondent should do nothing until he saw him again. At the next meeting the delegate told de Blowitz that he would supply him with a copy secretly the day before the Congress was due to end.

De Blowitz now began to importune Bismarck for an advance copy. Naturally, Bismarck refused, saying that he could not make an exception of one correspondent for fear of enraging the others. De Blowitz passed round Bismarck's latest letter of refusal among his colleagues, and professing pique at such treatment announced that he would not stay in Berlin to report the end of the Congress.

The delegate honoured his undertaking, and produced a copy of the Treaty, but without the Preamble. This de Blowitz managed to obtain from another source on the evening before the day on which the Treaty was to be signed; and as soon as he had telegraphed it to London in cipher, he took the train as he had announced, much to the surprise of the other correspondents.

An hour or two before the signatures were put to the Treaty the people of England were reading the text of it in **The Times**; and before the diplomatic storm broke, de Blowitz was safely outside the Prussian frontiers.

It was a brilliant coup, which served to enhance the already tremendous reputation of **The Times's** correspondent. The anonymity of the delegate who had helped him to achieve it he honoured for all time, and his name is still unknown. Why he was prepared to forswear his oath to secrecy to help de Blowitz can only be a matter for surmise.

The operation, though not strictly falling within the pure definition of espionage, deserves to be recorded here, for it carried all the hallmarks of a brilliantly executed espionage mission.

BIBLIOGRAPHY:
Memoirs — Henri de Blowitz (London, 1903).

BND
(Bundesnachrichtendienst)
West German Federal Intelligence Agency.

West Germany was recognised as a sovereign state — the German Federal Republic — in April 1956, whereupon

79

the organisation headed by General Reinhard G e h l e n (q.v.) became the official German Intelligence Service (BND). At the beginning it retained its old staff, its former organisation and its former headquarters. It was quickly discovered however, that as it was now responsible for all the intelligence activities it would need intense expansion. Not only were more agents required but a staff of economists, scientists and political specialists, to analyse and evaluate not only agents' reports but information drawn from published material. This latter accretion of intelligence sources — provided by a systematic study of foreign publications and literature carried out by university study groups and from visitors to Iron Curtain countries — which was a new concept of intelligence as far as Gehlen's organisation was concerned, soon outstripped what might be called the pure intelligence apparatus.

The BND is responsible for collecting military, political and economic intelligence on a world-wide coverage. It also keeps a close eye on the activities of foreign intelligence organisations working outside their own countries.

The General Directorate, situated at Pullach, near Munich, has three main divisions — subversion, counter-intelligence and foreign intelligence,—which are subdivided into territorial units. It has a permanent staff of five thousand. It is connected to a network of organisations, some of them international, through a variety of contacts such as German embassy staffs, the personnel of trade delegations, delegates to international conference, members of learned societies — cultural, economic, scientific and so on — staffs of banks which operate internationally, industries and travel agencies.

Information is also fed to it from American satellites, some of which consist of military communication intercepts originating in the Iron Curtain countries. This enables the BND to know the whereabouts of every unit of the armed services of those countries.

In fact, it is a highly efficient example of an intelligence organisation modelled on modern lines, employing all the latest scientific and technological aids, from computers for code-breaking to infra - red rocket - launching detection devices.

At its head, until his retirement in 1968, was General Gehlen. He was responsible, as is his successor, only to the Federal Chancellor through the chief of the Chancellery. A parliamentary committee, however, exerts a measure of control, though the extent of the control is debatable; however, it approves the senior appointments to the service, and the budget currently running in excess of $16\frac{1}{2}$ million dollars annually.

The present chief is General Gerhard Wessel, who has gained wide intelligence experience under Gehlen, and is a specialist in Russian affairs, the Russian armed forces, and the KGB (q.v.).

BONNESEN, Edith (Danish agent, World War II).

Edith Bonnesen, well known throughout the Danish Resistance by her operational name Lotte, was working in the Ministry of Transport at the time of the German invasion of Denmark. She began her work for the Resistance by engaging in the activities of the underground press. In 1942 she was arrested by the Gestapo three times on suspicion, but each time was released for lack of evidence against her, though on the last occasion she spent eight days in prison. It was quite clear that it would only be a matter of time before the Germans did eventually put her away, so she gave up her job and went deep underground, living in a variety of apartments scattered about Copenhagen.

In July 1943, she met Duus Hansen, leader of an SOE network in Copenhagen. He had recently returned from a visit to Stockholm where it had been agreed that he should set up his own radio organisation, building sets and training operators. Hansen asked her to join him and gave her the task of finding as many appartments and other posts suitable for transmitting as she could and to search for radio material. Later she became his cipher expert. She also recruited operators for him from among the marines, and gave them instruction in coding and decoding.

Duus Hansen had a "letter box" (q.v.) in a textile office

in Copenhagen. Crystals were expected from London, and the message came that they had arrived while Hansen was out. Lotte, therefore, decided to collect them herself. (1)

While she was at the office a telephone call came from someone whose name she did not recognise, and a little while later, as she was discussing this with friends there, wondering if it was part of a trick—as it later turned out to be — the Gestapo arrived. They found the package with Lotte's name on it, but she felt that so long as she could deny she was Lotte there was some hope for her. Skilfully and without being noticed, she left all the compromising contents of her handbag about the room.

The Gestapo, however, decided to arrest her and she was taken to an office in the Shellhus, a large building near the centre of Copenhagen, which the Gestapo had taken over. She hoped desperately that she would be recognised by someone in the little crowd of spectators outside the Shellhus, who would warn Hansen what had happened to her.

She was taken to a room on the fourth floor, and left in the charge of a drunken Danish policeman. Every few minutes odd Germans would enter the room and gloat, "Now we have Lotte."

Eventually she was interrogated, but insisted on her cover story, until the Gestapo infuriated by her obstinacy, ordered her to be taken down to the cellars, where torture was to be applied.

For some inexplicable reason the Danish policeman took her to an office on the second floor, and told her to wait for him there. Worried by the thought of what she might reveal under torture, for besides knowing all about Duus Hansen's organisation she was well acquainted with Fleming Muus, another Resistance leader, she decided she must escape if possible.

Going to the door, she looked out into the corridor, and finding it empty, closed the door behind her and began walking away as casually as she could. She did not take the lift, choosing instead the staircase. On the first-floor landing she heard two Ger-

(1) Crystals are specially prepared pieces of quartz which, when inserted in a radio transmitter determine the wavelength on which the set transmits.

mans approaching. If they were Germans who knew her, then it was finished. But good fortune was with her. They were strangèrs, and as they went downstairs she followed close behind them.

In the entrance hall stood a large German guard. She saw at once that he had recognised her as the woman brought in some time before. But she kept on behind the two Germans. As she walked down the last few steps, the guard walked by her side. It seems that he was undecided, however, for he said nothing, and presently turned back.

Outside, she made a mistake. Forgetting that a wire barricade barred progress to the left, she turned in that direction, and was compelled to turn back and go once more past the main entrance. She expected to see Germans running out of the building in search of her at any moment, but her luck still held.

Back at the apartment she found Duus Hansen very angry with her for having been so long in bringing the crystals. When she explained how she had escaped from Gestapo headquarters in the middle of Copenhagen in broad daylight, Hansen's quiet comment was, "That was good, Lotte !"

BORCH-JOHANSEN, Major Eigil (Danish Resistance leader, World War II).

In civilian life Eigil Borch-Johansen was the managing director of a coastal shipping company. After the Occupation of Denmark he was, therefore, singularly well-placed for carrying out illicit activities, since he was one of those who, because of business relations with Sweden, was able to make frequent visits there.

In the latter part of March 1940, Borch-Johansen was a member of a Danish shipping delegation to Berlin. From the negotiations, which revealed disproportionate shipping shortages, he read the first signs. As he travelled back to Copenhagen, where he arrived on 3rd April, he noted all he could of intelligence significance, which included German minelaying activities.

As soon after the invasion of Denmark as possible, he visited Stockholm and gave all the information he had

83

been able to gather to another prominent Dane who had been able to establish himself in the Swedish capital and who was the liaison link between Occupied Denmark and the Danish Government-in-exile — Ebbe Munck. Besides the results of his own observations, he took with him information provided by a number of similarly-placed friends and acquaintances. Thus, his reports included information on the U-boat construction at Hamburg; and later, information supplied by a friend in Rotterdam.

Being so well placed for visiting Stockholm, it was suggested that Borch-Johansen should pool his results with the Danish military Resistance organisation, known as the Princes, and act as courier for them. This he agreed to do, and was given the operational name of The Duke. But from the very beginning he was never entirely in sympathy with the policy of the Princes, and this lack of sympathy created occasions when the Duke acted on his own initiative, with outstanding results.

Borch-Johansen was also the man called upon to organise the escape of the former Danish Foreign Minister, Christmas Moller and his family to England. Early in the year, the German hatred and fear of Moller had prompted them to institute a campaign to remove him from the government, which was so successful that he was compelled to resign his membership of Parliament also.

When this happened, the British Government suggested that since the ambassador in London, Count Reventlow, had resigned when the Prime Minister had visited Berlin in December 1941, there ought to be a prominent Dane outside Denmark whom all free Danes could respect and in whom they could have confidence. Christmas Moller was the obvious choice, and he agreed provided his wife and family could escape with him.

The Duke accepted the task of arranging the escape. He approached the skipper of a small coastal vessel carrying lime from a port in Jutland to Sweden. Between them, he and the skipper built into the boat a secret cabin capable of hiding three people. The escape was successfully carried out in May 1942, and on his arrival in London, Moller was at once elected Chairman of the Danish Council, a kind of shadow government.

Shortly afterwards SOE asked Borch-Johansen to arrange a "reception committee" to receive the first "drop" of Danish agents. From then on he became more and more involved in Resistance operations.

Unfortunately he was compromised when another agent was discovered by the Danish police. He was arrested, but managed to escape through a lavatory window and disappear underground. Six months later he escaped to Sweden and from there went to London, where he remained until the Liberation in 1944, as adviser to SOE.

BIBLIOGRAPHY :

The Undaunted — Ronald Seth (London, 1956).

BORTHMAN, Abraham see under **Soviet American Network.**

BOSS (Bureau of Special Services).

Though BOSS is a branch of the New York City Police Department, it co-operates very closely with the CIA (q.v.). It concentrates chiefly on the activities of Cuban exiles in the city, and also keeps a close watch on black militants who may be in touch with China or Cuba. In some aspects it resembles the British Special Branch of Scotland Yard, the headquarters of the London Metropolitan Police, who co-operate with the British counter-espionage service.

BOSSARD, Frank Clifton (Englishman s p y i n g f o r Russia).

Frank Clifton Bossard, the posthumous son of a joiner, was born at Driffield in Yorkshire, on 13th December, 1912. The widow moved to Hull, where, at the age of six, her son began to attend the Mersey School. In 1921 Mrs Bossard became housekeeper at a public house in the village of Gedney in Lincolnshire, and in 1923 she married a farm worker of Gedney called George Lester. Bossard attended the village school, and was ambitious to go on to grammar school; but his step-father's financial situation did not permit it, and he left school to become, at fourteen, an assistant in a shop at Long Sutton.

He developed a keen interest in radio, and by the time he was sixteen had built his own wireless receiver. In 1933 he took a special course in radio at Norwich Technical College.

In the political field he became strongly attracted by fascism and nazism, and visited Germany and Austria. In Innsbruck he was sent to prison for being unable to pay his hotel bill. Helped by friends in England, he returned to Lincolnshire and obtained a job as a radio engineer.

His ambition to lift himself above his social station, involved him with people better off than himself, and in 1934 he received a sentence of six months' hard labour from the King's Lynn magistrates for passing a dud cheque.

In December 1940, Bossard joined the RAF, and was eventually commissioned in the radar branch. He was demobilised in 1946 with the rank of Flight Lieutenant (Captain), having served in the Middle East. He married in 1951 an attractive young woman half his age. After a brief period as a lecturer at the College of Air Services at Hamble, Hampshire, he obtained an appointment as assistant signals officer at the Ministry of Civil Aviation, later being promoted to staff telecommunications officer.

In December 1951 he was seconded to the War Office as senior intelligence officer with the Scientific and Technical Intelligence Branch in Germany. Four years later, in the spring of 1956, he was transferred to the Ministry of Defence Overseas Liaison Branch of the Joint Intelligence Bureau, with the rank of attaché at the Bonn Embassy. This post carried Second Secretary status, and Bossard's duties were to interrogate prominent scientists, engineers and technicians who escaped from the East.

With a generous official entertainments allowance at his disposal Bossard began to drink heavily. Still trying to impress with his own importance, he gave out that he was an "undercover man".

He possessed all the qualifications that Russian espionage is always on the look-out for; in fact, he was a stereotype of one category of Russian ideal agent. He held a position which gave him access to secrets and secret documents; he was always short of money; he was unstable; a weak character ripe for blackmail.

According to his own statement, he was first approached by the Russians in London in 1961, when a man calling himself Gordon got into casual conversation with him in a pub. By this time he had become so desperate for money, that he was running a small business in coins on the side.

After more meetings, at one of which the man who had revealed himself as a Russian agent, paid him £250 without Bossard having provided any material, he agreed to hand over photocopies of documents which would be of interest to Soviet espionage.

He was provided with no fewer than nine "letter-boxes" plus one reserve. One was in a broken drain-pipe on an estate at Weybridge, in Surrey; another was a creeper-covered beech-tree off a bridal path near Leatherhead, in Surrey; yet another was in a silver birch-tree with three trunks at Woking, also in Surrey. Which "letter-box" to use, was indicated to Bossard by the playing of certain tunes on Moscow Radio at 7.45 a.m. and 8.30 p.m. on the first Tuesday and Wednesday in each month.

From 1961 to 1965, Bossard worked undetected. It was a very lucrative assignment; the last payment he received amounted to £2,000.

On Friday, 12th March, 1965, Bossard took a room at the Ivanhoe Hotel, in the shadow of the British Museum, in the name of J. Hathaway. He went up to this room at 12.50 p.m. As he left it at 2.15 p.m. he was stopped by Detective Superintendent Wise of the Special Branch, who said to him, "I have reason to believe that you have committed an offence against the Official Secrets Act. Will you please accompany me back to your room?"

Bossard, who appeared to be quite unmoved, agreed. In his briefcase were four Secret files belonging to the Ministry of Civil Aviation. In a blue suitcase were found a camera suitable for photographing documents, some spools of film — one of which contained photographs of the documents in the brief-case — a magnifier, a diary, particulars of the "letter-boxes" and gramophone records of the tunes which might be played over Radio Moscow.

Describing how he worked, Bossard said, "I selected files on guided weapons, used them in my office, took them to an hotel room and photographed suitable extracts during my lunch period. The equipment was kept in the Left Luggage office at Waterloo Station and I removed it when I needed it."

At Bossard's home at Stoke d'Abernon, Surrey, the police found a portable radio transmitter-receiver.

Brought to trial at the Old Bailey on 10th May, 1965, Lord Chief Justice Parker sentenced Bossard to twenty-one years' imprisonment. It is estimated that he received a total of £15,000 from the Russians during the four years he worked for them; but what he provided — details of Britain's secret guided missiles —was cheap at the price.

BIBLIOGRAPHY :
The Great Spy Ring

—Norman Lucas, chapter 18 (London, 1966).

BOYD, Belle (Confederate agent, American Civil War).

Belle Boyd was one of a number of women agents employed by the South. Though the daughter of a Northern official, she had been born and brought up in Virginia, which apparently imbued her with sympathies for the South.

A beautiful girl, who already had the gift to charm men who had knowledge of military significance, she was seventeen when the War broke out, and was living with her mother in Martinsburg, just within the Virginia borders. When Northern soldiers arrived there in July 1861, they attempted to fly the Northern flag over the Boyds' house. Mrs. Boyd objected, however, whereupon one of the Northern troopers spoke to her in a bullying tone, and violently thrust open the door which she was attempting to shut.

Objecting to the way in which the soldier was treating her mother, Belle drew a pistol and shot the man dead on the spot. Such was the chivalry of the times that the subsequent inquiry found that the young girl was guilty of justifiable homicide and released her.

She entered upon her espionage activities shortly afterwards, beginning when the quartering of Northern officers in her home provided her with information which she recognised would be useful to General "Stonewall" Jackson, commanding the Southern armies.

Realising the urgency of her intelligence, and having failed to persuade any of her male acquaintances to carry it to the General, she set out herself. Her journey took her through Northern lines already under heavy fire. Undaunted, however, by the shells bursting about her, she reached the Southern lines, and as a result Jackson was able to turn almost inevitable defeat into victory.

From now on she continued her unofficial spying, and soon became the talk of the North. Her continued success made her brazen, and weakened her security, and one day she made a very serious mistake. She gave a report she had made for General Jackson to a Northern agent disguised as a Southern soldier. The soldier delivered the report to his superiors instead. A Northern agent called Cridge, a man unlikely to be affected by her feminine wiles, was sent to bring Belle to Washington.

She was a difficult prisoner, but again the chivalry which persisted towards women even when they were proved spies, came to her aid. She could not have been seriously searched, otherwise the twenty-six thousand dollars concealed in the trunks which she had been allowed to bring with her, would have been found. Finally she was exchanged and returned under escort to Richmond, where she was received with bands playing and flags flying.

BIBLIOGRAPHY :

History of the United States Secret Service — Lafayette Baker.

Belle Boyd in Camp and Prison, written by Herself (New York, 1865).

BOYER, Professor Raymond see under **Soviet Canadian Network.**

BREWSTER, Caleb see under **Tallmadge Network, The.**

BUKKENS (Dutch agent, World War II) see under **Giskes, Col. H. J.**

BULME, Fernand and Paul (French traitors, World War I) see under **Roquebert, Francois.**

BURDIUKOV, Lev see under **Munsinger Affair, The.**

BURGESS AND MACLEAN (British traitors, post World War II).

Guy Burgess, an open homosexual, went up to Trinity College, Cambridge, in 1930, and became a near neighbour of Harold "Kim" Philby (q.v.) who had come up the previous year. He had the qualities with which to have made a brilliant academic career, but after taking a first class in Part I of his honours degree examination, he gradually faded out as a scholar.

In June 1943 he visited Soviet Russia. He carried with him letters of introduction which he had obtained through a prominent member of the Astor family. On his return his friends noticed that his former enthusiasm for Marxism had greatly declined,

and in a very short time he had swung over to the Right. He tried to get a job in the Central Office of the Conservative Party, and joined the Anglo - German Fellowship. His ambition was to enter the Civil Service, but he had gone up to Cambridge late, and was too old.

In October 1936, through the good offices of the famous historian G. M. Trevelyan, he was able to leave an unhappy job as a journalist on the London **Times** and join the BBC. There he produced a weekly political programme called **The Week at Westminster,** in the course of which he made some very useful political contacts. Among these was a future Minister of State at the Foreign Office, Hector McNeil, a contact which was to be very significant later.

All this time he was blatantly carrying on his homosexual activities and in the summer of 1938 was arrested as the result of an incident in a lavatory at one of the London railway termini. This was the first of a long series of incidents. At the same time he was indulging in frequent violent bouts of drunkenness, which were to become notorious.

In January 1939 he was offered a job with one of the intelligence services which were then having a mushroom growth — Department D of the Secret Intelligence Service, where he was joined later by Philby, a friend from his Cambridge days. He remained in Dept. D until it was disbanded in 1941, when he returned to the BBC.

In 1944, however, he achieved his ambition to enter the Civil Service, by joining the Foreign Office News Department. Two years later, when McNeil became Minister of State, he invited Burgess to become a member of his staff.

Hoping to become a permanent Civil Servant, after a time Burgess moved to the Far East department, then briefly to a department dealing with black propaganda. He was not a success in either, and his personal habits and homosexual activities alienated many who might have helped him. He was continually involved in some incident — once receiving an official reprimand — so it must have been surprising to many who knew him that in November 1950 he should be posted to the British embassy in Washington. It was an extraordinary appointment because Burgess made no secret of his anti-American sentiments.

Kim Philby had already taken up his post in Washington as liaison between the British SIS and the American CIA, and for a time Burgess lived in Philby's house.

In Washington, Burgess's behaviour became so extreme that the American authorities began to suggest he was **persona non grata** with them. London took the hint, and Burgess was recalled.

Now, while at Cambridge, Burgess had made another friend, Donald Maclean, son of the former Minister of Education, Sir Donald Maclean. Maclean was an undergraduate at Trinity, where he studied Modern Languages. In 1933 he obtained a good second class in Part I of the Modern Language degree examination, and announced to his family that on leaving Cambridge he intended to become a teacher in Russia. He had become interested in Marxism which he accepted without reservation.

In the summer of 1933, however, he suddenly told his family that he had given up the idea of going to Russia, and was going to aim at joining the Foreign Office. He eventually passed the Foreign Office examination.

His first post was in Paris, but in 1938, he was recalled to the Foreign Office, where he remained until 1944, when he was appointed First Secretary to the British embassy in Washington.

Maclean was also something of a Jekyll and Hyde character. Normally polished, amiable and obviously a skilful diplomat, at times he had bouts of heavy drinking, during which he became dangerously physically aggressive. This latter behaviour became progressively worse after he had been transferred from Washington to Cairo in 1948. There his behaviour became such a public scandal that in 1950 he had to be recalled. But instead of being dismissed from the Foreign Office he was placed under psychiatric treatment and promised a new post when he was recovered.

In January 1950 it became known to British counter-espionage that there had been a leak to the Russians of high secret Foreign Office intelligence dealing with nuclear armaments. The investigation that followed narrowed the field of possible culprits to one man — Donald Maclean.

By this time, however, the Foreign Office had honoured its promise and on 8th November, 1951, he became head of the Foreign Office American Department. In this post he had access to highly important information and it is extraordinary that with MI5's investigation in progress he should have been appointed to it at this time. But soon the sands of his good fortune began to run out.

On 7th May, 1951, Guy Burgess arrived back in England in disgrace from Washington. By this time, MI5 were convinced that Maclean was the man who had given the information to Russia, and he was being followed everywhere he went during the day by two MI5 agents.

On 25th May, the Foreign Secretary, Herbert Morrison gave the security forces permission to interrogate Maclean. The decision had been delayed for some weeks because though MI5 was convinced Maclean was their man, they had no direct, positive evidence, and the only way this evidence could be obtained was by breaking Maclean down and making him confess. The security officers had argued among themselves whether Maclean was, so to speak, ripe for picking. At last it was decided that he was.

The 25th May happened to be a Friday, though why this should be allowed to influence the course of events can only be described as a British idiosyncrasy. It was decided that Maclean's interrogation should begin the following Monday.

Now among those who knew the course events were taking was Kim Philby in Washington. There is now no doubt at all that Philby warned Burgess in some way that their friend was about to be interrogated.

Philby had intended to go that evening to the continent for a holiday with a young American whom he had picked up in the **Queen Mary**

on his way home. He had bought two tickets for passages in the steamer **Falaise** sailing from Southampton to Brittany that very night.

When he received Philby's warning, he told the young American that the holiday would have to be postponed as he had a friend who was in serious trouble, and he was the only one who could help him. He hired a self-drive car, and early in the evening he drove down to Maclean's house at Tatsfield, not far from London. The two men had dinner provided by Mrs Maclean, and then drove in the hired car to Southampton where they caught the **Falaise** by the skin of their teeth.

From that moment they disappeared. Everyone was convinced that they had disappeared behind the Iron Curtain, but they had covered their tracks so well this could not be absolutely certain. However, in 1953, Mrs Maclean, who was on holiday in Switzerland with her three children also disappeared.

The first break came when Vladimir Petrov (q.v.) defected in Australia in April 1954. One of the things he disclosed was that Burgess and Maclean had been recruited into Soviet intelligence while at Cambridge in 1933. When this news was made public in England, the Russians produced the two traitors at a press conference in Moscow. Both denied that they had ever been Communist agents.

Burgess died in Moscow on 30th August, 1963.

There is no doubt at all that Maclean, like Philby, passed a vast mass of highly important atomic information to Russia. At one time he had a pass to the American Atomic Energy Commission's building in Washington where he could wander about at will. According to a letter written in 1956 by Senator James Eastland, chairman of the Senate Internal Security Committee Maclean "had an opportunity to have access to information shared by the three participating countries in the fields of patents, declassification matters and research and development relating to the programme of procurement of raw material from foreign sources by the Combined Development Agency, including estimates of supplies and requirements". If his opportunities were not quite so extensive as Philby's, they certainly provided him with the highest-grade information.

Burgess was not in the same category as either Philby or Maclean, and had he not chosen to run with Maclean he might not have been suspected.

The Burgess and Maclean affair was a great blow to British intelligence prestige. Heads rolled in the Foreign Office and the security services, and relations between Britain and America became so strained that Washington threatened to cut off the British from information in the atomic field. But worse was to come, and the article on Harold "Kim" Philby should now be consulted.

BIBLIOGRAPHY :
The Great Spy Ring
—Norman Lucas (London, 1966) Chapter 6.
The Missing Diplomats
—Cyril Connolly (London, 1953).

BURTAN, Valentin see under Dozenberg, Nicholas.

BYTCHKOV, A. E. see under Munsinger Affair, The.

CANADIAN SPY CASE see under **Gouzenko, Igor.**

CANARIS, Admiral Wilhelm (Chief of the Abwehr, German Military Intelligence, WW II).

Wilhelm Canaris was born at Aplerbeck, near Dortmund, in 1887. He joined the German Navy, became a U-boat commander, and after the World War I was transferred to the personal staff of the Minister of the Army, as naval ADC. In March 1920, Canaris supported the Kapp **putsch,** and when this attempt to overthrow the republic failed was transferred to Kiel in a shore job which he held until 1922, when he was posted to the cruiser **Berlin** as first lieutenant. In 1924 he was appointed to the staff of the Admiralty as a specialist officer, and in 1928 went back to sea, being promoted commander in the following year. From 1931 to 1932 he was chief of staff at Kiel, which was followed by the command of the old battleship Schlesien.

With the seizure of power by Hitler in 1933, Canaris was promoted captain and given command of the naval base at Swinemünde. In 1934, on the sudden retirement of Captain C. Patzig, chief of the **Abwehr** (q.v.) he was recommended for the post, and took up his duties as chief of military intelligence on 1st January, 1935.

Under the Nazis, what had been a modest intelligence organisation now began to expand rapidly. Hitler looked upon the intelligence services as instruments whereby he could execute his political policies, and provided the Abwehr with practically limitless funds.

When Blomberg had to resign as Minister of War in 1938 as a direct consequence of having made what the Nazi leaders regarded as an unsuitable marriage, the Defence Ministry was replaced by the High Command under Keitel. Canaris and the Abwehr thus became subordinate only to Keitel, and through him to Hitler himself. Since he was also the senior officer, after Keitel, on the High Command, he also became chief of staff to Keitel.

95

This concentrated an enormous power in his hands when added to the power of his position as chief of intelligence.

As chief of intelligence, however, he encountered many difficulties which sprang from the fact that Himmler had established not just one rival intelligence organisation, but two — the Gestapo and the Sicherheitsdienst. There was consequently much overlapping of activities, which vitiated the total German intelligence effort, and a rivalry which was all the more fierce since Himmler's chief of intelligence was "Butcher" Heydrich until his death at the hands of Czechoslovak resistance, an utterly ruthless man who had a strong dislike for Canaris personally.

Canaris, as the best-informed man in Germany by virtue of his position, was convinced that Hitler's policies must inevitably lead to war. He believed, too, that this war would destroy not only the Nazis but Germany as well. Since he had no desire to disappear himself in the maelstrom, he began to seek alternatives. On the other hand, he gave Hitler loyal

service despite his political opposition, and he protected the security of Germany with great thoroughness.

Unfortunately, there were also flaws in his character which did not make him the ideal spy-master. He was a bad judge of character; allowed himself to be influenced by gossip; and he made demands on his subordinates which affronted their moral principles and thus undermined their performance in many cases. This led, as it inevitably had to, to personal quarrels, resentment and much petty jealousy within the small group at the top of the Abwehr. In time, by an erosive process, the intrigues affected the overall efficiency of the Abwehr, and led to its liquidation in 1944, when Canaris fell victim to Hitler's vengeance, on unsupported evidence that the Admiral had been connected with the 20th July Plot on Hitler's life.

This trumped-up charge was merely an excuse for removing him, for since 1942 Hitler had become dissatisfied with Canaris's performance as chief of the Abwehr, and for a long time seriously considered getting rid of him. This was not due entirely to the incompetence of the Abwehr, who had made one or two considerable blunders, but arose chiefly out of the personal dislike of the Admiral in the Sicherheitsdienst and Gestapo chiefs. One incident in 1940 gave rise to the suspicion that Canaris might be in treacherous communication with the enemy. The Sicherheitsdienst had intercepted two radio messages from the Belgian ambassador to the Vatican in which the ambassador had given the exact date of Hitler's intended attack on Scandinavia, Holland and Belgium. This clearly indicated that there was a traitor in high German military circles, and because Canaris had attempted to stave off the outbreak of war through western contacts he had in diplomatic circles accredited to the Vatican, suspicion fell on him.

Subsequent investigation by the Sicherheitsdienst brought forward no conclusive evidence of Canaris's connection with the Belgian ambassador, and the matter fizzled out, but the suspicion remained. In 1943 he was suspected again, in connection with some serious sabotage which had taken place in Italy.

Once more he was investigated, and this time definite evidence was forthcoming that Canaris, who wished to get Italy out of the war, had been deeply involved. Schellenberg, chief of the Political Intelligence of the SS, was able to present to Himmler a thick dossier of evidence against the Admiral. For some reason, Himmler did not pass this file to Hitler. Nevertheless, the Führer had become so dissatisfied with the Abwehr's performance, for which he blamed Canaris, and at last decided to remove him. This he did in the early months of 1944. The official reason was that the conduct of the war now demanded a unified intelligence service. In the reorganisation which followed, a small remnant of the Abwehr remained, under the command of Colonel Hansen.

Hansen was a friend of the young Count Klaus von Stauffenberg, leader of the 20th July Plot, and became involved in the plot. This was used as an excuse for the arrest of Canaris after the assassination attempt failed. He was arrested by Schellenberg on the first Sunday in August.

Schellenberg has written in his **Memoirs,** "The evidence against (Canaris) was certainly sufficient to satisfy the People's Court, under its blood-thirsty President Freisler, of his guilt. In July 1944 two dispatch cases containing incriminating documents had been discovered in a safe in one of Canaris's offices outside Berlin." No proof, however, that Canaris had put them there or knew about their contents was brought forward, but he was found guilty and sentenced to death. Again Himmler acted with the quixotic unexpectedness to which he was prone from time to time, and which makes him an interesting character. He was still sufficiently powerful to protect Canaris from the death sentence, and the Admiral was sent to a concentration camp at Flossenberg in Bavaria. In March 1945, Kaltenbrunner and Hitler jointly signed the order for Canaris's execution, and this time the sentence was carried out.

A legend has grown up in certain journalistic circles that Canaris operated as a British agent for much of the time that he was chief of the Abwehr. No evidence for this has ever been brought forward; but I have a theory of my own—that he might have been the high-ranking contact in the inner councils of the Nazi leadership who supplied Rudolf Rössler with the fantastic intelligence which Rössler passed on to Moscow for much of the war.

BIBLIOGRAPHY :

Chief of Intelligence — Ian Colvin (London, 1951).

Memoirs — Walter Schellenberg (London, 1956) Chapter XXXVI.

Downfall of the German Secret Service—Karl Bartz (London, 1956) Chapter 1.

CAPMAN, Agatha see under **Soviet Canadian Network.**

CARR, Sam see **Kogan, Schmil.**

CARRANZA, Lieutenant Ramon.

In 1898 the United States second-class battleship **Maine** was blown up in Havana Harbour. Relations between Spain and America had been strained for some time, and an incident like this seemed perfect for detonating the explosion which most observers believed must come.

A Congressional Committee was set up to inquire into the **Maine** disaster. The committee called as witnesses the American Consul General in Havana, Fitzhugh Lee, and the captain of the battleship, Captain Charles D. Sigsbee, both of whom testified that they were convinced that the Spanish authorities were responsible for the explosion. Immediately this testimony was given, the Spanish naval attaché in Washington, Lieutenant Ramon Carranza, challenged Lee and Sigsbee to duels, which the authorities naturally banned.

The Congressional Committee accepted the testimony of the consul general and the **Maine's** captain and others, and war was declared. The Spanish minister, Señor Poloy Bernabe, was handed his passports and left with his staff for Madrid, going by way of Canada. Lieutenant Carranza accompanied the minister, but only as far as Montreal, where he remained, ostensibly to wind up the affairs of the legation.

Carranza rented a house in Tupper Street, Montreal, and a suite in a Toronto hotel, and this extravagance brought him to the attention of the Secret Service of the American Treasury, whose chief function was to keep an eye on counterfeiters and forgers. They were the only agents which the American government could call on when it wished to investigate the activities of individuals such as Lieutenant Carranza.

It did not take the Treasury agents long to discover that Carranza was, as they suspected, engaged in espionage. At Toronto a Treasury agent was able to rent a room next to Carranza's suite and overheard him engaging the services of an American, a naturalised Englishman called George Downing, who also went under the name of Harry Rawlings. Downing had been a yeoman aboard the US armoured cruiser **Brooklyn,** and it was clearly this which made him appear suitable to Carranza for carrying out a mission to Washington to attempt to discover the movements of American warships. Apart from this, Carranza knew nothing about Downing and made no effort to test his suitability as an agent.

The American agents followed Downing to Washington, and on the way struck up an acquaintance with him and secured specimens of his handwriting. Taking the cover name of Alexander Cree, Downing visited the Navy Department almost as soon as he arrived, and while there he obtained from a friend who was a cipher clerk a most important piece of intelligence. When he left, he returned to his lodgings, from which he emerged after an hour, and was seen to post a letter.

With the collaboration of the Post Office officials, this letter was seized by the agents. It was addressed to Frederick W. Dobson, at a Canadian address, and was in plain language. It informed Dobson that a cipher message had just been sent by the Navy Department to San Francisco, ordering the cruiser **Charleston** to Manila with five hundred men and replacements of machinery for repairs to Commodore George Dewey's squadron.

A warrant for Downing's arrest was issued, and he was put in a military prison to await trial. He hanged himself before he was brought to trial. Carranza's first attempt had failed, and for the reason that the untrained Downing had committed almost every mistake it was possible to make.

Carranza, however, was by no means disheartened by this failure, but what he now did in his efforts to recruit agents demonstrated his own unsuitability as a spy-master. His scheme was a fairly complicated one. By offers of good financial rewards he attempted to persuade Canadians and other neutrals to volunteer for service with the American forces in the guise of adventurers. As soon as these volunteers arrived in Cuba or the Philippines, having learned as much as they could about the strength of the Americans, they were to go over to the local Spanish commanders with their information. Each was to be given a gold ring inscribed **Confienza Augustina,** as a means of identity by the Spaniards. This scheme, too, failed. It did not produce a single recruit.

By this time becoming mildly frantic, Carranza engaged the services of a Canadian private detective agency to find recruits for him. The Canadian agency were not long in producing two down-and-out young Englishmen, whom Carranza dined well and wined better. Under the influence of this treatment they agreed to Carranza's proposal, but when they sobered up, one had second thoughts. He reported what had happened to a former commanding officer, who arranged his passage back to England on a cattle boat, while the CO revealed all to the American consul, who immediately informed Washington.

The detective agency, however, proved as persistent as Carranza, encouraged no doubt by the latter's gold supplies. But American agents were keeping a close watch. They had arranged for the scrutiny of all telegrams sent to Montreal and Toronto telegraph offices near military bases or training camps in the United States, and vice versa.

Presently a man calling himself Miller tried to enlist at the American camp at Tampa. Among the telegrams scrutinised by the agents had been one from him to Montreal, and a reply to him signed "Siddall". Siddall was tracked down, tending a bar in Montreal. He admitted that he had lent his name to the private detectives working for Carranza in return for a substantial fee. Miller was at once arrested, and died some time later of typhoid fever in prison.

The second of the first two recruits now turned up at Tampa and tried to enlist. He was detected by the gold ring he was wearing, and he, too, was arrested and imprisoned.

A letter from Carranza to Miller was also intercepted, and this and other evidence of the Spaniard's violation of Canadian neutrality was presented to the Canadian authorities, who requested him to leave their country at once.

In all the history of espionage there is scarcely a more glaring example of an incompetent spy-master. But Carranza cannot be made to shoulder all the blame. He was untrained in espionage, and he apparently lacked any natural instinct for it.

BIBLIOGRAPHY :
The Story of Secret Service
—R. W. Rowan (London,
1938) Chapter 56.

CARRE, Mathilde (alias The
Cat). (French double-agent
World War II.)

Mathilde Carré was the
daughter of a military family
whose father had been
awarded the Legion of Honour in World War I. She was
recruited into the Interallié
network by Captain Romain
Czeniawski, (code-name Armand) in the autumn of 1940,
where they set up their first
headquarters in the rue du
Baubourg St Jacques, Paris.

Interallié quickly grew, and
eventually became a network
covering the whole of German Occupied France.
Mathilde Carré, first given
the code-name Lily, and later
the Cat, became one of
Armand's most enthusiastic
and hardworking assistants,
her work consisting of helping him prepare reports for
London made up of material
supplied by his numerous
agents.

Early in October 1941,
Sergeant Hugo Bleicher
reported to German Intelligence in Paris that a young
French woman had been
trying to obtain information
from the workers at a Luftwaffe fuel depot. The Abwehr
(q.v.) sent a Captain Erich
Borchers to Cherbourg to see
Bleicher, and after a talk with
him, they arrested the young
woman, Christine Bouffet,
who admitted working for a
British agent known as Paul.

Paul was arrested on 3rd
November. He was Raoul
Kiffer, Amand's chief of the
D Sector of Interallié. On
being told he had been
betrayed, he broke down.
From the information he
gave them, they were able
to trace Interallié's hideout.

Bleicher's natural flair for
counter-espionage work was
recognised by the Abwehr,
who secured his transfer to
Abwehr HQ. He was to
become the most successful
spycatcher the Abwehr ever
had.

Bleicher's first task was to
destroy Interallié, with the
help of Kiffer, who became a
most enthusiastic informer.
Twenty-one members of Section D were arrested, and
early in the morning of 17th
November, 1941, Bleicher led
a raid on the network's
Paris HQ arresting Armand

on the spot, and, when she arrived three hours later, the Cat. Armand, beyond admitting that he worked for the Allies, would tell the Germans nothing, even under torture, so Bleicher decided to work on the Cat and another woman. This woman, a young widow called Renée Borni, was of little help, so the Abwehr agent concentrated on the Cat.

She was taken from prison and set up in a suite in the Hotel Edward VII, which the Abwehr had requisitioned for their HQ. At their first meeting over a meal of black-market luxuries, Bleicher told the Cat that if she would help him, he would try to save her friends from the firing-squad. It was an old gambit, but it worked. He also promised to pay her sixty thousand francs a month.

The Cat agreed, and within a few days all Armand's helpers were arrested one by one. Interallié was completely destroyed.

Along with the agents, Bleicher also captured four radio transmitters. He proposed to his chiefs that the arrests should be kept secret, and the transmitters operated to give London the impression that Interallié was still active. In this way they would receive all the signals from London, which would tell them a good deal about British intentions, and so on; and by sending false, but plausible information, be able to confuse London considerably.

After an initial hesitation, Bleicher's superiors agreed to try the scheme. The Cat knew all the British codes, transmission schedules and security checks, but even so, the plan succeeded beyond Bleicher's wildest hopes.

In the early days the Cat had introduced to Armand a lawyer called Maître Brault. Bleicher decided not to arrest Brault, hoping that by not doing so they would be put on the track of other SOE agents. Using the Cat as his contact with the unsuspecting Brault, Bleicher achieved this, too. Brault introduced her to Pierre de Vomecourt a veteran SOE agent to land in France — who had difficulty at this time contacting London. Vomecourt asked the Cat to arrange to send some messages for him via an Interallié transmitter, which the Cat agreed to do. The outcome of these messages was a summons from London for Vomecourt to return there for consultations. Bleicher decided to let Vomecourt go, because he believed the agent would make a favourable report on Interallié.

A pick-up by Lysander was arranged, but before it took place, Vomecourt's suspicions were raised regarding the Cat. By one or two questions she asked, he was convinced that she was working for the Abwehr, and decided to try to warn London. The warning, unfortunately did not get through.

By this time also, the Germans were becoming apprehensive, believing London might have discovered the deception being played on them by information supplied by the Cat. They then hit upon a bold plan. If they sent the Cat to London with Vomecourt, providing she was genuinely working for the Abwehr, she would obtain all the information she could about SOE and come back and tell them.

While they were awaiting transport to London, Vomecourt directly accused the Cat

of working for the Germans. Tearfully she broke down and confessed. Vomecourt, however, decided to trust the apparently repentant Cat, and with German help to reach England.

After two fiascoes, they were eventually picked up by a motor-torpedo-boat off the coast of Brittany on the night of 26th/27th February, 1942, Vomecourt naturally informed SOE of the Cat's role with the Abwehr, and SOE planned that she should be treated as though her story were true. In her eagerness to prove her genuineness, she once more turned traitor and gave SOE the names of all the Abwehr officers she had met, all she knew of the Abwehr organisation, and a German code.

Vomecourt returned to France in April 1942, but shortly afterwards he was arrested, and sent to the fortress prison at Colditz. (He died in Paris in 1965.) SOE believing Vomecourt would have revealed to Bleicher that London knew of the Cat's treachery — which he had not — imprisoned her, and after the war handed her over to the French authorities. In 1949 she was tried and sentenced to death, but the sentence was commuted to life imprisonment. She was released in September 1954, and now lives in a provincial town in France under an assumed name.

BIBLIOGRAPHY :

Inside SOE — E. H. Cookridge (London, 1966).

J'ai été la chatte — Mathilde Carré (Paris, 1959).

CENTRE, The.

This is the Russian term for Soviet intelligence headquarters in Moscow. It has now come to mean the direction of Russian espionage, as well, in such phrases as "The Centre gave him instructions . . . ." or "The Centre were pleased with the results."

The term includes both the GRU — military intelligence — and the KGB — all other forms of intelligence.

CHAMBERS, Whittaker

(Self-confessed secret agent for the Russians).

On 3rd August, 1948, Whittaker Chambers, a 30,000 dollar-a-year senior editor of **Time** magazine, appeared before the House Committee on Un-American Activities in Washington DC, and de-

clared that Alger Hiss among others, had been a secret Communist between 1935 and 1937, when he had held high posts in the US Administration.

Chambers revealed that he had himself been a member of the American Communist Party for some years, and that between 1935 and 1937 he had belonged to the Communist "underground", acting as go-between between the secret Communist group, known as the Ware Group, to which he alleged, Hiss belonged and the Russian network in Washington. He claimed that he had collected their Party dues from the Ware Group and passed on to them Russian instructions. In 1937, he claimed, he had defected from the Communists, and after the Molotov-Ribbentrop Pact was signed in August 1939, he had gone to the Assistant Secretary of State, Adolph A. Berle, who was responsible for security, and had told him what he was telling the Committee now. Roosevelt, however, had laughed at his charges and nothing had been done.

Hiss, who had trained as a

lawyer, and who had had a brilliant career in Government Service — as secretary of the Nye Committee on Munitions in 1935, assistant general counsel in the Solicitor - General's department, assistant to the Assistant Secretary of State, director of the Political Department of the State Department, a member of Roosevelt's delegation at Yalta, and first Secretary-General of the United Nations — was in 1948 President of the Carnegie Endowment for International Peace.

Immediately he heard of Chambers's charges, he telegraphed the Chairman of the House Committee denying that he had ever been a Communist and that to the best of his knowledge he did not know Chambers and had never met him in his life. He also asked for an opportunity to repeat his denials under oath before a public hearing of the Committee.

His request was granted, and on 5th August he appeared before the Committee for this purpose. Chambers was not present, and Hiss asked for a confrontation so that he might settle once and for all whether he had ever

met Chambers, whose current photographs in the press he did not recognise. Chambers had told the Committee that Hiss had not known him as Chambers, but only by his "underground" cover-name of Carl. To this Hiss had replied that he knew of one or two Carls, but also knew their surnames. He had never known anyone simply as Carl.

The Committee found themselves in something of a quandary. They could not understand why a man in Chambers's position should make such damaging accusations, thereby laying himself open to the very serious charge of perjury were his statements found to be untrue; but at the same time Hiss had been so forthright and frank in his denials that it was difficult to believe he was lying.

In an attempt to find a solution, therefore, the Committee decided to question Chambers in secret session to try to discover whether his claim to have been on very intimate terms with Hiss between 1935 and 1937 could be substantiated by his knowledge of Hiss's private life which such a close friend must have. So

Chambers was summoned to appear before a sub-committee in New York.

At this meeting Chambers declared, among other things, that he and his family had stayed in an apartment rented by the Hisses for several weeks until the lease expired (the Hisses had moved to another house); that he and his wife and child had stayed on various occasions with the Hisses in their later houses; that Hiss was an amateur ornithologist and had told him of once seeing a rare bird—a prothonotary warbler; that Hiss called his wife Dilly, and she called him Hilly; that Hiss had donated an old Ford car to the Party; that Hiss had taken his stepson, Timmy Hobson, from his school, where his fees were paid by his father, and sent him to a cheaper school so that the balance of the fees could be donated to the Party; that the Hisses owned a golden cocker spaniel; that Hiss as a small boy of twelve had bottled spring-water and sold it; that Hiss's mother had lived in Baltimore; that the Hisses slept in single beds; and so on.

The Committee was amazed by the abundance of small details which Chambers put forward. By asking Hiss identical questions and comparing the two sets of answers they would soon be able to discover which man was lying.

Eleven days later Hiss was also called before the sub-committee and the same questions were put to him. His answers, which once more he supplied with utter frankness, confirmed Chambers's story in many details, though they disproved it in others.

Ever since Chambers's first accusation Hiss had been racking his brains trying to identify Chambers, and, by degrees, a doubt had crept into his mind about the truth of his denial of ever having known Chambers. He recalled now a man called George Crosley who, in 1935, had gone to him, when he was counsel for the Nye Committee, claiming to be a free-lance journalist who was searching for information on which to base a series of articles on the Committee's work. This man Crosley had been very slovenly in his dress and had had exceptionally bad teeth. But the current photographs of Cham-

107

bers did not remind him of Crosley, and, besides, Chambers flatly denied ever having used the name Crosley. At his secret interrogation on 16th August, Hiss had mentioned this man Crosley to the Committee, describing the man as he remembered him, and stating how he had let Crosley have the use of his flat on 28th Street for the remainder of the lease, after he had moved to P Street. He charged Crosley the actual rent, but Crosley had never paid anything. In fact, he had borrowed small sums from Hiss from time to time, which he had never paid back; though on one occasion Crosley had given him a fine oriental rug, which, he said, had been given to him by a wealthy patron. Hiss also said that the Crosleys had stayed a couple of nights in the P Street house, but he maintained that the last time he had seen Crosley was in July 1935.

As a result of the secret hearing on 16th August the Committee decided to confront the men in person, and the date was fixed for 25th August. The very next day, however, Hiss was summoned to the Commodore Hotel in New York, and there in another secret session, was confronted with Chambers. When Chambers admitted to having had extensive repair work done to his teeth, Hiss declared he was satisfied he was the man he had known as George Crosley.

He challenged Chambers to repeat his accusation outside the privilege accorded by the Committee, so that he might sue him for slander.

On 25th August the two men confronted one another in public session in Washington. Chambers, still denying that he had called himself Crosley, now expanded his "evidence" to support his claim that he had been an intimate friend of the Hisses. He repeated his former claims and then made the following among others, (1) that he had given Hiss the rug on the orders of his Russian chief as a token of Soviet Russia's appreciation of Hiss's work for the Party, (2) that when he had broken with Communism he had gone to Hiss and implored him to do the same, but Hiss had refused "with tears in his eyes", (3) that the Hisses had taken him on various trips by car, on one of which they had visited Harry Dexter White, another accused, and asked him to break with Communism, and (4) that Hiss had lent him 400 dollars in the autumn of 1937 to buy a car.

Hiss still denied all the charges, stated categorically that he had never taken Chambers on the trips and that Chambers had never asked him to break with Communism.

Unfortunately for Hiss the Committee had secured evidence which showed that he had signed over his old Ford car in July **1936** — he still claimed not to have seen Chambers after July **1935** — and that he had withdrawn 400 dollars from his bank account at the time Chambers said he had loaned him this amount.

The Committee now believed that they had sufficient evidence to support a charge against Hiss of "guilt by association" with Chambers. In subsequent proceedings the **main** points in this theory of "guilt by association" were :

(1) the prothonotary
warbler

(2) the old Ford car
(3) the rug
(4) the 400 dollar loan.

At the close of the 25th August hearing, Hiss again challenged Chambers to repeat his charges outside the protection of the Committee.

Two days later Chambers did so on a nationwide radio broadcast, **Meet the Press.**

Hiss's lawyer was in Europe, but immediately he returned Hiss issued a writ for libel against Chambers.

Up to this point Chambers claimed that the Ware Group was a subversive group plotting to overthrow the US Government and that he had left the Communists in the autumn of 1937, having last seen Hiss at Christmas 1937.

Under American law in civil actions the plaintiff has the right to conduct what are termed Pre-trial Hearings. At these hearings, which are conducted by the plaintiff's lawyer in his office, only the principals and the chief witnesses are heard. The ordinary rules of evidence, of examination and of cross-examination do **not** apply.

Hiss claimed this right, and the pre-trial hearing opened in Baltimore on 8th November, 1948 in the office of William Marbury, Hiss's attorney.

Hiss's attorneys had done a good deal of research into Chambers's antecedents and had come up with a good deal that was disreputable. The information included evidence that Chambers had been dismissed from Columbia University for publishing pornography, that he had been dismissed from the New York Public Library for the theft of books, that he had lied all through his life, up to and during the Committee hearings, and much more besides.

At the close of the first day Marbury challenged Chambers to produce any letters or other documents that he had had from Hiss or Mrs Hiss. At the opening of the next day's hearing Marbury asked Chambers if he would produce such papers and Chambers replied through his attorneys that he had not yet searched everywhere where such papers might be. His attorneys impressed upon Chambers that if he had any papers he must produce them, as he stood in grave danger of losing the case.

The hearing was adjourned until 16th November.

On 13th November Chambers went to New York to visit his wife's nephew, Nathan Levine. With Levine he went to the house of Levine's mother where, in the bathroom, Levine took from a recess near a dumb-waiter, a large dusty envelope which Chambers had given into his keeping in 1938.

Chambers took the envelope into the kitchen, and, he subsequently claimed, while Levine was sweeping up the mess in the bathroom, he opened it and there discovered papers "which I had forgotten existed".

He returned that night to Baltimore. Next morning he went to his attorneys and told them he had discovered papers. They returned with him to his farm and he handed them 65 pages of copies or précis of State Department documents which he claimed, had been taken out of the State Department files by Hiss and copied by Hiss or Mrs Hiss and handed to him. He had photographed them and passed the photographs to the Russians. There were also four notes in Hiss's handwriting.

In other words, he was now accusing Hiss of espionage. **This was the very first time he mentioned espionage.**

His explanation for having the papers was that when he defected he was afraid that SMERSH might attempt to murder him, and he had kept the last messages Hiss had given him as a "life-preserver".

The typewritten papers were not the only contents of the envelope. There were also three rolls of microfilm. One of these was badly light-struck, but the others contained photographs of more State Department documents.

The House Committee, hearing what had happened, sent its representatives to Chambers, and when he intimated that he had not handed his lawyers all the contents of the envelope, they subpoenaed the rest. Chambers then led them to a pumpkin patch and from a hollowed out pumpkin melodramatically produced the rolls of microfilm.

When Eastman Kodak experts were called in to identify the date of the manufacture of the film, they stated that they had been made in **1945.**

This produced a really bad moment for Chambers, because all the documents were dated in the first three months of 1938. He contemplated suicide and did, in fact, make an unsuccessful attempt. However, Eastman Kodak came back to say they had made a mistake and the film could have been manufactured in 1937.

The production of these documents on the face of it overwhelmingly testified to Hiss's guilt, not merely of having been a secret Communist, but of having been a spy. Though he appreciated this, Hiss denied the new accusations and instructed his lawyers to inform the Department of Justice of the situation.

A Grand Jury in New York, which had been convened to investigate charges of Communist infiltration of the Administration, summoned Hiss to appear before it. On 15th December, 1948 they indicted him on two charges of perjury in that he had declared under oath that he had not seen Chambers after July 1935.

Now, the production of the documents made it necessary

111

for Chambers to revise his story, since all the documents were dated January-March 1938 and he had up to the first day of the Baltimore pre-trial maintained that he had defected in the autumn of 1937; and since also up to this date he had maintained that Hiss and the Ware Group had **not** engaged in espionage.

The first point he met by claiming that after eleven years his memory had been at fault, and that he had actually defected on 15th April, 1938; the second point he countered by declaring that he had not wished to hurt a friend until that friend had shown that he was intent on ruining him.

His story now ran that all that he had told the Committee of his friendship with Hiss was true, but, in addition, he had to explain the espionage set-up between Hiss and the Russians.

He now declared that he was the go-between for two or three sources as well as Hiss. His Russian contact he named as a Colonel Boris Bykov.

He had introduced Hiss to Bykov in a Brooklyn movie theatre in 1936, and Bykov had asked Hiss to betray State Department documents to Russia, to which Hiss had agreed.

Thereafter once a week or ten days, Hiss had taken home documents, Chambers had called at Hiss's house for them about 6 p.m., taken them to Baltimore, where they were photographed by Felix Inslermann, after which, between 1 a.m. and 2 a.m. Chambers had returned them to Hiss at his Washington house, and Hiss had replaced them in the State Department files next morning, before they were missed.

There came a time, however, when Bykov announced that Moscow was dissatisfied with the volume of Hiss's traffic, and it was arranged that Hiss should take home documents every night and should type copies of them or make précis. As Hiss was no typist, Mrs Hiss, who was also a Communist, undertook the typing, which she did on an ancient Woodstock machine which she had taken over from her father, Thomas Fansler, in 1932 or 1933. Chambers collected the typed pages, photographed them and afterwards burned them.

Hiss was brought to trial on 31st May, 1949. Before the trial both the FBI and the defence had conducted searches for the old typewriter, which the Hisses had given to one of their coloured maids at the time of one of their frequent moves. It was the defence that found it, in the possession of a coloured removal man, Ira Lockey, who had taken it in part payment for a job, as his daughter was learning to type.

Specimens of the typing alleged to have been done by Mrs Hiss on this machine were discovered by the FBI. Comparisons of these with the Chambers typewritten documents proved, according to the experts, that the Chambers documents had been typed on the machine — Woodstock 230099.

At the trial the prosecution introduced all Chambers's evidence before the House Committee to prove "guilt by association", to bolster their case of Hiss's guilt as supported by the documents.

The defence, on the other hand, introduced evidence which cast considerable doubts on Chambers's charge that Hiss had handed him the documents. They put forward a State Department official, Julian Wadleigh, who had admitted being one of Chambers's contacts and who estimated that he had passed to Chambers at least 400 documents. With one or two exceptions he could have passed all the Hiss documents. (The four notes in Hiss's handwriting could have been retrieved from his waste-paper basket.)

Despite all the proof that Chambers was an extraordinary liar who had committed perjury over and over again, on 9th July, 1949 the Jury announced that it was strung and a new trial was ordered.

The second trial began on 7th November, 1949, and ended on 21st January, 1950. This time the Jury pronounced a verdict of Guilty on both counts, and Hiss was sentenced to the maximum — five years.

His appeal was thrown out, as was his application for a new trial, and on 22nd March he surrendered to the Governor of the Federal Penitentiary at Lewisbury, Pennsylvania. He was released on ten months' probation on 27th

November, 1954.

While he was in prison, Hiss's defence continued their researches. They discovered that it was possible to commit "forgery by typewriter". A typewriter was produced capable of reproducing all the idiosyncracies of Woodstock 230099.

As a result of these investigations, Hiss applied for a new trial. This, too, was refused.

At present Hiss is working as a representative for a firm of stationers in New York, still searching for evidence which will prove his innocence. Chambers died on 9th July, 1961.

Few cases have so attracted the attention of the American people, who were almost evenly divided into pro-Hiss and anti-Hiss. Twenty years after Chambers's first appearance before the House Committee it is practically impossible to discuss the case in the United States without rousing strong passions.

BIBLIOGRAPHY :

Witness — Whittaker Chambers (London, 1952).

In the Court of Public Opinion — Alger Hiss (London, 1956).

The Strange Case of Alger Hiss — the Earl Jowitt (London,   ).

A Generation on Trial — Alastair Cooke (London, 1951).

Friendship and Fratricide — Meyer Zeligs (London, 1967).

The Sleeping Truth — Ronald Seth (London, 1968).

CHAPIN, John see under Soviet American Network.

CHARLOTTE see under Vanhoutte, Marie-Louise.

CHURCHILL, Peter (British agent, World War II).

Peter Churchill was one of the early agents of SOE's French Section. In January 1942, he landed from a submarine in the south of France carrying money and instructions to groups of French resistance already existing in the area between Marseilles and Lyons. After making a short reconnaissance, he returned to London.

Not long afterwards he was back again in the south of France, his mission, to act as liaison between the various groups and London and to help with the landings from submarines of wireless operators sent out by London. After another visit to London, he was landed by parachute in August 1942 near Montpellier as leader of a team, to organise and co-ordinate supplies to the Resistance groups in the area.

In November 1942 he was joined by Odette Sansom (q.v.) who landed by felucca, and had been told to report to him en route to Auxerre. Mrs Sansom was a radio operator, and as his own operator was badly in need of a rest, she agreed to help him temporarily while her route was being planned. Eventually he was able to persuade London to allow him to retain her services.

In February, 1943 Churchill returned to London for consultations and returned on 15th April, this time landing by parachute above Annecy. He was met by disquieting news. Mrs Sansom had been approached by a German Abwehr officer, who had recently arrested in Paris a trusted colleague of theirs, Jean Marsac. The German had given his name as Lieutenant Bleicher — which was in fact his real name; he was

a very successful Abwehr officer who intervened in the lives of many of SOE's agents, rarely to their advantage. Apparently Bleicher had been able to convince Marsac that he had genuine proposals for peace negotiations between the anti-Hitler elements and the Allies. All he needed was contact with London, and it was on the strength of this that Marsac put him in touch with Mrs Sansom.

Mrs Sansom was suspicious and cautious, and to play for time had sent a courier back to Marsac with Bleicher. While waiting for advice from London, she took the precaution of making plans for dispersing the team, had sent a newly arrived British agent to safety and had said nothing about Churchill's imminent return.

When he heard her story, Churchill decided that they must get away, but before they could do so, Bleicher reappeared with a posse of Gestapo and seized them both. After two or three weeks in local prisons they were taken to Fresnes. On the way they were able to communicate with one another, and agreed that they should

115

claim to be husband and wife.

After interrogation and some torture, Churchill was transferred to a concentration camp in Germany, from where he was liberated at the end of the war.

Churchill died early in 1972.

BIBLIOGRAPHY :

Of Their Own Choice—Peter Churchill (London, 1952).

The Spirit in the Cage—Peter Churchill (London, 1954).

Duel of Wits—Peter Churchill (London, 1957).

SOE in France—M. R. D. Foot (London, 1966).

CIA — The US Central Intelligence Agency.

The official description is as follows :

CIA Washington DC

Phone 351-1100

Director : Richard Helms

Deputy Director : Vice Admiral Rufus L. Taylor, USN.

Creation and Authority :

For the purpose of co-ordinating the intelligence activities of the several Government departments and agencies in the interest of National Security, the Agency, under the direction of the National Security Council :

1. Advises the National Security Council in matters concerning such intelligence activities of the Government Departments and Agencies as relate to National Security.

2. Makes recommendations to the National Security Council for the co-ordination of such intelligence activities of the Departments and Agencies of the Government as relate to the National Security.

3. Correlates and evaluates intelligence relating to the National Security and provides for the appropriate dissemination of such intelligence within the Government using, where appropriate, existing agencies and facilities.

4. Performs, for the benefit of the existing intelligence agencies such additional services of common concern as the National Security Council determines can be more efficiently accomplished centrally.

5. Performs such other functions and duties as related to intelligence affecting the National

Security as the National Security Council may from time to time direct.

The present Director Richard McGarrah Helms was sworn in on June 30th 1966.

He was born on March 30th, 1913 at St David's, Pennsylvania. He spent the last two years of Prep. School education in France and Germany and is fluent in both languages. As a journalist with United Press in Germany, he covered the 1936 Olympics there and had an interview with Hitler.

Later he became national advertising manager for the Indianapolis "Times" and subsequently became a "model Civil Servant". In 1965 the National Civil Service League gave him an award for "significant contribution to excellence in Government".

He has no politics, and regards himself — and is — a technician.

He was a Naval Officer attached to the OSS (Office of Strategic Services) during World War II. He worked in Germany under Allen Dulles and stayed in Intelligence after the War.

His salary is 30,000 dollars a year.

His predecessors were :
Admiral William Raborn 1965-66
John A. McCone 1961-65
Allen Dulles 1953-61
General Walter Bedell Smith 1950-53

As Director of CIA Helms also acts as Chairman of Board of entire US Intelligence Community —
CIA
Defence Intelligence Agency
National Security Agency (making and breaking of codes)
Intelligence Branches of Military Services
State Department Bureau of Intelligence and Research
Atomic Energy Commission
Federal Bureau of Investigation

In addition to his Deputy— Vice Admiral Taylor — the Director also has a Deputy Director for Intelligence — R. Jack Smith; and a Deputy Director Plans (until 1967 Desmond Fitzgerald) being part of the controlling officials of the CIA's four main divisions :
Plans
Intelligence
Research (Technical and Scientific Matters)

117

Support (Equipment, Logistics, Security, Communications)

Although the CIA was established in order to handle Foreign Operations only, by 1964 home front activities necessitated a special section known as the Domestic Operations Division (DOD) and was established under the direction of Tracey Barnes, who was formerly an OSS Captain during the war and had worked closely with Dulles.

Locations

The Headquarters was built at a cost of 46 million dollars and is "located on a 125 acre tract forming an inconspicuous part of a larger 750 acre government reservation . . . chosen as the one location, among many sites inspected in detail, most adequate for safeguarding the security of CIA operations . . . This site, with its isolation, topography and heavy forestation, permits both economical construction and an added measure of security safeguards."

It is at Langley, Virginia. The Director of CIA occupies the innermost sanctum

(7th floor office, Door 75706).

The present Headquarters was occupied in 1961 and before this the Agency was housed in a complex of buildings at 2430 E Street in the Foggy Bottom section of Washington.

The Headquarters of DOD (Domestic Operations Division) is described as "the huge Madison Avenue-style secret CIA office, a block from the White House". This is 1750 Pennsylvania Avenue, Washington.

There is also a mysterious CIA "Building 213" at the Naval Gun Factory in SE Washington, completed in 1964 at an estimated cost of 10 million dollars.

CIA offices listed throughout the States are :

New York	Miami
Chicago	Pittsburg
Los Angeles	Houston
Boston	St Louis
Detroit	New Orleans
Philadelphia	Seattle
San Francisco	Denver
Minneapolis	

Staff and Recruitment

There are about 10,000 employees at Langley, and this, with branch and overseas employees brings the total to well in excess of 15,000 full-time staff. This does not include the thousands of sub-agents, local informants and CIA-financed cover organisations.

Nearly half of its employees have served for more than 15 years and 75% of its professionals are over 35 years of age.

Educational Backgrounds of Professional Employees :

- 35.5% Sociological Sciences
- 24.3% Business Administration
- 19.7% Physical Sciences and Mathematics
- 10.5% Engineering
- 5.3% Biological and Life Sciences
- 4.7% Intelligence and Military Science.

CIA employees s p e a k and read more than 100 languages.

- 38% of CIA professionals speak one foreign language
- 18% of CIA professionals speak two foreign languages
- 14% of CIA professionals speak three or more foreign languages.

A majority of all CIA employees have baccalaureate degrees, 5% hold Ph.D's. These were awarded by 700 colleges and universities in the USA and 60 universities abroad.

The CIA has 281 major fields of specialization, the six most representative being :

> History
> Political Science
> Business Administration
> Economics
> English
> International Relations

Function

The CIA's missions are accomplished, not by flashy triumphs of espionage, but by an enormous amount of painstaking work.

It is not a secret organisation. CIA has the responsibility of reporting to the President, the Secretaries of State and Defence and other senior national security advisors on events abroad. Its staff reads everything that comes into official Washington and covers the American and foreign press. They distil information into brief, accurate reports, arrange it in context, and present it

119

in concise, non-bureaucratic English. Each top policy officer exercises a priority call on CIA's services, and each is entitled to have his specific interest satisfied in the terms most convenient to him. Research staffs of CIA are supported by extensive source materials and a library of 116,000 volumes.

One typical office requires from its members "sensitivity to developing trends and ability to synthesize from political, economic and military intelligence, support for judgements regarding the intentions and capabilities of foreign govts. . . ." The work of such an office is required by USIB (United States Intelligency Board) which meets regularly every week (and more frequently in crisis) under the chairmanship of the Director of CIA.

The USIB is made up of the advisory councils of CIA : G2, A2, the ON1, the State Dept., the FBI, the Director of Intelligence of AEC, and more recently the Head of the Defence Intelligence Agency (co-ordinating work of the Army, Navy, Air Force Intelligence).

Research staffs and departments must, at all times, be ready for "crash estimates" an example of which is described by the Director of CIA in 1956, Allen Dulles.

"One of these occasions," Dulles writes, "was the Suez crisis of Nov. '56. I had left Washington to go to my voting place in New York when I received early on election eve a message from General Charles B. Cabell, Deputy Director of CIA. He read me a note from the Soviets which had just come over the wires. Bulganin was threatening London and Paris with missile attacks unless the British and French withdrew from Egypt. I asked General Cabell to call a meeting of the intelligence community (USIB) and immediately flew back to Washington. The USIB met through the night and early in the morning I took to President Eisenhower our agreed estimate of Soviet intentions and probable courses of action in this crisis."

This is an example of US involvement in an international crisis and the role played by CIA in advising policy, but similar involvement is more frequent in specific US policy. "Each time the National Security Council is about to consider a certain policy — let us say a policy having to do with Southeast Asia — it immediately calls upon the CIA to present an estimate of the effects such a policy will have," President Truman has written in his memoirs.

But the CIA also has departments where research staff are responsible for surveying foreign scientific literature, space technology and missile systems, and a department of specialists who study the Art and Science of Photogrammerty (critical interpretation and analysis of aerial photographs).

In this latter respect CIA was embarrassed by the U2 incident when Francis Powers (q.v.) was shot down over Russia whilst taking such photographs on May Day, 1960. President Eisenhower assumed responsibility but the organising of it was a CIA project and ushered in a new era in the history of espionage.

On its active side CIA is organised into Regional Divisions, each of which is responsible for espionage in clearly defined geographical areas. It is the headquarters at Langley which analyses and interprets incoming traffic from the field supplied by the Regional Divisions and correlates all information into an overall espionage picture.

It was the Russian Division of CIA which was presented with the problem of keeping an eye on the ballistic missile programme of the Soviet Union. The extreme difficulty of this project was due to the size of the country, the strict security and the consequent great difficulty of getting within range. Based on the experience of the RAF during wartime, tests were made with the latest photographic equipment and high-flying planes.

Bases were applied for under NATO regulations and the CIA obtained facilities in Turkey and Pakistan. A CIA air espionage cell was established in Incirlik, Turkey, under the command of Colonel Shelton, USAF. Powers, the pilot, had been signed on contract to the CIA (signing the American Official Secrets Act) and was required to keep his enlistment a secret. If broken, the penalty is 10 years' imprisonment and/or a fine of ten thousand dollars.

Powers was shot down over Sverdlovak on May 1st, 1960. The CIA had hoped to be covered in this eventuality by equipment fitted to the U2 plane to blow it up if detected, but CIA pilots were not sure of time allowed for their own escape or whether they were to be destroyed with the plane.

The U2 affair placed both the Director of the CIA and his organisation in an embarassing position, and posed the question of the powers of the Director and the role of CIA. "Has he powers over and above the politicians? Is there a serious flaw in the conception and organisation of the CIA for the man at the top must be omnipotent in this field of activity, and politicians untrained in espionage are the last people who should be allowed to interfere?"

More recently the case of the spy ship "Pueblo" has caused similar embarrassment to the U2. Senator Milton Young (Committee member supervising CIA operations) said that he was "greatly disturbed about revelations at 'Pueblo Court of enquiry'". He is pressing for destruction

equipment to be fitted to all intelligence ships.

But Richard Helms, Director of CIA took the unusual step of issuing a statement that the CIA had nothing to do with the "Pueblo". In disavowing the CIA's part in the affair Helms exposed a raw nerve. His Agency, the Pentagon Intelligence Agency and the National Security Agency are constantly engaged in inter-departmental feuding.

There would appear to be considerable influence on the CIA from the American Establishment, and there has been a desire to build up the kind of "Secret" network which exists in Britain. When President Roosevelt originally sought advice on how to centralise US Intelligence in 1940, he sent General Donovan (q.v.) (later head of wartime OSS) to England to study the British system, and when in 1948 for the first time ways were sought to conduct covert operations in peacetime, the initial reaction was not to turn to Congress, but to wealthy friends for money and approval.

The list of distinguished persons who have taken part in CIA cover activities reads like the roster of the American Establishment, that informal coalition of lawyers, businessmen and financiers who silently determine the course of public policy in the United States. Some of the distinguished names are :

MORRIS HADLEY
One time head of Carnegie Foundation permitted his family's Rubicon Foundation to be used as CIA conduit.

ELI WHITNEY
                DEBERVOISE
Former Department High Commissioner in Germany, one of the principal officers of a CIA conduit.

FRANCIS T. PLIMPTON
Former US Deputy Representative to the UN was Director of Foundation for Youth and Student Affairs, a recipient of CIA funds.

ARTHUR AMORY
                HOUGHTON Jr.
President of Metropolitan Museum of Fine Art and Trustee of Rockefeller Foundation.

JOHN HAY WHITNEY
Former Ambassador to Great Britain and owner of New York "Herald Tribune" was founder of Whitney Trust, financed in part by CIA.

Finances

The Agency's spending is monitored by the International division of the Budget Bureau, which controls the CIA's total appropriation but is not in a position to exercise fiscal control over individual operations. As of 1967 the CIA was 1,500,000,000 dollars a year. The total US Intelligence expenditures, including aerial reconnaissance (planes and satellites) comes to 4,000,000,-000 dollars annually. Now CIA expenditure exceeds that of Department of State.

CIA — Divisions

Intelligence

A highly specialised form of scholarship. 80% of its information comes from "open sources": technical magazines, foreign broadcast monitoring, scholarly studies, propaganda journals, and data produced by visible branches of the Government as the US Information Agency. The Intelligence Branch prides itself on its independence from operational problems.

123

Plans

This division is in charge of the CIA's cloak-and-dagger activities. It controls all foreign special operations such as the Bay of Pigs and Guatemala, and it collects all of the agency's covert intelligence through spies and informers overseas. Allen Dulles was first Deputy Director Plans, and Richard Helms in 1962. Both subsequently became directors of CIA.

Research

This division is in charge of technical intelligence. It provides expert assessments of foreign advances in science, technology and a t o m i c weapons. U2 photographic research came under this.

Support

This is the administrative arm of the CIA. It is in charge of equipment, logistics, security and communications. It devises CIA special codes, which cannot be read by other branches of the Government.

World Situation checklists

The CIA provides the President with a daily top-secret checklist of the major world crises. Copies go to the Director of Central Intelligence and the Secretaries of State and Defence. Top-ranking men of the Intelligence Division get to work at 3 a.m. to read the overnight cables and compile it. The checklist was presented to President Kennedy by Major General Clinton and to Johnson by McGeorge Bundy. Special procedures are established to ensure that the President can be reached instantly in the case of emergency. An Indications Centre is manned 24 hours a day by CIA personnel, the Pentagon and the State Department.

Morality of the CIA

A contrast in the approach and basic principles of espionage between the Communist countries (Russian KGB, etc.) and the CIA has been of concern to many Americans, but at basic level there can be little difference. The most extreme action, the bloodiest deed, can be justified on the ground of "higher morality". The Cold War philosophy that the end justifies the means.

Lenin said : "A Communist must be prepared to make every sacrifice and, if necessary, resort to all sorts of schemes and strategems, employ illegitimate methods, conceal the truth." This philosophy, running counter to America's image of itself, is the opposite of speeches made by Presidents Eisenhower, Kennedy and Johnson on the morality of America's purpose. However, as Eisenhower's Director of CIA, Allen Dulles, saw no contradiction in his activities and the dictates of morality. And Richard Bissell, deputy director of plans to Dulles explained that CIA men "felt a higher loyalty and that they are acting in obedience to that higher loyalty". He conceded that agents sometimes took action that was "contrary to their moral precepts" but contended that "the morality of, shall we call it for short, cold war is so infinitely easier that the majority never encountered this as a serious problem".

The threat remains to many Americans that if their vision is to be sustained, they must guard against the easy rationalisation that everything can be excused in defence of the American Way of Life. (CIA's involvement in domestic issues.)

The Russian attitude towards CIA's subversive activities has been set out in **Pravda** which claimed that the CIA planned a major campaign of espionage and ideological subversion against Russia and East European countries. **Pravda** described this as a change of tactics. The CIA habitually used cultural exchange programmes and tourist trips to mask their espionage. But new secret CIA plans now call for provocation and blackmail of citizens of Communist countries aimed at pushing them towards betrayal.

It is not unusual for the CIA to contact Americans about to go behind the Iron Curtain as tourists. In addition to approaching legitimate tourists, the agency has also planted its own tourists behind the Iron Curtain occasionally with disastrous results. For example Air Force Veterans Mark Kaminsky and Harvey C. Bennett, both of whom were caught.

In the American hemisphere it is an open secret that the CIA supplies money and weapons to anti-Castro Cuban factions who operate in the Carribean. Castro has repeatedly accused CIA of raids and plots to overthrow him.

CIA officers sometimes operate overseas under Embassy or commercial cover recruits "agents" locally to feed him information. The most valuable information often comes not from a trusted agent, but from the occasional highly placed defector from the opposition camp.

A delicate aspect of the CIA's work is the care and protection of its colony of important defectors who have fled the Communist world. On a CBS television interview Dulles called defectors "one of the two or three most important sources of intelligence".

The President's Foreign Intelligence Advisory Board.

This was formed largely owing to public unrest over the powers and scope of CIA activities.

It was established by Executive Order 10938 of May 4th, 1961 to advise the President with respect to the objectives and conduct of the foreign intelligence and related activities of the United States which are

required in the interests of foreign policy and not defence and security. It is the duty of the Board to conduct a continuing review and assessment of all functions of the CIA and of other executive departments and agencies having such or similar responsibilities in the foreign intelligence and related fields and to report thereon to the President.

BIBLIOGRAPHY :

US Govt Organisation
　　　　Manual 1968-69.
Central Intelligence Agency— Allen Tully (London, 1962).
The Craft of Intelligence — Allen Dulles (London, 1963).
The Espionage Establishment —Wise & Ross (London, 1968).
A Close Look at CIA — Jeanette Sotokdos in "American Education" May '68.

"CICERO" (World War II).

In 1939, Hitler appointed Franz von Papen, a wily career diplomat, to be German ambassador in Ankara, Turkey. Von Papen's espionage record in World War I — he had been involved with Mata Hari — had not been outstanding. Nevertheless, he

126

was cunning, and a born conspirator; not in the same class as his friend Canaris, but not far behind. The combination of von Papen and his proximity to the Middle Eastern oilfields could only spell excitement for British Intelligence in that theatre.

Von Papen arrived in Ankara accompanied by a large staff of diplomat-spies, and very soon he had Afghanistan, Syria, Iraq, Saudi Arabia, the Lebanon, Egypt, Morocco, Algeria and Tunisia under his surveillance. He achieved his best results in Persia, and was so successful that eventually the British had to intervene with military force.

The most romantic and certainly what could have been the most valuable success he achieved was in the grand tradition of E. Phillips Oppenheim. Nor was it his fault that the information he presented to the Nazi leaders in Berlin should be rejected by them entirely as false, and planted on a too credulous agent. For they actually held in thier hands the decisions of the Teheran Conference, and the details of Operation Overlord, the invasion of Europe.

The British ambassador in Ankara was Sir Knatchbull Hugesson. Sir Knatchbull was also a career diplomat, one who maintained the highest traditions of his profession, whose integrity could never once be called in doubt, an English gentleman.

Sir Knatchbull was employing as his personal valet at this time a man thought to be an Albanian, known to the world now as Cicero, the code-name given him by von Papen, "because his information spoke so eloquently." Whatever else Cicero might have been, he was certainly proficient in his everyday profession.

One evening Cicero called at the house of von Papen's attaché and announced that for a consideration he was prepared to hand over the most secret documents which were communicated to the British ambassador. His "consideration" was so formidable, however, that even von Papen was unable to strike a bargain without consulting Berlin. Nor was Cicero prepared to hand over a sample role of film as a token of good faith.

After a certain amount of haggling, the two parties

127

came to an arrangement, and for several months Cicero did, in fact, supply photostats of the most secret documents, which, as I have already hinted, included the minutes of the Teheran Conference, held in the winter of 1943, at which Churchill, Roosevelt and Stalin met for the first time and decided on plans for 1944, and the details of the plans for the allied invasion of Europe. In exchange the Germans paid him a total of £300,000 in sterling notes.

After a time it began to be apparent to British embassy officials that there was a leakage, and security officers were sent to Ankara to investigate. Cicero read the signs and disappeared.

He had achieved his success by acquiring in a way which has never been discovered, impressions of the keys and the combination of the embassy safe. He was already an expert photographer, so the rest was easy.

Fortunately for the Allies, Berlin was quite convinced that the documents had been planted by the British Secret Service, and decided not to act on them. It would be intriguing to know the reactions of the Nazi leaders when events proved Cicero's documents to be genuine.

The story has a pleasant twist, of which only an expert teller of espionage tales would have thought — the Germans paid Cicero in £5-notes which they had forged themselves. When he tried to pass them after the war in the South American republic to which he had retreated, Cicero was arrested for uttering counterfeit.

When the story by L. G. Moyzisch, the German attaché who had been Cicero's go-between with the Germans, was published in London by Messrs Wingate, doubts were cast on its veracity, and as a renowned ambassador had been named, questions were put to the Foreign Secretary in the House of Commons. Mr Ernest Bevin in his answer was compelled to confess that the story was factual.

A year or two after Moyzisch's account was published, the well-known London publisher André Deutsch published a book entitled **I Was Cicero** by a man who called himself E. Bazna. Internal evidence indicates that whether he was writing under his true name or not, E. Bazna was certainly Cicero. For some years he disappeared from the international scene, but a year or two ago it was reported that he had died in poverty.

BIBLIOGRAPHY :

Operation Cicero — L. G. Moyzisch (London, 1948).

I Was Cicero — E. Bazna (London, 1953).

Memoirs — Walter Schellenberg (London, 1956) chapter 35.

CLEMENS, Hans see under **Felfe, Heinz.**

CLISSMANN, Helmut (German Abwehr agent intended for operations in Eire during World War II).

Helmut Clissmann had made his first trip to Dublin as a student in 1930. He made friends with some of the leaders of the IRA (the illegal Irish Rupublican Army). After he had completed his studies, he returned to Eire and opened branches of the German Academic Exchange Service in Dublin, Cork and Galway. He married Elizabeth Mulcahy, who came from a respectable Republican family.

After a few years he returned to Germany, and at the outbreak of war was Director of the German Academic Exchange Service in Copenhagen. On leaving Eire, he had got in touch with the Abwehr and told them that there were developments taking place in the IRA which could be useful to Germany. Since official policy at this time was no involvement in Irish affairs, he was turned away. In 1940, however, when this was changed, he was called into the Abwehr in the capacity of adviser on Irish affairs. He passed through the Abwehr's training school — which went under the cover of the Special Duty Construction Demonstration Company 800 in Brandenburg — he was selected to undertake a mission to England via Eire.

His mission was connected with Operation Sea Lion, Hitler's plan for invading England. Clissmann was to make his way from Eire to England with the help of the IRA, and there recruit guides in the Kent coastal areas for the Brandenburg Regiment whose role was to capture Dover wearing British uniforms. If he found he could not get to England himself, he was to try to carry out his mission from Eire.

Clissmann, who was accompanied by a radio-operator, was to land in Sligo Bay from the cutter **Anni Braz-Bihen,** navigated by a man called Christian Nissen, well-known in international ocean racing circles, who had made a trip to Eire in an attempt to land saboteurs destined for work in England. This second attempt was also to fail in consequence of the bad weather which was responsible, too, for the postponement of Sea Lion.

Clissmann's next assignment was given him in 1941, when he was ordered by the Abwehr to accompany a small team of three to Eire, there to set up a "listening-post". The trio were to act as contacts between the Irish government and the German Army, should the British and Americans attempt to occupy Eire, and to organise guerilla warfare should this occupation succeed. This operation, given the code-name **Caprey,** was postponed again and again and finally cancelled.

Things began to warm up a little and, finally, in the late summer of 1941, the Germans decided that "something must be done about Ireland", Clissmann was attached to Ribbentrop's special representative for Eire, Dr Veesenmayer, and on his behalf conducted negotiations with the Irish ambassador in Madrid. Again, nothing came of this undertaking. This failure marked the end of Clissmann's employment by the Abwehr on operational missions.

CODES AND CIPHERS

From the beginning of his history, it would seem, man has had a need to convey his thoughts to selected others in such a way that none outside the circle may read what he had to say. This need has developed, over many centuries, the now very extensive subject of codes and ciphers.

The categories of people who have to make secret communications are many and various. Outstanding among them are the fighting services, the diplomats, and, naturally, spies.

Ciphers range from signs and pictures that guide the tramp and gipsy to the ordinary cipher writing used for amusement or business, the cryptograms of criminals and those much more sophisticated ones used by governments and diplomats.

There are numerical and alphabetical ciphers, syllable and word ciphers, stencil and blackline, and numerous others. In the numerical, letters of the alphabet are replaced by one or more fixed numbers. In the simplest letter cipher, one letter stands for another. In the syllabic system, certain syllables in the written message have a value of their own, previously arranged between the correspondents. In word ciphers, the writing consists of two parts, the second of which contains the key. In stencil ciphering, a stencil is laid over the paper.

If there is a need on the part of some to communicate in code and cipher, there is the counter-need in others to decode these secret messages. Governments lead in both categories. If a government can know exactly what another government, with whom it is negotiating or towards whom it is hostile, is committing to secret writing it can be both forewarned and forearmed. So there are code breakers, men who, without

knowing the key to the code or cipher, can solve it. The existence of code breakers has automatically meant the invention of more complicated and sophisticated codes, which have become progressively more sophisticated and complicated as the code-breakers have kept up with them. The highest-grade diplomatic codes of the twentieth century are encoded and decoded by machines. A famous example is the Japanese so-called Purple code, which was broken by American cryptanalystic early in World War II who were able to similate the Purple Machine (q.v.) by which it was encoded and decoded.

Codebreaking has provided many exciting episodes in history. Most famous among the codebreaking organisations are the British Room 40, which operated in World War I, and the American Black Chamber which was brought into being by H. O. Yardley (q.v.) in the 1920's. The exploits of Room 40 included the interception and decoding of the famous Zimmermann Telegram (q.v.) which brought America into World War I, while interceptions of German Admiralty signals and their decoding led to the naval Battle of the Dogger Bank in 1915. Yardley was the first to discover the principles of Japanese coding procedures, which gave the American government a distinct advantage in the Naval Disarmament Conference of 1922, while the successor of the Black Chamber, the Signal Intelligence Service, solved the Japanese diplomatic codes in the period leading up to Pearl Harbor, which enabled Washington to read the secret reports of the Japanese negotiators to Tokyo.

Besides the government and the armed forces, important commercial undertakings also use codes for communicating their secrets. These commercial codes are likely to be less complicated. Nevertheless, in the highly competitive industrial world of the twentieth century, the use of codes is expanding rapidly.

After the diplomatic codes, clearly the most important use of codes and ciphers is by spies. The codes used by spies must be based on simpler principles than diplomatic codes, for the simple reason that the spy cannot carry around with him a bulky key or a cipher machine. He must be able to commit his code to memory, and various codes have been devised which allows this to be done. Perforce, however, though complicated to the uninitiated, because their principles have to be so simple that the agent can memorise them, they are easily solved by the codebreaker. The use of such codes can only be justified by the hope that they will not fall into the hands of the super-codebreakers.

The code most used by agents during World War II was that known as a **double transformation type.** It was simple enough for the agent to be able to memorise it; yet complicated enough to take the code-breakers several weeks to decipher it.

Each agent had his own personal key phrase. e.g.
THANKS FOR NOTHING
The letters were numbered off from left to right beginning with the first letter of the alphabet as follows :

```
T  H A N K S F  O  R  N  O  T  H I  N G
15 4 1 6 7 14 2 11 13 9 12 16 5 6 10 3
```
The message was written down across the page, one letter under one figure, etc.

```
15  4  1  8  7 14  2 11 13  9 12 16  5  6 10  3
 R  E  N  D  E  Z  V  O  U  S  T  H  I  R  D  F
 R  I  D  A  Y  I  N  M  O  N  T  H  U  N  D  E
 R  C  L  O  C  K  A  T  N  A  I  N  R  A  I  L
 W  A  Y  S  T  A  T  I  O  N  A  T  S  E  V  E
 N  P  M
```

Begin with column 1, the letters read downwards are written across the page, thus:

NDLYMVNATFELEEICAPIURSRNALEYCT etc.

These letters are then written across the page under the figures, and the resulting columns again read downwards:

```
15  4  1  8  7 14  2 11 13  9 12 16  5  6 10  3
 N  D  L  Y  M  V  N  A  T  F  E  L  E  E  I  C
 A  P  I  U  R  S  R  N  A  E  E  Y  C  T
```

Etc.

After the second reading, the letters are split up into groups of five, and transmitted by morse code.

Cryptology is a fascinating subject, and if any reader wishes to know more about it, he can do no better than consult a truly monumental work called **THE CODE-BREAKERS** by David Kahn.

BIBLIOGRAPHY :

The Codebreakers — David Kahn (London, 1966).

COHEN, Elie (Israeli agent, post World War II).

Cohen was a fervent Zionist from his youth until the day he died. He lived only for the furtherance of the Zionist cause, and it was in pursuit of the devouring passion, that he was recruited in Israel's intelligence in 1959.

After several months of rigorous training he was given a new Moslem identity and a name to go with it — Kamil Amin Taabes. He was then sent to Syria to study the Syrian dialect and accent.

The cover-story devised for "Taabes" was that his family had emigrated to Argentina. Cohen already spoke fairly good Spanish. At the end of 1960, he was sent to Buenos Aires to establish his new persona. A half million Arab immigrants, among them thousands of Syrians, live in Buenos Aires, and it was hoped that Cohen would find among them someone who could provide him with political contacts in Damascus.

He stayed six months in Argentina, and then returned to Israel taking with him numerous letters of introduction to Arabs in Syria and the Lebanon.

In Tel Aviv he was given his final instructions. He was to work in Damascus, and his mission was to supply Israel with all the information he could gather, first, about the Syrian army, its strength, equipment, organisation, personnel and activities inside Syria; and second, about the Syrian economic situation. He was to send urgent information by radio, and was provided with a miniature transmitter the size of a cigarette packet, hidden in the double bottom of an electric mixer. He would use an ordinary radio set for a receiver.

On 1st January, 1962, Cohen boarded the **Astonia** at Genoa, bound for Beirut. From there he made his way to Damascus, and established himself in an apartment in a large block opposite the Syrian army headquarters.

Cohen sent his first message to Tel Aviv at 9 p.m. on the evening of 12th February, 1962.

In his role as Taabes, he posed as a moderately well-off young businessman who had made money abroad, and had patriotically returned to invest it in his own country. His letters of introduction proved very useful, and within a short time he had a growing circle of Syrian friends.

One of the outstanding features of Cohen's operation was the speed with which he established himself in Damascus. Within weeks he was sending to Tel Aviv a surprising volume of accurate and very valuable information. He had even toured the Syrian-Israel border with a nephew of the Syrian chief of staff, which gave him important intelligence regarding Syrian strong points, gun-sites, the type of equipment available to the Syrian army and so on.

After six months, he was recalled to Tel Aviv for consultations. On his return he gave a party, to which another guest brought George Seif, chief of the radio and press sections of the Syrian Ministry of Propaganda and Information. The two men subsequently became very friendly, and Seif would spend hours in Cohen's apartments relating anecdotes about the regime, all of which were grist to the spy's mill.

Seif was a great womaniser, and on some of his activities in this field, he was accompanied by Colonel Salim Hatoum, commander of the crack Syrian paratroopers. Seif brought

Hatoum to Cohen's apartment, and Cohen thereafter made it available for the amorous adventures of the two men.

Hatoum's opinion of the men in power was not flattering, and he was not reticent in expressing his views. He also talked freely about the army and its strength. He played a leading part in the coup of 9th March, 1963, which put the Baath party in power. Cohen was thus drawn into the group of the men at the centre of these changes.

Among these was the appointment of El-Hafez to the post of Minister of the Interior. El-Hafez had been military attaché in Buenos Aires during Cohen's stay there, and, in fact, had advised him to return to Syria. As Minister of the Interior, El-Hafez was responsible for the Syrian counter-espionage service.

Shortly after the coup, at an even wilder than usual party in Cohen's apartment, Hatoum introduced another staff officer, Colonel Salah Dalli, prominent in the Baath party. From now on Dalli also used the apartment, and appears to have been as indiscreetly talkative as Hatoum and Seif.

To maintain his Taabes role, in 1963 Cohen paid a visit to Buenos Aires. He returned with a cheque for 10,000 dollars for Baath party funds, and a mink coat for the wife of the party leader— provided of course, by Israeli intelligence.

Between February and October 1964, on three separate occasions Cohen was provided by his friends with the opportunity of seeing at first hand, the growing strength of the Syrian army along the Israeli border. From these visits he obtained vital and invaluable information.

All this time he was transmitting twice daily to Tel Aviv. Unknown to him, however, his transmitter was causing interference to the transmitters and receivers of a number of foreign embassies in the vicinity. The Indian embassy found this interference extremely annoying and towards the end of 1964 made a complaint to the Syrian authorities.

An investigation was carried out, and though nothing unusual was discovered, the interference continued, which forced the Syrian counter-espionage to conclude that someone was using an illegal transmitter in the area. After consulting Russian technicians working in Damascus, the Syrians bought a mobile Direction-Finding unit from Moscow.

Cohen had two transmitters, both battery powered. The Syrians discovered by chance that the Russian D/F-ing equipment gave its best readings of the interference when there was an electricity blackout. This naturally led them to the conclusion that the illegal transmitter was battery powered, and they arranged for black-outs to be made.

One of these was for the early morning hours of 21st January, 1965. Unfortunately, because Cohen had no lights burning in his apartment at the time, he was unaware of the black-out, and he transmitted his latest messages happily to Tel Aviv.

Nor did he have the opportunity of discovering the black-out when he switched on his mains receiver, for at that moment Syrian counter-espionage agents burst into his apartment. He was taken so completely by surprise that

he had no time to jump from his fourth storey window, as he had always planned to do were he in danger of discovery.

Hundreds of people, most of them innocent, were rounded up in the weeks following Cohen's arrest. Among them was George Seif, who did not have the immunity enjoyed by Hatoum and Dalli.

Cohen, after hours of interrogation and torture, during which he gave away nothing, was brought to trial on 28th February, 1965. On 9th March the trial ended, and on 8th May sentence was pronounced — death. The president of the military court which tried him was Colonel Dalli and a member was Colonel Hatoum.

At 3.30 a.m. on 19th May, Cohen was publicly executed in the main square of Damascus, Martyrs' Square. Ten thousand people filed by his body before it was cut down and buried in the Jewish cemetery in Damascus.

BIBLIOGRAPHY :

The Spy From Israel — Ben Dan (London, 1969).

COPLON, Judith (American Communist who spied for Russia, post World War II).

In December 1949 it came

to the knowledge of the FBI through a thoroughly reliable source, that the Soviet Embassy in Washington had come into possession of a number of most secret documents emanating from the FBI itself and from the Department of Justice. The information was incomplete and the only idea that could be given of the nature of the documents was that they contained particulars of certain known foreign agents, diplomats and American Communists. The information also gave an indication that the supplier of the documents might be a woman who worked in the Foreign Registration office of the Department of Justice, and who had formerly been employed in the office of the same Department in New York.

Only one woman in the Foreign Registration Office in Washington fitted this description and the FBI began investigations to eliminate or convict her.

Judith Coplon was a college graduate of twenty-seven, attractive to look at, keen on her work which dealt with external and internal security matters, and marked out for promotion. This came her way when she was appointed to a £1,750-a-year post in May 1948, after she had received the commendation of the Attorney General for a piece of brilliant political analysis.

She came of good family. Her father was a well-to-do manufacturer, who was something of a philanthropist. Mrs Coplon was quiet and retiring.

Judith had formerly lived in an apartment at 2634 Tunlaw Road, Washington, DC, where her landlord and neighbours described her as a quiet, intellectual type who never brought men home. Recently, to be nearer her work, she had moved to a one-roomed apartment in Jefferson Hall, McClean Gardens.

After a month of probing and surveillance all that the FBI could discover was that Judith saw many men.

The following week, however, Judith Coplon asked her chief, William Foley, to let her see the most secret report on Russian agents in America, as she needed it in her work. Foley knew that she was being watched by the FBI and stalled, and immediately telephoned the FBI.

J. Edgar Hoover, the FBI chief, called on Foley, bringing with him a faked letter marked most secret, in which it was stated that three Soviet agents working in the Amtorg (the Russian Trade Organisation in America) were really FBI agents, who were shortly to be submitted to a loyalty test. Hoover asked Foley to give this letter to Judith and ask her to work on the case, arguing that if she were really in league with the Russians she would warn her friends.

This was done. On Friday, 14th January, 1949, Judith asked her chief to be allowed to leave at the end of the morning, so that she might have a long week-end. Foley gave her the permission she sought and when she took the one o'clock train to New York, she was surreptitiously accompanied by four FBI agents.

Arrived at the Pennsylvania Station, Judith went to the ladies' room, where she stayed three-quarters of an hour, and when she came down put her bag in a cloak-room, visited a book-stall, and then went to a drug-store where she ate a sandwich at a counter. After this she went by underground to 191st Street, Manhattan.

It was dark when she ar-

rived there, and the street lamps were already lit. She walked down the street for about ten minutes, and then stopped and looked in the window of a jeweller's shop. She stayed looking in the window for about seven minutes, clearly employing an old, well-worn espionage trick —watching what was going on in the street in the reflections in the glass.

Presently a well-dressed, dark, well-built but short man appeared. He did not speak to her, but when he walked away, she followed him, and they went into a restaurant, where they occupied the same alcove. The FBI agents who had followed them in, were unable to hear what they said, however, because they continuously fed nickels into a juke-box, the noise from which covered their conversation.

They stayed in the restaurant for about an hour, during which Judith talked animatedly, and she was still in an excited condition when they left and took the underground again.

As the train was about to pull out of 125th Street station, the man suddenly got to his feet, squeezed through the closing doors, and was away with only one FBI man after him. His security was good. He did not know he was being followed, but he was leaving nothing to chance. By taking a series of taxis, trams and buses he succeeded in throwing off the FBI agent.

From his appearance the FBI men were convinced that this man was a Slav, and that he might possibly be a member of the staff of the Soviet consulate-general in New York. Working on this assumption agents were posted outside the Russian offices, and at ten o'clock they saw their man entering the building. An hour later he came out, and took the underground to his apartment on 64 West 108th Street, where, through the porter, he was identified as a Russian engineer working for the United Nations Architectural Department, going by the name of Valentine Gubitchev.

The FBI now advised Foley to make it impossible for Judith Coplon to have access to the most secret documents, and she was transferred to another office. She did not go without demanding to be told why, only to receive the reply that her new job had to be done, and that she was the person most suited to do it.

When she had accepted the inevitable, however, she was undeterred. Every day she visited her old office, and gave much needed assistance to her successor, in this way still having access to the files.

It was on 18th February that she did make another move. Repeating her previous procedure, she took the two o'clock train to New York. This time the New York agents took with them a woman agent, who followed her to the ladies' room, and then on to the underground.

The woman agent, accompanied by a male agent, followed her, and she led them once more down the street. She turned out of Broadway into one of the side-streets and it was there that Gubitchev met her. They were together only a very few minutes, and though it was too dark to see, the agents were convinced that papers had been passed. Once more the man evaded pursuit.

On 3rd March, Judith again asked for the half-day off and went to New York to spend

139

the week-end with her father and mother. During the following week she asked if she could see some of the most secret files. Foley asked her if she remembered the three Amtorg men who were FBI agents acting as Soviet agents. He now had more information on the case, he said.

This information included a letter from J. Edgar Hoover to the Assistant Attorney General, purporting to set out that Amtorg had recently been making inquiries about some instruments called geophones which measure blast pressures. A few of these geophones had been manufactured in connection with the original atom tests. Mr Hoover asked the Attorney General's advice as to what would constitute a violation on the part of Amtorg.

The letter was a trap devised to settle once and for all whether Judith Coplon was passing information to Soviet agents.

Very shortly after her interview with Foley, she went again to New York. Once more there was a repetition of all that had happened on previous occasions, with only a very few unimportant vari-

ations. But this time the FBI struck. Both of the quarries tried to escape, and almost succeeded. At last they were arrested at 16th Street and Third Avenue.

They were taken to FBI headquarters in New York and searched. Gubitchev had on him one hundred and twenty-five dollars, but nothing incriminating. Judith had nothing on her person, but in her handbag was found a sealed advertising circular for nylons. When this was opened the agents discovered inside copies or résumés of thirty-four most secret documents, including Hoover's letter to the Attorney General about Amtorg, and a covering note explaining that she had been unable to get a copy or even more than a quick glance at the FBI's most secret report on Soviet and Communist intelligence activities in America.

Judith denied everything; but the evidence against her was too strong. At her trial she stated that she was in love with Gubitchev whom she had first met in the museum of Modern Art. He had told her he was married, but she hoped to become his wife as soon as he got his divorce. The jury were not sympathetic to her and the verdict was, more or less, inevitable.

She was found guilty under the Treason Act of stealing Government documents and of conspiracy against the United States and imprisoned. Gubitchev was deported.

BIBLIOGRAPHY :

The Web of Subversion — James Burnham (New York, 1954).
Forty Years of Soviet Spying — Ronald Seth (London, 1965).

COURIERS.

In normal espionage organisations a network is comprised of a number of cells. In each cell there are a number of agents, each of whom has a specific task to perform spying-wise.

At the head of a network, is a network chief. He coordinates the efforts of the network, and knows who the agents serving under him are and what their tasks entail. In a network which has good security, none of the working agents should know the identity of their chief, so that, if they are caught they cannot compromise him and through him other cells in the network.

The chief maintains contact with the agent by means of a courier. A courier is a go-between between the chief, and either the cell-leader or each individual agent. He, or she, collects the individual's reports and carries to each agent the chief's instructions.

In effect, the courier is a messenger. He takes no other part in the spying activities of the network for which he works. On the other hand, his role is of the greatest importance, far exceeding the functions of the usual messenger-boy.

He has it in his power to compromise the whole network, for he alone, besides the chief, knows the identities of all, or most of the agents — according to the type of cell organisation employed — and of the **chief.** He, and he alone, is in a position to compromise the chief, unless the chief employs a go-between between him and the courier, which is not a widespread practice.

The courier, then, is a Number One target for counter-espionage agencies. To avoid their snares he must devise a method of operating that is as foolproof as possible, and his appreciation of security and his practice of it must be one hundred per cent.

Indeed, his role is probably more arduous than that of any other member of the network.

Although couriers have been replaced to some extent by other means of contact since the end of World War II, they still play an occasional role, particularly in the Russian organisation, eg in the Gordon Lonsdale case (q.v.).

COVER-NAME.

When an agent goes into the Field — ie, when he embarks on his actual operation — he almost invariably assumes the identity of either a real or fictitious person. In doing so he adopts a name to fit his new character; if he is impersonating a real person, even if that person is dead, he adopts that persons name; alternatively he takes a fictitious name. Both are known as his **cover-name.**

Thus Gordon Lonsdale was the cover-name of the Russian spy, K. T. Molody, the director of the Portland spy ring.

The term should not be confused with the **Operational Name** of an agent. An agent is allotted an operational name by which he is always referred to by his chiefs, the members of his own network, if they have cause to use it and know it, in order to identify the agent without using either his own name or his cover-name. Thus Alek was the operational name of the British-Russian agent Alan Nunn May.

An operational name is also accorded to a network.

CUT-OUTS.

A cut-out or go-between is an intermediary, employed to make contact between the chief of a network and an agent or a potential agent or supplier of information. He is used to protect the identity of agents and others from becoming known outside a very restricted circle.

D

DAVIES, Henry see under **Pinkerton, Allan.**

DEFOE, Daniel (Father of the British Secret Service).

One morning in the spring of 1704, Robert Harley, Lord Treasurer of England, received a long communication which he had been awaiting for some time. Though it was unsigned, he knew who the writer was — an ex-convict who had recently been released from Newgate Prison at Harley's intercession with Queen Anne. The document described in great detail — it can still be read in the original in the Manuscript Room at the British Museum — a scheme which would allow Her Majesty's Ministers to keep themselves fully informed of what men and women in all walks of life and in all parts of the country thought of them and their acts. It was, in fact, a blueprint of a secret service which would cover the whole of Great Britain.

Harley was just the man to whom such a scheme might appeal, and the formulator of the scheme could not have found a more sympathetic ear. Harley liked secret scheming, and took great pleasure in wielding power unseen. One of his contemporaries, Earl Cowper, said of him, "He loved tricks, even where not necessary, but from an inward satisfaction he took in applauding his own cunning. If any man was ever born under the necessity of being a knave he was."

As he read through the document, Harley realised at once that to have at his disposal the services of an intelligence organisation such as that described would be extremely useful to him. It was almost overwhelming in its comprehensiveness. It would provide lists of all the gentry and families of rank in each county and note where their political sympathies lay. It would report on the character and morals of the clergy and local magistrates. The strength of the political parties would be a subject of the most searching investigation. There would be a widely flung intelligence system in Scotland.

Earl Cowper might with equal justification have applied the words he spoke about Harley to the author of the scheme, Daniel Defoe, who was to achieve lasting fame with a novel he was to write some fifteen years later, entitled, **The Life and Strange Surprising Adventures of Robinson Crusoe.** Up to 1704 his life had been troublesome and adventurous. Beginning as a very successful City merchant, he had made a considerable fortune while he was still in his early twenties. Then he had joined the Duke of Monmouth's Rebellion in 1685, and had narrowly escaped death at the hands of Bloody Jeffreys, a fate which overtook three of his former school-friends who had the misfortune to be caught.

His extravagance lost him a large part of his fortune, bad business deals, some of them very shady, lost him even more, and eventually, when he was thirty-three, he had been made a bankrupt. Powerful friends, however, came to his aid, and through a series of extraordinary events he became a personal friend and private adviser of William III,

whom he greatly admired. He had the gift of writing political pamphlets, and it was one of these which was responsible for his being gaoled shortly after Queen Anne came to the throne. While serving his sentence, Harley had found him, talked to him, been impressed, and persuaded Anne to release him.

Defoe was a man of great energy and drive, and once having set his hand to a project, he drove forward until he succeeded or was overcome. So, when Harley asked him to set about organising his intelligence service he began laying his plans at once, beginning by making an experimental journey in the south-eastern counties of England in the summer of 1704. In July he wrote to Harley, "I firmly believe this journey may be the foundation of such an intelligence as never was in England." A belief which was proved very soon to have its counterpart in fact.

Within a short time, by making similar journeys which took him throughout the whole of England, he had covered the country with a network of agents, whom he chose for their intelligence, their understanding of what was required, and their ability to carry out instructions secretly.

At the beginning of the eighteenth century travel was so difficult that the remoter parts of England were farther away from London than New York is in these days of air travel. News of events happening in Newcastle did not reach the Government in London until several days after they had occurred, often not at all. If the Government was to be a strong Government, it must know quickly what people thought of it, and have knowledge of any plots for its overthrow.

Defoe's agents reported immediately to his central office in London all anti-Government sentiments and the identity of those who voiced them. He instructed them to report things which might seem unimportant, for he recognised that it is the cumulative effect of intelligence which is the medium to its achievements. Soon his tentacles reached out secretly outside the boundaries of England, to Paris, Toulon,

Brest and Dunkerque, where he set up branch offices.

Defoe was a natural spy. The methods which he introduced are still used by intelligence services all over the world. He insisted that the true identity of his agents should be absolutely secret. Men must not know, indeed must not have the slightest suspicion that a man is a spy. If he is going to do his work with any success, the spy must be able to move openly and freely. He must appear to be an ordinary harmless citizen, and if he is a stranger or foreigner he must appear to have a very sound reason for being where he is and doing what he is doing.

When Defoe was travelling about the country organising his network, he used the cover of travelling salesman or merchant. He did actually buy and sell goods. And this is a cover still widely used by secret services.

He was well-known for his political writings, so it was essential that when he went on his journeys no one should know that he was Daniel Defoe. He, therefore, adopted two operational names,

Alexander Goldsmith and Claude Guilot.

His cover stories were always carefully thought out. His methods for getting his information to London were always secret and reliable.

Defoe's greatest personal triumph was achieved in connection with the Union of Scotland and England. The Scots and English crowns had been united when James VI of Scotland succeeded Elizabeth I as James I of England, but the two countries had remained two separate entities. No serious attempt was made to unite the two administrations until the reign of Queen Anne. By 1706 negotiations between the two Governments had been set out in an Act of Union. The two parliaments had to ratify this act, and though there was unlikely to be any opposition from the English Parliament, trouble was expected from the Scots parliament.

Defoe had realised this for some time, and had been trying to persuade Harley to allow him to go to Edinburgh to see at first hand what was happening. For some time Harley ignored this request,

but at last in the autumn of 1706 he agreed. Then he insisted that Defoe should depart with such haste that he gave him no time to discuss several important facets of the mission. Indeed, there was only just time for Defoe to "kiss the Queen's hand" before setting out.

Harley's instructions to him were definitive. He was to go to Scotland not merely as an agent to find out what was happening, but to be active in furthering the English cause. He was to take the greatest care that he did not give the impression that he had come to Scotland as anyone's agent. "You came there on your own business and out of love to the country," Harley told him.

Defoe was to report to Harley once a week, but his letters must be unsigned. Harley would meet expenses out of his own pocket, though Defoe would have liked to have been paid out of public funds. He had already had experience of Harley's uncertainty and dilatoriness in money affairs, and knew that this might embarrass him — as, indeed, it did.

Defoe set out on 13th September, travelling under the name of Alexander Goldsmith until he had crossed the border. Then he reverted to his own name, arguing that if he were ever discovered and denounced operating under a fictitious name he would be done irreparable harm. His cover stories were numerous, and suited to the company he was in. To merchants he made out that he had come to build ships, or explore the possibility of starting a glass factory or a salt works, as he foresaw a ready fortune to be made by Scots merchants as soon as the Act was ratified. To a merchant from Aberdeen he was interested in the woollen trade; to one from Glasgow he was a fish-merchant. In lower company, he had come north to escape the results of financial embarrassment. To ministers of the Kirk he was about to embark on a new metrical version of the Psalms. To ministers of the Government he was preparing to write a **History of the Union,** and, as he wrote to Harley, "Under the pretence of writing my history I have everything told me". (He did, in fact, write his **History,** which was published in 1709.)

When he let it be known that he wished to buy a house and land, and settle in Edinburgh with his family, the Commissioners sought his advice in planning the arrangements for operating the trade between the two countries.

At last on 18th January, 1707, the Scots Parliament ratified the Act, and the English parliament followed suit. It received the Royal Assent on 6th March.

When Defoe heard that the Royal Assent had been given, he asked Harley to be allowed to return home. He was fully justified in making this request, for no other single Englishman could have claimed truly to have done more by his own efforts to make the Union an accomplished fact. His work on this mission was a tremendous contribution to the welfare of his country and deserved to be specially rewarded. But as often happens to successful agents, he was ignored, and it was only after several months of pleading, when at last he was penniless, that Harley recalled him.

147

Harley's dismissal in 1714 deprived Defoe of the protection of his master, which in those days, could be a very serious matter for a protégé. But Defoe was not the man to be worried for long by such a turn of events.

He wrote to Lord Chief Justice Parker that if the new Ministry could use his services, he would be pleased to carry on. Parker submitted Defoe's offer to Lord Townshend, the chief Minister, who knew of Defoe's espionage abilities, and offered him the mission of gaining control secretly of the newspapers antagonistic to the Government. Defoe accepted, and was soon in a position in which he could stop any news harmful to the Government from being printed. Very soon other anti-Government papers were asking his advice, and little by little he was given wider and wider powers until the editors were under a promise to him not to publish anything he vetoed.

Defoe carried on this work for several years, and was never once the object of suspicion, until on 25th October, 1718, one of the editors, Mist, of the Jacobite newspaper

The Journal, published a letter criticising the Government's handling of Anglo-Spanish relations without submitting it first to Defoe. When Mist was summoned before the Secretaries of State, he tried to put the blame onto Defoe. Defoe was, in the event, exonerated, but the incident caused a rift between him and Mist, which was not healed until Mist apologised several weeks later.

In June 1720, Mist repeated his indiscretion, and this time was imprisoned. From now on, it would seem, Defoe gradually relinquished his connections with the Government. He was now sixty, which was a considerable age for the eighteenth century.

He lived on for another ten years. Shortly before his death he suddenly disappeared. On 12th August he sent to his son-in-law a letter headed, "Written about two miles from Greenwich, Kent." In it he complained of "the blow I received from a wicked, perjur'd and contemptible enemy," and signed it "Your Unhappy D.F."

Though they searched for

him, his family were unable to find him, and never saw him again. He died in a cheap lodging-house in Ropemaker's Alley in the parish of St Giles-in-Cripplegate on 26th April, 1731, and was buried in Bunhill Fields. No one followed his hearse; none of his family or his friends knew he was dead.

The only notice of his passing appeared some time later in a small journal edited by his son-in-law. It was brief and cold : "A few days ago died Daniel Defoe Senior, a person well known for his numerous writings."

The reason for his disappearance, it has recently been discovered, was the re-emergence of an old money trouble. **Robinson Crusoe** and his other novels had made him well-off; he could have easily paid off the ancient debt; but in his old age he had grown miserly.

BIBLIOGRAPHY :

Defoe — James Sutherland (London, 1937).

DEGRAIS, Francois (Outstanding seventeenth century French secret agent).

Marie Madeline Marguerite, Marquise de Brinvillers, was the daughter of Dreux d'Aubray, civil lieutenant of Paris, and was married in 1651 to the Marquis de Brinvillers. Introduced to Godin de Sainte-Croix, a cavalry officer, she became his mistress in 1659. To stop the scandal, d'Aubray had Sainte-Croix imprisoned in the Bastille on a **lettre de cachet.** There he acquired the art of poisoning from an Italian and on his release persuaded the Marquise to poison her father, and her two brothers in order that he and his mistress might inherit the whole of the family wealth.

When the crimes were detected, the Marquise managed to escape to Germany, where she took refuge in a convent near Liége, outwardly repentant. The French government, however, were determined on her punishment, and detailed their outstanding agent, Francois Degrais, a "good looking, insinuating man of gentlemanly exterior", to go after her and bring her back.

Degrais went to Liége in the disguise of an abbé, and obtained admission to the convent. Before long he had established excellent relations with the Marquise, and one day suggested that they should drive out into the country together and have breakfast together at a country inn. She agreed, and when the carriage arrived at the inn she was arrested by a number of Degrais' officers.

During the journey to Paris the Marquise tried to kill herself on two or three occasions. Degrais instructed one of his men to profess sympathy with the Marquise to stop further attempts. The man was successful and won the confidence of the Marquise to such an extent that she gave him letters to pass on to her friends. When these were later perused they were found to contain what amounted to a confession to the three murders.

She was tried and found guilty. Mme de Sévigné, the famous French seventeenth century letter-writer, recorded "She died as she had lived — with resolution. On the way to the scaffold she asked only that the executioners might walk between her and Degrais, the scoundrel who had betrayed her."

BIBLIOGRAPHY :
Mme de Sévigné, her Letters
150

and her World — A. Stanley (London, 1946).

DE HAAS (Dutch agent, World War II) see under **Giskes, Col H. J.**

DEHNERT, Josef see under **Linse, Dr, The Kidnapping of.**

DELDONCK, Lucelle see under **McKenna, Marthe.**

DELILAH
(Agent provocateur).

The first famous female spy of the **femme fatale** type was Delilah. Round about the year 1161 BC, the Israelites, having displeased Jehovah again, found themselves under the domination of the Philistines. One of the Judges of Israel at this time, was a man called Samson, who had been born at the intervention of an angel to a mother who, after many years of marriage had proved barren. Announcing to her that she should at last have a child, and that it should be a boy dedicated to Jehovah, the angel also told her that Jehovah would use him as the instrument for throwing off the Philistine yoke.

Samson was something of a Hercules. As a youth he performed great feats of strength, and as he grew to manhood he directed his strength against the Philistines. When he reached marriageable age, much to his parents' surprise, he told them that there was a certain Philistine girl he wished to marry. They did not know that Samson was acting under the direction of Jehovah, and tried to dissuade him. But he persisted, and his father eventually gave his consent.

Though the Philistines might have had much the same objections to the match as Manoah, for intermarriage between people of different religions was not encouraged, they saw other possibilities in such an alliance, and allowed it to go forward.

At the wedding feast Samson set the Philistines a riddle. If they guessed the answer within seven days he would give them thirty sheets and thirty changes of raiment; if not, they were to give him thirty changes of raiment and thirty sheets.

The riddle was a difficult one and no one was able to guess the answer. The Philis-tines, therefore, came to Samson's wife and threatened that if she did not discover the answer for them, they would take reprisals against her family. She succeeded in cajoling the answer out of her husband; and when, at the appointed time, the Philistines came with it to Samson, he was so angry that he killed thirty of them to provide the thirty changes of raiment in settlement of the wager, and deserting his wife, returned to his father's house.

When the wound to his vanity had healed, however, he decided to return to his wife. But when he arrived, he found that his father-in-law, believing he hated her because of his desertion of her, had given her as a concubine to Samson's best friend; and Samson refused to be consoled with his wife's younger sister, whom his father-in-law urged him to take in exchange.

More angry than ever, Samson caught three foxes, tied lighted torches to their tails and stampeded them among the ripe standing crops of the Philistines, destroying not only them but the olive-yards and vine-yards as well.

151

When the Philistines made inquiries and discovered the reason, they killed Samson's wife and her father. This enraged Samson more than ever, and he killed large numbers of the Philistines.

Then the Philistines sent three thousand men to Judah to fetch Samson and bring him in chains to Timnath. The men of Judah, frightened by this show of strength, went to Samson and bound him with new ropes and handed him over to the Philistines. They, seeing him helpless, as they thought, taunted him, and this roused his anger to such a pitch that he broke the ropes binding him, and with the jaw-bone of an ass, which was conveniently handy, as his only weapon, he killed a thousand of them, and the rest fled.

Samson now increased his operations against the enemies of his people, performing prodigies of strength against them; and the matter came to the point where it was clear that something out of the ordinary would have to be done if they were ever to rid themselves of the disastrous results of the giant's turbulent strength.

Now, it was quite clear that Samson was more than ordinarily susceptible to female beauty. Whether they actually put Delilah directly in his way is a matter for debate; but the results of her intervention being what they were, there is little point in devoting time to a solution of this aspect of Samson's downfall. He saw her, was attracted by her beauty and succumbed to her physical charms.

Delilah was certainly, from the moment of her first physical contact with Samson, an agent of the Philistine leaders, charged with the Mission of discovering the secret of her lover's strength. Samson was a Judge, or ruler, of Israel, and therefore cannot have been devoid of a certain measure of intelligence. He must have known Delilah's secret role, otherwise he would not have given false answers to her early attempts to wrest his secret from him. He knew quite well that he had been chosen by Jehovah as the instrument for freeing his people from the domination of the heathen conqueror, and must have appreciated that this freedom was concentrated chiefly in him.

The writer of the account in the Book of Judges excuses his surrender to Delilah's daily importunities by suggestion that she had wearied him "so that his soul was vexed unto death". But there can be little excuse for his not leaving her as soon as he had evidence of her intentions — and this she had supplied unequivocally on more than one occasion — and making certain that the temptation of her sexual charms was physically removed by setting a great distance between them. It is possible, however, that his refusal to do this was due not entirely to his infatuation for her, but that he had fallen into the trap which is so often set for the agent — overconfidence in his own ability to meet all contingencies. The most sympathetic view to take of the whole rather sordid business is that Jehovah had ordained that the fall of the Philistines should be achieved in the way that it was eventually achieved.

Delilah, however, completed her mission successfully and received her promised fee of eleven hundred pieces of silver. She owed her success to her physical attributes. She set the example for the **femme fatale** spy, and proved that no matter how strong in body or mind an agent-opponent may be, he has his Achilles heel, if only opportunity and time are allowed for its discovery. The only hope for the male agent against his female opponent of this type is never to allow himself to come within the limits of physical temptation.

BIBLIOGRAPHY :

The Book of Judges, chapters 13 to 16.

D'EON, Chevalier d'Eon de Beaumont (Eighteenth century French agent).

On 5th October, 1728, a son was born to a Burgundian aristocratic family, who was given, among other names, those of Geneviève Louise. It was perhaps a mother's unfulfilled wish for a daughter which gave him two feminine Christian names, and was the reason for her subsequent clothing of him, between the ages of four and seven, as a girl; though until a post-mortem examination was made, many of his contemporaries believed there to be other more potent reasons.

The young d'Eon, however, grew up to be an excellent fencer at an early age, and he added to this practical art a precocious knowledge of civil and canon law, which procured for him the degree of doctor, and a call to the Bar at an age when most other young men were beginning their higher studies. His skill with the foil and rapier quickly gained him the position of prévôt of the fencing school of his native town; and a thesis on the finances of Louis XIV brought him to the notice of Louis XV.

The rivalry between France and England was concentrated at this time in the German state of Hanover. The king of England, George II, was also ruler of Hanover, and France, in alliance with Prussia, was plotting to expel him.

The English standing army was virtually non-existent, and in order to protect Hanover, George would have to rely on mercenaries. But these were not so numerous in Europe now as they had been, and the English king was attempting to persuade the Russian empress, Elizabeth, to supply him with several thousand Russians in return for a subsidy of half a million pounds.

It was in Louis' interest, therefore, to prevent this arrangement but the English ambassador and his agents were so active and skilful, that it was made impossible for any French representatives to approach either the empress or her ministers. In the circumstances Louis felt compelled to take extraordinary measures, and these involved enlisting the services of the Chevalier d'Eon, who must somehow break through the English blockade and present France's views to the Russian ruler. D'Eon embarked upon his mission with all the skill of the master agent.

He set out from Paris disguised as a young woman, posing as the niece of his travelling companion, a certain Chevalier Douglass, and calling himself Mlle Lia de Beaumont. The mademoiselle was travelling for her health.

D'Eon and Douglass went to considerable effort to disguise their destination, going first to Sweden, then to Germany and on to Bohemia, before they eventually turned towards St Petersburg. Arrived there they entered the home of a French international banker called Michael.

Douglass was working under the "cover" of a fur trader, hoping thereby to find a means of introducing his "niece" to Russian Court circles. But he had no success, and, as the mission was becoming desperate, it was d'Eon who made the acquaintance of the vice-chancellor, Voronzoff, who presented him to the empress.

Elizabeth, who was interested in all things western, was enchanted with the beautiful young French girl, who could tell her about France and the scandals of Louis XV's Court; and it was not very long before Mlle de Beaumont was appointed Reader to her imperial majesty.

If anyone had been able to take his eyes from the charms of the French girl, he would have noticed that wherever she went, she carried with her an elegantly bound copy of Montesquieu's **L'Esprit des lois.** This book had been given to her by the French king on the eve of her departure. Hidden in it was a letter to Elizabeth in Louis' own hand, inviting the empress to enter into a secret correspondence with him. At the first convenient opportunity d'Eon handed this letter to Elizabeth, and whether she was so captivated by the skill of the young man, or by the young man himself — for he discarded his disguise when he was sure of success — at all events, she acquiesced in Louis' proposals, and d'Eon's mission succeeded. Before long the English ambassador was having to report to the king that it was impossible to induce the empress to put her hand to the treaty which had once seemed to be assured.

Louis was so delighted with d'Eon's triumph that he granted him a considerable annuity, and employed him on many diplomatic missions, some open, some secret. His activities took him all over Europe, and brought him to England.

In London he was accredited as the secretary of the French ambassador, the Duke of Nivernais. Louis was at this period trying to arrange a treaty which would immunise France from English attack until such time as he felt himself sufficiently prepared to go to war. D'Eon's part in this was to supply Louis with accurate copies of confidential instructions to the English negotiator, the Duke of Bedford.

It would appear that the Chevalier came into possession of these documents in a very simple way. An official of the Duke of Bedford called one day on the French ambassador, carrying under his arm a portfolio which he would not let out of his possession. This immediately roused d'Eon's interest, and he plied the official with wine until he was no longer alert. Thereupon d'Eon removed himself and the portfolio to a neighbouring room and copied all the secrets which it contained, subsequently restoring it, unnoticed, to its owner. The use to which this information was put by his masters was such that the Duke of Bedford resigned, believing that he had been betrayed by Lord Bute, the Prime Minister, and favourite of the new King, George III.

D'Eon was now more in favour with Louis than ever before, and this inevitably brought him under the displeasure of Madame de Pompadour. D'Eon had been raised to the rank of minister in London, and in co-operation with the famous French officer, de la Rozière, had successfully undertaken a survey of the Channel coast defences of England, preparatory to a French attack. Then suddenly he found himself replaced.

D'Eon's reaction was violent. He held copies of his correspondence with Louis and Louis' own letters to him, all dealing with Louis' proposed invasion of England. He threatened to publish these documents. Louis made all kinds of promises at one time suggesting that he should return to France in female disguise, so that he might be given further secret missions. D'Eon refused, and sought political asylum in England, which was granted.

D'Eon retired to a quiet obscurity, but the long arm of French vengeance time and again threatened him, until at last he came out into the open and made public the details of the private war in which he was engaged. He began with only the least important parts of the correspondence, but when this only acerbated the attempts of his enemies either to assassinate him or entirely to discredit him, he retaliated by publishing more of the letters.

In France he was sued for libel, lost, and was outlawed. Louis XV died, but d'Eon's influence was still too dangerous for the French to leave him alone. An agent as brilliant as d'Eon was, therefore, despatched to London to deal as effectively with the Chevalier as he had recently with Theveneau de Morande.

For the account of Caron de Beaumarchais' handling of d'Eon in the article under BEAUMARCHAIS **supra.**

After succumbing to Beaumarchais' blandishments and handing over the letters, d'Eon returned to France, and spent eight years from 1777 to 1785 living there as a woman. He· then returned to England, where he passed the remaining twenty-five years of his life.

He lost his complete fortune in the French Revolution, and to support himself opened a **salle d'armes** in the Royal Borough of Kensington (London). There, dressed always as a woman, and known as Mlle la Chevalière d'Eon de Beaumont, he taught the young Regency bucks the art of swordsmanship.

The problem of his real sex aroused tremendous controversy and heavy bets were made in White's and Boodle's. D'Eon did nothing to settle the question. He even ignored challenges and consequent insults, and would give no sign of his true gender.

When he died on 21st May, 1810, at the age of eighty-two, a number of influential gentlemen, who stood to gain or lose heavily on wagers they had made, engaged a doctor to make an examination which would settle the controversy once and for all. To the pious horror of the lady with whom d'Eon had shared a house during the last five years of his life, the doctor found the body to be that of a fully equipped male.

BIBLIOGRAPHY :

The World's Greatest Military Spies — George Barton (London).

DESTRELLES, Marussia
(French traitress, World War I).

"The well-known Parisian actress, Mlle M a r u s s i a Destrelles, was found yesterday morning, unconscious in the bedroom of her hotel in Geneva. Despite every effort it was impossible to revive her. The deceased appears to have taken an overdose of veronal. Mlle Destrelles was in evening dress, lying on her bed, which was strewn with flowers."

So ran the brief announcement of Marussia Destrelles' apparent suicide in the Swiss newspapers one morning in 1916. The facts as quoted were true with one exception; the overdose of veronal had been administered to her without her knowledge.

Marussia Destrelles was a Rumanian by birth, French by adoption. She was not a great actress; she played leading roles in second-rate provincial theatres.

During 1916 she began to make frequent visits to Switzerland, which eventually brought her to the attention of French counter-espionage. Investigation revealed that one of her brothers was in a Swiss prison having been convicted as a German spy. In consequence, a closer watch was kept on her, and it was soon discovered that she was in the pay of the German **Abwehr.**

She seems to have become aware that the French were on her trail, but finding that flight was out of the question, she did the next best thing in the hope of putting the French off the scent — she offered to work for French intelligence.

Ostensibly her offer was accepted, and a trap was laid for her. An officer interviewing her, left her alone in his office having placed on his desk a list purporting to be of the names of agents working for the French. She was given sufficient time to herself to allow her to copy at least part of the list.

One name near the top of the list was genuine — that of a man suspected of treachery by the French. Three weeks later this man was arrested and shot by the Germans; a fact which, in the French view, pointed to the guilt of Marussia Destrelles.

To be rid of her, French intelligence arranged for it to become known to the Germans that she had offered her services to France. The Germans took rapid action. A young officer was designated to liquidate her. He invited her to dine, and she accepted eagerly. Before the dinner he sent a bouquet of roses to her room.

Towards the end of the meal, the young man complained of feeling unwell, and suggested that they should retire to her room, and order coffee and liqueurs there. She agreed. While she was preoccupied he slipped a lump of sugar impregnated with veronal into her coffee. She took one sip and collapsed.

Laying the unconscious woman on her bed, he strewed over her the roses he had sent her, hoping that they would encourage the notion that she had killed herself. If the Swiss police had any suspicions they kept them to themselves.

BIBLIOGRAPHY :
The Secret Services of Europe — Robert Boucard (London, 1940).

DEUXIEME BUREAU.

A widespread popular misconception designates the Deuxième Bureau as the French Secret Service. Were this to be true, it would be the strangest intelligence service in the world, for it lists its telephone number in the Paris directory.

On the other hand, it is intimately concerned with intelligence, and indeed exercises a very important function. It centralises and interprets intelligence for the French High Command.

To allow it to exercise this function it is fed by two other organisations : the **Service de Renseignements,** which is, in fact, the French Secret Service; and **counter-espionage.** They are collectively known as the Special Services.

In peace-time, the Special Services keep very much in the background but in war-time they emerge as the Fifth Bureau of the French General Staff. Their function is to carry out espionage and to protect France's secrets from foreign spies.

In the period of imminent threat of hostilities, and naturally, after the outbreak of hostilities, the **Deuxième Bureau** assumes a role second to none in importance for the protection of France. It is on their appreciation of the situation as it appears from the analysis of intelligence from all sources on which the French High Command bases its strategy and tactics almost solely in the initial period, and on which it places great reliance thereafter.

In 1958 the French intelligence services were reorganised, and emerged in a form more suited to moslem countries. Two major services were set up; the Service de Documentation Extérieure et de Contre-espionage (SDECE) and the Direction de la Securité du Territoire (DST). The SDECE functions more or less along the lines of the American CIA (q.v.) while the DST is the equivalent of the British MI5, the counter-espionage service.

Since its re-organisation the SDECE had been involved in a number of cases which have tarnished its image considerably. It was shown to be deeply involved in the kidnapping and subsequent murder of the Algerian leader Ben Banen. When this case was ultimately made public, the repercussions came very near to toppling de Gaulle's government.

In recent years, too, there have been grave suspicions that the SDECE has been infiltrated by Soviet agents. This was highlighted by the revelations of Philippe de Vesjoli, for 13 years head of French intelligence in America.

In April 1968 de Vesjoli declared that in 1962 President Kennedy had sent to President de Gaulle a personal letter in which the American president stated that a source in which he had every confidence had informed him that the French intelligence services, and even de Gaulle's Cabinet had been penetrated by Soviet agents. Kennedy offered every assistance in verifying these statements.

Though his first reaction was to shrug off Kennedy's letter as pure fiction, de Gaulle nevertheless sent to Washington General de Rougemont who was attached to the French Prime Minister's office as director of the second division of the national defence staff and had responsibility for cooperating the various branches of military intelligence.

On arrival in Washington, de Rougemont avoided all contact with his French friends there, and went straight to the Americans, who told him that Kennedy's source was a very high-ranking former KGB (Russian intelligence) officer, who had lately defected. The Americans had given the Russian the code-name Martel.

De Rougemont questioned Martel for three or four days and was shaken by the details concerning the SDECE and DST which the Russian gave him. As a result both services organised a combined team of expert interrogators who were sent to Washington to interrogate Martel.

Quite early on in his questioning Martel asserted that French KGB agents in NATO headquarters in Paris were so well placed that if Moscow asked for any NATO document whatsoever, even the most secret, these agents could produce it in two or three days. He continued that Moscow had almost a complete set of NATO top secret documents.

The French interrogators, hoping to trap Martel, had a series of NATO documents sent to Washington, among which were a few that had been fabricated. Martel could not identify all the documents, but those he did were authentic.

The French team ·were shaken, but they were more shaken still when Martel described to them in **detail** the reorganisation of the French security services which had been carried out in 1958, even including the names of French officers who were in charge of certain operations.

For two weeks the French interrogators questioned Martel in depth, and returned to Paris with hundreds of pages of statements made by him. As a result, investigations were put in hand.

When these gave rise to further questions, the team flew back to Washington. The new interrogations of Martel opened up other avenues of investigation. For example, Martel declared that the Ministry of the Interior, the French department of NATO, the Ministries of Defence and Foreign Affairs had all been penetrated by KGB agents; that a certain politician who had held high posts in de Gaulle's government was a KGB agent; that a network known as Sapphire, consisting of almost a dozen French intelligence officers, were KGB agents operating i n s i d e SDECE itself; that SDECE was forming a new section to spy on America's nuclear and other technological advances, all of which information would eventually reach Moscow.

The French investigations were continued for some time, but then seemed to fizzle out. As far as the expert observer could see little or nothing that Martel had disclosed was acted upon. The relief of France's allies must have been great when a year or two later de Gaulle decided to withdraw France from NATO.

BIBLIOGRAPHY :

Second Bureau — P. J. Stead (London, 1959).

DESMAREST see under **Réal.**

DISCH, William see under **Zilbert, Mark.**

DODINGTON, G e o r g e **Bubb, Lord Melcombe** (died 1762).

Bubb Dodington, a Lord of the Treasury, was a connoisseur of Italian antiquities. He made his first visit to Rome in August 1732, and made the acquaintance of that other great connoisseur Cardinal Albani (q.v.) with whom he kept up a correspondence over many years.

To him Albani passed much of the information about the activities of the Old Pretender (Prince James Edward Stuart, known to his friends as King James III) who had made Rome his base, and was the magnet of Jacobite exiles. The British Government were anxious to know every move of the Pretender's Court, its intrigues and intentions, in order to be able to meet any threat to the Crown and administration of England, such as a repetition of the Rebellion of 1715, which the Jacobites might plan.

In other words, Dodington was one of the go-betweens between the British Government and their Eminent Informer.

DOIHARA,
Lieutenant-General Kenji
(Chief of Japanese Intelligence).

Kenji Doihara was the son of an ancient and well-to-do Japanese family. He was an ambitious young man of more than ordinary ability, much attracted by State

Shintoism, the State religion, and confident that if he could only find the right channels he could do much to assist his country in achieving the mastery of the world, which the Third Tenet of State Shintoism required. The problem was, however, to make the contacts which would be instrumental in bringing him to the notice of those in authority.

His tortuous, subtle mind eventually hit upon a way of achieving this. He was a very keen photographer. He had a beautiful younger sister, aged fifteen. Somehow he was able to overcome her natural scruples of modesty for which Japanese women are renowned, and persuaded her to pose for him naked. The films he developed and printed himself, and saw that they were exceptionally fine and well suited to his purposes; so he enlarged them and sent the enlargements to one of the Imperial princes, with the suggestion that he would find a no more beautiful girl in all Japan.

He had read the prince's character well. The prince agreed with him, and suggested that the sister should enter his household. But the Doihara family was of such lineage that though the prince's proposal could not be denied, at least the position which the girl was to have was not to be a menial one. The prince agreed once more. He could not marry the girl unfortunately, as he was already married, but he could and would make her his First Concubine. So the girl went to live in the palace.

When she had been there a few weeks, Doihara called on his sister and, rather to his astonishment, found her supremely happy. The prince showered presents upon her. When he was at home he rarely left her side, there was nothing he would not do for her.

Watching her carefully to judge her reaction, Doihara said quietly, "Sister, there is something you could do for me."

Anxious to prove that she was not exaggerating, the girl replied, "Anything you ask, I promise you."

"Tell the prince," Doihara said, "that I speak nine European languages and four Chinese dialects without a trace of an accent. Tell him

163

that there is much I could do for the divine Emperor and for the fatherland if only I could be sent to China in a responsible position. The prince has great influence with the government, and he could arrange it if only he knew what I am capable of."

"Is that all, brother? This very night the prince shall be told what a brilliant brother I have," his sister laughed. "He will have to promise to send my brother to China, otherwise I shall be too tired to entertain him for a long time. Have no fear, brother."

As he made his way from the palace, Doihara was well pleased with his success. The most difficult part of his plan had clearly been to persuade his sister to pose for him naked. If that part of his plan had misfired, it would have been too terrible to contemplate. But he did not allow things to misfire; and now he only had to wait until the summons came.

The summons was not long in coming. Within a few months General Honjo, of the high command, was sent to Peking as military attaché and Kenji Doihara, commissioned in the rank of major,

was assigned as his assistant.

There was very little to choose between the characters of Honjo and Doihara. Both were entirely ruthless, utterly without moral scruples or values, and relentless if daring plotters.

Doihara had already thought out his plan. His basic scheme was to create a kind of moral desert on the Asian mainland. His slogan would be **Asia for the Asiatics,** though for **Asiatics** one should read **Japanese.** He would accomplish his plan by undercover means, undermining by plots, sabotage, assassinations, the promotion of vice of every kind, by bribery and corruption, the influence of the Chinese republican government both in China and Manchuria.

As a beginning he would use the contacts which his position as assistant military attaché gave him. Before long one of the high-ranking Chinese officials, who was not one of his "men" but who saw what was happening, was able to say "Doihara probably has more Chinese acquaintances than any living Chinese engaged in the most intense political activity."

Within a short time of his arrival in Peking he was in the thick of intrigues with a movement called Anfu, which was so powerful that it controlled the Chinese government. Soon it began to be rumoured that certain members of Anfu had sold concessions in Manchuria to the Japanese without the government's consent or even knowledge. Riots broke out — actually organised secretly by Doihara — and the president's palace was attacked. Appearing now in the other part of his dual role of agitator and saviour, Doihara arrived at the palace in time to rescue the frightened president from the mob, by means of a laundry basket, and lodge him in the Japanese embassy. From that time, the president was never again his own master, and indeed the turmoil in which China was writhing made him only too glad to lean on his self-appointed advisers, Honjo and Doihara.

The importance of Manchuria for the Japanese lay in the fact that it was the nearest part of the mainland to Japan, and a place which would facilitate the execution of a later phase of the Japanese master plan, the domination of southern China. By the control of Manchuria they could build up forces of men and supplies of material there and use it as a springboard for the next step, the conquest of the five northern provinces. In its present state of internal insecurity it should fall an easy prey to outside, meaning Japanese, influence.

As time went by, Doihara realised that he was wasting his time in China, for he now believed that he was tackling the problem from the wrong end. He must first work for the annexation of Manchuria. When Manchuria was in Japanese hands, the five northern provinces would not present a great problem.

Even so, he appreciated that Manchuria would never be absorbed as easily as Korea had been annexed. In spite of its inherent weakness there was an army which was not too badly equipped and supplied; and, just as important, it had a bold determined leader in Marshal Chang Tsolin.

During the Russo-Japanese war, Chang had offered himself as the ally of the Japanese, and as a reward, when the war was over, the Japanese obtained for him, from the Peking government, a pardon for his previous acts of banditry, and appointment as governor of his native province of Fentien, in Manchuria.

But Chang was a born war lord, and could not be satisfied with the governorship of a province; so in 1922 he left Manchuria with his army and joined in one of those strange local wars which happened to be raging about Peking. Unfortunately he backed the wrong side and his army was defeated by the forces of the war lord Wu Pei-fu. Thereupon he retired to Manchuria, where he declared the independence of the three eastern provinces and set himself up as their ruler.

He quickly revealed himself as a most admirable administrator, though at the same time he emerged as a ruthless, pitiless autocrat, destroying everything and everybody who opposed him. Nevertheless, under his rule the three provinces flourished and were rapidly becoming a

rich prize. To the chagrin of the Japanese, however, Chang now found that he could get along very well without them; and if they were going to be foolish enough to intervene, he would not hesitate to fight them.

Doihara had the measure of Chang, and sought permission from Tokyo to go into action in his own particular way, on the clear understanding that he must have **carte blanche** and be assured of the necessary funds.

By this time, Doihara's reputation stood high in Tokyo, and he was given everything he asked for. He was now to prove himself a natural spy and spy-master. He had the peculiar vision, the tortuous mind, the relentless hardness, the pitilessness, that the successful spy-master must have.

He formed several secret services. The largest was known as the combatant secret service, which was composed of 5,000 criminals who had fled from Russia after the Revolution. Other forces were composed of White Russians, and there was a vast army of 80,000 Chinese renegades, called

Ch'ang mao tao, the long-haired sect, who were willing to carry out Doihara's orders in return for his support. For while concentrating on Manchuria, he did not neglect China, and particularly the five northern provinces, which were scheduled next after Manchuria for Japanese tutelage.

Besides these hordes of operatives, who were used more for sabotage, assassination and the stirring up of strife than for purely intelligence purposes, Doihara employed many other nefarious, and in some cases unmentionable, devices.

To his way of thinking, addiction to opium was a virtue, abstention a vice. He converted the Chinese so-called clubs into combinations of saloon, gambling house, brothel, and opium den, with the accent on the latter. He employed traffickers in opium, who travelled throughout Manchuria and China, visiting every village fair, where they set up booths for tuberculosis cures. The medicine was either opium or an opium derivative. Once the unfortunate victims had become addicts,

it was but half a step to becoming the slaves and informers of Doihara, who controlled the supplies of the drug.

At his request, Japanese cigarette manufacturers began to make a new brand of cigarette, known as the Golden Bat. The sale of the Golden Bat was prohibited in the mother country; they were for export only. Doihara controlled their distribution in Manchuria and China. In the mouthpieces were concealed small doses of opium or heroin, and many unsuspecting purchasers were thus gathered into Doihara's ever-growing army of addicts.

The more vicious of Oriental gentlemen attain, so they believe, the greatest orgiastic release in sexual intercourse with Occidental women. Doihara accepted this as a ready-made weapon with which to weaken further the peoples against whom he was warring in his own strange way.

In Mukden and Harbin and other satisfactory locations he set up brothels in which the prostitutes were all White Russians. The source of supply was a plentiful one, for no fewer than 100,000

167

White Russians had fled from Siberia into Manchuria after the Revolution. They came with nothing; they remained with nothing. In a brothel they were at least sure of their day-to-day food and a roof, and happy oblivion when they were not on duty, for with every six pipes of opium they sold to clients, they received one for themselves gratis.

It was a terrible thing that Doihara was doing here. He set about deliberately to destroy half a continent with drugs and depravity of every kind. The success he had was even more terrible.

But even this was not enough for the Japanese. In 1926, in order to remove Marshal Chang from the Manchurian scene, they persuaded him to have his revenge on Peking. Supplied with weapons by the Japanese Chang took his armies to the capital and sat down to besiege it for two years. But during these two years Kuomintang armies swept over the whole of China. Under the able direction first of the Communists and then of General Chiang Kai-shek, by 1928 they had reached

Tsinanfu. By now the Japanese, under their various concessions, had a considerable army in Manchuria, and were in control of the Tsing-tao-Tsinan Railway, and at Tsinanfu they offered considerable resistance to the Kuomintang forces.

Realising what was happening, Marshal Chang's oldest and best friend, General Wu Shu-chen, whom he had left as regent in Manchuria, begged Chang to return home urgently if he did not wish the Japanese to seize his country. This did not suit the Japanese at all, and Doihara arranged for the train in which Chang and Wu were travelling to be blown up, and the two men were killed along with a large number of their ablest officers.

For the next three years Doihara and his hordes plotted, assassinated, raised riots, dug deeper and wider their wells of depravity in vain. At last the Japanese government saw that it would achieve its ends only by direct use of force, and in September 1931 startled the world by its full-scale invasion of Manchuria, which it attempted to pass off by describing it as the Manchurian Incident.

On 19th September, 1931, the Japanese captured Mukden; on 3rd February, 1932, Harbin fell to them. A fortnight later they declared the independence of Manchuria and set Henry Pu-yi, the last Emperor of China, on the throne.

With the Manchurian Incident closed, Doihara turned his attention fully to the next phase of the plan. This was to detach the five northern provinces of China from Peking, and turn them into a second puppet state which would act as a base for the main project of seizing the whole of China. He himself went to work on men of high rank. Some of them resisted his bribes and his promises, but some fell for him. Among the latter was Huang-sen, an official of the Central Bank of China.

Not long after Huang fell in with the agents of Doihara, he was appointed the secretary of General Chiang Kai-shek. When the Japanese became more violent in their threats, Chiang called a council of war, at which were present only General Feng and General Pai and the trusted secretary, Huang.

The generals planned to trap a large flotilla which the Japanese had anchored in the Yangtse River at Hankow. In some way the Japanese got wind of what was going to happen, and when the Chinese forces arrived they found no ships. Chiang immediately ordered an investigation, and this revealed that his secretary had confided the plan to Ito Soma, alias Kenji Doihara, and he paid the supreme penalty.

It was only by executions and ruthless counter-espionage that Chiang was able to resist to any degree the espionage of Doihara. In 1938, after the next phase of the plan had begun to operate, Chiang had to execute eight divisional commanders who were discovered to be Doihara's agents. It is said by reliable sources that more high-ranking Chinese officers were executed in the first six years of the war for dealings with Doihara than for any other military offence of extreme gravity.

The confusion which this one man spread among the

enemies of Japan and the assistance which his own government and armies received from his activities will never be entirely evaluated, since he spread his nets so wide that they could never be pulled together again. He was, however, to meet the end which his nefarious practices merited.

After the war, by then lieutenant-general, he was arraigned by the Allies as a war criminal and executed. He is the first spy-master on record to be tried for the crimes of his agents and pay the penalty for the responsibility which he had for those crimes.

BIBLIOGRAPHY:

Secret Servants: The Story of Japanese Espionage — Ronald Seth (London, 1957).

DONOVAN, Major General William J., ("Wild" Bill) Director of American Office of Strategic Services, World War II, see under **OSS.**

DORONKIN, Krill S. see under **Hirsch, Willi.**

DOURLEIN, Pieter (Dutch agent, World War II) see under **Giskes, Col H. J.**

DOWNING, Sir George (English intelligence chief in Holland, 17th century) see under **Thurloe, John.**

DOWNING, George see under **Carranza, Lt Ramon.**

DOZENBERG, Nicholas (Russian agent in America, between wars).

Nicholas Dozenberg, a Latvian immigrant, was appointed Resident Director of the networks in the United States in 1930. He had joined the American Communist Party in its early days, and had been recruited into espionage in 1927. His chief task was to set up the American-Rumanian Film Company as cover for Soviet espionage in the US. A branch in Bucharest was also to act as cover in that country.

Very early on the plan ran into trouble. A hundred thousand dollars were required to back the Rumanian branch, and at this time the Soviet Union did not have this sum to spare in American currency, so it was decided to make some. An initial run of counterfeit dollars was made in Cuba and Brazil, where they passed muster. On the strength of this Dozenberg was instructed to arrange for 100,000 dollars to be put into circulation in New York.

This he did with the help of a Russian-born doctor, Valentin Burtan. Burtan became the vice-president of the American-Rumanian Film Company. Burtan had among his patients a certain non-Communist German, E. Dachow von Bülow, who tried to make a living gun-running to South America. Since Burtan had rescued Bülow from time to time from financial difficulties he had a certain hold over him, and he now demanded a **quid pro quo** from the German — assistance in circulating the counterfeit dollars.

Bülow did not hesitate, and suggested a scheme which ought to have been foolproof. A friend of his was the Guatemalan Minister of Finance, who, he believed, for a certain consideration, would switch 100,000 counterfeit dollars for 100,000 real ones in the vaults of the National Bank of Guatemala. Everything began very well, but suddenly Guatemala City fell silent. Undeterred, Bülow now proposed to engage the services of another friend, a private detective operating in Chicago called Smiley. Smiley agreed to co-operate, and organised a band of distributors.

All was going smoothly when one of the distributors was caught passing counterfeit bills. He talked, and so, when arrested, did Smiley. Only Dr Burtan held his tongue. In 1934 he was brought to trial, sentenced to fifteen years and fined 10,000 dollars.

Dozenberg escaped abroad, and was sent by The Centre to Rumania. In 1939 he defected, returned to America, served a short term in prison for trying to obtain a passport by making false statements, changed his name and vanished from the espionage scene.

BIBLIOGRAPHY :
Soviet Espionage — David Dallin (New York, 1955).

DRONKERS (Dutch traitor, World War II).

Dronkers, a member of the Dutch Resistance, was captured by the Gestapo, who brought pressure to bear on him by threatening to kill his family if he did not fall in with their wishes. He agreed, and the Abwehr sent him to England to act as an agent. His cover was that of "refugee", and he was set adrift in a small boat near the English coast, so that he might be picked up by British coastal patrols.

This happened on 18th May, 1942. He was taken to London, where he was interrogated by the Dutch Security Service operated by the Dutch Government-in-exile. They declared that they were satisfied that he was a genuine refugee.

He suggested that he should broadcast from Radio Orange, the BBC service sponsored by the Dutch government. His over-eagerness roused the suspicions of British security officers, and a trap was laid for him. He was brought to the microphone to read messages which he had prepared, so he said, for friends in Holland. In them were concealed code words.

As he turned from the microphone, he was told that he would be detained. In fact, he had done no harm for the microphone had been dead.

At his trial at the Central Criminal Court, in London, in November 1942, he admitted that he had been instructed to obtain information concerning invasion plans of the Allies. He was hanged at Wandsworth Prison, London, on 14th December, 1942.

DUBOIS, Alice, cover name of Louise de Bettignies, Allied agent in World War I.

When the Germans invaded Belgium and northern France in 1914, Louise de Bettignies was a governess in Lille. Caught up in the throng of refugees she eventually reached England, and there attracted the attention of British intelligence officers.

An expert linguist, intelligent above the ordinary, she had kept her ears and eyes open during her flight, and the information she was able to give as the result of her observation, suggested a course to which, when it was put to her, she readily agreed.

So instead of going home to her mother in St Omer, in unoccupied France, she returned to Lille via France, under the cover name of Alice Dubois.

In Lille she soon found many of her former friends who were willing to risk their lives if only they might be given some work which would provide them with active opposition to the invader, and at the same time be of assistance to the Allies. In a very short time she had organised a system of agents, all amateurs like herself, men and women, who, as they moved into action, began to provide Allied intelligence with a flow of information which grew in bulk and importance as they achieved their rhythm.

Alice's chief assistant was a young shop-keeper, Marie-Leonie Vanhoutte, cover name Charlotte. To enable them to move about the countryside without raising suspicions, Alice travelled in home-made lace, and Charlotte in home-made cheese.

In time of war, up to this period, there have always been pockets of neutrality close to the territories of the combatants, and centres of espionage are set up there. Among the most important of these in World War I were Holland and Switzerland, and in World War II, Switzerland,

Sweden, and most important of all Lisbon, Portugal.

With the German establishment of their front line in northern France, Alice's channel for passing her information was Holland. It was, of course, forbidden for anyone to cross from Belgium into Holland, but there were points along the frontier where it was possible for a bold and resolute agent to cross.

These journeys Alice and Charlotte made themselves, for it was always her policy to undertake the most dangerous missions rather than endanger the lives of subordinates. For a time, until the Germans tightened up their control of the frontier, Alice and Charlotte made a weekly trip by day into Holland.

Undaunted by the increasing vigilance of the Germans, she discovered one place where she could cross the frontier in safety; but it meant swimming a canal. Alice was a strong swimmer, but Charlotte could not swim a stroke. So they kept an old kneading-trough under a nearby bush — it had been contributed by a Belgian baker — and in this C h a r l o t t e crouched, while Alice, swimming, pushed her and the trough.

This kneading-trough was a clever ruse. Had a boat or canoe been found under a bush, the Germans would at once have been suspicious. But a discarded kneading-trough was more than likely to pass unnoticed. Her other methods of passing information were equally cunning, and until now unknown to espionage. Balls of wool, children's toys, artificial limbs, spectacle rims, bars of chocolate, sausages — she used them all.

Among her little band of operatives was a chemist called de Geyter, who was not only a brilliant forger, but an inventor of secret inks. There was also a cartographer named Paul Bernard (q.v.).

German counter-espionage sooner or later had to become aware of the superior forces opposing them at this particular point, and the counter-measures they introduced were inevitable. They banned practically all civilian travel, and insisted on travel permits. They stopped trains between stations to inspect the permits. Alice and Charlotte once trapped like this, climbed out of their carriage which was towards the rear of the train, and crawled underneath the coaches until they reached the first one. Taking their seats there they knew they would be safe, because the Germans never varied their habit of starting always with the first coach and working towards the rear.

To avoid the ever-tightening net thrown over her activities Alice now employed children as couriers. So far as I can discover this was the first time that children were used in espionage. These child agents were mostly boys of eleven, twelve or thirteen, who would not cause any German reaction except a frustrated anger engendered by normal boyish pranks. Alice used them chiefly to carry forged passes between one agent and another. There was a considerable shortage of "papers" now, for de Geyter and Bernard could not keep pace with demands. Charlotte would go into the forbidden zone on her papers, and be met by a small boy, who hid the papers in the linings of his trousers, scampered past the controls unchallenged and delivered them to Alice, who would then join Charlotte with their aid.

The strain of such dangerous activity takes its toll of the strongest. Alice gave herself no respite, and as a consequence she became ill. But she refused to acquiesce to suggestions that she should take a rest.

The Germans presently began to make arrests, and to execute without hesitation all those against whom there was the faintest shadow of proof of illegal activity. The pressure on Alice's group soon became so great that to safeguard them she decided to disband them. Even then she and Charlotte carried on, working as they had never worked before.

Her employers should have disciplined her, insisting that she retired, for tiredness and strain are bound to weaken the strongest agent's resistance to opposition. If she did not withdraw to safety, disaster would overtake her sooner or later.

And so it happened!

Alice had just crossed into Holland, and there came to Charlotte within a short time, two messages, one from Alice announcing her safe arrival, and another in an unknown hand telling her to go at once to a certain small, isolated inn. Despite misgivings, Charlotte went at once to the inn, fearing that if she did not go it would imply fear or guilt.

Outside the inn she was met by a stranger, an obvious German posing as a Belgian, who realised her worst fears by questioning her about Alice. She denied that she knew anyone called Alice Dubois, and eventually returned home, no attempt being made to prevent her.

In the early hours of the morning, German a g e n t s searched her house and arrested her. Immediately a message was sent by former collaborators to Alice in Holland, telling her what had happened and begging her to stay where she was.

Unfortunately she was already on her way back before the message could reach her. The Germans did not arrest her at once but shadowed her for several days, and at last struck as she visited Tournai in search of vital information.

Alice and Charlotte were

tried together and condemned to death. However, the world-wide outcry against the shooting of Edith Cavell which had recently occurred, saved them from the firing squad, and they were sentenced, Alice to twenty-seven years' imprisonment, Charlotte to fifteen.

Charlotte lived to be released on the Allied victory; but Alice died in Cologne prison on 17th September, 1918.

BIBLIOGRAPHY :
Louise de Bettignies —
Antoine Redier (London, 1922).

DUCIMETIERE, Rose

(French traitor, World War I).

Rose Ducimetière was nineteen in 1914, a working girl living in Paris with a cousin. Shortly before the outbreak of World War I she met a waiter called Walter, who said he was Swiss, but was, in fact, German, and fell head over heels in love with him. She left her cousin's home, and went to live with her lover in an attic in the faubourg St Martin.

They had not been together long before he made her leave the dress-maker in the rue Saint-Honoré, for whom she was working, and take to the streets. Her pitch was the boulevard Sebastopol, which, in war-time, was a scene of constant bustle as soldiers of all ranks hurried towards the gare de l'Est. Rose found her business booming.

At the end of the day, she would return to Walter and would tell him about some of her clients, saying casually, as though she were merely trying to make conversation, "I was told today by a man in the 137th Regiment that important troop movements are going on at Noisy-le-Sec."

Walter was quick to appreciate that this was the kind of information which might interest someone so much that they would be willing to pay cash for it. While he was still wondering how he could make contact with such a person, he saw one day in a newspaper an advertisement which read, "Reliable correspondents wanted in Paris and large French towns. Easy work needing only a few hours a day. 500 to 1,000 francs a month. Complete discretion. Write P.O. Box 128, Central Post Office, Geneva."

Walter wrote to Box 128, and shortly afterwards was invited to go to Geneva to interview the advertiser. The latter described himself as the editor of a military review. He wished to be kept informed, he said, of the new techniques of modern warfare, and needed detailed information of every kind relating to the French army in order to write articles and so on for his review. He approved the kind of information with which Walter could provide him, and they struck a bargain.

In his turn, Walter ordered Rose to question every soldier who bought her favours about his unit and his destination, and to get any other military information she could out of him. She also offered to become the "little god-mother" of the officers she picked up, and was thus able to keep up correspondence with them, asking innocent questions such as the losses of a recent action, the morale of the troops, and so on. All the information she gleaned in this way eventually found its way to Box 128.

When Italy entered the war, the editor of the **Swiss** **Military Review** instructed her to join the nursing service on the Italian front, while Walter returned to the neutral safety of Switzerland. In October 1916 she returned to Paris, and became a nurse at the Val de Grace hospital.

She had not been there long when one of her reports to Walter though written in invisible ink, was detected by the censor. She was arrested, confessed, tried by court martial and sentenced to death. President Poincaré, however, in view of her youth, transmuted the sentence into one of imprisonment for life.

BIBLIOGRAPHY :
The Secret Services of Europe —Robert Boucard (London, 1940).

DUKES, Sir Paul (British agent in Russia immediately after the Revolution).

After living in Tsarist Russia for several years, Paul Dukes was a member of the Anglo-Russian Commission when the Revolution broke out in 1917. Then, surprisingly, in the following year he was training Boy Scouts in Samara under the auspices of the American YMCA, a strange change of activity which has not been satisfactorily explained. The Commission had returned to England, but Dukes was still in the employ of the Foreign Office, and it is difficult to see how he could be working for the American YMCA at the same time.

While in Samara he visited Moscow, and there received an urgent telegram recalling him to England. He set out at once via Archangel, and from there embarked on the ten-day journey round the North Cape to Bergen, and from there across the U-boat infested North Sea to Newcastle.

On arrival in London, he was taken, with a certain amount of mystery, to an office not far from Trafalgar Square and interviewed by a colonel who informed him that he was to be offered the post of chief of British intelligence in Russia. The Foreign Office believed that very soon foreigners would be barred from entry into the new Soviet Union and that England and the Bolsheviks would soon be at war. So they wanted to have someone in Russia who would keep them informed of developments.

Dukes accepted the appointment without hesitation, but he did protest that he was only an amateur and had no inkling of the techniques of espionage. He was reassured when he was told that there would be a little time for training. Whatever training he did receive could not have been extensive, for three weeks after his arrival in England, he was on his way back to Russia.

For the next three years he directed British intelligence in the Soviet Union with a brilliance which betrayed in him natural qualities and other qualifications rarely surpassed in British espionage. He was courageous, clear-thinking, quick-acting, a master of disguise, fearless in taking the initiative, and he had a keen appreciation of security. In addition, he knew the language and the customs and thought-habits of the people as though he were one of them.

He was working under very different conditions from those radio-pampered among us who operated in World War II. In order to get his information out of Russia, he had to employ couriers to carry it to the British chargé d'affaires in Helsinki. Each time he had to choose men who could be trusted, and who were prepared to risk their lives.

On many occasions Dukes made the journey himself. Then the risks were doubled, for having got out of Russia he had to get back again. His account abounds in exciting and hair-raising descriptions of incidents which happened to him on those and other occasions.

Besides his espionage activities, Dukes helped many Russians who had been listed as enemies of the régime to escape to safety. To do so, he took many risks, but his courage and his audactiy served him well. Many spies of World War II could have learned much from Dukes's example, and would probably still be alive.

Russian counter-espionage was fully aware of his presence in their country, and the nature of his activities, and every member of the OGPU and police were on constant watch for him. But by using different names, moving ceaselessly from place to place, and never sleeping twice in the same house, he avoided capture.

He was the only British agent to be knighted as a direct reward for his active spying.

BIBLIOGRAPHY :

Red Dusk and the Morrow — Paul Dukes (London, 1932).

DULLES, Allen see under **Central Intelligence Agency.**

DZERSHINSKY, Felix (Chief of Russian Intelligence).

Felix Dzershinsky was a former Polish aristocrat, the son of a great landed family. As a student he joined the S o c i a l i s t Revolutionary Party, which he left after a short time to become a member of the more ideologically acceptable Social Democratic Labour Party. When the Bolsheviks and Mensheviks parted company in 1903, he cast in his lot with Lenin and the Bolsheviks, and it was to Dzershinsky that Lenin turned in 1917 to organise the formation of a secret service.

Dzershinsky's first task was to seal off all lines of communication which he did so successfully that a number of the members of the Kerensky government only learned that they were no longer in power some hours after the Bolsheviks had taken over. From that moment Dzershinsky applied himself to his work with an almost frightening speed. Only six weeks after the Bolsheviks had seized power, he raised his organisation from a mere subcommittee, to the status of a commission — the Extraordinary Commission for the Struggle against Counter-revolution and Sabotage; **Chrezvychavnaya Komissiva,** from whose initials it derived its popular designation Cheka, often spelt Tcheka (q.v.).

Dzershinsky had gained his experience of clandestine activity as a revolutionary in the role of courier, maintaining contacts between the revolutionary underground movement in Russia and the exiles abroad. He was, in fact, a natural spy, and this combined with considerable powers as an administrator, permitted him to establish Soviet intelligence on a firm foundation. The fact that it had grown into an unwieldy giant must not be attributed to Dzershinsky, but to the machinations of Beria and other chiefs whose personal ambitions made such a vast organisation necessary to protect them against the hundreds of thousands of enemies they inevitably made.

It was at Dzershinsky's suggestion that the Cheka's name was changed to GPU, the initials of the Russian for State Political Administration. The excesses of the Cheka during the Civil War, which ended in the winter of 1921, had resulted in such hatred for it among every stratum of the Soviet Russian community that it was felt that if a change of name were effected, and the Cheka were apparently to disappear, the people would become less hostile towards it.

Twenty-two months later, the name was changed again — to OGPU, United State Political Administration, with Dzershinsky still at its head. He died on 20th July, 1926 and was succeeded by Vyacheslav Menzhinsky.

EFRON, Serge see under **Reiss, Ignace.**

EISLER, Gerhard (Russian agent, Resident Director in US).

In the early days of the Soviet Union, the Russian resources in foreign currency were so small that it was difficult to spare any for the financing of espionage abroad. Russian intelligence, therefore, hit upon the plan for obtaining the necessary currency by producing counterfeit money. The forgery department of the Cheka made extremely good counterfeit 100-dollar bills, and these were distributed throughout the world through the crypto-communist bank of Sass and Martini in Germany. The Sass and Martini Bank deposited the forged bills with the Deutsche Bank, who issued them without having checked them, since in the past the Sass and Martini Bank had had a considerable reputation in the banking world.

From Germany the bills began to find their way into the United States. The first discovery of the forgeries was made by the Federal Reserve Bank in New York in December 1929, but it was many months before the source of the notes was discovered. In the meantime, the forged bills continued to make their appearance in different parts of the world, and by the time the situation was brought under control altogether ten million dollars had been changed for legal currency.

The man behind this operation was Gerhard Eisler, who was working in Berlin at the time. Eisler was the son of a lecturer in philosophy at Vienna University. His sister, better known as Ruth Fischer, had led the German Communist Party in the 1920s, but later quarrelled with Stalinism and forsook Communism.

In his early days in Germany, Eisler was involved in many plots against the members of the German government. Using the cover-name of Edwards, he visited the United States, but after a few months was recalled to organise Soviet espionage networks in the Scandinavian countries, from his base in Germany.

With the advent of the Nazis Eisler moved to France, and from there organised escape routes for Communist agents trapped in Vienna and Prague. With the fall of France he was himself trapped and interned. He might have fallen into the hands of the Gestapo had not the American embassy in Paris, for reasons best known to themselves, gone to his assistance, secured his release, and provided him with a visa for America.

Immediately he arrived in the United States he took over the direction of the networks there. He lived in a comfortable penthouse in New York and as Hans Berger occupied offices in Lexington Avenue on behalf of the fictitious Anti-Fascist Refugee Committee.

When his activities were discovered after the war, he was summoned before a Congressional Committee, and as a result of his behaviour there was sentenced to one year's imprisonment for contempt of Congress. He was released on bail of 23,000 dollars, put up by the Civil Rights organisation pending appeal. For a time he remained in America, but as the time for his appeal approached he decided to skip bail and boarded the Polish liner **Batory,** which was due to call at Southampton.

The American authorities, on learning this, appealed to the British to arrest and extradite him. The British complied with the request, but when he was taken off the ship at Southampton and brought before the Bow Street, London, magistrate, the magistrate rightly ruled that contempt of Congress is not an offence in British law and therefore not extraditable, and Eisler was released.

He rejoined the **Batory** and sailed to Gdynia. In Warsaw he was put up as a martyr of imperialist persecution at one of the peace congresses which were common occurrences in the Iron Curtain countries in the 1950s. A short time afterwards he became Deputy Minister and Chief of Propaganda Services of the East German People's Republic. He has been out of the picture for a number of years now.

BIBLIOGRAPHY :
Soviet Espionage — David Dallin (New York, 1955).

ENGLANDSPIEL see under **Giskes, Col H. J.**

ERDBERG, Alexander see under **Red Orchestra, The.**

ERICKSON, Eric (Allied agent, World War II).

Eric Erickson was born in Brooklyn, New York, in 1889. He left school early, worked in various oil-fields in Texas and as a pipeline walker for Standard Oil. At the age of 28 he enrolled at Cornell University, but his courses there were interrupted by service during World War I. Afterwards he returned to the university and completed his engineering studies. After a number of years in the Far East representing oil interests he went to Sweden and decided to set himself up in business there, as an oil importer. He subsequently renounced his American citizenship and became a naturalised Swedish subject.

At the beginning of World War II, he was approached by the American ambassador to Moscow, Laurence Steinhardt, with a suggestion that he should work for American intelligence, keeping an eye and reporting on German synthetic oil production. Though under no patriotic obligation, Erickson agreed to do so.

It would seem that the worst part of his mission was his having to pretend that he was a rabid pro-Nazi, thereby incurring the hostility of his former friends and the Swedish business world.

With various colleagues, among whom was Prince Carl Bernadotte and several German businessmen, he carried out his mission from 1941 to 1944. He made many visits to Germany during this time, gleaning valuable information about German oil production. His greatest coup was in persuading Himmler to set up an oil refinery in Sweden. In this connection he was able to visit and study all the important German synthetic oil plants. The intelligence he thus gained was invaluable to the Allies.

BIBLIOGRAPHY :
The Counterfeit Traitor — Alexander Klein (London, 1958).

ERNST, Karl (German agent, World War I).

Some time before the outbreak of World War I, the German Kaiser Wilhelm II paid a visit to his uncle King Edward VII of England. Up to this time, German Military intelligence had had little interest in England, since the English standing army was so puny that the United Kingdom could never be a threat to the powerful military might of Prussia. On the other hand, Britain was the greatest naval power in the world, and so became an object of interest to German Naval intelligence.

So it was that during this particular visit of the Kaiser to London, one of his entourage, a Captain von Rebeur-Paschwitz, known to be a leading member of German Naval intelligence, paid a call on a little third-class hairdresser in the Caledonian Road, London. It so happened, that one of the recently formed MI5's agents had been detailed to keep an eye on Rebeur-Paschwitz, and followed him to the barber's shop. Naturally he was curious to know why such an aristocratic Prussian should visit such a down-at-heel establishment.

The owner of the business was a man called Karl Ernst. Technically Ernst was a British subject, because although both his parents were German, he had been born in London, and at the time that Rebeur-Paschwitz visited him, he had been occupying the same premises for sixteen years. He had no record with the police. That was all that was known about him.

More puzzled than ever now, MI5 began to examine Ernst's mail to see if it would yield any clue. It yielded not one clue, but such a spate of them, that this simple act of censorship formed the basis of what turned out to be a most spectacular counter-espionage success.

Ernst, it was discovered, was the chief "letter-box" for a network of German spies which covered the whole of the British Isles. He received batches of instructions for these agents from German Naval intelligence headquarters, already sealed in envelopes, addressed and sometimes even stamped with English stamps, and all he had to do was to put them in a pillar-box. He also received the spies' replies, which he despatched to Germany.

In a very short time MI5 knew the names and addresses of twenty-six German agents scattered throughout the country. All that it had to do was to sit back, and note the instructions sent to these spies and how they complied. This was just as well, for MI5 at this time was composed of four officers, three investigators and seven clerks; fourteen men altogether, though by the end of the subsequent war the personnel numbered eight hundred.

Since the information which the spies were sending home was not important, it was decided to leave them alone, the argument being that if they were rounded up now, the Germans would replace them and the task of trying to locate a new ring would place too much of a strain on the man power of MI5.

The ring now installed were a normal selection of unimaginative Germans, trained to The Book and unable to go outside their terms of reference. They were plodding and methodical. Every situation had been foreseen except two — what was to happen if British counterespionage were to catch one of their number; and what they were to do if war did break out between Britain and Germany.

The head of the ring was a man called Gustav Steinhauer, who operated from the safety of Ostend, though he made periodic visits to his agents. Steinhauer was a former private detective, and it was the old story again of the detective promoted spy — inability to rise above his detective training and adapt himself to the exigencies of espionage techniques. Naturally, he did not look upon himself as a failure, even after the seizure of all his agents. He referred to himself always as The Kaiser's Master Spy, and after the war published a book of reminiscences with that title.

In the last weeks of July 1914, Steinhauer came to England to warn his agents of the imminence of war between Germany and England. He also came on a mission of his own.

This mission provides a good example of the strange

workings of German intelligence. Since 1909, that is, for five years, Great Britain had been engaged in building Scapa Flow into a naval base large enough to take the whole of the North Sea Fleet at one time in its natural, sheltered harbourage in the Orkney Islands, north of the Scottish mainland. Yet, not until a week before hostilities broke out did they send Steinhauer to investigate it.

Before he went north, however, Steinhauer went round to his agents issuing warnings. To his surprise, most of them laughed at him. They had, they argued, been working in close contact with the British for a number of years now, and they were quite certain that the British would never fight.

On a visit to another barber called Kronauer, at Walthamstow, in northeast London, Steinhauer was convinced that he was being shadowed by the English police. Taking flight he informed Kronauer of the approaching conflict in a code so simple that a child could have "broken" it; but what is more incredible, **he sent it on a postcard,** and despatched similar warnings

to various other agents whom he had no time to visit in person.

He then hurried north and at Scapa Flow, posing as a fisherman, he took rough soundings with a specially knotted fishing-line. Almost at once, he dashed south again, only pausing at Edinburgh to warn his agent there, a music-hall pianist called Georg Kiener. Then MI5 lost track of him, and a day or two later he reappeared in Hamburg.

On 5th August, 1914, the second day of the war, with synchronised movements, detectives visited seven addresses in the London area, and arrested Ernst and six other agents. Meanwhile the Chief Constables of the counties where the other spies were located had received telegrams and simultaneously with the London arrests fourteen more spies were seized.

Otto Weigels at Hull, who had been one of those who had laughed loudest at Steinhauer, and Schappman at Exeter were among the five who managed to escape. And so, at one swoop German Naval intelligence in Great Britain was eliminated.

The Defence of the Realm Act had not been passed when these arrests were made, so that the captured agents could only be interned for the duration of hostilities, with the exception of Ernst, who was a British subject by birth-place. He was sentenced to seven years' penal servitude.

A final point of interest remains. For his services Ernst had been paid the princely sum of £1 a month.

BIBLIOGRAPHY :

MI5 — John Bulloch (London, 1963).

FARNSWORTH, John S.
(American traitor, spied for Japan between the wars).

John S. Farnsworth was born in Cincinnati, and graduated from high school at the top of his class. During his last years at school he developed an ambition to enter the US Navy, and on leaving school he obtained an interview with his congressman, who was impressed by the boy and secured a place for him at the Naval Academy at Annapolis.

At Annapolis, though he seemed to concentrate more on women and drink than he did on his studies, he passed out in 1915 with a brilliant mark.

Farnsworth served in destroyers in World War I, but in 1922 his interest turned to flying and he returned to Annapolis to study nautical aviation. From Annapolis he continued these studies, in 1923, at the Massachusetts Institute of Technology, and when he left there he was promoted lieutenant-commander and posted to a teaching appointment at the Navy Air School at Pensacola, Florida. After a time there he commanded the Squadron Base at Norfolk, Virginia.

Farnsworth's charm made him not only very attractive to women but popular with a wide circle of people. He married a society girl, well above his social station, and his attempts to keep her in the style to which she had been accustomed, and to repay the hospitality they received, ran him into debt and he began to borrow. Getting deeper and deeper into financial difficulties, he eventually borrowed from a naval rating, and when pressed to repay, refused. The result was a court-martial; found guilty, he was dismissed the Service.

It is one of the unfortunate consequences of cases like this that such an entry in a man's record is indelible. Farnsworth's attempts to obtain civilian employment always failed as soon as he had to confess that he had been dismissed from the Navy. It can perhaps be understood that after repeated failures to procure a means of livelihood he felt he was being hounded by the authorities.

In desperation he offered his expert knowledge of aviation to Peru, China, Brazil and Russia. None was interested. Then he turned to Japan.

The Japanese were interested, but not in a technical adviser. Perhaps he would consider other employment in which his knowledge and background would be of great use?

Farnsworth first came to the notice of Captain William Puleston, Chief of the Office of Naval Intelligence (ONI), early in 1934.

A few days previously Farnsworth had paid a call on a former Navy friend, Lieutenant - Commander Leslie Gehres, of the Navy Examining Board. For some time now it had been known in Navy circles that Farnsworth had been haunting old Navy friends, hoping, it seemed, that his past might be forgotten and that he might be re-employed.

While Farnsworth was with him, Gehres was called from his office for a few moments, and when he returned he asked his visitor to excuse him as he had some urgent work to deal with. Farnsworth left.

Within a short time Gehres found that a copy of **The Service of Information and Security,** a highly confidential document, printed especially for a very limited number of high-ranking Navy officers, was missing from his desk. Perturbed at not being able to find it, as a last resort, after questioning his staff, he telephoned Farnsworth and asked him if he had, by any chance, picked up the book by mistake. Farnsworth replied that he had, and would return it the following morning, which he did.

Being a good officer, Gehres made a report of what had happened. It was this report which found its way to the ONI.

Captain Puleston called for the Farnsworth dossier, and found that since he had left the Service he had been divorced, had remarried, and that his second marriage was now running into difficulties. But more significant, he also discovered that Farnsworth was no longer short of money, but almost any day could be found flashing hundred-dollar bills.

This was strange, because he had confessed to Gehres

and other naval friends that he had no employment. How, then, could he live for days in the New Willard, a luxury hotel in Washington, never getting any further than the bar ? Where did his money come from ?

His bank account revealed nothing.

ONI's experience with another ex-Navy man caused Puleston to wonder whether Farnsworth might not be getting his money from a similar source — the Japanese. So, when he began to look around for Farnsworth's Japanese contact — supposing he had one — his attention was attracted to the Japanese naval attaché in Washington, Commander Ichimiya.

Commander Ichimiya lived at the Alban Towers, a block of service apartments. From the maids at the Alban Towers, Puleston learned that they were never allowed to go into two rooms in the commander's suite. They also spoke of a strange acrid smell seeping under the doors of these rooms from time to time, which suggested photographic activity.

But Farnsworth and Ichimiya never seemed to meet.

190

Yet when Ichimiya's bank account was studied it was found that he regularly received large sums of money over and above his normal salary, and whenever he paid in one of these cheques, he also withdrew the greater part of it in new hundred-dollar bills.

Since the ONI was very much understaffed, Puleston decided to ask the FBI for assistance. The FBI put a twenty-four-hour watch on Farnsworth, but for a time they were unable to gather evidence that he was in any way connected with the Japanese.

Presently, however, they got their break. Farnsworth paid a visit to Annapolis, and there called on Lieutenant-Commander James E. Mather at his home, staying for more than an hour. When he left, FBI agents visited Mather and asked what Farnsworth had wanted.

Both the commander and his wife were above reproach. They told the FBI that Farnsworth called on them from time to time, and, believing his protests, because they were loyal Navy people themselves, and could understand that the Navy was in his blood, they had tried to make him happy by talking about Navy affairs. When, however, the FBI agents suggested that Farnsworth might be involved in espionage, though it came as a great shock, the Mathers were able to read sinister implications into his visits to them.

On several occasions, for example, while Mather had been out of the room, Farnsworth had questioned Mrs Mather closely on various matters affecting the Navy which a non-naval, even an ex-naval, man would not have asked. In fact, this had happened on this very visit.

Almost as soon as Farnsworth had arrived he had begun to ask questions about a new destroyer, the USS **Baddlitt,** very recently commissioned, and purported to have the very latest innovations in construction and equipment. Noticing the deterioration in Farnsworth's physical appearance since the last time he had called, and reading the all-too-obvious signs of excessive drinking, Mather had evaded answering the questions. But when, presently, he left his wife alone with Farns-

worth, Farnsworth had said to Mrs Mather, "Please tell me about the **Baddlitt !** I've just got to know !"

Since registering in Annapolis at the Carvell Hall Hotel, Farnsworth had made a telephone call to a Washington ex-directory number. This was suspicious; but all the more suspicious was the fact that he had given the operator a false name. The man who had answered angrily said that he had the wrong number; but the man had spoken with an unmistakable Japanese accent.

When the number was traced it was found to be that of Commander Ichimiya. But Ichimiya had been recalled to Japan, and his apartment at the Alban Towers had been taken over by his successor as naval attaché, Commander Akira Yamaki.

And so the FBI learned definitely for the first time of Farnsworth's connection with the Japanese.

Now, the recall of Ichimiya and his replacement by Yamaki had been carried out with such secrecy that no one in American government circles was aware of the change until Yamaki had installed him-

191

self in the Alban Towers. The reason for the secrecy could only be surmised.

Farnsworth's action in telephoning the Washington ex-directory number led the FBI to check on his other visits to Annapolis, where he always stayed at the Carvell Hall Hotel. He had been to Annapolis seven times in the last two years, they discovered, and each time he had telephoned this same number at least once a day. On one occasion he had made three calls in four hours.

The FBI investigations were now extended, with the result that a picture of Farnsworth's movements over the past three years was built up. He had been to Boston, Philadelphia, B a l t i m o r e , Norfolk and New York. In every instance he had called Ichimiya in Washington.

In Boston, early in 1933, he had telephoned a second number, that of a Japanese called Sato, who was officially described as correspondent of Domei, the Japanese news agency. Sato lived in Morrison Street in Washington, and since he was seen only in the highest official circles he was looked upon as a semi-

official representative of the Japanese government.

One of Sato's closest companions was Yamaki, it was now discovered. They dined together frequently in the leading restaurants in Washington, but when they parted each went to his own home. Nor were they ever known to meet again the same evening.

Then an FBI agent learnt from a maid at the Alban Towers that Sato often called on Yamaki at four o'clock in the morning, using the rear entrance, and staying until dawn. Thinking that perhaps Farnsworth might also be using the back door to visit Yamaki, a permanent watch was set on it. But there was no result until 5th March, 1936.

Slowly, but inexorably, the FBI ground on, and presently they had obtained evidence which would be capable of proving Farnsworth a spy. A m o n g the information which came to them was that during the last three years Farnsworth had constantly visited commercial photostating firms in Washington. When employees of these firms were questioned, they were unable to recall details of the material which they had processed for him, though they could say definitely that the work was always connected with naval matters. He had always waited while the photostating was being done, had paid on the spot, and had taken away with him all the copies and the originals.

Extending this line of inquiry to other cities, photostat operators in Norfolk and Baltimore recognised Farnsworth's photograph. They, too, recalled that he described himself as a naval officer who needed immediate copies of certain official documents.

Remembering the testimony of the maids at the Alban Towers concerning Ichimiya's ban on their entering two rooms of his apartment, and of the odours which sometimes seeped under the doors, the FBI began to wonder whether he might not also have been engaged on such work. With increasing satisfaction they found that within a month of Ichimaya's arrival in Washington in 1933, two photostating machines had been delivered to him at the Alban Towers.

By this time enough evidence against Farnsworth had been collected to justify his arrest, for, besides the obvious contact existing between him and certain Japanese, interrogation of naval ratings and officers who had been approached by him revealed that unwittingly he had been supplied with a great deal of information. He had been told for example, the effectiveness of every gun in the Navy, and the vital performance records of the aircraft-carriers **Ranger** and **Saratoga.**

But the FBI were held back by the authorities from making their kill. By the time Farnsworth had to be arrested to avoid a scandal, he had ceased to be an active spy, Commander Yamaki was safely back in Tokyo, and Sato was working innocently in New York.

Commander Yamaki's decision that Farnsworth was no longer to engage in any espionage activities on behalf of the Japanese, and, even more, his withholding of money from Farnsworth were about the biggest blunders the Japanese secret service ever made in America, and perhaps elsewhere.

The publication in July of long prison sentences on another ex-naval traitor had an effect on Farnsworth that this man's arrest had not had. That night he went out and got very drunk indeed — on money he had had to borrow.

The following morning he went to the National Press Building on Fourteenth Street NW, where he took the lift to the offices of the Universal News Service, a Hearst subsidiary. There he was interviewed by John Lambert, chief of the Washington office, and was passed on by him to Fulton Lewis Jr.

The entirely impecunious Farnsworth, besides being in search of money, was now bent on establishing justification for his collaboration with the Japanese. It had at last struck him that he, too, might have been watched by counter-espionage agents.

His story was an ingenious one, and had the FBI been unaware at this time of the true damage he had done they might have been deceived by it. He told Fulton Lewis that he had been pretending to spy for the Japanese in an attempt to find out the extent of their espionage activities.

He had not told the authorities what he was doing, because he hoped that if he did a good job it might lead to his reinstatement in the Navy. He offered Fulton Lewis the story for 20,000 dollars.

Lewis refrained from asking him why he had come to him now instead of going to the ONI, and playing for time he said that he could not himself authorise the payment of so large a sum as 20,000 dollars, but would have to consult his chief. Perhaps Farnsworth would call back the following day?

As soon as Farnsworth had gone, Lewis informed the police, and the FBI, arguing that it would be dangerous to the security of the nation to leave the ex-officer at liberty any longer, obtained the consent of the authorities to his arrest. He was taken into custody a few hours after he had left the National Press Building.

It was February 1937 before the US Attorney General had his case against Farnsworth ready. The indictment included specific charges of having visited the Navy Department in August 1934 and January 1935, and the Naval

194

Academy at Annapolis in April 1935, for the purpose of obtaining code and signal books, sketches, photographs, blue-prints, maps and models.

To his defending attorney and to all who came into contact with him Farnsworth protested his innocence, as he had done to Fulton Lewis Jr, and the FBI. But at the last moment he changed his mind and entered a plea of **nolo contendere.**

On 23rd February, 1937 he was sentenced to four to twenty years in a Federal penitentiary.

BIBLIOGRAPHY :

Passport to Treason — Alan Hynd (New York, 1943).

FAUCHE-BOREL see under **Montgalliard, Comte Maurice de.**

FAUQUENOT-BIRCKEL Affair, The (World War I).

In August 1914, Marie Birckel, a young schoolmistress living with a family in Lorraine, decided to return to her parent's home at Variscourt, near Château-Thierry, as the German forces invaded Lorraine. She was slightly built, with dark brown eyes, and intelligent above her years. Somewhat ironically, that part of Lorraine where she had worked was soon cleared of the invaders, whereas Château-Thierry was occupied by the Germans until almost the end of the war.

Mme Birckel, a widow, was the village schoolmistress, and when the mayor and other leading men were called to the colours, she found herself de facto in charge of the little community. When the Germans arrived, she was so calm and firm, that they readily consulted her about the various problems that arise from occupation. Unfortunately, she died within a few weeks of dysentery, leaving her daughter alone with two young nephews under her care.

Marie, however, had inherited her mother's strength of character and courage. The Germans had left her with only one room, and one day when she returned from a visit and found her younger nephew, who was ill, shivering outside and a party of soldiers playing cards in the room from which they had evicted him, she took him back into the room, sat him beside the fire, and told the Ger-

195

mans to leave at once. They obeyed without argument.

Early in 1915, she and all the other civilians in the area were sent into districts unoccupied by the Germans. Before she left, Marie made a careful note of every tiny item of information about the German forces she could acquire. These she passed on to the French Military intelligence, who were so impressed by it that she was called to headquarters in Paris. She volunteered to return at once to Variscourt as a spy.

To do so, it was decided that she would travel via Folkestone to Holland, and from there to Variscourt. On her way through Folkestone she made contact with the Mixed Bureau (q.v.) who briefed her on the organisation of the Allied secret service in Belgium. She arrived in Holland in February 1916.

The crossing of the frontier between Holland and Belgium was a difficult and risky business. By this time the Germans had erected an electrified wire barrier, to touch which meant instant death. Fortunately this barrier did not run the entire length of the frontier, but even the

wire-free country presented great obstacles in the form of canals and dykes. However, on the outbreak of war the peace-time smugglers of the region had offered their services to the Allied intelligence services as guides, and it was one of these who was detailed to lead Marie into Belgium.

On the first attempt she fell into a canal and almost drowned, but at the second, on 15th May, 1916, she was successful. Accompanying her and the guide was a young French agent, Emile Fauquenot, who was in charge of the Maastricht information centre. He had his misgivings, however, about the guide who had been allocated to the operation, but could do nothing about it. His misgivings seemed to be well-founded when, after several days in which Marie gave no sign that she had reached her destination, it was learned that she had been arrested not long after she had reached Liége. Investigation showed that without doubt she had been betrayed.

Marie was confined in the Saint-Leonard Prison in Liége. Under the most strenuous interrogation she refused to answer any question put to her.

Emile Fauquenot was the son of a French father and Belgian mother. Aged seventeen, he was on holiday in Belgium at the home of some cousins when war broke out and he was caught by the invasion of the country. Within a short time, however, he managed to reach France, and though under-age he volunteered and joined an infantry regiment. The initiative he had shown in escaping from Belgium attracted the attention of his superiors, and in some way French intelligence heard of his exploits. By May 1915 he had been seconded to the SR, and though only eighteen had been put in charge of the Maastricht information centre.

On 1st July, 1915 — two months after Marie's arrest— he, too, was caught and it was clear that he had been betrayed. He was taken to the Saint-Leonard prison, and was able to organise ways of communicating with Marie.

In September they were brought before the same court martial, and sat together on the prisoners' bench, where they fell in love with one another. Fortunately, the Dutch authorities pleaded with the Germans on their behalf, chiefly on account of their youth, and King Alfonso of Spain personally provided their counsel. Instead of the death penalty, they were sentenced to life imprisonment.

Despite the fact that he was constantly moved from cell to cell, Fauquenot, who proved himself one of the most difficult prisoners the Germans ever held, at last managed to escape on 28th March, 1918. In July 1918 the Germans, fearing that Fauquenot might attempt to rescue her, moved Marie to a prison in Germany, from which she was released after the armistice in November.

The French government bestowed on her the Croix de Guerre, the citation reading, "A young girl inspired by the highest patriotism. After spontaneously asking to perform a particularly dangerous mission in invaded territory, she succeeded in penetrating the enemy lines. Arrested and imprisoned, she proved her high conception of duty by facilitating for more than two years, while in prison, the accomplishment of the mission entrusted to another person, showing throughout her long detention the greatest energy and courage."

Fauquenot received the same award. "After asking to perform a particularly dangerous mission in the enemy lines," the citation went, "since 1915 he has rendered important services with complete devotion. Caught in a trap, he fell into the hands of the enemy on 1st July, 1916. Imprisoned he succeeded, by his doggedness and daring, first of all in continuing from prison the mission entrusted to him, then in escaping on three occasions in the most perilous circumstances. Having at last regained his liberty he managed to outwit his pursuers and performed his mission until the armistice. A young man admirable for his patriotism and high conception of duty."

Within a few months of the armistice Marie Birckel and Emile Fauquenot married. The British government awarded both with the OBE and the French government with the Legion of Honour to celebrate their devotion to duty and the occasion.

198

BIBLIOGRAPHY :
Agents secret, l'affaire Fauquenot-Birckel — Paul Durand (Paris, 1937).

FEDERAL BUREAU OF INFORMATION (FBI)
Counter-espionage role of.

Established in 1908, as the detective service of the Department of Justice, the FBI's functions were originally the investigation of violations of the law. This is still its major role. It is concerned with crime as it affects the United States as a whole, as distinct from individual state offences which are the responsibility of the state police.

Shortly before the outbreak of the Second World War, it was given the added role of a counter-espionage service, in which it is comparable with the British MI5 and the French C-S, and indeed with any counter-espionage service organised on a national basis. In this role, the FBI has figured prominently in all the major espionage cases that have occurred in America since the end of the war.

FELFE, Heinz Paul Johan
(Russian double-agent, post World War II).

Heinz Felfe was born in

1918, the son of a policeman. Later he joined the SS, rose to the rank of Obersturmführer (lieutenant) and worked in RSHA (q.v.) all through World War II. At the end of the war, because of his membership of the SD (SS security service) he was arrested and interned in Canada. In 1946, however, he was released, and after a time found work in the Ministry of All German Affairs, where he informed on refugees from East Germany. Presently he also became an informer for British intelligence in the University of Bonn, when he enrolled as a law student. Because of his usefulness both to the German government and the British he was eventually classified, in the de-nazification process, as **uninvolved,** this despite the fact that he had served several years in the notorious SD.

Hans Clemens had been a captain, Haupsturmführer, in the SS, in which he first began service in 1931. With the accession of Hitler he was appointed head of the Dresden branch of the SD. In 1938, he was sent to Switzerland as an agent provocateur. As a reward for successful service, he was transferred to RSHA, in which he served throughout the war. At the armistice he tried to escape to Switzerland, but was caught, subsequently tried as a war criminal, but acquitted. While serving at RSHA he had become a close friend of Felfe.

Erwin Tiebel had been deputy mayor of Radeburg near Dresden. During the war he joined the SS, but never rose above the rank of corporal. He rehabiliated himself quickly after the war, and after a period as a labourer, became manager of the firm of building contractors that employed him.

Clemens was released from his Italian gaol in September 1949. While in prison Tiebel had pressed him to go and stay with him as soon as he was free, and Clemens's first act was to accept the invitation. While he was staying with Tiebel, he received a letter from his wife, who was still living in Dresden, now in the Soviet Zone of Germany, suggesting he should go there and meet some of her Russian friends.

199

Clemens made a favourable impression on the Russians and he was eventually enlisted in Soviet intelligence. He was given the assignment of investigating the possibility of his joining an intelligence organisation in the West. In addition, he was required to try to persuade his friend Heinz Felfe, now working for the Gehlen organisation, to become an agent for the Russians while continuing to work for the West.

Clemens and Felfe met early in 1950, at a very propitious moment for Clemens, for Felfe was dissatisfied with German intelligence methods which were no challenge for a man of his cunning. He accepted Clemen's proposal that he should work for the Russians with alacrity. In return, through the good offices of ex-SS Colonel Krichbaum, now a personnel officer for the Gehlen organisation, he was able to insinuate Clemens into the Gehlen set-up. Within a few months Felfe also had joined the Gehlen organisation.

Felfe and Clemens were now in positions in which they could supply the Russians with first-grade intelligence from the West. Their one need was a go-between, and who else could be more suitable than the respectable businessman, Erwin Tiebel. Though he never drew the same thrill from espionage activities that Felfe and Clemens did, Tiebel had no hesitation in joining his old friends.

Felfe, helped by a steady flow of "material" from the Russians quickly made a tremendous impact on his superiors in the Gehlen organisation, and within a short time he became chief of the Russian counter-espionage department. Thus, Felfe, the Russian spy, was responsible for the West German effort to thwart Russian espionage.

Because of his position as chief of a department of the BND, Felfe also received reports from the other two German intelligence services BfV (q.v.) and military counter-espionage. In addition he knew the names and code-names of all BND agents operating in Russia, copies of their reports and a record of the instructions passed to them.

All this information passed to the Russians enabled them to warn their agents whenever the BfV prepared to pounce.

Felfe photographed all the documents which passed through his hands. He and Clemens later admitted that they had passed 15,000 photographs of top secret documents from West German intelligence records and twenty spools of tape-recordings to Russia. Most were delivered by Tiebel, though special couriers from the East did come forward from time to time.

Felfe and Clemens also made journeys to the East, to obtain from the Russians genuine intelligence material which would enhance their positions as Western agents. The Russians played their part in this so well, that before long Felfe was put in charge of the Russian counter-espionage section of the BND.

All went well, and might have continued to do so for far longer than the eleven years during which the trio operated, had not an agent for the Russians, Günter Mannel, defected to the West in the autumn of 1961. Mannel brought with him a suitcase containing hundreds of secret documents and some tape recordings. Besides identifying fifteen other Soviet agents working in the West, Mannel's contribution also disclosed the true roles of Felfe and Clemens.

Felfe was arrested on 6th November, 1962, at Pullad in possession of an attaché case containing fourteen rolls of films and a miniature tape. Clemens was arrested in Berlin next day, and Tiebel shortly afterwards.

Their trial began on 8th July, 1963, and when it closed Felfe was sentenced to fourteen years and a fine of 140,000 marks, Clemens to ten years and a fine of 140,000 marks, and Tiebel to three years and a fine of 4,000 marks.

The case, which almost brought about the fall of General Gehlen also resulted in the complete reorganisation of the BND.

BIBLIOGRAPHY :
The Secret War For Europe—
Louis Hagen (London, 1968).

FIELDING, Xan (British agent in World War II).

Xan Fielding was born in India in 1918, and educated at Charterhouse (where he was a

Classical Scholar) and at Bonn and Munich universities in Germany. Before the war he travelled extensively in Greece and the Mediterranean. In 1939 he was commissioned as an officer in the Intelligence Corps, and not long afterwards was seconded to SOE, by whom he was posted to Crete to assist in the organisation of Cretan Resistance.

In February 1944 he was recalled from Crete after two years in the field. He then applied for a transfer to the French Section of SOE, which was granted. Early in August 1944, he was parachuted into southern France and joined the network in the Basses Alpes led by the outstanding British agent Francis Cammaerts (q.v.). He had not been long in France when he was arrested with Cammaerts, and placed in Dignes prison, from which he was rescued by the astounding woman agent, Christine Granville (q.v.) only hours before the two men were due to be executed.

His next assignment was in Indo-China, where he operated until the end of the war with Japan. He was awarded

the Distinguished Service Order for his outstanding Services.

BIBLIOGRAPHY :
Hide and Seek — Xan Fielding (London, 1954).

FOOTE, Alexander (Englishman who spied for Russia before and during World War II).

Alexander Foote was born in 1905, the son of a middle-class English family. After World War I, like many other young men of his age, the unsettled times made him restless, and for some years he drifted from job to job. He then became attracted to Communism, but never joined the British Communist Party.

During the Spanish Civil War he applied to join the International Brigade. He was accepted and in December 1936 he went to Spain, where at the headquarters of the Brigade at Albacete, he was allocated to the British battalion, and was placed in charge of battalion transport. He served two years in Spain, and while on leave in London he was told that he had been chosen for a dangerous assignment abroad, if he were willing to take it.

Foote accepted the assignment with alacrity, though he had no idea of the nature of the work he was to be asked to do. He was told to go at once to Geneva, Switzerland, where, on the day following the day of his arrival, he was to contact a woman outside the General Post Office. He was given passwords and made the contact satisfactorily.

Over coffee in a nearby cafe, the woman introduced herself by her cover-name Sonia, and arranged further meetings with him. During these meetings over the next few days, she gave him his instructions. He was to go to Munich in Germany and there prepare reports on certain aspects of German politics. At the end of three months he was to return to Geneva with the results of his studies.

He passed this test satisfactorily, and only then was he given any indication of what his real assignment was. He was to become radio-operator for a Soviet network operating in Switzerland under the Resident Director (q.v.) Alexander Rado (q.v.).

This network was one of the smallest and least important of the Russian networks at the time that Foote joined it in 1938. Up to 1937 it had had at its head a good-looking woman of thirty, known as Vera. At the end of the war she was promoted to the Swiss Section at The Centre in Moscow, became involved in the Canadian Spy Case (q.v.) and was liquidated by SMERSH. During the war the Swiss network was to become one of the most important of all Russian networks.

Vera was succeeded by a number of good agents, the best of whom was Sonia, whose real name was Ursula-Maria Hamburger, the first Soviet agent ever to operate a radio transmitter in Switzerland. Her husband, Rudolph Hamburger operated in the Far East and was arrested in China. When this occurred Maria had been sent to Switzerland to reorganise the German networks from there. When Foote met her, she was living in a rented villa at Caux, near Montreux, from where she transmitted to Moscow.

When war broke out, Sonia was instructed to withdraw all

203

her agents from Germany, but she was to remain in Switzerland and instruct Foote and another Englishman in radio procedure. The former German agents were, for the most part, absorbed into the Swiss network.

Foote proved an apt pupil, not only at acquiring radio techniques, but at appreciating the value of other espionage techniques, particularly security. For a time he lived in Montreux, acting as Sonia's radio operator.

In August 1940, Foote was ordered by The Centre to go to Geneva, there to instruct a man called Edmond Hamel in Morse and radio procedure. Sonia's transmitter was moved to Hamel's apartment above his radio shop at 26 rue Carouge, Geneva, and Foote began to instruct Hamel, who did not prove a very apt pupil.

Sonia now disappeared from the scene, at last obtaining The Centre's permission to go to England. Foote's duties in instructing Hamel were taken over by the other Englishman, and Foote himself was ordered to Lausanne, and to establish himself there, with the object of understudy-

ing Rado, so that he might take over the duties of Resident Director should Rado ever get into trouble.

He had some difficulty in setting himself up in an apartment in Lausanne, chiefly on account of the Swiss laws which prohibited foreigners from renting apartments, instead of living in hotels. He eventually overcame this, however, and settled down in a self-contained apartment in a large block at 2 Chemin de Longeraie, Lausanne. Another obstacle he had to surmount was yet another Swiss regulation which forbade the erection of outside wireless aerials. This he also overcame, managing to convince the Swiss authorities that he was homesick for England and found listening to the BBC broadcasts a great consolation, and this he could only do with an outside aerial.

Until the day on which Hitler launched his invasion of Russia, Foote found the life of a secret agent in Switzerland, leisurely and pleasant. He was required to transmit two schedules only each week, and the messages he was required to pass were few and short. He used the time in establishing himself in a small circle of acquaintances, to whom he represented himself as a man of means, something of an eccentric, who was living abroad to escape Hitler's bombs over England.

Shortly before the launching by Hitler of **Operation Barbarossa** a man called Rudolf Rössler (q.v.) who was to prove himself to be one of the greatest spies of all times, had approached Rado with the offer of top-grade intelligence. At first, The Centre was sceptical of Rössler's claims to be able to supply information of such importance, but it was not long before Moscow realised that every single item he sent was reliable. Anxious to retain his services, they were prepared to fulfil every condition he laid down, and in fact no other Russian spy has ever been so generously treated financially by the Centre. Since Rössler produced a constant flow of intelligence, Foote's duties consequently became more onerous.

The Swiss authorities were fully aware of the existence of Rado's network, and so was the German **Abwehr's** network which was also operating in Switzerland. The Swiss counter-espionage organisation known as **Bupo,** however, was prepared to take no action against it so long as its activities did not overtly flout Swiss neutrality. This was fortunate for Foote, because in the middle of 1943 he was denounced to the Swiss by two former Russian agents, George and Joanna Wilmer, who had defected to the Germans.

The **Abwehr,** on the other hand, were anxious to put the network out of commission, and since the Swiss were clearly not prepared to do so, they began to chase Rado and at the same time kept up a constant surveillance of his radio-operator and mistress, Margaret Bolli. Rado was aware of this and for the time being took her transmitter from her, and passed the traffic she would have carried to Foote.

Despite Rado's warnings, the **Abwehr's** trap for Margaret Bolli, which they baited with a handsome young agent called Hans Peters, caught its hoped-for victim. While she was in bed with Peters one evening, Abwehr agents unceremoniously and thoughtlessly interrupted their lovemaking and abducted her. In view of this the **Bupo** decided that, for the sake of appearances, they must take some action against Rado and his colleagues, and they began by arresting the Hamels. This left the network with only one operator—Alexander Foote.

These events threw Rado into a panic, for shortly before the Hamels' arrest, he had deposited all his financial records, copies of the messages he had sent to Moscow, and, worst of all, his code book, in their flat, and these would obviously be found by the Swiss.

The **Bupo** did not yet know of the existence of Rado. They believed that Foote was the head of the network, and in assuming this they were not far wrong, for Rado decided to go into hiding in Berne and begged Foote to take over the direction of the network.

Unfortunately, the **Bupo** decided that the time had come to move against Foote. During the night of November 19th/20th, 1943, while he was in the middle of his regular transmission to Moscow,

they forced their way into his apartment. The door was stronger than they had believed it would be, and gave them considerable trouble. In the few moments this gave him, Foote was able to burn his papers and so damage his transmitter that it would no longer work.

Foote was interrogated, but betrayed nothing. He was kept in prison for ten months while the **Bupo** prepared their case against him. He was then told that as there was no evidence against him of having spied on Switzerland, he could apply for bail while awaiting trial by a military tribunal, provided he would sign a statement that he had been spying for the Soviet Union. This Foote refused to do, but a compromise was reached, and he was released on giving surety for himself in the sum of 2,000 Swiss francs.

Foote went at once to Lausanne, and having made certain that he was not being watched, he contacted the Swiss Communists who told him that Rado and his wife had not been caught, and had left for Paris only a few days earlier. (By this time France had been liberated.) He then got in touch with his agents, who told him, that despite everything that had happened, their sources were still intact. This decided him to follow Rado to Paris, to ask the Russian embassy there to contact The Centre for him and ask them for instructions.

In Paris he found that Rado had only just contacted the embassy though he had been in the city some days. Rado was in a highly nervous state, as he had every reason to be, for it had been through his extremely lax security that the network had been compromised.

Both men were summoned to Moscow for "consultations", and they left Paris in a Russian aircraft on 6th January, 1945. As the battle for Germany was still being hotly contested, the aircraft was routed via Cairo. While they were waiting in Cairo, Rado, who was now more nervous than ever, for he knew what fate was in store for him in Moscow, disappeared. Foote went on to Moscow alone, and there he had a very tough time convincing the Director of The Centre that he had not been

double-crossing them, for at this time, the Russian High Command was obsessed with the idea that the British had been trying to hold up their advance into Germany by supplying them with false intelligence, through Foote.

Eventually, Foote was able to clear himself and was able to persuade the Director to give him a new assignment, chiefly because the Canadian Spy Case, which compromised so many Russian agents in many parts of the world, and touched off a purge in The Centre, made it necessary for the Russians to forego their rule that once an agent has been arrested he cannot be used again for at least five years. So, in March 1947, Foote, under the cover name of Major Granatov, arrived at Berlin airport en route for Argentina.

His handling by The Centre had made him disillusioned with Russian intelligence and with Communism as well, and he had left Moscow intending to defect at the first opportunity. While waiting in Berlin, he crossed into the British Sector.

He asked for, and was granted permission to return

to England. After all, he had not occasioned any harm to the West by his spying for Russia. Until his death in the early 1960s, he lived in England, working as a clerk and living as inconspicuously in this role as he had conducted himself as a spy.

Without doubt, though he had brought off no spectacular coup, Alexander Foote was one of the most successful agents ever to serve Russian intelligence.

BIBLIOGRAPHY :

A Handbook for Spies — Alexander Foote (London, 1949).

The Art of Spying — Ronald Seth (London, 1957).

FOUCHE, Joseph (French spy-master).

Joseph Fouché was born in Nantes on 31st May, 1758. Disregarding the family seafaring tradition, Joseph, displaying an unwonted intellectual ability for a Fouché adopted a gentler career. Having received and profited by an education from the Oratorians, he joined the Order in the preliminary degrees, and was very early appointed to be a teacher of physics and mathematics, and an inspector of schools.

During a tour of duty in Arras, he met Carnot and Robespierre and from them learned about and approved the principles of revolution. Finding that he had gifts as an orator, he renounced his orders, and was elected chairman of the **Amis de la constitution** in Nantes. But he was not an extremist, and with a nice appreciation of future developments, he married the daughter of a wealthy bourgeois.

When, in 1792, elections for the National Convention were announced. Fouché put himself forward as a candidate. The commercial and seafaring community of Nantes, where his liberal views and his connections by marriage, met with approval, made him their representative, and he set off for Paris. He was thirty-three.

It was not long before he changed his policy and became one of the loudest callers of Jacobin airs, and was harsh and vehement in his advocacy of Louis XVI's execution. Nor was it long before his ambitions became even better defined.

In 1794 he was one of the

chief architects of Robespierre's downfall, for he saw in his former friend a rival whose continued existence would block his own progress. Five years later he had achieved the position he believed would best allow him the means of fulfilling his ambitions. He was made minister of police.

By this time the system of French police had become an intricately organised and extremely powerful force in French life. It was operating on such an extensive front, that no one was safe from it. The force was entirely manned by outcasts and rouges, all determined to make the most for themselves out of their connections and activities.

Fouché understood them well. But he brought to his office a genius which raised the performance of the men under him to a level unprecedented in the history of espionage in any country up to this time.

If the Committee of Public Safety had felt the need for an extended system of police, Napoleon had an even greater need, as all tyrants have, of knowing what was going on in every corner — and hole — of his realm. A competent judge of men, he recognised in Fouché the right man in the right position, and confirmed him in his post as minister of police. They were to quarrel later, but this event also accrued to Fouché's benefit.

Fouché's right-hand men were Réal, inspector-general of police, and Desmarest, chief of the Division of Public Safety and of the Secret Police. These two men worked together in the closest concert, understanding one another's aims so perfectly that they were almost indispensable complements of each other. They were not endowed with the same capacity of duplicity as their chief was, but as administrators they were vastly superior.

Their technique was also a great advance on that of any of their predecessors. They had what they called the Test of Fidelity, under which they chose as spies those unfortunates who had committed crimes for which they were yet unpunished; or they organised matters so that the men they chose who started with clean records, should be trapped into committing a felony. In both cases, they were threatened that if they betrayed their masters in the slightest degree, punishments would be pronounced. Thus they inspired a kind of loyalty by **force majeure,** or more simply, blackmail.

Fouché, in contrast to his precursors, held the theory that it was knowledge and not the threat of death or the ability to inflict it, which was the source of power. Réal and Desmarest were in full agreement with him, and in their processes used a technique until this time employed by those wishing to make their victims divulge their knowledge. Instead of the rack, the thumbscrew, the bastinado and the branding-iron, they sought to undermine the morale of those who were brought to them, by a deceptive appearance of friendliness. There was no bullying. In its place they led the unfortunates to believe that they were among friends; and no one was more surprised when they found themselves nevertheless led to the guillotine. And if this technique did not work, they were thrown into cells, where they were subjected to methodical physical degradation and psychological torture which reduced them to such a weak state that when they were again brought up for interrogation they did not know what they were saying.

Fouché's tentacles stretched not only into every corner of France, but reached out to wherever the enemies of the régime happened to be. No one could escape him, not even Montgalliard who, in accordance with the technique, had supplied himself with a Test of Fidelity par excellence.

By 1810, Montgalliard was in prison for debt, and it looked as if he would remain in prison for the rest of his life. Realisation of his predicament encouraged him to write to Fouché offering to do anything that the minister of police might set him to do, if only he might be freed and provided with the means of subsistence.

Fouché immediately agreed. Montgalliard's debts, to the extent of 78,000 francs, were paid, and he was granted an income of 14,000 francs a year, which he earned by political spying.

Napoleon, all this time, had

not been unaware of the debt he owed to his minister of police. He had made him a member of the Senate and duc d'Otranto. This recognition Fouché deserved, and deserved well, for his control of the foreign spies with whom his master's realm was riddled, was masterly. Perhaps there is no better example of how this mastery was achieved than the case of the Secret Committee.

There was serving in the political police a man called Charles Perlet, who for his Royalist tendencies, had been sentenced to a period on Cayenne from which he returned to find his family destitute and himself compelled to take any employment. He was, of course, an excellent subject for Fouché, because he, too, provided a ready-made Fidelity Test.

Perlet, who had suffered on account of his Royalist sympathies, was just the man who could make contact with Bourbon factions abroad, and under Fouché's orders he opened a correspondence with a group in Berlin. The real and primary object of this operation was unspectacular. That it developed into

what it did was not accidental, but the intelligent outcome of a resourceful mind which recognised the opportunities provided by an expected turn of events. At the beginning, then, Perlet was given the task merely of luring Fauche-Borel (**see under** Montgalliard, Comte Maurice de) back to Paris.

At this time, Fauché-Borel, who had been imprisoned on being betrayed by Montgalliard, had escaped from the Temple prison, but had been recaptured. Confined this time in La Force prison, a description of which defies words, he had promised Fouché that in return for his liberty, he would be a loyal servant of the minister of police. Fouché accepted his offer, and sent him to Berlin to keep an eye on Royalists there. It was not long before there came into his hands a document which was of tremendous value to the Bonapartists. It was a declaration by Louis XVIII of Napoleon's "crime" in accepting the crown of France, but devised in such terms that it was designed to be a rallying call to all Royalists everywhere, and particularly in France.

Fauche-Borel told Fouché that he had obtained his copy from the original, but he failed to tell him that he had had ten thousand copies of it printed for his own use, and was smuggling them into France. Immediately Fouché discovered this treachery, he ordered Fauche-Borel to be apprehended, but his quarry managed to escape to London.

To counter the effects of Fauche-Borel's private activities, Fouché conceived the idea of the Secret Committee. The basis of the idea was the supposed formation of a provisional government among the supporters of Louis in France, who would be ready to take action the moment the tyrant had been overthrown by a Royalist uprising. He sent Perlet to Berlin to tell the Royalists there about it, and his news threw them into a flurry of excitement. They accepted Perlet as their intermediary with the (non-existent) Secret Committee without question, and discussed at great length in their clandestine correspondence with him — all of which Fouché read and thus gained a shrewd idea of Royalist

potentialities — the details of the plan they had for the uprising.

Sooner or later the news of the Secret Committee was bound to reach Fauche-Borel. Immediately this happened, Fauche-Borel, believing himself destined to play an important role in Louis' restoration, began to bombard Perlet with questions, requesting particularly a list of names of the members of the Secret Committee. Perlet retorted that it was far too dangerous to commit such information to paper, and suggested that Fauche-Borel should come secretly to Paris to meet the Committee. But Fouché's plan did not come off; Fauche-Borel was too old a hand to fall into a trap like that. The risk, he said, was far too great for him to undertake such a mission.

Perlet's correspondence had completely deceived not only Louis himself, but the British government, and when the latter suggested to the point of insistence that a reliable negotiator should go to Paris to meet the Committee, Fauche-Borel put forward his nephew, Charles Vitel, a gallant young soldier.

Fouché, by the way, had allowed himself to be named as a member of the Committee, and when Vitel arrived in Paris he was carrying a letter to the supposedly enlightened minister of police, in a hollow cane. Immediately on arrival, Vitel was arrested and shot as an English spy.

It might be thought that the failure of their agent to return would have made the expatriate Royalists at once suspicious. But no such thing happened, and the Committee "continued to operate", until Fouché, seeing that nothing would eventually be achieved by it, ordered Perlet to withdraw. Even so, when the Restoration was at last accomplished, the Royalists made exhaustive inquiries about the Committee.

Not long after Fouché had closed the operation down, he fell victim to Napoleon's whim. Not quite without warning, he found himself out of office. He made no protests, but he did something which seems to indicate that he had a devilish sense of humour.

He put on full-dress uniform to welcome his successor, General Savary (q.v.) in his office; but it was an office completely devoid of files or records of any sort. Fouché had been minister of police for a dozen years, and the knowledge he had acquired by virtue of his position had made him the most powerful man under the emperor. In fact, without this knowledge, in the form of records, Napoleon was shorn of much of his power. At least, that was how Fouché saw it.

There may have been an idea at the back of Fouché's mind, that when Napoleon realised that no successor could carry on without the records, he would have to reinstate him. But Napoleon was not the man to be blackmailed in this way.

When General Savary found that the police archives were empty, he immediately informed Napoleon. The emperor sent to Fouché, resting in his country-house prior to setting out for Italy, where he had been given the governorship of Illyria, ordering him to restore all ministerial documents. Fouché returned the answer that he knew too many secrets concerning the disreputable activities of the

213

Imperial Family to be given orders.

Further messengers were sent. To each of them Fouché gave the same reply. In an excess of zeal, undoubtedly misplaced, he had burned all the documents.

Worked into a dreadful fury by these answers Napoleon sent the chief of his own personal police — a private force outside the authority of Fouché — to put his papers under seal. Although he had removed all the valuable ones to a private and secret place, Fouché at last saw that he had gone too far, and wrote an apology to Napoleon. But the Emperor would not be mollified, and banished Fouché to Otranto.

After the battle of Leipzig, seeing that Napoleon's power was on the wane, he prepared to desert to the Bourbons in earnest, and after 1815 he was restored by them to the police ministry. In the following year, however, he was arrested and tried for his part in the execution of Louis XVI, declared a regicide and exiled. He died in Trieste on Christmas Day, 1820.

BIBLIOGRAPHY :

Life of Joseph Fouché — Stefan Zweig (London, 1930).

FOX, Montagu (British Admiralty agent, 18th century).

On 16th June, 1780, the Spanish ambassador at The Hague called upon his colleague, the French ambassador, the Duke de la Vauguyon, unexpectedly, to tell him that a young Englishman, who called himself Montagu Fox, was waiting at the Spanish embassy in the hope of making the acquaintance of La Vauguyon. He entertained this hope, the Spanish ambassador explained, because he had a proposition to make which, if he were genuine, would provide the Spanish and French governments with high-grade British naval intelligence.

The Spanish ambassador had seen one of the documents which Fox had brought with him, and believed it was authentic. On hearing this, La Vauguyon decided to appease his curiosity and accompany his colleague to his embassy to meet the young man, determined nevertheless to keep an open mind until his doubts had been set at rest.

On the way the Spanish

ambassador told La Vauguyon something about Fox's background, as described to him by the Englishman. He had, he claimed, taken part in the riots which had broken out in London a few weeks earlier at the unconscious instigation of Lord George Gordon. He had been with the mob which had broken into the house of Lord Sandwich, First Lord of the Admiralty, where he had come upon some secret government documents. He had done so, he said, so that he might be able to prove his bona fides to their excellencies.

La Vauguyon had expected to find Fox to be somewhat of a ruffian; instead he found him a well-spoken, well-educated and quite elegantly dressed young man, who presently intrigued him even more by announcing that he was in reality the intermediary with their excellencies for a group of the British Opposition led by Charles James Fox. These gentlemen, he went on, had reached the conclusion that the infamous government of Lord North could only be brought down if the Royal Navy were deprived of much of its power.

This could be done by the French and Spanish navies the more easily if the two governments were given access to reliable information about the projected movements of the British fleets. This information his friends were in a position to supply.

After some questioning La Vauguyon was convinced of Fox's genuineness, and undertook to consult his Foreign Minister, the Comte de Vergennes. Fox suggested that he should go to France to put his scheme to the minister in person.

From the very first moment Vergennes was suspicious, but he did agree to receive Fox, and the young man met him at Versailles. What passed between them did nothing to relieve Vergenne's suspicions, who warned La Vauguyon to proceed with the utmost caution.

La Vauguyon believed his chief to be wrong, and reached an agreement with Fox for the supply of documents. So at intervals, Fox disappeared and returned with copies of secret Admiralty memoranda and reports and instructions to the commanders of squadrons. For the next year he kept up his supply.

Then, strangely enough, he slipped up. He had been promising for some weeks to produce the original of a letter from the Spanish Minister of Marine, the Count de Castejon. Finally pushed to produce something, he presented La Vauguyon with a document purporting to be this letter, but signed **Casteconde.** This was too much even for the French ambassador, who at last admitted that he had been deceived by Fox and suggested to Vergennes that the mountebank should be arrested and imprisoned. Vergennes gave orders for this to be done, but Fox evaded the traps set for him and disappeared from the pages of history as abruptly as he had entered them.

Montagu Fox was, in fact, an Admiralty secret agent. The documents he handed over to the French government were extremely skilful falsifications of true reports, so altered as to give information exactly opposite to that contained in the real documents. The whole operation was a brilliantly conceived and executed espionage mission.

BIBLIOGRAPHY :
The Spy in Silk Breeches — Ronald Seth, (London, 1968).

FRAHM, Hans (Russian agent operating in West Germany).

Hans Frahm was a sports writer and a Communist, who organised a small cell operating in Kiel. He was already working for the Russians when he met Harald Freidank, who was in charge of the British-sponsored press service in Kiel. He recruited Freidank and found him so useful that when the British dispensed with the latter's services in 1952, he was loth to lose him, and promised to find him another job with an East German press agency with offices in the British zone.

Frahm took Freidank to Berlin and there introduced him to a Russian agent, who persuaded Freidank to carry on with his spying. Freidank agreed and was given an assignment in Hamburg. There, however, he went about his task so assiduously that he attracted the attention of the

British security forces, who arrested him. He disclosed the Kiel cell, and Frahm was arrested.

Frahm killed himself in prison while awaiting trial. Freidank was given the light sentence of one year's imprisonment.

FRANCILLARD, Marguerite (French traitress, World War I).

Marguerite Francillard was an eighteen-year-old dressmaker in Grenoble. Pretty and vivacious, she attracted the attention of a German agent who was operating under the cover of a commercial traveller for a French silk firm. She fell for his charms and allowed herself to be persuaded into acting as a "letter-box" (q.v.) for him. She made several visits to Switzerland to take him reports left with her by other German agents.

As the result of denunciation to the French C-S, she was shadowed and eventually arrested in Paris in possession of a report from a German agent which she had gone to the capital to collect. She was imprisoned in the St Lazare prison, in cell No 12, the same cell that Mata Hari had occupied. There her conduct was exemplary, and her piety was for some time afterwards a popular topic of conversation among the prisoners and guards who had known her.

On 10th January, 1917, she was driven through a downpour of rain to the execution ground at Vincennes. Throughout this cruel journey she wept uncontrollably, but when she was bound to the stake, she refused the bandage for her eyes, and met the firing-squad with calm courage.

BIBLIOGRAPHY :
The Secret Services of Europe — Robert Boucard London, 1940).

FRANCKS, Wolfgang (German agent in Palestine in World War I).

For some years before the outbreak of World War I, Wolfgang Francks had lived in a number of British colonies. But though he may have looked and talked like a British colonial, he remained constantly faithful to Germany, and when war broke out he returned to his native country. He volunteered, for the Army, and after a brief period in a routine post, he offered to go to the Near East as an agent.

In 1916 the Turks had embarked on a campaign to wrest Egypt from the British, and achieved several initial successes. But in the middle of 1917, General Allenby was put in command of the Expeditionary force to Egypt, and by slow degrees pushed back the Turks, who were the Allies of the Central Powers.

Francks arrived in Palestine, then under Turkish suzerainty, at this critical time for the Turks. He not only spoke English perfectly, but a number of colonial variations equally well. He came supplied with a variety of British uniforms, and it was not long before he was penetrating British camps and fortifications in the guise of a staff officer. His impersonations were perfect, and though the British were aware of a leakage of information which often compelled them to change their plans at the last moment, Francks was never once challenged. Despite the valuable aid he gave to the Turks, they were eventually compelled to re-

treat from Palestine, and Francks returned home, and was lost to sight.

BIBLIOGRAPHY :

The Atom Spies — Oliver Pilat (London, 1954).

FREIDANK, Harald s e e under **Frahm, Hans.**

FUCHS, Klaus (Russian atom-spy).

The detection of Dr Klaus Fuchs was the outcome of a bad blunder made by the Soviet delegate at a meeting of the United Nations Atomic Energy Commission, who let it be known that Russia had access to atomic secrets which the United States believed were absolutely safe. The hunt was at once on. It was clear, from the admission of the Soviet expert, that the information could not have come from Nunn May (q.v.) another traitor and atomic-spy, and this being so, it was equally clear that the Canadian Spy Case investigations had not uncovered all the agents involved.

By a process of elimination, the FBI narrowed their search down to two or three possibilities, one of whom was Fuchs. Fuchs had come to

England as a refugee from the Nazis. He was a brilliant young physicist, and on account of the shortage of this category of scientists when the various atomic projects got under way, it was not long before he had been recruited into one of the British teams, working first in Glasgow and later in Birmingham under another German refugee, a former acquaintance of his, Rudolf Peierls.

Fuchs had fled from Germany because he was an anti-Nazi and in Nazi Germany many anti-Nazis had unfortunately turned to Communism. What was not discovered by the British security authorities was that as a student the young physicist had been a member of a secret underground Communist group of professional men; nor did they discover that he had not been in England long before he made contact with the Soviet network directed by Semion Kremer, secretary to the Russian military attaché in London.

Fuchs met Kremer first as early as May or June 1942, and during the eighteen months until Fuchs was sent to work in the United States, he handed to Kremer copies of his monthly reports.

Fuchs arrived in America in December 1943 and was assigned first to Columbia University, New York, and then to the atomic bomb plant at Los Alamos. In America Fuchs maintained contact with Soviet espionage through the American spy, Harry Gold of Philadelphia (q.v.), and until he returned to England in the middle of 1946 he regularly passed top secret information. On his return to England he went to work at the Atomic Energy Establishment at Harwell, under Dr Cockcroft, reopened his contact with the Soviet network in Great Britain, and continued to hand over vital information.

Late in 1947, however, he began to have doubts about Russian policy and intentions, and soon he was failing to keep appointments with his Soviet contacts. But by then the wheels of fate were beginning to turn against him.

It was not until 1949, however, that the Americans were able to put the British on Fuch's tail. He was watched, but like Nunn May, did not betray himself. When, however, Special Branch officers eventually confronted him, he too made a full confession. He was tried and sentenced to fourteen years' imprisonment.

BIBLIOGRAPHY :

The Atom Spies — Oliver Pilat (London, 1954).

FURUSAWA, Dr Takashi (Japanese agent operating in America pre-World War II).

On an October day in 1933, a Japanese was knocked down by a car in a Los Angeles street, and killed. Documents on his body revealed that his name was Torii and that he was a language student. Another document disclosed, however, that Torii was also a lieutenant-commander in the Japanese Navy. This might not have aroused any suspicions at all, for a Japanese naval officer might have a perfectly legitimate reason for learning English.

When he was run down, however, Torii had been carrying a briefcase, which was locked. Since the police knew the victim's identity and where he had been staying, they had no cause to inspect

the case. All that remained to be done was to inform the Japanese consul, arrange the formalities with regard to handing over the body, and prepare the evidence for the coroner's inquest.

But before any of these things could be done the police received a telephone call from a compatriot of Torii, a Dr Furusawa, the proprietor of a private nursing home situated at $117\frac{1}{2}$ Weller Street, Los Angeles. There were two things about this call which made the police suspicious. The afternoon editions in which the accident would be reported were not yet on the streets; so how had Dr Furusawa learned of Torii's death. The second thing was the anxiety expressed by the doctor, not on account of Torii's death but for the safety of the brief-case.

He was assured that the brief-case was safe, and that it would be handed in due course to the Japanese consul. It did not require a psychologist to recognise the relief in the doctor's voice when he thanked the police for the news.

But the attention of the

police was now focused on the brief-case. Why did the doctor regard it as so far more important than the life of the unfortunate Torii? The case was opened, and after a cursory glance through its contents the FBI were called.

In themselves, the contents of the case did not present a serious threat to the security of the United States. Certainly, to learn that Lieutenant-Commander Torii in his role of language student was a spy contained the elements of a shock; but it was decided that no action should be taken at this point purely on the basis of the contents of the case. Instead, a little watchfulness might produce more important results. So the contents were photographed, and the case relocked and handed over intact to the Japanese consul.

But what was Dr Furusawa's role? If Torii was a spy, where did the doctor fit in? The investigations of the FBI were to unearth some curious facts.

Dr Takashi Furusawa had lived in the United States for several years. He had, in fact, graduated from Stanford University. While still a student he had met his wife, Sachiko, a beautiful woman, with an outstanding personality and a lively mind. They had met when she was working as a waitress in a Japanese restaurant in Little Tokyo, the Japanese quarter of San Francisco. How she had got there was part of a pathetic story.

At the age of fifteen she had married a commander in the Japanese Navy, a man much older than she, and consequently with a different outlook on many things from his child-bride. After five years of what were to her boredom and frustration, she left him and took a passage to San Francisco, where she got work as a chambermaid in an hotel, then as a waitress in the restaurant where Furusawa met her. They fell in love, and when she had obtained a divorce from the commander, they married.

The doctor's early years in his profession were not easy. Gradually, however, his outstanding ability, both as a physician and a surgeon, became more and more widely appreciated. He was eventually elected President of the Southern California Japanese

Physicians' Association, and not long afterwards President of the South California Fishing Club, an honour bestowed in recognition of his prowess as a fisherman, which only slightly exceeded his prowess at golf.

He was, therefore, a man of high professional reputation, respected and popular. Just the sort of man to attract a spy-master looking for a local cell-leader in Los Angeles.

Coming to Los Angeles in 1930, he rented 117½ Weller Street, which thereafter became known as the Medical Building. His establishment was a private nursing-home to which, theoretically, any patient might apply for treatment. It was perhaps a little strange, therefore, that no resident of Los Angeles, either American or Japanese, ever became a bed-patient there.

The Medical Building was frequented solely by Japanese, who arrived from more distant parts of America, stayed at the nursing-home two or three days only — during which time they never ventured outside its doors — and when they did leave were taken either to Los Angeles or San Francisco docks, where they arrived just in time to board a Japanese liner sailing for Japan.

Yet, apart from his duties as President of the Japanese Physicians' Association and of the Fishing Club, his rounds of golf and his angling expeditions, Dr Furusawa's duties at the Medical Building seemed to preclude his taking a very prominent part in the public and social life of Los Angeles.

Mrs Furusawa, on the other hand, devoted much time to public works. She was a very active member of the South California Federation of Women's Societies; she was an officer of the Koysan Buddhist Temple Women's Society; she was a founder member of the Los Angeles branch of the Women's Patriotic Society of Japan, whose headquarters were at 7425 Franklin Avenue, the official residence of the Japanese consul.

For the time being there were no facts, beyond Furusawa's interest in the brief-case of Torii the spy, to connect him and the nursing-home with Japanese espionage. The FBI were not in a position to afford personnel to keep 117½ Weller Street under constant surveillance, but they did put a fairly tight watch on it, and were to discover a good deal that was as serious as it was alarming. One disclosure was of a link between German and Japanese agents, and between the east and west coasts.

In September 1933 a certain Count Hermann von Keitel arrived at the Medical Building. It did not take the FBI long to discover that Keitel was a high-ranking German naval officer, and in consequence he was followed wherever he went. It was through him that the FBI discovered the identities of other spies, both German and Japanese.

The FBI were watching, though from a distance, a party which Dr and Mrs Furusawa gave for their guest two days after his arrival at the Kawafuku Tei, the well-known Japanese restaurant in Los Angeles; and they noted among other guests several Japanese attachés. Indeed, Japanese attachés appeared to have a particular liking for the count, for during his stay at 117½ Weller Street attachés in Los Angeles, San Francisco, Seattle and Portland — all of them places important in the life of the US Navy — visited the Medical Building.

The Furusawas must have felt very secure, because on the eve of von Keitel's departure they gave him another party, at which the guests included not only attachés, but Momotu Okura, commandant of the South California Imperial Veterans' Association, a body which was controlled by the Japanese government. Okura was now a citizen of the United States, and his son, Kiyoshi P. Okura, was an examiner for the Los Angeles Civil Service Commission.

Keitel stayed in Los Angeles, off and on, for about a year before returning permanently to New York. Here, naturally, the FBI continued to watch him. The first thing they discovered was that he was on intimate terms with Roy Akagi, manager of the New York office of the South Manchurian Railway. So Akagi was added to the list of those under surveillance, and this uncovered the fact that he was frequently in the company of George Gyssling, the German vice-consul in New York. Gyssling, who was only twenty-eight and a typical Nazi, had made himself extremely unpopular in America for his outspoken criticisms of conditions during the depression.

One evening towards the end of December 1933 Akagi, with the FBI on his tail, went to the Foreign Press Association offices at 110 West 57th Street. He did not go into the building, but waited in the entrance, where he was presently joined by Chuzo Hagiwara, the New York chief of Domei, the official Japanese news agency. The two men then went straight to 5 East 66th Street, which was a very exclusive German club. The watching FBI agents noted that they were admitted without difficulty, and concluded that they had been expected. Shortly afterwards, Gyssling, accompanied by two other Japanese entered the club, and close on their heels came Count von Keitel.

On the west coast the Furusawas were being kept very busy, Mrs Furusawa particularly so. Whenever a Japanese liner arrived at Los Angeles she would hurry to the pier to welcome certain Japanese officers, whom she would entertain lavishly at the Kawafuku Tei. Shortly before the liner was due to sail she would hurry down to the pier again and go aboard. Each time she would be carrying a brief-case when she went on board, and each time she came ashore she would be empty-handed.

The FBI were confident that they could obtain evidence of specific espionage if the Administration would only allow them to raid $117\frac{1}{2}$ Weller Street, but permission was refused them. For some obscure reason, the US authorities were reluctant to do anything which might upset the Japanese. As a result, the Furusawas continued to operate until shortly before Pearl Harbour, when they left Los Angeles for Tokyo, with incensed FBI men watching them from the pier.

BIBLIOGRAPHY :

Betrayal From The East — Alan Hynd (New York, 1943).

GAPON, Father (Agent of the Imperial Russian **Ochrana**).

Father Gapon was a Russian priest whose sympathies lay with the revolutionary movement in Russia at the beginning of the twentieth century. He led the procession of workers to the Winter Palace on Bloody Sunday, 22nd January, 1905, when imperial troops fired on the workers killing a number of them.

From his behaviour subsequent to this event, it is quite obvious that even if he had become involved with the workers from the best of motives there was no deep-rooted altruism in him, and what there was quickly withered. He had emerged from the events of Bloody Sunday the hero, but his character was basically shallow, and the adulation went to his head. Everywhere he was feted and money for his "workers' movement" — of which he was really the only member—was showered upon him. He went abroad, where the same treatment was accorded him and his real weaknesses rapidly began to show themselves. He was a gourmandiser and a womaniser on no mean scale, he squandered his funds on gambling at Monte Carlo and on riotous living in Paris. Inevitably he sickened his former supporters; equally inevitably his money ran out; and when it did he returned to St Petersburg where he was an easy prey for anyone who could pay well and wished to make use of his services.

Among those who sought his acquaintance was a popular journalist called Manasevich-Monoilov, who was also an agent of the Prime Minister Witte's private secret service. Manasevich-Monoilov immediately appreciated that Gapon was ready to do anything for money, and introduced him to Ratchkovsky, chief of the St Petersburg Ochrana (secret police).

Ratchkovsky saw the possibility of transforming the priest into a second Azeff, and skilfully began to win him over by flattery. The government, Ratchkovsky told Gapon, were sorry about what had happened on Bloody Sunday, that the shooting had been the result of a sad misunderstanding, and that it would like to obtain the Father's valuable services because of his relations with the workers. Specifically they would like him to organise a labour movement on peaceful lines which would educate the workers along paths that the government sincerely believed would in the long run serve all their aspirations.

Gapon was deceived with an ease which surprised even Ratchkovsky who believed that he had summed up the man's purely mercenary character correctly. There were several meetings in exclusive, expensive restaurants — always in private rooms — and by degrees Ratchkovsky drew the priest into his net.

Referring to his own advancing years, Ratchkovsky told Gapon that Russia had great need of men like him. Soon he, Ratchkovsky, would be retiring and if Father Gapon would agree to help the police now by revealing what he knew of revolutionary activities, he might stand a good

226

chance of succeeding him as chief of the Police Department.

For his part, Gapon, while responding favourably, let Ratchkovsky know that the cost of his services would be very high indeed. They were in fact so high that Ratchkovsky had to apply to the Minister of the Interior for authorisation to spend such sums on the project. But despite the fact that Ratchkovsky was able to tell the minister that Gapon was a close friend of an engineer called Rutenberg, who had close connections with the Socialist Revolutionaries, the minister decided to seek the advice of the chief of the Moscow Ochrana, a Colonel Gerassimov.

Gerassimov did not at all share Ratchkovsky's enthusiasm for the scheme. For one thing his information was that Rutenberg was a sincere revolutionary and not at all the type of man who would be prepared to betray his comrades for money. Because of this the minister suggested that Gerassimov should meet Gapon and have a chat with him, and a meeting was arranged which only served to strengthen the Colonel's doubts. In the end, however, Ratchkovsky had his way and Gapon was authorised to approach Rutenberg, who at that time was in hiding from the police.

Despite the fact that on Bloody Sunday, he had lain by Gapon's side in the snow as the bullets of the Tsar's soldiers rained over them, and had helped to draw up the famous petition to the Tsar, Rutenberg was at once made suspicious of the priest's motives by his ham-fisted presentation of his cover-story. This, concocted with Ratchkovsky's help, was that he, Gapon, had made contact with Ratchkovsky whom he intended to use for his own revolutionary aims.

But Gapon had not as-similated the details of his story, and there were so many contradictions in it that Rutenberg at once believed that Gapon was in contact with the police for reasons very different from those he had put forward. If he were right, Rutenberg argued, then his comrades would be in danger, and to protect them by find-ing out all he could about the priest's true aims, he pretend-ed to go along wih him. He played his part much more convincingly than Gapon played his. In no time at all he had succeeded in extrac-ting from Gapon the inform-ation that Ratchkovsky was prepared to pay a very high price indeed for news of the Socialist Revolutionaries' pro-posed campaign of Terror.

Having told the Party chief of Gapon's planned treachery, Rutenberg went to Helsinki where, since Finland had recently been granted in-dependence, Azeff had es-tablished the headquarters of the Battle Organisation of the Party, as the terrorist sec-tion was called. Azeff's re-sponse was unequivocal: "Gapon ought to be killed like a snake." He suggested that Rutenberg should invite him to a certain restaurant for dinner and as they were driving back through the forest in a sleigh provided by the Battle Organisation he should stab the priest and throw his body out.

Unfortunately this simple solution was not feasible. Though he had lost the re-spect of the revolutionaries, Gapon was still worshipped by the workers. This being so, the Central Committee of the Party decided that his death had to be arranged in such a way that the extent of his treachery was made clear to the masses. At the same time Ratchkovsky was also to be liquidated.

So, Rutenberg, acting on instructions to continue to "co-operate" with Gapon, returned to St Petersburg and told the priest that he had finally decided to work with him. Gapon's next concern was for Rutenberg to meet Ratchkovsky, and indeed the latter was impatient for the meeting to take place. After some hesitation it was fixed for 17th March, 1906, in a restaurant.

However, Gerassimov had been keeping an eye on Rutenberg and had become very suspicious of his recent movements; so in the afternoon of the 17th the Colonel telephoned Ratchkovsky and advised him not to keep the appointment. Ratchkovsky's first reaction was to believe that Gerassimov was being too suspicious and ultra-careful, but he did at length agree to take his advice. Not long afterwards it began to be clear that he had some-

what inexplicably changed his mind about the whole affair, for it was evident that he had lost interest in both Gapon and Rutenberg.

This change was no mere accident. It would have been in the interests of Azeff's continuing safety for Ratchkovsky to die, because, of all the members of the Police Department, its chief was the only one to regard Azeff with suspicion. He had learned of Azeff's real role in the Battle Organisation from a police informer called Tatarov, and now he had heard the same thing from Gapon. He had doubted Tatarov, and just when he was beginning to wonder whether Gapon's confirmation might not contain an element of truth, he received a letter from Azeff warning him of a plot to kill him.

This combined with Gerassimov's warning, cooled his ardour for the project though he shrank from taking action against Rutenberg. Azeff's change of front, on the other hand, was typical of him. He never missed an opportunity of warning one of his police chiefs of danger threatening them for he had learned that ruthless though they might be they were always less inclined to believe the worst if they had been personally saved. At the same time Azeff was fully determined that Gapon should be removed, so to overcome the complication of the Central Committee's decision to kill both the priest and the policeman, he undertook the responsibility for the whole operation.

By this time, too, Rutenberg was beginning to lose his nerve. He had no stomach for the double killing, and seizing on this Azeff urged him to lose no time in bringing Gapon to justice.

In order that the workers should be disillusioned about their favourite priest, Azeff planned that Gapon should be "executed" after a trial. An empty villa on the outskirts of St Petersburg was rented, and there in the early evening of 10th April, 1906 the workers chosen to act as judges were concealed in a room divided from its neighbour by only a thin partition. Shortly afterwards Rutenberg arrived and was presently joined by Gapon. The latter had been inveigled there in the belief that they were to settle the terms on which Rutenberg would be prepared to betray the Battle Organisation. The two men went into the room adjoining that where the judges were hidden.

Gapon was in an angry mood on account of Rutenberg's inability to bring himself to a decision, and when the engineer still showed signs of uncertainty he spoke harshly and loudly.

"Twenty thousand roubles isn't bad money," he cajoled. "I can't thing why you're behaving like such a fool."

Rutenberg retorted that what he could not stomach was that if the men he betrayed were caught they would hang. Gapon replied that that was their bad luck, and he tried to reassure Rutenberg by telling him how very skilful Ratchkovsky was, so that he need not fear for himself.

Presently Rutenberg could stand no more of it, and striding to the door between the two rooms, he flung it open, and called in the judges. They had heard every word through the thin dividing wall, and had hardly been able to contain themselves. Now they burst in and threw themselves upon the priest who, recognising some of his former friends among them, fell on his knees and begged for mercy.

His pleas were in vain. While Rutenberg hurried away sobbing, unable to wait to see the task completed, they slipped a noose of rope round the priest's neck. The riding end of it was flung over a hook which they had fixed near the rail for drying clothes, and a few seconds later Gapon's body was jerking spasmodically, high in the air. They stayed until he was dead, and then quietly left the villa.

Rutenberg hurried at once to Helsinki to tell the Battle Organisation and was puzzled and pained by Azeff's denial that he had given permission for Gapon alone to be executed, or that he had been informed in advance that this was to happen. He told the Central Committee quite firmly that if anyone accepted Rutenberg's word and rejected his, he would regard it as an insult. No one did, and Rutenberg found himself accused of flouting Party discipline and of slandering one of the most respected members of the Central Committee, (Refer to **AZEFF, Eugene**). The Party also denied responsibility for Gapon's death and Rutenberg was so overwhelmed by this desertion that he left the revolutionary movement for good.

BIBLIOGRAPHY:

Azeff: the Russian Judas — Boris Nikolaeevsky (London, 1934).

The History of Azeff's Treachery — A. Ratayev (London, 1928).

GARRY, Lieut B. A. H. see under **Khan, Noor Inayat.**

GEE, Elizabeth see under **Portland Spy Case, The.**

GEHLEN, General Reinhard (Director of West German Intelligence).

The heads of the German espionage agencies were known to the British from the beginning of World War II, but only one of them escaped publicity. He was Reinhard Gehlen, who from 1942 to the end of the war, as chief of the Army High Command Foreign Armies East Department, was in command of all anti-Soviet espionage operations.

Until 1968 this quiet Prussian ex-general was director of the West German espionage service. He still tried to preserve his incognito. By his 6,000 subordinates he was known as Number 30 or The Doctor; and he resolutely refused to be photographed. As his work took him for the most part in close proximity with the East-West border, he went everywhere accompanied by two armed bodyguards, carried a gun himself, and never travelled twice in the same motorcar.

How this former Nazi general with a fondness for obscurity had become one of the most powerful of West Germans is a fascinating story.

On 9th January, 1945, Gehlen made what was to turn out to be his last personal report to Hitler. On leaving the Führer, he summoned his staff to meet him in his steel and concrete underground room at the Maybach headquarters of the Army High Command, at Lossen, near Berlin. At this meeting he told his staff that the time would soon come when the Maybach HQ would have to be evacuated. Thereafter, they would be on the run. This meant that files would have to be abandoned, and he, therefore, was instructing them to begin a review of all material immediately. The unimportant was to be destroyed, the important was to be microfilmed in three copies, and the originals then destroyed.

The men he then divided into three groups. Each group was to be responsible for one complete set of microfilms, which was to be kept in a watertight container, to which was fixed a mechanism that would destroy the contents if any unauthorised person tried to open it.

If they were overrun, each group would go into hiding separately and would hide the container. If surrender was necessary, they would give themselves up only to the Americans. They were to disclose nothing to their captors about their work unless he gave them permission to do so in writing.

By the time the microfilms were made, the Russians had reached the River Oder, and Gehlen decided that the time had come to move. With all his staff and the three contain-

231

ers, he moved down into Bavaria, into what Hitler had termed The Redoubt, where his armies were to make their last stand. At the village of Mossbach Gehlen ordered the men to split up and carry out his instructions. He and his group climbed on foot up into the mountains, to the now notorious Schliersee, a bottomless lake where many other espionage agencies had already sunk cases of secret documents and millions of pounds' worth of forged Bank of England notes.

They did not stay by the Schliersee, however, but continued to climb until they reached the Blendsalm, where Gehlen had already arranged a well-supplied secret chalet. There they awaited the Americans.

Gehlen did not go down the mountain to meet the Americans when they shortly appeared in the valley. He decided to wait until the Americans found him. A week passed before a party of GIs surrounded the chalet, and Gehlen, unlike other Nazi chiefs, did not attempt to disguise himself nor undervalue his importance.

He produced his paybook and papers to prove that he was Lieutenant-General Reinhard Gehlen, chief of the anti-Soviet espionage organisation. But the NCOs and officers were not interested in army generals; they were after high Party officials, war criminals, Gestapo and SS men; and to his surprise and chagrin, Gehlen found himself ignored.

Now Gehlen had taken these steps deliberately with one end in view. He was the son of a Prussian officer — who had later become a publisher — and at the age of eighteen, in 1920, had joined the new German army, the Reichswehr, as an ensign. The German generals had overcome western opposition to the formation of the new army by playing on the Allies' fears of Bolshevik Russian expansion, and Gehlen had seen all that had happened and remembered it.

By 1944 he knew that Nazi Germany was defeated, and he was quite certain that when hostilities ended, the uneasy alliance of the West and Soviet Russia would break up. He was also a patriotic German and a career soldier, and was as eager that the

Germany that arose out of the ashes of the old should have an army as were the generals of 1918. He saw that an instrument for achieving this would be a repetition of the 1920s tactics of playing on Allied fears of Russia, and he planned to exploit and exacerbate the situation to achieve this end.

Through his own espionage service, he knew that the American Office of Strategic Services (q.v.), which at this time represented America's major espionage effort, had not yet even begun to consider building up a network in Soviet Russia, against the day when the breach would come. He argued, therefore, that if he could offer the expert services of himself and his organisation to the Americans, they would eagerly accept the offer, and once he had begun to operate for them, the resurgence of the German army would be assured or his name was not Reinhard Gehlen.

So his consternation and chagrin at being ignored by the officers of America's Central Intelligence Corps can be understood. Had he misjudged the Americans? Was his plan going to fail?

Several weeks went by, during which the Americans continued to show no interest in him at all. But there was a certain General Patterson, employed by intelligence, who was desirous of discovering how German espionage had been organised and how it had worked. General Patterson had requested to be allowed to interview all high-ranking German espionage experts, and so came to meet Gehlan in Wiesbaden.

General Patterson now relates that during their interview, it was Gehlen who asked the questions. Apparently the general's answers satisfied Gehlen that his fortune had changed, that here was an influential American officer to whom he could reveal his plan.

When General Patterson had taken a first quick glance at the microfilms of German espionage documents and captured Russian documents containing secrets of the Soviet's espionage establishment and learned of the hidden teams of experts, he saw much farther than his own academic interests. Within a short time Gehlen and his

233

reunited staff were installed in the US intelligence headquarters at Frankfurt-am-Main, busily engaged in preparing papers on every aspect of German and Russian espionage, on Gehlen's instructions holding nothing back.

It was not long before American intelligence officers were coming to the Germans asking for help in interpreting this or that item of information, or the best way of coping with this or that problem.

Now, the microfilming of the documents and the hiding of his staff of experts had not been all that Gehlen had done. He had also ordered large numbers of his agents to stay where they were in the territory which was to become the Soviet Zone. Gehlen suggested, and Patterson readily agreed, that he should get in touch with some of these agents to see whether they had been able to gather any information that might be useful. Before long, the volume and value of the information coming in was truly impressive, and Gehlen's interpretations were so shrewd that Patterson's chief in the Pentagon was eager

to meet this German general.

The outcome of a visit to Washington was the crowning of all Gehlen's planning. He agreed to form an intelligence service which would get information from behind the Iron Curtain, on certain conditions. First, his staff would be exclusively under his command; second, no members of his service would be required to work against Germany's national interests; third, when Germany regained her sovereignty, his organisation would be handed over to the German government; fourth, in the interim, the Americans would finance his organisation on a fixed Dollar budget.

The Americans in their turn agreed to these conditions. To begin with, they granted him an annual sum of three and a half million dollars. They provided him with a headquarters at Pullach, near Munich, handing over a small housing estate consisting of twenty or so one- and two-family houses, where his staff and their families could live, protected by a high boundary barricade of barbed wire. Even the children were not allowed to leave the compound and a special school was built for them.

The staff of his former organisation who had accompanied him were not sufficient for the new organisation, so he recruited former members of the General Staff, among them Lieutenant-General Heusinger, his old chief. Nor were his agents numerous enough for his needs, and here he went to former members of the SS Sichersheitsdienst and the Gestapo, giving as his excuse for doing so that the Russians were using large numbers of their men to spy in the Westtern Zones and that by employing former colleagues he could more easily penetrate the Russian espionage and counter-espionage services.

Both sides to the agreement meticulously kept its conditions, and when West Germany became an independent state, Gehlen's organisation became its espionage agency. General Heusinger left him to become the first inspector-general of the new German army, and then chairman of the Standing Military Committee of NATO. Chancellor Adenauer habitually referred to Gehlen as "**mein lieber General**".

Gehlen's organisation has brought off several spectacular and highly important espionage coups. One of the most impressive of these was his planting of an agent in the office of Ernst Wollweber, Gehlen's opposite number in East Germany.

Gehlen chose for this mission an agent called Walter Gramsch to whom he gave the cover-name B r u t u s . Gramsch and Wollweber had known one another in Nazi days, when both were members of the Party. Wollweber was not to know that Gramsch had subsequently undergone a similar change of heart as he himself had, though Gramsch's sentiments had led him to espouse democracy.

Wollweber had b e e n appointed chief of the Transport Commissariat in the Soviet Zone in 1946 — both he and Gramsch had been Nazi transport experts — and Gehlen had sent Gramsch to Wollweber to ask for a job and had been taken on. Within a short time Gramsch had become the director of the department of Fleets and Harbours, and was able to supply Gehlen with highly valuable information concerning Soviet troop and shipping movements, and about the espionage agency for which Wollweber's Transport Commissariat was the cover.

Gramsch worked in this important position for seven years without Wollweber ever having the slightest suspicion of him. Then in November 1953 he received instructions from Gehlen to flee immediately to the Western Zone of Berlin. No one was more surprised than Gramsch. He did not know that one of Wollweber's agents, a man called Geyer, had done exactly the same thing and had penetrated Gehlen's organisation, in which he had risen to a post of great importance — director of one of Gehlen's networks in East Germany, with thirty West German agents under his control. Geyer remained in this position for a year, during which he learned a great deal about Gehlen's organisation. Then he prepared a coup which would result in the arrest of the network of which he was director. He knew, however,

that he would reveal his own position, so when everything was ready, he fled to the East. As soon as Gehlen heard of this, he did everything he could to save his agents. He was successful in a number of cases, one of which was Gramsch.

Gehlen's most spectacular success is one that has generally been attributed to the American CIA (q.v.). This was obtaining a copy of Krushchev's Stalin-denunciation speech in 1956. It was the unabridged text of the speech as delivered by the Russian leader to the secret session of the Supreme Soviet, and was procured by a Russian working for Gehlen.

Gehlen's organisation now covers not only East Germany and Russia proper, but every Iron Curtain country, and stretches through the Balkans, Greece and Turkey to Persia and the Middle East. The organisation has one characteristic which is original. A very large number of Gehlen's radio operators suffer from some serious physical disability. He has chosen them because, he argues, cripples will not be called up for military service and will be able to remain at their posts after war has broken out.

Gehlen's organisation is now a fully comprehensive one. It not only collects information from agents but has departments for the interception of radio messages and cipher-breaking, the interrogation of travellers, the study of Russian newspapers and scientific, technical and economic periodicals, and for the analysis and evaluation of all information. It is, without doubt, one of the most formidable espionage services working today, and Gehlen, so far at least, seems to have been able to break away from the inflexible conduct of espionage which characterised German spying from Wilhelm Stieber (q.v.) until the present day.

Gehlen retired in 1968 and was replaced by Lieutenant-General Gerhard Wessel.

GEHRTS, Erwin see under **Red Orchestra, The.**

GEMPP, Colonel.

Gempp was the first Director of the **Abwehr** in the post-World War I period. He had been a member of the **Abwehr** under Colonel Nicolai. He was replaced by Captain Patzig of the German Navy, when Hitler came to power in 1933.

GERMAN SPIES in Spain in World War I.

The **Abwehr** organised three intelligence bureaux in Spain during World War 1. The first, directed by Lieutenant von Krohn, of the Navy, was at 17 Calle del Prado, in Madrid, which had as its cover a Press agency called Officina de Informacion; the second was sited in Barcelona, and was under the command of Colonel von Rolland; while the third, of which General von Schultz was in command, was at San Sebastian.

The Allies were equally active in Spain, and bent all their efforts to hinder the activities of the Germans. Their first success came not long after the outbreak of hostilities, when they were able to inform the Spanish authorities that the German consul at Carthagena was violating Spanish neutrality. He was caught in the act of supervising the refuelling and

237

revictualling of the submarine U-6, was arrested and declared **non persona grata.**

What the Allies were really aiming at was to induce Spain to abandon her neutrality and join the Allies. In high places it was believed that the addition of Spain to the ranks of the Allies would be a considerable boost to civilian and military morale. In addition to harrying the Germans, the French and British governments entered into off-the-record negotiations with the Spanish government with the long-term aim of winning the Spanish over, and the immediate advantage of allowing the Allies to send their troops through Spain to North Africa .

German violations of Spanish neutrality took place almost daily. To avoid being sunk, the Spanish had to ask German permission for their merchant ships to leave port, Spanish territorial waters were full of German warships, which in order to take on supplies or make repairs, did not hesitate to enter Spanish ports under the pretence that the were defecting, only to slip away when their object had been achieved un-

der cover of darkness.

King Alfonso was the main obstacle to Spain renouncing her neutrality. Neither the Court nor the Clergy had a great regard for France, and the Spanish ambassador to Berlin, in every telegram he sent, drove home his opinion that the Central Powers must be victorious.

Aware, naturally, of the Allies' activities the Germans brought every propaganda weapon they could devise into play. The most important newspapers in the country were won over, largely by the largesse distributed by the Banco Transatlantico, a subsidiary of the Deutsche Undersee Bank. They maintained a sustained demand for the continuation of neutrality.

At Barcelona, von Rolland anticipated a German victory by publishing a magnificent volume commemorating the event. It was called **Amistad Hispano Germana,** and distributed free in tens of thousands. The frontispiece consisted of a portrait of William II facing one of Alfonso over the caption, "Friends of yesterday, today and tomorrow."

When the Banco Transatlantico's funds began to run low, neutral ships came into Spanish ports laden with bullion to restore them. The Allies prevented this happening whenever possible. The Dutch freighter **Tubantia,** bound for Spain, sank in mysterious circumstances in the Straits of Dover. Some of its cargo of Edam cheese floated ashore, and when these were salvaged and cut open, they were found to contain gold coins.

To counteract the intrigues of the **Abwehr** agents, the Allies sent scores of their own, notably among the businessmen and merchants whom they encouraged to smuggle into France as much contraband material as possible.

On one occasion when the French commissariat found itself in urgent need of 4,000 mules, circus owners, gipsies and similar wanderers were rounded up and instructed to go into Spain, buy mules wherever they could find them and smuggle them over the Pyrenees to France. When the Toulouse powder-works was in danger of closing down, because of a shortage of industrial alcohol, Allied

agents arranged for supplies from new distilleries, the crops of Spanish vineyards were bought up and transport was obtained regardless of cost.

Von Rolland reacted like the Prussian he was. He instructed his agents to intimidate those who collaborated with the Allies in any way by threats of violence and dynamite.

One of his observation-posts in Barcelona was in the Calle Santa Anna. From there he published a periodical pamphlet called **La Vérité,** printed in French, and purporting to be the work of French dissidents. The following is an extract from one number :

People of France! Under pressure from England our leaders are preparing a new winter campaign. The last offensive having failed miserably, they are thinking of undertaking another — next Spring.
Where are we going, Frenchmen? Where is France heading? We no longer have the strength to continue this useless struggle. The submarine

blockade is rebounding on us.

The Spectre of Famine is already accompanying the Spectre of Death in our towns and countryside. If we do not obtain peace immediately, France will meet an irreparable and certain fate.

Von Rolland had worked in espionage for many years before he took over the Barcelona network. He had lived in Spain since 1911. By 1914 he had established his posts, and had spent much of his time, when he was not inventing codes, travelling along the coast-line of Spain selecting secluded inlets where German U-boats might take refuge in time of need. Occasionally he visited France, ostensibly in connection with the hobby of which he was passionately fond — collecting stamps; in reality, to probe the reserve supplies of the French Army.

For as long as the war lasted, the struggle between the Allied and German secret services raged with an intensity rarely encountered in espionage records.

GERSON, Captain Vassily Vassilijevich (Russian agent of World War I).

In 1916 the Austrian High Command became aware that the Russians were receiving correct information about the movements of their forces and their weak points. They posted the best men in their counter-espionage service to try to discover the source of the leakage, and when they failed, they instructed Major Karl Nowolny of the intelligence service to try his best to solve the problem.

In the course of his investigations, Nowolny visited a medical unit at the front near San, at the foot of the Beskides Mountains, between Sanok and Przemysl, in Galicia, where Sisters of Charity were acting as nurses. One of the patients, on being questioned by Nowolny, loudly sang the praises of one of the nuns, Sister St Innocence, who watched over them throughout the long hours of the night, comforting them, making them laugh with the stories she told of her convent in Vienna.

Instinctively, the major asked to be allowed to interview this model nurse, and was at once struck by her noble bearing and her smooth, kindly features. Her feet, which peeped from under her long habit, however, seemed to him to be just a little large. But when he inspected her identity papers, he could find nothing wrong with them.

He could not get the woman out of his mind, however, and inquired of the Medical Superintendent what kind of nurse she was.

"One of the best, devoted, intelligent," he was told. "She is full of compassion and kindness, and her selflessness has become a byword. All her off-duty hours she spends with the patients, writing their letters for them, questioning them about their homes and their families. I've just recommended her for the Red Cross Gold Medal; she deserves it more than anyone else here."

Appearing to be impressed, Nowolny asked the Superintendent to summon Sister St Innocence to his office so that he might congratulate her. A few moments later the sister arrived, and quietly asked how she could help him.

For reply Nowolny suddenly appeared to collapse, and as he staggered and fell, it was into the arms of the nun, who caught and held him easily, despite the fact that he was a heavy man. When she suggested that he should lie down until he had recovered and began to unbutton his tunic, he made a rapid recovery.

"Strip!" he ordered her, sternly.

The Superintendent began to protest, believing that Nowolny must have taken leave of his senses. But Nowolny drew a whistle and in answer to a blast on it guards came running.

"Strip her!" he ordered them.

When Sister St Innocence stood naked before them it was clear that Nowolny's intuition had not deceived him.

When Nowolny demanded "her" name, "she" replied, "I am Captain Vassily Vassilijevich Gerson, of the staff of General Dimitriev."

For five months Gerson had lived in his nun's habit. From the men who were constantly passing through the unit, he learned from his kindly questioning of them, not only about their families and lives at home, but was able to piece together the whole picture of the Austrian dispositions on that sector of the front. Messages found in his habit were ample proof of his espionage activities, but he had been as good as dead from the moment that his true sex was revealed.

GERSON, Harold see under **Soviet Canadian Networks.**

GESTAPO, Counter-espionage role of.

Though constituted as an internal security police force, it was not long before the Gestapo was playing a major role as a counter-espionage agency. In this it was not manifesting a purely Nazi determination that the Party should be committed in every field of national enterprise. During the Kaiser's times, the **Abwehr** (Military Intelligence) had been responsible for counter-espionage through its Department III.

Despite this organisation, however, the **Abwehr** had never at any time had full freedom to take all measures necessary to protect the Reich from acts of sabotage and espionage. An agreement between the Ministry of War and the Ministry of the Interior, dated 1869, provided that it was the duty of the police to deal with spies, and though the **Abwehr** had not been lax in counter-espionage measures, the police had always claimed the right to intervene when they believed it to be necessary.

This situation was drastically changed when the Gestapo came into being. The agreement of 1869 was invoked and was recognised as valid by the **Abwehr,** and from that time onward, the function of Department III was restricted to protecting the security of the armed forces alone. The Gestapo took over every other counter-espionage function. Its position was not unlike that of the American FBI.

GILMORE, John alias **Hirsch, Willi** (q.v.).

GISKES, Colonel H. J. (Chief of **Abwehr** counter-espionage, Holland in World War II).

On the night of 9th March, 1943, a young Dutchman, Pieter Dourlein, with two companions, Bogaart and Arendse, made their third attempt to drop into Nazi-occupied Holland. On the two previous occasions, ground mist and an aircraft damaged by flak had made their efforts abortive. This time, however, they succeeded.

Dourlein, who had dropped as second man of the stick, was caught up in a tree. Unfastening his parachute harness, he let himself fall the six feet or so to the ground and hid in nearby bushes, his revolver in his hand. As he had floated down he had seen the flashed signals of the reception committee on the dropping-point. Now he waited until at last he heard someone calling his code-name, Paul. He went forward to meet them, and was welcomed heartily by three men, who took him at once to the leader of the reception committee. There he found Bogaart and Arendse, who had also landed unhurt.

The leader was as happy to see them as the other members of the committee had been, and offered them a swig of whisky and an English cigarette. For some reason, the agents were told,

it was necessary to wait an hour or two before they could go to Ermelo, to meet the chief of the network they had come to join.

Before they eventually set out for Ermelo, the leader of the reception committee asked the agents to hand over their weapons. They would get them back, naturally, but they might have to pass Germans on the way, and if they were searched and weapons found on them it might be very serious. The agents could understand that, and handed over their revolvers. The reception committee had already taken charge of fourteen containers of supplies which had been dropped with them.

The leader then asked if he might see their identity cards, explaining that those which Special Operations Executive had recently been supplying were so bad that they were a positive danger rather than a help. Theirs were no better, it seemed, and the man said he would arrange for new ones to be supplied to them. For this, however, they would have to tell him their real names. The Germans were now checking identity cards

243

by the national register, therefore they must have names in the register, and their own names were as good as any.

SOE, however, had always stressed that their agents must never, in any circumstances, reveal their true identities to anyone whomsoever, not even their colleagues. So before acceding to the leader's latest request, the men discussed the situation privately among themselves. If all that the leader had said were true, and clearly he was in an unassailable position to know, then SOE headquarters in London must be hopelessly out of touch with the real conditions in the Field; and not only out of touch, but incompetent as well. So they decided to give their own names.

At last they began to move off. They had split into three groups, one agent accompanied by two members of the reception committee. They had not gone far when suddenly their guides threw themselves upon them, pinioning their arms behind them, and handcuffing them before they had recovered from their surprise. This done, at a signal a number of

men appeared from the surrounding trees and bushes. In perfect Dutch one of these men informed the agents that they were in the hands of the German counter-espionage.

The three men were then put into separate cars and driven to a villa a few miles from Utrecht. Each was taken to a different room and searched.

Dourlein, like his companions had on him an address in Switzerland concealed in the false bottom of a matchbox. His searcher seemed to be expecting to find it, and seeing the astonishment on Dourlein's face was at pains to surprise him even further.

He told the agent the address of a supposedly "safe" house in Rotterdam to which he had been directed, and the names of Dutch and English instructors at the training schools in England through which he had passed during the last six months. Every detail was correct.

After being given something to eat, Dourlein was strapped onto a stretcher, though nothing was wrong with him, and taken to a large college building at Haaren which had been converted into a Gestapo prison. After a further search he was handed over to the coding specialist.

Dourlein at first denied having a code, until at last the German exclaimed that he would show him something to cure his obstinacy. Taking him up to the second floor of the building he led him into a corridor in one wall of which were a number of doors. Lifting the cover over the spy-hole in each door, the German made Dourlein look into the room beyond. This he repeated, going from door to door, until all had been covered. And here, among the forty men confined in these rooms, Dourlein saw friends with whom he had trained, and who had dropped before him.

"Some of them have been here a year," the German told him.

Downstairs again, the German asked him to decode the Swiss address, and when Dourlein said he could not remember the details of the code, promptly and without any hesitation deciphered it himself.

For forty continuous hours Dourlein's interrogation last-ed. During the whole time it became clearer and clearer to the agent that there was practically nothing about SOE's Dutch section in England which the Germans did not know, even such small details as when a certain officer shaved off his mous-tache. Worse still, it was quite evident that the Germans were controlling the radio communications with England.

As he lay on his bed in his cell between long periods of further interrogation, Dour-lein was able to establish contact with prisoners in ad-joining cells by tapping in Morse on a radiator pipe. But the more he and his friends discussed the situation, the further away an explana-tion of what had happened seemed to be.

One thing was quite clear, however; somehow England must be informed. The prob-lem of how this was to be done seemed as insoluble as the problem of how it had happened.

At last after six weeks, Dourlein's interrogation end-ed. By this time he had reach-ed the conclusion that the only possible solution was for one of them to escape and try to reach England. And how to escape from a Gestapo prison?

His cell-mate Bogaart, whom he joined when the Germans stopped questioning him, told him that such an attempt would be virtual suicide. Nevertheless he began to consider various plans.

At intervals new prisoners were brought in. Not all the prisoners were agents. On the floor below were many Dutchmen, among them prominent citizens, all held by the Gestapo on charges of resistance or no charges at all. Now and again, some of them would be selected as hostages and shot as reprisals for sabotage or the killing of a German soldier. Some-times, however, one might be released.

While pondering his plan for escaping, Dourlein succeeded in making contact with the lower floor, and in passing a message addressed to SOE in London, which it was hoped a released prisoner might be able to relay.

The message read : "Entire organisation in German hands stop even radio communications stop all agents captured now at Haaren stop Dourlein

and Bleker."

The message did get through and reached Colonel de Bruyne, chief of the MVT, a Dutch organisation working with SOE in London, on 23rd June, 1943. Unfortunately, in transit it had been so corrupted that the version received in London read : "Eight para-chutists among whom Doulin and Drake were arrested many weeks ago. Code-word Marius known to enemy."

It made no sense at all to Colonel de Bruyne, but he warned SOE that no more agents should be dropped until the position had become clear. Other messages had been sent by members of the Dutch underground, and one agent, Dessing, had sent a message from Belgium stating that some transmitters were in the hands of the Germans. SOE, however, chose to dis-regard these warnings, and in the case of Dessing, suggested to the Belgians, that he was not to be trusted and should be regarded with suspicion.

In the middle of June, 1943, Dourlein and Bogaart were moved to another cell, where they were joined by an agent called van der Bor, and had soon established communication with their neighbours on each side. Of these neighbours, only one, Ubbink, agreed at once to try to escape. From then on, Dourlein and Ubbink began to study possible ways and means in seriousness.

Communication between the two men was by means of a small hole under the washbasin in the cell which they had managed to scrape through the wall. Now no longer having to use the laborious method of tapping out Morse messages on the radiator pipes, they were able to discuss their ideas more exhaustively and eventually decided on a plan.

Above the cell door was a window on a hinged sash opening inwards. By unpicking a thread from his mattress and measuring the window with it, Dourlein discovered that it was large enough to allow him to pass through it if he took off his outer garments. Ubbink made a similar discovery.

The windows, however, were nailed down, and for a fortnight with infinite patience, the two men worked at loosening the nails, enlarging the holes so that the nails would go back into position easily but at the same time remain undetected during the occasional German inspection.

Once through the window they would be in the corridor outside the cells. They would then hide in a lavatory until night-time, when the number of guards was not so large as during the day, and escape out of the building by letting themselves down from a first-floor window. For this they would require a thirty-six foot rope strong enough to take the weight of a man; and this presented a major difficulty.

Twice a week, however, they were given shaving-tackle in their cells, and with the razor they cut strips from the undersides of their mattresses, which they plaited to make a strong rope. They would be able to loop it round a bar and draw it down after them, thus delaying discovery of their escape.

Having studied the habits of the guards they decided that the best time for their attempt was just as the evening ration of food was being distributed. The food was brought round on a trolley which made a good deal of noise, which, in turn, would cover up any noise they might make. The corridor was L-shaped, and there was a time when the guard distributing the food would be in the other arm of the L and so be unable to see them emerging from their windows and make for an empty cell which they knew to be nearby. As the guard returned with the empty trolley, they would follow him in stockinged feet to the lavatory.

There were great risks attached to the scheme, but both men were willing to run them. For their attempt they chose a moonless Sunday night, the 29th August.

The hours of Sunday dragged by with the two men's nerves on a knife-edge of suspense. Their cell-mates pleaded with them to give up the attempt, but they refused to consider it.

In the event, everything went well for them. After the guard had passed they crept from the empty cell to the lavatories and shut themselves in one of the compartments. As they waited there, from time to time a guard came and rattled on the door, and one of them would call out,

Besett — engaged.

For six hours they crouched in the constricting cubicle, wondering if their absence from the cells would be discovered. A few minutes before midnight, a thunderstorm broke over the prison, and gave them more confidence than anything else so far.

At the height of the storm they decided to make their next move. Taking the blackout down from the lavatory window, and removing most of their clothes, they tied the latter in bundles, attached them to the end of the rope, and lowered them to the ground outside. Then, waiting until the searchlight had swept the window, one at a time they squeezed through the bars and slid down the rope.

Pulling the rope down after them, bent double they ran over to the shadow of the chapel, hurried into their clothes and disposed of the rope. Without incident, though not without excitement, they negotiated the barbed-wire entanglement and the moat-like ditch which ran round the outer perimeter of Haaren, and set out for Tilburg, six miles away.

They had an address in Tilburg where they might expect help, but when they reached it they found it was a chemist's shop and no one answered their knocks. This was a set-back. It was only half-past five in the morning, and they would have to wait until eight o'clock when the shop opened.

People were beginning to appear in the streets, and they realised that they must get under cover before they attracted unwelcome attention. They entered a Catholic Church, intending to throw themselves on the mercy of the priest. The priest received them coldly at first, but they were able to convince him that they were not German **agents provocateurs,** and he handed them over to a policeman, who in turn passed them to a farmer out in the country near Moergestel, and within a short distance of the prison.

The policeman was, in fact, a former police inspector called Van Bilsen. At the beginning of the Occupation he had refused to co-operate with the Nazis and had resigned. His case is a sad one, for he did so many wildly extravagant things without the intervention of the Germans that Dutch Resistance became suspicious of him and eventually liquidated him. His loyalty has been vindicated since the war ended and the illegal newspaper he organised is now a legal one and pays his widow a pension.

At the time he arranged the safe hiding for the fugitives Van Bilsen was a porter in a factory. He returned from work one day, and produced a handbill which was being distributed by the Germans. It announced the offer of a reward of 500 guilders (£50) for information leading to the capture of Dourlein and Ubbink who it alleged were wanted by the police for "robbery with violence".

After two weeks in the attic of the farm, Van Bilsen had them driven into Tilburg and there handed them over to a man called Vinken, who led them to a house in the middle of the town. For several days they stayed with their new hosts, a Mr and Mrs Lauwerrijssens, during which time their impatience to be on their way began to fray their tempers.

Van Bilsen and Vinken had sent a message to England on their behalf and they were waiting for a reply. But the message had had to be routed by Belgium and Switzerland and it was taking a long time. When, after several weeks, the answer arrived it was not encouraging. It asked Dourlein and Ubbink to make their way to England, if they could, or at any rate to a neutral country where they could be helped.

After much discussion, they decided to attempt to reach England by way of Belgium, France and Switzerland. With great difficulty Van Bilsen procured papers, but the money for the journey remained the most difficult problem and was eventually solved by Ubbink's brother. In some way he was able to transfer money to a bank in Paris, providing it from his own resources.

They had escaped from Haaren prison on 29th August, 1943. It was not until 11th November that they were in a position to start out on their long and dangerous journey to England.

Van Bilsen took them to Antwerp, but from then on,

armed with only two addresses, one in Paris, the other on the Swiss frontier, they had to make their own way. Helped by an odd assortment of people across Belgium and into France, they arrived safely in Paris where they were to collect the money transferred by Ubbink's brother.

They had been given the address of a small hotel in the rue de la Fayette, run by a Fleming who would ask no questions. But when they called at the Banque de France next day, there was no money. Nor was there the next day, nor the next, nor the next. The little money they had ran out. They were hungry and had no money to pay the hotel. In desperation they planned to waylay and rob a German soldier if the money had still not arrived. But when they called at the Banque, it was there. The following day they took the train to Belfort, the nearest point to Maiche on the French side of the Swiss frontier, whither they had been directed.

Arrived at Belfort they found it to be the centre of a prohibited area on account of the activities of the local French maquis. But their good fortune continued and they eventually arrived at the address at Maiche. The following day the maquis put them over the frontier into Switzerland and safety.

In Berne they were welcomed by the Dutch military attaché, General van Tricht, who took down all the details, and sent a full account of what they were able to tell him to London, at the same time asking London what was to happen to the agents and suggesting that he could send them to England via the south of France and Spain.

SOE requested that they be sent to London, and after four days rest Dourlein and Ubbink set out once more on a dangerous, risky journey across France, from contact to contact, and on into Spain, suffering a good deal physically. Held up in Spain by a variety of causes, at length they arrived at Gibraltar, from where they were sent to Bristol, where they arrived on 1st February, 1944, five months after their escape from Haaren.

At Bristol they were met by a Dutch-speaking English officer from Military Intelligence, who took them to London. They asked this officer to let them speak to their Dutch chief, Colonel de Bruyne, but he refused their request. After interrogation by British intelligence officers, they were taken to Guildford where they continued to be held incommunicado. It was becoming more and more obvious that they were not trusted. Ubbink was practically told openly that he was working for the Germans.

After all they had attempted and suffered, their reception greatly affected them. They wrote letter after letter to Colonel de Bruyne, begging him to help them. The Colonel replied telling them not to worry, he was doing all he could for them.

For three months the interrogation continued and then gave place to accusations. Then in May, without any explanation, they were transferred to Brixton prison, in London.

A week after the invasion of Europe had begun, Dourlein and Ubbink were released. Dourlein was reduced in rank from sergeant to Corporal. SOE had no further

251

use for him. But the war was not over, and he joined the Dutch Air Force and saw active service as a corporal gunner with Squadron 320.

Ubbink had held the temporary rank of Lieutenant (3rd Class) in the Royal Netherlands Navy. This was taken from him and he returned to his former service, the Dutch Merchant Navy.

Nevertheless, for all their sufferings, both physical and mental, Ubbink and Dourlein were fortunate. In 1944, 48 of the former agent-prisoners of Haaren were shot in Mauthausen concentration camp. They represented nearly all the agents whom SOE had sent to Holland in twenty months of 1942 and 1943. Besides Ubbink and Dourlein, only two other agents involved in what is now generally known as the **Englandspiel,** the England Game — survived.

What lay behind this cynical appellation? Were Dourlein and Ubbink would-be traitors? Was their story a fabrication.

When the war was over the people of Holland were naturally anxious to know the truth of what had happened to the agents of Haaren; and when it was revealed that all except four had been executed in Mauthausen, rumours began to circulate. These rumours were wild and various, but among them was the suggestion that Britain had betrayed the agents in order to play a deeper game. The newspapers took up the question and public indignation mounted to such heights that the Dutch Parliament ordered a Parliamentary Commission to be set up under the chairmanship of L. A. Donkers, who was later to become Minister of Justice. The Commission, with the most searching care, questioned a vast number of witnesses, probed and sifted the evidence, and eventually published their conclusions.

At the head of German Military Counter-espionage in Holland—(Department III of the **Abwehr**) — was a certain Colonel H. J. Giskes. At the head of the Gestapo's department of counter-espionage was Josef Schreieder. Both these men had the same idea, the seed of which had probably been sown by their capture of one or two agents. The idea came to the two men independently, but when their efforts began to bear fruit, they worked well together.

It will facilitate the recounting of the tragedy if certain points are made plain at once. First, it is clear that SOE instructed its Dutch agents that if caught and compelled by the Germans to divulge their codes, they should not resist. Therefore, it cannot be held against the agents that they followed this instruction. Second, though the agents might divulge their codes, SOE forbade them to disclose their security checks. The security check is the normal procedure in ciphering. (**See under** SECURITY CHECK.)

It must be stressed that the security check is almost as important as the message itself. Contrarily, it must be admitted that a number of agents, among them some Dutch, in the stress of their dangerous work, were careless about using their security checks. But the security check was so important that any message without it should have been suspect, and no excuses accepted; and it should never be referred to in radio correspondence by either side.

This is one of the simpler finer points of espionage technique, and should have been known to SOE instructors and relentlessly inculated by them into their pupils. It should have been equally relentlessly inculcated into those officers responsible for the executive side of every section. It is a major item in security, which is the agent's Staff of Life.

Another point was what is known as "handwriting". It has been known at least since World War I, that every radio operator's technique of tapping out Morse is as distinctively individual as his calligraphy. It can be stated that Morse "handwriting" can be recognised at once by those receiving it, and that it can only be copied with as much difficulty as actual handwriting is forged.

It is essential that these points should be borne in mind during the recounting of **Englandspiel**.

Among the agents caught by Scheieder's Gestapo agents was a certain van der Reyden. This agent had been sent by SOE against the advice and wishes of the temporary chief

253

of the Dutch Military Intelligence Bureau, known as the CID. Van der Reyden was arrested on 13th February, 1942.

It was part of van der Reyden's mission to instruct the agents working in the Netherlands gathering information for CID. He had to teach them the double transposition system of coding (**see under** CODES AND CIPHERS), which was widely used throughout SOE. After his arrest van der Reyden quickly gave the Germans the particulars of his code to the limit of the instructions which had been given him, that is, all particulars except his security check.

The Netherlands Commission comments at this point: "If the agents for missions in the Netherlands had been properly selected, the case of van der Reyden might have been prevented. Obviously the English SIS — the actual British Secret Service, which worked independently of SOE and was more concerned with intelligence than with sabotage — chose him solely for his excellent abilities as a wireless operator. The CID's

position at that time, its small voice in these matters, and the undesirability of this situation are best characterised by the fact that van der Reyden was sent over against the chief of CID's wishes."

The arrest of van der Reyden and the information gained from him, while not a decisive factor in bringing about what followed, certainly encouraged Schreieder to persist with his idea.

On 6th March, 1942, Colonel Giskes had better luck. On that day his men arrested Hubertus Lauwers, and three days later, Lauwers's chief saboteur, Taconis.

Lauwers and Taconis formed the second team; the first sabotage team sent into Holland by SOE had been dropped on 7th November, 1941. Since 3rd January, 1942, Lauwers had been in radio contact with London, but his organisation had been penetrated by German agents of the type called "confidence men" or V-men, generally Dutchmen working with the Germans, and Lauwer's transmissions had been intercepted by the German Military Police. SOE's second sabotage team was thus put out of action, and so discreetly that no news of it reached England.

Also in accordance with his instructions, Lauwers gave his code, but not his security check, to Giskes. He also agreed to operate for the Germans, being certain in his mind that as soon as the absence of his security check was noted SOE would know what had happened.

Lauwers made his first transmission to England on behalf of the Germans on 12th March, 1942. This transmission began what has become known as the **Englandspiel**, or rather that part of it which Giskes called **Fall Nordpol** (the North Pole Case).

On the night of 27th/28th March, 1942, Giskes caught his first victim who was arrested immediately he had dropped. SOE had announced the arrival of this agent over Lauwers's wave-length. On the following night four other agents were dropped, and early in April, three others, without the knowledge of **Englandspiel.** Their names were Ras, Jordaan, Andringa, Molenaar (killed in the jump), Kloos, Sebes and de Haas.

On 27th April a message from SOE arrived for Taconis, Lauwers's saboteur, and also fell into Giskes's hands, telling him to go "to the tobacconist in Haarlen to contact Pijl". Pijl was the cover-name for agent de Haas who was one of those dropped in April without Giskes's knowledge. The Germans sent a V-man to the tobacconist's who by chance met Andringa. Andringa introduced the V-man to de Haas (Pijl) and both were arrested on 18th April, 1942.

On account of Molenaar's death, Andringa had been sending his messages by Jordaan. Jordaan connected Sebes, Ras and Kloos, and consequently Giskes was able to eliminate the entire group.

With Jordaan's transmitter, Giskes opened up a second contact with SOE. Before he was arrested on 3rd May, Jordaan had by chance heard of Ras's arrest on 1st May, and had informed SOE that he was replacing him by a wireless operator already living in Holland. Like Lauwers, Jordaan had not given his security check to the Germans. Presently, a message came from SOE to Jordaan

telling him to teach his new wireless operator his security check. When the Germans received this message naturally they forced Jordaans to reveal his security check. This was the first the Germans knew about the use of security checks by SOE agents.

After 9th May, 1942, all SOE agents in the Netherlands were in the hands of the Germans. Giskes now controlled all radio connections with the SOE. Between 29th May and 23rd July, five more agents were arrested as soon as they landed. The last, van Hemert, brought an order for the Taconis group to destroy the transmitter of Kootwijk radio station. Thereupon Giskes staged a mock attack on Kootwijk, reported failure to SOE and sent similar accounts to the Press. SOE were so delighted with the "activities" of Taconis's group (who were under arrest) that one of them was awarded a decoration, and instructed to go to London to receive it. The Germans staged his journey via France, where he was "unfortunately arrested in the presence of some members of the Resistance".

One day the Germans blew up a useless ship in the Maas, near Rotterdam, a n d announced it to England as a sabotage success. Actual sabotage acts by Dutch groups, and accidents in the army and navy were also reported as successes by the SOE groups (under arrest).

The Dutch organisations in London, the BVT (Office for the Preparation for the Return to the Netherlands) and the MVT (Military Preparation for the Return) had had nothing to do with any of the agents mentioned so far. Neither before nor after the arrests did a single report from them reach MVT, who were merely aware that SOE had radio contact with the Netherlands.

In the meantime the BVT had sent agent Jambroes and his wireless operator Bukkens, to Holland on the night 26th/27th June, on a mission connected with what is known as the Holland Plan. The plan had been drawn up by SOE in collaboration with the BVT, and had, as its main aim, the organisation of a Resistance Movement for which it would supply arms and equipment.

The intention was to make

the Resistance group known as the **Orde Dienst** (OD) a link in the organisation of the Holland Plan, by using a number of its members to carry it out. The Netherlands were to be divided into seven regions, and 1,070 men were to be formed into small groups of energetic men who would receive instructions from England as well as the necessary material. In the event of an Allied invasion, these groups were to disorganise the enemy's rear as much as possible, and attempt to prevent the arrival of reinforcements. To do this it would be necessary to interrupt communications between Holland and Germany and Holland and Belgium for at least seventy-two hours from the moment of invasion. The 1,070 members of OD would discontinue all other Resistance activity and be completely detached from OD in a separate organisation.

An agent was to be sent to Holland to make the necessary contacts with OD, and Jambroes was the man chosen for this very important task. The weakest point of the plan was, clearly, entrusting its execution entirely to one man instead of to a group of agents, each of whom would have been responsible for one part of it, none of them knowing the full details.

The arrival of Jambroes and Bukkens was announced by SOE over one of the **Englandspiel** "lines", and both men were arrested at the moment they landed. From that moment the Holland Plan was doomed to failure.

Very skilfully the Germans developed on paper the organisation which Jambroes should have set up with the help of OD and were so successful in deceiving SOE that that organisation sent all the agents and material applied for, all of which, without exception, fell into the hands of the Germans. In the second half of 1942 the Chief of the Imperial General Staff, Sir Alan Brooke urged Colonel de Bruyne, the Dutch head of the MVT, the organisation now responsible for the Holland Plan, to speed up the formation of his organisation. It was obviously considered that some sort of arrangement might be made to induce the Germans to retire from the Netherlands early in 1943; hence the need for speed.

On 24th/25th September, agent Jongelie was dropped into Holland with a communication from the Dutch Prime Minister saying that the Dutch Government was in favour of co-operation between OD and the political parties. The Germans had a shrewd idea that Jongelie had come for a special purpose, but nothing they could do would make him reveal one word. To overcome this difficulty, Giskes informed London that Jongelie had died of concussion. (He was among those who later met their deaths at Mauthausen.)

Altogether, thirty-seven agents were dropped in connection with the Holland Plan, the last on 21st/22nd May, 1943. Giskes seized the lot as soon as they landed.

Whenever London requested the return of an agent, as they did several times for Jambroes, when the Germans could no longer produce plausible excuses for non-compliance with this request, they staged Journeys via France, during which the agents became "lost".

The **Englandspiel** involved far more than the complete frustration of the Holland Plan. Its repercussions were felt over a far wider field of SOE and other espionage activity. Thus, an agent, Niemeyer, of SIS, was compromised and arrested because an SOE agent, van der Giessen, was sent with money for him. The arrest of Niemeyer, however, did not compromise SIS, since the Germans were more interested in military intelligence and had no desire to risk their particularly fruitful connection with SOE merely to develop their activities in a wider field. There was also the case of the woman agent, Beatrix Terwindt, who was sent to Holland by MI9. Unfortunately for her, SOE undertook to drop her for MI9, and she, too, fell into Giskes' hands. She was met by a reception committee to whom she made various communications before they arrested her, but subsequently she resisted all attempts to make her reveal her codes.

The Dutch organisation, MVT, knew nothing about these agents whom SOE and others sent to Holland for their own purposes. The investigations of the Dutch Parliamentary Commission reveal a curious state of affairs. The officers of MVT had nothing to do with ciphering matters, indeed they had no voice at all in matters of communication, which were dealt with by the British authorities without consultation with the Dutch.

The Dutch in London began to be suspicious early in 1943, that something was wrong in Holland, though they had no idea what it was. At all events, Colonel de Bruyne refused to send any more agents for the Holland Plan after 21st/22nd May. A month later Dourlein and Bogaart's very corrupt message reached London, and though it could not be understood, it did at any rate confirm that Colonel de Bruyne had acted wisely. Then several other events took place which made it more certain that there had been the deepest penetration of SOE groups in the Netherlands.

There was, for instance, the unmasking of the V-man Ridderhof. When requests from London, for someone to be sent who could inform them of conditions in the Netherlands, became so urgent that they could no longer be disregarded, Giskes induced a member of the Resistance called Knoppers to undertake the journey. Knoppers acted in good faith. He had been approached by Ridderhof, who, on 13th July, 1943, set him on his way via a route through France and Spain, by which, as a ruse to give an additional air of genuineness to the **Englandspiel,** he had helped American and British airmen to escape. Knoppers arrived in London on 11th September, but when questioned appeared to know nothing about the OD.

After much serious discussion, it was decided to send Knoppers back to Holland. He did actually arrive over the country but weather conditions prevented his dropping. A little later it became apparent that Ridderhof was, in fact, George van Vliet, who had recently been identified as a traitor.

In December, Dourlein and Ubbink had arrived in Switzerland and the Dutch Military attaché there had sent their report urgently to London. By his time, however, it had become clear to those in London that several "lines" had been penetrated.

The **Englandspiel** began to lose its value for Giskes, therefore, in the autumn of 1943, especially after the exposure of Ridderhof/van Vliet. Deliveries of material became less and less, and by the end of the year had ceased altogether.

On 1st April, 1944, Giskes announced the end of the game with the following message :

> Messrs Blunt, Bingham and Successors Ltd London. Recently you have been trying to do business with the Netherlands without our assistance STOP We think this rather unfair in view of our long and successful co-operation as your sole agents STOP But never mind, whenever you come to pay a visit to the Continent you may be assured that you will be received with the same care and result as all those you sent us before STOP So long.

Blunt and Bingham were the former and actual chiefs respectively of the SOE Dutch Section.

As a result of their investigations, the Dutch Parliamentary Commission rejected the suggestion that there had been any treachery on the part of any Dutchman or Englishman connected with it. They gave their conclusion that several of the Dutchmen were not the right men for the work, and criticised the arrangement whereby the Dutch organisations in London had no voice in the policy of communications and certain other activities carried out by SOE, that is, the lack of full communication between them. There did develop a greater collaboration later; and after the end of the **Englandspiel** SOE were successful in putting agents into Holland who did magnificent work.

The point which puzzled the Parliamentary Commission is one which must puzzle all who read the story: How was it possible that the **Englandspiel** could be operated successfully for the incredible period of twenty-months?

The Commission asked Giskes and Scheieder if they had any clue. Giskes had to confess that he was, and always had been, as puzzled as anyone else.

When reduced to simplicity, the problem revolves round the question of the security checks for the codes.

As part of their investigations, the President of the Commission visited London, and there questioned Major-General Sir Colin Gubbins, Chief of SOE, and six officers concerned with the Dutch Section and three officers of SIS. From these they learned that SOE and SIS each had a separate receiving station. At these stations the messages from all agents all over Europe were received. Messages from the Dutch agents were deciphered and sent in full to the Dutch sections of SOE and SIS. The Dutch MVT received only paraphrases of those messages referring to the Holland Plan. The messages were sent to SOE and SIS marked according to whether or not the security check had been included. The MVT paraphrases did not have such a note.

Though SOE could not produce the messages, **declaring that all the hundreds of thousands of messages received from all parts of Europe had been destroyed a few days after VE-Day,** the Commission were satisfied that Lauwers had not revealed his security check to the Germans. Lauwers's transmissions had started the **Englandspiel.** Giskes knew nothing about the security checks from 12th March, 1942, until the middle of May, 1942, when SOE sent the message telling Jordaan to teach his new operator his security check.

The Commission expressed their amazement that such a message could have been sent by radio.

Even after May, 1942, not all the agents handed over their real security checks. Dourlein, for example, gave one that had been discarded and replaced before he left England. Because there were only half a dozen survivors, it was not possible to discover how many agents gave false security checks. On this point the Commission states: "Concerning the security checks ... they think it improbable that agents who were parachuted into occupied territories and who were willing to risk their lives for their

261

missions had disposed of the genuine security checks; they admit that one cannot take it for granted that men of such courageous disposition would not have tried to deceive the enemy. The Germans even considered this possibility during the course of the **Englandspiel,** but as everything went on as they wanted it, they had to assume that the genuine security checks had been handed over."

They also criticised the nature of Lauwer's security check. It consisted of making a striking mistake in the sixteenth letter of the message, or in the multiples of sixteen. It was a bad check when messages normally arrived corrupted.

Giskes was surprised that no control agents had been dropped during the whole of the **Englandspiel.** A control agent is one who is dropped without announcement, and his mission is to see that all is well. Giskes also wondered why it did not occur to the SOE authorities to ask why certain CID agents had not been tried by a German court after their arrests. When it appeared that these agents were not doing any work,

262

and when no reports concerning their trials were received, it ought surely to have aroused the suspicion that something extraordinary was the matter. They also thought that this should have applied to SOE sabotage agents. The Commission points out, however, that during a certain period there was not a single information agent in the Netherlands, whereas all SOE and SOE/MVT agents were in prison.

The Commission was surprised that all SOE agents all over Europe should have used the same type of code. Once the principles of a code are in the hands of experts, it is not very difficult for them to break any message received in it.

The Commission noted that the majority of agents had no other means besides their security checks, by which to identify themselves. They mention that Giskes had admitted being told by one agent that he had to send a check message, and he immediately signalled to England that the man was dead. He was afraid that the agent's check message would arouse suspicions in London, since he could not be sure of the correct meaning of the message.

"This example shows clearly," says the Commission, "how well this system might have worked. In the absence of such checking methods the Commission sees an indication of short-comings on the side of the Netherlands as well as of the British authorities concerned. It may be put forward that the Dutch authorities had no voice in the matter of communications, to which the Commission would reply that in any case the Dutch authorities could have made certain pre-arranged plans for their agents. In that case the Netherlands authorities should have insisted upon being shown the agents' messages and they should have made this a condition for sending or refusing to send agents."

There was also the question of the "handwriting". It was revealed that the tape recording of agents' "handwriting" was not employed by SOE until mid-1943. "But still," the Commission comments, "it must be assumed that the persons concerned could have been more careful and that certain random tests made by the operator-instructors who had taught the respective agents might have shown that one man was operating several lines or that the person who sent a certain message had not been trained in England."

For this was what had happened. One of Giskes's operators took over from Lauwers in mid-October 1942, and yet another operated several "lines" without any consequences to the playing of the **Englandspiel.**

On 14th December, 1949, the British Foreign Office addressed to the Chairman of the Dutch Parliamentary Commission of Inquiry a statement giving a summary of the conclusions which they drew from their own inquiries. Paragraph 13 of this statement says:

13. The various and searching inquiries held by his Majesty's Government into the failure of Special Operations Executive (SOE) operations in the Netherlands during 1942 and 1943, leaving aside such errors of judgment as may have occurred in the course of their conduct...

on which the Dutch Commission comments :

In spite of all this, it is the opinion of the Commission that a number of inadequacies which have been found may not be qualified as "errors of judgment", as they are called in the Statement of the British Government, but that they are blunders, in some cases even grave blunders. However, as has been shown in previous explanations the Commission excludes any thought of wilfulness or bad faith.

The Commission also found that the Netherlands authorities had to bear part of the responsibility for what had happened. In the cases of Dourlein and Ubbink the Commission were forthright in expressing their opinion.

After the two men's escape from Haaren, Giskes sent a message to London saying that he thought the two agents were working for the Germans. This, to a certain extent, justified the British action in imprisoning them. The Dutch authorities, however, should have used more strenuous efforts on their behalf.

However, the Commission failed to comprehend why Dourlein had to be deprived of his temporary rank after his return to Britain which was preceded by the young man's escape from Prison in Haaren and his formidable journey via Belgium, Switzerland, France and Spain. The Commission cannot understand that it was not possible to find a way by which this enterprising young man would have been allowed to keep his temporary rank . . . with regard to Ubbink's rank, the situation was somewhat different, but still it is the opinion of the Commission that the attitude of the people concerned was far from tolerant. Certainly Ubbink's achievements were not less impressive than Dourlein's. Furthermore the Commission fails to understand why these two men have not been given decorations. It is the opinion of the Commission that the authorities concerned are seriously at fault.

It is the Commission's opinion that the reasons given by the British authorities (i.e. the impending Invasion would not allow them to take the slightest risk of penetration by German agents, and the two men's cases were not yet entirely cleared by Security) for the imprisonment of Dourlein and Ubbink must be accepted ... Nevertheless the Commission believe that it would have been fitting and proper to inform the men of these circumstances and in so doing to relieve them of the idea which had been worrying them since their release from prison, namely, that even then they were not thought to be fully reliable.

The seal of the two men's clearance from all suspicion, however, was publicly set on their achievements when on 6th October, 1949, both were made Knights of the Fourth Class of the Military Order of William, for having distinguished themselves "in action by outstanding deeds of courage, enterprise and loyalty".

The catastrophe of the **Englandspiel** was turned to tragedy when forty Dutch agents were executed at Mau-

thausen on 6th and 7th September, 1944. The only relief in the whole unhappy story is that the final aim of the Germans in playing **Englandspiel** was frustrated. This aim was to discover what were the military plans of the Allies with regard to the invasion of Western Europe, and especially in the Netherlands. Giskes, Schreieder and the other German witnesses informed the Commission that never during the twenty months in which the **Englandspiel** operated, was any military information given them by London.

A tragedy though it was, the **Englandspiel,** taken in its proper perspective, was merely an incident in Dutch Resistance. It did, however, prevent the normal growth of that Resistance, but when, at last, it was discovered and an end put to it, thereafter the Resistance Movement in the Netherlands began to develop rapidly and became a really effective instrument against the Germans.

This story of the **Englandspiel** has been recounted under the entry for Colonel H. J. Giskes rather than under **The England Game** or **Op-**

265

eration **North Pole,** because in this writer's view, despite the errors and shortcomings of SOE, the operation was a triumph for the German counter-espionage services, and for Colonel Giskes especially. Once it had begun, the slightest small error might have jeopardised its continuation. The closest study of Colonel Giskes's handling of the operation discloses no such error. Each move was carefully thought out and executed, and for that Colonel Giskes must be given all credit.

BIBLIOGRAPHY :

London Calling North Pole — Colonel H. J. Giskes (London, 1953).

Inside North Pole — P. Dourlein (London, 1953).

Schreieder und die Spione — L. D. Gerson (München, 1950).

GOERGEN, Edmund (Agent of Luxembourg Resistance, World War II).

Edmund Goergen is an artist of outstanding original power, though nowadays he devotes much of his skill to restoring ancient paintings for museums and churches. During World War II, however

266

he was employed at Radio Luxembourg, where he organised a small cell for gathering intelligence. He had radio contact with London, and a **teleprinter** link with Berlin.

Some 15,000 young Luxembourgeois were called up into the Wehrmacht, and among them was a young friend of Goergen's, who was posted to guard some strange underground installations at Peenemünde. While home on leave the young soldier talked to Goergen about these installations, and was able to describe them with great accuracy. Goergen appreciated the value of such information to the Allies, though he had not, at any time, a clue to their significance.

Goergen transmitted the information to London. Many intelligence groups have claimed the discovery of the German flying-bomb base at Peenemünde; but the strongest claim for providing the first information about them is that of Luxembourg intelligence.

Goergen was caught eventually by the Gestapo and sent to Mauthausen concentration camp. He survived by a miracle, and brought home with him, as a constant reminder to all, a series of brilliant drawings he made in this notorious camp.

GOERTZ, Captain Dr Hermann (Inter-war and World War II German agent).

On 29th August, 1935, there landed at Harwich a certain Dr Hermann Goertz, who described himself as a lawyer-author and the purpose of his visit the study of law cases in Cambridge and London. In actual fact, he was a highly trained intelligence officer, whose experience dated from the First World War.

Goertz had not been in England long before he joined forces with a nineteen-year-old German girl, who had arrived in England a few weeks earlier. He bought a powerful motorcycle on which, with the girl riding pillion, he toured the countryside, wherever there were to be found Royal Air Force stations. On points of vantage he would set up an easel and under the pretence of landscape painting, he sketched the layout of the airfields and their defences.

On 11th September he rented a bungalow at Broadstairs,

on the Kent coast, until 26th October. But on 24th October he and the girl left the house and telegraphed the owner that they would return in two days. But they did not come back, and the owner, becoming suspicious, informed the police.

The bungalow was searched by Special Branch officers, who found hidden among Goertz's clothes, a sketch of nearby Manston RAF airfield with various points explained by marginal notes. This was enough for them to apply for a warrant for his arrest should he ever come back.

He did return, but alone, on 8th November, landing again at Harwich from the Hook of Holland. He was arrested immediately. The arrest was kept secret for eleven days, for the Special Branch hoped that the girl, Marianne Ewig, would eventually follow. But she did not.

Goertz was tried at the Central Criminal Court. He pleaded not guilty, but he was sentenced to four years penal servitude for making a sketch of an airfield likely to be of use to an enemy.

Why Goertz had made his

sudden dash to Berlin was never revealed. When asked whom he had seen in the German capital, he replied, "I dare not answer."

Goertz's blundering was typical of so many German agents. Counter-espionage had not been interested in him at all until his sudden disappearance on 24th October. They might never have been suspicious of him had he behaved more circumspectly, and particularly if he had not left in the bungalow the sketch of Manston.

He was destined to be the victim of his own or others' blunders until he eventually put an end to his own life. During World War II he was sent by the **Abwehr** to make contact with the pro-German elements of the IRA in Eire. He was parachuted into Northern Ireland by mistake, and his radio, which was attached to another parachute, went adrift and he was unable to find it.

He eventually made his way to Eire, but when he arrived he found that the internal struggles of the IRA made all his plans impossible to fulfil.

He made contact with a number of highly placed Irish politicians, senators and "high Catholic dignitaries" among them, and must have believed himself immune from arrest. On 27th November, 1941, however, the house in which he was living in Blackheath Park, in the Dublin suburb of Clontarf, was raided and he was seized. He was interned in Athlone Camp for the remainder of the war.

In September 1946, the internees of this camp, including Goertz, were told that they were to be given the right of asylum in Eire. A little later they were released, and most of them moved into Dublin, and there tried to make a living. Goertz lived with some sisters called Farrell, and in February became secretary of the **Save the German Children Fund,** an Irish relief organisation for German children.

On 12th April, 1947, he was rearrested, together with the other two Abwehr II agents, Günther Schütz and Dieter Gärtner, and imprisoned in Mount Joy prison. They were to be deported to Germany and handed over to the Allies. Though assured again and again that he had nothing to fear in Germany, he swallowed potassium cyanide, and died at 11.15 a.m. on 23rd May, 1947. He was buried in Deans Grange cemetery, Dublin, three days later, his pall the Nazi flag.

BIBLIOGRAPHY:

Germany and her Spies — S. Theodore Felstead (London, 1940).

German Military Intelligence —Paul Leverkühn (London, 1945).

Spies in Ireland — Enno Striphan (London, 1963).

GOLD, Harry see under **Soviet American Network.**

GOLDSMITH, Alexander — (cover name of **DEFOE, Daniel,** q.v.).

GOLLNOW, Herbert see under **Red Orchestra, The.**

GORIN, Mikhail (Inter-war Soviet agent in USA).

Mikhail Gorin arrived in America sometime in 1936, as an employee of Amtorg, the Russian trade organisation, from where he was transferred to Los Angeles as manager of Intourist, the Soviet State Travel Bureau. In Los Angeles he made contact with an American naval intelligence officer, Hafis Salich, who, in the course of his official duties had access to secret information about Japan.

Salich, who was Russian-born, at first refused to have anything to do with Gorin. Gorin, however, following customary Soviet techniques of blackmail, reminded Salich that he still had relatives in Russia, who would be sent to Siberia if he did not co-operate. Subsequently, Salich passed to Gorin secret Navy documents, many of which referred to Japanese espionage.

Salich handed over sixty-two intelligence documents before Gorin made an extraordinary blunder, all the more strange because he was a highly trained and experienced agent. He left some of the documents in a suit which he sent to the cleaners, who at once reported their find to the Office of Naval Intelligence. Both men were arrested.

At FBI headquarters Gorin broke yet another rule of espionage. He asked permission to telephone the Russian embassy in Washington. His request was granted, and he was put through to the ambassador, Constantin Oumansky, from whom he requested instructions.

Oumansky, highly perturbed by Gorin's arrest, sent the Soviet vice-consul in New York, who was actually an NKVD agent, to see Gorin in Los Angeles goal, and himself called on the Secretary of State, Sumner Welles, to whom he protested about Gorin's arrest, claiming that it was not strictly legal.

When Welles said he could not understand the ambassador's argument, Oumansky left him and went to see Loy Henderson of the European Affairs Division of the State Department, to ask that Vice-Consul Ivanushkin might visit Gorin. Though an American-Russian agreement provided that American citizens arrested in Russia could be held incommunicado for the first three days of their arrest, and the US Administration had taken it that the agreement conferred reciprocal rights on them, Henderson gave his permission.

In the weeks before Gorin was brought to trial, Oumansky made several attempts to bail him, but the State Department refused to intervene, as Gorin had no diplomatic immunity. When subsequently tried, along with Salich, in May 1939, Gorin was sentenced to six years' and Salich to fours years' imprisonment.

The Soviet authorities at once entered an appeal on Gorin's behalf, and for the next two years the case meandered through the appeals machinery. Ultimately the court of appeal upheld the verdict of the court of first instance.

BIBLIOGRAPHY :
Soviet Espionage — D. J. Dallin (London, 1955).

GORSHKOV (Soviet agent in Canada) see under **Gouzenko, Igor.**

GOUZENKO, Igor (Soviet agent in Canada during World War II).

On 7th September, 1945, the Authorities in Ottawa became aware of Igor Gouzenko, a cipher clerk in the Soviet embassy. They became aware of him because he pleaded with them for protection on behalf of himself, his wife and small son, stating as his reason for making the request the possession of documentary proof of a Russian spy-ring operating in Canada, on account of which he feared for his life.

Gouzenko had been in Canada for two years, during which time he had had the opportunity of seeing what the democratic version of freedom really is. He liked what he saw, and preferred it to the Russian concept; so much so that he underwent a sincere change of heart and made up his mind to have nothing more to do with the Soviets and their works.

When he left the Soviet embassy on the evening of 5th September, 1945, it was for the last time. He had already planned what he was going to do; and he took with him in his brief-case a number of secret files which would uncover almost completely the Russian espionage organisation in Canada.

He went straight from the Soviet embassy to the offices of a leading Ottawa newspaper, told them his story, offered them his proofs—and found himself shown to the door. They did not believe him.

He returned home, and being well aware of what would happen as soon as the Soviet officials noted his absence coupled with the absence of the files — which could only be a matter of hours — he spent the next day going from government department to government department, only to meet with the sort of humouring that is shown to the crank or the idiot. Late in the afternoon he visited the newspaper once more; and met with a similar rebuff.

Going home again — in what state of mind can be guessed — he locked himself and his family in their flat. Almost at once there was a knock on the door. He signalled to his wife to be quiet and pretended they were out; but their little four-year-old son ran with a clatter across the parquet floor. The man at the door heard the noise and called out, and Gouzenko recognised the voice of one of the chauffeurs at the embassy. The man went away when he received no reply.

When he had gone, Gouzenko went out on to the balcony and there made contact with his next-door neighbour, a Sergeant Main of the Royal Canadian Air Force. He told the Sergeant he was afraid for his life, described what had happened, and asked Main to give him and his family shelter for the night.

Main believed him, and took the Gouzenkos in. Later they were transferred to the flat of another neighbour. Then Main went in search of the police. Two police-officers came and questioned Gouzenko, and agreed to keep the block of flats under observation.

About half-past eleven Main heard voices outside in the corridor. Thinking it was the police returning, he went to his own door and saw four men in the act of breaking into Gouzenko's flat. He gave the signal for help which had been pre-arranged with the watching police, and when the latter arrived they found the four men ransacking Gouzenko's home.

When questioned the men said that they were officials from the Soviet embassy, and that they had the permission of a colleague who was away in Toronto, to enter the flat to get some important papers. The policemen sent for their inspector, who arrived and asked to see the men's papers, which they showed without

protest. Asking them to remain where they were, he went outside to make some inquiries. While he was gone the men left, the watching police making no attempt to stop them.

On the 8th September the Canadian Department for External Affairs received a note from the Soviet embassy explaining the visit of the embassy officials to Gouzenko's flat, stating that Gouzenko was a common thief who had stolen a sum of money from the embassy, and complaining of the behaviour of the police who had refused to recognise the diplomatic immunity of the officials. The embassy requested the Canadian authorities to take all measures to arrest Gouzenko, so that he might be deported to Russia, as a "capital criminal".

On the morning of the day before, however, Gouzenko had told his story to the Canadian Mounted Police, and handed over his documents. This time he was believed; and the authorities, considerably shaken, found themselves in possession of particulars of what has been described as "the largest and most dangerous spy-plot ever known in the Dominion in peace or war".

Igor Gouzenko's disclosures revealed, for the first time, the methods and techniques of Soviet spying; and these were made public in the Report of the Royal Commission which the Canadian government subsequently set up to probe the affair.

The choice of Gouzenko and his training followed the normal pattern of all Soviet agents employed abroad.

He was born in 1919, received a primary and secondary education, and joined the Young Communist League at seventeen, but was never a member of the Communist Party. (In fact there are only six million Party members out of a population of 172 million.) On leaving school he entered the Moscow Engineering Academy, with the intention of joining the Army as an engineer officer.

At the Academy his outstanding ability attracted attention, and when he had been screened by the NKVD — as the security service was then known — he was sent to a special General Staff school, where for five months he was trained in general intelligence subjects, and eventually allocated to cipher work.

He completed his training in 1941, was posted to the Main Intelligence Division of the Red Army, served for nearly a year at the front, and was then chosen for service abroad. During the next six months he underwent the closest surveillance by the N KVD who watched him at all times for his habits and behaviour under the following headings: partiality for the opposite sex, indulgence in alcohol, financial stability, any tendency towards loquacity and observance of security regulations. If the NKVD found that he was not "safe" in any one of these respects, his services in any branch of Soviet intelligence would have been barred for the NKVD was the final authority in these matters. Thus, though Gouzenko was never employed at any time by any branch of Soviet intelligence except the Red Army, it was on the decision of the security police that he was adjudged suitable agent-material.

Even then the Red Army could not send him abroad at

will, but had to seek the approval of the Chief of the Foreign Branch of the Central Committee of the Communist Party or one of his assistants. It will thus be seen that the Party has the final word in such cases.

This approval was forthcoming, and Lieutenant Gouzenko of the Red Army arrived in Ottawa in June 1943, as cipher clerk on the staff of the military attaché, Colonel Zabotin, officially described as a "civilian employee". In the cipher department he worked in a room of his own, which not even the ambassador, Mr Zaroubin — later ambassador in London — was allowed to enter. There he enciphered and deciphered messages between the military attaché and the Director of Military Intelligence in Moscow.

In the cipher department of the Ottawa Soviet embassy there were five sections :

1 The NKVD (Secret Political Police) sending its own, messages to NKVD headquarters in Moscow.

2 The embassy section, sending the messages of the ambassador and his staff to the Commissar-iat of Foreign Affairs in Moscow.

3 The political Section (Politbureau), communicating directly with the Central Committee of the Communist Party in Moscow.

4 The Commercial Section, communicating with the Commissariat of Foreign Trade in Moscow.

5 The Military Section of military intelligence, communicating with the Director of Military Intelligence in Moscow.

Each section worked independently of the others, and had its own ciphers. A peculiar feature of the arrangement — and this is true for all Soviet missions abroad — was that the only ciphers open to the ambassador were his own and those of the Commercial attaché. The Royal Commission found that Ambassador Zaroubin was neither aware of, nor responsible for any of the activities of his military attaché, nor of the NKVD and the Politbureau.

The head of the NKVD in Ottawa was a man called Vitali G. Pavlov. His rank was that of Second Secretary, and therefore subordinate to the ambassador. Yet he had his own ciphers. His functions included watching and reporting to Moscow on the members of the embassy staff. The head of the Political Section also had the rank of Second Secretary, but he was equivalent in authority to the ambassador.

Colonel Zabotin had at his house in Ottawa apparatus for photographing documents. From the same address he operated a very efficient espionage system which covered the whole of Canada.

Practically everybody and everything had a "cover" name. Gouzenko's was Klark, Zabotin's was Grant, Lt Gousev, a door-keeper, was Henry, Captain Gorshkov, a chauffeur, was Chester; Canada was called Lesovia, the Soviet embassy, the Metro, the NKVD, the neighbour, the spy-ring itself, the Net, passports were known as Shoes. This giving of "cover" names is not particular to Soviet espionage, but is general practice (see Covernames) The Soviet Union perhaps carries it several phases further than is normal among services elsewhere.

One of the most important features of the Soviet espionage system is the Fifth Column of local Communist Party members. When the Royal Commission had completed its work, and criminal proceedings were set in motion, no less than eighteen members of the Canadian CP or people in sympathy with Communist principles, were arraigned. (Seven were acquitted and one disappeared.) Some of these agents, like Fred Rose, the Canadian Member of Parliament, and Sam Carr (See under **Kogan, Schmil**) were openly professing Communists; others like Nunn May were secret sympathisers.

Zabotin received his directives from the Director of Military Intelligence in Moscow, to whom he passed his reports and results. The Director's instructions were comprehensive, among them being to obtain information on the technological processes and methods employed by the Canadians and English for the production of explosives and chemicals, information concerning the transfer of American troops from Eur-

275

ope and the Pacific, and the locations of army, army corps and divisional headquarters, instructions to take measures to obtain particulars as to materials of which the atomic bomb was composed, its technological process and drawings, to obtain from the National Research Council models of developed radar sets, photographs, technical data, periodic reports characterising radar work carried on by the Council and future developments planned by the Council, to obtain a sample of uranium 235 and details of the plant at Chalk River, Ontario, and the processing of uranium. These were among the twenty-one distinct requirements which covered a range so wide that practically nothing was overlooked.

That Zabotin succeeded well enough to achieve the high approval of his chiefs, is shown by the fact that in August 1945 he was awarded two important decorations—the Order of the Red Banner, and the Order of the Red Star.

The colonel was a methodical and thorough man. He kept a dossier on each agent which contained every possible detail about the man or woman serving him. The Royal Commission said this of his methods of recruitment :

One of Zabotin's main objects when he started his operations was to recruit persons willing to supply secret information. A belief in, or sympathy with, or a susceptibilty to the Communist ideology was a primary requirement in the persons to be recruited. The ingenuity that is shown in the methods employed to get prospective agents into the "Net" indicates that the system has been thoroughly worked out to cover all eventualities. The way in which persons who were in a position to furnish secret information, or who might be used as contacts, and who had some inherent weakness which might be exploited, were selected and studied, clearly establishes this. The methods of approach varied with the person and with the position. Zabotin's chief recruitment officers, without whose assistance he would have been helpless, were members of the Canadian CP, and certain of its associated bodies.

The method of recruitment followed a pattern. First of all, one of the Communist leaders would suggest a possible agent to Zabotin, who would make a local check with the help of the NKVD Section. If the NKVD's report was satisfactory, Zabotin reported to his director in Moscow. The director would then check, from his own resources, and would then pronounce his agreement or veto. Sometimes acting on his own information, the director, though thousands of miles away in Moscow, would suggest certain potential agents to Zabotin for specific tasks, which indicates that the director had another channel of information besides Zabotin, and this may have been the Politbureau, which not only watches its own agents but everybody else's.

Everyone who came into contact with Soviet officials was considered from the point of view of his potentialities as an agent. Was he in financial difficulties? Had he an extravagant wife? What were his personal tastes? To what sort of information would he have access? For what sort of task would he be suitable? This kind of information, and much more besides was all recorded in The Index, kept in The Centre in Moscow, along with such intimate details of people all over the world who might at some time be useful in the espionage field.

Time after time the director urged Zabotin to extend the Net, and since prestige in public service, in the Soviet Union as well as in the democracies, is based on the number of subordinates a chief has, Zabotin was zealous to succeed. If it had not been for Gouzenko's defection it is impossible to say how it might have developed.

All this information about Soviet espionage techniques was supplied by Gouzenko. What he revealed was to shake not only the Canadian government, but the US Administration as well, for Zabotin's network was but part of a larger network which covered atomic development in the United States as well. (See under **SOVIET CANADIAN NETWORK**).

Zabotin remained in Canada for some time after

Gouzenko's defection. He did not know how many papers his cipher clerk had handed over to the Canadian authorities, because a great number of the records had been marked up in the registers as officially burned. For their part, the Canadian authorities were prevented from acting quickly, because in all the Gouzenko documents, agents were referred to only by their cover names, and these took many months to identify. Not until arrests began did the Centre close down Zabotin's headquarters in a secret wing of the Soviet embassy at 285 Charlotte Street, Ottawa. Zabotin and all his staff were recalled to Russia, and subsequently Zabotin was sentenced to four years imprisonment for not realising that he had a disillusioned Gouzenko on his staff.

BIBLIOGRAPHY :

The Soviet Spy System — John Baker White (London, 1948).

The Great Spy Ring — Norman Lucas (London, 1966).

GRAMSCH, Walter (West German agent) see under **Gehlen, Reinhard.**

GRANVILLE, Christine — (Allied agent World War II).

Christine Granville was born Countess Krystyna Skarben, the daughter of a Polish aristocrat. Shortly before the outbreak of World War II she married a young Polish writer. They were in Kenya when hostilities began, and the husband flew home to Poland to join the colours. He was never heard of again.

Instead of remaining in the safety of Kenya, Christine made her way to London, and offered her services to the British authorities, who passed her to SOE. The latter were impressed by her qualities and sent her off on her first mission.

Shortly before the outbreak of the war, the Poles had invented a new anti-tank gun, which was capable of piercing the armour of a tank at two hundred yards. The Allies had nothing like it and since it was a great advance on any anti-tank gun they had, they decided to get the plans of it, out of Poland. This was Christine's assignment.

She made her way to Hungary, and from there crossed into Poland, with the aid of Andrew Kowerski, an officer in the Polish army who had managed to escape when the Germans overran his country. On her first trip to Poland, Christine was unsuccessful, but she was fortunate to make the acquaintance of Ludwig Popiel, also exiled in Hungary, who told her that while he did not know where the plans of the gun were, he had buried one of the few models produced in the grounds of his family estate before he had escaped.

Despite the risks inherent in returning to Poland, and especially to his family home, Popiel agreed to go and get the gun. After an extremely difficult journey across the mountains, and many narrow escapes, he succeeded in bringing the gun to Budapest.

Christine remained in Hungary, from which she made several journeys into Poland for the purpose of gathering information about conditions there under the German occupation, until after the Germans overran that country

also. In the autumn of 1941, however, she and Kowerski were betrayed to the Germans.

They made their escape and after a hazardous journey across Greece, Turkey and Palestine they reached Cairo, where they reported to the Middle East HQ of SOE. SOE had no employment for them, but both so importuned the British authorities, that eventually Kowerski was sent on an assignment to Italy, and a little later Christine was parachuted into Vercors, in the Rhone valley to act as courier to the Vercors maquis leader Colonel François Cammaerts.

She served with Cammaerts until the liberation, running risks which would have daunted many courageous men, and often finding herself in the greatest danger of arrest by the Germans. Nothing, however, deterred her.

When Cammaerts, Major Xan Fielding (q.v.) and an American OSS officer, named Sorenson were arrested in Digne, and were on the point of being executed, Christine rescued them. She went to Digne prison and so browbeat the commandant, who could have arrested her and shot her with his other prisoners, that he agreed to let the men go.

When hostilities in Europe ended, Christine returned to SOE in Cairo. They had no further use for her, and demobilised her. She returned to England penniless and without work. After a number of jobs as a shop assistant she took the post of stewardess on the liner **Winchester Castle,** plying between England and South Africa.

On board was a steward called Dennis Muldowney, who fell in love with her. She did not reciprocate, and later in the evening of 15th June, 1952, he followed her to the hotel in London where she was staying between voyages, and shot her dead. Muldowney was hanged for her murder two months later.

For her courageous services during the war, Christine Granville was awarded the George Medal.

BIBLIOGRAPHY:

SOE in France — M. R. Foot (London, 1966).

Some of My Favorite Spies— Ronald Seth (Philadelphia, 1967).

GRANVILLE, Captain Clive (British agent, World War I).

Clive Granville had been brought up in Germany, and had been educated at a German university. His knowledge of the German language and customs was perfect.

It so happened that he bore a striking resemblance to a Prussian junker, a rich landowner with large estates in Belgium, called Albert von Schultz. Schultz was in Belgium when the Kaiser's troops overran the country, and was kidnapped by a number of Belgians. Three days later Granville enlisted in the Wehrmacht and was commissioned. He rapidly rose to the rank of Captain.

He was able to gather much high-grade intelligence in the course of his military duties. The network controlled by the famous woman agent Marthe McKenna, a Belgian married to an Englishman, acted as couriers for him. Probably better known as Special Duty Agent Three-three, Granville, despite many narrow escapes, survived the war.

BIBLIOGRAPHY:

My Master Spy — Marthe McKenna (London, 1932).

GRAUDENZ, Johann see under **Red Orchestra, The.**

GREENGLASS, David see under **Soviet American Network.**

GREEN HOUSE, The see under **Stieber, Wilhelm.**

GROOS, Major see under **Schragmüller, Dr Elsbeth.**

GRU

Glavnoye **R**azvedyvatelnoye **U**pravlenie — Chief Intelligence Administration of the General Staff (of the Red Army) i.e. military intelligence.

The GRU — which, like the KGB, has been known by a variety of names in the course of it existence — was created by Trotsky, who intended it to be **the** espionage agency of the Soviet government. Its first chief was Jan Berzin, an outstanding organiser of forceful personality, who rose to the rank of general, and like so many Russian intelligence chiefs who escaped liquidation by other means, was ultimately arrested, tried and executed during the 1937 Purge.

The GRU, whose head-quarters are said to be at Arbatskaya Ploshehad, in Moscow, is organised on much the same lines as other military intelligence organisations. It has four divisions, the First Division controlling espionage abroad. The First Division is subdivided into eight sections :

1. Western Europe
2. The Middle East
3. America, the Far East and India
4. Technical intelligence, notably weapons
5. Acts of terror abroad, sabotage, kidnapping etc.
6. False documents and new techniques of espionage
7. Intelligence operations in the military districts on the frontier.
8. Codes and ciphers.

All GRU officers are graduates of the Military Academy of the Red Army. It operates abroad through the military attachés, who are generally in charge of espionage networks in the countries to which they are accredited.

The GRU recruits its agents and trains them in its own schools, but its personnel and agents must be vetted by the KGB before being finally engaged. There has never been a clear division of activities between the GRU and its great rival the KGB, and often their activities overlap. An attempt was made in 1947 to combine the GRU and the KGB in one central agency, on the lines of the American CIA, but the experiment was a failure and the former system was reverted to.

The GRU has been the agency behind some of the outstanding spy cases of the post World War II era. It was in charge of the Canadian and American Atomic Spy rings, blown by Igor Gouzenko (q.v.) in 1945, the Rudolf Rössler (q.v.) and Alexander Foote (q.v.) network which operated from Switzerland during World War II and it recruited the outstanding spy Richard Serge (q.v.) who operated in Japan from 1956 to 1942, while more recently Colonel Rudolf Abel (q.v.) has been its most outstanding agent.

GUBITCHEV, Valentine (Soviet Agent) see under **Coplon, Judith.**

GUILOT, Claude — covername used by **Daniel Defoe** (q.v.).

HAHN, Peter (German agent in Britain, beginning of World War I).

A censor in British Postal Censorship, examining outgoing newspapers and parcels, found among them a newspaper bearing an Amsterdam address which was included in the List of Suspected Addresses. The addresses on this list — always in neutral countries—were either known to be or believed to be the addresses of German intelligence "letter-boxes" (q.v.), and anything addressed to one of them was to be held up and submitted to British counter-espionage.

When the censor closely inspected the newspaper before him and could find no ink or pencil marks on it which ought not to be there, he passed it at once for chemical tests. These tests revealed a brief message written in English in a chemical ink — "C has gone north. Am sending from 201." MI5 were at once informed and a Special Branch inspector was detailed to find out what he could.

The inspector had only one clue to help him. The paper was postmarked "Deptford", a suburb of London. Taking a long shot, he contacted the Deptford police and asked for a list of all the streets which had a house numbered 201. He was told that in all of Deptford, there was only one — No 201 High Street.

On investigation, 201 High Street was found to be the shop of Peter Hahn, baker and confectioner. German by birth, Hahn was a naturalised British subject. Asked if he had ever written anything in the margin of a newspaper which he had then sent to an address in Amsterdam, he denied that he had done so. However, a search of the premises brought to light an old shoe-box in which was a bottle of chemical ink and a special pen. Still Hahn refused to say a word.

Inquiries in Deptford were then instituted, and neighbours of Hahn recalled that he was frequently visited by a tall, well dressed man of distinguished bearing, who was generally thought to be a Russian. The Deptford boarding-houses were then visited, and when these produced no trace of such a man, the inquiries were broadened to include all London boarding-houses, which presented the Special Branch with quite a formidable task.

Eventually the landlady of a boarding-house in the Bloomsbury district, not far from the British Museum, told the police that she had a Russian gentleman called Müller as one of her boarders. He was at present away, having announced that he was going to Newcastle-upon-Tyne on private business.

The Newcastle police set a watch on the central railway station, and within a few days arrested Müller as he was about to board a train for London. From their interrogation of Müller, MI5 discovered that he was a German agent of considerable experience, who specialised in naval intelligence. But for Hahn's doubtless well-meaning interference, he might have gone undiscovered for a long time, if, indeed, he had been discovered at all. For his means of communicating

his information to **Abwehr** headquarters was extremely ingenious, as well as being quite new. He inserted advertisements in English provincial newspapers — articles for sale, rooms to let, articles wanted — according to a prearranged code, and mailed the papers containing them to various "letter-boxes" in Holland and Scandinavia.

Müller had been born in Libau, Lithuania, from which he claimed Russian domicile. Well-educated and with polished manners, he spoke English without a trace of an accent. He was strikingly good-looking, and his successes with young women, about which he was inclined to boast, were understandable. Before the war he had made his somewhat precarious living wandering about Europe promoting a number of schemes, none of which really came to anything.

Shortly before the outbreak of World War I he had offered his services to the **Abwehr,** who, when he was able to produce several items of high-grade intelligence, took him on their strength, giving him the assignment of collecting naval intelligence in Britain. He had drawn Hahn into his net, chiefly because he needed a "letter-box" himself. Hahn, who had been on the point of going bankrupt, agreed to help.

Because he was a naturalised British subject, Hahn could have been hanged for treason; instead he was given seven years hard labour. Müller was treated as a regular Abwehr agent, and was sentenced to death.

After his execution at the hands of a firing squad in the moat of the Tower of London, British intelligence officers continued to send messages in his code to the Abwehr, all naturally containing false information. Before the Abwehr discovered that this information was worthless, they had sent the dead Müller four hundred pounds.

BIBLIOGRAPHY :

My Experiences at Scotland Yard — Sir Basil Thomson (London, 1935).

HALE, Enoch see under **Tallmadge, Network, The.**

HALE, Nathan (American agent, War of Independence).

Sometimes regarded as the Father of American espion-age, Nathan Hale presents something of a paradox and a mystery, for little or nothing is known of his mission or the circumstances which led to his capture by the British.

George Washington appreciated very well the value of intelligence (see under **Tallmadge, Major Benjamin),** for in his youth he had witnessed the defeat of the British General Edward Braddock at Fort Duquesne (now Pittsburgh) by the French on 13th July, 1755, a defeat stemming solely from Braddock's failure to discover the strength of the French at the fort.

Twenty years later, British headquarters were at New York, and Washington was eager to know how many troops were in the town and how well supplied they were with weapons and ammunition. How he came to choose Nathan Hale is unknown, for there seems to have been a conspiracy of silence which has helped to hide the facts. There was no mention of him in contemporary American history until Hannah Adam published **The History of New England** in 1799, almost a quarter of a century after Hale's execution. Miss Adam

285

wrote, "So far Hale has remained unnoticed, and it is scarcely known such a character existed. It is said that the spy passed in civilian guise to Long Island, examined every part of the British Army, and obtained the best possible information respecting their situation and future operation."

Some authorities have suggested that because he penetrated Long Island as an unarmed American civilian, the British took no interest in him since they were interested only in armed Americans. Others say that he went under the "cover" of a schoolmaster, and that when he was questioned, answered that as a schoolmaster he believed in obedience to the law, and that he had sworn allegiance to the king which he could not in conscience forswear. He had come to Long Island to escape persecution by his companions on this account, and hoped to receive the protection of the British.

When he fell under suspicion or why is equally unknown for certain, though it is believed that he was trapped as he attempted to pass through the defences on his way back to General Washington at the conclusion of his mission. It is suggested that at the crucial moment he faltered and allowed his anxiety to betray to the British that he was a spy.

He was hanged sometime in September 1776. His death was reported to Washington by Captain Montressor, Royal Engineers, ADC to General Sir William Howe, who came through the American lines under a flag of truce to do so. Montressor did not report any details of Hale's capture and treatment by the British, but it subsequently became known that the British Provost Marshal Cunningham had denied the condemned man both a clergyman and a Bible, and notes of farewell, which Hale had written to his mother, to his sisters, and to a young Connecticut woman he was hoping to marry, Cunningham tore up in Hale's presence, saying, "The rebels ought not to know that they had a man in their army who could die with that much firmness."

It was believed that Washington's subsequent refusal to reprieve Major John André (q.v.) was motivated by revenge for Hale's death.

BIBLIOGRAPHY :

The Two Spies — Morton Pennypacker (New York, 1932).

HALL, Rear-Admiral Sir Reginald (Director of Naval Intelligence, World War I).

Admiral Hall was one of the most brilliant spy-masters in the history of British espionage. Unfortunately, the history of the activities of British Naval Intelligence during World War I has still to be written. There have been a number of books purporting to give accounts of the Department's exploits, but it must be said that many are based on conjectures. Nevertheless, it is clear from the remarks made by famous naval autobiographists who were his contemporaries, that Admiral Hall was outstanding in his role of collecting and collating information which made many of the Royal Navy's victories possible.

HALL OF PLEASURABLE DELIGHTS, The.

The Japanese, when organising their first espionage service, consulted the great Prussian spy-master, Wilhelm Stieber (q.v.), many of whose innovations they adopted and adapted. The Hall of Pleasurable Delights, which they established in Hankow, was modelled on Stieber's Green House (q.v.) in Berlin, but it was much more attractive than its prototype.

Within the Hall every oriental version of all the vices could be experienced. Set up originally for the purpose for which Stieber had founded the Green House — the obtaining of intelligence by blackmail from decadent Chinese notables — its second function was to serve as a meeting-place for agents operating in Sinkiang and Russian central Asia.

Once he had entered The Field the agent was never again to contact any of his superiors directly, except on their instructions. Any agent who had a report to make was to go to the Hall of Pleasurable Delights, engage the services of a prostitute and hand to her his report. She would know what to do with it, and there is no more secret place for handing over a report than a bed.

But the Hall of Pleasurable

Delights had a third purpose.

In the West, on these days, it is the fashion to discount sex as a weapon of espionage. Gone, they say, are the days of Delilah and Mata Hari. Men, they say, are now more conditioned to sex, and are unlikely to reveal their secrets under its influence. Then, in the next breath they contradict themselves, and forbid their agents to indulge in sexual promiscuity while engaged on a mission, since there is no greater danger to security, and no influence more certain to undermine judgment.

The Japanese, on the other hand, have never been so muddle-headed.

They knew that if they laid upon their agents an injunction to abstain from making love they would be obeyed, so deep-rooted was the discipline, the devotion to duty with which their men were imbued. But they knew, too, that enforced celibacy of this kind can be harmful to a man's morale, particularly when the opportunity is to hand. So, in the Hall of Pleasurable Delights they prepared their agents for every variation from the norm of conventional sexual behaviour he might be likely to encounter, and taught him special skills by which he might acquire the confidence of women able to aid him in his mission.

BIBLIOGRAPHY :

Secret Servants — Ronald Seth (London and New York, 1957).

HALPERIN, Isador see under **Soviet Canadian Network.**

HAMBURGER, Ursula - Maria see under **Foote, Alexander.**

HARNACK, Arvad see under **Red Orchestra, The.**

HAUKELID, Knut (Norwegian Resistance leader, World War II).

Since before the war, Norsk Hydro, the State hydroelectric authority, had established in a valley near Rjukan, in the Hardanger Vidda, a barren, mountainous, sparsely populated region situated just south of a line Oslo-Bergen, a plant for the production of deuterium oxide, or heavy water. The amount produced was small, for it was a complicated process requiring a whole year to complete.

It is by now generally known that among its various uses, heavy water is an ingredient in the fearfully complicated manufacture of the atomic bomb. When the information arrived in England as early as May, 1940 that the Germans, before the conclusion of the campaign even, had ordered Norsk Hydro to raise its output to three thousand pounds annually, the Rjukan plant became an object of special attention of the British espionage network already established and operating in southern Norway. The position did not become serious, however, until the beginning of 1942, when the Germans increased their demand to ten thousand pounds annually. This created a situation about which something had to be done, and SOE (q.v.) were requested to do it.

The Norwegian Section of SOE, to the command of which Colonel J. S. Wilson had been appointed on 1st January, 1942, had two strokes of good fortune to assist them. In Section IV of the Supreme Command of the Norwegian armed forces was one of the greatest experts on Norwegian industry, Professor Leif Tronstad. Tronstad knew in detail all the complicated equipment used in the production of heavy water, and the layout of the plant at Rjukan intimately. He was, therefore, able to describe the most vulnerable points which, if successfully attacked, could put the plant out of production permanently.

The other stroke of luck was the arrival in England early in March 1942, of Einar Skinnarland. Skinnarland had been one of a small band of Norwegians who had captured the small coastal steamer **Galtesund,** and escaped in her to Aberdeen. His importance lay in the fact that he had an intimate knowledge of the Rjukan area and counted among his friends certain engineers at the heavy-water plant who were loyal patriots.

SOE gave Skinnarland a crash eleven-day course and on 28th March, 1942, he was dropped back over the Hardanger Vidda. The period between his departure and his return had been so short, that his absence had not been noticed.

Skinnarland was to prepare the way for a small party of four agents, specially trained to direct an attack on the plant. This party, given the code-name Grouse, was to be dropped during the April moon-period. Unfortunately the weather prevented the drop, and the onset of the "white nights" forcibly postponed the operation until 19th October, 1942.

In the meantime, so serious was the situation regarded by the British War Cabinet that an independent raid had been prepared. Thirty specially trained engineer troops were to be put on to the Hardanger Vidda in two gliders, put the plant out of action and escape to Sweden.

This operation, which had the distinction of being the first British glider operation of the war, was attempted on 19th November, 1942. The first aircraft cast off its glider just north of Stavangar town. In the appalling weather conditions, the glider crashed into a mountain-side, killing the two pilots, the commander of the detachment and seven of his men outright. Others were seriously injured, and 290

all the survivors were caught by the Germans. The injured were taken to Stavangar hospital, where they were poisoned, their bodies weighted with stones and thrown into the sea. The five uninjured were taken to Grini prison, and at dawn on 18th January, 1943 were shot as spies.

The Gestapo justified this action by the discovery in the glider of civilian clothes in which the men were to have escaped to Sweden, a move on the part of those responsible for the operation which was criminally foolish.

The other glider's towing aircraft was unable to find Rjukan, and turned for home. But the tow-rope became so heavily iced up that it snapped and the glider landed north-east of Helleland, in the mountains. Three of its occupants were killed in the landing, and the remainder captured, taken to the German camp at Egersund, and shot a few hours later.

SOE now prepared a second party, code-named Gunnerside, to go to the aid of Grouse. The leader of Gunnerside was Captain Knut Haukelid, who was later to plan and execute the operation against Rjukan. Haukelid after a period of unorganised activity following the Norwegian capitulation had been summoned to Stockholm, whence he was flown to England.

After two false starts, Gunnerside was dropped on the Hardanger Vidda, and joined forces with Grouse. As soon as practicable, they planned an attack on the plant.

The Germans had considered that fifteen men were sufficient to protect the plant, so inaccessible was it. Haukelid's party numbered nine, which he split into two sections, one to carry out the placing of the charges, the other to cover the first. Every move was carefully worked out beforehand. Every man knew exactly what he must do.

The guards gave no trouble, but the demolition party met with more formidable obstacles than they had been led to expect, and though the operation was carried out according to plan, in Haukelid's own words, when "at last there was an explosion (it was) an astonishingly small, insignificant one'. Nevertheless, the "little bang at Vermork" had put the high-concentration installation completely out of commission, so it was thought.

With the exception of Haukelid and a companion, Gunnerside retreated to Sweden. Throughout the remainder of the winter and the following summer, Haukelid worked with Milorg (the Army Resistance organisation). Then in the summer of 1943, it was found that the attack had not been so successful as at first had been supposed. After four or five months of feverish work, the Germans had succeeded in getting the plant into production again.

The Allies now decided to try bombing, and both British and American raids were made. Though these were not very effective, the Germans decided to move the plant to Germany.

London asked for another attack on the plant, but the German arrangements had gone so far forward that there was insufficient time to organise one which would be worthwhile. Haukelid, therefore, suggested that the best

291

solution would be to wait untill all the drums of heavy water were on the Tinnsjö ferry, to which London agreed.

Lake Tinnsjö lay to the east of Rjukan, a few miles away. A railway connected Rjukan with the north end of the lake, and a train ferry joined the north end to the railway which ran to the sea. It was this route which the Germans had decided to use.

Dressed as a workman, Haukelid reconnoitred the ferry and worked out a plan. Sunday, 20th February, 1944, was the day chosen by the Germans for the removal of the heavy water. During the night Haukelid and his companion boarded the ferry, persuaded the night watchman to hide them as fugitives, and when he stowed them in the depths of the boat, they immediately began to lay a charge of explosive calculated to blow eleven square feet out of the ship's side, so as to make her sinking inevitable. The fuses were set for eleven o'clock on Sunday morning, by which time, if all went well, the ferry would be over the deepest part of the lake. This done, they with-

292

drew, making the excuse to the watchman that they had forgotten something at Rjukan so important that they must risk going back for it.

Everything did go well. The ferry sank, carrying with it not only the precious heavy water — all that remained of Norwegian supplies — but four Germans and fourteen innocent Norwegians. But Haukelid comforted himself for the latter with the thought that the Allies had sacrificed fifty-six lives, thirty-four in the glider operation and twenty-two in the bombing raids.

There is no doubt that Haukelid's attacks on the Norwegian heavy water maintained the Allies' initiative in the production of the atomic bomb. But for the courage and loyal devotion of him and his men, the outcome of the war might easily have been different.

BIBLIOGRAPHY :

Skiis Against the Atom — Knut Haukelid (London, 1954).

HAYHANEN, Eugene see under **Abel, Rudolf.**

HEILMANN, Horst see under **Red Orchestra, The.**

HELMER, Captain Fritz (Abwehr agent, World War I).

Before the war Fritz Helmer had joined the Abwehr and proved himself an outstanding agent, and he continued to acquit himself in this role throughout the war. He was the main driving force behind the seduction of the Russian Minister of War Soukhomlinov, and personally supervised the courier service between the Russian traitor and the Abwehr. In 1916 he personally decided the issue of a battle by blowing up single-handed a bridge of the highest strategic importance in Galicia.

When the armistice was signed he was in Latvia. There he raised a company which he placed at the disposal of Baron von Manteuffel, the millionaire-agitator. He led this company against the Soviet forces advancing on Latvia, and with his handful of men succeeded in holding up the advance-guard for several days.

When the treaty of Versailles was signed, France requested Germany to recall Helmer. For the first time in his life, he refused to obey an order, and taking out Latvian papers, he assumed the rank of general in the Latvian army. Dressed in a Ruritanian uniform, and heavily bedecked with decoration, he recruited fresh troops from among the Latvian peasants, trained them and provided them with machine-guns and armoured cars paid for by Manteuffel.

He seems to have succumbed to delusions of grandeur, for he had plans for marching across Germany with his "army" and attacking France or alternatively of rebuilding the empire of the Tsars.

He eventually decided upon the latter, and with the aid of eight German generals and twenty colonels of the former Wehrmacht, he invaded Northern Latvia and marched into Estonia, where he defeated Estonian troops after a brief battle.

When he ran out of money, he designed his own and printed it. The notes soon became a collector's item, however, for they had a currency for just three weeks.

The Allies, piqued by the antics of this secret agent turned general, sent forces to

293

the Baltic States. These trained soldiers quickly routed the "army" of General Helmer. He took refuge in flight, and, disguised as a beggar, succeeded in reaching a Danish port. Hearing that rebellion had broken out in Morocco against the French, he decided to offer his services to Abd el-Krim, who welcomed him enthusiastically.

He set out for Tangiers, representing himself as a correspondent of certain German newspapers, and obtained a passport to cross France. Unhappily for him, he had not been in Morocco long, when a convoy in which he was travelling was ambushed by French troops and he was wounded. He disappeared from hospital, and the next heard of him was a message from the Berlin police to the French government, announcing that they had arrested him in the capital on a charge of plotting against the state.

HELMS, Richard McGarrah (Chief of American Central Intelligence Agency, 1966).

Richard McGarrah Helms was appointed Director of the Central Intelligence Agency (CIA) (q.v.) in June 1966. He was the first career intelligence officer to be appointed to the post.

He began his intelligence career during World War II, when he had served, as a naval officer attached to the OSS (q.v.), in Europe. After the setting up of the CIA, Helms was one of a small number of OSS men to be brought into it. His first post was as deputy head of the Plans Division. When the head of the Division resigned over the Bay of Pigs fiasco in 1962, Helms was promoted, but found that he was still playing second fiddle, in effect, for at the same time a new post was created — that of Executive Director — senior to him.

HEREWARD the WAKE.

Hereward, called the Wake because he evaded many traps to catch him, was a Saxon landowner in Lincolnshire. After the Norman Conquest, he became leader of the Saxon Resistance movement and conducted a guerrilla war against William's forces, covering a period of some five years, operating chiefly in

East Anglia, whose fenlands, with their treacherous swamps, gave him a very high degree of protection.

During his operations he personally imitated the tactics of Alfred the Great in his struggle against the Danes. He assumed many disguises, sometimes dressing as a woman, and entered the Norman camp where he gathered much useful intelligence about the enemy's intentions. It was this espionage that was largely responsible for his being able to hold out against the Normans for so long.

In 1071 he was betrayed by the monks of the monastery at Ely. One of them guided the Norman forces through the little known paths through the fens to his stronghold. Hereward's forces were annihilated, but history has not recorded the fate of their leader.

He is the subject of a romantic novel by Charles Kingsley, first published in 1866, and now a minor English classic.

HILBOLING, Jacob and Hendrika see under **Wenzel, Johann.**

HIRSCH, Willi (Soviet agent, operated in America in 1950s).

Willi Hirsch was born in Kassel, Germany, on 6th January, 1908. When the family moved to Munich in 1922, Willi was sent to live with his aunt, Mrs Chamberlain, in Philadelphia. In 1932 he married Dorothy Baker, giving his name as John Gilmore, aged 32, born in Philadelphia.

Mrs Hirsch had left-wing sympathies, and was an active member of the Friends of the Soviet Union, and shortly after their marriage he was given the post of art editor of the society's magazine, Soviet Russia Today. In 1936 the magazine sent him to Moscow, whither he travelled on a false passport made out in the name of Sidney Joseph Chamberlain. On his return from Moscow, he resigned from the staff of the magazine, and concentrated on a career as a medical illustrator.

Despite the fact that he had never become naturalised, he was called up during World War II, but never actually drafted. After the war he and his wife separated, and he went to live in Greenwich Village. There he met Ruth Davis, an ex-WAC who had served in the Far East as an aerial photographer. She was a divorcee, and soon they had established an intimate relationship. She nursed him after a heart attack and when he had recovered they began work on a book called **New York, City of Magic,** which was to be illustrated with aerial photographs. At the same time he was rapidly establishing himself as one of the leading medical illustrators in America, his work frequently appearing in such magazines as **Life, Collier's** and the **Saturday Evening Post.**

In 1956 he was living in an apartment in 30 Fifth Avenue. In another apartment in the same block Dr Jesus Maria de Galindez, an outspoken critic of the Dominican dictator, Rafael Trujillo, lived. On 12th March, 1956, Galindez mysteriously disappeared. Three months later, Hirsch moved into the now empty apartment, an event which brought him to the attention of the FBI investigating the Galindez case.

On the face of it, Hirsch seemed above suspicion, but as the FBI probed into his background certain disturbing facts came to light. He called himself Dr Gilmore, but, the FBI discovered, he did not hold the Ph.D. he claimed. In 1949 he had contact with the Soviet mission to the United Nations. Thirdly, he had been collecting aerial photographs all over America. Lastly, his name was not John Gilmore.

On 26th November, 1956, the FBI approached him personally. He readily admitted that his name was not Gilmore, and disclosed his real one. He also gave the true facts about his birth and upbringing, and subsequent activities in the United States. Since his change of name, his contact with the Soviet mission and the collecting of aerial photographs were not crimes, the FBI had no grounds on which to proceed against him. They did, however, decide to keep him under surveillance.

The interest of the FBI did not seem to have any effect on his future activities, even when they called him for a second interview in March 1957. Still the FBI had an uneasy feeling about him and continued to watch him. In this way they knew when, while passing through Chicago, he telephoned an old friend, William D. McCuaig, and asked if he "would like some real money". When McCuaig asked how, Hirsch explained that he had some friends overseas who were hiring agents all over the country. The phrase "friends overseas" made McCuaig suspicious. He knew enough about the Hirsch-Gilmores to assume that these friends were Russians. Before the FBI contacted him, McCuaig went to them.

In October Hirsch telephoned McCuaig again and said he was coming to see him. They met on 24th October, and dined together at the Tropical Hut Restaurant, Chicago. At dinner McCuaig was told that he would be well-advised to be on the winning side before the events that were soon going to turn the world upside-down actually took place. Hirsch also took leave of his senses, and informed McCuaig that he had been a Soviet agent for some time, and had been very well treated by them. A senior

Soviet agent, he went on, was arriving in Chicago the following day especially to see McCuaig. Under instructions from the FBI McCuaig agreed to the meeting.

The following afternoon, Hirsch met McCuaig in the lobby of the Sherman House Hotel and introduced him to a foreigner whom he called Peter. Over a drink in a nearby drugstore, Peter asked McCuaig his views on the Hungarian revolt and about Russia in general. McCuaig's answers satisfied Peter, who asked him to obtain maps of the Chicago area showing the military installations.

Before they parted Peter arranged to meet McCuaig alone at the drugstore at 10 o'clock. They had breakfast in Holloway's Cafeteria, and then went for a drive in McCuaig's car. On the drive Peter talked almost without pause. He told McCuaig that if ever he had to introduce him to anyone, he should describe him as Peter Stephens. He also revealed that he was Russian, lived in New York, had formerly lived in England, and had a son and two daughters. He told McCuaig that Hirsch would

297

no longer be his contact, and that future meetings would be in New York. The work might be dangerous, he warned, but the rewards would compensate. Before they parted at the railway station, Peter gave McCuaig two hundred dollars in cash, and instructions for their next meeting.

Now Peter, when describing his family, had told McCuaig that his younger daughter was two months old. This fact made it possible for the FBI to identify him as Igor Yakovlevich Melekh, chief of the Russian translation service at the UN's Office of Conference Services.

Early in November, before McCuaig kept his next appointment with Peter, he received a visit from Hirsch, who told him to do nothing more until he received fresh instructions. The FBI, however, asked McCuaig to keep the rendezvous as planned. Unfortunately their prearranged scheme went awry, for there was no vacant seat next to Melekh at the counter in the Savarin Restaurant. However, Melekh saw McCuaig, got up, paid his bill and left. McCuaig followed

him, and outside the restaurant, Melekh greeted him effusively. McCuaig replied that he was glad Melekh was pleased to see him, because after Hirsch's call he had wondered whether he ought to keep the rendezvous. It was now Melekh's turn to be confused. When he had recovered his speech, he told McCuaig that he would meet him later at the Cleveland Station in Brooklyn at nine o'clock that evening. If he was not there, he would be at the same place the following evening.

Watching FBI agents had spotted another Soviet agent nearby — Krill S. Doronkin, ostensibly an editor in the public information department at the UN. Doronkin, who had entered the United States two years earlier, had also been seeking aerial photographs.

On leaving McCuaig, Melekh had gone to Doronkin, and together they walked the streets of Brooklyn for about on hour, apparently in search of Hirsch but not finding him. Melekh kept the next appointment, complimented McCuaig on keeping the previous rendezvous, told him to carry

298

on as though nothing had happened, and gave him instructions for their next meeting. They had a number of rendezvous over the next few months, until Melekh failed to appear at one in March 1959, which had been set up in Woolworth's, in Allerton Avenue, in the Bronx.

Now, Doronkin had recruited a Canadian, to collect aerial photographs, and the Canadian had become, like McCuaig, a double-agent. On 15 January, 1959, the US Mission to the UN had delivered a note to the Secretary-General asking f o r Doronkin's dismissal on account of his espionage activities. When Soviet intelligence knew that Doronkin had been "burnt", they obviously assumed that his presence at the Melekh-McCuaig meeting in the previous November might have compromised Melekh-McCuaig, and this was probably the reason for Melekh's failure to appear at Woolworth's. In fact, McCuaig and Melekh never met again. Strangely, throughout the remainder of 1959, Hirsch kept a regular rendezvous at Second Avenue and Sixty-eighth Street, Manhattan, every second Friday, despite the fact that no contact ever turned up.

The next step in this odd affair came on 27th October, 1960, when it was officially announced that Hirsch and Melekh had been arrested on charges of espionage, **though they had not met for a year and nine months.** The only possible explanation for this long delay is that the FBI hoped that both men would lead them to other Soviet spies.

The Soviet authorities tried desperately to persuade the US to free Melekh, but made no comparable move on Hirsch's behalf. Hirsch was unable to raise his bail and remained in gaol; Melekh's wife, however, put up the amount set for her husband— 50,000 dollars.

In the event, however, neither man was brought to trial. Attorney-General Robert Kennedy requested the Judge to drop the charges against them, as the result of consultation between the State Department and the Department of Justice. Conditions were attached — both men were to leave the country forthwith. Melekh left on 8th

April for Moscow; Hirsch, with his wife — on 21st July, 1961. According to his wife, Hirsch died not long after.

BIBLIOGRAPHY :

The Espionage Establishment —Willand Rose (London, 1968).

HISKEY, Clarence see under **Soviet American Network.**

HISTIAEUS of MILETUS. Though espionage rivals prostitution for the distinction of being the oldest profession in the world, the ancient leaders had no permanent system of espionage, but appointed their spies for specific missions as the need arose. There are in the pages of recorded history several examples of resorts to espionage stratagems, which lend considerable weight to my contention that sucsessful spying is largely a matter of commonsense. Take, for instance, the story of Histiaeus of Miletus recounted by the Greek historian Herodotus, known as the Father of History, who died in the closing years of the fifth century BC.

Histiaeus, who was something of a tyrant, was given the task of guarding the pontoon-bridge over the Danube when Darius I of Persia invaded Scythia in 513 BC. Miltiades the Athenian, who was sharing the assignment, proposed at one crucial point, that the bridge should be destroyed, but Histiaeus opposed this and was rewarded by the Persian king for doing so, by being made ruler of Mitylene. But he had not long been in this new rôle when he excited Darius's suspicion that he intended to set up an independent kingdom in Thrace. To circumvent this, Darius invited Histiaeus to visit him at Susa, and when Histiaeus arrived there, refused to allow him to return to Mitylene.

Growing weary of what amounted to captivity, Histiaeus began to plot a revolt in Ionia, with a relative called Aristagoras, hoping thereby to bring about his release. He was, however, faced with some difficulty in communicating with Aristagoras secretly owing to the restraint in which Darius was keeping him. In his attempt to discover some safe method, he hit upon the idea of shaving the head of one of his slaves, pricking the message on the skin of the man's bald scalp, waiting for the hair to grow again, and then sending him to his co-plotter.

The stratagem succeeded and the revolt broke out in Ionia; and Histiaeus was released by Darius on offering to go and put it down.

HOFFMANN, Lothar (Russian agent, inter-war period).

Lothar Hoffmann was a Russian agent of long standing working in Germany between the wars under the cover name Sanger.

In 1928 the Germans laid down the keel of the first cruiser permitted to them under the terms of the Versailles Treaty. Since the tonnage was limited by the treaty the German designers had devoted much time and ingenuity to make up for it. It was an obvious target for Russian espionage, and in the spring of 1929 a small cell of Russian agents had been exposed.

Over the next year German counter-espionage had no further successes, but in February 1930 Hans Schirmer, a well-known Communist writer, wrote a letter to the chief of the espionage division of the Communist Party Centre in Hamburg in which he said that he had formerly worked in the Hamburg naval dockyard and so was in a position to supply information of interest which he could obtain through contacts he still had in the yards.

Before making contact with him, Hamburg asked him to be more explicit. This he refused to be unless he could talk face to face with an accredited representative of the espionage division. So Herbert Sanger (Lothar Hoffmann) was sent to see him.

Hoffmann was an agent of considerable experience, and when the first cell had been compromised in 1929, he had been sent to Hamburg to organise a cell to replace it. He was a professional spy, and this makes his contact with Schirmer difficult to understand.

At their meeting Hoffmann told Schirmer that the espionage division already had very good sources of information in the naval dockyards, but they would appreciate very much information on the political leanings of naval officers and men. The men parted without anything definite having been decided, though Schirmer was given an address to which he could write if the need arose.

Months went by and Hoffmann made no attempt to get in touch with Schirmer. This seems to have upset the writer, for in October 1930 he went to naval counter-espionage and told them that he had been in touch with Hoffmann. At the same time he offered to co-operate with them to expose Hoffmann, and this offer was accepted.

On counter-espionage's instructions Schirmer wrote to Hoffmann saying that he had in his possession documents of considerable interest. Hoffmann reacted with alacrity, and during the next few months he met Schirmer who handed over to him counterfeit documents prepared by naval intelligence.

In the meantime counter-espionage had investigated Hoffmann and discovered what his activities were, and the identities of his agents. In May 1931 they pounced and arrested the cell complete with its leader. Unfortunately this success came too late to prevent the Russians from learning every detail of the

302

Cruiser's extremely sophisticated equipment.

BIBLIOGRAPHY :
Les Espions de la paix — Paul Allard (Paris, 1935).

HOOVER, J. Edgar.

Appointed Director of the Federal Bureau of Investigation (FBI) in 1924, J. Edgar Hoover was still in that post in 1969. He led the FBI throughout the war with the gangsters during the prohibition period in the United States, and the success of the campaign made him internationally famous.

He was an able lawyer and criminologist, and turned the FBI within a period of months from the subject of music hall jokes into a famous national institution. By keeping free from party politics, he had at no time drawn upon himself even a half-hearted smear of being corrupt.

When President Roosevelt decided that the FBI should take over counter-espionage functions, Hoover readily agreed, though he had the doubtful example of Allan Pinkerton to remind him that espionage and counter-espionage work are very different from the ordinary detection of crime and criminals. In this field, under his guidance, the FBI has greatly enhanced its reputation as a whole.

Perhaps somewhat naturally, in view of his success, Hoover has tended to become an autocrat during the later period of his directorship of the FBI.

Hoover died in April 1972.

HOUGHTON, Harry see under **Portland Spy Case, The.**

ICHIMIYA, Commander Yoshiashi see under **Furusawa, Dr Takashi.**

INDEX, The. (Department of Russian Intelligence) see under **Gouzenko, Igor.**

INTERCEPTS

Though British intelligence had made excellent use of wireless interecepts during World War I—e.g. The Zimmermann Telegram (q.v.) — it was not until the late 1930s that the interception of radioed messages from special listening stations was introduced on a large scale. The United States led in this field. The US Navy had such interception stations at Bainbridge Island; Winter Harbour, Maine; Corregidor and Guam; Amagansett, Long Island; and Jupiter, Florida, among others. The US Army had stations at Hancock, New Jersey; Fort Sam, Houston; Panama; Honolulu; Fort Mills, Manila; Fort Hunt, Virginia; and in Rio de Janeiro. Unfortunately, intercepted coded messages were often delayed in transit to Washington for so long that when they arrived they were useless; e.g. two Army intercepts in the week before Pearl Harbor did not reach Washington for eleven days. On the other hand, the intercept service missed very little. Between March and December, 1941, only four out of 227 messages sent by the Japanese delegation in Washington to Tokyo were missed.

Interception has now become the responsibility of NASA's (q.v.) satellites and ships like the **Pueblo.** The Russians use the same techniques with their **Cosmos** satellites.

ISRAELI SECRET SERVICE

Like all good intelligence services, the Israeli Secret Service shuns all publicity, and does so so effectively that it is difficult to obtain any extensive information about it. On the other hand, it is very apparent from the success of Israeli military operations in recent years that it is an extremely efficient service, the more so since it has so short a tradition of operations.

Historically, the ISS is a descendant of the defence organisation called Hashomer (the Watchman), which was formed by settlers in Palestine at the beginning of the present century for defence against hostile Arab activities. As the struggle for the creation of an independent Jewish state gained momentum a number of clandestine organisations, the majority of them committed to guerilla activities against the Protecting Power, came into being. Among these were Hagganah (q.v.), Irgun and the Stern Group.

The Chief of these organisations was Hagganah, which was a rich underground army with units in every town, village and settlement in the country. Hagganah naturally set up its own intelligence organisation and in doing so joined with Hashomer, the combination becoming known as Sherut Yediot or "Shay"— Intelligence Service.

When Israel became an independent country Shay, and the intelligence sections of Irgun and Stern, were all brought into a reorganised central intelligence service. This new service, set up in 1950, is organised in five main branches.

(1) The Intelligence and Research Service (Mossad) whose agents operate abroad.

(2) The Army Intelligency Service (Modi'in), in traditional military intelligence service whose interests lie in the military activities of Israel's enemies.

(3) The Internal Security Service (Sherutei Habitahon), the equivalent of the British MI5, i.e. counter-espionage within Israel.

(4) The Research and Information Department of the Foreign Office which collects political intelligence.

(5) T h e Investigation Branch of the Police, which resembles in function the British Special Branch of the Metropolitan Police, which arrests and prosecutes foreign agents after they have been identified by Sherutei Habitahon.

Mossad, from the espionage angle, is, of course, the most

important of the branches. It has its agents in all hostile Arab countries — and elsewhere — and is responsible for such operations as the tracking down and kidnapping of Adolph Eichmann.

The ISS as a whole is directed by a chief who is responsible only to the Prime Minister and Minister of Defence. From 1953 to 1963, the chief was Isser Harel, who resigned as the result of a disagreement with Prime Minister Ben-Gurion. It was he who planned the Eichmann kidnapping and who discovered the presence in Egypt of a team of former Nazi rocket experts after the Suez Incident of 1956.

Compared with other intelligence agencies the personnel of the ISS numbers no more than a few hundreds, including active agents. The agents themselves are mostly recruited from Israeli nationals. Training in all branches of espionage activity is of an extremely high standard. As in most other intelligence organisations, the employers — and this includes agents — are paid at Civil Service rates—about £60 (144 dollars) a month, with appropriate increases for length of service.

BIBLIOGRAPHY :

The Spy From Israel — Ben Dan (London, 1969) Chapter 5.

IVANOV, Peter see under **Soviet American Network.**

JAMBROES (Dutch agent, World War II) see under **Giskes, Colonel H. J.**

JENGHIZ KHAN, The Espionage System of.

In the year 1162 AD there was born to a pretty chieftain in Northern Mongolia, a son who was to succeed his father while he was still a boy. From the year 1177, when he was only fifteen, until his death fifty years later in 1227, there was scarcely a month when he was not engaged in fighting somewhere on the Asian continent, from the China coast to the far shores of the Black Sea.

In 1202 he won his first notable victory when he defeated Oungh Khan of Keraites, and from that time he pushed forward with his conquests so effectively that four years later, 1206, he was able to proclaim himself Khan or Emperor of Mongolia, calling himself Jenghiz Khan, Jenghiz meaning **the perfect Warrior.**

Between 1213 and 1215, he almost completed the subjugation of the northern provinces of China, and further strengthened his position in the latter year — the year of the signing of Magna Carta by King John of England at Runnymede — by marrying the daughter of a former Chinese emperor.

He then turned his attention towards the west and by 1219 had brought under his rule all the nations as far west as Turkestan and Bokkara not far from the frontiers of modern Afghanistan. He pressed on westwards, through Samarkand, and, though diverted southwards for some years bringing his armies down to Lahore in India, he struck north again, up through Georgia until he came to the very gates of the Western World. Trouble in China alone deflected his intended invasion of Europe, and he died as he was returning from putting down a revolt in China on 24th August, 1227.

This great oriental conqueror is almost without equal. Hitler's conquest of almost the whole of Europe pales into insignificance beside the exploits of Jenghiz Khan. Even Alexander the

307

Great can scarcely match him, though his armies penetrated far into the east. Without parallel in history, too, is Jenghiz's record of inhumanity. To the slightest resistance he retaliated with wholesale massacres so horrible in scale and conception that the mind revolts at them.

Conquest on such a vast scale, even in the Middle Ages, when armies were less numerous and arms more simple, and against inferior opponents, could not have been possible without careful planning and strategy, and Jenghiz Khan, as much as Alexander and all the great conquerors, relied on spies to furnish him with the strength and dispositions of his enemies' forces.

His chief and most numerous type of agent was the travelling merchant. Chosen from men of all kinds and many nationalities but with the common factor of intelligent observation, these merchant-spies went in advance of the Khan's columns, and while they did their business with the unsuspecting traders of Kashgar and Samarkand, Kabul and Peshawar,

they looked and noted, sent back their information, and Jenghiz came and conquered.

Among the Khan's able commanders were two men whom he first employed as spies. In 1221, these men, Subutai and Chepe Noyon, now generals, had together brought the rule of Jenghiz as far east as the Crimea and had advanced into Southern Russia as far west as the River Donetz; and had quickly established an elaborate information service to discover the weak points of European stability, which lay in the great trading rivalries of Genoa and Venice. Upon the undertaking that the Genoese traders should be expelled from the Crimea, the Venetians gave the Tartar generals every assistance, many of them acting as agents.

But a long way back, both these generals, as young officers, had been among the most successful of Jenghiz's agents; and it was from the Great Khan himself, in these early days, that they learned their technique of campaigning when they had risen to the rank of general.

Subutai, in his role as an agent, had once acted the provocateur. He appeared before the commander of a rival Tartar force saying that he had deserted Jenghiz, and was willing to join them. He was so successful with his false information that the Tartars were completely surprised when the main body of Mongols, whom Subutai had said were nowhere near, fell upon them.

When the emperor of China asked the Khan for help in his campaign against the Sung of Southern China, Jenghiz sent Chepe Noyon with a cavalry force. Soon after Noyon's return the Mongol emperor launched his attack upon China, basing his strategy on the intelligence brought back by his subordinates.

So great was the Khan's reliance on espionage, that when he laid down, for the guidance of his generals, the basic principles for successful invasion, his second precept was the sending out of spies.

BIBLIOGRAPHY:

Milestones in Russian History —Ronald Seth (Philadelphia, 1968).

JOB, Oswald (British traitor, World War II).

Oswald Job was born at Bromley, in Kent, in 1885. He had been living in France for some years, when the Germans overran the country in 1941, and was interned by them in the civilian camp at St Denis, just outside Paris.

In October 1943 he entered the British embassy in Madrid, saying that he had escaped from St Denis and almost by a miracle reached safety. His appearance lent colour to this story, for naturally a fragile-looking man, his internment had made him more fragile-looking still.

Interrogated by Security officers attached to the embassy, Job described his education at an English Public School and his subsequent life, citing several well-known French men and women in support of his story of how he had opened a language school in Paris after the death of his parents, and there taught English to aristocratic families. Luckily for him, one of his interrogators had been at the same school in England, and this much eased his position. He was feted by the embassy, given

309

new clothes and good food, and forwarded to London.

Here he repeated his story, but this time in fuller detail. This revealed that he had been an idler and waster, who had spent his inheritance in riotous living and been adjudged bankrupt before he started his language school.

What he concealed, however, was that shortly before his "escape" from St Denis, he had acquiesced in training by the Nazis for a spying mission in England, and that he had been protected on his journey to Spain by SS officials, and through Spain by other German agents.

Job was cleared by Security, and took modest lodgings in Bayswater in London, supported by National Assistance. But according to their custom, counter-espionage continued to keep their eye on him for a time. So they came to discover his penchant for letter-writing. Day after day he posted numerous Red Cross letters to his friends interned at St Denis. These letters were examined and tested — and revealed that between the lines were messages in invisible ink, snip-

310

pets of "careless talk" likely to be of interest to the enemy.

He was visited by Special Branch officers, who in spite of his protests searched his room and discovered nothing, until the attention of one of them was attracted to a large bunch of keys, which was a curious object for a man to carry who had no cupboards or suitcases. When the keys were examined they were found to contain, in their hollow shafts, all the materials for invisible writing.

Tried at the Old Bailey (the Central Criminal Court, London) Oswald Job was found guilty of treason and hanged at Pentonville prison, London, on 16th March 1944.

BIBLIOGRAPHY :
The Meaning of Treason — Dame Rebecca West (London, 1949 edition).

JOHN, Otto (Chief of West Germany's BfV Post World War II).

Otto John was born in Marburg an der Lahin, Germany, in 1909. Shortly afterwards John senior, who was a civil servant, was posted to Wiesbaden, where Otto spent most of his youth. From the advent of Nazism, John was a convinced, if often silent, opponent of Hitler and his followers.

In 1933 he joined Lufthansa, the German civil air-line, and made friends with his departmental chief, Klaus Bonhoeffer, brother of the famous anti-Nazi Pastor Dietrich Bonhoeffer, a member of the resistance group led by Judge Dehnanyi. Under the influence of the Bonhoeffers, John took up clandestine anti-Nazi activities.

When World War II broke out, John's job in Lufthansa exempted him from service in the armed forces. He was also able to travel abroad, and from 1942 onwards, was in constant contact with British and American intelligence in Lisbon and Madrid, keeping them au courant with the activities of the resistance group.

In 1944 he told them of the plans to assassinate Hitler. He was in Berlin at the time of the attempt, but managed to escape to Madrid and on to Lisbon, from where he was flown to England by the British. There he joined the staff of Sefton Delmer's Black Propaganda organisation.

When this came to an end shortly before the end of the war, John joined the Central Office of Germany and Austria (COGA) to work for the Prisoner of War department. He had just begun this work when he heard that his brothers Hans and Klaus Bonhoeffer had been shot by the SS on the eve of the Russian entry into Berlin the previous April.

In 1949, having set himself up in London as a consultant in German and international law, he married Mrs Lucie Mankowitz, better known as Lucie Manen, the opera singer. As a law consultant he was engaged by the legal department of BAOR to help in the preparation of the trials of Field Marshals Manstein, Rundstedt and Brauchitsch, and Colonel-General Strauss.

Not long afterwards, President Heuss of West Germany, who was related to the Bonhoeffer family and an old friend of John's, invited him to visit him in Bonn. While there it was proposed to John that he should become chief of the newly formed BfV, the Federal Office for the Protection of the Constitution (q.v.). There was a good deal of opposition from reactionaries in Germany to the proposal, and even his English friends thought it would be inadvisable for him to return to Germany, since many Germans would object to the part he had played in the trial of Field Marshal Manstein. John, however, felt he could not refuse, and after some delay Chancellor Adenauer formally approved the appointment.

The BfV experienced a number of teething troubles. In the political and social climate of Germany at this time, added to the fact that John and his chief assistants had had no practical training in counter-espionage, was not surprising. At the beginning of 1954 John submitted recommendations for the reorganisation of the BfV in the light of the experiences of those early years.

On 15 July, 1954 John and his wife travelled to West Berlin where five days later John attended a memorial service for the victims of the 20th July Plot, among whom was his brother Hans. After this service, at 7.30 in the evening, John left the Hans Schaetzle Hotel where he was staying to keep an appointment with a Dr Wohlgemuth at the latter's apartment. John had first met Wohlgemuth during the war when the doctor was assistant to the famous surgeon Professor. The object of John's visit now, was to get from Wohlgemuth a certificate which would enable a friend to obtain a pension.

The official West German version of what happened at the apartment is John's own account. It differs from the version given by Wohlgemuth.

According to the first, John took a taxi to Wohlgemuth's surgery at the corner of the Kurfürstendamm and Uhlandstrasse, and found the doctor just finishing his dinner. While waiting for Wohlgemuth, John was given a cup of coffee, and they then went together to the doctor's private apartment.

As they were going Wohlgemuth remembered he had to collect some papers for his accountant. This displeased John, who was already late for dinner himself, but before he could protest he suddenly began to feel very sleepy.

When he came to he was in a darkened room, lying on a

couch. He could see through an open door three Russians and a nurse sitting in the next room. After a few minutes one of the Russians came to him and asked him how he felt. John asked for a glass of water and inquired about Wohlgemuth, who, he was told, was operating at the hospital. He then asked what the Russians wanted.

"You are to work for us," one of them said. "The General will give you details when you see him tomorrow."

When the General arrived next day, he told John that the Russians had watched his career closely and admired his stand towards former Nazis who had tried to obtain prominent positions. They also understood that he disapproved the re-arming of Germany, and they wanted him to go to the East and continue the struggle for peace alongside them.

John decided to play for time and appear to co-operate without divulging vital secrets. (This was in accordance with instructions to all BfV agents should they fall into Russian hands.) He told the General so and the General went away assuring John

he would be given every assistance.

The first step in collaboration was to be a speech made by John to the international press about peace and co-operation between East and West. There were some difficulties over the text, but eventually it was agreed, and the conference was called for 11th August, 1954, at the Press House in East Berlin.

The conference was televised. Between three and four hundred journalists attended, among whom John recognised his old friends Sefton Delmer of the **Daily Express,** Gaston Coblentz of the **New York Herald Tribune** and Karl Robson of the American **News Chronicle.** Between John and his audience sat two rows of East German security men.

There was nothing new or startling in John's speech, and when he sat down the journalists were invited to ask questions. Usually at press conferences John replied hesitantly to questions; now, however searching the question, he answered promptly and succinctly — as though he had been well primed beforehand.

313

When the conference was over Delmer, Coblentz and Robson asked if they might have a word with their old friend. To their surprise they were invited upstairs, where a buffet had been prepared. As á result of John's guarded replies to further questions Delmer was convinced John had been kidnapped.

A few days later John was flown to Moscow, where he was treated as a VIP visitor. Early in September he was taken to Garga, on the Black Sea, where a Colonel Mikhailov presently arrived, and with two assistants began to interrogate John in great detail, though when John analysed them the questions were, in fact, routine.

At the end of some weeks, John was returned to Moscow where he was again treated as an honoured guest, then on 12th December, 1954, he was suddenly flown back to East Berlin. There he was given an office and two secretaries in the headquarters of the East German Committee for German Unity, where he was required to write articles on German re-unification and letters attacking anti-Communist articles in the West German press.

Albert Norden, chief of the committee, had expected John to provide him with first-class propaganda. John, however, proved a broken reed, for, in fact, he had no journalistic ability whatsoever. After some frustrating weeks Norden told John to stop trying to compose articles and concentrate on writing letters to West German personalities inviting them to talks on re-unification.

During this time John seemed content with his lot and his easy life. He was, however, planning to escape back to West Germany at the first favourable opportunity.

John was allowed to visit the Press Club, and there he made friends with a Danish journalist, Hendrick Bonde-Hendriksen, to whom he managed to convey that he was planning to escape, and would try to do so from the University Library.

At this time, John was spending a good deal of time in the Library, allegedly writing a thesis on International Civil Law. He was accompanied there by two guards, and he was hoping that they would become bored

314

by having to wait for him for hours at a time and grow careless, and he would be able to escape from one of the two entrances.

Early in December, John said to Bonde-Hendriksen, who had decided to help him and had told him so, "I shall finish my researches at the Library on 12th December. Perhaps we could have a drink early in the evening. Why not wait for me at the main entrance?"

On 12th December, in the late afternoon, John asked the guards to drive him to the Library. As usual they took him to the rear, where Professor Nathan, with whom he said he had an appointment, had his rooms. John got out, leaving his case in the car, and said he would be back in a minute or two. He walked straight through the Library to the main entrance, where Bonde-Hendriksen was waiting for him with a car. A few minutes later they were at the Brandenburg Gate check-point. The policeman on duty, seeing the Danish number-plate on the car waved them through.

John was hurried from Berlin to Walm, near Bonn. There he recounted to the Federal Prosecutor the story set out above. To his surprise, he was arrested on a charge of treason, and on 12th November brought to trial.

Wohlgemuth refused to attend the trial, but in a written statement put forward his version. According to this, which is now the official East German version, he met John in Cologne on 9th and 10th July. During conversation John complained of the appearance of neo-Nazism and his own impotence to influence the course of events. Wohlgemuth suggested he should meet survivors of the 20th July Plot then living in East Berlin and offered to arrange a meeting to take place while John was in Berlin for the celebrations. John agreed. They arranged a password for the plan, which they would use when they telephoned one another. The word was **Nelson,** which, according to John's version, was the name of the widow whose pension claim John was supporting, and for which he needed Wohlgemuth's certificate.

John and Wohlgemuth had a telephone conversation on

17th July in which they arranged a meeting. A tape-recording of this conversation was made and Wohlgemuth supplied the court with a copy. The Nelson certificate was mentioned, but the reference neither proved nor disproved the doctor's story of the password.

On 20th July, John arrived at Wohlgemuth's surgery about 7 o'clock. He drank a cup of coffee and then went **voluntarily** with Wohlgemuth in his car, by which they crossed into East Berlin. The doctor parked his car at the Charité Hospital and they walked to the Dorothe cemetry where Hans John was buried. They were met there by a Dr Schneider, who took them by car to a villa in Weissensee, where they had dinner with a number of high-ranking Russian and East German officials. There were speeches about German unity and the brotherhood of those who had resisted nazism. As the evening wore on John consumed more and more alchohol, and began to grow maudlin with self-pity. Later still, he declared his intention not to return to the West, and then slumped across the table

in a drunken stupor. Wohlgemuth was so afraid that he would be blamed for John's defection that he fled to the Soviet sector of Berlin with his girl friend Anne-Marie, where he was given a position at the Charité hospital.

No other witness supported Wohlgemuth's testimony. It came down to John's word against Wohlgemuth's. The court, whose judges, by English standards at least behaved in a very strange manner, harassing John even more than the Chief Public Prosecutor, chose to believe the doctor. The prosecution demanded only two years hard labour; the court doubled the sentence.

John was released on 28 July, 1958. In December, Wohlgemuth, who had by this time returned to the West, was arrested and charged with having treasonable contact with the East. At his trial John confronted him. He made a very poor impression against the play-boy doctor's suave persistence that he was telling the truth. He was found **not** guilty.

Since his trial several Russian defectors have declared that Wohlgemuth had worked for East German intelligence. In 1967 sworn statements by defecting Russian intelligence officers to the effect that they had known of the plot to kidnap John, led to an application for a retrial. The judicial committee considering this evidence has not yet given its decision.

Since his release John has been living in Austria, devoting his time and energies to trying to clear his name.

BIBLIOGRAPHY :

Black Boomerang — Sefton Delmer (London, 1956).

The Secret War for Europe— Louis Hagen (London, 1968).

JONGELIE (Dutch agent, World War II) see under **Giskes, Col H. J.**

JORDAAN (Dutch agent, World War II) see under **Giskes, Col H. J.**

JOSHUA the son of NUN.
In about 2400 BC, Moses, the Israelite leader, in preparation for the occupation of Canaan, sent forward a party of spies under the command of Joshua the son of Nun. This story, which is the first reference in the Bible to spies, is told in the Book of Numbers, chapter 13.

"And Moses sent them to spy out the land of Canaan and said unto them, Get you up this way southward and go up into the mountain, and

1) see the land, what it is:
2) whether it be good or bad;
3) whether it be fat or lean;
4) whether there be wood therein or not;
5) and bring of the fruit of the land;
6) and the people that dwelleth t h e r e i n, whether they be strong or weak;
7) whether they be few or many;
8) what cities they be that they dwell in;
9) whether in tents or in strongholds."

Though these instructions were laid down for a band of twelve spies sent out on a specific mission, they embody the basic requirements of any spy sent out at any time since, and on any general mission.

Moses' spies spent forty days on their mission. They returned bringing evidence of the products of the country; a huge bunch of grapes which it took two men to carry on a staff between them, pomegranates and figs.

They reported to Moses and Aaron immediately. "We came unto the land whither thou sentest us, and surely it floweth with milk and honey, and this is the fruit of it."

Nevertheless, they warned their leaders, the people there were strong and they lived in walled cities of great size. The Amalakites lived in the south, the Jesubites and Amorites in the mountains, and the Cananites between the sea and the river Jordan. They had done their job thoroughly.

Joshua had divided up the twelve into parties each of which he had sent in a different direction. Caleb, who had led one of the parties, gave it as his opinion that the children of Israel stood a very good chance of overcoming these peoples, but there were others, who had gone elsewhere, who gave contrary advice.

"The land that we have searched is a land that eateth up the inhabitants thereof," they said. "And not only that, but all the people we saw were of great stature, and we saw the children of Anak there, which come of the giants;

and we were in our own sight as grasshoppers, and so we were in their sight."

The Anakim were a tribe of "giants" who lived in the mountains of Hebron in south Canaan. They are identified by some as nomad Cushites from Babel, which in Genesis is connected by popular etymology with Babylon.

This rift in the opinion of the spies upset the Israelites a good deal, and they murmured against Moses and Aaron, and began to suggest that they should depose their leaders, appoint new ones, and return to Egypt.

Joshua, who had supported Caleb's point of view, and Caleb himself, rent their clothes when they heard this, and cried out again to the people that they could surely conquer this land, flowing with milk and honey. But the people would not listen to them, and they and Moses and Aaron were only saved from death by stoning by the sudden manifestation of Jehovah in the Tabernacle.

It was a Jehovah in one of his angriest moods, and wearily He asked: "How long will this people provoke me? I will smite them with the pestilence and disinherit them."

Moses' reaction to this threat reveals all the deep cunning of the spy-master **par excellence.**

"If You do that," he replied to Jehovah, "the Egyptians will get to hear about it, and they will tell these people, and they will say: 'Despite all the wonders and miracles that their God did in Egypt, when He brought them to the very boundaries of the Land He had promised them, His power was not great enough to give it to them. So, as an easy way out, He killed them all.' But if you will forgive the people and help them to possess the land you have promised them, you will greatly enhance your reputation among the heathen."

In spite of its cunning, the answer was of course, a valid one, and Jehovah saw the strength of it; and because Caleb had not wavered in his support of Him, he should have the most prosperous part of the new country. Nevertheless, Jehovah persisted in meting out a modified punishment. All those who had been against going into Canaan should wander about the wilderness for forty years, one year for each day the spies had spent on their mission, and when they themselves were dead, only then should their children enter the land. So all except Caleb and his tribe of Judah, and Joshua with his tribe, the Ephramites, worked out the sentence.

There is probably a moral in this story which it would behove all agents to note.

KAN Mai, Colonel (Chinese espionage chief in Africa).

The Chinese Communists have made strenuous efforts to obtain a foothold in the emergent nations of the African continent, and have used espionage as a means of establishing their influence there with the help of subversive techniques. Ghana was one of the centres of Chinese espionage activity until the overthrow of Kwame Nkrumah in 1966. One of the specific charges against Nkrumah was that he had permitted the Chinese to set up six espionage schools to train operatives for the subversion of neighbouring countries.

With regard to Africa, Mao has declared that when the Congo falls to Communism, the rest of Africa will fall. For the fulfillment of this policy, Chinese espionage has concentrated on stirring up trouble throughout the Congo region, from headquarters in Brazzaville, in former French Congo, situated in the Chinese embassy there.

In charge of the operation was Colonel Kan Mai, ostensibly First Secretary. He organised and ran two training camps for Congo rebels, with the object of using the guerrillas thus produced to overrun the territory of the former Belgian Congo, now called the Democratic Republic of the Congo. The operation came to nothing, however, when, in 1966, the two Congos buried the hatchet.

K'ANG Sheng (Chief of Communist Chinese Intelligence).

K'ang Sheng, born in 1899 son of a rich landlord, turned Communist in early manhood, and became a member of the Chinese Communist Party in 1925. In 1927 he was drafted into the Party's intelligence organisation, and has worked in intelligence ever since.

He was lost to sight for eight years after World War II, though it is now clear that he had considerable influence on Communist affairs behind the scenes. When he did emerge from this obscurity it was as a powerful member of the Politburo and leading policy maker for higher education.

Since the rift between China and Russia he has become even more prominent, as chief of Chinese intelligence, which is closely modelled on the Russian organisation. In addition to controlling — through the Department of Social Affairs — the espionage and counter-espionage agencies, he is also responsible for internal security.

KANTOR, Solomon see under **Zilbert, Mark.**

KAO Liang (Chinese Communist agent in East Africa).

Under the cover of chief correspondent in Africa of the New China News Agency, Kao Liang has been active for some years in fermenting trouble in East Africa.

He was behind the Zanzibar coup in 1964, having supplied money and arms to Sheik Abdul Rahman Mohammed, the leader of the revolt, and Foreign Minister in the new regime. He also tried to stir up trouble in Mauritius, Réunion and Kenya.

He has, however, somewhat vitiated his influence by his overlavish distribution of money. He is now recognised by most African governments for what he is.

KATZ, Otto (SMERSH agent).

Otto Katz was fifty-two when he was hanged in 1952 in the Great Purge of the Czechoslovak Communist leadership. His place among this somewhat elevated company was strange, for he was not a general, nor had he ever held high government or Party office. At his trial he was listed as André Simone, a journalist on the staff of **Rude Pravo,** the official Communist n e w s p a p e r; though in the announcement of the hangings his real name was disclosed, and he was described as "an agent of Jewish bourgeois nationalists." In fact, he had been a Tcheka agent for the last 24 years.

Katz was the son of a wealthy textile manufacturer of Prague. Reared in luxury, he was given a first-class education. He was a friend of Kafka, and this gave him ambitions to be a great writer himself. He lacked only one thing — the requisite talent. Nevertheless, he launched one literary venture after another, and with the backing of Louis Katzenellenbogen, a millionaire whose wife was the well-known German actress Tilla Durieux, he produced some of his plays, all of which were failures.

When Katzenellenbogen had lost somewhere in the region of two million Marks in the seemingly bottomless pit of Katz's ambition, he retired. Since Katz senior had lost his fortune during the post-war inflation period, by 1928 Katz himself was penniless, and it was necessary for him to look for work. Communist friends arranged for him to receive an invitation to visit Moscow. There Russian intelligence suggested that he should spy for them, he agreed and after a short course of training he returned to Berlin a Tcheka agent.

The leader of the German Communist Party at this time was Willi Münzenberg, who was a brilliant organiser, and a very wealthy man, having made the greater part of his personal fortune from his work for the Party, for he controlled the Communist publishing organisation in Germany which printed and distributed all the Party's newspapers, magazines and pamphlets in that country. He was regarded with suspicion by the leaders of the Soviet regime for several reasons. They did not approve of the fact that he was rich, and they approved even less of the way in which he had acquired his wealth. But perhaps they objected most of all to his individualism which had led him to refuse the official Stalinist line put out by Moscow on several occasions.

In fact, the time arrived when the Kremlin decided that Münzenberg should be watched; and the man chosen to watch him was Otto Katz.

When Hitler came to power, Münzenberg was too well-known as a Communist leader to remain at liberty or alive, so he went into exile in France. Katz accompanied him, pointing out that he was in just as much danger because he was a Jew. Separated from direct contact with the GCP, Münzenbergs' influence on it weakened, and Moscow decided that he need no longer be permanently watched. Katz was given the new assignment of go-between for The Centre and the Communist networks in Spain. This job demanded frequent visits to Paris, and on these visits he was required to see what Münzenberg was up to.

When the Nazis overran France, Pétain, at the request of Stalin, arrested Münzenberg and confined him in an internment camp. The French Communists believing that it would not be long before he was liquidated, arranged to free him and send him to America, and in all good faith they consulted SMERSH agents in Paris as to the best way of doing so.

One day in June 1940 Münzenberg was successfully extracted from the camp. A couple of days later, however, a French farm-worker found his body hanging from a tree. It looked as if he had committed suicide within a few hours of leaving the camp, and that was the official verdict. But the question that all his friends asked was, what sort of man is it who commits suicide within hours of getting free, especially when he believes he is on his way to safety? The answer did not tally with their assessment of Münzenberg's character as they knew it. Though no specific proof has ever been produced that Katz was the SMERSH agent responsible for his former friend's murder, there are many Communists who believe that he was Münzenberg's killer, for it was Katz who, according to Frau Münzenberg, "brought to safety the two men who escaped with my husband."

In France Katz adopted the cover-name of André Simone, and it was in this name, after the death of Münzenberg, that he obtained a visa from the American embassy in Lisbon. He had not been long in the United States, however, when the FBI discovered that he was organising Communist cells among film actors and producers in Hollywood. Unfortunately, he was forewarned, and made his escape to Mexico, from where, in 1943, he went to Moscow. When the Red Army "liberated" Czechoslovakia in February 1945, the head of the Tcheka mission which accompanied it was Colonel Otto Katz of the NKVD.

Three years later, Katz was Chief of the Czech Government Information Service, and it was he who issued the announcement of Jan Masaryk's death on March 9th, 1948. The recent investigations of the Czech government into Masaryk's alleged suicide revealed that Katz played a sinister part in the plot to murder the Czech Foreign Minister.

It is also believed that it was this role which was responsible for his being included in the Purge of 1952. He had tried to use his knowledge of the part played by others in the drama to enhance his own power.

BIBLIOGRAPHY :

The Executioners — Ronald Seth (London, 1967).

KAULLA, Baroness de (Prussian agent, late 19th century).

Sex as a weapon of espionage has rarely been used on any scale except in the case of Japanese espionage which made extensive use of brothels and perversion as a means of gathering information from the habitués and addicts. Where sex has been used it has been applied in certain specific cases where the object of attention has been considered vulnerable both in his judgment and in his discretion when subjected to the

sexual blandishments of a well-chosen agent.

The example of this thesis which springs most readily to mind is Delilah. The case involved the French General de Cissey and a beautiful young German baroness, Madame de Kaulla.

General de Cissey had been taken prisoner during the Franco - Prussian War of 1870-1. He was treated with the respect due to his rank, given a villa in Hamburg, and granted a certain amount of freedom. Soon he had settled into a pleasantly diverting routine in which the Baroness Kaulla played a prominent, consolatory role.

When the war was over, General de Cissey was released and returned to Paris, where presently he was appointed Minister of War. By 1875 France was already beginning to think of revenge. The armed forces were being reorganised; the Chief of Staff was planning the campaign to come.

The Prussian Chief of Intelligence, Wilhelm Stieber (q.v.) learned what was happening and summoned the baroness to him. He hoped she would agree to renewing her acquaintance with General de Cissey. She would find it very rewarding, he could promise her. The baroness knew enough of Stieber to appreciate that his request was a command.

Within a few weeks, plentifully supplied with money, the baroness had installed herself in a luxurious apartment in Paris and had reopened the frantic idyll of Hamburg with the ancient Minister of War. Every evening, as soon as his work was done, he hurried to her apartment. Often he was weary with grappling with the plans which must be prepared, often perplexed by the problems which confronted him without any visible solution. His mistress received him with an embrace, drew off his coat, put up his feet, and brought him a glass of champagne. Then sitting on a footstool beside him, she would soothe his hot brow with her cool hand, while he discussed his problems and France's plans with her. It was more banal than even these words are!

Unfortunately for the lovers, French counter-espionage investigated the baroness and discovered that Stieber

and she had met. That was enough. Saved by the necessity to protect the Minister of War from scandal, she was deported to Prussia with all speed. But C-E had worked too slowly. Mme Kaulla had already done all that Stieber had required of her.

KEMPEI TAI, The (The Japanese counter-espionage service).

In 1939 the Japanese Diet passed a new anti-espionage law which provided for much wider application of the death sentence. At the same time there was a tremendous expansion of the counter-espionage services.

By means of exhibitions which displayed what the Japanese authorities believed to be the devious and criminal activities of foreign spies, the public were educated to an even higher pitch of awareness of the danger of enemy agents. Hundreds of posters in the streets, anti-spy weeks, even anti-spy days were promoted. Anti-espionage slogans were printed on match-boxes and there was scarcely a shop-window which did not exhibit either a slogan or a poster.

325

The press, the radio and the speeches of officials constantly encouraged every Japanese man, woman and child to be on the look-out for foreign spies, and to report the smallest suspicious incident. By these means the whole population was lashed into an unprecedented hatred of all foreigners; and behind it all was the Kempei tai, the secret military police, or counter-espionage service.

The Kempei tai, like the Nazi German Gestapo, had always been the most powerful and the most hated of all Japanese institutions, and the most feared, both by the Japanese at home and later by the people of the occupied territories. It derived its power, for the most part, from the semi - independent position which it held within the army.

Though it was organised as a combat arm of the army, it was commanded by a Provost Marshal General, who was directly responsible only to the Minister of War. In Japan itself, though its authority ran directly from the Minister of War to the commander, the Ministries of the Interior and of Justice had occasional and not very serious supervisory powers. Of the rest of the authorities, the Navy alone appeared able to keep a check on it, for we find the Minister of the Navy issuing instructions dealing with the Kempei tai control of navy personnel.

All the members of the Kempei tai were hand-picked volunteers from the army, and in peacetime were required to have six years' military service before they could be eligible to make application. The standards of intelligence, education, facility in the learning and speaking of languages, and of health and physique were extraordinarily high. Since successful counter-espionage requires an intimate knowledge of enemy countries, candidates were often drawn from the Foreign Office, embassy and consulate staffs.

Those fortunate enough to be honoured by membership of the Kempei tai were given one year's training at special schools. The instruction given in these schools was comprehensive, and among the courses provided were law, languages, espionage and counter-espionage techniques, horsemanship, fencing and unarmed combat, invisible writing, shadowing, and entering and leaving buildings. There was also equally extensive field-training. Students were sent to carry out exhaustive investigations of the organisation and production methods of Japanese industries, from which they were expected to return undetected. As a further test of their skill, they were made to disguise themselves and go to places where they were well known.

In 1945 it was estimated by American intelligence that the Kempei tai, including the occupied territories, was comprised of 70,000 men, of whom 24,000 were officers. These figures applied only to Japanese members, and if the numbers of native recruits in the occupied territories were added, the total would probably be doubled.

The Kempei tai were entitled to wear regular army uniform with special insignia, which consisted of a flower-like star surrounded by leaves. When working in plain clothes the agents frequently wore a button resembling a chrysanthemum on the underside of a coat lapel.

Besides its counter-espion-age functions, the Kempei tai was responsible for army discipline, and in this it had supreme power. A member of the force could arrest a member of the army up to three ranks higher than himself. He could decide and carry out punishment in the field. To demonstrate his superiority he might dress with complete disregard of uniform regulations and refuse to salute; and to emphasize his special standing he was released from all routine duties.

Wherever the Kempei tai was, whether in the Home Islands or in the occupied territories, its most important function was counter-espionage. To perform this function efficiently, by their own standards, its members haunted all hotels, post offices, railway stations, piers and other public places. The supervised photographic supply shops, cafes, brothels, theatres and cinemas, and, perhaps rather curiously, sweet shops.

They regulated the sale of electrical appliances, arms, drugs and explosives. They vetted canteen waiters, government contractors and the employees of all the important industrial undertakings. They kept a constant shadow on every foreigner who entered the country from the moment he stepped ashore to the moment he left; and they did this so thoroughly that they boasted that they could tell, if asked, how many times a day an individual went to the lavatory. They exercised a censorship of the press, radio, literature and the theatre.

Bearing all these many and varied functions in mind, it can readily be understood why the membership of the Kempei tai had to be so large. But for all its many thousands of agents, it could not function with anything like a hundred per cent efficiency without outside help.

They used informers, who either volunteered or were pressed into service, and controlled them by threats or blackmail. Yet like the Gestapo's reputation when it was at its peak, the reputation of the Kempei tai seems to have been founded largely on the myth which it deliberately built up around itself, of being omnipresent and omniscient.

Thus, then, stood Japanese espionage and counter-esp-

ionage after only fifty years of existence. Vast beyond the dreams of any spy-master in the history of espionage anywhere in the world up to 1930, both counter-espionage, as well as espionage, were to become even more vast as the tempo quickened towards the final showdown in the pacific.

For the Kempei tai the showdown was in effect a swansong. It was one of the first Japanese institutions disbanded by the American Mikado McArthur when he undertook to teach the Japanese a lesson they would never forget any more easily than they would forget the atomic bombs on Nagasaki and Hiroshima.

BIBLIOGRAPHY :

Total Espionage — Curt Reiss (London, 1941).

Secret Servants — Ronald Seth (London, 1957).

KHAN, Noor Inayat (British agent, World War II).

The last place one would expect to be the birthplace of a British agent is the Kremlin. Nevertheless, Noor-un-Nisa (Light of Womanhood) Inayat Khan was born there on 1st

January, 1914. Her parents were an Indian musician and mystic, Inayat Khan, a descendant of Tipu Sultan, The Tiger of Mysore, and an American woman, formerly Miss Ora Ray Baker, a relation of Mrs Baker Eddy.

The presence of Noor's parents in Russia was due to the fact that Inayat Khan had been charged by the Murshid, the chief of the Sufi sect of Moslems, to make Sufism known to the West. Going first to New York, then to France, shortly before the outbreak of World War I, he arrived in Russia, where he achieved a great success. When the Revolution seemed imminent, he brought his family west again to London, where he remained until 1920, then moving back to France and settling his family at Tremblay, north of Paris, while he went to Geneva where he was to found the International Headquarters of the Sufi movement. In the following year, he moved his family to Wissous, south of Paris, and himself toured Belgium, Holland and Germany.

In Holland he met a wealthy Dutch widow, who offered to buy a house for the family. Inayat Khan selected one at Suresnes, on the outskirts of Paris. While on a visit to Delhi in 1927 he died of pneumonia, and his widow was left with the burden of bringing up her two sons and two daughters alone. This she decided to do in France.

After attending the Collège Moderne des Filles in Suresnes and the Ecole Normale de Musique de Paris, Noor studied at the Sorbonne, intending to take a **Licence** in the psycho-biology of the child. Overwork caused a breakdown, and after a recuperative period in the south of France and Spain and a visit to Italy, in 1937 she entered the Ecole des Langues Orientales, in the university of Paris, where she studied for two years.

In the following year, Noor obtained her **Licence,** and then began to contribute, with success, articles and stories to the children's page of **The Sunday Figaro,** and to the Children's House of Radio-diffusion Française. In 1939 the London publishers, Messrs Harrap, issued **Twenty Jakata Tales.** With the war already looming, she now founded, with the aid of a

French publisher, a new children's newspaper, called **Bel Age.**

When war broke out, she took a course of nursing and first aid with the French Red Cross, believing that nurses would be in great demand as hostilities developed. It was the humane work which could be undertaken by those who by creed could not accept combatant service.

But as the Germans came west, Noor and her family found that they could not remain outside the conflict, and in 1940 she, her mother and sister came to England. The battle for France was at its height, and it was only after several days delay that they reached England.

After a very short time, during which Noor was trying to decide how best she might serve the Allies, she obtained a post in a maternity home for officers' wives, Her work here, however, did not satisfy her, and in November 1940 she volunteered for the Woman's Auxiliary Air Force (WAAF, now WRAF). Towards the end of the following year she applied for a commission in intelligence. She was accepted, selected for a secret course in instruction in signals, and became one of the first WAAF wireless telegraphists.

Then one day, quite unexpectedly, she received a request to attend an interview at the War Office with a Captain Selwyn Jepson, whose job it was to find people, in the Services or among civilians, who might be suitable for work with SOE. Jepson put to her, without any attempt to gloss over the risks, the suggestion that she might become an agent for SOE. Noor accepted the suggestion, and she was seconded on 8th February, 1943.

Because of her experience in radio, she was chosen to be a wireless operator. But before she had completed the full course, the radio operator of a network in Paris, who had for some time been pleading with London to send him some assistance, now made such urgent appeals for help that he could not be ignored.

The French Section of SOE had no fully trained operator whom they could send. And then they thought of Noor. She was told to stand by.

The callousness of this

decision inspires me with anger and dismay, even after these many years. Some of the things Noor did in all innocence illustrate only too well how untrained she was in security. In all my writing on espionage, I have never tired of stressing over and over again, that an agent's existence depends, as to ninety per cent, on his personal security behaviour. In France on those rare occasions when tea is drunk, it is the custom to put the milk into the tea, and not, as is general in England, the tea into the milk. Noor had picked up the English mannerism, and no one had corrected her. It is by such small points that an agent is compromised. On one occasion she passed to another agent with whom she rendezvoused in the Luxembourg Gardens, in the middle of Paris, a map of a site where supplies were to be picked up; and she did so in full view of the public, and of any Gestapo agent who might have been in the vicinity. She left her note-books in which were particulars of her code and coded messages, lying about the rooms of the flat where she was staying, for anyone to pick up and read.

She was a highly intelligent young woman, and if she had received adequate training in these aspects of security, it is fairly certain that she would not have committed such serious lapses as these. On the other hand, M. R. Foot, in his official history **SOE in France,** has recorded, "A fellow agent who trained with her put it still more directly: 'a splendid vague dreamy creature, far too conspicuous —twice seen, never forgotten — and she had **no** sense of security; she should never have been sent to France." In my personal view, very few agents were sent into the field who held their lives so dangerously in their hands.

Given the operational name of Madeleine, and the cover-name of Jeanne-Marie Regnier, Noor was landed by Lysander somewhere near Le Mans on the night of 16th June, 1943. There had been no reception committee to meet her, and help her over the first awful hours on enemy territory. She had to make her way to Paris alone, to a flat at 40 rue Erlanger, Auteuil. She carried only her handbag; her clothes and transmitter were to follow later.

She arrived at the flat and was admitted by a young Frenchman, Lieutenant Henri Garry, chief of the network known as **Cinema.** She completely puzzled Garry, and his fiancée Mlle Nadaud, who was present, by not saying the password for some time. She too was in a quandary, for she had been told that her contact would be an elderly woman. When Garry opened the door to her, she imagined this lady must be out.

When her belongings and transmitter arrived by parachute a few days later, the package containing her clothes burst and they were scattered over a tree, and collected only with difficulty.

Cinema was attached to a group of networks which had one of its working headquarters in the National School of Agriculture at Grignon, to the northwest of Versailles. Commander of the group was a British officer Francis Suttill, code-name **Prosper.**

A fortnight after Noor's arrival, on 1st July, the School of Agriculture was raided by the Gestapo and the SS. The director of the school, M. Vanderwynckt and one of his colleagues, a M. Douillet — both of whom were later executed by the Germans — were arrested with a number of other. Noor was not there, but she arrived while the raid was in progress. She had been told not to go there that day, but had received some very urgent material for transmission to London.

She left her bicycle against the wall, but as she went forward, she sensed that all was not well. As she came nearer she recognised the SS men, about eighty of them who had been sent on the raid, and quickly withdrew without being noticed.

It soon became apparent that this raid on Grignon was only one incident in the largest German counter-espionage operation of the war. Cells and groups and organisations, not only in Paris but in the provinces also, were completely obliterated by the arrests. The Germans must have been in possession of the most detailed information about practically the whole of SOE's networks in France.

It was a catastrophe. Since

332

Noor, of all her group, was the sole survivor, the chief of the French Section, Col Buckmaster, told her she must return to England, and that he would send an aircraft to pick her up. She decided, however, that she must stay, and for the next three months she carried almost the complete burden of radio work in Paris.

She seemed to have learned a good deal about security in a very short time, for she took pains to find safe places from which to transmit, changing her lodgings and transmitting posts frequently. Those who knew her during this time say that she always appeared to be in a hurry, always nervous until she was sitting at her transmitter.

The decision to stay in France was an act of supreme courage, for she was a timid creature. An officer who watched her being questioned in mock-Gestapo raids while she was training has said that she seemed terrified, and emerged from such ordeals deathly pale and trembling. One would have thought that, with so everwhelming a catastrophe happening to all her colleages within so short

a time of her arrival, she would have gladly accepted the order to return to England and safety.

During the next two or three months she had many narrow escapes. Once when she was travelling on the Metro with her transmitter in a suitcase, a German soldier asked what she had in the case. Without hesitation, she replied that it was apparatus belonging to a film projector. Even when he insisted on inspecting it she noted at once that he was obviously not acquainted with this kind of radio set, and said a little testily that he could see she was speaking he truth "because of all the little bulbs".

On another occasion a German officer came upon her unexpectedly while she was fixing her aerial from a tree on the pavement to her window; and the officer helped her to tie the wire to the tree.

She was betrayed to the Gestapo in the middle of October, by an unidentified Frenchwoman for the equivalent of £500. She was arrested in her flat, and her transmitter and notebooks removed any necessity for denial on her part that she was an agent.

In captivity she refused to speak, and asked that she might be shot quickly. She made one attempt to escape on her own, a dangerous project, which together with her resistance to all attempts to obtain information from her, won her the ungrudging admiration of her captors.

She was kept in a cell on the top floor of the Gestapo headquarters in the avenue Foch. Two other agents were also imprisoned there at the time. Somehow they made contact with Noor, and together they planned to escape. They were successful in leaving the building, but had not gone far when an air-raid warning sounded. When this happened all prisoners were checked and so Noor and her companions' absence was very quickly discovered. Within a short time they were recaptured.

The Gestapo chief now had to treat her as a highly dangerous prisoner, and applied for her transfer to Germany. She was taken immediately to Pforzheim, where the prison governor, at considerable risk to himself, refused to obey an order to keep her

perpetually in chains.

She remained for ten months in solitary confinement, in this prison, and on 13th September, 1944, with three other women British agents, she was taken to Dachau concentration camp, where all four were executed.

The citation of the posthumous award to her of the George Cross ends with these words:

Assistant Section Officer INAYAT-KHAN displayed the most conspicuous courage, both moral and physical, over a period of more than twelve months.

Moving as this tribute is, it hardly has the edequacy to describe the supreme courage and self-sacrifice which this young woman brought as her contribution to the Allied victory.

BIBLIOGRAPHY :

Madeleine — Jean Overton-Fuller (London, 1952).

KHEIFETS, Grigori see under **Soviet American Network**.

KHOKHLOV, Captain Nicolai (SMERSH agent, defected to West 1954).

During World War II Nicolai Khokhlov was engaged in guerrilla activities behind the German lines. As Oberleutenant Wittgenstein of the German Secret Field Police, he had played a leading part in the liquidation of the notorious Nazi Gauleiter of Minsk, and had then worked as a partisan in the Minsk area, in Eastern Poland and in Lithuania. In 1945 he had been sent to Rumania to organise paramilitary and guerrilla activities in preparation for the possibility of the Communist satellite states being overrun by the Allies (which did not happen).

In the course of his career he acquired a Polish passport, Rumanian citizenship and Austrian documents. Subsequently he served in the Austrian and German sections of Russian intelligence. During his later interrogation by US security officers, he claimed that Lieutenant-Colonel Pavel Sudaplatov, who commanded SMERSH in 1942, has assigned to him the task of assassinating Franz von Papen, the Nazi ambassador to Turkey, but that he had refused.

In October 1953, Colonel Lev Studnikov, commander of SMERSH's murder squad, summoned Khokhlov, whom he considered to be one of his star operators, and gave him the task of "executing" Igor Okolovits, head of the Society of National Unity (NTS), which had its headquarters at Frankfurt-am-Main, in West Germany. The NTS had been highly successful in spreading anti-Russian propaganda among the men of the Red Army and Communist officials in Austria and East Germany. The Kremlin regarded Okolovits as the brains behind this success, and he was classified in MGB files as "the most dangerous enemy of the Soviet regime," hence the order for his liquidation, which had been signed by Georgi Malenkov, then prime minister of Russia, and Nikita Kruschev, First Secretary of the Party.

A short time after his interview with Studnikov, Khokhlov went to the SMERSH school at Karlhorst, in East Berlin, and there selected two assistants. They were both

East Germans; Hans Kugovits and Kurt Weber small-time spies working for Russia in Germany. When he had received The Centre's approval of his choices, Khokhlov took the two men to Moscow, where they were given the special training required for the assassination of Okolovich.

This training was completed by Christmas 1953, and the three men returned to East Berlin. Before leaving Moscow, Khokhlov was told by Colonel Studnikov that if he did a good job he would be recommended for a high decoration and promotion.

His orders required Khokhlov and his two assistants to go first to the SMERSH school at Baden, in West Germany, going by a roundabout route which would take them through Vienna. Kugovits and Weber set out first together, and when they arrived safely in Baden, Khokhlov flew to Vienna, to wait there for Moscow's go-ahead. These orders arrived on 8th February, 1954.

Immediately on receiving them, Khokhlov instructed the two assistants to proceed to Zurich, in Switzerland, where

he joined them on 13th February. Again they separated, Weber and Kugovits going on to Frankfurt by train, where they re-encountered Khokhlov four days later.

It was at this point that a strange transformation took place in Khokhlov's mental attitudes. The root cause of this change was his wife, Yanina Timashkevits.

Yanina was a Uniat Christian, brought up in a Christian family, and her faith was still unimpaired by Communist pressures. It is surprising, to say the least, that the MGB should have approved of Khokhlov's marriage to her, for they have always regarded Christianity as an insidious enemy of Communism.

Khokhlov was influenced by his wife's beliefs, and became a secret Christian, and when their son was born, he was given Christian baptism. The two young people were very much in love with one another, and when he received his first assignment to murder since his marriage to Yanina, Khokhlov found himself in a truly terrible dilemma. As a Christian — and he could not renounce his Christianity without jeopardising his relationship with his wife — Khokhlov could not deliberately take the life of another man. But if he refused, SMERSH would unhesitatingly kill him, and, if they did not similarly punish Yanina and their son, would probably imprison them for life.

While Kugovits and Weber had been training in Moscow, Khokhlov had been given leave, which he had spent with his wife and son. During this leave he told Yanina of his problem, and she told him firmly that he must not only refuse to obey a criminal order, but take active steps to prevent the murder of Okolovits. She was not afraid of what would undoubtedly happen to her and the boy if he took this step, she assured him calmly, and this and her powerful courage took effect in Khokhlov's mind. He arrived in Frankfurt firmly decided to defect to the Americans and tell them the whole story.

On arriving in Frankfurt, however, he had qualms about the kind of reception the Americans might give him, so he went to Okolovits instead. He called at Okolo-vits flat on the evening of 18th February, 1954, and blurted out the whole story to him. At Okolovit's suggestion they went together to the American security forces.

The tremendous impact Khokhlov's defection would make throughout the world, including Soviet Russia, was at once appreciated by the Americans, and plans were laid for extracting Yanina and her son from Russia before any announcement was made of his defection. He was, therefore, told to carry on as though nothing had happened, for it was well-known that SMERSH always kept their assassins under constant surveillance when on a mission.

It was to avoid this surveillance that the subsequent meetings of Khokhlov and the Americans read like something out of a James Bond novel. The rendezvous took place in a lavatory in the Frankfurt Opera House, and in a dressing-room backstage.

Following American instructions, Khokhlov ordered Kugovits and Weber to go to Augsberg to pick up the special weapons which were to be used to murder Okolo-

337

vits, and to deposit them in the Left Luggage at the Frankfurt main station. This they did, and the Americans subsequently retrieved them.

Again acting on American orders, on 25th February Khokhlov went to Kugovits and Weber and told them that he had defected to the Americans and advised them strongly to do the same. Without argument, they went with him and formally asked the Americans for political asylum.

When the Americans inspected the special weapons which SMERSH had provided for Okolovits's assassination, these created almost as great a surprise as Khokhlov's decision to defect. There were pistols shaped like cigarette-cases, which operated electrically so that when they were fired they made no sound beyond a very slight plop. The projectile was not an explosive bullet, but a poisoned pellet which killed instantly.

Before Khokhlov's defection the West had had no certain evidence that SMERSH existed. Now not only was there proof, but full details were available of their methods. Nor was this all, Khok-

hlov also knew a great deal about Russian espionage networks in Europe. He was able to give names and network headquarters, with the result that the whole of Soviet espionage activities in Europe were disrupted. For, not knowing exactly the extent of Khokhlov's revelations, The Centre called in a large number of operatives, and since there were no replacements immediately available, espionage efforts in Europe were greatly curtailed.

Unfortunately the plans to get Yanina Khokhlov and her son to the West did not succeed. On 2nd June 1954 it became known that she, her son and her fourteen-year-old sister had been arrested and imprisoned. All subsequent efforts to secure her release have failed.

BIBLIOGRAPHY :
The Executioners: The Story of SMERSH — Ronald Seth (London, 1967).

KIEBOOM, Charles van den.
The first German spy to be executed in Britain — in December 1940 — in World War II. With two companions he landed by parachute carrying

a radio transmitter. All three were captured shortly after landing.

The Germans were ahead in short-wave radio development, and the sets the three would-be spies brought with them greatly speeded up British short-wave radio development.

KIENER, Georg see under **Ernst, Karl.**

KISLITSYN, F. V. see under **Petrov, Vladimir.**

KLAUSEN, Max see under **Sorge, Richard.**

KLEIN, Wilhelm (German agent operating for Russia, 1950).

In 1950, the British arrested Wilhelm Klein, whom they caught spying on their airfield at Gatow, near Berlin. Like almost every other agent caught in West Germany since the war, Klein was prepared to talk.

He confessed he had served several sentences for burglary, and was of the type that most espionage-agencies normally shun. He revealed that he had been given his assignment by the chief of one of the Soviet networks in Germany, a Captain Grabowski. He boasted that he had been able to obtain important information about the British Army of the Rhine (BAOR), and about military objectives, such as bridges, tunnels, barracks and other strategic installations, most of which he had been able to photograph.

BIBLIOGRAPHY :

Soviet Spy Net — E. H. Cookridge (London, undated).

KLOOS (Dutch agent, World War II) see under **Giskes, Col H. J.**

KNISPEL, Erwin see under **Linse, Dr, The Kidnapping of.**

KNOPPERS (Dutch agent, World War II) see under **Giskes, Col H. J.**

KNUTH, Maria (German agent for Russia, post-war).

Maria Knuth, aged 42, was separated from her husband, the well-known writer Manfred Knuth, when she was recruited by Karl Kunze and his mistress Luise Frankenberg to work for the Polish espionage agency in 1948. Kunze and Frankenberg had been instructed to organise a network in West Berlin, and this they did from the cover of an art gallery, gathering into their net those West Germans who were anti-Allies and willing to engage in espionage. When they had formed their network, lover and mistress moved on to Frankfurt to set up a headquarters from where the network was to be controlled. Maria Knuth was left in Berlin to act as a "letterbox" (q.v.) for the network.

The ring-had not been in action long when Kunze killed himself. He had been well supplied with funds by the Polish agency, and besides treating his agents extremely liberally, he had spent even more on himself and his mistress. Polish headquarters had discovered what was going on, and were about to demand a reckoning. Kunze was forewarned, and did the only honourable thing that the Prussian officer he had once been could do.

Maria Knuth was brought from Berlin to take Kunze's place. She soon showed herself to be an excellent agent, and under her leadership the network soon became one of the most successful working in West Germany.

When West Germany was incorporated into NATO in 1950, an intelligence agency was set up to keep track of Soviet networks operating in West Germany. It was called Amt Blank.

Maria Knuth was instructed to penetrate this agency with her network, and made the first attempt to do so personally, by applying for the post of secretary in the Amt. She was turned down because she lacked the necessary shorthand ability.

In fact, the task proved a very difficult one, and it was not until 1952 that any success was achieved. A Knuth agent called Hauer introduced Frau Knuth to a man called Petersen, who claimed to be an Amt Blank agent. Before she employed him, Frau Knuth, as required by standing regulations, applied to Polish headquarters. She was warned that Petersen might be a plant, but was given permission to go ahead with extreme caution. She was so cautious, in fact, that within a few weeks she had become Petersen's mistress.

Polish headquarters had been right to believe that Petersen might be a plant, for he was, in fact, a West German agent. For some time he supplied the network with high-grade counterfeit material. At the same time he learned every detail about the network's operations, and in 1953 the West German authorities having decided that they had all the information they required, arrested every agent in the network.

Frau Knuth by this time had developed secondary cancer. Though she submitted to two operations while awaiting trial, she knew that she had not long to live. She made no attempt to defend herself, declaring only that she had done what she had done because she wished to prevent the re-arming of Germany.

BIBLIOGRAPHY :
Forty Years of Soviet Spying — Ronald Seth (London, 1965).

KOBOLOV, Bogdan see under **Red Orchestra, The.**

KOCH, Robert (G e r m a n agent operating for Russia, 1953).

One day in 1953 a West German blacksmith reported to the British authorities that a certain Werner Berg had attempted to induce him to collect secret information by offering to pay him 700 Dm a month, a sum equivalent to £60. Berg was watched, and he led the security forces to a cell led by Robert Koch, which was comprised of three men and two women. Koch was a commercial traveller who frequently crossed into the Soviet Zone on business, which was a perfect cover for him.

The cell operated in the Lüneburg Heath and Brunswick areas. The former was the most important testing ground of BAOR's experimental services, where tanks and other new equipment were put through their paces. It was controlled from headquarters in Brunswick.

The key members of the cell were undoubtedly the two women. One of them was engaged to marry a British officer, from whom (it is suggested without his knowing) she was able to supply details of the testing programme. The other, Erika Krüger, was a telephone operator on the switchboard at the large camp at Münster, by virtue of which post she was able to gain access to reports and photographs. When arrested, the former talked, and the charges against her were consequently dropped. Berg was sentenced to five years, the remainder to four years, with the exception of the leader Robert Koch, who evaded capture.

BIBLIOGRAPHY:

Forty Years of Soviet Spying — Ronald Seth (London, 1965).

KOENEN, Heinrich see under **Red Orchestra, The.**

KOGAN, Schmil (alias **Sam Carr**) see under **Soviet Canadian Network.**

KONDRATIEV, Ivan see under **Reiss, Ignace.**

KONO, Torchichi (Japanese agent in America between Wars).

In the early days of his prosperity, the famous film-actor Charlie Chaplin had employed a Japanese valet and handyman named Torchichi Kono. In 1933 Kono was no longer in Chaplin's employ;

in fact he had left the comedian several years before.

In the intervening period, however, he seemed to have found for himself a much more lucrative source of income, for he was now living in an expensive apartment in Bronson Street, Hollywood, and owned two motor-cars, in one or other of which he would sometimes drive up to $117\frac{1}{2}$ Weller Street, Los Angeles (see under **Furusawa, Dr Takashi**), ordering it to wait while he went inside. When the American embassy in Tokyo was asked if they could supply any information about him, they were able to report that he owned a very fine estate on the outskirts of the capital, which he visited for a few months every year.

One day in May 1934 Kono was seen to be in a great hurry — so great in fact that he drove through several sets of traffic-lights. He did not stop until he had reached Dr Furusawa's nursing-home. He stayed with the doctor about a quarter of an hour, then at midnight he took the express to San Francisco. Next morning he went by taxi to Stanford University, and was seen to enter one of the men students' hostels. It was assumed that he was visiting a Japanese language student, one of the few who did actually attend a place of learning.

From the university he returned to the station, where he took the day express back to Los Angeles. He drove straight to 117½ Weller Street and stayed the night there. Next day he boarded a transcontinental express to Chicago. In Chicago he took another express for New York and there went at once to the apartment of a known Nazi agent, Count von Keitel (see under **Furusawa, Dr**). Keitel and Kono emerged from the apartment in time to catch the midnight train to Washington, where they visited Commander Yoshiashi Ichimiya (see under **Furusawa, Dr**), the Japanese naval attaché, with whom they stayed for several hours, and then returned to New York on an overnight train.

On the following day Kono began his journey back to Los Angeles, seen off by Keitel. When Kono's train had departed Keitel went straight to the offices of the Southern Manchurian Railway, where he stayed for some time with another suspected Japanese agent.

Though the FBI was convinced that Keitel and his various Japanese contacts were engaged in espionage, they could not take the necessary steps to procure the necessary evidence, for the State Department had placed a ban on all activity which might annoy the Japanese. It was a frustrating time for Edgar J. Hoover's organisation, who in addition to having their efforts curtailed by US government policy, were also short of agents. Over the next five or six years, Kono swam into their orbit briefly and then swam out again.

One of these occasions occurred in 1940 at the San Francisco World's Fair.

A sideshow at the Fair was called the "Candid Camera Artist's Model Studio". For a small fee an amateur photographer might enter and take pictures of the attractive nude girls provided for this purpose.

The man who had conceived the idea, and who was employed to take charge of it at the Fair, was a well-known American music hall artiste called Al Blake. Blake had a

343

most remarkable muscle control, and would often pose in the windows of tailors' shops alongside the dummies; the public would be asked to compete for a prize by picking out the living model. Blake's ability to control his movements in this way had earned him the title of King of the Robots.

One afternoon in 1940 there came into the Candid Camera Studio a thickset, fiftyish Japanese with the inevitable camera slung round his neck He took his quota of photographs, and then walked over to Blake and reminded him that they had met in 1917 when Blake was appearing in Charlie Chaplin's film **Shoulder Arms.** Without this reminder Blake would not have recognised Chaplin's former valet, Torchichi Kono.

The two men exchanged personal histories for a few moments, and as Kono was on the point of leaving he remarked that it was a pity Blake was not still in the navy for if he were he could have made a good deal of money. Before Blake could ask him what he meant, the little man had gone.

They did not meet again until March 1941, when they bumped into one another, one day, on Santa Monica Boulevard, in Hollywood. They walked along together for a short distance, and Blake, carefully watching Kono for any reaction, casually remarked that conditions in the American music hall being what they were, he was seriously thinking of rejoining the navy.

Kono showed considerable interest in Blake's proposal, and asked him if he had friends in the Navy who would help him to get back. On the spur of the moment Blake invented a very good friend aboard the flag-ship USS **Pennsylvania,** then on the Hawaiian station.

After a little more conversation, Kono invited Blake to dine with him that evening in his apartment on Bronson Street. Not wishing to seem over-eager, Blake invented a prior engagement, and eventually agreed to lunch with Kono at the Kawafuku Tei restaurant, two days later.

Over this meal Kono probed Blake more deeply on his intention of rejoining the Navy, and Blake played up. Kono then asked Blake the name of his friend in the **Pennsylvania,** and after a show of reluctance Blake said, "Jimmie Campbell."

That same evening Kono telephoned Blake and asked him to meet him in a furniture store the next morning. Puzzled still, but now excited, Blake agreed to do so, and at that meeting, after a good deal of spy-fiction precautions Kono told him to be at the corner of Sunset Boulevard and Wilton Street at noon without fail, where "a very important man would speak to him".

When Blake arrived at the rendezvous he found Kono already waiting, but he studiously avoided making any sign of recognition. Presently a large sedan drew up to the kerb, and at a faint sign from the Japanese, Blake got into the rear seat, followed by Kono.

At the wheel was another Japanese, who introduced himself, as he drove them out to Hollywood hills, as Yamamoto. He said he was interested in Blake's proposal to return to the Navy, and asked Blake to tell him as much as he could about Jimmie Campbell.

At first Blake refused to answer, inquiring why he should talk about his friends to a stranger. Calmly Kono soothed him, and appearing to be reassured, Blake insisted that if he agreed to join forces with the Japanese there must be definite arrangements, particularly with regard to money.

Yamamoto was silent for a few moments after Blake's outburst, and then asked if he would be prepared to go to Hawaii. Blake replied that he was prepared to go anywhere provided the financial considerations were attractive enough. Yamamoto said that Kono would arrange the financial details, but that all he would have to do would be to go to Hawaii and persuade Campbell to give him certain information. They then drove back to Hollywood, and on parting Kono told Blake that he would be getting in touch with him in a few days.

In the intervening time Blake discovered that he was being shadowed by the Japanese, and for the first time he realised that he had got himself into a very difficult position. Blake had no intention of playing the traitor, but he was now faced with the difficulty of making contact with the Office of Naval Intelligence (ONI) without the Japanese knowing.

While he was trying to puzzle out how he might accomplish this, Kono telephoned and arranged a meeting. At this encounter Kono told him that if he were prepared to leave for Honolulu within the week he would receive 2,500 dollars and expenses. A further 5,000 dollars would be paid to him when he had delivered the information Yamamoto wished him to obtain from Campbell.

These proposals made contact with the ONI more imperative than ever. But as soon as he got into the street he saw that the Japanese were still there, ready to fall in behind him. Eventually he solved his problem by going into a cinema and asking the manager to let him out by a back door.

At the ONI, Blake told Lieutenant Leo P. Stanley all that had happened. Stanley asked if he were prepared to co-operate with the ONI by doing whatever the Japanese requested him to do. Blake

agreed and Stanley said that the ONI would at once put an agent on board the **Pennsylvania** to impersonate the nonexistent Campbell. When they had laid further plans Blake returned to the cinema, went in by the back door, remained for the rest of the performance, and when he came into the street again saw the patient Japanese were still sitting in their car waiting for him.

By the time the Japanese had made the necessary arrangements for his passage to Honolulu, the ONI had discovered that Yamamoto was in fact Commander Itaru Tachibaka of the Japanese navy. He had been educated at the Japanese Naval Academy and the Naval War College in Tokyo, had been commissioned as a lieutenant-commander, and been rapidly promoted to commander. He had arrived in the United States in 1930, and had enrolled at the university of Pennsylvania, where he had studied American history and American foreign relations. When he had completed these courses he transferred to the university of Southern California in Los Angeles. For several years he had been travelling constantly up and down the Pacific coast meeting prominent Japanese.

Blake's departure was delayed for a week, because the liner sailing for Honolulu was full. His new instructions were to take passage in the **President Garfield,** of the Dollar Line, sailing the following week.

Two days before Blake was due to sail Yamamoto met Kono in a hat-shop in Los Angeles, and while they had tried on hats, they had held a whispered conversation. Leaving the shop separately, Yamamoto returned to the Japanese consulate, while Kono went to 117½ Weller Street, where he remained until it was dark, and then emerged accompanied by two other Japanese. The three men had then gone straight to the Red Mill brothel, where they stayed until it was time to catch the night train to San Francisco.

In San Francisco Kono's companions had met two Germans, and with them boarded the **President Garfield** shortly before she sailed with Blake aboard.

In Honolulu Blake met the counterfeit Campbell, and between them, following ONI instructions, they concocted a bulletin of information among the lines laid down by Yamamoto, but so contrived that though it was false it appeared authentic enough.

When Blake returned to Los Angeles, Yamamoto asked him if he would be prepared to return once more to Honolulu. Blake's suspicions were slightly roused when Yamamoto began to haggle about money, but he did agree to go.

Blake engineered another meeting with the ONI, who told him that they had discovered that in fact the Japanese had no further use for him and intended to liquidate him in Honolulu. But he was urged to return since it was essential that the Japanese should not yet become suspicious about the "information".

After several extremely uncomfortable days in Honolulu, Blake could stand the strain no longer. Throwing off his shadows, he reached the airport and was able to reserve a seat on the next flight to Los Angeles. Yamamoto troubled him no more.

The Japanese had sent

Blake all the way to Honolulu for one specific purpose — to obtain information about the speed, equipment, armament and performance of one battleship. On the face of it, it appears to be a tremendous expenditure of time and effort compared with the results that could possibly accrue from it, even supposing he were entirely successful.

Yet this episode is indicative of all Japanese espionage effort in the United States. Their language students, night-club owners, doctors, dentists, brothel-keepers and traitors were all engaged in exactly the same kind of activity. They had not been planted there, in their hundreds, even thousands, to find out any closely guarded top secret of the US Armed Forces. Were something of this order to be achieved, so much the better, but the main object of Japanese espionage in the United States was to gather a mass of information about every conceivable facet of American naval and military accomplishment and intention. No matter how trivial it might be, it must be collected, reported, classified and

filed for future reference.

Collecting, reporting, classifying are, of course, a feature of all intelligence work. It is the small pieces, probably unimportant-seeming on their own, which provide the vital pattern when collected together. But the individual agent must be trained to recognise, until it becomes an instinct, the correct interpretation of isolated minutiae.

The Japanese failed to do this. They collected, apparently being more interested in bulk than in quality, vast mountains of trivia which, however, they might be put together, could never amount to much of importance. A large proportion of their material was not only unimportant but based upon misinformation. This often led to really vital items being lost in an ocean of rubbish.

But they kept at it in the United States, believing that because they had defeated the Russians in 1904 and taken over Manchuria due largely to the intensive espionage preparations they had made, they would gain the same success in America. It was not so much the times that had changed in the past fifty years however, but the fact that they never really understood the American character. It was this which was to save America from any great harm in the long run.

A few weeks after Blake's final return to Los Angeles, Kono sailed for Japan and never returned. A couple of months later still, and the Japanese attacked Pearl Harbor.

BIBLIOGRAPHY :

Betrayal From the East — Alan Hynd (New York, 1943).

KOUDRIVTZEV, Sergei see under **Soviet American Network.**

KOVALIOV, N. G. see under **Pertov, Vladimir.**

KRASSILNIKOV, Rem see under **Munsinger Affair, The.**

KREMER, Semion see under **Fuchs, Klaus.**

KROGER, Peter and Helen see under **Portland Spy Case, The.**

KRONAUER, Ernst see under **Ernst, Karl.**

KRUGLOV, Sergei (Russian director of intelligence).

Sergei Kruglov was appointed Minister of the Interior after the death of Stalin, when that ministry was combined with the Ministry of State Security. It has been suggested that his appointment was a reward for past services as a "trigger man", for he is in no way a distinguished member of the Party or the Soviet government clique.

He joined the Red Militia as a constable, and slowly climbed the ladder until he was promoted colonel and commander of the Kremlin guard. He has the unique distinction of having survived five of his Tcheka chiefs, two of whom were executed, three of whom died mysteriously. It is believed that he personally shot Marshal Tukhachevsky, Chief of the General Staff, who was liquidated in the Great Purge of the Red Army in 1937. Shortly afterwards he was made an honorary lieutenant-general and Deputy Commissar for Internal Affairs.

He was in charge of the security arrangements for the Yalta, Teheran and Potsdam

349

Conferences, for which he was made an Honorary Knight of the British Empire by the British government and given the Legion of Merit by the US government.

After the fall of Beria the leadership determined that one man should never again be in charge of the secret services. For this reason, in April 1954, the chairmanship of the Committee for State Security was detached from the Ministry of the Interior's responsibility and given to A. I. Serov (q.v.).

On 1st February 1956, Kruglov was dismissed from his post as Minister for Internal Affairs by the Praesidium of the Supreme Soviet. Since then he has faded out of the picture.

KUCKHOFF, Adam see under **Red Orchestra, The.**

KUHN, Ruth (Agent for the Japanese in Hawaii).

Ruth Kühn was the daughter of Bernard Julius Otto Kühn, to whose wife she was born in 1917. Bernard Kühn was a friend of Himmler, chief of the Nazi SS and Gestapo; Leopold, his eldest son, was private secretary to

Dr Joseph Goebbels, Minister for Propaganda and Enlightenment.

Early in 1935 Goebbels gave a gala-party for his staff at the Ministry. As Leopold Kühn had no fiancée or particular girl-friend, he took with him as his partner, his sister Ruth.

Ruth was a very beautiful girl, and had about her a freshness and an air of innocence which immediately attracted the lecherous Goebbels to her. When she was presented to him, he held on to her hand just a little longer than was necessary, and later in the evening asked her to dance with him. Though dwarfish and club-footed, Goebbels could exude an irresistible charm. Ruth Kühn fell before it and within a few weeks of this first meeting, though only seventeen, had become his mistress.

Ruth was only one of a number of mistresses which the doctor found necessary to provide him with sexual excitement. Women were fascinated by him and plunged headlong into affairs. But his sexual palate was so jaded that the excitement of a new encounter soon wore off, and the current mistress was rejected.

What happened exactly to Ruth Kühn is now likely to remain a permanent mystery. When Goebbels suddenly tired of her, he not only cast her off but decided she must leave Germany.

The head of the Geopolitical Department of Berlin University was General Haushofer, whose son Karl was one of Goebbels's closest friends. Haushofer had had close connections with the Japanese espionage authorities since 1914, and, as good fortune would have it, at the very moment of Goebbels's break with Ruth Kühn the Japanese had asked if they could be given some assistance in acquiring the services of Europeans for their espionage organisation. One of the great difficulties with which the Japanese spymasters have always had to contend has been the physical characteristics of their countrymen, which makes them conspicuous in any area outside their own theatre and among any people but those of eastern Asia.

The coincidence of Tokyo's request with the predicament in which Goebbels found himself could not have been more fortunate. When Goebbels explained his problem to his friend Karl Haushofer, Karl's father could say that he could use not only Ruth but Ruth's family. Nothing could have been more satisfactory for the doctor, because it removed the embarrassing girl literally to the other side of the world.

So it came about that the Kühn family, with the exception of Leopold, who remained at his post in Berlin until he met his death on the Russian front, arrived in the Pacific.

Their cover was Dr Kühn's supposed "Interest in the Japanese language and the ancient history of the Hawaiin Islands." They gave every appearance of being a typically united Teutonic family. Certainly they aroused no suspicions in the minds of anyone who ought to have been curious about a German family transplanting themselves in Hawaii, so many thousands of miles from the Fatherland. Not even the travels of Ruth and her father to the adjacent islands caused a single eyebrow to be raised.

Indeed, it would seem that the Kühns had everything in their favour. Friedel Kühn, the doctor's Frau, was plump and bespectacled and treated her husband with the respect that has always been one of the good qualities of German women. But she had the pigeon-hole type of mind which could sort and evaluate and store away even small details of military significance. While she seemed to be concerned only with the welfare of her family, she disarmed those who would have been on their guard had they ever begun to suspect what her true role was. Even when she left Hawaii for two fairly long periods her absence merely provoked expressions of commiseration for the family whom she was temporarily deserting. Yet, had the interested authorities known, each time she was visiting Japan as a courier, carrying secrets of United States naval and military defences in the Hawaiian Islands.

Her encounter with Goebbels had not affected Ruth's physical appearance in the least. In fact, as she grew older, so her beauty increased. She was fond of tennis and swimming, and was an exquisite dancer. These accomplishments soon brought her invitations to every social event, and the majority of these gave her contacts with American naval officers who unwittingly provided her with extremely useful information.

The Kühns were in the service of both the Germans and the Japanese, though the latter were unaware of their contact with the Nazis. Copies of all the information they supplied to the Japanese consuls in Hawaii, who were their contacts, they sent to Ribbentrop's intelligence via General Haushofer.

Early in 1939 the Kühns moved from Honolulu to the quieter Pearl Harbor. There is no hotter bed of gossip than a woman's beauty parlour, and either the Kühns or their superiors decided to take advantage of this. As Ruth was very skilful at making herself up, and as there was no amenity of this kind for the Navy wives in Pearl Harbor, there was nothing strange to be seen in her opening a beauty parlour. This new venture marked the intensification of Japanese espionage in the southern Pacific.

The success of the beauty parlour was as overwhelming as it was instantaneous. At a meeting with Otojiro Okudo, the vice-consul at Honolulu, the specific requirements of the Tokyo spy-masters were explained to the Kühns. Their chief assignment was to supply precise details of the US naval forces in the Pacific, with their exact locations and dates of departure and arrival at any given spot, and with particular reference to Pearl Harbor.

The Kühns next step was to work out a simple code and light signal system by which they could transmit their information from the attic-window of a small house which they had rented above Pearl Harbor direct to a Japanese agent. The pace was now increased at such a rate that personal contact with the Japanese, as frequently as changes in the dispositions of US naval units now made desirable, was dangerous. The signal-system eliminated this risk.

The system was tried out on 2nd December 1941, and was a complete success. Otojiro Okudo now came himself to Pearl Harbor, and was able to transmit by radio to Japanese Naval intelligence, via his consul-general, the exact location of all American warships in Hawaiian waters.

As the Kühns, father and daughter, watched the Pearl Harbor base filling up during the next few days they had great difficulty in keeping their mounting excitement in check.

When, at 7.55 a.m. on Sunday, 7th December 1941, the Japanese launched their attack on the naval base, the Kühns were at their posts. Throughout the attack they signalled to Okudo which American ship had been hit. Okudo in turn signalled them to the commander of the Japanese fleet.

Towards the end of the attack, two American naval officers noticed the flashing lights coming from the house, and went to investigate. They caught the Kühns in their attic, still flashing their messages.

The Kühns were eventually brought to trial. The doctor, his wife and Ruth all attempted to claim the leadership of the little ring. The Americans accepted the doctor's claim, and he was sentenced to

353

death. Frau Kühn and Ruth were imprisoned.

The doctor made a bid to save his life by telling all he knew about Axis espionage in the Pacific. The Americans must have found his information valuable, for on 26th October 1942 his death sentence was commuted to fifty years' imprisonment.

BIBLIOGRAPHY:

Secret Servants — Ronald Seth (London and New York, 1957).

LAELIUS, Roman commander, espionage role of (203 BC).

In 203 BC Rome was at war with Carthage, and in North Africa the brilliant young Roman Scipio Africanus, was facing one of Carthaginian Hannibal's strongest allies, Syphax, King of Numidia. Scipio had decided that if his own armies were to be reasonably sure of success, Syphax must first be eliminated. He did not know, however, the exact strength of the Numidians, nor the disposition of their defences.

With a display of cunning not at all in tune with the chivalrous conduct of war, Scipio proposed to Syphax an armistice with the aim of arranging peace terms, while in fact intended that his negotiators should gauge the strength of Syphax's army and note the nature and disposition of his defence works. Since skilled soldiers would be required to collect this information. Scipio was faced with a difficulty, for if

Syphax saw that the Roman deputation was composed of military men, he would undoubtedly become suspicious. After a good deal of consideration, Scipio eventually solved the problem by the appointment of civilians who had accompanied the Roman armies, and sending skilled soldiers with them in the disguise of slaves.

That Syphax would be suspicious was fully substantiated by his stipulation that the Roman deputation and their attendants, civilians though they were, should remain within the compound allotted to them and that if they wished to move about the camp at all, they must be accompanied by Numidian officers.

In command of the "slaves" Scipio had sent his great friend and general, Laelius. Confronted with the restriction on his movements, Laelius instructed the deputation to draw out the discussions as long as possible, so that he might try to devise some way of obtaining the information for which he had come. But as day after day passed, neither opportunity nor plan presented itself, until eventually the head of the delegation said firmly that he could play for time no longer. Laelius begged for twenty-four hours more. If he had not succeeded by then, he would give up.

As he sat among his "slaves" trying desperately to conjure up some scheme, suddenly one of the horses neighed loudly and reared, possibly under a more than usually vicious attack from a fly. As one of the men ran to the horse to quiet it, Laelius was suddenly inspired.

Calling his men about him, he told them that they were surreptitiously to provoke the horses began to stampede. They would then appear to be trying to quiet them, but they were, in fact, to increase the provocation until the horese began to stampede. They would chase after the animals, ineptly attempt to catch them, but all tl e while edge them nearer and nearer to the Numidian defence works, and if possible inside them.

The plan succeeded. The horses, with the "slaves" in pursuit, entered the defences, and by the time they were caught, not a detail of the Numidian fortification system was unknown to the Romans.

The following day the negotiations were broken off. A short time later Scipio attacked Syphax, set fire to the defences, and so completely routed the Numidians that they were compelled to withdraw to their own country. They were still licking their wounds, when Scipio and Hannibal met on the battlefield of Zama, and the contest ended with the permanent defeat of Carthage.

BIBLIOGRAPHY :

Stratagemeticon Libri III, by Sextus Julius Frontinus, governor of Britain, 75 AD.

LAURENT, Colonel.

Colonel Laurent was chief of the French **Deuxième Bureau** between the wars. In 1933, in consequence of the Aeropostale Affaire, he was forced to give evidence in public in the Court of Assizes.

Aeropostale was the state-subsidised South Atlantic Airline Company, which became involved in a typically bizarre French case involving false contracts, forged telegrams and secret commissions. The **Deuxième Bureau** was introduced into the scandal when it was disclosed that two French agents of the Ministry of War were involved in the dirty business, and it was proved that they were paid regularly by the counter-intelligence agencies of both the Ministry of War and the Air Ministry at the same time.

LAUWERS, Hubertus (Dutch agent, World War II) see under **Giskes, Col H. J.**

LEGAL RESIDENTS.

This is a term used in Communist espionage circles to denote agents of the KGB and GRU who have as their cover a post in their embassies or trade missions. Agents, like Colonel Abel (q.v.) who work on their own and have no connection with any official set-up, are known as ILLEGALS. LEGALS have diplomatic immunity and do carry out the duties of their cover-roles. They are generally attachés, but may be chauffeurs or receptionists.

LETTER-BOXES

Letter-boxes are a regular feature of espionage techniques. They are of two kinds; human and "dead".

Their function is to act as a repository in which agents may leave their reports or receive their instructions without having to contact their superiors in person. The agent sends his report by post to, or leaves it by hand on the human letter-box, who then forwards it.

The dead letter-box may consist of any convenient hiding-place which is not likely to be inspected by persons other than the agent to whom they are allotted. They may be the hollow trunk of a tree, behind a loose brick in a wall, the inside of a flower-pot, a disused drain-pipe, and so on. The letter-boxes allocated to Frank Bossard, the British traitor, by Soviet intelligence in London provide some good examples.

According to Norman Lucas in **The Great Spy Ring** (page 257), "At the time off the arrest, Detective Superintendent Alfred Wise of the Yard's Special Branch had found in Bossard's wallet a list of 'dead letter boxes'. There were nine boxes and one reserve, referred to by the letters A to C, E to I and K to P.

"Box A was a broken drain pipe alongside a fence on an

estate at Weybridge, near Silvermere Lake; a creeper-covered beech tree off a bridal path near Leatherhead was identified as DLB 'C'; DLB 'E', a triple-trunked silver birch tree, near a 'No Litter' sign at Woking. A Forest Green site was DLB 'F' and 'H' was discovered at Blackheath."

The Public Prosecutor told the Court at Bossard's trial that on the first Saturday of January 1962 Bossard made a collection and found in DLB 'A' developed 35 mm film and £300 in cash. By applying a magnifying glass to the six-inch length of film Bossard was able to read his instructions for the future.

Soviet espionage are very fond of "dead" letter boxes. They crop up in practically every case involving Soviet agents.

LEW, Elizabeth van (Northern agent, American Civil War).

The American Civil War produced circumstances and opportunities peculiarly suited to women spies, and both the North and the South were greatly aided by the activities of their women agents. Most famous of all those for the North was unquestionably Elizabeth van Lew.

Elizabeth van Lew had been born in Virginia in 1818. Having finished her schooling in a select seminary for young ladies in Philadelphia, she returned to her parents' home in Richmond, where she lost no time in rousing first the anger of the neighbours and then their pitying contempt by her violent anti-slavery sentiments. Nor was she a theorist, but was prepared to free all the van Lew slaves and to try to purchase the parents of these slaves owned by other families.

Between 1861 and 1865 this woman of the South rendered more service to the North than almost any other agent. Surrounded by people of hostile views, suspected, and rightly, of helping Negroes and refugee Northern soldiers, she was never, it seems actually suspected of being a spy. She collected information but never took the risk of forwarding it personally. For this work she organised a network of five posts, the first of which was her house in Richmond. Between these posts relays of her servants carried her messages.

She was completely ignorant of all espionage techniques. This was no handicap, however, for she was a natural spy. Having procured military passes for her black servants, whom she sent to the family farm outside Richmond, she hid her reports in baskets of eggs or fruit. A young dressmaker who worked for her sewed reports into her work. She placed in the house of Confederate President Jefferson Davis a young Negress whom she had had educated, and trained her to repeat all she heard at the President's table.

Despite their ideas, which were considered eccentric, Elizabeth and her mother were nevertheless regarded still as distinguished women and continued giving hospitality to the civil and military leaders of the South. These influential men no doubt protected them, for the newspapers constantly drew attention to the "scandal" of their activities, and they often ran the risk of being lynched.

Elizabeth gathered much of her intelligence in the military prisons where she went to carry comforts to the Northern prisoners of war. These men, while being passed after capture through the Southern lines, were often able to observe the equipment, dispositions, and moral of the Southern armies, and sometimes even picked up news of the Southern leaders' intentions. These they communicated to Elizabeth in the whispered conversations she had with them, or by faintly underlining words in books she let to them.

In the library of the van Lew house there was a large fireplace on either side of which stood a large brass lion. In one of these lions she hid her messages, and the maid whose duty it was to clean the room would extract them, and take them to the farm. Less than twenty-four hours later, by way of the other posts, they would be in the hands of the Northern leaders.

The four years of war were nerve-wracking one for Elizabeth and her mother, for they were in constant danger of being found out. If they were not, it was because Elizabeth insisted always on observing the rules of security. When at last peace came, General Ulysses Grant sum-

359

med up her achievements in these words: "From her I received the most valuable Intelligence that ever came from Richmond throughout the entire conflict."

This being so, it might be thought that she would have received some sign of gratitude from those she had so greatly helped. She had spent the whole of the family fortune on her work, but she claimed from the government only 15,000 dollars — and did not receive a single cent. Grant did nominate her for the postmastership of Richmond, but that was all. The people of the South neverforgave her for her "treason" and refused to have any contact with her. When Grant's term of office as President came to an end, she even lost the postmastership. Thereafter she lived in very straitened circumstances, for she had no means beyond a small pension given to her by relatives and friends. She died forgotten in 1900, aged 72.

BIBLIOGRAPHY :
The Story of Secret Service—
R. W. Rowan (London, 1938) chap. 42.

LIEDTKE, Harry see under

Linse, Dr, The Kidnapping of.

LINSE, Dr Walter, The Kidnapping of.

Dr Walter Linse, a prominent German lawyer, was acting President of the Association of Free German Jurists, affiliated to the World Federation of Free Jurists, whose aims are to expose the more outrageous evils committed under the cloak of Communist law, and to offer some protection to the victims of arbitrary arrest, secret trial and sentence by "administrative process" to iniquitous terms of imprisonment or confinement in a labour camp. In this work it was succeeding so well that in 1952 SMERSH received orders from the Kremlin to arrange the kidnapping of its prominent members. SMERSH went into action at once, and since the President of the German Association was in Sweden they selected for their first victim the acting President, Dr Linse.

Linse lived in the American sector of Berlin, in an apartment at 12a Gerichtstrasse, in the suburb of Lichterfelde. Every morning promptly at

7.30 he left his apartment and walked to his office, and SMERSH decided to seize him as he emerged and set out on his constitutional.

As the abduction was to take place in broad daylight, a group of seventeen thugs was earmarked to carry it out. Four were eventually selected for the main roles. These four were Harry Liedtke, 22, who had been serving a sentence for robbery with violence when recruited by SMERSH; Herbert Novak, 27, who was serving a life-sentence for murder; Erwin Knispel, 27, who was serving sentences for eighteen separate crimes; and Josef Dehnert, 22, serving a sentence for burglary.

The abduction was timed to take place on 8th July, 1952, within a few yards of Linse's home. On 7th July, Liedtke, who had passed from East into West Berlin, a few hours earlier, hired a taxi driven by Wilhelm Woiziske, and asked to be taken to Senefelderplatz, in the Soviet sector. As West Berlin taxi-drivers were not keen to cross into the Soviet sector, Liedtke offered Woiziske a 20 Mark tip.

Shortly after they had passed the check-point, Liedtke leaned forward and dropped a carton of a hundred American cigarettes on the seat beside the driver. Woiziske thanked him.

As soon as they drew up in the Senefelderplatz, German police ran over to the taxi shouting, "So you're the smugglers of American cigarettes," and arrested both men. At police headquarters the driver was locked in a cellar, but no attempt was made to interrogate him, a fact which puzzled him until he learned sometime later the reason for the seizure of his taxi — the "borrowing" of its West Berlin registration plates for the car which the kidnappers planned to use the following morning.

A few minutes before 7.30 on 8th July, Liedtke, Knispel, Dehnert and Novak, driven by Knispel, drew up in the SMERSH saloon carrying Woiziske's number-plates, not far from Linse's house. Promptly at half-past seven the doctor emerged, puffing vigorously at his pipe, and set out for his office.

As he approached the parked SMERSH car, Liedtke and Dehnert got out, and Dehnert went up to Linse. An eye-witness later said that Dehnert appeared to ask Linse for a match, for he had an unlighted cigarette between his fingers, and Linse put his hand into his pocket.

While the doctor was fumbling in his pocket Liedtke, who had gone behind him, struck him a blow over the head with a sandbag. Linse was clearly a tough gentleman, for he was not knocked out, as had been intended, so Liedtke dropped his blackjack, and seized him round the waist while Dehnert took his legs. Together they carried the struggling Linse to the car and tried to bundle him in. This proved not to be easy, and to quieten his struggles Nowak leaned out of the car window and shot him in the legs. The shot had the desired effect, but Knispel was in such a hurry to be going that he drove off at speed with one of the lawyer's legs protruding from the partly shut rear door.

As the car sped down the Drakenstrasse it was closely pursued by the driver of a small van who had witnessed the incident. The kidnappers saw that they were being followed and Liedtke threw several tetrahedral "nails" in the car's path to try to stop it. When these had no effect, Nowak leaned out of the car window and fired two shots both of which hit the van, which had now been joined by a police patrol-car. Though both the van and the police-car kept up the pursuit, they were hampered from gaining on the SMERSH car by the morning rush-hour crowds, and eventually the kidnappers crossed safely into the Soviet sector through a check-point the barrier of which had been already raised for them.

Later in the day taxi-driver Woiziske was released and escorted back to West Berlin. He was told where he would find his taxi. It was at the place, unharmed and with its number plates refixed.

Because of Dr Linse's prominence and the audacity of the kidnapping the Western press headlined the crime and the American authorities made an immediate protest to the Soviet authorities. From the very beginning the Russians denied all knowledge of Linse's whereabouts.

Subsequently the Americans made frequent representations. For eight years demands for information and denials went back and fourth between the West and Russia. Suddenly in June 1960, the Russians suddenly performed one of their famous **volte-faces.** The Russian Red Cross informed the German Red Cross that "Walter Linse died in a Russian prison camp on 15th December 1953."

BIBLIOGRAPHY :

The Executioners — Ronald Seth (London 1965, New York, 1966).

LINTON, Freda see under **Gouzenko, Igor.**

LODY, Carl Hans (Abwehr agent, World War I).

At the beginning of World War I, England was a naval power only, and for this reason, within the sphere of interest of German naval intelligence. Steinhauer's network had been under its control when British counter-espionage eliminated it within a few hours on 5th August, 1914. Naval intelligence cast about, a little wildly, for just one spy to place in England to keep watch on the British Fleet, and could not find a suitable professional agent. They had to ask for a volun-

teer, and Lieutenant Carl Hans Lody stepped forward.

Lody was not even a professional sailor, but he had been a guide for the Hamburg-Amerika shipping line, and he knew Great Britain well. He spoke English fluently with a marked American accent.

Now it happened that at this time a certain Charles A. Inglis, an American citizen, was visiting Berlin, and had cause to go to the German Foreign Office for an extension of his visa. Unaccountably the highly methodical Wilhelmstrasse mislaid his passport; and when they apologised profusely, the American embassy issued him with a new one, which the Germans visa-ed gratis.

Not long afterwards, in September 1914, Lody arrived in Edinburgh on Mr Inglis's lost passport, in which his photograph had been substituted for the American's. Almost on arrival he sent a telegram to an Adolph Burchard in Stockholm.

It was a strange telegram, for in it Lody expressed his hostility towards Germany, a sentiment which one normally expresses by means of the four-penny post rather than the expensive cable. It drew suspicion to him at once.

So did his behaviour, and for this he was in no way to blame. German naval intelligence had been so anxious to get him to England that they made no attempt to train him, despatching him without any knowledge even of the most rudimentary principles of security, in complete ignorance of codes, and unsupplied with secret inks.

He stayed for a few days in an hotel, and then moved to a boarding-house. Then he hired a bicycle and rode round the countryside, taking a particular interest in the naval base at Rosyth. He drew even more attention to himself by the vast number of questions he asked about naval matters. Altogether his behaviour was not the normal behaviour of a tourist.

Lody communicated the information he acquired by letters so the same Adolph Burchard in Stockholm. He wrote five letters and only one of them was permitted to reach its destination because it confirmed the rumour that Russian soldiers with snow on their boots had landed in Scotland.

From Edinburgh to London, thence to Liverpool and Dublin counter - espionage trailed him. He was en route for the naval base at Queenstown when he was arrested. His last letter to Burchard completed the proof that the judges would require to convict him of espionage.

Lody was brought to England and lodged in the Tower of London, the traditional prison up to this time for all spies and traitors. On 30th October, less than two months after his first arrival in Edinburgh, he was brought before a general court-martial, sitting in London's historic Guildhall under the presidency of Major-General Lord Cheylesmore. Representing the Crown was a young barrister Archibald Bodkin, who later acquired national fame as the Director of Public Prosecutions. Lody was defended by George Elliott, one of the leading barristers of the day.

He was charged with communicating information about British military preparations to Berlin, and the Crown based its case on a note-book containing naval information, copies of letters to Burchard and to a certain Karl Stammer, and a forged passport, all of which had been found in his baggage when he was arrested. His reports were described as accurate in observation and clear in expression, the best that MI5 had so far come upon.

From the moment of his arrest, Lody conducted himself with great courage and dignity. He put forward no defence. He refused to compromise anyone connected with his mission. Mr Elliott, addressing the court, declared, "I am not here to beg mercy for him. My client is not ashamed of what he has done. Many would gladly do for England what he has done for Germany, and may be doing at this moment. Whatever his fate may be, he will meet it as a brave man."

His bearing at his trial made a very great impression on his nine judges, but at this time they could not do other than pronounce sentence of death on him. On 6th November he was taken out to face a firing-squad in the moat of the Tower, and to the very last moment his calm and courage did not desert him.

Before the bandage was put over his eyes, he said to the Provost Marshal, Lord Athlumney, his principal goaler, "I don't suppose you would care to shake hands with a spy?"

"No, I don't think so," Lord Athlumney replied. "But I shall be proud to shake hands with a very brave man."

And Lord Baden-Powell, himself an agent of distinction, has written, "In the Lower House (the House of Commons) they spoke of him as a patriot who had died on the battle-field for his country."

BIBLIOGRAPHY :

My Experiences at Scotland Yard — Sir Basil Thomson (London, 1935).

LONSDALE, Gordon see under **Portland Spy Case, The.**

LOUK, Mordecai (Post World War II).

On 17th November, 1964, a customs guard at Fiumicino airport, Rome, heard whimpering noises coming from a trunk labelled 'diplomatic mail' from the United Arab Republic Embassy in Rome to the Foreign Ministry in Cairo. It was about to be loaded onto a flight for Cairo. The trunk was accompanied by a UAR embassy official, First Secretary Abdel Moneim El Neklawy, who claimed that the noises were made by musical instruments.

After an argument, he and another man (probably First Secretary Selim Osman El Sayed) bundled the trunk onto a lorry with diplomatic number plates and drove off. They were chased and taken to the Italian police headquarters where the trunk was opened. Inside, drugged, bound and gagged, was a man whom the police later named as Josef Dahan, aged about 25, who claimed to have been abducted on Monday night, 16th November, from the Café de Paris in the Via Veneto.

The white trunk had been specially fitted out for a human body. It was lined with leather, had a tiny chair, a helmet for the head and metal clamps for ankles and neck. It was about $4\frac{1}{2}$ feet high and appeared to the police to have been used before.

The Egyptian Embassy de-nied any knowledge of the event. The two officials were taken into custody, but released on claiming diplomatic immunity. On 18th November they left for Cairo, having been declared persona non grata in Italy. The Italian authorities made a vigorous protest to the UAR ambassador, Ahmed Naguib Hashim, who deplored the incident but protested that no member of his staff had been present when the trunk was opened nor had they been allowed to phone the embassy. The Israel embassy also claimed to know nothing.

The London Times reported that the man had been in Italy since January, when he arrived ostensibly as a tourist. He had since been living in Naples where he was said to have been seeking work as a guide in a tourist agency. He was reported to speak ten languages, including Hebrew. He told the police that he was Mordechai Ben Masuud Louk, born 28 years ago near Tel Aviv. He entered Italy with a Moroccan passport and lived in Naples until 16th November when he went to meet UAR embassy contacts in Rome.

The UAR embassy accused the Italian police of replacing a trunk containing documents with that in which Louk was found. On 22nd November, Ambassador Hashim was called to the Italian Foreign Ministry and rebuked for the embassy's behaviour. The Italians started legal proceedings against four embassy staff involved in the kidnapping. Abdel Ismail Salem (First Secretary) was declared persona non grata. Another man, not a diplomat, was thought to have left Rome.

On 23rd November Louk was asked to return to Israel after being visited by the Israeli consul. He said he had deserted to Egypt in the Gaza area three years before, misled by Egyptian propaganda. Police stated he had belonged to an organisation 'for collecting information'. He left Italy on the 24th, after making a press statement denying having spied for Egypt or Israel. He was arrested on arrival in Tel Aviv for illegally crossing the border in 1961. On 26th November, 1964, he was remanded for 15 days on suspicion of 'contact with enemy agents' and 'passing information of security value to the enemy'.

Louk was brought to trial on 17th May, 1965. Now described as a carpenter aged 31, he pleaded not guilty on 6 counts, including State Security offences. The prosecution stated that he came to Israel in 1948, served in the army and established a family in Petah-Tikva. He became estranged from his wife in June 1961, crossed the border and gave himself up to UN guards asking to be handed over to the Egyptians. He later gave the Egyptian Intelligence information harmful to Israel's security.

On 9th September, Louk was convicted on all 6 counts. He admitted volunteering to spy for Egypt, but denied ever having actually done so. "Those hours in the trunk gave me a clear picture of how I should conduct myself in future in honest society,' he declared.

He contended that the Egyptians turned against him because he had not fulfilled his undertakings to supply information about the characters and weaknesses of Israeli pilots and sailors in Italy who might be blackmailed or en-

367

ticed into serving Egyptian Intelligence. The court dismissed this. Louk acknowledged crossing the border because he was dissatisfied with conditions in Israel and hoped for help in getting to Canada or Australia. He gave information to Egyptian Intelligence in Gaza and Cairo and in late 1962-3 volunteered to serve Egyptian Intelligence against Israel, as a device to get out of gaol. He had 6 months training in Cairo and was then sent to Naples where he received 75,000 lire (£50) a month, later only 50,000 from Egyptian agents. He claimed that he never intended fulfilling orders and stalled with the excuse that he had no work permit. The court replied that even the Egyptian Intelligence could not be so gullible as to pay him for a year and four months for nothing. He was sentenced to 13 years in prison.

Louk appealed against his sentence and on 29th April, 1966 the Israeli Supreme Court reduced the sentence to 10 years on the grounds that 'he had already suffered punishmen during his experiences'.

It has never been revealed why the Egyptians tried to smuggle him out of Italy in a trunk.

BIBLIOGRAPHY :

The London **Times.**

Corriere della Sera, Milan.

LUCIETO, Charles (French master-spy, World War I).

Charles Lucieto, one of the most successful of French agents of World War I, was valuable to his superiors because of his specialist knowledge of the manufacture of heavy ordnance and high-explosive shells. It was in this field that he achieved his greatest success.

The Germans first used poison gas on 22nd April, 1915, at Ypres. The method employed was to release the gas from cylinders when a favourable wind was blowing that would carry it across to the Allied lines. Initially, the use of gas in this way was a success, but the Germans had not taken into account the prevailing winds in Flanders, nor the suddenness with which they might change direction, and after they had experienced a gas cloud being turned back over their own lines by an abruptly changing breeze, with disastrous effects on their own men, the use of the gas cloud was discontinued.

To Lucieto this did not mean that the Germans had given up the use of poison gas as a weapon, and he became certain that he was right when he found the Badische Anilin und Soda Fabrik at Mannheim still working at high pressure.

Keeping watch on the B.A. S. Fabrik's activities, he noticed that their tank trucks were making for Krupp's munitions factory at Essen, so he now made this his centre. He did so at great risk to himself, because German counter-espionage was stronger there than anywhere in Germany.

He haunted the bars where master mechanics from Krupp's dropped in for their beer, and picked up some useful information from their gossip. But it was a friendship he struck up with an elderly security guard at the great munitions works which eventually brought him complete success.

Posing as a commercial traveller, with considerable patience he won the guard's confidence. Naturally, talk came round to the war, and Lucieto pretended to be pessimistic about the outcome for Germany. The old man argued with him, but Lucieto would not be convinced, and eventually the guard, anxious to prove his argument, brushed aside all thoughts of security and confided to Lucieto that experiments were being carried out with a new secret weapon — shells filled with gas which could be fired by ordinary field artillery.

To the old man's disappointment, this news only increased the French agent's scepticism. It irritated the old man, too, to have his word doubted, and in the end he undertook to let his new friend see for himself a series of experiments which were shortly to be made with the new weapon.

The experiments were carried out on a field range, and from the hidden vantage point to which the guard had led him, Lucieto watched the arrival of a large convoy of military motorcars. When the occupants of these cars had dismounted, he recognised among them no less a person than the Kaiser himself.

Two guns were used for the

369

experiment, a .77 field gun and a larger-calibre naval gun. Their target was a flock of sheep grazing on a slope a thousand yards away. The two guns were fired, and Lucieto noted that when the shells burst they did so with an effect quite different from that of ordinary shrapnel shells. After each burst a cloud of greenish-yellow smoke hung in the air and began to drift slowly toward the sheep, at last enveloping them. When eventually it was dissipated, nothing alive remained; even the grass was scorched black, and the earth looked as though it were covered with a rust-coloured deposit.

Lucieto was, of course, convinced by this visible evidence, but he decided that he must have some kind of tangible evidence before he could hope to convince the French military authorities. So he asked the guard if he could search for a fragment of one of the gas shells to keep as a souvenir. The old man, delighted that he had been able to prove to his friend that he knew what he was talking about, said it would be better if he looked

for it, and within half an hour of the Kaiser and his party leaving the range, Lucieto had a shell fragment in his pocket.

Three days later he presented himself at headquarters in Paris. He described what he had seen, and produced the fragment, on which laboratory tests were immediately carried out and supported everything he said. Before the Germans had produced the gas shells in sufficient quantities to put them in the field, the Allies had been able to supply their troops with efficient gas masks and had begun to make gas shells themselves.

Few exploits in espionage history illustrate more clearly the three chief rules which the really successful spy in the field must follow: to discover where the most valuable information is to be found; to obtain the information, if possible with proof, without its being suspected that he has done so; and to get his information to his headquarters with the least possible delay. It demonstrates also, that specialised knowledge is essential, for had not Lucieto been a munitions expert himself, it is more than likely that he would never have located the information, and even if he had, would not have been able to assess correctly what he saw happen on the range.

BIBLIOGRAPHY :
On Special Missions —
Charles Lucieto (London, 1925).
Some of My Favourite Spies — Ronald Seth (Philadelphia, 1968).

LUNAN, David see under **Soviet Canadian Network.**

MACKENZIE, Sir Compton
(British novelist; World War
I agent in Greece).

This distinguished novelist,
like many others of his trade,
— Somerset Maugham, Ian
Fleming, A. E. W. Mason, Len
Deighton among them—serv-
ed as a British agent. In World
War I he operated in Greece.

In 1933 he was arrested and
brought to trial at the Central Criminal Court, because
just before Christmas 1932 he
had published **Greek Memories,** an account of his experiences as an agent in
Athens in 1916. He was
charged with using material
he had acquired while he was
in the "service of the government" and contravention
of the Official Secrets Act in
that he had mentioned in his
book the names of some of
the people who had been connected with the secret service
sixteen years previously.

Sir Compton was found
guilty, and he was fined £100.
Greek Memories was seized
and withdrawn from publication.

MAKAROV, Mikhail see under **Trepper, Leopold.**

MAKAROV, Semion (Rus-
sian agent in Australia) see
under **Petrov, Vladimir.**

MANN, Horace.

Horace Mann was born in
1701, and entered the diplomatic service in 1738 in
Florence, where he assisted
the British Minister, Sir
Charles Fane. He had not
been in Florence more than
a few weeks, when Fane returned to England to attend
to some private business. He
never went back to Florence,
and in 1740 Mann was ap-
pointed to succeed him as
Resident to the Great Duke
of Tuscany.

The Young Pretender was
very active in Florence, trying to obtain help from the
Florentines for the Stuart
cause. Though Fane had been
reprimanded a short time previously by Lord Newcastle,
Secretary of State, for per-
mitting the Grand Duke to
receive the Young Pretender
privately.

The chief function of the
Resident at this time was to
organise a network of agents
whose task was to keep the

Stuart exiles under constant surveillance and report on their every move. As chief of this network, he fulfilled this assignment with great success. One of his chief informants was Cardinal Alessandro Albani (q.v.). He probably ranks third after Sir William Wickham and Sir Joseph Yorke, who were the great spy-masters of this type of the eighteenth century.

BIBLIOGRAPHY :

Connoissuers and Secret A-gents — Lesley Lewis (London, 1961).

MANNEL, Günter see under **Felfe, Heinz.**

MARLOWE, Christopher (English playwright and agent, 16th century).

In the spring of 1587 the duc de Guise, leader of the French Catholic party, was being active in attempts to rescue his niece Mary Stuart, Queen of Scots, from the clutches of the English Queen Elizabeth I. It was Guise's plan to offer hospitality to English students who might have Roman Catholic leanings, but who were not yet admitted to the Faith, at the Jesuit stronghold in Rheims, having as its ultimate intention the employment of these young men in plots against Elizabeth.

Sir Francis Walsingham (q.v.), Elizabeth's spy-master, became aware of what was happening at Rheims, and decided to plant an agent in the seminary to obtain detailed information of the conspiracies being plotted there, which he was sure would be intensified after the execution of Mary.

The agent he chose for this mission was a young Cambridge student called Christopher Marlowe, who in February 1587, suddenly disappeared from the university without anyone knowing where he had gone. He reappeared again in July, also without explanation, and was arraigned by the university authorities for being absent without leave, and more seriously for having gone to the Jesuit seminary at Rheims.

In fact, Marlowe, at Walsingham's direction, had gone to Rheims and had entered the seminary as a potential Catholic student through the unsuspecting offices of the famous Jesuit campaigner,

373

Father Parsons, who according to his report to the general headquarters of the Society of Jesus had "at length insinuated a certain priest into the very university (at Cambridge) under the guise of a scholar or a gentleman commoner and have procured him help from a place not far from the town. Within a few months he sent over to Rheims seven very fit youths."

In the seminary Marlowe had been loud in his detestation of the Protestant Elizabeth, and having been screened, was admitted to the schemes which were being hatched there for the formation of an extensive Catholic Resistance movement in England. Having discovered the identities of the members of this organisation he returned to his master with their names.

The accusation of the university authorities that Marlowe had been at Rheims had been a shot in the dark, but it was so accurate that Walsingham, had to intervene to save his agent from attracting too much attention to himself. On secret and direct orders from the Secretary of State all charges against the student were dropped.

According to the traditional version of English history, Marlowe met his death as the result of a brawl in a tavern in Deptford, not far from Greenwich, on the Thames. It is certainly true that this was the manner of his death, but recent researches indicate that it is more than likely that he was the victim of an espionage assassination.

His untimely death at the age of twenty-nine in May 1593 removed a playwright of outstanding talent. Some hold that had he lived he would have rivalled Shakespeare; but this I personally doubt.

BIBLIOGRAPHY :

Mr Secretary Walsingham and the Policy of Queen Elizabeth — Conyers Read (London, 1925).

MARSHALL, William Martin (British traitor, post World War II).

William Martin Marshall, the son of a former bus-driver, was trained for the Merchant Navy. Not finding this career congenial, he withdrew half-way through his training, and went to a school for wireless telegraphy.

While doing his National Service, in 1948 he was posted to the Middle East as a private in the Royal Corps of Signals. When he had finished his eighteen months service, he remained in the Middle East as a civilian wireless operator, and was still in this post when he obtained a job with the British Foreign Office, and was sent to the embassy in Moscow.

Sometime before he had been attracted to Communism, but this seems to have been overlooked during his screening. Though a somewhat retiring young man up to this time, in Russia he changed, and soon was caught up in a small social whirl in which his companions were Russians.

In 1952 he was recalled from Moscow and sent to the diplomatic wireless station at Hanslope Park, in Buckinghamshire. Three days after his arrival in England he contacted the Second Secretary at the Russian embassy in London, Pavel Kuznetsov, who entertained him lavishly and frequently both in the capital and in its environs.

This brought him to the attention of the counter-espionage authorities, and a special watch was kept on him. His meetings in London parks and elsewhere were noted for three months, and then on the evening of Friday 13th June, 1952, he and Kuznetsov were arrested in St George's Park, Wandsworth, London, by officers of the Special Branch.

Because of his diplomatic immunity, Kuznetsov was released. Marshall was brought to trial, and though the evidence against him was largely circumstantial, he was found guilty and sentenced to five years' imprisonment.

BIBLIOGRAPHY :
Various newspaper cuttings.

MARTIGNAT, Etienne-Charles see under **Reiss, Ignace.**

"MARTIN, Major William" (**Operation Mincemeat** World War II).

With the capture of North Africa in 1942, the Allies had two alternative strategies, either of which would permit them to regain a foothold on the continental mainland of Europe. One was a landing in

Greece; the other, a landing in Italy. Largely because Churchill was convinced that Italy was "the soft under-belly of the Axis", the choice fell on her. During the preparatory period, the natural need arose for the Allies to try to deceive the Axis powers about where they intended to strike, and one attempt to do this was made under the somewhat macabre code-name of **Operation Mincemeat.**

As a **ruse de guerre** it was impeccable; the brainchild of a naval intelligence officer, Lieutenant Commander the Hon Ewen Montagu — later a Queen's Counsel — and some of his colleagues. Montagu and his team had been assigned the task of trying to find some means of diverting enemy attention from Sicily to Greece. At one stage in their deliberations, Montagu recalled that a short time before, someone had suggested dropping into France a corpse with a radio-transmitter attached to it to test the genuineness of certain German reports. The technical difficulties had seemed insuperable at the time, but provided certain conditions could be met, Montagu thought it might work this time.

The chief of these conditions was whether doctors could be deceived into believing that a corpse, if damaged in a certain way, had been the victim of an air-crash at sea. Montagu consulted Sir Bernard Spilsbury, one of the most eminent pathologists of all time. Spilsbury told him that if the conditions he described were observed, it would be possible, and the decision was taken to explore the matter further.

Montagu began his search for a suitable body, which proved more difficult than he had anticipated. Eventually, however, he came upon the corpse of a 38 year-old man who fulfilled Spilsbury's specification. The body was put into cold storage and the rest of **Operation Mincemeat** went into full preparation.

The body was to be put into the sea by a submarine off the Spanish seaside town of Huelva, where it was known an active German agent was based, who was very friendly with the local Spanish authorities. Montagu and his team were convinced that any documents found on the corpse of a British officer washed up on the beach at Huelva would certainly find their way to the Germans.

Who the corpse had been was unknown to Montagu. The cover-identity with which it was provided was as follows :

Name: MARTIN, William

Rank: Captain, acting major, Royal Marines.

Speciality: An expert in certain types of landing-craft.

Posting: On the staff of Louis Mountbatten, Commander - in - Chief Combined Operations on secondment to Admiral Sir A. B. Cunningham, Commanderin-Chief of the British Mediterranean Fleet.

Martin was to carry on him a top secret personal letter from General Sir Archibald Nye, Vice-Chief of the Imperial General Staff to General Sir Harold Alexander, Commander-in-Chief of the British 18th Army Group, in which Nye was to tell Alexander that it was hoped to make the Germans believe the Allies intended a landing in Sicily, the actual objection was Greece.

In addition to this skilfully contrived letter, Martin was to carry another letter purporting to originate from Lord Louis and addressed to Admiral Cunningham, in which Lord Louis hoped Martin would be the man Cunningham was looking for. There was also to be a third letter — from Lord Louis to General Eisenhower — in which the alleged writer asked General Eisenhower to contribute a message to be used in advertising in America in a pamphlet on Combined Operations. All three letters were to be carried in a brief case attached to Martin's body by a chain. (Had they been on the corpse their immersion in sea-water might have made them illegible.)

On the personal side, Martin was provided with a letter from his bank manager asking him to reduce immediately an overdraft of £79 : 19 : 2d., a letter from his father to lunch with his solicitor to discuss certain financial arrangements, one or two other letters, among them two love-letters from a girl called Pam, and a snapshot of her. There was also a receipt for a diamond engagement ring and other receipts, the stubs of two threatre tickets and various odds and ends.

Early in the evening of 19th April, 1943, HM submarine **Seraph** sailed from Holy Loch, in north-west Scotland, with its precious cargo. On 30th April the **Seraph's** commander informed Montagu that Major Martin had been put overboard at 04.30 hours that morning "in position 148° Portil Pillar 1.3 miles, approximately 8 cables" from the Huelva beach and had started drifting inshore.

Montagu had not long to wait for news of the success of part of **Operation Mincemeat.** The British naval attaché in Madrid reported on 3rd May that the body of a Major Martin RM had been picked up by a Spanish fisherman on 30th April. Montagu signalled the attaché on 4th May that Martin had had some very secret papers with him, and requested him to inquire if these had been recovered with the body.

The unsuspecting attaché contacted the Spanish Minister of Marine who told him that the documents had been passed through naval channels and would only reach Madrid via naval HQ at Cadiz. On 13th May, a fortnight after Martin's "landing", the Spaniards handed over all his belongings to the attaché intact.

Even at this point Montagu did not know if the plan had really succeeded. By degrees, however, from "information received", it became certain that the Germans had been told the contents of the three important letters. It was not until after the war that captured German documents revealed how successful the Operation had been. Among them were exact copies of the letters.

BIBLIOGRAPHY:

The Man Who Never Was — Ewen Montagu (London, 1952).

MARWEDI, Captain Friedrich Carl (Abwehr agent, World War II).

Captain Friedrich C a r l Marwedi was Director of Office I West in Abwehr II, the department of the German intelligence organisation which was responsible for contacts with discontented minority groups in foreign countries. He devised great plans for raising an IRA rebellion in Eire during World War II, which, however came to nothing.

Marwedi operated under the cover-name of **Dr Pfalzgraf.**

BIBLIOGRAPHY :

Spies in Ireland — Enno Stephan (London, 1963).

MATA HARI (German agent in World War I).

Without doubt the best-known spy in all the world is Mata Hari, The Eye of the Dawn.

Though attempts have been made recently to show that Mata Hari has been badly served by her biographies, I am not convinced of the arguments or the evidence brought forward by her apologists, and the story I shall recount is what may be called the "traditional" Mata Hari story.

At the height of her career she fostered the story that she was a half-caste Javanese, who had been trained as a temple-dancer in Malabar. It was a legend. Her parents were Dutch and her maiden-name was Margaret Gertrude Zelle. In 1895 she married an officer in the Dutch colonial army, called MacLeod, and went with him to Java. There a son and a daughter were born to them.

MacLeod was a brute, a sot, and an adulterer. He beat his wife and heaped upon her every indignity. The son died in infancy, it has been suggested of poison given him by a servant outraged by his father. It would seem probable that as a relief from the horror of her home life, Margaret MacLeod studied the Javanese erotic books and spent a good deal of her time watching performances of the dancing girls, because when she later came to Paris in the role of temple-dancer, she performed well enough to deceive many Oriental experts.

In 1901 she returned with her daughter and husband to Holland. The following year MacLeod left her, taking the little girl with him. This seems to have stirred a latent power in the mother, because for the first time in her life she went on to the offensive, and obtained a court order for the return of the child and maintenance for both of them. She got the child back, but no money from MacLeod, and after three unhappy and difficult years, in 1905 she left her daughter with relatives and disappeared — to reappear at the Musée Guimet in Paris, as Mata Hari, whose mother, a temple-dancer had died in giving birth to her, and who had been trained by the priests and dedicated to the god Siva in her mother's place. How she had come to Paris was not explained, and no one seemed curious enough to find out.

She was an immediate success, because her dances, so she said, demanded complete nudity. The term for her meant complete nudity except for breast-plates, which she wore to conceal flabby, pendulous breasts. Her beauty was, in fact, concentrated in her eyes and arms; her attraction in the eroticism of her olive-dark limbs.

Lovers came in their scores, and were drawn from such exalted families that she could afford to pick and choose. Her reputation spread to all the capitals of Europe, and she followed it to prove that she was all that rumour said

she was. In Berlin, Rome, Vienna and Paris she gave her favours to princes, dukes, ministers and generals — in return for enormous fees.

When she made her first appearance at the Musée Guimet she was twenty-nine. When she faced the firing-squad at Vincennes she was forty. In the intervening decade she had established herself as the leading prostitute in Europe, and held a fatal fascination for men right to the moment that she slumped lifeless against the stake. As a spy she was not one-hundredth part so successful.

Berlin had always shown her the greatest hospitality, but if she spied for Germany, it was only because the Germans had been the first to ask her. The French have always maintained that her operational number was H 21 and that the Germans only used this initial for their pre-war agents. Yet for the first year of the war, Mata Hari kept herself well away from every scene of military activity.

The first notice we have of her after 4th August, 1914, comes in a telegram from the Italian intelligence to the

Paris authorities late in 1915:

While examining the passenger list of a Japanese vessel at Naples we have recognised the name of the theatrical celebrity from Marseilles, named Mata Hari, the famous Hindu dancer, who purports to reveal secret Hindu dances which demand complete nudity. She has, it seems, renounced her claim to Indian birth and become Berlinoise. She speaks German with a slight eastern accent.

From the moment that that message reached Paris, Mata Hari was shadowed wherever she went, whether to Paris, London, Antwerp or Brussels. But for another year no Allied counter-espionage service could find any grounds for apprehending her. She performed her dances as before; she dispensed her favours as before. But she was never furtive; never displayed any fear.

Then, almost by chance, French counter-espionage discovered that she was sending her reports to Germany by neutral diplomats, upon whom she now was concentrating, and who were exempt from censorship. Even so, the evidence available would not have satisfied a court.

One of her former lovers had been a Russian, Captain Maroff, who had been permanently blinded w h i l e fighting. Maroff was now at Vittel, and Mata Hari applied for a permit to go to the Vosges to nurse him. Not believing her reasons for wanting to go, the French granted the permit and she was more closely watched than ever before.

Again she disappointed French counter-espionage. It is conceded now that of all the many men with whom she was intimate the only man she ever loved was Maroff. Thwarted and desperate the French decided that the only way they could rid themselves of her was to deport her.

To their secret amazement, on being told of this decision her nerve seemed to break. Vehemently she protested that she had never spied for the Germans, but that if the French wished to use her services, she knew many high-ranking Germans and it would be very easy for her to obtain much important information.

The French pretended to believe her and sent her first to Brussels to one of her former inamorato, General von Bissing, Governor-General of Belgium. Before she left they gave her the names of six Belgian agents to whom she was to pass von Bissing's secrets. But she had been in Brussels only a short time when one of the six was arrested by the Germans and executed.

The move in sending her to Brussels was not an exceptionally good one, because it was easy for her to pass, with German help, to neutral Holland, whence she made for neutral Spain, most surprisingly via England. The behaviour of British intelligence on her arrival is equally surprising. She was taken to London where she was questioned by Sir Basil Thomson, chief of the Special Branch, to whom she admitted being a spy, but in the service of France. Sir Basil states that he said to her, "Madame, if you will accept the advice of one nearly twice your age, give up what you have been doing."

With this sound advice she was permitted to continue her journey to Spain, where she made contact with the German naval attaché and the military attaché, from whom she received her instructions. The Germans had realised by this time, however, that she was compromised so hopelessly that she was no longer of any use to them. She was also extremely expensive, and German secret service funds were running low.

She did not appear to have any idea of her danger, and went back to France fearlessly. The French knew she was coming, because the Germans, when they issued her instructions, had deliberately used a code which they knew the French had broken.

On arrival in Paris she stayed at the hotel Plaza-Athenée in the avenue Montaigne. The Germans had told her that the sum of fifteen thousand pesetas would be paid to her by a neutral legation. She collected the cheque but did not cash it at once, and it was in her possession when the French arrested her.

She was brought before a court-martial on 24th July,

1917. She was defended by the distinguished French barrister, Maître Clunet, who was one of the few who belived that she would be acquitted. The president of the court opened the proceedings by questioning her about the sum of thirty thousand marks which she had received from von Jagow, chief of the Berlin police, on the outbreak of the war.

"He was my lover," she answered, "Thirty thousand marks was the fee for my favours."

That was the explanation she gave for all the large sums of money she had been receiving for years. The court cited all the high-ranking Germans with whom she had been to bed — General von Bissing, the Duke of Brunswick, the German Crown Prince, and naval and military attachés engaged in espionage. She countered by calling as witnesses Jules Cambron, the permanent secretary of the Foreign Office, and a former Minister of War and others equally exalted.

"I am not French," she declared, "so what is to prevent my having friends of any nationality I choose? If I wrote to high-ranking Germans it was only because they wrote to me and I returned their endearments, but nothing more. My letters that were sent in diplomatic bags were letters to my daughter in Holland."

She became confused only when the Commissioner for the French Government, Lieutenant Mornet, began to question her about her offer to spy for France.

"I told the French authorities," she retorted, "many places in Morocco where German U-boats call to refuel. It was very useful information, I am told."

"No doubt," Mornet replied. "But how could you know these things if you were not in contact with German intelligence chiefs?"

She launched into a long explanation, which became more and more muddled as she went on, until she realised this herself and broke off.

"After all, I am not French. I have no duty towards this people."

The trial, held **in camera,** lasted for two days, but she was condemned before it began.

Her lawyers fought desperately for her reprieve, but the President of the Republic refused to consider it. So did Queen Wilhelmina, who was pressed by her prime minister, Mijnheer van der Linden, one of Mata Hari's former lovers, to sign a petition to M Poincaré.

Mata Hari was sentenced on 25th July, and the sentence was not carried out until 15th October. She comported herself with great calmness and courage to the last, refusing the bandage for her eyes, and faced the firing-squad with such composure that she attracted the admiration of her executioners.

It is said that her courage sprang from the fact that she had been told that her execution was to be "arranged"; that the rifles would contain only blanks; and that afterwards she would be spirited away to safety by powerful friends. But there is no evidence for the story.

BIBLIOGRAPHY :

My Experiences at Scotland Yard — Sir Basil Thomson (London, 1935).

Crime Reporter — Georges du Parcq (an intimate friend of Mata Hari) (Paris, 1936).

MATSUI, Dr Yochuchi (Japanese agent in Central America, between the wars).

It is doubtful whether any nation except Japan would have opened an espionage campaign, even in Central America, by attempting to teach the Mexicans to fish **scientifically.**

One of the experts in the Japanese conception of scientific fishing was Dr Yochuchi Matsui, who arrived in Mexico in 1935 by a special arrangement between the Japanese and Mexican governments. Matsui may have intended to give the Mexican Pacific fishermen the benefit of his knowledge, but he had another and more important reason for coming to Mexico. When he had paved the way, he was to attempt to persuade the Mexican government to give permission for the establishment of a colony of Japanese "fishermen" at San Gabriel Bay, on the southernmost tip of the peninsula of Lower California.

Not long after his arrival Dr Matsui made the acquaintance of a Captain Manuel Camiro. Camiro was already aware of the doctor's chief assignment, and undertook to act as his inter-mediary with the Mexican government.

Since his first attempts at explaining scientific fishing met with little success with the Mexican fishermen, who had no fault to find with their own methods, he decid-ed to concentrate his efforts on achieving his chief ob-jective. So, with Camiro, he moved to Guaymas, the little fishing-port about half-way up the east coast of the Gulf of California.

At Guaymas, Matsui and Camiro began to entertain the local officials in a compara-tively lavish style, to prepare the ground for meeting more important and influential government officials later on. But when the latter were en-countered they proved to be disappointingly unco-opera-tive.

Their lack of co-operation sprang from the fact that in San Gabriel Bay a consider-able number of Mexican pearl-fishers were already en-gaged in a lucrative business. Not unnaturally, the pearl-fishers saw in the Japanese proposal a threat to their own livelihood, and the govern-ment divined that it would

most certainly mean a loss of revenue for them. By an arrangement between the pearl-fishers and the govern-ment the pearl-fishers made a most vigorous protest of which the government was bound to take note officially.

But Camiro and Matsui were persistent and patient men, and for three years they entertained, but were no nearer to reaching their goal than they had been at the beginning.

It was Camiro who lost in-terest first, and this loss of interest was prompted by a message conveyed to him by the San Gabriel Bay Pearl-fishers Association. A full meeting of this body was held on 19th December, 1938 and resolved unanimously that if Captain Camiro continued his efforts on behalf of Dr Matsui he should be per-manently removed, and that this decision should be made known to the captain im-mediately.

Knowing his countrymen well, Camiro at once left Guaymas, and wisely never showed himself there again.

Matsui, however, stayed on, for Guaymas had for some years been the headquarters of Japanese espionage on the west coast of Central America.

BIBLIOGRAPHY :
Honorable Spy — J. L. Spivak (New York, 1939).

MAUGHAM, W. Somerset
(World-famous British author, secret agent World War I).

W. Somerset Maugham, the world-famous author, served as a secret agent in Switzerland during World War I. It has never been disclosed in what capacity he served, nor what his assignment was. It is widely believed, however, that his famous spy-novel, **Ashenden,** is a thinly disguised account of his own exploits.

MAXIMOVICH, Vasili and Anna (Soviet agents in France, World War II).

Vasili and Anna Maximovich, were the children of a Russian nobleman who had emigrated to Paris after the defeat of the White Russian forces in 1922. Their mother did not accompany them, and when their father died, they were placed in the care

386

of the Bishop of Paris, Monsignor Chapital. Vasili, on growing up, became an engineer, Anna a doctor specialising in psychiatry and neurology.

In view of their antecedents, it is strange that the Maximoviches became attracted to Communism. On the outbreak of World War II, Anna, who had established a home for mental patients from the profits of which she financed the fellow-travelling Union of Defenders, was arrested. When she was able to produce bona fide patients, she was freed. Vasili, on the other hand, was interned, in October 1939, in a camp at Bernet, near Toulouse. There he stayed until the Germans overran France, when he was released by the Germans on agreeing to act as interpreter for a German general of anti-Nazi leanings.

Not long after he had joined the general's staff, Vasili was contacted by Leopold Trepper (q.v.) the Resident Director of the French networks, and very soon was supplying Trepper with a constant flow of high-grade material. Soon he added to his sources by offering marriage to a forty-four-year-old maiden lady. His German chiefs approved, and Vasili was given permission to visit the Military Administration HQ as often as he wished. This was a source unrivalled except perhaps by the sources of Rösseler in Switzerland, and Sorge in Tokyo (q.v. both). His wife also proved another source, she willingly agreed to pass on to him all that her gossiping girl colleagues—she worked for the Military Adiminstration — related.

The information which Vasili forwarded to The Centre through Trepper included reports on the French attitudes to their uninvited guests, the whole lay-out of German military economy both in France and the other occupied countries, the seriousness of the manpower situation, and the location of concentration camps. Secret documents were "borrowed" for a few hours, photographed and returned before they were missed, while "blanks" of almost every form used by the bureaucratic Germans were to be had for the taking.

Vasili gathered round him a group of useful contacts, into which he drew his sister Anna. With Trepper's aid she had set up a new clinic on the demarcation line between the Occupied and Unoccupied Zones. This clinic was an extremely useful rendezvous for clandestine operators on account of its position. In addition, through Vasili's contact with the Military Administration, German officers began to seek treatment from Anna for nervous complaints, and they provided another source of information.

All went well until the breakup of the networks in Belgium and Holland. This in turn affected the working of the French network, and eventually Trepper was arrested. Perhaps his greatest treachery was his betrayal of the Maximoviches and all their networks. Their arrests destroyed all the networks based on Paris, and indeed all Soviet networks in France except for that led by Victor Sukulov (q.v.) operating in the Marseilles area.

BIBLIOGRAPHY :

Soviet Espionage — David J. Dallin (New York, 1955).

MAY, Dr Allan Nunn (British atomic scientist who spied for the Russians during and after World War II).

Dr Allan Nunn May was one of a group of British research physicists sent to Canada with Dr (now Lord) Cockcroft in July 1944 to work on the Atomic Energy Project at Montreal and Chalk River. Up to his arrival the Russian atomic spy-ring operating in Canada (see under **GOUZENKO, Igor**) had been unable to carry out its instruction from The Centre to obtain a sample of uranium 235. Only a short time after Nunn May's arrival he was approached by one of the Russians, and by 9th August, 1945, Colonel Zabotin, head of the ring, was able to report to Moscow the date of the first atomic-bomb test, the daily output of uranium 235 at Clinton, and had obtained a sample of uranium 233 (sic), all from Alek, Nunn May's operational name.

After giving details of an electronic shell used by the Americans against Japanese suicide-pilots, Nunn May returned to England in September, 1945. Zabotin had known of his impending return, since May, and had informed Moscow, and the following cipher telegrams were exchanged :
(Grant is Zabotin's operational name)

To Grant   30.7.45
Reference No 218
(22.7.45)

Work out and telegraph arrangements for the meeting and password of Alek with our man in London.
Grant
31.7.45
To the Director
We have worked out the conditions of a meeting with Alek in London. Alek will work in King's College, Strand. It will be possible to find him there through the telephone book.

Meetings : October 7.17.27 on the street in front of the British Museum. The time, eleven o'clock in the evening. Identification sign : A newspaper under the left arm. Password : Best regards to Mikel (Maikl). He cannot remain in Canada. At the beginning of September he must fly to London. Before his departure he will go to the Uranium Plant in Petawawa district where he will be for

388

about two weeks. He promised, if possible, to meet us before his departure. He said he must come next year for a month to Canada. We handed over 500 dollars to him.

22.8.45

To Grant

Reference No 244

The arrangements worked out for the meeting are not satisfactory. I am informing you of the new ones.

1. Place:

In front of the British Museum in London, on Great Russell Street, at the opposite side of the street, about Museum Street, from the side of Tottenham Court Road, repeat Tottenham Court Road, Alek walks from Tottenham Court Road, the contact man from the opposite side — Southampton Row.

2. Time :

As indicated by you, however it would be more expedient to carry out the meeting at 20 o'clock, if it should be convenient to Alek, as at 23 o'clock it is too dark. As for the time, agree about it with Alek and communicate decision to me. In case the meeting should not take place in October, the time and day will be repeated in the following months.

3. Identifications signs :

Alek will have under his left arm the newspaper **Times,** the contact man will have in his left hand the magazine **Picture Post**.

4. The Password :

The contact man : "What is the shortest way to the Strand?"

Alek : "Well, come along, I am going that way."

In the beginning of the business conversation Alek says, "Best regards from Mikel".

Report on transmitting the conditions to Alek.

18.8 Director 22.8.45
Grant

As a result of the disclosures of Igor Gouzenko, a general round-up of agents connected with the Canadian ring began on 15th February, 1946. On that day, Commander Burt, chief of the Special Branch, called on Nunn May at Shell-Mex House, in London, where the scientist was then working. The commander asked him if he thought that there had been a leakage of secret atomic information while he had been in Canada. Nunn May replied that he had never heard of such a leakage and denied that he had ever been approached by Soviet agents.

Commander Burt did not stay long, but he had Nunn May closely watched for the next five days, during which Nunn May did nothing to betray himself. In the meantime, however, more information reached the commander from Canada, and he paid a second call at Shell-Mex House. Quite bluntly he told Nunn May that he had reason to believe that he should have met a Russian contact near the British Museum, but had not gone to the rendezvous. At this Nunn May, even before any mention could be made of arresting him, said he wanted to confess everything.

In a subsequent statement, Nunn May gave the reasons for his treachery. "I gave and had given," he said, "very careful consideration to the correctness of making sure that the development of atomic energy was not confined to the USA. I took the very painful decision that it was necessary to convey general information on atom-

ic energy and make sure it was taken seriously."

It must be understood that this statement was made by a man facing the most serious charge after murder. But the implication is nevertheless there. Nunn May decided that he was behaving correctly in making sure that the development of atomic energy was not confined to the USA because of his ideological sympathies with Communism. The evidence proved that he had gone much further than conveying general information, but it also revealed that he had not done so for financial gain, but for ideological reasons. All he received for his vital information was 700 dollars and two bottles of whisky.

But there were indications too that Nunn May had not been contacted by one of Zabotin's agents out of the blue. He denied knowing the names of any of the agents with whom he was involved, and the statement he made carefully avoided implicating Russia, Soviet officials in Canada, and the Communist parties of Britain, Canada and America. This appears to be the behaviour of the well-

390

trained and disciplined spy, not an absolute tyro in the techniques and ethics of espionage.

Nunn May was tried at the Central Criminal Court at the Old Bailey in London in March 1946. He pleaded guilty to the charge of having "communicated information to unauthorised persons likely to threaten the security of the State" and was sentenced to ten years' imprisonment.

In 1952, having earned full remission for good behaviour, he was released. He returned to his wife, Viennese-born Dr Hildegarde Broda, deputy medical officer of health at Cambridge, and his seven-year-old son. In January, 1962 he obtained the post of professor of Physics in the University of Ghana, West Africa, where he now lives with his family.

BIBLIOGRAPHY :

The Soviet Spy System — John Baker White (London, 1948).

The Atom Spies — Oliver Pilat (New York, 1952).

MAZERALL, Ned see under **Soviet Canadian Network.**

McCONE, John A. (Chief of the American Central Intelligence Agency, 1961-1965).

General John A. McCone was appointed to succeed Allen Dulles (q.v.) as Director of the Central Intelligence Agency (CIA) (q.v.), when Dulles retired in 1961. He held the post until 1965.

McCUAIG, William D. see under **Hirsch, Willi.**

McKENNA, Marthe (Allied agent, World War I).

Marthe McKenna's maiden-name was Cnockaert. She was born in 1892, the daughter of a Belgian farmer, who, at the outbreak of World War I was living at Westroosebeke, in southwest Belgium. In August 1914, Marthe, then a young woman of twenty-two, was on holiday at the farmhouse from the university where she was studying medicine.

The small but valiant Belgian army under its gallant commander-in-chief, King Albert, was quickly crushed under the weight of the Wehrmacht, and the Cnockaert family, father, mother and daughter — the three sons had joined the colours on the first day of the invasion — were plunged into the horrors which characterised the advance of the German armies. The Cnockaert farmhouse had been used by French troops as a strong-point. In its walls loopholes had been made for French rifles. But when the Germans arrived, they insisted that Cnockaert père had himself fired upon them, and ordered the house to be burned down and the farmer roasted alive in the cellars. The house was burnt, but the farmer managed to escape by breaking out of the cellars at the back of the house, which was unguarded.

As the line pushed forward, Westroosebeke became a rest base and medical clearing centre. Marthe joined three nuns who had come from Passchendaele and converted a large house in the village into an emergency Hospital in which they treated German and Allied wounded. But it was not long before the spy-mania of the Germans convinced them that the nuns were signalling to the Allies at night with lights in upper floor windows. Despite the good work the nuns were doing and the shortage of medical assistance, they were ordered to leave the village within three hours.

Marthe spoke excellent English and German, as well as French and Flemish, and had been so useful to the invaders as interpreter and nurse that she was allowed to stay. She was helped by eleven of her country-women, including her mother, and by the beginning of December 1914, these twelve were the only civilians left in the village.

It was not long, however, before Marthe's eleven assistants were also suspected of spying, and moved further back behind the lines. Once again, she was allowed to remain, and it was not until January 1915, when the Allies made a temporary advance, that the German Kommandant decided that Westroosebeke was no place for a woman, and sent her to Roulers with a glowing letter of recommendation to the authorities there. The Germans had appreciated her services both in the hospital and as an interpreter, and had shown her the greatest deference at all times. Now she was provided with a protective escort as far as the town, which is situated about fifteen miles northeast of Ypres, and had at that time about 27,000 inhabitants.

In Roulers Marthe found her mother, and they were offered hospitality in the house of a prominent grocer. Within a short time they found M Cnockaert, who had been taken away from Westroosebeke with all the men of the village soon after the arrival of the Germans and his escape from his proposed funeral pyre. Under an assumed name he had spent some time in prison for a minor offence, and since his release had been working for a farmer on the outskirts of Roulers, with whom he was lodging.

The morning after her arrival in Roulers, Marthe reported, as she had been instructed to do by the Westroosebeke Kommandant, to the hospital on the Menin Road which had been set up in the premises of Roulers College. Here she remained until her arrest two years later, towards the end of 1916.

About a fortnight after joining the staff of the hospital, she returned to her lodgings after night-duty, and was talking with her mother in the kitchen, when the back-door creaked on its hinges and slowly began to open. It was early morning and no one was about. The two women, a little frightened, swung round, and saw in the doorway an old friend, Lucelle Deldonck, whom they had given up for lost after her disappearance from Westroosebeke shortly after the village was captured.

Lucelle was middle-aged and grey-haired, and as she came in with her fingers to her lips, there were deep lines of exhaustion on her face. She revealed herself as a British agent, and before she left, she had enrolled Marthe for similar work. The young woman had had no hesitation in accepting her friend's suggestion. Telling Marthe that she would receive instructions in a day or two, Lucelle slipped away as secretly as she had come.

A few days later Mlle Cnockaert was handed a message by an aged vegetable woman, Canteen Ma, as she was called by the Germans and Belgians alike. She was a popular figure, and was allowed to wander freely in the town and countryside. This made her an admirable courier.

The message she passed to Marthe was a summons to an out-lying farm that evening. There she met Lucelle once more and from her received instructions.

In her position as nurse at the Roulers hospital, Marthe would come into contact with Germans of all ranks from whom she would be able to gather information about troop movements, military formations, artillery concentrations and positions, supply dumps and other important intelligence. She was to make her reports in a simple but efficient code, and hand them to another agent known as No 63.

To contact No 63 she was to go to an alley-way leading off the Grand' Place, and on the fifth window on the left down this alley she was to tap three times, pause, then tap twice again. She would receive her instructions for special missions from Canteen Ma.

Mlle Deldonck also told her of an Allied organisation of agents known as Safety-pin Men, so called because their means of identification was two white-metal safety-pins fastened to the under-side of the lapel of jacket or coat. If any agent identifying himself in this way ever came to her lodgings she was to persuade her landlady to shelter him for as long as he wished to remain. With a final warning to be on her guard against German counter-espionage agents, known as **Berlin Vampires.** Lucelle dismissed her.

Entirely without training of any sort, Marthe now embarked on a career of espionage which showed her to possess those natural qualities which are essential for a spy who is to hope for any success at all. That she was able to operate so successfully for nearly two years in these circumstances reveals her to be in the front-rank of agents of World War I, male or female. That she ultimately fell into a simple trap which a trained agent would have avoided, in no way detracts from her record. As soon as she knew that she was caught, she wondered at her own simplicity.

Admittedly, she had much to help her. Her skill as a nurse in the face of a grave shortage of medical staff, combined with her natural kindness, which prevented her from showing any rupugnance she might have felt at having to minister to her enemies, made her much appreciated by the Germans, who treated her as one of themselves There were incidents, of course, when attempts were made to induce her to have sexual intercourse with some of her patients and the German orderlies. But she resisted them all, even when she spent four days in Brussels with a colonel in an attempt to discover the date and time of a proposed visit of the All Highest to Roulers, which, after all her efforts, was cancelled at the last moment. She had many narrow escapes, too, when it seemed as if the enemy had really awakened at last to what she was doing.

Once she had initiated her flow of information, she kept it up with a regularity that, in the face of all her difficulties, was amazing. She allowed nothing to stand in the way of passing her reports. Often the demands on her courage would have daunted many a so-called strong male. The mental strain in which she constantly lived out to have broken her.

She very quickly developed a sense of intelligence value, and was soon volunteering information. The majority of this was received enthusiastically, but once when she came upon something really big, she knew the disappointment of rebuff, and of being ignored — because she was a woman.

In the middle of March 1915, M Cnockaert was offered a small café in the Grand' Place, the owner of which had decided to take his family to safety further back from the lines. Marthe encouraged her parents to buy the property, because she realised that it would widen the scope of her sources of information. So farmer Cnockaert transformed himself into café proprietor.

Not long after the family moved into the cafe, three German officers were billeted on them. They made an odd trio. Two of them were captains, one of whom was red-haired, large and florid, and known as Red Carl, and the

395

other a thin, middle-aged be-spectacled man called Teich-mann; while the third, Lieu-tenant Otto von Promft, was young, fair-haired and hand-some.

The two older men insisted upon sharing the same room, saying they had much to dis-cuss. They were an interesting and rather sinister couple, and had already roused Marthe's interest before Otto, who should have known better, since he was on counter-espionage detail him-self, let fall some unguarded remarks.

Almost simultaneously there arrived in Roulers a large number of metal containers which seemed to fit in with no known type of military operation. These containers were dumped outside Roulers and were under constant guard.

Two of Marthe's contacts were an Alsatian, Alphonse, who had been pressed into service as an ambulance driver, and Stephan, a Pole, a friend of Alphonse, who was employed as a clerk in the brigade orderly room. Both were Safety-pin Men.

Stephan was the more use-ful, since one of his duties was to open and sort all letters and other communica-tions and place them before the adjutant. But in this particular case it was Alphonse who brought the first clue concerning the mysterious containers. He had it from one of the men guarding the dump, that they held chlorine. Marthe dis-covered that the two captains billeted at the Café Carillon were chemists. She was quite certain that there was a con-nection between chlorine and chemists, but could not see the significance. Nevertheless, she forwarded the informa-tion via No 63 and received a reply to the effect that she would be better employed collecting information of troop movements and supply dumps. In other words, not to waste time in nebulous, even wild speculations.

Then Stephan brought the news that both Red Carl Sturme and Teichmann were taking a great interest in the weather. Sturme had even been up in a balloon to make observations.

One day while the three officers were out of the house, Marthe was able to study the weather charts which the captains had left in their room. Details of some of these together with a summary of the rest, she sent to the Allies, and again received a rebuff.

If they had taken notice of what they considered useless intelligence, especially a report on roughly made cotton-wool pads which had been issued to all Germans in the area, the subsequent tragedy might have been averted. As it was the first German gas attack on the Passchendaele Ridges on 22nd April, 1915, took the Allies completely by surprise.

For the rest of the year, and well into 1916, Marthe Cnockaert continued her spying and nursing. She had by this time been awarded the Iron Cross by the Germans for her devotion to duty, and held the respect of her superiors at the hospital. She supplied routine information about troop movements during all this time, and her intelligence regarding supply dumps led to many of them being destroyed. She located a secret telephone between a priest behind the Allied lines and German intelligence, and put it out of action single-handed. She had also helped many Allied soldiers to escape to Holland, often running considerable risks to do so, and supplying the necessary funds from her own pocket.

Many of her contacts were rounded up. No 63 disappeared, and so eventually did Canteen Ma. Lieutenant von Promft attempted to make her spy on British agents for the Germans — and had his brains blown out by Safety-pin Men as a result. By making the duty officer at Roulers airfield drunk, she was able to re-route his report on a new type of fighter aircraft, so that Stephan could copy it. All the time she was experiencing narrow escapes and it often seemed that they must end in her exposure.

An then came the day in October 1916 when Alphonse announced that he had been giving a good deal of thought to a supply dump situated in the town. In 1914 a shell had landed in the grounds of the hospital and left a large crater. Alphonse had noticed that at the bottom of the crater as though pierced through stone-work was a dark hole which he explored with several others, and found that it led to what seemed to be a secret passage, so long that it had no end.

Shortly after this, a wooden hut had been built over the crater, and he had forgotten about it, until one day not long ago, he had bought in a second-hand book-shop an old history of the town, which spoke of an ancient sewer that at one time ran through the town, emptying into the river. He believed that the underground passage he had found was this sewer.

From the description in the book, he was certain that the sewer ran under or near to the supply dump in the town, and if they could judge the distance correctly and open up the sewer within the bounds of the dump, they might be able to destroy the stores. Marthe was enthusiastic. She had a small supply of dynamite which she had taken from a dying British agent; and Alphonse could produce some fuse and detonators.

They laid their plans carefully. The chief difficulty, after they had calculated the distance from the hospital to the dump — a distance which

Alphonse judged to be about three kilometres—was to camouflage the hole which they would have to make inside the dump. When investigations were made after the explosion it would never do for there to be a gaping hole leading to an underground passage. The hole was therefore to be covered by a wooden lid which in turn was covered with wet concrete and earth.

They embarked on this perilous undertaking the following evening, and everything went well for them. It took them three strenuous evenings to complete their preparations. On the third evening they placed their bombs skilfully, lit the fuses and made their escape. When Marthe reached home, the dump was burning so fiercely that firemen could not control it.

The following morning Marthe discovered that she had lost her gold wrist-watch, which had her intials engraved on it!

Shortly afterwards a new matron and nursing staff arrived at the hospital. They proved to be antagonistic towards her, and this eventually led to her dismissal; which meant the curtailment of her sources of information.

It was towards the end of November that she fell into the trap.

She saw on the notice-board of the Kommandantuur in the Grand' Place a list of property purported to have been taken from a thief who had recently been caught. Among the items described, she recognised a description of her watch. Believing she must have lost it in the street and the thief had picked it up, she went next morning to claim it.

The German security forces moved at one. Neighbours came in throughout the morning to say that they had been closely questioned about her. At three o'clock agents arrived and searched her home, and found in her room two coded messages which she had concealed behind her wash-stand until she had time to pass them on.

She was arrested and charged with espionage. Several attempts were made to make he reveal her contacts, but she refused to speak. She even refused the services of a Prisoner's Friend at her court-martial; and only made a short speech justifying her actions.

She was condemned to death. As Sir Winston Churchill wrote in his foreword to her own account of her exploits, "By all the laws of war her life was forfeit. She did not dispute the justice of her fate."

But the doctors at Roulers hospital had pleaded for her, and because she had been awarded the Iron Cross for her services, the sentence was commuted to life imprisonment. She was released at the armistice after serving nearly two years.

And the watch that had been her downfall?

Some children playing on the site of the dump had discovered the camouflaged lid. By ill fortune a German agent happened to be passing at that moment. He lifted the lid and discovered the passage, and on exploring it found that it came out in the hospital grounds.

A little time later, a German soldier who was also exploring the passage came upon the watch near the opening at the dump end of the old sewer.

German counter-espionage

had been suspicious of Marthe for some time. The combination of the watch with M.C. engraved in the back and the entry to the sewer being in the hospital grounds, was too much of a coincidence. Nevertheless, the trap had been set, and she had walked into it. The discovery of the messages in her room finally sealed her doom.

She was awarded the French and Belgian Legions of Honour and the British — a mere mention in despatches. A few months after her release she married a British officer, who had been on the receiving end of her operation throughout all the time she carried on her amazing work.

BIBLIOGRAPHY :
I Was a Spy — Marthe Mc-Kenna (London, 1932).

MELEKH, Igor Y. see under **Hirsch, Willi.**

MEY, Pieter van der (Dutch agent, 16th century).

"If I take Alkmaar," wrote the Duke of Alva to King Philip II of Spain, his master, "I am resolved not to leave a single creature alive; the knife shall be put to every throat."

Though unaware of this threat, the Dutch defenders of the city knew only too well the reputation of the Spanish general, and though their hope of holding out successfully was slim, they determined to die dearly.

They had one ally, however; the sea, held back by the dykes so laboriously built to keep it out. If the sluices could be opened and the dykes breached, so that the country round the city was flooded, Alva would have to withdraw his army. But they could not carry out the plan without the consent of their neighbours, and to obtain it, they would have to send a messenger to William the Silent, their leader.

Such a messenger would have to pass through the Spanish lines. If caught, he would undoubtedly be killed.

A carpenter, called Pieter van der Mey, hearing what was required, volunteered to make the attempt. He was successful in getting through, but William had an idea that might avert much of the damage that wholesale flooding of the country would cause.

He wrote a dispatch to the

people of Alkmaar promising to open all the dykes for miles around. It was in eloquent terms; though all the crops and cattle would be lost, this would be a small sacrifice if it would save the people of Alkmaar from Alva's butchery. He gave the dispatch to Mey, telling him that he was to drop it as he passed back through the Spanish lines in a place where it must be found by the enemy. At the same time he sent orders to the Governor of the provinces, Sonoy, telling him to open one or two of the dykes which would flood the land in the neighbourhood of the Spanish lines.

The ruse worked. The dispatch fell into Alva's hands as intended; Sonoy opened the dykes; and Alva, believing that the Dutch leader intended to carry out his threat and flood the whole of the country, ordered his forces to retreat.

BIBLIOGRAPHY:
The Rise of the Dutch Republic — John Lothrop Motley (New York, 1856).

MfS (East German Ministry of State Security).

The Communist agitation and seditious activity against the Bundeswehr, (the West German Armed Forces) and the Federal Government's defence policy are carried out mainly by the 'Independent Departments' of the 'Political Administrations' of the Soviet Zone's Ministry of National Defence and Ministry of State Security. The methods used included the dissemination to a carefully selected group of people of counterfeit information concerning call-up and rejection, letters from Bundeswehr units, certificates, NATO literature, etc. Usually only experts can tell the letter-head, stamp and signature from the real thing. The Soviet Zone's Ministry for State Security and the secret Military Intelligence Service (Administration for Co-ordination) have established their head offices in East Berlin and have stationed there a staff totalling more than 4,000.

Since the inception in 1953 this very large apparatus for espionage and intelligence has developed into an instrument of those in power in the Soviet Zone, whose tentacles stretch out far beyond the Soviets themselves. At the end of 1953, the most efficient and best-trained collaborators in this organisation — which is mainly drawn on for Intelligence tasks in the Soviet Zone — were drawn together in one organisation. Today within the framework of the Chief Administration Reconnaissance they form the cadres of the foreign espionage service in the MfS — Ministry of State Security. Since 1st November 1957, the head of the Ministry of State Security has been Colonel-General Erich Mielke. He has repeatedly claimed to be the murderer of the Berlin Police Captains Anlauf and Lenk in 1931.

Under the Ministry of State Security are 16 Bezirk (administrative regions) which in turn have more than 220 Kreis (Administrative districts) subordinated to them. The MfS has a full time staff of about 13,500, of whom more than 3,000 are active in East Berlin alone.

The main offices are situated in a group of buildings on Normannenstrasse, Berlin-Lichtenberg. It also maintains numerous offices in other parts of East Berlin.

Headed by Major-General Markus Wolke the Chief Administration Reconnaissance has the task of penetrating particularly important ministries and other public bodies and offices in the Federal Republic and the other west European countries, and of collecting "secret political intelligence" issued by governments hostile to the East German Government, apart from gathering general up-to-date information.

The emphasis of these operations is on institutions in the Federal Republic though other penetration operations are directed towards those of the other Nato Powers.

The East German MfS is estimated to employ 10,000 agents. The HUA (Chief Administration for Intelligence) has 800 personnel in East Germany and an estimated 20,000 agents in West Germany.

BIBLIOGRAPHY:

East Berlin: Main Centre of Agitation and Sedition.
(West German Embassy, London, 1962).

MGB see under **Russian Intelligence Organisation.**

MI5.

The branch of the British intelligence organisation responsible for internal security and counter-espionage at home. Officially it is known as the Security Service. Its Director is directly responsible to the Prime Minister. MI5 has no powers of arrest. (See SPECIAL BRANCH).

MI5 came into being at 10 a.m. on Monday, 23rd August, 1909, and consisted for the first year of its existence of one man, Captain Vernon Kell. It was first known as the Special Intelligence Bureau, and was formed expressly on a suggestion of Kell's prompted by the knowledge that German spies were operating in England and that there was no machinery for counteracting their activities.

From those early days, MI5 expanded until it costs £7½ million a year to run. Kell remained Director — later he was promoted Major-General Sir Vernon — until 1924 officially, but according to his widow (he died in 1942) he was at the head of the department until 1940.

BIBLIOGRAPHY :

MI5 — John Bulloch (London, 1963).

MI6.

The branch of British intelligence which carries out espionage all over the world. It is what foreigners refer to when they use the phrase the British Secret Service. It is the most secret intelligence organisation in the world.

Historically speaking, it is a direct descendant of Sir Francis Walsingham's (q.v.) intelligence service in the reign of Elizabeth I and of Daniel Defoe's intelligence service, though Defoe's service carried out its operations mostly within the confines of the British Isles, and had MI5's function of protecting internal security.

MICRODOT.

The invention of microphotography, i.e. photographing objects on very small negatives, brought to espionage a very welcome innovation in the realm of passing secret documents. Up to this time, ordinary photography had been used, which, owing to both the cumbersome equipment required and the necessarily large size of the negative was not satisfactory method from the security point of view.

The use of the microdot is microphotography taken to the very limits of smallness. The microdot-making equipment is small and easily concealed, while the resulting negative is so tiny that it can be used to "dot" an "i" in a harmless letter without being detected.

MIXED BUREAU, The.

The Mixed Bureau was a combined operation by British and French intelligence and counter-intelligence. It had its headquarters at Folkestone, on the Kent coast opposite the Pas de Calais, and its function was to screen all refugees fleeing from the German advance into Belgium and Northern France. By skilful interrogation of the diverse crowds who passed through its corridors it obtained much useful intelligence. It also kept a look-out for potential agents, and one or two of its protegés became spies of note, e.g. Louise de Bettignies.

MIASOIEDOV, Commandant Serge Nicolaivits (World War I).

Miasoiedov was personal assistant to the Russian Minister of War, Soukhomlikov, who entered into secret communication with the Germans during World War I. Miasoiedov was also the lover of Madame Soukhomlikov.

He came of an aristocratic Russian family, but was a born rogue. He joined the Russian cavalry on leaving school, but had not been long in the army when he was involved in a card scandal and dismissed from his regiment. From that time on he led the life of an adven'urer. He joined the gendarmerie, and was given the rank of captain at Wierzbolovo, in Poland. There he quickly became the protector of a band of Jewish smugglers, whom he deserted after a time to set up his own smuggling organisation while still retaining his official appointment as commander of the Wierzbolovo post. In three years he had acquired a considerable fortune through these activities, and began to live up to his reputation as a millionaire. He was a handsome man, and the most noble ladies of Russia seemed to have fought for the doubtful honour of becoming his mistress.

In 1913 he sought and was granted an interview with Kaiser Wilhelm, during which he undertook, in return for a considerable reward, to spy on Russia on Germany's behalf. His offer was accepted. His next step was to place himself in such a position that he could learn Russia's military secrets.

Since he never did anything by half measures, he seduced the beautiful young wife of General Soukhomlinov, Russian Minister of War. When they married she was twenty, the General was sixty-three. Through his mistress's good offices, Maisoiedov was appointed to the personal staff of the Minister, and soon became his right-hand man, and the keeper not only of his chief's secrets but of Russia's as well. All the latter he passed to the Germans, and later encouraged Soukhomlinov to enter into a secret agreement with them.

MIYAGI, Yotoku see under **Sorge, Richard.**

MIYAZAKI, Toshio see under **Thompson, Harry Thomas.**

MOE, Thorvald see under **Rinnan, Henry Oliver.**

MOLENAAR (Dutch Agent, World War II). see under **Giskes, Col H. J.**

MOLODY, K. T. real name of **LONSDALE, Gordon** see under **Portland Spy Case, The.**

MONITORS.

This is a very specialised technique of intercepting radio-telephone conversations, even though the two persons speaking are using a scrambling device, which makes a nonsense of vocal sounds though the voices come through the telephone receivers quite normally.

The Abwehr (q.v.) had a monitoring station at Brest, in France, during World War II which was able to "monitor" most of the Churchill-Roosevelt conversations.

MONTGALLIARD, Comte Maurice de. (19th century French double-agent).

405

Even Montgalliard's personal appearance was revolting. He had a Bergerac nose, a chin like the toe of a boot, one shoulder higher than the other, and a hump on his back.

He had a proper claim to the aristocratic "de", though his family name was Roques and the title was assumed. He began life as an officer, but did not care for campaigning, and resigned his commission after a longish tour of duty in Martinique. He married the goddaughter of the absentee Bishop of Bordeaux, in whose small circle of sycophants he enrolled himself. After his marriage he made progress in his ambition to play a part in the political activities of France.

He became a Royalist secret agent, had a part in planning Louis XVI's flight and spent a good deal of his fortune on behalf of the imprisoned Queen. His name was on the list of proscribed aristocrats, but after a visit to England he returned to France in safety, and this could only mean that he was now working for the Revolution.

After further visits to Austria and London, he returned to the Continent and met the Prince of Condé, commander of the remnants of the Royalist army. Condé's forces consisted of about five thousand French volunteers, drawn up on the right bank of the Rhine. Penniless, the Prince relied on Austria for a parsimonious financial support which practically accomplished the extinction of his army through starvation. Opposed to it on the left bank of the Rhine were the even more tattered armies of the Revolution under the command of the famous soldier, Charles Pichegrue, among whose pupils at the Brienne military academy had been a certain Bonaparte. Pichegrue had been a divisional commander since 1793, and in the two years between then and January 1795 he had gained a reputation in the field by his victories over the Dutch allies of Austria.

It was Montgalliard's bright suggestion to Condé that he should attempt to buy over Pichegrue. The money to do this would be obtained from the English who had already expressed their willingness to support any opposition to the

Revolution.

Condé agreed, and not only was the English promise to provide the money for the purchase of Pichegrue honoured, but they actually showered Condé with gold to an amount which allowed him to revictual his forces, settle arrears of pay, and still leave a balance of half a million livres and open a credit account in his name to the tune of three and a half million.

Montgalliard was not so foolhardy as to suggest himself for the attempt on Pichegrue's virtue. Instead he chose a deputy, the Swiss bookseller Fauche-Borel (q.v.) who agreed to undertake the mission on the promise of a reward of a million livres, the directorship of the Royal Presses, the Inspectorship-General of the Libraries and the Order of St Michael when Louis XVIII returned to his throne.

Fauche-Borel was a tyro in such espionage matters, but he had a natural flair for the work. But he was also fortified by vast sums of money provided by the English chargé d'affaires in Switzerland, William Wickham, who was in charge of British intelligence in southern Europe. Pichegrue, however, proved incorruptible and was relieved of Fauche-Borel's importunities by the issue of a warrant by the Directory for the latter's arrest as a spy for the emigré and foreign armies of France.

Fauche-Borel believed that Montgalliard was responsible for the exposure of his rôle, and as it happens, he was right. When Montgalliard had put the suggestion to Condé, it had been his intention to control the English bribe to Pichegrue, and to deduct during its passage through his hands, a substantial commission. Fauche-Borel, however, had exceeded his instructions from Montgalliard, and was in direct contact with the English, who were giving him money in large amounts without the services of an intermediary, which meant no commission for Montgalliard.

Seeing that he was receiving no recompense, Montgalliard promptly transferred his services to the other side. His first step was to betray Fauche-Borel, and in so doing compromise Pichegrue which he did by the aid of forged documents. Pichegrue

407

was removed from his command.

Making his way to Venice Montgalliard assured the French minister there of his desire and intention henceforward to serve France. He then went to d'Antraigues, Louis XVIII's representative, and declared to him his devotion to the Bourbon cause. But he needed money and the only way now open to him to obtain it was to blackmail Condé

Announcing that he was about to abandon politics for ever and return to France, he suggested that it would be dangerous for him to do so with Condé's secret correspondence to him during the Pichegrue negotiations in his pocket. Condé agreed to pay him twelve thousand francs for the letters. Montgalliard pocketed the Prince's draft for that amount and also the papers which were the object of the agreement.

Fauche-Borel, temporarily unemployed, set out in pursuit and caught up with Montgalliard in an hotel in Neufchatel. The meeting was a stormy one, but Fauche-Borel recovered the papers and sent them triumphantly to Louis XVIII.

Not long afterwards, Joseph Fouché, Napoleon's chief of intelligence, (q.v.) came into Montgalliard's life. By 1810 the **soi disant** count was in prison for debt, and it looked as if he would remain in prison for the rest of his life. Desperate, he wrote to Fouché offering his services in any capacity if only he were set free and his subsistence assured. Fouché arranged matters and Montgalliard was granted an income of 14,000 francs a year, which he earned by political spying.

With the Restoration of the Bourbons he was once more placed in a predicament from which he tried to extricate himself by insisting that he had been Napoleon's captive and that at heart he had always been a Royalist. But the Royalists did not believe him, and thereafter he faded out of the picture.

His fate during his last years, and the circumstances of his death history does not reveal.

BIBLIOGRAPHY :
Two Royalist Spies of The French Revolution — G. Lenotre (London, undated).

Souvenirs du Comte de Mont-galliard — Clément de Lacroix (Paris, 1859).

MORASAWA, Chiyo (Japanese agent in Central America between wars).

In 1937 there were no less than forty-seven Japanese barbers in Panama City and eight in Colón.

Panama City is at the Pacific entrance to the Panama Canal; Colón is at the Atlantic entrance.

In Panama City they were concentrated round the highly select and exorbitantly expensive avenida Central and the calle Carlos A. Mendoza. There were so many of them that they formed a union, the Barbers' Association, to which no barber who was not Japanese was admitted, though Japanese fishermen were made welcome. The meetings were held in a second-floor room at calle Carlos A. Mendoza 58.

The founder of the Barbers' Association was a barber's assistant named A. Sonada. The Japanese consul in Panama, Tetsuo Umemoto, attended the meetings regularly, and he and Sonada sat side by side, facing the rest of the

members. Sonada's position could be partially gauged from the fact that the consul never sat until the barber's assistant was seated. But whenever one other member was present, neither Umemoto nor Sonada would sit until he was sitting down. This man's name was T. Takano, and he owned a very small business in a less wealthy district, at avenida B 10.

Another important member of the Association was Katarino Kabayama, a soft-spoken, mild-mannered businessman in late middle-age, who lived at calle Colón 11. Kabayama had not always been a businessman. In his younger days he had been a barefoot, tattered fisherman. But even then, when he had gone aboard a Japanese warship visiting Panama in his tatters, he had been piped aboard, while the assembled crew had come to a smart salute. When he had left, after a two-hour interview with the commander he had been piped over the side. Then he had rowed back to his fishing-boat.

Apart from the barbers' shops, there were other Japanese-run establishments.

Rather out of the ordinary was a shirt-shop which used to be on calle 10A, between the avenida Herrera and the avenida Amador Guerrero. The owner was an attractive oriental lady who called herself Lola Osawa.

Lola's real name was Chiyo Morasawa, and she had arrived at Balbao from Yokohama as long ago as 24th May 1929 in the liner **Anvo Maru.** As soon as she landed she disappeared from the public view, and it was not until a year later that she reappeared at the other end of the canal, in her shirt-shop.

Lola's husband lived with her in rooms over the shop. He had entered Panama illegally, for his passport contained no visa. He gave out that he was a merchant. In fact, he was a reserve officer in the Japanese navy. He and Lola specialised in photographing all objects of military importance in the canal zone, and they operated without interruption for more than ten years.

BIBLIOGRAPHY :

Honorable Spy — J. L. Spivak (New York, 1939).

410

MOSCOWITZ, Miriam see under **Soviet American Network.**

MOUGEOT, Jacques
(French agent, World War I).

Jacques Mougeot was the son of a former Minister of Posts. Wounded early in the war, he had just left hospital when he was summoned to the Ministry of War and asked to go to Switzerland and there organise an "Information Service" to spy on the activities of German agents in that country.

Mougeot accepted the assignment though he had had no espionage training. He set up his headquarters in the Château de Bellegarde at Thonon-les-Bains, on Lake Geneva, and there surrounded himself with Frenchmen who, to the local population, appeared to be refugees from military service. Soon Mougeot had established an organisation which was able to report in detail the activities and intentions of the numerous German agents operating in Switzerland.

All his agents were amateurs, which makes his achievements all the more remarkable. Among them was a talented organist, a former Sous-Préfet, a businessman from Metz, and a well-known French manufacturer.

Unfortunately his wounds had seriously undermined his health, and Jacques Mougeot died shortly after the Armistice.

MUNDAY, Anthony (Elizabethan playwright and agent)

Anthony Munday, a minor Elizabethan playwright and actor, entered Walsingham's secret service and was sent to Rome in 1578 to spy upon the English seminary there. On his return the following year he was appointed to the staff of Topcliffe, the chief official torturer, as an interrogator.

MUNSINGER AFFAIR, The.

Victor Spencer was born in England, but emigrated to Canada with his parents as a child. He grew up into something of a social misfit, a lonely man who flirted with Communism, and wanted above all else to ease the lot of mankind. He was, however, a failure at almost everything, even Communism, for he was expelled from the Candian Commu-

nist Party in 1946.

He worked in the Post Office at Vancouver, and it was there, in 1956 that he was first contacted by Soviet intelligence. A year or two later he became a KGB agent under the persuasion of the Resident Director, Lev Burdiukov. Between 1960 and 1963 he flew to Ottawa seven times for meetings with Burdiukov and two other KGB agents, A. E. Bytchkov and Rem Krassilnikov, both of whom were attachés at the Soviet embassy.

In 1960, the KGB gave Spencer the assignment of visiting cemeteries in Canada and taking photographs of tombstones. From the inscriptions on the tombstones the KGB produced false documents for their "illegals" — that is, agents who operated under false identities.

In time his activities attracted the attention of the Canadian counter-espionage authorities. Under their interrogation he revealed the details of his work for the KGB. By this time he was seriously ill with cancer, so he was not brought to trial. He was, however, dismissed from the Post Office and deprived of his pension rights.

Though this might have appeared to be an unusually lenient treatment of a traitor, the Canadian Conservative Party attacked the Liberal government on the grounds that it had mishandled Spencer's case and violated his rights.

In retaliation, the Minister of Justice declared that several Ministers of the previous Conservative Government had been intimate with a beautiful East German blonde named Gerda Munsinger, who, the Minster claimed, was a Soviet spy. From this announcement a tremendous scandal blew up, especially when Gerda Munsinger was discovered in Munich by the **Toronto Star,** to whom she admitted that she had been on rather more than friendly terms with various Canadian Ministers.

The Conservatives attempted to defend themselves by charging the Minister of Justice with the intention of starting a Communist witchhunt on McCarthy lines. Whereupon Prime Minister Lester Pearson ordered a Commission of Inquiry to be set up to probe the affair. As a result, Gerda Munsinger's background was brought to light.

She had been born in East Germany, at Königsberg, where her father taught in a Communist Party school. In 1947 she was recruited into Soviet espionage, and sent to West Germany to operate. In 1949 she was arrested by the West German police, to whom she admitted that she had spied for the Russians. In 1952, she applied for a Canadian visa. The Canadian authorities refused her application on the grounds that she was a self-confessed spy and "a common prostitute, a petty thief and a smuggler".

Undaunted, she married a sergeant in the US Army called Michael Munsinger, but the United States also refused her entry on the same grounds as the Canadian authorities had. Munsinger divorced her in 1954.

In the following year, somehow she managed to slip into Canada undetected. In September Pierre Sevigny, Associate Minister of National Defence made her acquaintance in Montreal where she was working as a call-girl, and entered into "illicit sexual relations" with her. The Minister of Trade, George Hees, also had a brief contact with her of the same kind.

In 1960, sponsored by Sevigny, Gerda Munsinger applied for Canadian citizenship. Sevigny naturally had no inkling that Gerda Munsinger was in fact Gerda Heseler, who had earlier been refused entry into the country. The Royal Mounted Police, however, did discover this important fact, and informed Prime Minister Diefenbaker of it. Diefenbaker summoned Sevigny and told him that he must cease his association with the woman forthwith, not on moral grounds, but on grounds of national security. Nevertheless he did not remove Sevigny from his post.

When these facts were made public, reaction was nationwide, and the scandal reached almost the proportions of the Profumo affair in Britain, in 1963. Victor Spencer, who had been the fuse which had touched it off, died while the Commission was sitting.

BIBLIOGRAPHY :

Report of the Commission of Inquiry Into Matters Relating to One Gerda Munsinger (Ottawa, 1966).

MUNSINGER, Gerda see under **Munsinger Affair, The.**

MUUS, Fleming B. (Danish Resistance leader, World War II).

From the beginning Danish Resistance suffered from lack of good agent-material. The men available were courageous in the extreme, but courage alone is not enough to keep a Resistance organisation in existence. Consequently, numbers of agents were constantly being caught, and this, unfortunately, included the leaders.

In March 1943, there arrived on the Danish underground scene a new leader, Fleming B. Muus. Muus was quite different material from that which, for the most part, had come SOE's way so far. He possessed a brilliant and flexible mind, and outstanding courage. Denmark should never forget the debt she owes him for his work between March 1943 and December 1944; a remark which will be amplified later.

With Muus and his party was dropped the first material ever to be sent to Denmark, with the exception of a minute

413

quantity delivered for a proposed operation against the ferries in early 1942. The reception was arranged by a wealthy Jutland landowner named Junke. who lived near Randers.

Muus at once began to display his flair for organisation. Admittedly he was more favourably placed than earlier leaders had been. He came with a programme which met Danish Home Front (the central Resistance organisation), and the Home Front responded as they had always wished to respond.

Setting up his headquarters in Copenhagen, Muus applied himself vigorously to his task. Among the most formidable of his achievements was his winning over The Princes to the principle of sabotage, against which they had steadfastly set their faces from the moment of their inception. They were, in fact, a purely intelligence-gathering organisation.

He also made contact with the Danish police with the satisfactory outcome that thereafter he received advance information of intended German moves against Resistance. He was then able to take suitable evasive action.

Under Muus's leadership the SOE network grew with amazing speed. Reception points were set up all over the country, and reception teams were trained. Men who never before had had any connection with Resistance, were now drawn into it, and so increased the potential of the organisation.

In the autumn of 1944 Muus was compromised to such an extent that he had to leave the country. His place as leader was taken over by Ole Lipmann.

In January 1945, Muus and his wife arrived in London. He was received by King George VI and made much of by the SOE chiefs. However, like many successful men, he had made a number of enemies, and they now began to plan his disgrace.

Such was the influence of these men that they persuaded SOE to call Muus to account for every penny which had been sent him for his network in Denmark. The accounts he did produce failed to satisfy auditors, especially as the sum unaccounted for was a fairly large one.

The implications — though

totally unfounded were obvious — that Muus had applied the missing kroner to his own use. After the war a Danish commission was set up to inquire into the affair. Clearly Muus had not kept his books meticulously; how can a Resistance leader working in constant danger of his life be expected to do so? For this he was reprimanded, but the inquisition found no evidence at all of misappropriation. Nevertheless there was a certain element of scandal attached to the affair, and alone among the Danish leaders Muus received no recognition for his work.

It is a sad commentary on human nature that a man's immeasurable acts of patriotism and courage should be allowed to be obscured by petty jealousy to the extent that he is deprived by an unjustified slur of his justifiable place in the history of his country.

BIBLIOGRAPHY :

Inside SOE — E. H. Cookridge (London, 1966).

NELSON, Steve see under **Soviet American Network.**

NETWORK.

An espionage network consists of a number of cells. A cell consists of three or more agents none of whom knows more than one other agent in the cell. Each cell has a chief who issues orders from the network chief to and gathers reports from the other agents in the cell.

If there are more than three members in a cell, which happens only rarely, the cell chief may use a cut-out or courier to collect reports or issue orders. Similarly, the network chief employs a cut-out as a go-between between himself and his cell chiefs. No cell knows of the existence of any other cells in the network.

This arrangement means that the fewest number of people in a network and cell know one another, and is designed as a security measure. If an agent is captured and the organisation of the cells and the network has been effi-

ciently carried out he cannot compromise more than one, or at most two, of his fellow agents.

Besides his cut-out man, the network chief has the services of a radio operator.

A network is set up to cover a certain area. A cell is established to investigate one of the various intelligence interests in that area. The cell members are chosen for their expert knowledge of the subject they are required to investigate. How they carry out their assignments is a matter for them to decide.

NICOLAI, Colonel Walter (Director of Abwehr, World War I).

Colonel Walter Nicolai is the most famous of Abwehr directors, after, probably Admiral Canaris. He was appointed to the post shortly before World War I, and retained it until he was replaced by Colonel Gempp (q.v.) in 1921.

According to Captain Ellis M. Zacharias, deputy director of US Naval Intelligence, contemporary with Nicolai, the Colonel "was a ruthless and unscrupulous spy-master, devoted to Secret Service work with the unconditional devotion of an ascetic monk."

Despite the importance of his post, Nicolai, who was a General Staff major when appointed, was never promoted above the rank of Lieutenant-colonel.

BIBLIOGRAPHY :
The German Secret Service —
Walter Nicolai (London, 1928).

NIEMEYER (Dutch agent, World War II) see under **Giskes, Col H. J.**

NIGHTINGALE, Matthias see under **Soviet Canadian Network.**

NKRUMAH, Kwame (Exiled President of Ghana).
With the help of the Chinese, Nkrumah established an espionage school in his home in Accra, where potential agents from the Ivory Coast, Upper Volta, Congo and Togo were taught espionage and sabotage techniques. The Chinese instructors were supplied by the School for Revolutionary Techniques in Nanking, while Algerian instructors were sent from Marna to demonstrate the practical applica-

tion of revolutionary techniques. Nkrumah died early in 1972.

NKVD see under **Russian Intelligence Organisation.**

NORTH POLE, Operation see under **Giskes, Col H. J.**

NOWAK, Herbert see under **Linse, Dr, The Kidnapping of.**

NOWOLNY, Major Karl see under **Gerson, Capt V. V.**

NSA — **National Security Agency (American).**
The NSA engages in top secret cryptography and electronic espionage. Into their headquarters are filtered the secret messages from agents the world over and reports from secret interception stations which function day and night to pick up communist messages. The NSA headquarters are at Fort Meade, Maryland 20755, 22 miles from Washington DC, in a mass of concrete and steel buildings behind tall, barbed wire fences, guarded by armed marines.

The National Security Agency is the USA's most

417

secret organisation and it is correspondingly difficult to obtain much information about it. The President of the United States is solely responsible for **all** security, both internal and external. Although there are advisers and councils, the ultimate responsibility is his alone. The late President Kennedy often quoted :

Bull-fight critics ranked in rows
Crowd the enormous plaza full;
But only one man is there who knows,
And he's the man who fights the bull.

In 1947, as a provision of the National Security Coun-President Truman established the National Security Council. The members included the President as chairman, the Vice-President, the Secretaries of State and Defense, and other officials. Although the 1947 Act had provided a unified defense department, the Joint Chiefs of Staff were not members of the Council but were frequently invited to attend meetings. In 1952, when Eisenhower became President, one of his first

acts was to put into operation an organisation that would be responsible to the Council for providing all the information that body could want. This organisation was NSA.

The official statement issued at the time of the U-2 trial contained the following:

In accordance with the National Security Act of 1947, the President has put into effect since the beginning of his administration, directives to gather by every possible means information required to protect the US and the Free World against surprise attack and to make the necessary preparations for defense.

Under Eisenhower, the National Security Council became the maker of policy definitions, but Kennedy thought the whole apparatus too cumbersome and called smaller meetings.

The official constitution of the NSA is as follows : it is an agency under the Department of Defense, under the direct control and authority of the Secretary of Defense who is the Executive Agent. It was formed for the per-

formance of highly specialised technical functions in support of the intelligence activities of the US, with two primary missions :
intelligence/information security

The NSA's functions are as follows :

1. To outline plans of security for the US.
2. Organising, operating and managing the activities and facilities for the production of intelligence information.
3. Organising and co-ordinating the research and engineering activities of the US Government in support of agencies with assigned functions.
4. Regulating certain communications in support of Agency missions.

The NSA works very closely with all other government departments particularly the Transportation and Communication Department.

The NSA features in several books about spies and individual cases. There can be no doubt that they were behind the U-2 flight and working on the same pre-mise it is possible to conclude they had more than a passing interest in the recent Pueblo Affair. An official statement issued at the time of the U-2 affair, declared :

Programmes have been developed and put into operation including extensive aerial surveillance by unarmed civilian aircraft, normally of a peripheral character but on occasion by penetration.

In 1960 two technicians defected from the NSA.

In 1958 a very ordinary man called Jack Dunlap was posted to the NSA as a chauffeur. He gradually amassed large amounts of money and although he joined the NSA boat club (rather an exclusive set-up for senior personnel) with his own speed boat, no one questioned his source of income. He visited his 'book-keeper' every week and returned loaded with money. In answer to all remarks he said he had been left money in a will. It was not until the possibility of his posting somewhere else, possibly abroad, made Dunlap resign from the army and re-apply for his post as a civilian that anyone became suspicious. Security tests revealed him as a risk but before anything could be proven against him Dunlap attempted to take his own life and succeeded at the second try by sitting in his car, the engine running, and a hose pipe running from the exhaust, on July 22, 1963. Although a suicide and a traitor he was buried with full military honours.

The NSA does not seem to have held much appeal for novelists. Their work would seem to be too technical and too backroom to have mass appeal. They are the body which makes use of information acquired by agents in the field. They do not appear to send out or recruit agents themselves, and hence lack the glamour of other security agencies, such as the CIA.

BIBLIOGRAPHY :

US Government Organisation Manual **The Great Spy Ring** — N. Lucas (London, 1966).

OGPU see under **Russian Intelligence Organisation.**

OKURA, Otojiro and **OKURA, Shibenobu** see under **Furusawa, Dr Takashi.**

ONDEDEI, Bishop of Fréjus (Cardinal Mazarin's spymaster).

When the Italian Cardinal Mazarin succeeded Cardinal Richelieu as chief minister of France in 1642, he replaced Richelieu's director of espionage, Father Joseph du Tremblay (q.v.) with his own favourite agent, a man called Ondedei. Ondedei was not of the same calibre as du Tremblay. He based his system more on the defensive principle; by which is meant that his espionage was directed more to the protection of the Cardinal than for the prosecution of his policy. Nevertheless, it played a leading role in firmly establishing the Bourbons on the French throne.

OPPENHEIM, Major G. (Chief of British Intelligence, Rotterdam, World War I).

Oppenheim was consul at Frankfurt-am-Main prior to 1914, where he made many friends. When war broke out, he was transferred to Rotterdam, and was able to convince the Germans that he was remaining in the service of the British only to betray them. He ingratiated himself with the German Minister at The Hague, Rosen, who arranged with him that all his important official communications should be carried as far as the frontier by King's Messenger (the official British government couriers) on the grounds that they would thus be safe from the prying eyes of British agents who were extremely active in Holland. The volume of important intelligence which Oppenheim gathered by means of this arrangement was considerable.

As chief of the Rotterdam office, Oppenheim was in charge of British networks in Belgium and northern France. One of his main concerns was getting his agents' reports safely through the frontier zone, which was always

421

heavily guarded. For some time he resorted to a somewhat macabre method.

Under ancient treaties, a tiny area of Belgian territory, known as Baer-le-Duc, is enclosed completely in Dutch territory — a Belgian island in a Dutch sea — in the province of Brabant-Septentrional. It, therefore, could not be occupied by the Germans during the war, without violating Dutch neutrality. This isolation of Baer-le-Duc gave Oppenheim his idea.

When a Belgian died in a village near the Belgian-Dutch frontier it was suggested to the deceased's family that they should seek permission from the Germans to arrange for burial in Bar-le-Duc. Many families agreed, for they patriotically preferred for their loved ones to be buried in ground not under the German heel.

As a rule the Germans made no difficulty about granting permission, on two conditions — that the family deposited a large sum of money which would guarantee their return to Belgium, and that the coffin should be examined by a German doc-

tor before it was taken across the frontier.

This latter condition called for some ingenuity in using the coffins as receptacles for intelligence reports, nevertheless, over a period of two years Oppenheim successfully used this method of transport.

Unfortunately, the Germans were tipped off about what was going on, and one evening their counter-espionage raided a house in Anvers just as a corpse was being placed in its coffin, under the supervision of a German doctor. They searched the coffin thoroughly, but without success. Then they turned their attention to the corpse itself. They did this so successfully that the tube containing the reports which had been thrust down the dead man's throat was found. Thereafter burials at Bar-le-Duc were forbidden.

OSLO SQUAD, The (Norwegian Resistance, World War II).

On 2nd May, 1945, Oslo, the capital of Norway, seethed with rumours, and the people could contain their excitement only with difficulty.

422

For five years the Norwegians had suffered the degradation and perils of German Occupation. Now it seemed as if Liberation, longed for, though sometimes despaired of, was only a matter of days. Nevertheless, the occupation forces were still in control and appeared to be quite unperturbed by what was happening to their comrades in other parts of Europe. Their commander had let it be known that whatever happened elsewhere he and his men would fight on in Norway.

When the Allied spring offensive promised success from its beginning, the leaders of the Norwegian Home Front began to prepare themselves for the role which had been allotted to them. But besides maintaining order until the Allies and the King and government-in-exile arrived there were other duties to be performed, among them making sure that traitors and war criminals did not escape the penalties of their treachery and barbarity.

In the archives of the Department of Justice and of the Police Headquarters was all the evidence. The Germans were certain to destroy this evidence before they eventually capitulated; it was the obvious and sensible thing to do. The Central Leadership of the Home Front, therefore, decided that this must be prevented, and put their views before one of their groups of saboteurs, the Oslo Squad.

The Oslo Squad was led by a young man called Gunnar Sonsteby, who worked under the cover-names of Kjakan, or No 24. Sonsteby made contact with the Secretary of the Department of Justice, and discussed with him ways and means of removing the archives to the safe-keeping of the Home Front.

It was clear from the beginning that the operation would be one of the most difficult the Oslo Squad had so far undertaken. The archives weighed two tons, and the removal of so much paper would require the use of a lorry, which, parked outside the main entrance — the most suitable place for the purpose — would be within fifty yards of Police Headquarters.

Undeterred by this, Sonsteby made his preparations. A few days after the meeting with the Secretary of the Department of Justice, he approached a constable who was a member of the Police Headquarters guard. From him he discovered that the same guard was also responsible for protecting the Department of Justice. The precautions taken by the guard were very effective. The main doors were securely locked and bolted. Inside was a guardroom where, within easy reach of the guard, was an alarm which alerted the whole building and Police Headquarters. Patrols were constantly on the move outside.

The Home Front had especially requested that there should be no bloodshed. To enable Sonsteby to acquiesce with this request, the official in charge of the guard duties was able to arrange for two men willing to co-operate to be on duty at the time of the attack.

On this basis a plan was drawn up whereby three men were to enter the Department of Justice and put out of action the porter and any of the officials who might be working overtime. At a signal the van carrying the men responsible for the operation

on Police Headquarters was to drive through the gates. From men in the two Departments, Sonsteby's squad knew the exact location of the papers. Two hours would be sufficient to complete the operation if all went well.

At six o'clock on the evening of 2nd May, Sonsteby, armed with passes supplied by the State's Police, went to the door of the Department of Justice in Akers Street, and was shown into the guardroom. The two guards were told what was happening and knew what to do.

With three of Sonsteby's men dressed as policemen, and accompanied by the Secretary of the Department of Justice, they went to the caretaker's quarters and told him that they were searching the building. The man could understand that, but he could not so readily comprehend why he and his family had to be placed under guard. In the other offices they found three officials working overtime, and them they also escorted to the guard-room. The Secretary then opened cupboards and drawers with his keys, revealing the files.

The signal was given, and a

424

van bearing the name of **Kristiania Express Office,** a removals company, drove up to the entrance of Police Headquarters. From it jumped six men led by two of Sonsteby's best lieutenants, Olsen and Houlder, who made their way quickly inside.

Two policemen on duty at the telephone switchboard surrendered without protest, and the six men then split into groups of three. One group took over the switchboard, while the other went in search of an armed guard known to be patrolling the third floor, who must be prevented from raising the alarm. When they found him he was too nervous to speak, let alone shout.

Within three-quarters of an hour the two tons of paper were loaded into the van, and as they could not open a half-ton safe belonging to the chief official of the Police Department, they trundled it noisily down from the second floor and into the van, which then drove on to the Department of Justice.

There Sonsteby and his party had already removed another half-ton of documents and two smaller safes

into the corridor. These, too, were loaded with all speed into the van.

In the meantime, three other men had visited the chief official of the Police Department and tricked him into handing over the keys of his safe. Within ten minutes of the completion of the operation the contents of the safe were being added to the other archives.

If this was one of the most audacious operations of Norwegian Resistance, it was also the last important one. For within a week the German commander had changed his mind about prolonging the struggle from Norway, and his forces, well-disciplined to the last, were surrendered peacefully.

Gunnar Sonsteby had carried out several daring operations of this nature in the two years before hostilities ended. About a year earlier he had become an almost legendary figure then he sabotaged a German computer.

In May 1944, the Germans announced a compulsory call-up — the first — of three age groups. This had to be resisted at all costs, and the best way of doing it, Sonsteby suggested, was to prevent the issue of the call-up cards.

It had been discovered that in order to send the cards out quickly, the Germans had commandeered a special type of tabulating machine from the firm of Watson Norsk A/S. There were only half a dozen of these machines in Norway, and the Home Front rightly realised that if they could be destroyed, the call-up would be disorganised and delayed for a long time, if not permanently.

The call-up cards were taken by the Germans under heavy guard from the office of the Labour Service to Watson's, and there punched by the machine. The easiest method would have been to smash the machine with hammers, but this would have brought suspicion on the firm and their employees who were expert operators of the machine. In order to avoid reprisals as far as possible Milorg (military intelligence) had for some time been conducting their sabotage in such a way that it looked as if it had been carried out by parachute saboteurs dropped specially. It was decided to

use this technique on this occasion.

On 19th May, the Germans in Oslo indulged in one of their favourite pastimes, the lightning check, or snap control, as it was called. Without warning they would cordon off an area of the city and the papers of everyone caught in the net would be examined. Those whose papers were not in order, or who, for some reason, roused the suspicions of the Germans would be arrested. These checks were primarily aimed at trapping agents and saboteurs infiltrated from abroad, but they rarely succeeded in this object.

Whenever the Germans carried out a check, the rest of the population at once made for their houses, and stayed there until the all-clear. While the streets were deserted on 19th May, Sonsteby and the Oslo squad went into action. They broke into the offices of Watson Norsk and blew up three tabulating machines found there.

To make quite certain that the call-up should be entirely ineffectual, the day before the men were due to register the offices in Akers Street were

426

also blown up. Unfortunately, however, the Germans had found another tabulating machine in the back room of an insurance company's headquarters. The Oslo Squad made the same discovery but when they went to attack it the alarm was raised and the attempt had to be abandoned. The Germans then placed the machine under a guard of ten men. Undeterred, the Oslo Squad returned to the attack, and though the machine was not completely destroyed it was so badly damaged that it took months to repair.

Not believing in half measures, though others might have termed them full measures, the Oslo Squad turned their attention to the offices of Astrup, the chief of the Labour Directorate, where many dossiers were kept. They were so tenacious that though six attempts failed, a seventh, in which the whole of the Squad took part, succeeded in the partial demolition of the offices and archives.

Taking their cue from these activities and obeying the instructions of the central leadership, the young men affected by the call-up went into

hiding in the forests and mountains and in the remoter parts of the country where they were not known. This presented the Home Front with a colossal problem of feeding the refugees.

A new rationing period was about to begin and the Germans decreed that those who did not present themselves for registration would not receive a ration card. At the request of the Home Front, Sonsteby and his men again went into action. They had a contact in the printing works in which the new cards were being produced, and from him obtained vital information which was to enable them to carry out an operation in Oslo which matched the raid of the Department of Justice in audacity.

About 9.30 on the morning of 26th July, 1944, a large covered van carrying seventy-five thousand new ration cards, drove out of the main entrance of the printing works on its way to distribute its load to the various Food Offices. Beside the driver sat a guard, and two others were in the back with the cards.

As the van drove out into the street, a grey Ford saloon

427

did likewise, and since it had the right of way, the driver of the van was compelled to brake. Simultaneously, Sonsteby leapt on to the running-board of the van, and thrust a revolver into the driver's face, ordering him to drive on as though nothing had happened. Two of Sonsteby's colleagues had made a similar entrance into the back of the van.

Outside the city the cards were transferred to a Milorg van, and the driver and his companions were given the option of being bound and gagged, or helped over the border into Sweden. Two chose Sweden, two to be bound.

This action was the climax of the forced-labour situation. Out of 80,000 men affected by the call-up only 300 were brought in by the Germans.

BIBLIOGRAPHY :

The Undaunted — Ronald Seth (London, 1956).

OSS (Office of Strategic Services — American wartime espionage and sabotage organisation).

On 13th June, 1942, President Roosevelt issued a Presidential Order which stated that henceforth the Central Office of Information, which had been set up in July 1941 "to collect and assemble information and data bearing on national security . . . and will analyze and collate such materials for the use of the President" would cease to exist, and that its place would be taken by the Office of Strategic Services, which would "collect and analyze strategic information (and) plan and operate special services" under the direction of General "Wild Bill" Donovan, the President's adviser on intelligence. Though the Order may have seemed vague as to the OSS's functions, both Donovan and Roosevelt knew that it was intended to be more than a bureau for the collection of information. It was, in fact, to be responsible for intelligence, sabotage and relations with the Resistance movements then rapidly growing up in Occupied Europe.

There was some resistance to the formation of the OSS from the Services intelligence chiefs and from J. Edgar Hoover of the FBI, despite the fact that Roosevelt stated specifically that the OSS was only to function in countries

428

outside the western hemisphere. Donovan, however, was able to overcome all opposition with one or two exceptions, notably General Douglas MacArthur, who throughout the war would not permit the OSS to work in any area commanded by him.

In 1940 Roosevelt had sent Donovan on a fact-finding tour of Europe. While in Britain, the authorities had shown him SOE (Special Operations Executive) (q.v.) which had been brought into being not long before for just the same purposes as the OSS, and which was making rapid development. Donovan had been greatly impressed by SOE, and he modelled OSS on it.

The British "by generously baring to Donovan their most sacred secrets . . . were certain they were gaining a direct line to the White House." (Alsop and Braden in **Sub Rosa,** New York 1946). This may have been a motive, but it was not the sole motive for the British offering and giving Donovan the full benefit of their experience in organising OSS, which they did. The British are, by nature opportunists, and they believed that in helping the Americans to build up an equivalent organisation in the US, they would be greatly increasing the success of their own aims of building up behind the German lines secret armies against the day when the great liberating forces would land on the Continent of Europe. This also applied to their harrying of the Germans by acts of sabotage while waiting for the great day to come.

Under Donovan's brilliant administration, the OSS expanded rapidly. He drew into it experts of every kind, and courageous young men who were not afraid to risk their lives, if only they were permitted to do something really worthwhile for the war effort.

By the time the American forces were ready to come physically to Europe, the OSS was ready to go into action, sometimes alongside and sometimes independently of SOE's plans and policies. But the co-operation of the two organisations was always close, and their combined effectiveness was proved when, after D-Day, the underground armies which they

429

had helped to raise, train and equip rose in the Germans' rear and made an outstanding contribution to their defeat.

The OSS operated in the Far East and in the Pacific, except in the area commanded by General MacArthur, as well as in every occupied country in Europe.

It was disbanded at the end of the war, and was succeeded by the Central Intelligence Agency (CIA—q.v.).

BIBLIOGRAPHY:
Sub Rosa — Stewart Alsop and Thomas Braden (New York, 1946).

PAKHOMOV, Ivan (Russian agent in Australia) see under **Petrov, Vladimir.**

PAPEN, Franz von (German career diplomat and politician).

During the First World War Franz von Papen was German military attaché first in Spain and then in the United States. As such he was connected with German military intelligence activities in those countries.

He was the contact with Mata Hari, while in Spain, and through carelessness he exposed the sabotage network of Captain Von Rintelen in the United States.

After having been Chancellor of Germany for a brief period, when he paved the way for the succession of Adolf Hitler to that high post, he served as ambassador in various countries. During the Second World War he was appointed ambassador to Turkey, where he was again involved in espionage activities, particularly in Operation Cicero (q.v.). While serving in Ankara he narrowly escaped an attempt to assassinate him by SMERSH, (q.v.), the murder squad of Russian intelligence.

PARRY, Dr William (Elizabethan agent).

According to Lord Burghley, Elizabeth I's Secretary of State, Dr William Parry, Member of Parliament, ex-convict and adventurer, was one of the most dangerous of all Walsingham's agents. Burghley mistrusted him, for he had evidence of his double-dealing, and eventually formulated a plan to remove him. He proposed to Parry that he should suggest to Edmund Neville, one of the prominent Roman Catholics, a plot to assassinate Elizabeth. Neville who was too astute to fall for such provocation, reported Parry's suggestion at once to Burghley. Burghley, despite Parry's protests that the Secretary himself had planned the trap for Neville, had Parry arrested, tried for conspiracy to murder the Queen and had him executed.

PAVLOV, Col Vitali (Russian agent).

Colonel Vitali Pavlov is Russia's most ubiquitous secret agent. He served in America, Canada and in Australia, and figures in the great spy cases connected with those countries.

PENKOVSKY, Colonel Oleg V. (Russian defector) see under **Wynne, Greville.**

PEPER, Maurice see under **Wenzel, Johann.**

PERLET, Charles see under **Fouché, Joseph.**

PETROV, Vladimir (Russian agent in Australia, who defected).

The defection of Vladimir Petrov in Australia in 1954 caused a world-wide sensation on a par with that which had attended the defection of Igo Gouzenko (q.v.) in Canada in 1945.

The Australian Government had not recognised the Soviet Union diplomatically until 1942, but from that moment Soviet espionage had launched a full-scale attack on the sub-continent. The network was first organised and led by Semion Makarov, who had as his chief assistant the official Tass news-agency correspondent, Feodor Nosov.

The Australian network was developed on traditional Russian espionage lines. Local Communists and fellow-travellers in government service formed the main sources of information. There was one group, particularly, which worked in the Ministry of External Affairs and which passed on documents relating to Australian and British foreign policy.

The war years was a period of considerable and successful activity. After the war, however, when the former attitudes towards Japan and fascism began to mellow, and when the Amerasia case in America (q.v.) and the Nunn May case in Britain (q.v.) awoke the public awareness to the menace that Russian spying had become, the network began to run into serious difficulties.

After the end of hostilities, Makarov had been replaced by Valentin Sadovnikov. Unfortunately, in 1949 Sadovnikov committed the unforgivable sin — in The Centre's eyes — of staying the night at the home of some Australian acquaintances. He was recalled and replaced by Ivan Pakhomov, who turned out to be indolent by nature and not very keen on his job. Within a very short time he was replaced by Vladimir Petrov.

Pétrov was posted to the embassy in Canberra with the rank of Third Secretary, but his real function was that of Resident Director, or chief of the network in Australia. His wife Evdokia, who accompanied him, was also employed by the NKVD, and acted as a clerk in the embassy.

By the time that Petrov arrived, the network had reached almost rock bottom, chiefly through lack of sources, for the original sources were no longer available and those who had taken their places were not compliant. Though Petrov explained the situation very carefully to The Centre, before very long they were beginning to criticise him, too.

Probably to put more life into him, they sent him an assistant, F. V. Kislitsyn. Kislitsyn's stay was short, however, because he was no more successful at producing results than Petrov was. The same applied to his successor N. G. Kovaliov, and when they recalled him, they blamed Petrov for his failure, "because of the absence of your positive guidance."

From this time on The Centre's criticism began to increase. Again doubtless in the hope of spurring him on, they ordered him on 6th June 1952, in a long instruction, to prepare for the outbreak of another world war. They set out the measures he should take to prepare for this new conflagration.

The result of this mounting criticism, however, had just the opposite effect that The Centre intended it to have—it engendered in Petrov a growing bitterness. He expressed his feelings fully on one occasion to Mikhail Bialogusky, a Polish immigrant, whose acquaintance he had made since coming to Australia. He believed Bialogusky to be a pro-Russian member of the Russian Social Club—in fact, the Pole was an Australian counter-espionage agent.

When, shortly after Stalin's death in 1953, Lavrenti Beria (q.v.) the head of all the security forces in Russia for fifteen years, and the most

433

feared and hated man in the Soviet Union, was liquidated by the new régime, it was hinted that the reason for his removal was that he had organised a plot to overthrow the other members of the new set-up. In some weird and wonderful way Petrov was implicated in this plot, and this, combined with the adverse reports on his work by his ambassador, was used as an excuse to recall him in the spring of 1954.

On 3rd April he disappeared. For some reason he had not taken his wife into hiding with him, and when he did not reappear within a few days, Moscow ordered her to be repatriated. The aircraft in which she was being flown home landed at Darwin airport to refuel, and she, with her bodyguard of three or four Soviet agents, was taken to the terminal building. Her progress had been noted by Australian counter-espionage, and somehow or other her husband was able to speak to her on the telephone. At Canberra and on landing at Darwin, she had behaved quietly, but after speaking to her husband she changed. She cried out to Australian officials that she did not want to go back to Moscow and that she wished to be granted asylum.

The bodyguard seized her and tried to rush her across the tarmac to the waiting Russian aircraft, but Australian officials intervened and were able to free her and take her into their protection. Interestingly, some Australian photographers and television cameramen happened to be present, and the struggle was visually recorded. As a result, within a few hours the world knew of the defection of this high-ranking member of Soviet espionage.

Petrov's defection coming so soon after Gouzenko's, especially since it was blazoned round the world with not very edifying photographs attached, was more than The Centre could take. The Soviet embassy broke off relations with Australia and closed its Canberra embassy.

The information and documents Petrov had been able to take with him when he left the embassy — the documents included letters to and from Moscow dating back to 1952, which he was supposed to have burned — added yet more knowledge to the West's picture of the working and policies of Soviet espionage. The case did much to bring home to the man in the street the skill of Soviet espionage penetration, and it roused the authorities everywhere to yet a further tightening of their own internal security.

BIBLIOGRAPHY :

Soviet Espionage — David J. Dallin (New York, 1955).

The Great Spy Ring — Norman Lucas (London, 1966) Chapter 7.

PHELIPPES, Thomas (Elizabethan cryptographer).

One of Sir Francis Walsingham's chief concerns as chief of Elizabeth I's secret service was protecting the Queen from Roman Catholic plots to assassinate her, and particularly those in which Mary Queen of Scots was deeply involved. Even after her arrest and internment Mary made strenuous efforts to communicate with her sympathisers, and was, in a way, successful. The correspondence, which is still preserved in the Record Office, involved the use of codes and ciphers. Few of Mary's letters got through without falling into the hands of Walsingham, for whom they were decoded by Thomas Phelippes, who was an expert without equal among his contemporaries.

Phelippes other distinction in the history of espionage is as founder and proprietor of a private espionage agency, which he established after the death of his patron. So far as can be traced, Phelippes's agency was the first of its kind in the world.

PHILBY, Harold "Kim" (British traitor, defected 1963).

Harold "Kim" Philby was the son of Harry St John Bridger Philby an eccentric officer of the Indian Civil Service. Kim Philby was born at Amballa, India, on New Year's Day, 1912.

St John Philby was an Arabist of distinction, and in that role he was caught up in Britain's attempts to stir up an Arab revolution against Germany's Turkish allies during World War I. After the war he joined other eminent Arabists, among them T. E. Lawrence, in believing that Britain reneged on her promises to the Arabs. He went to live in Saudi Arabia, where he became a Moslem and took a second (Moslem) wife. He subsequently became famous for his exploration of that part of the Arabian desert, known of the Empty Quarter. He died in Beirut in 1961, his last words being: "God, I'm bored."

There were strong emotional ties between the older Philby and his son, and there is no doubt that his father never ceased to warn Kim against trusting in the good faith of the British Establishment. Many people believe that it was St John Philby's influence which played a considerable part in Kim's extraordinary career.

In 1929 Kim Philby became an undergraduate at his father's old college, Trinity, Cambridge. He was a fair-haired, well-built youth of 17 with a stammer.

In the very early '30's a left-wing movement was just beginning to become perceptible in Cambridge. During the 1931 General Election campaign Kim Philby gave his support on the hustings to the Labour Party. Shortly thereafter, however, possibly as a result of Ramsay Macdonald's so-called betrayal of the Party, he swung over to the extreme left.

Among Philby's friends at Cambridge was a fellow student at Trinity, and old Etonian, Guy Burgess (q.v.), and a student at Trinity Hall, Donald Maclean (q.v.). He formed a particular attachment for the blatantly homosexual Burgess, but if there was any physical relationship between them, it was a passing phase, for Philby soon revealed himself as blatant a heterosexual as Burgess was homosexual. The friendship of the three, however, was to be life-long; and it was a superb example of dramatic irony that it should be Burgess who led to Philby's eventual downfall.

During his vacations at Cambridge, Philby made extensive travels in Eastern and Central Europe, often by motorcycle. Already on the extreme Left of British Socialism, what he saw of the early Nazi terror made him an ardent Communist. Not only that, but he came into contact with Russian intelligence, and according to his own admission to his children who visited him in Moscow after his defection, it was at this time that he was given the task of penetrating British intelligence; a task, as will be seen, which he pursued with diabolic skill and devastating success for thirty years.

In February 1934 Philby married Alice Friedmann, a divorcee a year and a half older than himself, an Austrian Jewess. Alice Friedmann was already a Communist, and has remained so all her life. Shortly after their marriage, the Philby's came to live in London, when Philby became sub-editor on the liberal **Review of Reviews.** It was the first step in a carefully thought-out campaign to cover up their Communist sympathies.

Philby's chief method of carrying out this campaign was to adopt an extreme Right Wing stance. He condoned the Nazi regime in Germany, and joined the Anglo-German Fellowship; and when the Spanish Civil War broke out in 1936 he obtained a job as a **Times** correspondent with Franco's forces. When the war was over he was awarded a decoration by Franco.

It is thought that he began his espionage activities during this period, but for the British, in the hope that whatever he did might stand him in good stead later. Whether this is true or not the outbreak of World War II in 1939 saw him as No 1 correspondent for the **Times** with the British Expeditionary Force in France, a job he held until the retreat from Dunkirk brought him back to London.

It was at this juncture that he realised his secret ambition to penetrate British Intelligence. Almost immediately on his return to London he asked to join Department D of the Secret Intelligence Service (SIS) in which his friend Guy Burgess had been working for some time.

Department D, which was concerned with sabotage, subversion and propaganda was wound up in 1941, and its functions taken over by the recently formed Special Operations Executive (SOE). SOE trained Philby as an agent, but because of his stammer it was decided ultimately not to put him in the Field, though he had come through his training brilliantly. Because of this, Philby was recruited to work for

Section V of the SIS. He was really in at last.

The British Secret Services at this time consisted of two quite separate organisations: MI5, set up in 1909 and still in 1940 in the charge of its first chief, Colonel Vernon Kell; and MI6, which was created half-way through World War I, with Captain Mansfield Cumming in charge MI5 was concerned with counter-espionage in British territories; MI6 was concerned with espionage in foreign countries. After World War I both departments were "civilianised", MI6 becoming the SIS. In 1937 Admiral Cumming died and was succeeded by Colonel Stewart Menzies, Eton and the Life Guards.

Department D had been set up after Munich, and its disbandment in 1941 was a blow to the prestige of SIS, which had no control at all over SOE. The Venlo incident, when two SIS agents were kidnapped by the German Abwehr was an even more serious blow, for in one of the agent's brief case the Germans found a list of the names of most of the British agents operating in Europe, who were promptly seized.

The SIS was hampered in its attempts to recover its reputation chiefly because it was manned by officers of low calibre. The top scholars, like Menzies and his chief assistants, came from aristocratic families and were the backbone of London's most elite clubs. Family connections, social background — school, regiment and clubs — were the more sought after qualifications.

Under these men a second kind of recruit served. These were mostly drawn from ex-members of the Indian Police, who were not of the intellectual calibre of the British Civil Service. Though they had had practice in keeping an eye on Indian nationalist leaders, they were not really qualified in secret service techniques, and the Venlo Incident highlighted this.

Section V, which had been set up to organise counter-espionage in foreign countries, was commanded by Major Felix Cowgill, an "Indian", who was as unlike his subordinates as it was possible to be. These were wartime amateurs taken from the ranks of novelists, journalists, university dons and other intellectuals. Neither side was happy working with the other.

Philby's arrival in Section V, to take up an executive post was hailed by the top-brass and SIS as a scoop. He did not belong to the ranks of the clubmen, nor was he an intellectual, and it was felt that he would weld the two factions in a way no other man could.

This was before the days of "positive vetting". Philby had gone to a good school, Westminster, and a good college at Cambridge, so he must be all right from the clubman's point of view. It is doubtful whether those in charge of SIS were aware of his Communist leanings as a young man. If they were, it was probably thought that he had obviously got rid of that nonsense, otherwise he would not have taken up his extreme Right Wing stance during and after the Spanish Civil War. Had he not been very successful as a **Times** correspondent? Well, the **Times** would not have taken on a shady character.

One thing alone saved SIS from the same sort of shake-up that had been meted out to MI5 and Department D in 1940. This was SIS's code-breaking unit run by Captain Edward Hastings RN at Bletchley, in Buckinghamshire. The code-breaking exploits of Room 40 in World War I had not been forgotten by the Germans. Determined that they should not be repeated, they had developed a machine cipher which they were sure the British could not break. Unfortunately for them a U-boat was captured intact, with its coding machine. The capture was successfully kept a secret. Within a short time Hastings' unit was reading all the German codes. This, too, was kept a deadly secret, and whatever else Philby was able to pass to the Russians during this period, he did not pass any material from this quarter. Though few knew it, it was the success of the Bletchley unit which was responsible for SIS remaining untouched.

In 1944, Section V moved from its country headquarters at Praed Green, back to London. About this time, Philby manoeuvred to take over charge of Section V himself. He was able to persuade Colonel Vivian that Major Cowgill should be moved on and sent to Germany on police work. Philby's plan, however, failed to work because Graham Greene, the novelist resigned rather than have anything to do with such conspiracies.

However, even better things were in store for Philby. It was decided, now that the end of the war was in sight, to revive the Soviet counter-espionage section of SIS, which had lapsed when Russia became our ally. Philby was appointed to lead this section. Philby, in his role as Russian spy, could hardly have believed his luck.

Within a year and a half the Soviet counter-espionage section had been so revived by Philby that more than a hundred were on its staff. It was already gathering together a huge amount of information on Communist and front-organisations in the West. Through Philby, everything it knew, the Russians knew, too.

After the war many people who had been recruited into SIS during the emergency were clearly unsuitable for a peacetime organisation. A

general inspection of the Foreign Office and its off-shoots — of which SIS was one — was carried out by Sir Harold (now Lord) Caccia in 1946, and all the undesirable elements were weeded out. Philby was not one of them. In fact, in that year he was awarded the OBE.

Early in the summer of 1946 Philby went for the first time into the Field. Under the cover of a First Secretary, he was sent to Turkey and worked in the passport control office in Istanbul in the British Consulate-General. What exactly his mission was in Turkey has never been revealed, though there are indications that he was in contact with Communist agents there.

His next step upwards brought him to the most vital period of his career as a double agent. In October 1949 he was posted to Washington to act as liaison officer between the SIS and the American Central Intelligence Agency (CIA) (q.v.). He was thus at the very centre of Western intelligence, for at this time relations between the SIS and CIA were closer than at any other period.

Since he was SIS's expert on Soviet counter-espionage, he helped the CIA to form a similar section. As he passed on to Moscow all that the SIS learned, so now he passed on all that the CIA were planning to do to counter Soviet spying.

Now, while Philby had been playing so successfully his role of Soviet spy at the heart of British and American intelligence, one of his Cambridge friends, Donald Maclean (q.v.), had been pursuing a similar role. Maclean had also spent some time in Washington shortly before Philby arrived, and during that time had had access to American atomic secrets, all of which he had passed to Moscow.

Maclean, however, was a very different character from Philby, and in Cairo, where he had been sent after Washington, he began to crack up.

By chance, this deterioration occurred at a time when he had become a principal suspect in an alarming series of atomic information leakages. That such leaks were occurring had become evident to SIS and CIA in 1948, and after two years of investigation by Western security offi-cers, the net was beginning to close in on him.

This was known only to a very small circle of men, one of whom was Philby.

Maclean's behaviour in Cairo eventually became so scandalous that he was re-called. The Old Boy network, of which he was a member, prevented his being dismissed, and instead, he was given leave to undertake a course of psychiatric treatment, with the promise of re-employment as soon as he had recovered.

Somewhat staggered by this, the security officers nevertheless tenaciously con-tinued their investigations, and in May 1951 came into possession of evidence that practically proved that Mac-lean had betrayed vital infor-mation to the Russians. Faced with this evidence, the Establishment's hand was eventually forced, and For-eign Secretary Herbert Mor-rison gave the order on 25th May that Maclean was to be interrogated. The 23rd May was a Friday, so it was decid-ed to do nothing until the fol-lowing Monday.

Philby, in Washington, was informed of this decision when he was asked to relay it to the CIA.

There is no doubt that it was he who passed the warning to the third member of the trio, Guy Burgess.

At midnight, Burgess and Maclean boarded the steamer Falaise at Southampton and crossed to Europe. There they disappeared, to turn up later in Moscow.

Now, if Burgess had not defected with Maclean, it is fairly certain that Philby would have been able to continue as a double-agent for several years longer than he actually did. It was clear to all concerned that Maclean must have been warned that he was to be interrogated, and a search for the warner pointed to a fair number of possibilities, of whom Philby was one.

He might still have got away with it, however, had it not been for the fact that Guy Burgess, who since the war had been employed by the Foreign Office, and was on the staff of the Washington embassy when Philby arrived there, had moved into Philby's house in Washington shortly before he was recalled, like Maclean, for scandalous behaviour involving homosex-

uality. This fact made Philby one of the six or so prime suspects.

A team of security officers was flown to Washington to question Philby, the upshot of which was that Philby was removed from his post as liaison officer with the CIA.

At this time, and for several years previously, there had been vicious feuding between the SIS, which had escaped post-war reconstruction, and MI5. MI5 were in charge of the investigations, and this automatically brought the SIS men to his defence. Once again the Old Boy network came into play.

But though SIS could protect him, Philby had to resign from his Foreign Office cover job. Nevertheless, by the end of 1951 he was back at a very important post in the Field — in Cyprus.

None of these things prevented MI5 from continuing with their investigations in depth into Philby's activities. These were completed in 1952, and the results were so formidable that Philby was summoned home to face a very strange procedure — a secret trial with no judge. This trial lasted for three days, and when it finished, the most embarrassed party was not Philby, but the security forces. Philby returned to the Field, this time to Turkey once more.

But the tenacity of the security forces still sent them in relentless pursuit, and two years later, in 1955, the whole matter was brought to a new head when Colonel Marcus Lipton, MP, under the immunity of the House of Commons, actually named Philby as the "third man" in the Burgess and Maclean affair.

Colonel Lipton's intervention compelled the government to take public cognisance of the affair. Once more the Old Boy network came to Philby's aid. Foreign Secretary Harold Macmillan on the advice of the SIS told the House that nothing could be proved against Philby.

Six months later Philby was once more on the payroll of SIS. In April 1956 he began to establish a new cover for himself. The Foreign Office approached the Sunday **Observer** and asked if it would be possible to appoint Philby its correspondent in Beirut, the capital of Lebanon. So

Philby returned ostensibly to journalism, arriving in Beirut in September 1956.

In Beirut his customary charm soon made him very popular. He made many official contacts, particularly at the British and American embassies. What his worth was in terms of practical intelligence either to SIS or the Russians it is difficult to assess.

Philby spent five years in Beirut. He might have been there longer had George Blake (q.v.), the Russian spy, not been arrested in 1961. Philby realised that his days were numbered, and yet, despite the fact that Blake made a full confession, the authorities were slow to move.

It is a fact that shortly after Blake's confession was taken, an SIS agent came to Beirut and told Philby that there was now definite evidence that he was working for the Russians. Philby admitted it apparently, but still nothing was done. From this moment, however, he began to show signs of cracking up.

It seems that the reason why no move was made to bring him to justice was because it would have meant a sensational trial. It was decided, therefore, to try to force him to take refuge behind the Iron Curtain.

To this end a team of SIS men descended on Philby towards the end of 1962. They submitted him to an ordeal of interrogation that had the desired effect of breaking his nerve.

On 23rd January, 1963, while a guest at a dinner party in Beirut, Philby vanished. Six months later, on 30th July, the Russian newspaper **Izvestia,** announced that Philby who had held a "leading position in British intelligence, has been granted political asylum in Moscow."

The British government did not entirely escape the public sensation they had tried so hard to avoid. At long last a reorganisation of SIS was undertaken. Many heads rolled, but the Service was now put on a sound footing, and ever since has been working hard to retrieve its reputation.

Philby, despite his thirty years of treachery, has to be classified as one of the great classic spies of espionage history. It is impossible to evaluate his espionage performance, which, at the very least,

was superb. The skill, the nerve and the cunning with which he built up his cover and was able to sustain it for so many years, working as he did, at the very heart of British intelligence, is unrivalled so far in the modern annals of spying.

BIBLIOGRAPHY :

Philby: The Spy Who Betrayed a Generation — Bruce Page, David Leitch and Phillip Knightley (London, 1968).

PINKERTON, Allan (Private detective, director of intelligence to Lincoln).

As the quarrel between the South and the North gathered impetus and it began to be plain that the differences would ultimately have to be settled by a trial of physical strength, both sides did not fail to appreciate that an espionage agency could have an important rôle in the struggle. Neither side, however, had any trained agents, and though before the conflict was finally resolved both antagonists were to produce many courageous and successful agents, at the beginning there was much groping and learning by hard experience.

The situation was already explosive when Abraham Lincoln was elected to the White House in 1860. The Secessionists saw in Lincoln their greatest enemy, and before the elections had sent a number of agitators to the Northern states to spread anti-Lincoln propaganda. When this was unsuccessful and Lincoln was elected, it was decided that he must be prevented ever from reaching the White House.

The prominent men of the North were not unaware of the South's machinations, and when rumours of projected violence reached them, it appeared to them that the South's chief objective would certainly be the destruction of the newly laid Philadelphia - Wilmington - Baltimore railway, since by doing so they could completely isolate the nation's capital from the Northern states.

As a precautionary measure the railroad company's president, Samuel Felton, summoned a Chicago private detective who was already beginning to enjoy a considerable reputation. His name was Allan Pinkerton, and he was a former native of Glasgow, Scotland, who as a young man of twenty-three had emigrated to America in 1842.

After a conference with Felton in the last week of January 1861, Pinkerton went to Baltimore, where it was believed the headquarters of the Southern conspirators had been established. There he took a house in the name of K. J. Allen. He was accompanied by one of his most outstanding assistants, Timothy Webster.

Although Webster was a native of New Jersey, he could assume a Southern accent to perfection. Pinkerton also summoned another brilliant detective, Henry Davies, a former inhabitant of New Orleans, where he had made the acquaintance of some of the prominent Southern leaders.

It was Davies who made the first contact with the plotters. He had received information that a certain young man named Hill was in contact with the clandestine organisation, and under the cover-name of Howard, Davies concentrated his eff-

445

orts on Hill, whom he eventually persuaded to introduce him to the chief plotters as a strong sympathiser. In this way, too, he discovered that Marshal Kane, chief of the Baltimore police, was also a Southern sympathiser and had let it be known that he would do nothing to prevent an attempt on Lincoln's life that might be made in his territory. Davies so won the confidence of the plotters that he was authorised to attend the meeting at which Lincoln's assassin would be selected.

The conspirators conducted themselves in the best traditions of melodrama. About thirty men had been summoned to the meeting, each of whom was required to swear a solemn oath not to reveal to anyone anything that happened at the meeting, and particularly the man successful in the lottery was to keep his rôle to himself, as a deadly secret.

All having been sworn, the chairman of the meeting produced a box in which, he said, there were twenty-nine white balls and one red one. The man who drew the red ball was to carry out the killing.

446

So that there should be no risk of defection by the assassin-elect, the chiefs had, in fact, placed eight red balls in the box.

As soon as possible after the meeting, Davies informed Pinkerton of what had happened, but so well had the rank and file of the plotters observed their oath that he could not tell who had drawn a red ball. Pinkerton took the next train to Philadelphia to contact his other agent, Webster, who had joined a gang of watchers voluntarily organised to protect the railway at its most vulnerable points. It had not taken Webster long to discover that the majority of the gang were Southern sympathisers in league with the Baltimore plotters, who intended to destroy the railway. The signal for them to do this was to be the public announcement of Lincoln's death.

By this time the President-elect had set out on a slow journey by special train toward Washington, where he was to be inaugurated. He was accompanied by his private secretary and six friends. He arrived in Philadelphia on 21st February, 1861, and, on the insistence of certain of his chief supporters, he agreed to see Pinkerton. When he had heard the detective's story, though he could not understand why anyone should wish to kill him, he put himself in Pinkerton's hands.

Although he had no definite information about where the plotters intended to attack, Pinkerton was convinced that the attempt on Lincoln's life would be made in Baltimore, where there were two railway terminals, which made it necessary for through-passengers to Washington to be drawn, in their railway carriages, through the streets by horses from one terminal to the other. Lincoln was that night the guest of honour at a dinner in Harrisburg, from which, having made a short speech and pleading fatigue, he retired early. Samuel Felton had a special train ready outside the town to which Lincoln and his party, joined now by another of Pinkerton's agents, Mrs Webster, posing as Lincoln's sister, were immediately taken, and it set off for Philadelphia.

The regular night train from Philadelphia to Baltimore had been held up on the excuse that important papers were to be carried by the guard to Washington. Arriving at Philadelphia, Lincoln and his party were hurried secretly to sleeping cars at the rear of this train, and the journey to Baltimore began.

Pinkerton had organised another party of watchers from among trustworthy employees of the railway, which he had placed under the command of Davies and Webster. Their ostensible object was to guard the bridges along the route while actually being on the alert to counter any move by the other watchers. As each danger point was passed a signal was made by hooded lantern to Pinkerton, who stood on the rear platform of the train.

Baltimore was reached in safety. But now came the most dangerous part of the whole journey — the crossing from one terminal to the other. Pinkerton had planned the operation so well, however, that the plotters were completely unaware that Lincoln was on the train. Indeed, they had no suspicion that their intentions had been discovered until the news-

447

papers next morning revealed the conspiracy in full detail.

When he had heard of the plot, Lincoln had given orders that none of the men was to be arrested or punished in any way. They did not know this, of course, and by the evening of the following day, Pinkerton was able to report that not one of them remained in Baltimore.

Allan Pinkerton's handling of the affair had been a brilliant piece of detective work, and when war broke out not long afterwards and Lincoln was convinced of the need for an espionage service, it was natural that he should turn to the detective to organise it.

In the months that followed, Pinkerton's organisation, while served by outstanding detectives, suffered one set-back after another, which culminated in the capture and execution of Webster (q.v.) and others. Indeed, it quickly became apparent that as a director of intelligence Pinkerton was a complete failure. He himself knew it, but the North could find no one to replace him until Lafayette Baker (q.v.) proved himself to be one of the most brilliant spies in

448

history, and when tested, an equally brilliant director of intelligence.

BIBLIOGRAPHY :
The Spy of the Rebellion — Allan Pinkerton (New York, 1877).

PONTECORVO, Dr Bruno (Atom traitor, post World War II).

Bruno Pontecorvo was an Italian. He had been a pupil of the famous Italian scientist and Nobel Prizeman, Enrico Fermi, until, in 1927, he went to work in France under two famous Communist scientists, Longevin and Joliot-Curie, both now dead. In France he joined a group of extreme left-wing Italian refugees.

When the German invasion of France was imminent, Pontecorvo fled to America, where he arrived in the summer of 1940. Early in 1943 he was sent to Canada, to work on the atomic projects there. After the end of the war, he remained in the United States until 1949, when he was assigned to work in England.

In 1949 a reformed Communist friend of the scientist reported Pontecorvo to the

American authorities, making a full disclosure of his activities and connections. The United States took no steps beyond warning the British, who for some inexplicable reason remained inactive. Two years later, while still working on secret assignments at Harwell and passing information regularly to the Soviet network in Great Britain, he applied for permission to take his family to the Continent for a holiday. Travelling by motorcar through France to Rome, they there took an ordinary airlines airplane to Helsinki. There they were met by Soviet officials and taken into Russia.

Along with Nunn May and Fuchs, Pontecorvo must share a large part of the responsibility for Soviet Russia's progress in nuclear physics. Until they betrayed the secrets of American nuclear advances Russia was almost ten years behind in her own researches. Much of the international tension which troubled the world scene in the fifties stemmed from the spying of these three men.

On 4th March, 1955, it became known for certain that Pontecorvo was working in Soviet Russia, On that day he held a press conference in the Academy of Sciences, which is housed in the former Summer Palace of the Tsars. He announced that he had become a Soviet citizen in 1952, and that his work lay in nuclear development for peaceful purposes. In 1954 he was awarded the Stalin Prize Second Class for his researches in high energy physics.

BIBLIOGRAPHY:
The Great Spy Ring —
Norman Lucas (London, 1966) Chapter 5.

PORTLAND SPY CASE, The.

When the United States Line's transatlantic liner **America** berthed at Southampton on 3rd March, 1955, among her eight hundred passengers was a Canadian called Gordon Arnold Lonsdale. At least he claimed to be a Canadian, and in support proffered to all who asked to see it a genuine Canadian passport.

Lonsdale disembarked at Southampton, and from there travelled to London, where he took a room in an hotel. For the next few days he

449

behaved like any normal tourist, visiting the sights, the museums and the art galleries, taking scores of photographs with an expensive camera, and buying souvenirs.

In addition, he did what many other Commonwealth tourists in London do, but which in his case was of special significance — he became a regular visitor at the Overseas League. The Overseas League is a kind of club, with headquarters at Overseas House on Park Place, a cul-de-sac off St James's Street, and within a few hundred yards of St James's Palace, and membership is open to any visitor to Britain. The clubhouse provides excellent drawing rooms and writing rooms, first-class restaurant facilities at moderate prices, billiards, table tennis and card rooms, as well as a gymnasium and an information service to assist its often bewildered members with help and advice.

Lonsdale made a point of going to Overseas House at least once and sometimes twice a day, and made a further point of getting to know the various officers of the club well. Without ostentation or direct reference, he let these officers know that he was well supplied with money; and they had no reason at all for suspecting that he was not what he was making himself out to be — a genuine, honest Canadian.

In May he took his next step, which was to rent a small furnished apartment in a luxurious modern block called The White House, not far from Regent's Park. The management required references and, as he had hoped during the time he spent winning their confidence, the Overseas League officials were only too pleased to help in this respect.

The White House provides all the services of a first-class hotel, with the addition of absolute privacy for those who want it. It is possible to live there for months without getting to know anyone beyond the chambermaid and the room-service waiter, if that is how you want it.

Lonsdale asked for an apartment on the sixth — the top floor — and was allocated one. He told the management that he liked to have a view from his windows, but

450

the request had an entirely different significance.

The apartment consisted of a small sitting room, a bedroom, a bathroom and a kitchenette with facilities for simple cooking, should the tenant feel so inclined. The rent was in the region of £20 a week, which is expensive in London for this type of accommodation.

He had not installed himself in The White House long, when he went on a fifteen-day cruise to Scandinavia. On his return he enrolled as a full-time student in Chinese at the School of Oriental and African Studies of London University, and completed two full sessions before leaving in June 1957.

He did not apply all his time to his studies, but made a wide circle of acquaintances. He was a fluent and well-informed conversationalist, and had a gay and charming manner that was practically irresistible. Women, particularly, were attracted to him, and he apparently could not exist without their company, for he had a succession of mistresses, all beautiful and young, and who all later testified to his kindness and

consideration, though his performance as a lover was nothing out of the ordinary.

Though no one had any idea what his financial resources were, it was evident that he was very well supplied with money. In fact, he had between £7,000 and £10,000 deposited in various branches of the Royal Bank of Canada. From time to time he transferred some of these funds to accounts he opened with London banks, and the bank managers were so satisfied with his financial standing that when, at one period, he required extra capital urgently, he was granted an overdraft of £2,500 without security.

For a prolonged stay in Great Britain, Lonsdale obviously needed some occupation if he were not to attract attention. Because of certain activities to which he was committed, however, it could not be just any occupation, but one which would give him legitimate opportunities for travelling about England and making visits abroad.

With some ingenuity, he got himself a job as a salesman for jukeboxes. He be-

451

gan by buying two of these machines which he sold for a handsome profit, but much more valuable than the money were the contacts he made. Before long, in certain London business circles he became known as a man with an eye for easy money and with a considerable flair for salesmanship.

Toward the end of 1955, however, an even better opportunity came his way. A Mr Peter Ayres was planning to launch a bubble-gum machine company at the seaside resort of Broadstairs, in Kent. Ayres had been introduced to Lonsdale by a mutual business acquaintance over drinks in a London bar and took an instant liking to him, and when he went on to talk about his experiences selling jukeboxes, which showed that he was certainly energetic, and had some good ideas for selling a product, it struck Ayres that he might be a useful business partner in his own new venture.

As a start, Lonsdale undertook to try his hand at selling bubble-gum machines, and in a very short time proved himself a master at it. His energy must have been considerable,

for at this time he was attending the School of Oriental Studies for five hours a day as well as managing other, and entirely secret, activities.

Lonsdale's success in selling bubble-gum machines impressed Ayres, who invited him to join his company. Lonsdale accepted the invitation, bought five hundred £1 shares, and became a director of the Automatic Merchandising Company Ltd.

This was a great step forward for Lonsdale, for it established him well and truly in the British social complex. To be able to call oneself a "company director" is extremely useful not merely in business, but in lay circles as well, for to the lay mind the phrase has a high status significance.

The bubble-gum machine business flourished. On Lonsdale's initiative it was decided to try to enter the European market, and he himself paid visits to France, Switzerland, and Italy. Though he did not get much business, he continued to make these visits arguing that it only needed time to break down resistance.

When he was not abroad he was energetically selling machines in London and elsewhere, and during these activities he met several men who were to attempt to interest him in money-making ideas. Some of these he took up, and in doing so sailed very close to breaking the law, but somehow he always managed to draw back in time.

All went well for Lonsdale for nearly four years. He had made many friends and enough money to pay for his now luxurious way of life. A flaw in his character, however, was soon almost to bring about his downfall — he became over confident in his selling ability.

He was quite convinced that Italy would be a rich customer for bubble-gum machines, and though a reconnaissance of the Italian market showed negative results, he was sure that time would change all that. By making reports so misleading that they could be termed false, he persuaded his co-directors to expand their production. But this time he was wrong, and soon the Automatic Merchandising Company was in serious financial difficulties from which it never recovered. In March 1960 it went into liquidation with liabilities of £30,000.

Lonsdale was clearly frightened by the turn events had taken. He could not afford to be involved in a public examination. Besides this, he was in considerable personal difficulties in connection with certain shady credit transactions, and his financial resources had dwindled to a minimum amount. For a time he disappeared.

He possessed a most extraordinary resilience, however. Within a few months he had recouped his losses and straightened out his affairs. On 24th February, 1960, he became a director of the Master Switch Company which had procured the patents in a switch designed to immobilise a motorcar completely and to protect it from theft. But there were difficulties of production and not a single switch had been marketed when he was removed from the British scene by far more serious difficulties of another kind.

Now at the very time that

453

Lonsdale was forming the Master Switch Company, a naval security officer at the Admiralty Underwater Weapons Establishment at Portland had begun to take an interest in a certain civilian clerk employed by that establishment, which is engaged on highly secret work connected with the detection of nuclear submarines.

The clerk's name was Harry Houghton. He was fifty-four, and for twenty-three of those years he had served in the Royal Navy, rising to the senior non-commissioned rank of master at arms. In 1945 he retired from the service with a pension of £250 a year for the rest of his life. But he was still a comparatively young man, only forty-one, and £250 does not go far in these days, so he looked around for employment and obtained a post as a civilian clerk in the Admiralty, where he quickly impressed his superiors.

In 1951 he was sent to Warsaw as writer (secretary) to the British naval attaché there. It was an important post, for it gave him regular access to all the classified material sent to and collected by the attaché.

Houghton adapted himself well to life in the capital of an Iron Curtain country and scarcely missed attending any of the numerous parties which the employees of diplomatic missions organise for their relaxation, or similar functions organised by the Polish authorities.

Unhappily for him, he began to run into domestic difficulties. His wife, whom he had married in 1934, objected to his frequent bouts of drunkenness and this led to frequent quarrels, some of them in public. What was going on reached the ears of authority. Warsaw was no place for a scandal, so Houghton was recalled after fifteen months.

On his return to England, the Admiralty committed one of those strange actions of which governments are guilty from time to time. Houghton had proved himself to be unworthy of a position of trust by his behaviour in Warsaw, and ought to have been given a "safe" post. Instead, he was appointed to the Underwater Weapons Establishment with access to all the information about the later developments in ASDIC — underwater radar — information for which the enemy would pay much.

After a time Houghton and his wife separated, and he became friendly with a colleague, a Miss Ethel Gee. When the friendship developed into an intimacy which neither troubled to conceal, Mrs Houghton divorced her husband.

Houghton had by this time left the Admiralty quarters which had been provided for him, and had bought a cottage in a nearby village. After the divorce, he began to make improvements to the cottage 'and completely refurnished and decorated it at a cost of some hundred pounds. He also bought a new motorcar.

Now, the naval security officer and Houghton used the same pub for drinking, and what had attracted the attention of the security officer to Houghton was the amount of money the civilian clerk spent on his drinks. He knew that Houghton's salary was £750 a year and his pension £250, making a total annual income of £1000, but it looked very much as if he spent far more on drinks than he could afford on this salary.

Under regulations, the security officer could make no investigations himself, and he had no definite evidence to base an official report on, but he had as an acquaintance a detective officer in the local police force. Introducing the subject of Houghton casually into a conversation, he did nothing more, but waited for the results which he confidently expected would follow.

Within a short time the results were forthcoming. They showed that Houghton was spending more on drink than he received in salary, that he had paid for the improvements to his cottage and for his new motor car in £1 and £5 notes.

This was sufficient for counter-espionage to be called in.

It was March 1960, and from then until 1st January, 1961, MI5 with the help of the Dorset police, kept a record of every single movement made by Houghton and Miss Gee.

This surveillance disclosed that at frequent intervals, usually on a Saturday afternoon, Houghton sometimes accompanied by Miss Gee travelled

455

by train to London and there met a man whom it was not difficult to identify as Gordon Lonsdale. Nor was it difficult to discover that Houghton invariably handed a package to Lonsdale and received a package in return. Nor was it a problem to imagine what was going on.

However, for nine months MI5 made no move, other than to tail Lonsdale, Houghton and Miss Gee everywhere they went, and gradually definite evidence of espionage was acquired. MI5 then contacted the Special Branch of Scotland Yard — since they had no power of arrest themselves — and Superintendent George Smith was put in charge of the final operation.

On 7th January, 1961, the 12.32 train from Salisbury ran half an hour late, and arrived at 2.45 p.m. instead of 2.15 p.m. A bowler-hatted man carrying an umbrella, hearing the announcement over the station loudspeakers, turned away from the barrier of platform 14 and began to stroll casually through the station hall and outside into the Waterloo Road.

At intervals along the way

456

he spoke in quiet undertones to a man. "Half an hour late," he said, without pausing in his slow stride. Fifteen times he spoke the words until he finally reached a motorcar parked near the famous London Shaksperean theatre, the Old Vic, and told Superintendent Smith.

The train arrived at 2.45 and from it stepped Houghton and Miss Gee. On leaving the platform, Miss Gee went to the ladies' room while Houghton bought a newspaper and glanced at the headlines. When Miss Gee returned they walked together out of the station into the Waterloo Road. Ahead of them walked the bowler-hatted, umbrella-carrying man, and as he passed, each of the fifteen agents prepared for the final phase of the operation.

Then came a sudden moment of surprise. For months Houghton and Miss Gee had been met at Waterloo, and during all that time their behaviour had followed a consistent pattern. Now, however, the pattern dramatically changed.

Outside the station a No 68 bus was just pulling away

from a stop. Hand in hand, Houghton and Miss Gee made a dash for it and managed to board it. But one agent was near the stop and seeing what was happening, also jumped onto the moving bus.

As the bus approached a noisy street-market just off the Waterloo Road, the two Admiralty clerks disembarked. So did the agent, the only one of the fifteen who could hope to complete the operation successfully.

For twenty-five minutes Houghton and Miss Gee walked aimlessly through the market, then made their way back to the Walworth Road, where they boarded another bus to take them back to Waterloo.

Meanwhile, Superintendent Smith had instructed his agents to remain where they were, and he himself remained in the motorcar. A short time after Houghton and Miss Gee had disappeared, a motorcar driven by Lonsdale drove up. He got out and crossed to the Old Vic, where he stood studying the posters.

Arrived back at Waterloo, Houghton and Miss Gee crossed the road towards the Old Vic. Miss Gee was carrying a straw basket and might have been any housewife out with her husband for an afternoon's shopping.

As Houghton and Miss Gee approached, Lonsdale glanced at them and when they had passed fell in behind them, while behind him followed Superintendent Smith and behind him and on the opposite pavement a dozen of his agents.

After about fifty yards Lonsdale caught up with Houghton and Miss Gee. There were "surprised", affectionate greetings, and Lonsdale courteously took Miss Gee's basket.

At this moment Superintendent Smith hurried forward, passed them, and turned, blocking their path.

"Wait a minute!" he said. "You're all under arrest."

The other agents moved swiftly in, and before the three had recovered from the shock, they had been hustled into three motorcars and were being driven to Scotland Yard.

At Scotland Yard, after the usual cautions, Smith turned to Lonsdale to question him, but before he could speak,

Lonsdale, relaxed and smiling, said, "To any question you might ask me, my answer is 'no', so you need not trouble to ask." Through subsequent long hours of attempted interrogation, he steadily maintained silence.

Houghton's first words were, "I've been a bloody fool!" Miss Gee's, "I've done nothing wrong!"

In the straw basket were two parcels containing Admiralty documents; in Lonsdale's pockets two envelopes, one containing £125 which was Houghton's "salary", the other fifteen American 20-dollar bills.

Since he received no help from Lonsdale, Superintendent Smith decided to find out what he could from people who had been seen to meet him. For some reason which he cannot explain, Smith chose to make his first call at a bungalow in Cranley Drive, in the Middlesex suburb of Ruislip.

No 45 Cranley Drive was owned by a middle-aged married couple known as Peter and Helen Kroger. To acquaintances they were known to be Canadians who had lived for some time in Switzerland and had come to England in 1954 hoping that the climate would be more suited for Peter Kroger's health.

They had first taken a furnished house at Catford, another London suburb, and Kroger, an antiquarian book expert, had opened a second-hand bookshop at 190 The Drive, Catford. Eleven months later they brought the bungalow at Ruislip for £4000. Kroger closed his shop and henceforward carried on his business by mail from his house.

He devoted a great deal of his time to buying and selling books, and was well known and respected for his expertise in antiquarian book-circles in London. Apart from these activities, Kroger and his wife kept themselves to themselves, and had only a few friends and casual acquaintances.

That Superintendent Smith decided to call on them at all was due to the fact that while MI5 had had him under observation, Lonsdale had visited the Krogers frequently, and on several occasions had spent the week-end at their bungalow. The Krogers must know him fairly well, therefore.

Peter Kroger answered the Superintendent's knock, and when Smith identified himself, asked him in. Smith entered the bungalow accompanied by Chief Inspector Ferguson Smith and Woman Police Sergeant Winterbottom.

After a few preliminaries, Superintendent Smith asked Mrs Kroger if she would be willing to give him the names of guests who had visited the bungalow during the last six months. Mrs Kroger recited a list, but did not include the name of the most frequent visitor, Lonsdale. Smith knew at once from this that she was lying, and said that he would have to ask them to go to Scotland Yard for further questioning. Up to this moment he had had no suspicions concerning the Krogers.

Mrs Kroger made no difficulties. She put on a coat, picked up her handbag, and said, "As I am going out for some time, may I go and stoke the boiler?"

"Certainly," Smith replied, "but first let me see what you've got in your handbag."

Mrs Kroger refused to hand the bag over, and it took all Smith's and Woman Sergeant Winterbottom's efforts to prise it from her.

Inside the flap of the handbag Smith found a plain white envelope containing a six-page letter in Russian, a glass slide bearing three microdots, and a typed sheet of code.

Smith then told the Krogers that they were under arrest on charges under Section 1 of the Official Secrets Act.

The rooms and houses of all five prisoners were then searched and their bank accounts scrutinized. In Ethel Gee's lodgings were found a list of the numbers of eighteen classified pamphlets; all were missing from the Admiralty files at Portland. Another sheet of paper was a questionnaire dealing with twelve different subjects of research at Portland. Also found were £316 in £5 and £1 notes, savings certificates valued at £726, and share certificates to the value of £3703. She had an account with the Midland Bank in Weymouth in which, on 10th February, 1960, she had deposited £300 in cash. The Admiralty paid her £10 : 13 : 0d a week.

At Houghton's cottage at Broadway, the searchers

459

found three Admiralty charts with submarine exercise areas and locations for secret trials marked on them. Test pamphlets were found hidden in the radiogram. Five hundred £1 premium bonds were in a drawer in the living room. In a shed at the bottom of the garden they discovered a drum of paint powder, and buried in the powder £650 in six bundles of £1 notes.

But it was the Kroger's bungalow at Cranley Drive and Lonsdale's apartment at The White House that were most rewarding.

In the bungalow were found a Ronson table lighter containing signal plans covering radio transmission times and frequencies; equipment for making microdots; £354 in bank notes, 230 dollars in travellers cheques; 35.mm cameras and supplies of films; the bathroom convertible into a photographic dark-room. But the most important find of all was a long piece of electric wire attached to the radiogram. Tracing this back led to a trap door in the kitchen floor. When lifted, this revealed a cavity, and several feet under the floor was hidden a radio transmitter.

In Lonsdale's apartment, objects similar to those found in the bungalow were discovered. They included 3600 dollars and signal pads used for encoding messages.

The letter found in Mrs Kroger's handbag was one written by Lonsdale to his wife in Russia; the microdots were letters from the wife to Lonsdale.

The five spies were tried at the Central Criminal Court at the Old Bailey in London, on 18th March, 1961. The trial ended with Lonsdale being sent to prison for twenty-five years, the Krogers for twenty years each, Houghton for fifteen years and Ethel Gee for fifteen years.

During the course of the trial the Attorney General had made some surprising disclosures concerning the Krogers. Their real names were Morris and Lorna Cohen. Up to 1950 they were having regular meetings with Julius and Ethel Rosenberg (q.v.) the fanatical American Communists executed for treason and espionage in Sing Sing in June 1953. The FBI learned of this connection too late, for when they looked for the Cohens they had disappeared.

The FBI, in fact, lost all trace of them, and so did the security forces of other nations, until Colonel Abel (q.v.) was arrested as a Russian spy in 1957, and the Cohen's names came up again. In fact they had gone from the United States to Australia on forged passports. They stayed in Australia for three years, then moved from Australia to Switzerland and thence to England on forged Canadian passports in December 1954.

Now, The Centre had gone to great pains to provide Lonsdale with a cover story. Inquiries made by the Special Branch between his arrest and trial showed that there had been a real Gordon Lonsdale who had been born on 27th August, 1924, at Kirkland Lake, a village fifty-five miles northeast of Cobalt, in Ontario, Canada. His father was a Canadian who had variously worked as a farmer, a spare-time lumberman, and a general handyman; his mother was a Finn who had immigrated to Canada with her family a short time before she married Lonsdale.

Our Gordon Lonsdale had a Canadian passport when arrested, and it was a genuine passport. When the Canadian authorities were asked by the British to investigate the issue of this passport to Lonsdale in 1954, they discovered that it was obtained by means of a birth certificate which had been issued a short time previously in Cobalt.

The Canadian passport requirements are that an application shall be accompanied by a birth certificate and the names and addresses of two sponsors. Canadian birth certificates are issued by regional administration headquarters, and apparently if a man walks into an issuing office and can produce evidence in the form of letters addressed to him or some other mild form of identification, a birth certificate is issued to him without question.

The names and addresses of the sponsors given on the passport application form were genuine enough, but when questioned both said they had never heard of Lonsdale, nor were the signatures theirs. Their names were both in telephone directories, however. But the Canadian authorities had not checked with them before issuing the passport. Thus two procedural

461

lapses made it possible for Lonsdale to obtain a proof of identity which is accepted as valid the world over.

The real Lonsdale's father told the police that he had separated from his wife a year after the birth of their son, Gordon Arnold. Mrs Lonsdale remained in Canada until 1932, when she returned to Finland with the boy, now eight years old. Since then, Lonsdale senior had heard nothing of his former wife or his son, nor had anyone else.

The Canadian and British authorities believe that the real Gordon Lonsdale died sometime before his thirteenth birthday, that is, before 1954, and that his death and background were known to The Centre, who had reason to believe that his true fate was unkown except to them.

Genuine identification papers are obviously always more satisfactory than even cleverly forged ones; and in any case, in arranging things as they did The Centre were acting in their traditional way in acquiring genuine documentation for their agents. For this reason our Lonsdale arrived in Canada sometime in 1954 — though it is impossible to say

in what disguise, since lists are not kept recording the entry and exit of tourists and other visitors — and within a short time had acquired a genuine Canadian passport. Armed with such a document it was the easiest thing in the world for him to enter Great Britain, and since Commonwealth citizens were not at that time required to have either residence or work permits, no official trace of him would be recorded.

As the leader of a network, Lonsdale needed a cover that would give him freedom of movement, and he chose that beautifully vague one of "company director".

This trouble in providing Lonsdale with the best possible cover, is indicative of the great emphasis which the Russians place on security. In the early period of his activities here, Lonsdale himself showed a similar appreciation, and yet British counterespionage was able to break this enormously powerful network only because all five committed most serious breaches of security.

Houghton began it all by overspending, and so aroused the first suspicions. Even so, his breach of security need not have led to Lonsdale had Lonsdale himself not committed as flagrant breaches. The three spies always met at the same time at the same place on a Saturday afternoon. Lonsdale was the key man in the network — some British authorities believe he was a Resident Director, chief of a number of networks, not necessarily all of them in Britain — and not only ought he not to have met Houghton and Gee himself, but he should have used a series of go-betweens and stipulated that no meeting should ever be held twice in the same place. He ought never to have kept the money and other equipment in his apartment, concealed though it was.

And the Krogers were equally, perhaps even more, careless. They ought to have had a prearranged signal by which Kroger could have given immediate warning to Mrs Kroger that police were at the door, so that she could have destroyed the Russian letter and microdots, which she ought not to have had in her handbag in any case. It was also a fatal mistake to keep large sums of money in the house, and equally fatal to have left attached the electric cord which connected the radiogram to the transmitter under the kitchen floor, for without pulling the bungalow apart, the counter-espionage agents might never have discovered the radio.

Gee and Houghton were both guilty, too, in having in their rooms the pamphlets, lists of pamphlets, and other classified material. Certainly they were taken **in flagrante delicto,** but no spy can be sure at any time that the knock on the door does not herald the police acting on suspicion and nothing else, in which circumstances, provided the cover is good and there is no incriminating evidence, it is possible to escape.

It is surprising at first sight that Lonsdale should have been guilty of such lapses of conduct, the most serious of which was his having direct and frequent contact with the Krogers; though, having operated for five years without attracting suspicion or even the slightest attention, he may have grown over-confident, as he did in his cover-business operations. The fact remains, however, that the training and equipment sections of The Centre are also guilty of breaches of security.

It will be remembered that a Ronson lighter with a false compartment was found in the Kroger's bungalow; so, also, was a tin of Richard Hudnut "Three Flowers" talcum powder containing a false compartment, and a whisky flask made in three compartments, the middle one of which alone contained whisky. Exactly identical objects were found in Lonsdale's apartment. Obviously supplied by The Centre it would appear that such objects are mass-produced. In a case where only suspicion rests, the presence of these objects will at once attract attention. It is difficult to understand how such a careful, methodical people as the Russians can be guilty of such bad security.

The case also presents one final, but very interesting point. Lonsdale steadfastly refused to give the Special Branch any indication at all of his real identity. Only some years after he had been sent to prison was it discovered that his real name is Konon Trofimovich Molody. On the

other hand, as a result of their Canadian inquiries, the British authorities knew for certain that their prisoner calling himself Gordon Arnold Lonsdale was not the real Lonsdale.

During their investigations the Royal Canadian Mounted Police traced the doctor who delivered Mrs Lonsdale of her son. This doctor, Dr W. E. Mitchell, in 1961 practicing in Toronto, remembered the occasion very well, for he had had to travel many rough miles to reach the Lonsdales' lonely house. This helped him to turn up old records, and these showed that within a few days of the baby's birth it had been necessary for him to circumcise the boy. The Lonsdale arrested by the British was not circumcised.

Supposing Lonsdale, despite proof that he had forged the signatures of his sponsors for a passport, had doggedly persisted in stating that he was nevertheless the real Lonsdale, this difference would have proved that he was not. The incident seems to suggest that in the future when the identities of real people, living or dead, are assumed, unless it is definitely known that the cover man has not been subjected to this particular surgical attention, all male spies should be circumcised. The operation can be performed at any time in a man's life and many adult men do undergo it. This being so, it would be difficult — in fact, impossible — to prove when the operation had been performed. On the other hand, once the change has been made, the **status quo ante** cannot be restored, and the baby who was circumcised cannot become an uncircumcised adult. So carefully are covers prepared that this is not the somewhat far-fetched consideration that it may appear to be to a layman.

Molody-Lonsdale served only three years of his twenty-five-year sentence. In 1963 the Russians had arrested, tried and sentenced a British businessman, Greville Wynne (q.v.) for espionage.

At 5.15 p.m. on the afternoon of 22nd April, 1964, Wynne and Lonsdale were exchanged at the Heerstrasse checkpoint in Berlin.

BIBLIOGRAPHY :

Spy Ring — John Bulloch and Henry Miller (London, 1961).

POWERS, Francis Gary (The U-2 spy).

(This article is based in considerable part on the Russian transcript of the Powers Trial. Where I have quoted, except where otherwise noted, the extracts are taken verbatim from this transcript — RS.)

On the morning of May Day, 1960, in a small village a few miles from the industrial city of Sverdlovsk, in central Russia, a truck driver called Surin was enjoying the public holiday with a late breakfast. It was exactly 11 o'clock local time when the comparative peace of Surin's living-room was broken by the harsh, compelling noise of a jet aircraft which seemed to be flying more than usually low.

Curious, Surin put down his cup and ran out into the village street, and as he reached the roadway, there was a loud explosion. In the distance, in the direction from which the noise had come, Surin saw what looked like a column of dust rising up to the cloudless May sky, and as he watched it, he saw the tiny speck of a descending parachute.

At that moment his neighbour Chuzhakin, who had been visiting friends in a neighbouring village, pulled up beside him. He too had heard the explosion and asked Surin if he knew what it was. In reply Surin pointed up at the sky, and as they had no means of knowing who the parachutist might be, Chuzhakin suggested that Surin should get into his car and that they should go and see if they could give him any assistance.

As they came up to the spot where the parachutist had landed, another man, called Cheremisin, joined them and together they ran to help a fourth man, Asabin, who had arrived before them and was helping the airman to his feet and deflating the parachute. Asabin, who was an invalid, had gone up onto the roof of his house on hearing the jet aircraft, and from there had seen a column of dust rising some five kilometres from the village, and the descending parachutist. Asabin had served in the Red Air Force and knew how to deal with parachutes, so he had run to help.

The parachutist, a solidly built man of medium height with close-cropped hair greying at the temples and a birth mark on the left side of his neck, had pulled himself up and was swaying slightly dazed on his feet as Cheremisin, Chuzhakin and Surin ran up. He was dressed in a steel-coloured suit, a white helmet with the figure 29 painted on it, and brown shoes. In a holster at his belt was a long-barrelled pistol. Asabin removed the parachute harness and with the help of the others took off the helmet and the attached earphones. The Russians asked the airman who he was, and when he replied in a strange language they decided to take him to the local Soviet headquarters. So Cheremisin took away the pistol and Asabin a dagger which he noticed was also attached to the flying suit, and they led him to Chuzhakin's car.

Asabin wanted to know whether the flier had been alone or with companions, so he held up first one and then two fingers. The airman replied by holding up one finger and pointing to himself. As the car set off, Asabin inspected the dagger and saw engraved on it an inscription, which he recognised as being English, and he told the others. Presently, the airman indicated that he was thirsty and would like a drink, so at the next house along the way the car was stopped and water was got for him. He also mimed that he would like a cigarette and was given one.

State security officers had arrived at the local Soviet by the time the Russians and the airman arrived, and they handed him over. He complained of a headache, so a doctor was fetched and he was treated. Then he was taken to Moscow.

On 17th, 18th and 19th August he was put on trial in the Hall of Columns in Moscow on charges of espionage.

The Russian division of the American Central Intelligence Agency was presented with an extremely difficult problem when it was required to keep an eye on the ballistic missile programme of the Soviet Union. Russia is so vast that it is possible to site secret establishments far inland, in isolated regions which of themselves, and disregarding the strict and intensive security guard maintained on the establishments, make it ex-

ceptionally difficult for foreign agents to come within spying distance, even if those agents are able to penetrate Soviet frontiers, and escape the vigilance of counter-espionage. The movement of the individual in Russia is not so free as in the democracies, and if the would-be traveller is non-Russian, his movements are controlled, all of which adds to the difficulties of the spy, though it does not entirely frustrate him.

How then, might one keep a check on Russian nuclear activities, particularly in the preparation of missile launching bases, even a check which could give only vague indications of what was going on?

Now, the Lockheed aircraft designers and manufacturers had developed an aircraft capable of carrying out meteorological observations at very high altitudes. Perhaps recalling how successful Royal Air Force aerial reconnaissances had been in World War II in revealing rocket-launching sites, and other useful intelligence, it was not long before it occurred to the CIA that if this aircraft were married to the very latest developments in photographic equip-

467

ment, it would produce half an espionage unit — the other half being the pilot to fly it — which could fill the important gap in their spying on Russia.

An aircraft which could achieve heights of up to 70,000 feet was necessary, because only at this height could an aeroplane escape detection by Soviet Radar, or if it were picked up by radar, still be out of reach of Russian fighter aircraft. It was argued, it seems, that even if the Russians became aware of the flights, they could do nothing about them, for they would be unable to produce any proof that such flights were occurring, and the CIA would be able to deny that they were being made without fear of contradiction, or at least without fear of being proved guilty of lying. Also, it was argued that the Russians would not humiliate themselves by publicly admitting that their territory could be overflown with impunity by American aircraft.

Tests were made of the aircraft, the equipment and the technique to be employed, and they were found to be satisfactory. Thereupon the CIA

planned to go into action.

Under the membership rules of the North Atlantic Treaty Organisation (NATO), member states — and this for the most part means America — could apply for bases of one kind or another in any other member state, on the grounds of defence planning. Through the Administration, the CIA applied to Turkey for facilities at the air-base at Incirlik, near Adana, and to Pakistan for facilities at the Peshawar air-base.

At Incirlik, the CIA installed its air-espionage cell, under the command of Colonel Shelton, of the US Air Force. Known as Detachment Ten-Ten, it was manned by civilian and military personnel and equipped with Lockheed U-2s carrying highly specialised cameras capable of photographing the ground from a height of at least 68,000 feet. Pilots of outstanding ability were required to fly these very special aircraft and to work the fairly complicated equipment. Recruitment was confined to the service air arms, a number of whose pilots, specially selected because of their qualifications, were approached. Among those so approached in 1956 was Francis Gary Powers.

Powers had been born in Bourdyne, Kentucky, in 1929. He came of a working-class family; his father had first been a miner but was now a shoe-repairer in Pound, Virginia, as the result of an accident in the mines. It was his father's wish that Francis Powers should become a doctor, and at great sacrifice a higher education was provided for him at Milligan College, near Johnston City. When he graduated from Milligan, however, Powers did not go on to study medicine, but took a job as a life-guard at a swimming-pool. This proved only temporary work, and as his draft for military service was coming up, instead of seeking other employment he volunteered for the Air Force at the end of 1950. In 1952 he was commissioned in the rank of lieutenant and qualified as a fighter pilot. A year or two later he married.

As his period of military service neared completion, one day, he says, "I was notified that some people wanted to see me. I went for an interview. They told me that they had a very good job, and I had the qualifications for this. I was required to have training and to be away from the family overseas for some eighteen months. At that time I did not know what the pay would be, but they said there would be an increase over what I received before. The next interview was in the next day or so. I liked the sound of a flying job with more money, and I told them I would be willing to be away from home, and then they told me what would be required. I was to meet certain physical requirements, and pass a medical examination. I was up to the mark. I was given a special flying suit for high-altitude flights. This was tested in an altitude chamber, and I was told I would be paid 2500 dollars a month. I was told that my main duties would be to fly along the Soviet border and to collect any radar or radio information. I was also told there would possibly be other duties. I signed the contract and started my training."

Besides the contract, Powers also signed an agreement by which he undertook to keep his enlistment with CIA secret. He was warned that if he broke this agreement he would be liable to ten years' imprisonment and/or a fine of 10,000 dollars.

Given the cover name of Palmer, Powers was sent to Las Vegas airfield in the Nevada desert. Here he received instruction over two and a half months in handling the U-2 and in operating the equipment for intercepting radio and radar signals.

Having carried out high-altitude long-distance flights over California, Texas and the northern United States, Powers was sent to Detachment Ten-Ten at Incirlik. As cover, Incirlik was officially attached to the National Aeronautics and Space Administration (NASA) and Powers was provided by NASA with a certificate which entitled him to pilot United States Air Force aircraft.

Between 1956 and 1960, Powers, in company with the six other pilots who constituted the flying personnel of Detachment Ten-Ten, made a number of flights, chiefly along the Turkish-Soviet frontier. The flights were fairly evenly distributed among the pilots, and it would seem that because of the dis-

covery that Russian radar was of a much higher standard than had previously been thought, only shallow penetration was made into Soviet air space during this period. In 1959 and 1960, however, certain technical improvements were made to the U-2 equipment, and it was decided that a deeper penetration could now be attempted with reasonable chances of success.

Then, toward the end of April 1960, Powers and about nineteen others including Colonel Shelton, commander of Ten-Ten, went by air transport to Peshawar. On the evening of 30th April, the U-2 was brought from Incirlik to Peshawar, and Powers and one other pilot were instructed to hold themselves in readiness to make a flight into Soviet territory on the following day.

Fate seems to have played a decisive hand in apportioning the role of spy pilot to Powers. The original contract was for eighteen months, but was renewable for further periods of eighteen months if the pilot was willing and if the authorities considered the pilot still in the condition of physical and mental fitness which the flights demanded.

It will be recalled that when he was first approached and even when he signed his first contract, Powers had been told that his duties would be to make flights along the Turkish-Soviet frontier to gather radio and radar information, but that he might be required to undertake "other duties later". These "other duties" were not defined at the time, but he learned what they would be about six months later. This did not prevent Powers from renewing his contract in 1958. Indeed, because he had not been asked by that time to penetrate deeply into Russia, it seemed an extremely worthwhile job from the material point of view. As he said himself, "This was a good job with good pay, and I did not consider this job dangerous, that is at least not until May! As a result, from the material viewpoint, I lived well, my wife and I had anything we wanted and at the same time we were able to save." He had, in fact, been able to save about 15,000 dollars for the purchase of a house, and under an arrangement with the authorities whereby part of his salary was held by them until his contract was terminated, he had accumulated a further 30,000 dollars. (With the exception of a very few cases of magnificently outstanding spies who carried out espionage for foreign powers, there is no record of any agents of any nationality receiving such remuneration for their work. This was spying put on a really worthwhile basis, and the CIA are to be congratulated on being the first organisation to pay the "rate for the job.")

When his contract came up for renewal a second time, in 1960, Powers hesitated before signing on again. He very much wanted to obtain a flying post in a civilian capacity at home, he says at one point, but was unable to find one. At another time he says "I wanted to buy a good home and if possible to start a business of some kind . . . I would like to own a service station."

Probably it was a combination of these two factors which eventually overcame his hesitation, and he signed on for a further eighteen months not long before he was sent on his last mission.

471

The decision to renew his contract on this last occasion was the first move that fate made against him. The second was that, though another pilot besides himself was ordered to prepare himself for the flight, it was Powers who was chosen to carry it out.

Early in the morning of 1st May, Powers was awakened as he had been awakened many times before, while on the "alert flight" schedule, and was told to prepare himself to make a flight which would take him right across the Soviet Union.

This is how he described it. "On the morning of 1st May, I think it was three or four hours before the flight, I was awakened, given breakfast, and told that I was to fly today. Another pilot was awakened at the same time, and two and a half hours before take-off we started to breathe oxygen. Soon after that Colonel Shelton brought the maps and showed them to me. He told me this was the route I was to fly. It was the route on the maps found in my plane. He told me that he had some information about some airfields, and if I wanted to, I could put the places on my map. I wanted to do so and did mark some of them. There was also a place where he said I might see a missile launching site. I also put that down. There was one place where he thought there was something, but he did not know what. I also put that down. I was to follow the course of the route which was plotted on the map with red and blue pencils and to turn on and off the controls of the equipment over the points indicated on the map . . . The colonel also said that just in case anything should happen, he was giving me some packages with Soviet money (7500 roubles) and some gold coins, which I might use to bribe Soviet citizens to help me, if I needed help. They were put into my flying suit pockets. He also had a silver dollar coin which he showed me which had a needle installed in it. He said that there was no danger because no USSR aircraft or rocket could get to my altitude, but in case something happened and I was captured, the needle contained poison and, if I was tortured and I could not stand it, I could use the needle to kill myself."

Other instructions to Powers were that if he ran into difficulties he was to destroy his aircraft. At the subsequent trial eight expert witnesses were called to testify on various aspects of Powers's personal equipment and on the investigations carried out on the remains of the U-2.

In the event, when his aircraft went out of control, however, Powers was prevented by conditions from activating the destructor unit mechanism, as we shall see later.

According to Powers, in evidence at his trial, his mission called for him to fly from Peshawar, over Afghanistan, and into Russia, and then follow a route which took him east of the Aral Sea, northwest of Chelyabinsk, and over Kirov and Sverdlovsk, then northeast to Arkhangelsk, and on to Murmansk, then almost due west to Bodoe in Norway, where he was to land. He was to fly at his maximum altitude 68,000 feet, and at various points marked on the map he was to switch on and off the various knobs which operated the photographic and recording equipment. His radio callsign, to be used only on arrival at Bodoe or in case of emergency, was "Puppy 68."

When questioned at his trial by R. A. Rudenko, Procurator General of the USSR, about his knowledge of the equipment, Powers gave some interesting replies.

Rudenko: With what aim did you switch on the equipment?

Powers: I was instructed to do so. It was indicated on the map where the equipment was to be switched on.

Rudenko: Defendant Powers, you probably knew the purpose for which you had to turn on and off the equipment?

Powers: I could very well guess the purpose for which I turned on and off the equipment. If I was to be very exact I would say no.

Rudenko: I think that the defendant Powers did not doubt that this was a reconnaissance plane from the moment he started his flight?

Powers: No, I didn't doubt it.

Rudenko: On your plane, radio intelligence equipment and tape recordings of various Soviet radar stations were found. Is that correct?

Powers: I have been told so, but I don't know. In any case, I do not know what much of the equipment looks like except what I have seen here.

Rudenko: But you, defendant Powers, were trained enough to know that such equipment is designed for special spying flights?

Powers: I didn't know anything about the equipment before.

Rudenko: But you were sufficiently informed that this flight had espionage aims?

Powers: I saw no other reasons for such a flight.

Rudenko: Did you also make visual observations?

Powers: Yes.

Rudenko: Did you make corresponding marks on the map?

Powers: Yes. I remember making three marks on the map.

Rudenko: What marks were they?

Powers: First there was an airfield not indicated on the map. I defined as exactly as possible the bearings of this airfield. The second as I remember was an oil storage. In this case I made the mark through a thin layer of clouds. I was off course and did not know the exact position. The third was a big outfit indicating a lot of buildings.

Rudenko: You do not deny that you invaded Soviet air space in violation of the law?

Powers: No, I do not deny it.

Rudenko: Therefore, this intrusion pursued intelligence Espionage aims?

Powers: I did what the chart indicated.

Rudenko: Not knowing what the special apparatus was?

Powers: I never saw the apparatus.

Throughout his trial Powers gave the impression of being an honest young man, conscious of being in a most unenviable situation, in danger of losing his life before a firing squad, anxious to avoid that fate if possible by appearing to be helpful to the prosecution, and yet not prepared to be led into trapping himself into admissions which could particularly damage his defence.

In this passage, we see him following the technique of the

trapped spy; that is, admitting to what he knew his interrogator could prove, yet on points which the interrogator could not prove maintaining a firm attitude of denial. In March 1962, after Powers was exchanged for Colonel Abel, the Soviet spy, (q.v.) and returned to the United States, the CIA released a statement by its director, John A. McCone, which said, in part: "The pilots involved in the U-2 programme . . . were not selected or trained as espionage agents . . . Their job was to fly the plane . . . " Indeed, since Power's training period at Las Vegas lasted only two and a half months and was devoted wholly to learning to handle the U-2, it does not seem that he could have been given any training in espionage techniques, especially since he was posted to Incirlik as soon as his Las Vegas training was completed. This passage is of considerable interest — and there are other passages illustrating the same technique — for if Powers had had no training in general techniques, then he seems to have adopted this particular technique instinctively, a sign of keen intelligence. In any case, he is to be admired, and not at all criticised, as he has been criticised by certain "professionals", for allegedly being too helpful to his captors. Indeed, after his testimony before the Senate Armed Services Committee on his return to America, Powers was applauded, and the McCone statement said that he had faithfully carried out his instructions on how to act in the event of capture and had met "his obligations as an American."

That Powers had his wits about him during his examination by Roman Rudenko was also made very plain in his answer to the prosecutor's question immediately following the last one quoted above.

From the record, it is clear that Rudenko, who is an outstanding lawyer and an expert in examining witnesses, was trying to extract from Powers an admission that he had not only been spying but knew that he had been spying. Unfortunately for Powers, his maps had been recovered, and on these maps there were marks he had made. Powers realised, too, that he could not deny them, but was still prepared to make out the best case for himself. He could not have known — it is doubtful whether any but the most experienced witness could have known — that Rudenko had also a secondary motive in pursuing this line of questioning. One has said a "secondary" motive, yet, in fact, it was a primary motive of the trial taken as a whole — in other words, propaganda.

Rudenko had asked "You stated here and during the investigation that you switched the equipment on and off at definite points? and Powers had answered: "I did what the chart indicated."

Rudenko: Not knowing what the special apparatus was?

Powers: I never saw the apparatus.

Then came what Rudenko fully expected would be the **coup de grâce** of this phase of the questioning:

Rudenko: With the same ease you could have pulled a switch to release an atom-bomb?

It could indeed have been the **coup de grâce** which Rudenko hoped it would be, and with his first words, it seemed that Powers had accepted it as such.

"It could have been done," he said. Then with admirable presence of mind he went on, "But this is not the type of plane for carrying and dropping such bombs."

The official record of the trial comments at this point, **These words which Powers lets drop with amazing indifference, are received with indignation in the court room.** Perhaps those who were indignant did not hear Powers completely blunt Rudenko's shaft and utterly destroy all its propaganda value. This reply alone — "But this is not the type of plane for carrying and dropping such bombs" — redeems any error of judgement Powers might otherwise have made or be considered to have made during the course of his trial.

But to return to Powers's briefing for the flight.

When Rudenko and Powers's defence counsel, M. I. Grinev, had finished their questioning, various members of the court asked questions designed to clarify certain points. One of them, Major General of the Air Force A. Zakharov, acting as one of the two People's Assessors, asked, "How much time did

476

you spend in studying the route and the map?"

Powers: I had very little time to study the route and the map. I was briefed at the same time. All this took place between the time I put on the helmet until I started getting dressed, which was probably forty-five minutes before the scheduled take-off. It would be roughly one hour and fifteen minutes.

Zakharov: How much time did you spend preparing for the flight the first time you flew along the Soviet border in 1956?

Powers: I knew about this flight several hours before; if I remember correctly, it was the day before.

What these questions were designed to bring out is not clear. Powers's answers, however reveal that the time given him to familiarise himself with the route he was to take was just sufficient but not more, and seems to indicate that those in charge of it were satisfied that it was merely a straightforward flight from one point to another, with the pilot required merely to operate a few extra instruments. In other words, despite the fact that Powers was supplied with money and a means of killing himself, if he were in agony in an accident or under torture, and an alternative route if anything, barring his being shot down, went wrong at any point, it was not expected to be a flight beyond the capabilities of the pilot chosen to undertake it.

Powers took off about 5 a.m. Moscow time, and half an hour later was crossing the Soviet frontier. He did not know that from the moment he did so, his progress was tracked by units of the Russian anti-aircraft defences. As far as he was concerned, all was going well, and he was having no difficulties with his navigation. Two or three times he checked his position by his radio compass, using Russian ground stations once near Stalinabad and once near Chelyabinsk.

Four minutes short of four hours after take-off, he was approaching the large industrial centre of Sverdlovsk, about 1250 miles from where he had crossed the border, and had just finished making a turn when, "I saw, that is felt, a sort of hollow-sounding explosion. It seemed to be behind me. I could see an orange flash or an orange-coloured light behind me." He later said he was almost sure there had not been a direct hit on the plane. Within a few seconds, however, he realised that the U-2 was out of control and descending rapidly.

Testifying before the Senate Armed Services Committee after his exchange and return to America, Powers described the falling plane being whipped into an inverted spin, so that he was thrust outward by centrifugal force and hung against his seat belt rather than sitting in his seat. His first impulse was to activate the "destruct" switches, but this would have left him with only 70 seconds to get clear of the aircraft, and he was unable to use his ejection seat. Had he done so he would probably have lost both legs, which were wedged under the windshield. He succeeded, however, in releasing the cockpit canopy, and then found himself half-way out of the plane and connected with it only by his oxygen tubes. He tried to work his way back to the cockpit to throw the "destruct" switches, but was unable to do so because of

the G forces acting upon him and the sudden frosting over of his helmet face-plate in the cold outside air. Making several lunges, he managed to break free from the aircraft, and his parachute opened automatically.

When he left the U-2, Powers was at an altitude of some 14,000 feet. Later, testifying before the Senate Armed Services Committee he recalled, "I remembered I had a map in my pocket. I took out this map, looked at it, tore it into small pieces and scattered it in the air.

"I also thought of the coin with the poison pin in it. This had been given to me just prior to the flight, and it was my option whether to take this or not, and I chose to take it. I got to thinking that when I got on the ground, if I were captured they would surely find this coin, but maybe just the pin lying loose in the pocket would be overlooked, so I opened up the coin, got the pin out and just dropped it in my pocket."

Regarding this needle, CIA director McCone said in his statement: "In regard to the poison needle which was prominently displayed at the trial at Moscow, it should be emphasised that this was intended for use primarily if the pilot were subjected to torture or other circumstances which in his discretion warranted his taking his own life. There were no instructions that he should commit suicide and no expectation that he would do so except in those situations just described, and I emphasise that even taking the needle with him in the plane was not mandatory, it was his option.

The Soviet authorities did not announce the capture of Powers until 7th May, when Mr Krushchev announced it while addressing the session of the Supreme Soviet of the USSR. By that time, the authorities in Washington had in effect made themselves appear quite ridiculous by issuing statements which the Russians were in a position to prove to be lies. At this stage no announcement of any sort was necessary, and Allen Dulles must have appreciated this, but apparently had no power to override the politicians who, after Krushchev's revelations, made the situation even worse by issuing a series of contradictory statements.

First, an official spokesman of the State Department said that "in so far as the Washington authorities were concerned, there was no authorisation for any such flight as described by Mr Kruschev." This was followed by a statement by Secretary of State Herter that, in accordance with the National Security Act of 1947, since the beginning of his Administration President Eisenhower had put into effect directives to carry out intelligence operations against the Soviet Union, under which directives, programmes had been developed and put into operation providing for the incursion of American reconnaissance aircraft into the air space of the USSR.

This was an admission of government responsibility for the flight and was bad enough. But the situation was further worsened when President Eisenhower himself confirmed Herter's statement and took upon himself, as head of the Administration, full responsibility for the flight. However, what seems to have roused the anger of the Soviet authorities almost to breaking point was a television speech by Vice President Nixon in which he confirmed the statements of Herter and the President, and went on to declare that flights of American aircraft over the territory of the Soviet Union were a calculated policy of the United States and that they would continue.

To people experienced in espionage procedures, these statements came as a shock which for a time left them bemused. They could not understand how responsible men like Herter, Nixon and Eisenhower could behave in this way, which was contrary to all accepted practice. Admittedly, they could not deny that the U-2 had been on an espionage mission, but they could have remained silent, even if they felt that they could not deny governmental responsibility.

Purely from the espionage angle, any ground for defence which Powers might have felt able to put forward in mitigation of his act of espionage was completely knocked away by each statement that was made in Washington.

This is said, though it is known that filmed and recorded evidence in the remains of

the aircraft proved without a shadow of doubt that the U-2 was a "spy plane". The evidence of G. Istomin D.Sc. Tech., makes this quite clear. He testified:

A study of the remnants of the U-2 photographic equipment enabled the commission to establish that a wide-angle long-focus air camera model 73-B was installed on this aircraft for aerial reconnaissance photography. The name of the model of the camera is given on several company nameplates fastened to the camera body. The locks of the removable spindles of the film spools carry an inscription showing that they were made in the United States.

For its tactical and technical characteristics, the 73-B model is a reconnaissance air camera and its salient feature is that it is designed to photograph large areas from the air in the course of one flight. The air camera had a rotating lens for ensuring multistrip photography. In the course of the flight of 1st May, 1960, the air

480

camera was used for seven-strip photography consecutively through seven glass-encased aircraft windows in the skin of the plane. The lens cover was from 160 to 200 kilometers in width.

The camera was loaded with two films, each of which was 24 centimeters wide and about 2000 meters long. The films were placed parallel to the focal plane of the camera so that during each action of the shutter two films were exposed with a total size of 45 × 45 centimeters The supply of film in the camera made it possible to receive about 4000 paired serial pictures i.e. to photograph in the course of the flight of 1st May, a route of about 2187 miles . . .

The aerial photographs taken contain sufficiently complete and diverse espionage information regarding industrial and military installations located on the photographed territory and can be used both for espionage purposes and for compiling and correcting topographical maps and determining the co-ordination of military and topographical objects.

Thus the study of the remnants of the photographic equipment of the Lockheed U-2 aircraft which violated the state frontier of the USSR on 1st May, 1960, and the materials of the aerial photography taken from it, lead to the conclusion as to the reconnaissance nature of this equipment and the espionage purposes of the flight by this aircraft.

Faced with this evidence, Powers could scarcely put forward in his defence that he had lost his way. He had to admit, "I could very well guess the purpose for which I turned on and off the equipment."

Nevertheless, even taking into account the extremely difficult position in which Powers found himself, there were several courses he might have considered taking in defending himself. But when his President admitted that the flight was an espionage flight, what defence was there left to him except that he had been the tool of im-

481

perialist warmongers who had tempted him against his better judgment with large sums of money? And Powers did not sink to this.

Indeed, throughout the whole of his trial, he comported himself with a dignity and spirit which might have been found lacking in many another. All the way along the line, Powers was badly served — by his President and others who ought to have known better, by faulty intelligence which led him to believe that he was invulnerable, and by attempts just before the trial to accuse the Russians of having brain-washed or drugged him.

The Russians staged the trial with an eye to propaganda. The speeches of the prosecutor and the defence counsel and the wording of the indictment itself lost no opportunity to ram home the "lying deceit" of the American Administration and its "warmongering activities." A natural corollary of this was an ostensible sympathy for the prisoner, the poor tool of these "imperialist warmongers". This sympathy was indeed apparent. Taking into consideration the fact of the

extreme antagonism which is at the root of all Russian–American relations and the further fact that Power's defence had been wished on his counsel, since Soviet law requires the accused to be adequately represented, and though the defence counsel's participation in Power's defence could not redound to his credit among his fellow countrymen, one could expect him to make the most of the propaganda aspect and do nothing more to help Powers. Mr Grinev did make the most of the propaganda.

"I shall be right if I say that the Powers case is of international importance inasmuch as besides Powers, one of the perpetrators of a perfidious and aggressive act against the Soviet Union, there should sit and invisibly be present here in the prisoner's dock his masters, namely, the Central Intelligence Agency headed by Allen Dulles and the American military and with them all those sinister aggressive forces which strive to unleash another world war . . .

"The clumsy attempts of the United States' leaders to vindicate the unprecedented provocation they staged against the Soviet Union are so fresh in our minds . . . Speaking in the Senate Foreign Relations Committee, Secretary of State Herter described the statement issued by his department as a cover story prompted allegedly only by a humane desire, a desire above all to protect the pilot, that is, Powers. In this case, too, the United States Secretary of State did not speak the truth, since neither he nor his colleagues in the Eisenhower-Nixon-Herter administration thought of protecting Powers . . .

Yet the materials of the preliminary investigation have irrefutably established that the plane, piloted by Powers intruded into the air space of the Soviet Union on the orders of the American authorities who had instructions from the United States government to effect the intrusion or, as the statement of Secretary of State Herter says, to penetrate within the frontiers of other countries.

"In the given case the point is that the United States government has proclaimed systematic espionage intrusions within the confines of the Soviet Union an integral part of its national policy, in fact laying claims to some exceptional rights both with regard to the Soviet Union and to other states . . . In carrying out this policy, the ruling monopoly circles of America do not even stop at committing such actions which directly endanger universal peace, which are taken only when nations are at war.

"What I have said gives the defence the right to assert with complete confidence that the appearance of Powers over Soviet territory was not a manifestation of his own will but was predetermined by the will of the aggressive circles behind him, especially the Central Intelligence Agency of the United States headed by Allen Dulles, in the system of which Powers was a small pawn.

"In other words, though Powers was the direct perpetrator, he is not the main culprit, notwithstanding the fact that the case heard today is associated with his name.

"In this connection it is unfortunate that Powers alone is in the dock. If those who sent him to commit this crime were alongside him, there is no doubt that the position of my client Powers would be different and he would then hold a secondary place and consequently could undoubtedly expect a considerable mitigation of punishment."

Had Mr Grinev stopped there — and up to this point he had echoed the contentions of the Procurator General Rudenko — he could have argued that he had done his duty. As I have said, however, there was a natural corollary. Since it was the burden of his argument that the real culprit was the American Administration and its subordinate bodies, and that Powers was their tool, an appearance of sympathy with Powers would not be at all out of place. We have seen the first signs of it in the last two paragraphs which I have quoted above, but Mr Grinev developed it.

"It goes without saying that I do not absolve Powers from responsibility in arguing this way, but I want to emphasise and draw your attention to the fact that he committed this crime not of his own volition and reasoning, but on orders from above, on orders from his masters; moreover, he was not connected with any of them, except his direct superior, Colonel Shelton, and was not even informed of the plans they harboured in sending him to commit this crime. More than that, they deliberately misled him, assuring him that the flight over Soviet territory was absolutely safe and did not involve any risk. Thus defendant Powers testified: "I was informed that the Soviet Union did not possess the means to hit my plane." However, life corrected these assurances given by Colonel Shelton and others, and Powers, having run a deadly risk, is now, thanks to the vigilance of a unit of the Soviet rocket forces, faced with the necessity to answer for his actions to a Soviet court of justice. This to a certain extent lays emphasis on the place Powers held among those who are really guilty of the crime and who, in all fairness, should bear their punishment in full measure."

Again, Mr Grinev could have stopped there and considered he had done his duty. He went on, however, to try to enlist more than the

484

ostensible sympathy for Powers which the propaganda line required.

"Comrades Judges, deciding on the punishment for Powers, you cannot but take into account the testimony given by Powers both at the preliminary investigation stage and at the trial.

"Concerning his testimony Powers says : "I am doing my best to be honest ... I wish to be frank." And this cannot be denied him, because his behaviour during the interrogation shows that the explanations he has given are not just phrases, not an attempt to mislead the investigating bodies and the court, but are truthful and sincere. I do not know whether Powers has told the whole truth, but what he has told is the truth. Is it not a fact that everything that constitutes the substance and subject of his guilt, of the guilt of his masters, was reflected by Powers himself in his testimony given with all detail which, I repeat, leaves no room for doubt concerning the truthfulness and sincerity of this testimony ...

"If in some cases the testimony of Powers is reserved and if sometimes he is not too communicative, this is explained, Comrades Judges, by the fact that to this day he is still held captive by those forces who sent him to commit this crime ... Under all circumstances, proceeding from Article 33 of the Fundamentals of the Criminal Code of the USSR, such testimony and such behaviour of the defendant constitute circumstances mitigating his responsibility, and, as a rule, they serve as grounds for a more lenient attitude toward him, grave as his crime may appear."

This was farther than Grinev need have gone, and he seems to have realised it, for within a few minutes he was back again on to the propaganda tack, back again to placing the burden of guilt on the American leaders.

The passage, however, gives weight to the feeling one has that throughout the trial there was more sympathy for Powers than just the sympathy required by the line taken by the prosecution and the defence for propaganda purposes.

Rudenko's questioning, except for the propaganda passage in which he tried to get Powers to admit that for all he knew he might have been releasing an atomic bomb when he switched on his equipment, was confined to eliciting facts, and his final speech was devoted to a repetition of the facts and an elaboration of the propaganda line. When he did attack Powers personally, it was not in the ranting rhetorical terms to which one has become accustomed by previous show trials in Moscow.

"The defendant Powers," he said, "for whose crimes the American intelligence service paid so generously, is not an ordinary spy, but a specially and carefully trained criminal. All Powers's actions show that he is by no means a weak-willed and blind tool, a robot in the hands of the American Intelligence Agency and the Pentagon, whom they used for espionage, subversive activities and aggression. He is a dangerous criminal. He cannot plead that he was forced to carry out the order because he voluntarily sold his honour and his conscience, he sold himself for dollars, and undertook to carry out any criminal act, that is, he acted merely from mercenary and base motives. He did not commit his crimes only by a method which, as the law says when defining circumstances aggravating responsibility, was to the common danger, but by a method fraught with danger for millions and millions of people. He consciously committed a crime with consequences of a gravity which cannot be measured by the scale which we are accustomed to apply in determining the gravity of a crime ... I have every reason to ask the court to pronounce the supreme penalty on the defendant Powers. But, taking into account the defendant Powers's sincere repentance, before the Soviet court, of the crime which he committed, I do not insist on the death sentence being passed on him, and ask the court to sentence defendant Powers to fifteen years imprisonment."

The few questions put by the presiding judge and the two People's Assessors were all designed, whether consciously or not, to give Powers the opportunity to make points helpful to his defence.

Finally, discounting the propaganda value of a lenient sentence "proceeding", as the presiding judge said in pronouncing the verdict of the court, "from the principles of socialist humaneness," the sentence of five years less than the prosecutor had asked for seems to drive this point home.

And one last point. Attempts were made on the American side to contend that the U-2 had not been brought down by a rocket, but that it could not have been flying at 68,000 feet and was destroyed by aircraft. The reason for making this attempt seemed to be wishful thinking and did not do credit to those responsible, for it is a waste of time carrying out espionage if disagreeable information is not to be accepted. More than a waste of time, this attitude constitutes a grave danger, for it misleads those who rely upon espionage results to draw up counter-defensive measures.

More than once during the trial, Powers stated that when the explosion threw his plane out of control he was flying at 68,000 feet, and there was no reason for him to lie on this point. After the trial he issued a statement in which he confirmed that he was flying at maximum altitude, and that in his opinion, judging by what happened, he was brought down by a rocket.

It could be argued that the Russians would have the Amercians believe that they had perfected their ground-to-aircraft rockets by 1960 to such a state of performance that they could bring down aircraft at 68,000 feet. Their reasons for wishing to do so are obvious. But it would be criminally stupid to disregard Powers's statement. If nothing else has come of his efforts, he has not been a failure if he has demonstrated even this one point.

On this subject, CIA director McCone said in his statement summing up the investigation of the U-2 incident, "Some information from confidential sources was available ... Some of this information was the basis for considerable speculation shortly after the 1st May stories in the press that Powers's plane had descended gradually from its extreme altitude and had been shot down by a Russian fighter at medium altitude. On careful analysis, it appears that the

487

information on which these stories were based was erroneous or was susceptible of varying interpretations. The board came to the conclusion that it could not accept a doubtful interpretation in this regard which was inconsistent with all the other known facts and consequently rejected these newspaper stories as not founded in fact."

At first sight the novelty of the spy plane appeared to indicate that a revolution in espionage techniques had taken place — a revolution, moreover, that was in keeping with the strange events that are daily being enacted in the nuclear age, and which have already become so commonplace that we find ourselves genuinely unsurprised by them. A slightly closer investigation, however, almost at once shows that what the U-2 was aiming to achieve was no novelty at all but merely an improvement on techniques used by the Royal Air Force and other air forces in World War II.

The U-2 photographic equipment took stereographic photographs; but so did the RAF's equipment in the later stages of the war. The U-2

could photograph from heights which even today demand our admiration; but the RAF flew at heights which for those days was just as extraordinary. The U-2's function was to photograph secret installations, and that was exactly what the RAF did. The one thing the U-2 did, which the RAF did not do, was to record radio and radar signals.

So far I have not mentioned what I believe to be by far the most serious blunder made by the CIA in the whole affair. A Summit Meeting had been arranged in Paris for mid-May, and it seems either the height of folly or arrogance on the part of the CIA that it should have ordered a U-2 espionage flight to be carried out so near to this meeting. As it was, Krushchev, having arrived in Paris, refused to attend any meetings unless Eisenhower formally admitted that the flight of the aircraft was a purely espionage one and apologised publicly before the world for it.

While it is clear that Krushchev had ulterior motives for not wanting to be involved in a Summit Meeting at that time, he had to attend unless he wished to create a bad impression on world opinion. The flight of the U-2 gave him a heaven-sent opportunity for wrecking the meeting before it began, and reasons which he could justify. In addition, it handed to him on a plate, a propaganda opportunity, the size of which he could not have hoped for in his most euphoric dreams. He seized it with both hands, and at a now famous press-conference which he held in Paris he squeezed every ounce out of the situation. In so doing, he humiliated the President of the United States under the glare of universal arc-lights to a degree that the leader of a great nation has never before — or since — been humiliated. Certainly Eisenhower himself, and his vice president Nixon, and his Secretary of State and others contributed to the situation, and it was to be several years before the balance was redressed, when a fearless young man, who, himself, had suffered humiliation at the hands of the CIA over the Bay of Pigs incident in Cuba, turned the tables on Krush-chev and compelled the Russians to dismantle their rocket bases in Castro's island.

I have given Gary Powers so much space, chiefly because his case is unique in espionage history, and, in my opinion, is likely to remain so. Of secondary, though not of much lesser importance, is the picture it gives of the operation of Soviet Russian use of its legal processes in the cause of making propaganda.

POYNTZ, Juliet Stuart (American who spied for Russia, post-World War II).

Juliet Stuart Poyntz joined the American Communist Party in the middle of the 1920s. She was a woman of some intellectual ability, and had been educated at Barnard College, one of the leading American educational establishments. Though somewhat masculine in her physical make-up, she possessed considerable charm. She was a schoolmistress by profession, and was an able and persuasive speaker. All of which gave her a position of some prominence in a Party that was not noted for the distinction of its membership.

489

Roundabout 1935, when the Soviet espionage organisation had decided to increase its effort in the United States, and was concentrating on acquiring recruits from the ACP, Juliet Poyntz was persuaded to work for it. Following customary procedure in such cases, she left the Party, and was sent to Moscow for a course of training. On her return to New York, she was set up in a comfortable apartment in New York, provided with ample funds and was soon supplying her employers with high-quality recruits.

She carried out her work with devotion until Stalin began his purges in 1936 and 1937. In 1937 the Trial of the Seventeen, as it is called, in which Stalin rid himself of the chief of his remaining potential opponents, resolved the crisis in which she had been privately involved ever since the first of the Purge trials. Now she resigned from the GRU.

In taking this step she overlooked one of the basic principles of Soviet espionage philosophy, namely, that once a man or woman had been a member of the organisation he or she cannot be allowed

490

to resign and live. This is true for nearly all agents of the NKVD; it is specially true of agents like Juliet Poyntz who, on announcing their resignations, announce also their intention of "telling all."

Juliet Poyntz was fifty when she announced her resignation from the GRU. She left her apartment and took a room at the Women's Association Clubhouse at 353 West 57th Street, New York. She did not break entirely with all her Communist friends, and was often in the company of Stalinists, with whom she would argue with all her customary forcefulness.

One morning towards the end of May or the beginning of June — the exact date is unknown for reasons which will presently b e c o m e apparent — she disappeared. At this time she was busy working on her memoirs, and sometimes did not see her friends for several days at a time. On this particular morning, she left her room and went out. The exact time is not known, because no one saw her go. That she fully intended to return was evident, for she left the light burning in her room, she took nothing with her, she left her papers spread out on the table, and she left no note.

No trace of her has ever been found, though there have been several theories put forward. The only thing of which one can be certain, however, is that she was liquidated by SMERSH. Some evidence of this has been brought to light since. George Mink, with whom Juliet Poyntz had once been on friendly terms, was discovered to have been in New York at the time of her disappearance. It seems justifiable to argue that, leaving her room as she did, she had gone out to meet, not a stranger, but someone she knew. Mink, an American, was a known SMERSH agent. At the climax of the Spanish civil war, he had been openly accused of organising the murders of the prominent Italian anarchists Camillo Berneri and Barbieri.

Now, too, he was openly accused by the anarchist Carlo Tresco, of having kidnapped or murdered Juliet Poyntz. Tresco was supported in his accusation by Benjamin Gitlow, a former leading member of the ACP and a disillusioned Stalinist; and by Louis Budenz, of the American **Daily Worker,** who defected in 1946, who stated in his book, **This Is My Story,** that he was informed by a member of the Political Committee that Juliet Poyntz had been liquidated by SMERSH.

BIBLIOGRAPHY :

The Executioners — Ronald Seth (London, 1967).

I Confess — Benjamin Gitlow (New York, 1940).

This Is My Story — Louis Budenz (New York, 1948).

PROMFT, Otto von (Abwehr agent, World War I) see under **McKenna, Marthe.**

POZANSKA, Sophie see under **Trepper, Leopold.**

PUNTER, Otto (Russian agent, Pre- and during World War II).

Otto Pünter comes into espionage prominence as one of Alexander Rado's (q.v. and also under **Foote, Alexander)** principal go-between with Rudolf Rössler. Less well known is that his standing at The Centre was high as the leader of a group, known as the Pakbo Group, an espionage network which he had led in the 1930s.

Pünter had never been a member of the Communist Party, but from his youth had belonged to the Swiss Social Democratic Party. By profession he was a journalist, and at the climax of the feud between Communists and Socialists in the thirties, was one of the leading Socialist protagonists. He was an extreme anti-fascist, and for this reason gave his support to the Communists because they seemed to him to be more resolutely opposed to fascism than any other political ideology.

His non-Communist-anti-Fascist career had been an outstanding one. In the middle 1920s he had joined forces with the Italian anti-Fascist Randolfo Pacciardi, and helped to organise the sensational flight which, on 10th July 1930, dropped anti-Mussolini leaflets over Milan. He had joined the Spanish Republicans during the Civil War and had gone on espionage missions for them to Italy, to discover information about Italian shipments of arms to Franco. It was this which

492

brought him to The Centre's attention.

He gathered about him a group of some half-dozen like-minded friends, and when, in 1940, the GRU (Soviet military intelligence) approached him and the group, he and they undertook to work for Soviet intelligence. Known as the Pakbo Group (Pakbo was formed of the initials of the places from which the members of the group came) it became part of Alexander Rado's network. A little later he enlarged his group, and throughout the entire time he worked for The Centre, he was able to supply information second only in importance to Rössler's.

BIBLIOGRAPHY :
Soviet Espionage — David J. Dallin (New York, 1955).

PURPLE MACHINE, The.
During the 1930s, when the Japanese militarists were concentrating on the conquest of China, it was very much to the advantage of America to be able to read Japan's secret communications. When the State Department, in 1929, closed down H. O. Yardley's (q.v.) Black Chamber, the

Army decided to create the Signal Intelligence Service (SIS) appointing the superlative cryptologist William Friedman as its chief. It fell to SIS to break the very complicated code that the Japanese used during the vital period 1938 to post-Pearl Harbor Day.

To make a code as safe as possible from the code breakers, the more complicated it is the better. Since a complicated code requires much time and patience to encipher, machines are generally set up capable of producing the coded message in a fraction of the time that a human codeographer could do it. The same applies to the decoding process.

The Japanese used a roman-letter code, and to encode and decode used a machine which they called the Alphabetical Typewriter '97, and which the Americans called the Purple Machine. The Japanese Foreign Office installed an Alphabetical Typewriter '97 in all their major embassies in the late 1930s.

The breaking of the Japanese Purple code proved an extremely difficult task for the SIS cryptanalysts led by Friedman. For between 18 and 20 months they wrestled with the problem almost every hour of every day. Gradually they pieced it together, and as they did so they were able to deduce the construction of the Alphabetical Typewriter '97.

The first complete solution of the Purple code was made in August 1940. (It almost brought about the complete collapse of Friedman, who had a breakdown in December 1940, and after three and a half months in the Walter Reed General Hospital returned to SIS on a part-time basis.) By this time the Americans were able to build a machine which would decipher the Purple code, and which, though they had never had a glimpse of it, closely resembled the Alphabetical Typewriter.

The Alphabetical Typewriter had been adapted from the German cipher machine by the Japanese Navy, who had lent it to the Foreign Office who had modified it further. The "machine" itself was housed in a box placed between two Underwood electrically-operated typewriters, which were connected to it by 26 plugs plugged into a row of sockets called the plug-board. To encode a message the operator would consult a table of keys, plug in the connection for the key of the day, turn four discs in the box according to directions given in the table, and type the plain text on one of the typewriters. As he did so, the other typewriter, operated by electric impulses in the box, typed the coded version. To decode the cipher text was typed on one typewriter, and the other simultaneously produced the plain text.

Such was the intricate construction of the box's contents that a plain text letter, because of varying electrical impulses, was represented by a different cipher every time. The code thus produced was therefore extremely difficult to break, for the analyst gets no help from repeated ciphers which, in a less complicated code, represent the same plain text letters every time.

The development of the American Purple Machine followed much the same course as the solution of the code. Thus, when the code was finally entirely solved, the SIS were able to construct at once a prototype Purple Machine which matched in execution the Alphabetical Typewriter '97. From the beginning of 1941 the Americans were able to read all the most secret Japanese diplomatic communications. The value of being able to do so as Pearl Harbor came nearer and nearer can be appreciated without having to be detailed.

Why then did Pearl Harbor take the Americans by surprise? Because never in a single one of their messages did the Japanese refer to Pearl Harbor by name.

The historians of cryptology rate the construction of the Purple Machine as perhaps the most outstanding in the history of code-breaking.

BIBLIOGRAPHY :
The Codebreakers — David Kahn (London, 1966).

RABORN, Admiral William F. Jr (Chief of American Central Intelligence Agency, 1965).

Admiral William F. Raborn Jr succeeded General McCone as Director of the Central Intelligence Agency (CIA)(q.v.) on the retirement of the General in 1965.

Raborn had been prominent in the development of the Polaris missile. A bluff, hearty sailor, he possessed none of the finesse which the post of Director of the CIA — or any other intelligence organisation for that matter — demands. This was quickly appreciated, and after a short period of office he was replaced by Richard McGarrah Helms (q.v.).

RADO, Alexander (Russian agent pre- and World War II).

Alexander Rado was Resident Director of the Russian network which operated from Switzerland during World War II and whose members included Alexander Foote (q.v.).

He was an agent of wide experience, but in view of his later behaviour, it would seem that The Centre made one of its rare mistakes in appointing him to the very responsible position of Resident Director.

He had operated first in Germany, where he had been posted to the cover-job of Clerk in the Russian embassy in Berlin, and it was he who organised the defence of the men arrested in 1931 in a case very similar to the Arcos Case (q.v.) in Britain. In 1933 he was moved to Paris, where, as cover he founded the Geopress, a press agency specialising in maps and other material relating to current-events. In 1936 he was appointed Resident Director in Switzerland.

He lived in Geneva with his German wife Helene and their two small sons. He was greatly liked and esteemed by the circle of acquaintances in which he moved, and was certainly never suspected of espionage, let alone of being a prominent Soviet agent.

As an agent he had many faults. He was fond of good

495

living and this led him to indulge in activities of a private nature normally shunned by a first-class agent. In a crisis, too, he was prone to lose his nerve and become excited. Again and again he contravened the strict security rules imposed by The Centre, and it was his failure to keep the financial accounts of his network — which The Centre demanded of all its Resident Directors in meticulous detail — that eventually led to his liquidation, despite the fact that he was a veteran Old Guard Communist.

I have referred in the article on Alexander Foote to the fact that during World War II the Swiss counter-espionage organisation BUPO adopted a policy of **laisser faire** towards Allied espionage, provided the agents did not blatantly advertise their activities. If, however, the German Abwehr, which was extremely active in Switzerland, complained of any foreign agent, they felt compelled to proceed against him in the normal way. The Abwehr became very troublesome in this respect in September 1943, the BUPO, to avoid a diplomatic scandal, in October arrested several

members of Rado's network.

When this happened, Rado panicked and went into hiding, instructing Foote to take over the Resident Directorship. He remained in hiding throughout Foote's imprisonment, Otto Pünter (Pakbo: q.v.) keeping the network going. On his release from prison, Foote tried to reconstitute the network, since there was still no sign of Rado. When Rudolf Rössler (q.v.) met Foote after the 20th July Plot and told him that his sources were still intact, Foote decided to go to Paris, which by this time had been liberated, to seek through the Soviet embassy there, new instructions from The Centre, since his radio contacts had been destroyed.

Before leaving for Paris Foote learned that Rado and his wife had gone to Paris three or four weeks earlier. Foote had some difficulty in reaching The Centre through the embassy, but when he did he was instructed to go to Moscow for consultations.

Though he had actually arrived in Paris four weeks earlier, Rado now made his first contact with the embassy, and he, too, was ordered to Moscow. The two men left together in a Russian aircraft on 6th January, 1945, and were flown via Cairo to avoid the battle that was still raging in Germany. Accommodation for the overnight stay in Cairo was scarce, and when it was being discussed, Rado said he was prepared to share a room with Foote.

Until now the two men had practically no conversation. Foote had lost most of his respect for Rado, and Rado seemed to suspect Foote of personal hostility. Rado, in fact, was a very frightened man, and this Foote sensed when they were safely in their hotel room. Owing to a defect developing in the aircraft, it was necessary for them to stay a second night, and it was then that Rado confessed to Foote that he was afraid they would have a very difficult time trying to convince the Director that it had not been through any fault of theirs that the network had collapsed. Foote tried to argue with him, but the more Foote argued, the more depressed Rado became.

Presently he went out of the room. The next morning when the aircraft was due to continue its journey, Rado was not to be found; and Foote never saw him again.

The Centre were not long in discovering the whereabouts of Rado, and they applied to the Egyptian government for the extradition of "a deserter, living in Egypt under the name of Ignati Kulichev, a colonel in the Red Army." Rado was arrested, but refused to go to Russia, so an officer was sent to fight for his extradition, and eventually, in the summer of 1945, he was taken to Moscow against his will.

From the moment of his arrival there, it became a struggle for existence between him and Foote. Since Foote was able to prove the truth of much of his case, and the more Rado's case was probed the more apparent did it become that he had played fast and loose with the network's finances to his own private advantage, Foote was eventually vindicated.

Rado was tried secretly, but the outcome of the trial is unknown. Foote and his collaborators believe, however, that he was executed.

BIBLIOGRAPHY :

Handbook For Spies — Alexander Foote (London, 1949).

RADIO and RADIO OPERATOR.

The development of short-wave radio has revolutionised the passing of intelligence between the network and headquarters. It has made two significant differences in the technique and practice of espionage : first, it has speeded up the transmission of information, which makes it possible for valuable information requiring urgent action to be in the hands of those who use it with the minimum delay; second, it has placed the agent in almost instant contact with his headquarters, thus bringing him under the direct control of his superiors.

With regard to the first, speed in communcation between agent and headquarters is of the essence. The most valuable information can be rendered utterly useless if it is delayed in transmission. In former times, when a courier had to make long, difficult and perilous journeys to get the agent's intelligence into the hands of those who translated it into acts or action, not only was there a risk of its never reaching its destination, but so much time could elapse that events to which it might have been referring, could have passed.

With regard to the second, the fact that what amount to "conversations" can be held, makes the gathering of information a much more intensive task. Exact details of what is required of the agent can be sent to him direct, and can be much more fully expressed and certain of delivery than the very brief messages passed by word of mouth or in writing on a tiny scrap of paper via the courier. What is perhaps even of greater advantage to intelligence headquarters is that radio, having brought every agent under the direct control of his superiors, each individual's personal inclinations can be curbed, and if necessary, he can be given warnings either that he is on the wrong track, or that he has been or is in danger of being compromised.

The radio-operator, though

498

unknown thirty years ago, as an espionage figure has now become indispensable, and his role of first class importance. But if he is one of the espionage elite, his task is, nevertheless, highly skilled and dangerous.

It is normal in espionage organisation for agents to specialise in one particular branch of the profession. One man will search out military intelligence — and nothing else; another will concentrate on industrial plants — and nothing else; another will function as a courier — and do nothing else; the radio-operator functions only as a radio-operator. Even when concentrating on just the one task, his work demands of him the highest degree of security appreciation, apart from his technical skills. In these days of rapid direction-finding, so that it is often a matter of hours or days instead of weeks and sometimes months before the enemy can pin-point the whereabouts of a radio-post, the operator must be so expert at sending or receiving Morse that he spends only a few minutes on the air at any one time. Even so, it is essential that he

should not send more than one transmitting schedule from one specific post without long waits in between. This means that he must organise a series of "safe" addresses, which are not always easy to come by, for it is not enough that there shall be willingness on the part of patriots to house him, the house must be in an area free from obstructions that may interfere with the quality of transmission or reception.

Being constantly on the move, carrying one's radio-set with one, through enemy territory, can be a nerve-wracking business. Nervous tension can play havoc with transmitting ability.

If the operator is also an encoder or decipherer, or both, he has the added responsibility of making or breaking the coded messages without error. This can be an arduous task, one that adds to the strain of nerves already taut to breaking point.

If caught the radio-operator must display courage and determination to resist all forms of inducements, either pleasant or unpleasant, to co-operate with his captors. The story of Operation North Pole

499

(which will be found under **Giskes, Col H. J.**) demonstrates exactly what may happen if he cannot withstand the blandishments of deception, persuasion or torture.

Since World War II great advances have been made in the radio field, which have been made possible by the technique of putting communication satellites into orbit. A transmitter has been developed which can send signals to a satellite as it passes overhead. The satellite stores the information until it is passing over its home territory, when it sends it to special receivers, which record it.

Instruments which will transmit Morse at exceptionally high speeds have also been advanced since World War II. Before the war the equipment was cumbersome and could be operated only by expert operators. Now the equipment has been simplified to enable the average agent to operate it. Its significance is that a transmission can take so little time that direction-finding equipment cannot plot the position of the transmitter.

RAHAB the HARLOT.

Some thirty or forty years

after Moses had sent his twelve spies, led by Joshua the son of Nun, (q.v.) to spy out the land of Canaan, Joshua, by now the leader of a strong army, was prompted to acquire some extra territory, and being encouraged by Jehovah to do so, led his forces against Jericho.

There is no doubt that during his intervening career — a very successful one — Joshua had not forgotten the value of espionage which he had learned from Moses. On this occasion he certainly made good use of his agents.

Before throwing his men against Jericho he sent forward two agents who were to go throughout the land and into the city, and find out the strength of it and all these other things which are useful for a general to know when he is about to launch an attack.

While it is not suggested that all agents would behave on duty as these two behaved, they are by no means alone in what they did. The consolation of love, even in its most ephemeral form, is often not only the sole consolation an agent is able to permit himself, it may be the only means of easing the fearful strain of his work. This is not the place to go either into the psychological or physiological aspects of this thesis; attention is drawn to it merely because it would be unjust to these two men to condemn them out of hand for allowing themselves to be distracted from their duties.

At all events, they went to the house of a beautiful prostitute called Rahab.

Now, whether their identities had been discovered before they went there or whether they knew themselves to be pursued and thought that their pursuers would not search a brothel, is unknown. Whatever may have been their object in going there in the first place, it was not long before the king of Jericho's men were commanding Rahab to produce "the men who had come to her" because they were spies of the Children of Israel.

"It is quite true that some men came to me," Rahab said, "but it is not etiquette in my profession to ask the names of one's clients. In any case, they are not here now. Just before the city gates were shut, they left the city.

But which way they went, I don't know. If you hurry, though, you make overtake them."

Simple soldiers! T h e y believed her. And all the time she had hidden the two agents up on the roof, under stalks of flax.

As soon as the searchers had followed her advice and left the city in pursuit and the gates had been closed after them, Rahab went up to the roof, to the two men.

"My friends," she said, "I know that your commander is bound to conquer Jericho, but since I have shown you this kindness in helping you escape capture, I want you to promise me something in return. I want you to swear that when your armies come to take the city my father and mother, and my brothers and sisters shall not be killed, and shall be allowed to keep all they possess."

Relieved by their escape, the agents promised that her wishes would be granted.

"Our life for yours, if you do not utter one word about this business!" they told her, and she was satisfied with their word.

Conveniently Rahab's

501

house was built on the city wall. Now she made ropes of flax, and let them down by them to safety. Before they went they assured her once again that they would keep their promise.

"When you hear our armies approaching, collect all your family and their possessions into your house, and bind this piece of scarlet in your window. If any of you goes out of your house then, it will be his own fault if he is killed. But if you betray us after we have gone, then we shall be absolved from our promise."

"Very well," she said. "Let it be so."

So the two men let themselves down by the ropes, hid themselves three days in the hills, escaped pursuit and returned to Joshua and told him everything.

When he brought up his armies, surrounded the city and launched his attack, Joshua met no resistance. But before the attack was made, Joshua warned all his army that immediately they entered the city Rahab and her family were to be brought out into the camp of the Israelites. So that there should be no mistake, he sent the two spies in with the first troops, and made them responsible for the fulfilment of their promise.

When Rahab and her family were safely out of the city, Jericho was completely destroyed, and all its inhabitants killed.

The subsequent career of Rahab is doubtful. Some authorities, including the Bible, say that she became the wife of Joshua himself and started the family — with a son, Boaz — from which David and Jesus of Nazareth sprang. Others say that she married one of the two spies, and they were the parents of Boaz. But whichever version is accepted, Rahab was well rewarded. The Roman Catholic Church has honoured her with canonisation and celebrates her feast day on 1st September.

BIBLIOGRAPHY:
The Book of Joshua, chapters 2 and 6.

RAKE, Major Denis (British agent, World War II).

Denis Rake, the son of an opera singer and a **Times** correspondent, was born and brought up in Brussels. At the age of five he joined the Sarazin Circus as a child tumbler, and he was still with it when World War I broke out, whereupon his mother decided to return to England. Looked after by the Belgian Refugee Committee, when he was sixteen he was put through a course of wireless operating with Cable and Wireless.

After the war, he decided to make his career on the musical comedy stage, and was given a part in a company which was to perform in Athens. While in Athens he attracted the attention of a prominent Greek and became his lover. When this liaison came to an end, he returned to England and had a notable success on the English musical comedy stage. He was playing in the Ivor Novello production at Drury Lane in the spring of 1939, but left the cast in the June and went to Juan-les-Pins, from where he returned two or three days before World War II broke out.

In 1938, at the time of the Munich crisis, he had offered his services should war break out. He had told the authorities that as he had perfect French, he would like to be an interpreter. As a result on the first day of the war he was called up, and posted to the Royal Army Service Corps as an interpreter, going to France at once with the British Expeditionary Force.

On the Fall of France he managed to get back to England, where he was seconded to the Royal Naval Reserve, again as an interpreter. He was still serving in this capacity when in 1940, having overheard a conversation in a Portsmouth pub, he offered his services to SOE (q.v.) and was accepted by them to train as a radio operator.

Rake was one of the most unorthodox of trainee agents. He detested bangs, refused to have anything to do with explosives, would not submit to arms practice and finally refused to undergo parachute jumping training. But for SOE French Section's great shortage of radio operators, there can be no doubt that he would have had his services terminated before his training was complete.

On 14th May, 1942 he landed on the coast of southern France at Juan-les-Pins in a rubber dinghy from a felucca. He was destined to become the radio operator for a network operating in the Lyons area.

He had not been long in Lyons, having already experienced some surprising adventures, when he was betrayed by a young Frenchman. Before he was caught, he asked for and received London's permission to move out of the Unoccupied Zone into the Occupied Zone and join a network operating in Paris.

While crossing the Demarcation Line, he was arrested by the Germans and imprisoned in Rennes. He was helped to escape in a swill bin by one of the prison chaplains, and eventually reached Paris. The network he was to join had no spare transmitter, and as he had lost his own, the leaders of the network decided to go to Lyons to obtain a transmitter through the famous Lyons "co-ordinator", the young American woman journalist Virginia Hall. They took Rake with them.

Virginia Hall was able to provide them with a transmitter and the three men set off back again for Paris. At Limoges all three were arrested. The other two men were quite convinced that Rake had been the cause of their arrest, and when they met in prison refused to have anything to do with him.

From prison they were transferred to an internment camp, and when the Germans took over the Unoccupied Zone after the assassination of Admiral Darlan, the camp commandant set them at liberty. After more incredible adventures, Rake crossed the Pyrenees into Spain, where he was interned for a time in the notorious Miranda camp. He was then transferred to the more pleasant surroundings of Jaraba, where elite prisoners were interned.

Eventually, with the help of the British legation in Madrid he returned to England. For a time he acted as an instructor in SOE training schools. Once more, however, the French Section was in dire need of radio operators, and Rake agreed to go back again to France, this time to act as operator to Nancy Wake, the Australian woman co-ordinator in central France. One day, while travelling with his lover to arrange the reception of supplies from

England, they were ambushed by some Germans, and Alex Shokolovsky was mortally wounded, and died in Rake's arms. The party managed to fight their way out of the ambush, and Rake continued to serve with Nancy Wake until the liberation of France.

He was awarded the Military Cross by the British, while the French bestowed on him the Croix de Guerre with Palms, and appointed him a Chevalier of the Legion of Honour.

He now lives in London, where, until recently he was the caretaker in a block of apartments in fashionable Chelsea.

BIBLIOGRAPHY :

Rake's Progress — Denis Rake (London, 1968).

RAS (Dutch agent, World War II) see under **Giskes, Col H. J.**

REAL.

Réal was Inspector-General of the French police, and Desmarest was chief of the Division of Public Safety and of the Secret Police under the leadership of the Minister of Police, Joseph Fouché (q.v.). These two men worked together in the closest concert, understanding one another's aims so perfectly that they were almost indispensable complements of each other. They were not endowed with the same capacity for duplicity as their chief, but as administrators they were vastly superior.

REDL, Colonel Alfred (Austrian traitor, director of Austro-Hungarian pre-World War I espionage).

The desire for money seems to be the motive of most double-agents, though there are one or two examples which point to psychological unbalance. Both of these reasons are found working in the case of Colonel Alfred Redl, a homosexual who required money to allow him to practice his special tastes in easier circumstances than he could do on his pay as chief of the Austro-Hungarian **Kundschaftsstelle,** (counter-espionage). But even here, though homosexuality was the root cause, very soon the desire for money became the predominant obsession.

Redl had been born into a poor family and his career presents something of a minor miracle. When quite young he became deeply interested in military history and the technique of espionage; and he travelled a good deal and learned to speak several languages. As a career he chose the army, and the miracle happened when the poor boy, contrary to all traditions, was granted a commission.

His strong intellect and his professional keenness, which had been largely instrumental in performing the miracle, also brought him to the notice of General Baron von Giesl — in 1900 chief of the intelligence services — who within a very short time promoted Redl to be chief of espionage services.

Redl occupied this post for five years, during which time he brought off several outstanding coups, for he brought to the task a skill and daring which this kind of activity had never before known. Whenever he received a visitor, the visitor was photographed by carefully hidden cameras, no matter which seat he chose to sit in. The arms of the chairs and the cigarette box which Redl proffered him were treated with fingerprint powder and a record of all conversations was taken

on phonograph discs.

His success was so considerable that when von Giesl was promoted to command the army in Prague, he sought permission to take Redl with him. Permission was granted and Redl was promoted to colonel.

Redl was succeeded in Vienna by a certain Captain Ronge, who soon wearied of always having the example of his brilliant predecessor held up to him. He determined to surpass even the successes which Redl had achieved. One of the measures he introduced to this end was postal censorship. Two or three people only knew the real purpose of this censorship. Even to the censors themselves Ronge explained that their work was to catch contrabandists and enjoined them to keep a special watch on all correspondence coming from the frontiers.

Ronge's postal censorship paid rich rewards in intelligence information, but the greatest of all came in March 1913.

On 2nd March the attention of the censors was drawn to two envelopes addressed as follows: Opera Ball 12, Poste

Restante, General Post Office, Vienna. They carried the postmark of the frontier town of Eydtkuhnen. One of the envelopes contained the equivalent of £300 in Austrian bank notes, the other the equivalent of £400. They contained nothing else.

Resealed they were sent to the post office and a watch was kept to discover who came to claim them. There was a police station next to the post office, and an electric bell was installed so that the clerk at the Poste Restante counter could warn agents waiting in the police station when Opera Ball presented himself. Ronge detailed two agents to be on watch at a time throughout the hours of business. As soon as the bell rang they were to hurry to the post office and detain the man pointed out to them by the clerk.

The agents waited in vain until 24th May, then when the bell did ring on that day both of them happened to be absent from their office, contrary to orders. When two or three minutes passed without the agents appearing, the clerk handed over the envelopes to the customer, who

left the post office. The two agents almost collided with him in the doorway without knowing who he was, and when they were told and had dashed out to the street again, they were in time to see their quarry entering a taxi and driving off. One of them, however, had the presence of mind to take the taxi's number.

While they stood on the pavement wondering how on earth they were going to explain to their chief what had happened, one of those coincidences occurred which generally happen only in fiction — the taxi cruised by again. Hailing it, they learned from the driver that he had taken his fare to a fashionable restaurant called the Kaiserhof. They were driven at once to the Kaiserhof, only to find that their man was not there. But near the restaurant there was a taxi rank, and on making inquiries there, they learned that a man answering the description of the wanted man had been driven to the Hotel Klomser.

Now, while they were being driven to the Kaiserhof, they had carefully searched the interior of the taxi and had

507

found the suede cover of a pocket-knife. Armed with this they drove to the Hotel Klomser and arranged with the receptionist to ask all the guests if the cover belonged to them. While one of the agents kept watch in the hall of the hotel, the other returned to headquarters to tell Captain Ronge what had happened.

This agent had scarcely left when a guest went to the desk and announced that he was going out. The clerk asked him if the knife-cover belonged to him, and the man claimed it. To his astonishment the watching agent recognised the man as Colonel Redl, his former chief.

He telephoned hurriedly to Ronge, who ordered him to tail the colonel, and this expert soon discovered that he was being followed. He led the agent around most of the streets of central Vienna, and finally attempted to shake him off by dropping several fragments of paper. But the agent was an experienced man, and refused to be diverted by this ruse. All over Vienna Redl led his shadow, until realising, at last, that he could not escape him, he returned to his hotel. The agent

then returned to the spot where Redl had scattered the scraps of paper, gathered them up and carried them to Captain Ronge.

Now, when the agent had telephoned the identity of Opera Ball, Ronge believed the man was out of his mind. Nevertheless he hurried at once to the post office, and demanded to see the receipts which Opera Ball had had to give for his letters. When he compared the writing on the receipts with Redl's writing in the files of the **Kundschaftsstelle,** he knew the man was right.

He was now to receive his second surprise. When the scraps of paper were pieced together, they were found to be receipts for registered letters containing money to addresses in Brussels, Warsaw and Lausanne, all of which were on Ronge's own black list, a list prepared by Redl himself, of foreign intelligence agents.

Ronge reported at once to his superior, General von Ostromiecz, General von Giesl's successor as chief of the secret police, who hurried with his information to his superior, General von Hötzendorf, the commander-in-chief.

At the Klomser Redl had found a lawyer friend waiting for him, who reminded him that they were dining together. They dined in a private room at the famous restaurant, the Riedhof, and after dinner the friend telephoned to the chief of police. He told him that Redl seemed to be on the verge of a nervous breakdown, that he had confessed during dinner to a long list of delinquencies, most of which seemed to be the magnified figments of a tired mind. He wished to return to Prague at once, could the police chief arrange for him to have a companion on his journey?

There was no mention of treason or spying!

The police chief replied that at the moment he was engaged on an urgent case, but that if Redl would go to see him in the morning he would arrange something.

But already something had been arranged for Redl; and Geyer, the police chief, knew it.

The commander-in-chief personally selected four officers, among them Ronge, who were to go to Redl to induce him to confess the extent of his treachery. They arrived at the hotel Klomser at 11.30 p.m. and found Redl writing farewell letters. All that they wished to know, he said, they would find at his house in Prague. He asked to borrow a revolver, but none of the four had one. Within a short time, however, one of them returned with a Browning.

They left him then, and went to a nearby cafe. One had been left at the door of the hotel to keep watch. He was relieved every half hour.

At 5 a.m. Ronge called for one of his agents, and gave him a letter addressed to Redl which he was to deliver at once into the colonel's own hands. The agent was told what he might find, and was instructed to return without raising the alarm if in fact Redl was dead.

When the agent arrived at the colonel's room and received no answer to his knocks, he tried the door and found it would open. Entering, he found Redl dead on the floor, shot through the head, the Browning beside him. The agent returned to the cafe with the news. A few minutes later the telephone at the hotel rang, and the porter was requested to call Colonel Redl to the instrument. So it was the porter who gave the alarm of Redl's death.

The official announcement stated that the colonel had committed suicide while his mind was deranged due to overwork. The commander-in-chief had decided that Redl's treason must at all costs be kept secret, even from the emperor. But the truth came out in a way which added yet one other bizarre touch to the whole business.

Hötzendorf had appointed a commission of officers to go to Prague immediately he had heard that Redl was dead. There in the presence of the colonel's friend and chief, Giesl, the house was searched. The revelations were fantastic.

The house was richly furnished from top to bottom, the cellars contained the choicest wines, and during the last five years he had bought four very expensive motorcars. The searchers also found that he had received from Russia in the last nine months nearly £3,000. He had

bought a magnificent estate in 1910, and a large house in Vienna. The money he had received from Russia represented about ten times his pay as a colonel. Money was then more valuable than it is now.

To help them in their search the officers had taken to the house with them a locksmith called Wagner. It was a Sunday, and that afternoon Wagner was down to play for his local football team. On Monday morning his captain called on him to find out why he had not turned up the previous afternoon, and when he explained why, he also told what he had seen and heard at the house as he opened drawers and desks and chests — plans, photographs, large sums of money, maps and documents said to be Russian; and the stunned horror of the officers.

Now it so happened that Wagner's football captain was a sub-editor of the **Prager Tagblatt,** who that morning had received the official report from Vienna of Redl's suicide. Putting the facts together he was sure that he had hit upon the most sensational news item of the century. But he did not dare to use it, for fear that the authorities would suspend the paper and throw him into prison where his mouth would be sealed. But the people of the Empire were accustomed by the long imposition of censorship to read between the lines.

So he hit upon a plan which would tell those who read the **Prager Tagblatt** of Redl's treachery. He published a denial of non-existent rumours that Redl had been guilty of treason and espionage, adding that the officers who had come to Prague to search the colonel's house were doing so in connection with something quite different. But he also happened to be the correspondent of a Berlin paper, and two or three days later all Germany was resounding with the story of Redl's infamy, and through Germany the whole of Europe.

The effect of Redl's treachery was disastrous. For more than ten years Redl had been Russia's chief foreign spy. He had helped other Russian spies, and had denounced to the Russians Austro-Hungarian spies operating in Russia. At one point a Russian officer approached the Austro-Hungarian authorities with an offer to sell them the complete Russian plan for an attack on Germany and the Empire. As head of the secret service the plans came to Redl first of all. Thereupon he produced a false set of plans which would deceive no soldier, but which seemed to point to a Russian trick. He then returned the real plans to Russia, and received the equivalent of £5,000 for his "loyalty" to his employers.

The greatest act of treachery, however, was his sale to the Russians of a document known as Plan Three. Plan Three was the detailed plan of the Austro-Hungarian General Staff's proposed campaign for the conquest of Serbia, which had long been in the minds of the leaders of the Empire. It specified the points at which Serbia was to be attacked, how many divisions were to be disposed at the various points, exactly how many guns were to be used, and was illustrated with maps and charts. It represented the long considered strategy of Hötzendorf's brilliant Staff.

By its very nature it was a plan which could be improved

upon, and though the Austro-Hungarian General Staff attempted to vary it in certain particulars, these variations proved of no avail. The result was that when the 1914 War broke out and the attack on Serbia launched, the Serbian Marshal Putnik, with his relatively tiny army inflicted such losses on the armies of Hötzendorf that the Austro-Hungarians were rendered almost entirely ineffective allies for Germany.

But not only had Redl sold his country's military secrets to his country's enemies, he had also prevented his country from learning anything about her enemies' secrets. Thus neither the Austro-Hungarian nor the German General Staff knew anything about the formation of several new Russian army corps which took the Hapsburgs and the Hohenzollerns so completely by surprise in the early days of the war. If the Russian High Command had been only a quarter as efficient as Russian military intelligence the war might, indeed, have been over by Christmas.

Ronge was eventually promoted to major-general and director of secret services.

512

BIBLIOGRAPHY :

The Treachery of Colonel Redl — Major-General Maximilian Ronge (London, 1921).

RED ORCHESTRA, The.

The Red Orchestra was the name given by the Germans to Soviet networks operating in Germany, and later to all Soviet networks in Nazi Occupied Europe. It was derived from the espionage jargon terms given by the Russians to a radio-transmitter ("Music-box") and to a radio-operator ("Musician").

The original Red Orchestra (**Die Rote Kapelle**) was outstanding among all Soviet networks and was led by two brilliant men, Harro Schulze-Boysen and Arvad Harnack. The reputation which the network won was due entirely to these two men, for the remainder of the group were inexperienced in espionage techniques, and so undertrained that in a high-grade espionage organisation they would have been considered grave security risks. Despite this, however, they overcame most of their difficulties, and were liquidated only when they fell victim of the Abwehr's D/F (direction-finding organisation).

Schulze-Boysen was the son of an aristocratic German officer, who had served in the German navy in World War I and as Chief of Staff to General of the Luftwaffe Friedrich Christiansen, German commander-in-chief in Holland during the World War II. In his middle teens, Schulze had been attached to a right-wing anti-Nazi movement for a short time. Soon, however, he was moving to the other extreme, and in 1932, when he was 22, he was the spokesman for a young progressive group. For his activities with this group he was arrested and imprisoned by the Gestapo when the Nazis came to power. Thereafter he moved far over to the left and to Communism, though this did not prevent his becoming a member of the Ministry for Air, in which, at the time when he was leading the Red Orchestra, he was serving as an intelligence officer.

When he was 26, he married a grand-daughter of Prince Philip von Bulenberg, Libertas Haas-Heye, who was to be a great help to him when he began his espionage activities in 1936 — the year of his marriage — by giving German intelligence to the Spanish Reds. Later in this year he gathered round him a group of men of like political views. Though his sympathies lay wholly with the Soviet Union, he was never an orthodox Communist, for his emotional and somewhat unstable character would never have allowed him to follow blindly the dictates of Moscow.

Shortly before Hitler launched Operation Barbarossa, Schulze-Boysen was introduced to a Soviet agent on the staff of the Russian embassy in Berlin. This man had been sent to Germany to assist Bogdan Kobolov, who was operating under the cover of Counsellor of Embassy, in setting up the network that was to operate inside Germany after the inevitable outbreak of hostilities. This agent, Alexander Erdberg (it is believed that this was a cover-name), recognised in Schulze-Boysen the type they were looking for. For once The Centre made up its mind quickly,

513

and within weeks Schulze-Boysen had been appointed a member of the triumvirate that was to lead the group, the other two members of which were Harnack and a man called Adam Kuckhoff.

Harnack was very different from Schulze-Boysen. Ten years older, he was connected with a famous family of German philosophers. Having, like Schulze, first had right-wing leanings and then switched to Communism, he had become an orthodox Marxist. He had been a prominent member of a group of young German Communist intellectuals who had formed, in 1931, the Society for Study of Planned Economy, which had the full backing of Moscow.

In 1932 Harnack accompanied one or two members of the Society on a visit to Russia, and he at once attracted the attention of The Centre, who invited him to spy for Russia. He agreed, and with the exception of George Blake (q.v.) Soviet espionage has probably not been served by a more altruistic spy. On his return from Moscow, he applied for and obtained a post in the German Ministry of Economics, though how he passed his screening satisfactorily remains a mystery.

Harnack was a natural spy. Though he had received no training in espionage techniques, all through his ten-year career as a spy he consistently observed all the rules of security. He was so successful in concealing his secret activities that in his Ministry he was held up as a model of the conscientious, hard-working bureaucrat.

In the late twenties, while on a visit to the United States on a Rockefeller scholarship, he married a lecturer in economics, Mildred Fish. Though she was arrested when the Red Orchestra was eventually liquidated, it has never been proved that she took part in espionage activities.

Adam Kuckhoff was a prominent writer and producer in the theatre. When he joined the Red Orchestra he was in his middle fifties. He, too, had started out as an extreme right-winger, and had then switched to Communism with the advent of the Nazis. In his anti-Nazi activities he was assisted by his wife Margarete, who was employed in Rosenberg's race policy department.

These three gathered about them a motley group of about one hundred, of whom members of the old German Communist Party were prominent, though they exerted little influence. The rest were young Communists, ideologically unsound, but fanatical in their hatred of the Nazis. There was also a small group who did not know exactly what they stood for except that they were anti-Hitler.

Only a small fraction of the group carried out active espionage. This "inner" group, besides Schulze-Boysen and Harnack, the effective leaders, included Horst Heilmann, who worked in the decoding department of the Wehrmacht signals; Johann Graudenz, a traveller for a brake manufacturer who supplied the Luftwaffe, and who kept The Centre **au courant** with Nazi aircraft production; Erwin Gehrts, who was also working in a department of the Air Ministry; Herbert Gollnow, who had access to Wehrmacht counter-espionage secrets; Gunther Weisenborn, who worked with the national radio; and others who were firmly entrenched in the Foreign Office, the Ministry of Propaganda, the Ministry of Labour, the Berlin City Administration and other important departments. Few groups have surely possessed such potential for supplying their masters with the highest-grade intelligence, covering such a wide field!

The Red Orchestra was the only network operating in Germany, but there were in addition one or two single, independent agents also working. The most important of these was Hans Kummerow, a leading engineer and inventor, who had taken part in industrial espionage in the early twenties, and had passed to Moscow his inventions in primitive radar and chemical warfare. The Russians still considered him a useful man on the outbreak of hostilities, and since he had no means of communicating with The Centre, they sent him a radio operator. Unfortunately this poor fellow was arrested on landing by parachute, and talked; and Kummerow and his wife were executed in 1943.

Equally important was Rudolf von Scheliha, born of

515

an aristocratic family, a career diplomat of the old type. He was a rather unpleasant character. He had married a wealthy wife, but he had extremely extravagant tastes, particularly in mistresses, which despite his own and his wife's wealth ran him deeply into debt. It was then that he decided to sell his Government's secrets to the highest bidder. The British did quite successful business with him for a time, but dropped him when it was discovered that he was selling the same information to the Russians at the same time. The Russians were not so moral about it, and he continued to work for them, and might have gone on doing so without being compromised had not he, too, been deprived of his channels of communication when the Soviet embassy was withdrawn after the launching of Barbarossa. A radio specialist, Kurt Shulze (no connection with Schulze-Boysen) was attached to him, but by this time Scheliha was beginning to get cold feet, and proposed breaking off his relations with The Centre, lucrative though they were.

The Centre was reluctant to let him go, and arranged to send a courier by parachute to blackmail Scheliha. Before this they had had Scheliha "investigated" by Victor Sukulov. This was before Sukulov had been arrested and begun to collaborate with the Abwehr. Sukulov had had a meeting with Scheliha, and had arranged for Kurt Schulze to be his operator. Sukulov submitted a report in code to The Centre, but the Abwehr came into possession of it and were able to break it with the help of the Belgian traitor Wenzel. The Centre did not know this, nor were they aware that Scheliha's assistant Ilse Stöbe had been arrested, before they sent their blackmailer to Berlin.

The result was that a woman Gestapo agent, posing as Stöbe, was waiting in Scheliha's apartment when the blackmailer, H e i n r i c h Koenen, arrived. They had a revealing conversation before Gestapo officers arrested him. Stöbe had refused to talk, but Koenen agreed to collaborate, and Scheliha was arrested and he and Stöbe were executed on 22nd December, 1942.

The loss of the Kummerows and Scheliha greatly increased

the importance of the Red Orchestra, and for fourteen months the group more than compensated for the loss. They were able to send to Moscow information on the strategic plans of the German High Command, troop movements and the postings of Goering's air squadrons, the plans for attacks on British convoys to Russia, monthly aircraft production figures, the fuel situation of the armies in Russia and much more information of less importance, though nevertheless well worth having.

Ever since it had begun its operations, however, the Abwehr and the Gestapo had been noting the activities of clandestine transmitters within Germany and had instituted an intensive search for them. Now, at the same time that Victor Sukulov had been sent to find out what was happening to Scheliha, he had been required to contact the Red Orchestra to find out whether The Centre could give them any special assistance. He met Schulze-Boysen and Harnack in Berlin, and they told him that what they needed most were first-rate radio connections with

Moscow. These Sukulov provided, and then returned to Belgium, where he narrowly escaped being arrested and fled to France.

The Abwehr had its first break when it managed to track down a clandestine transmitter working to Moscow in Belgium. This led to the seizure of a second transmitter, of which Hermann Wenzel was the operator. Wenzel decided to collaborate, and with his help the Abwehr was able to decipher many of the Red Orchestra's communications to The Centre. Among these monitored messages was one to Sukulov instructing him to go to Germany to see Schulze-Boysen. In it Adam Kuckhoff's address had been given together with brief particulars of Schulze-Boysen and Harnack. As a result, Schulze-Boysen was arrested on 30th August, 1942, his wife a few days later, and the Harnacks on 3rd September.

Before arresting Schulze-Boysen, the Gestapo had tapped his telephone, and in this way were led to nearly one hundred other members of the "outer" group of the Red Orchestra. Within a few

517

days the Red Orchestra in Germany had ceased to exist.

The trial of the chief defendants began on 15th December, 1942. The Schulze-Boysens, the Harnacks and the Schumachers, Hans Copp, the radio operator, Heilmann, Gehrts, Kurt Schulze, the operator for Scheliha, Graudenz, Gollnow and Erika von Brockdorf were in the dock. Of these fourteen, eleven received death sentences, but Mildred Harnack and Erika von Brockdorf were given prison sentences. The death sentences were carried out within a few days of their being pronounced, the victims being hanged by having meat-hooks thrust through their throats from which they were suspended. Hitler was furious at the prison sentences on the two women. "Those who have come within the shadow of treason have forfeited their lives," he declared yet again, and ordered new trials. They, too, were sentenced to death and beheaded.

Of the remainder, the Kuckhoffs were tried on 3rd February, 1943, together with others. All were sentenced to death, but somewhat curiously, Frau Kuckhoff was re-

518

prieved. Altogether, just over fifty of all those arrested were executed.

The whole business of the Red Orchestra was surrounded with such secrecy by the Nazis — which indicates that the hangings by meat hooks were not meant as deterrents but were pure sadism at its extreme — that only after the war was over was the story of their trials and executions revealed. It is said that Walter Funk, Minister of Economics, had no idea that Harnack, who was a member of his Ministry, had been arrested until the eve of his execution.

BIBLIOGRAPHY:

The Red Orchestra — Gilles Perrault (London, 1968).

REISS, Ignace (Soviet agent between the wars).

Ignace Reiss was born in Poland in 1899. While still a youth he was arrested for Communist activities and sentenced to five years' imprisonment. On his release he went to Moscow, where he was trained and sent to the Ruhr and from there to Vienna, where he was again arrested and sent to prison. By the early 1930s he was so highly regarded by The Centre that he was appointed Resident Director of the French networks.

He was one of the Old Guard revolutionaries, and was sickened by Stalin's Purges of the middle Thirties, which removed the veteran Old Guard Bolsheviks, that he resigned from the espionage organisation, and wrote a letter to Stalin, which he issued to the European press, giving his reasons. He said among other biting things, "He who remains silent at this hour makes himself an accomplice of Stalin and a traitor to the cause of the working class and of Socialism . . . I am finished with everything. I am returning to freedom, to Lenin, to his teachings and his cause."

On receipt of this letter, Stalin summoned Yezhov, (q. v.) chief of intelligence, and ordered him to send not one, but three groups of SMERSH executioners to seek out and liquidate Reiss. Yezhov chose Colonel Mikhail Shpigelglas, second deputy to the chief of the Foreign Division of The Centre, to mount the operation.

Shpigelglas was a well-educated man, a graduate of the Faculty of Letters of Moscow University. On being awarded his diploma he had been congratulated by the Rector, Andrei Vyshynsky, later to be Foreign Minister, who offered him a teaching post at the unversity. Shpigelglas declined, explaining that he believed he might serve Russia better by becoming an official. To support this claim he wrote a thesis on William Wickham, chief of British espionage in Europe in 1795, who had been involved in the overthrow of the French commander, General Pichegrue. On the basis of this study, Shpigelglas was taken into the Foreign Division.

Shpigelglas ostensibly obeyed Stalin's instructions, and formed three groups of executioners. He did not however, send the three groups into Europe to search for Reiss, but gave this task to one, holding the other two in reserve.

Group one was led by a man called Roland Abiatt, who, known throughout Europe under a number of aliases, chose for this operation the name of François Rossi. Rossi had two accomplices; a man called Etienne-Charles

Martignat, and a woman called Gertrude Schildbach, an OGPU agent who normally operated in Italy.

Group two was led by Ivan Kondratiev who lived in Paris where he made himself out to be a White Russian exile. Group three was under the direction of Serge Efron, who, under the cover of a journalist, worked in France as an agent. The Rossi group was to lead the attack; if they failed, Kondratiev would go into action, and if they did not succeed, then the Efron group would take over.

As soon as he had sent his letter to Stalin, Reiss went underground with his wife and young son, since he knew that no man who has ever held the high position of Resident Director could defect and survive. To find him Rossi engaged the services of a young Swiss schoolmistress called Renata Steiner, who, an over-ardent Communist, had long been plaguing Moscow to let her work for Russia, only to have all her requests rejected. Her importunity, however, eventually proved too much, and in 1935 the Soviet embassy in Paris sent her to an organisation called the Union for the Repatriation of Russians to Russia, which was just another cover organisation. There she was introduced to Efron, and Efron introduced her to Rossi. It must be said at once that Steiner did not know why she had been given the assignment which was to end in the murder of Reiss.

It did not take SMERSH long to track down Reiss, whom it found in Holland. Steiner watched him there for a time, and then he disappeared. It was not until August 1937 that Rossi tracked him down again, living in Paris, but once more, before SMERSH could reach him, Reiss vanished, though not for long.

Within a few days Rossi received a clue as to his new whereabouts. Steiner was summoned and asked if she could drive a car and if she held a Swiss driving licence. On answering yes to both questions, she was given some money, and on 28th August left for Berne where Rossi was waiting for her. Rossi met her in Berne and took her to the Hotel City where rooms had been engaged for them. Almost at once they went to the Casino Garage, where Steiner hired a car in her name, leaving a deposit of 150 Swiss francs. On 3rd September she met Rossi at the garage. He was accompanied by a woman of his group, Gertrude Schildbach. All three of them went by car to Salvan, where Rossi left Steiner with instructions to keep watch at the railway station for the man on whom she had kept watch in Holland. As soon as she saw him, she was to telephone Rossi at the Hotel de la Paix in Lausanne and tell him, "Uncle has left."

On the second day she saw her man, accompanied by a woman and a child. She telephoned Rossi, who told her to go to Territet to find out where the woman and child lived. The first day in Territet she was unsuccessful, but in the late afternoon of the next day she saw the woman and followed her to a villa.

When she telephoned the news to Rossi, he was not at his hotel. Having no instructions about her next move, she stayed the night in Territet. Next morning, at breakfast on the hotel terrace, she read in the **Gazette de Laus-**anne about the discovery of a man's body riddled with machine-gun bullets in a car on the road to Chamblandes leading out of Lausanne. She forgot about it as soon as she had read it.

When there was no message for her by midday the following day, she began to wonder if something had gone wrong, and Rossi's continued silence began to make her nervous. So on 8th September she returned to the Hotel City at Berne.

There was no news of Rossi there, but before she returned to Paris she decided to go to the Casino Garage to ask if the car she had hired had been returned. She noticed that the clerk who attended her seemed a little startled by her question, before he went into the office to check. When he came back he told her that the car had been returned, and asked her to step into the office to collect the deposit. While she was waiting there, Swiss police drove up and arrested her. When she asked on what charge, she was told she was under suspicion of being an accomplice in the murder of the shot man whose body had been found in the hired car, now known to be that of Ignace Reiss.

Steiner was completely overcome by the realisation that she had been deliberately used to lead a man to his death, and made a full statement. But the information the police had so desperately wanted had come too late. Rossi and Schildbach had got clean away.

BIBLIOGRAPHY :

The Executioners — Ronald Seth (London, 1966, New York, 1967).

RESIDENT DIRECTOR.

Term given by Russian espionage to the head of a network. Ideally the Resident Director lives in and operates from a country bordering on that in which the network is operating. The idea behind this arrangement seems to be that if the network is compromised, the Resident Director is safe from arrest, since espionage against another power is not usually an indictable offence. In this way agents of long experience are safeguarded from mistakes made by subordinates.

522

REYDEN, van der (Dutch agent, World War II) see under **Giskes, Col H. J.**

RICHELIEU, Armand du Plessis, Cardinal (The espionage organisation of 17th century France).

Early in 1707, Daniel Defoe (q.v.), founder of the permanent British secret service, wrote from Edinburgh to his master Robert Harley, "I act the old part of Cardinal Richelieu. I have my spies and my pensioners in every place, and I confess 'tis the easiest thing in the world to hire people here to betray their friends."

Defoe had for some years previously been working as a secret agent for the Tory Government, and Harley had sent him to Scotland to forward the Treaty of Union between Scotland and England "by any means in his power". The point about this reference is that even at this short period after his death, Richelieu's prowess as a spymaster was fully appreciated, as in fact it had been during his life-time. He had given France her first organised system of espionage.

The son of a noble family in Poitou, Armand du Plessis, at the age of twenty, in 1605, was made Bishop of Luçon. Since he was under age, he went to Rome to obtain a dispensation from the Pope. This was granted two years later, and he was consecrated bishop in 1607.

Through the influence of Concini, the Queen's secretary, he became secretary to the King, and after Concini's murder in 1617, though his friends were banished, du Plessis was not, since he had the confidence of Marie de' Medici, the Queen Mother, who was acting as Regent for the young King Louis XIII. In 1662 he was made a cardinal; by 1624 he was virtually chief minister; and in 1629 he was officially confirmed in that post. In 1631 he was made Duke of Richelieu, by which name he is known to history. He was then forty-six.

Richelieu's policy as chief minister of France was to make his country great. This he set out to achieve by concentrating the power in the hands of the absolute monarch — assisted, of course, by his chief minister; by granting religious toleration as a means of overcoming domestic unrest, which had been retarding the progress of the country since the religious civil war policy of Catherine de' Medici during her regency, and the reign of her son Charles; and by taking control of international diplomacy from the Hapsburgs.

He was petty, cunning, mean and avaricious, and made a host of political enemies. But in his capacity as virtual ruler of France he had to deal with the constant attempts of Gaston of Orleans to usurp the throne between 1626 and 1632; and a similar conspiracy by the Duke de Cinq-Mars in 1642. His policy as thus outlined called for the whittling away of the power of the great nobles, who were still as powerfull in France as the barons had been in England in the reign of King John, four centuries earlier. Until this was achieved finally in 1630, Richelieu was unable to participate in the Thirty Years' War, which he chose as the best means of dominating the Hapsburgs. But when he was free to embark upon this course, for the next twelve years until his death in 1642, his history is a long succession of almost unrivalled diplomatic intrigues. When he died he had firmly established the autocracy of Louis XIV, le Roi Soleil, who epitomised his conception of kingly power in his famous phrase — **l'Etat c'est moi.** The ultimate outcome of the cardinal's policy was the French Revolution.

For any man in Richelieu's position, who adopted the policies which he adopted, a knowledge of what was going on in every part of the country, in every walk of life, was an absolute essential. To be really successful that knowledge had to be as complete as possible.

In his realisation of this, Richelieu recognised that the only way of achieving it was by a wide-spread system of espionage. It was no use employing individual agents and setting them specific tasks. It had to be an overall system in which there was a central office for sifting and correlating all the i n f o r m a t i o n obtained.

With such a heavy burden of State affairs, the cardinal could never have been able to control his organisation personally. He was, therefore, fortunate in having at his side a man who had all the qualifications of the perfect deputy spy-master.

The director of the cardinal's secret service was a Capuchin father, Joseph du Tremblay. He was a mild and gentle man in appearance and manner, but he possessed a subtle, intriguing mind which earned him from his contemporaries the sobriquet of **Son Eminence Grise** — the Gray Cardinal — which summed up his likeness to his master and the shadow from which he operated.

Not only did Richelieu cover France with his spies, but every European country as well. Every Frenchman who went abroad to teach dancing or fencing is said to have been in the cardinal's pay. The success of his intelligence is witnessed by the victories which Richelieu scored time after time over Gaston of Orleans, one of the greatest conspirators of all times. But perhaps his major triumph was the removal of the great soldier Wallenstein from his position of influence at the Imperial Roman Court.

Wallenstein had been born a Protestant, but had become a convert to Catholicism. Very early in his career he gave evidence of his great abilities as a soldier, and won the confidence of the emperor. He married a very wealthy widow who died not long after, leaving him vast estates. His wealth gave him power, which he increased by acting as the saviour of the empire again and again.

At the height of his power, backed by an army of Mercenaries who owed allegiance to none save him, he rescued Vienna from disaster in 1618; in 1626 he defeated Count Mansfeld, who was attempting to restore James I of England's son-in-law, Frederick, to his Electorate; then he pushed back Christian of Denmark, and secured the supremacy of the Roman Catholic cause. In doing this, Wallenstein was pursuing a policy of German unification in which religious toleration was to be the chief characteristic. But this policy was entirely frustrated by the Edict of Restitution in 1629, and Wallenstein retired to his estates.

It would be thought that as the power in a Catholic state Richelieu would have espoused the cause of the Catholic Allies opposed to the Protestant powers. As part of his policy to remove the international diplomatic leadership from the Hapsburgs, however, he had secretly become allied to the great Protestant leader, Gustavus Adolphus of Sweden.

The Catholic princes of Germany, Richelieu knew, were greatly disturbed by Wallenstein's position and influence over the emperor, so he devised a plan to remove him on this pretext, though his motive in doing so was that he considered this to be the most valuable contribution he could offer in support of his secret Swedish ally. Du Tremblay went in person to the Imperial court; and using all the secret knowledge gained from his intelligence organisation, and his natural powers of persuasion, it was he who was directly responsible for the Edict which caused Wallenstein's withdrawal from active support of the Catholic cause. During the two following years, Gustavus Adolphus had success after success, and to prevent

525

complete defeat, the emperor was compelled to persuade Wallenstein to return, which he effected by promising to repeal the Edict. His failure to keep his promise resulted in Wallenstein making overtures to the Protestants, whereupon the emperor charged him with treachery. The great soldier was murdered by some of his own soldiers in 1634.

The unusual characteristic of Richelieu's espionage system was that it was his own organisation. That is to say, it was not supported by, and therefore owed no allegiance to the State. Richelieu paid for his spies out of his own purse — though that purse was lined with the vast fortune derived from state funds — and they were in his personal service. Sir Francis Walsingham, Elizabeth I's spy-master, (q.v.) also financed his organisation out of his own pocket, but only because of his loyalty to a monarch so parsimonious that she would not allocate funds for a secret service when she had a subject ready to plunge himself deeply into debt in order to carry out his responsibility to protect her and the security of her realm.

526

BIBLIOGRAPHY :

Richelieu — K. Federn (Eng, trs, London, 1928).

Richelieu — Hillaire Belloc (London, 1930).

RICHER, Marthe (Allied agent, World War I).

Marthe Richer was the widow of Henri Richer, killed in action in May 1916. Her maiden name was Betenfeld, and she was born at Blamont, in the department of Meurthe-et-Moselle. As a young girl she had been attracted to flying and had become an experienced pilot. She spoke several languages fluently, and possessed an intelligence that marked her out from the ordinary run of young Frenchwomen of her time.

She was, in fact, just the type of woman that Captain Ladoux, chief of French military intelligence, was looking for to spy upon the German colony at San Sebastian in Spain. Within three weeks of her husband's death she had entered Ladoux's service.

In San Sebastian she made the acquaintance of a Dr Stephan, who, having revealed to her that he was connected with the Abwehr, suggested that she should become an Abwehr agent in France. Mme Richer told the doctor that she would consider his proposition only if his chief would receive her himself.

So great was the German need at this time that Captain Hans von Krohn, naval attaché in Madrid and chief of German espionage in Spain, agreed to her request. Before long von Krohn was head over heels in love with Marthe Richer, and she became his mistress. At the same time, however, Colonel Nicolai, chief of the Abwehr, insisted that she should earn her keep, and assigned her the task of discovering the production figures of the great Schneider armaments combine in Paris.

Before she left for Paris she was given supplies of the newest German secret ink. This was in the form of tiny capsules, each about the size of a flower seed. One dissolved in ordinary water would produce, as von Krohn proudly stated, "enough secret ink to write a book."

Arrived in Paris, Marthe Richer reported to the French counter-espionage, where no one would believe that she had become Baron von Krohn's mistress until she identified his photograph. The secret ink proved to contain colargolium, which when used in an invisible ink can be made visible only by a complicated process akin to developing a photograph.

After a reasonable period, Mme Richer returned to Spain armed with skilfully counterfeited information for von Krohn. A few days later she was able to send to the French details of the submarine U-52, which had been interned in Cadiz owing to an engine breakdown and to which she accompanied von Krohn on a visit of inspection. Ironically, she used one of the colargolium "seeds" which von Krohn had given her to make the invisible report she sent to Paris.

Her next mission from von Krohn was as courier to Buenos Aires carrying highly secret instructions to German agents in South America and a number of phials containing "enough chemical to destroy the whole of the Allies' wheat stocks in South America". Neither instructions

527

nor phials of chemicals were delivered, for she destroyed both on the voyage, having realised that von Krohn could not know for some time that his agents in the Argentine had not received either orders or phials, since communications between America and Europe were very slow.

She then put up a plan to the Fifth Bureau for flying von Krohn out of Spain into France and holding him as a prisoner of war. Ladoux vetoed the scheme, as he considered her too valuable where she was. She continued in her dual role as von Krohn's mistress and French agent for two years. But at last she grew tired of it, and for some extraordinary reason, had to disclose her deception to him before she left.

BIBLIOGRAPHY :
I Spied for France — Marthe Richer (London, 1935).

RICHTER, Karel (German agent, World War II).

Karel Richter, twenty-nine, landed by parachute just outside St Albans, in Hertfordshire, on 13th May, 1941. Before coming to England,

Richter had been one of "Butcher" Heydrich's assistants.

The 13th May was a Monday. All through Tuesday and Wednesday Richter hid in a small wood, where he concealed his radio and other equipment. After dark on Wednesday evening he emerged from the wood onto the road. He carried no suitcase and was suitably dressed for his surroundings.

He had not gone far, however, when he saw the dim, hooded headlights of a lorry coming along cautiously in the black-out. He kept straight on, so as not to arouse suspicions, and up to this point behaved like any good spy faced with his first test. But the lorry driver was lost, and seeing Richter, he called out to him to ask the way.

This was a situation with which Richter had not been taught to cope. Instead of saying he was sorry but he was a stranger in these parts — which would have been quite safe, since there were many evacuees in the country districts at this time — he lowered his head, mumbled some words which the driver could not hear, and hurried away.

A little farther on the driver met a War Reserve Policeman, Police Constable A. J. Scott, from whom he received the directions he required. In thanking the constable he said he was grateful to him, which was more than he was to the man he had just met up the road.

When the lorry had driven away, the constable wondered who it could be going for a walk in dark country lanes at night, and set off to find out. He had not gone far when he found Richter in a telephone booth. He recognised the German as a stranger to the district, and asked him who he was and what he was doing. Richter produced an identity card which appeared to be in order, but Police Constable Scott sensed that something about him was not quite right, and asked him to go with him to the police station. At the station the spy's answers added to police suspicions and on instructions he was taken to Canon Row police station in London, which is next door to Scotland Yard.

When he was searched he was found to be carrying English pounds and American dollars to the value of £500, a map of the eastern counties of England, and a pocket compass. He was also wearing three pairs of underpants, and two pairs of socks, and when asked to explain why he was wearing all these clothes in May, he could not.

After being tried at the Old Bailey, he was hanged at Wandsworth prison, in London, on 10th December, 1941.

BIBLIOGRAPHY:

They Came to Spy — Stanley Firman (London, undated).

RIDDERHOF (Dutch agent, World War II) see under **Giskes, Col H. J.**

RINNAN, Henry Oliver
(Norwegian traitor, World War II).

The most infamous of all Norwegian traitors was Henry Oliver Rinnan, who had an organisation of his own and even succeeded in infiltrating some of his agents into the Home Front (the chief Resistance movement). Many attempts were made by Milorg (the Army Resistance movement) to liquidate him, but his organisation was so skilful that none of them succeeded.

Rinnan had his tentacles spread over the whole country. At one time the Allies were considering a landing in northern Norway, and men and weapons had deen dispatched to prepare the way, arriving by boat from the Shetland Islands. One of Rinnan's agents discovered what was going on and passed the information to the Gestapo who, as a reprisal, seized at random thirty-four Norwegians, whom they shot, hoping thereby to terrorise the inhabitants of the vicinity into disclosing the identification of the men who had landed. They achieved exactly the opposite reaction, however, and only one of the men, a wireless operator of one of the groups, was caught and a few rifles discovered.

But Rinnan's men worked on, and when Captain Sjoberg, who had led the first groups, landed yet again, the Gestapo knew of his coming. Sjoberg was able to burn the hut in which he had cached his supplies just in time, but in the ensuing pursuit he and his men were overcome, he himself being m o r t a l l y wounded and dying before

the Gestapo could take him.

Other boats were met by waiting German patrol boats, warned in advance of Rinnan's organisation; parachutists were captured as they landed. But Rinnan himself can best be seen at work in an incident involving Thorvald Moe, a teacher at Vikna.

With the sea routes hopelessly compromised the Norwegian authorities after much discussion, decided to try to get arms, equipment and instructors through from Sweden. Thorvald Moe offered to organise this new route.

In the meantime, Rinnan, using the cover-name Olav Wist, had made contact with a man in that Resistance organisation which was responsible for helping Norwegian Jews escaping to Sweden. This man, somehow discovering Moe's activities, tried to bring the teacher and Rinnan-Wist together. Rinnan was proposing that Moe should work for him, but Moe was suspicious and was on the point of giving a definite No, when he was arrested by the Gestapo, to whom he had been betrayed.

The Gestapo tortured him for several hours without result, and he was then put into a motor-car and driven to Vollen prison. As the car pulled up before the prison, two men ran up. The door on the side of which Moe was sitting was flung open, and one of the men shouted, "Olav's wating on the corner in a car." While Moe jumped out the two men dealt with the Germans.

At the corner Moe found the car and Rinnan-Wist. He jumped in and was driven at high speed to a safe hiding, where he discussed the situation with Rinnan, who by now had convinced him, quite naturally, that he had a strong organisation and was on the "right side". It was agreed that Moe and his family should escape to Sweden by a route known to Rinnan, while Rinnan should take over Moe's work of getting the supplies and men in from Sweden.

Rinnan met a number of Moe's people, who had got to hear of the rescue and were much impressed by it. They were strengthened in their confidence in Rinnan when they heard that the Germans had telephoned the border guard, and told them that

Moe had escaped from the Gestapo with the help of a strong organisation believed to be armed. They did not know, of course, that the Germans had done this at Rinnan's instigation.

Moe and his family reached Sweden in safety, but fortunately the Norwegian legation in Stockholm were aware of Wist's true identity, and the ruse, arranged to get control of the men and supplies sent from Sweden, did not succeed. So strong was Rinnan's hold of the organisation in Ytre Nandal, however, and so complete was the confidence of the key men of the organisation in him, that they refused to believe the warnings sent to them.

With such a state of affairs, it was decided that no further operations could be carried out there. Rinnan made the position in the whole of the Trondelag area so difficult that eventually the central leadership of the Resistance had to treat the district as one that had "fallen away".

Fortunately there were few men of Rinnan's calibre willing to help the enemy. He was caught at the end of the war and executed.

531

BIBLIOGRAPHY :

The Undaunted — Ronald Seth (London, 1956).

Inside SOE — E. H. Cookridge (London, 1966).

RINTELEN, Captain Fritz von (German saboteur, World War I).

Captain Fritz von Rintelen, of the German Navy, was one of the pioneer saboteurs in the Western Hemisphere in the history of sabotage.

The United States preserved its neutrality for a much longer period in World War I than it did in World War II, but it did not favour the Allies any the less. The Germans would have had to be very unperceptive indeed not to have discovered quickly the aid that America was giving to their enemies, and when they did perceive it, they lost no time in sending to the United States an agent charged with preventing all the American aid possible from reaching the Allies, and by any possible means, Rintelen chose sabotage.

Fritz von Rintelen had entered the German navy in 1903, when he was twenty. When hostilities broke out he was on the Naval Staff in Ber-lin, and out of patriotism accepted the mission he was asked to undertake. Arriving in New York at the beginning of 1915, he pursued his activities for two years, until he was compromised by the German military attaché in Washington, Captain Franz von Papen (q.v.).

Rintelen organised his sabotage with great daring and skill. His success was greatly facilitated by the fact that American counter-espionage scarcely existed at this time. No one in the United States seems to have had the least suspicion that the mysterious explosions on board munitions-carrying ships, and the no less mysterious fires, were the work of this affable and distinguished man who was a member of a very exclusive club in New York, and who dined with many leading personalities.

Many of the devices supplied by the British to their saboteurs in World War II were merely perfected copies of Rintelen's inventions. The time pencil had been developed from his "cigar", which consisted of a tube of lead divided into two compartments by a copper plug. In one part of the tube was a mixture of sugar and potassium chlorate, and in the other sulphuric acid. The "cigar" was placed in a favourable position on board a munitions ship, which was at sea by the time the sulphuric acid had eaten through the copper plug and mixed with the sugar-potassium-chlorate to cause an immediate incendiary.

Other devices were made up to look like harmless tins of fruit and toys. Pieces of coal were split in two, the middle scooped out and filled with explosive, and it was then introduced into the ship's bunkers. One of Rintelen's agents even invented a primitive "limpet" charge which was used with much effect by British agents and Italian frogmen in the Mediterranean in 1944. The "limpet" was attached by magnets to the hull of a ship or its rudder. The movements of the ship caused acid to eat through a wire attached to a plunger which activated a detonator, which in turn fired an explosive charge. Rintelen and his agents used this weapon in many American ports.

Despite all their activities and their ingenuity, however, Rintelen and his network had only a very insignificant effect on the flow of war material to Europe. But, on the principle that every little helps, their efforts were not entirely wasted. It is quite certain that but for the indiscretion of Captain von Papen they would never have been discovered.

The military attaché very unwisely informed Berlin of Rintelen's achievements in a code so simple that he might just as well have used plain language. He also used the same code to announce Rintelen's temporary return to Germany. This last was intercepted by British intelligence, and when the Dutch liner **Noordam** entered the English Channel, she was stopped and searched, and Rintelen, despite his protests that he was on a neutral vessel, was arrested and taken off. All the British could do was intern him, but when they entered the war, the United States applied for his extradition. He was subsequently tried and sentenced to four years in the Atlanta Penitentiary.

By the time he had completed his sentence, the war was over, and instead of re-

533

turning to Germany, he settled in England where, at the beginning of World War II, he was again interned. He could console himself, however, with the thought that if he had continued his activities after the United States had entered the war, he would almost certainly have been shot if caught.

BIBLIOGRAPHY :

The Dark Invader — Fritz von Rintelen (London, 1933).

ROE, Austin (American agent, War of Independence) see under **Tallmadge Network, The.**

RONGE, Captain (later Major-General) Maximilian (Director of Austro-Hungarian intelligence) see under **Redl, Col A.**

ROQUEBERT, François.
(French traitor, World War I).

The Central Pharmaceutical Service of the French army had its headquarters in the outbuildings of the La Tour-Marbourg barracks, not far from the official residence of the Military Governor of Paris, General Gallieni. In the warehouses were stocks of drugs and other medicines, together with thermometers, all of which had been hastily requisitioned from the chemists' shops on the outbreak of war.

After a time, a general complaint went up from hospitals and medical units that there seemed to be an acute shortage of thermometers.

In charge of the thermometer department of the CPS were two brothers, medical orderlies of the 20th Section, Fernand and Paul Bulmé, both of whom enjoyed the confidence of their superiors. The Bulmé brothers were addicted to card-playing, and spent practically every off-duty moment in this pursuit, in a café not far from the barracks. Their partners were usually François Roquebert of no known profession or trade, and his friend, who called himself "Athos" — his real name was Sydney — who described himself as a professor of physical culture, and who lived at 4 villa Croix-Nivert. In fact, both were in the employment of the German Abwehr.

It was Athos who first

broached the subject of thermometers. As the four were playing cards one day he casually mentioned that he was on the look-out for thermometers, and then suggested that the Bulmé brothers could surely let him have a few, which would not be missed from the Army stores. Attracted by the excellent price Athos was prepared to pay, if "no questions were asked", the brothers agreed to "cooperate". Thereafter they provided Athos with a daily dozen or so.

At heart, Fernand Bulmé was a pacifist, and he had become a medical orderly as a preferable alternative to internment as a conscientious objector. He revealed this to his card-playing companions one evening, and this fact gave Athos another idea.

Why not reward his conscience, he suggested to Fernand, by blowing up the La Tour-Marbourg barracks? The CPS's warehouses contained large stocks of ether, chloroform and carbonic sulphate, all of which were highly inflammable substances. Set fire to these and the barracks would go up at the same time. There would

be no risk, and besides quietening his conscience he could also be well rewarded for it by Berlin. Athos knew a German who had friends in important positions in the German government, and he would see to it that they were not forgotten.

When Fernand agreed, Athos set out for Spain to contact his German friend with whom he would make the financial arrangements. None of the men knew that the **patron** of the café had caught snatches of their conversation and had informed the authorities. Even before Athos set out for Barcelona they had been under counter-espionage surveillance for some days.

On his return journey from Spain, Athos was arrested by counter-espionage agents as he crossed the Pyrenees by a smugglers' route. On him were found several letters in code addressed to another of his cover-names, M Dumas, 54 Rue de Bourgogne, Paris, a bottle of secret ink and a French-Spanish pocket dictionary. Counter-espionage had little difficulty in breaking his code, which was based on words taken from the dictionary — the first two figures of each group indicated the pages of the dictionary on which the words were to be found, and the last two the position of the word on the page — and soon had sufficient information to charge him with espionage and conspiracy to sabotage.

Athos broke down under interrogation, and confessed all the details to blow up and set fire to the La Tour-Marbourg barracks. He confessed that he was somewhat bitter against his German friend, who was none other than Colonel von Rolland, chief of the Abwehr bureau in Barcelona, who had reduced the 150,000 francs (£6000) by 20,000 francs, and stipulated that the money would not be paid until the barracks were destroyed.

Roquebert and the Bulmé brothers were court-martialled with Athos. The last three were sentenced to face a firing-squad at Vincennes; Roquebert to fifteen years' imprisonment to be followed by twenty years banishment from France. The court somewhat generously allowed his defence that he had been only an accessory before the fact.

ROSE or ROSENBERG, Fred (Soviet agent) see under **Soviet Canadian Network, The.**

ROSENBERG, Julius and Ethel (American traitors) see under **Soviet American Network.**

ROSSI, Francois alias **Abiatt Roland** see under **Reiss, Ignace.**

ROSSLER, Rudolf (covername Lucy) (Outstanding Soviet agent in World War II).

Rudolf Rössler, the son of a Bavarian forester, was for a time the editor of an anti-Nazi newspaper in Augsburg, Germany. In 1933 he moved to Switzerland to avoid the unwelcome attentions of Adolf Hitler, and there he became head of the publishing firm of Vita Nova in Lucerne, which had, naturally, a very strong anti-Nazi bias. Politically he was more anti-capitalist than anti-Communist. He was a member of **Die Entscheidung,** a leftist Catholic group.

He was introduced to espionage by his young friend, a Swiss called Xaver Schnieper, a journalist and also a member of **Die Entsheidung,** whom he had met shortly before going to live in Switzerland. In 1939 Schnieper was taken into the Swiss Army Information Service, and when asked if he could recommend anyone else, put forward Rössler's name.

When Rössler entered the ND (Information Service) in the autumn of 1939, it seems to have been on the understanding that he would not work exclusively for it, but for anyone else as well who were anti-Nazi and needed his services.

From the beginning of the war, the western Allies had exchanged intelligence, and when Russia was attacked, Russia, despite her reluctance to reciprocate, was included in the arrangement. In fact, Stalin ought to have felt a good deal of gratitude towards the Allies had he chosen to listen to them, for he received from Washington and Churchill warning of the imminence of **Barbarossa.** Why he chose to disregard the warnings is one of the minor mysteries of World War II; but he treated one of his own impeccable sources Richard Sorge (q.v.) in Tokyo, in the same way, and even refused to believe the exact date of the launching of the attack provided by Rössler.

Rössler had acquired the information from one of his German sources, and was granted permission by the Swiss ND to pass it on to the Russians. This he did via a friend, Christian Schneider, who contacted Rahel Dubendorfer, one of Rado's (see Rado, Alexander) principal go-betweens. This was Rössler's first contribution to Soviet intelligence, but from that moment he worked regularly for Rado's network, presumably with the knowledge of the ND and of British intelligence.

Until his death in 1962, Rössler adamantly refused to disclose who his contacts in Germany were, and much speculation has been rife, though without anything definite being discovered. That they must have been exceptionally highly placed in the German administration is obvious from the fantastic information with which they supplied Rössler. Indeed, more extraordinary information did not come the way of any spy in World War II.

537

Rössler's information was not only fantastic in its accuracy and importance, but of equally incredible bulk. One can sympathise with The Centre who at first believed it was too good to be true and suspected that the Nazis were playing a game with them. But as Rössler disregarded their scepticism and continued to send his information, by degrees The Centre accepted all he sent them at face-value and treated him in a most un-Russian fashion. They allowed him to set his own price, and he set a steep one, which they paid without haggling. He received the equivalent of £425 a month, which he insisted should be paid regularly on the due date, under the threat of no pay, no results. When the time came that for one reason or another, The Centre had difficulty in getting money to their agents in Switzerland, the Director's messages to him were almost pathetic in their pleading. For example, on 9th December, 1943, the Director radio-ed, "Tell Lucy he should not worry about payments; we will certainly pay our debts not later than January. We request him to continue giving us most important information. Director", and again on 8th January, 1944, "Please tell Lucy that he and his group will receive large payment as soon as possible. He should wait patiently and should not waste time and work at this important hour of the last battle against our common enemy. Director."

Lucy's service was regular, often daily, and his information concerned Hitler's strategy, the strength, composition and location of all German armed forces, and a good idea of what the Abwehr knew about Russian positions, strength and plans. He kept up this extraordinary flow until the debacle which overtook Rado's network in November 1943, when Alexander Foote was arrested and Rado deserted his agents and went into hiding, as a result of which the network disintegrated.

After the war Rössler refused to continue his clandestine activities either on behalf of the Swiss or the Russians. Most of the money he had received from the Russians and the Swiss he sank in Vita Nova, but Nova fell on evil days when the end of fascism brought the return of free speech to Germany and removed the necessity for such propaganda as he specialised in.

When the Russians heard that he was in straitened circumstances they suggested that he should revive the Swiss network, and he accepted the offer. He had retained those of his wartime contacts with had survived the war, and were now working in the new German administration. The Russians also approached Schnieper, who was constantly in financial difficulties due to his expensive tastes in women, and he joined Rössler. Other members of the network were Colonel Volf, a Czech officer operating a Czech network in Switzerland under The Centre's guidance; and Colonel Sedlacek, a veteran agent then functioning as Resident Director under the cover of military attaché at the Czech embassy in Berne.

Rössler's contacts were still able to supply high-grade information, relating not only to Germany, but to Great Britain, France, America and Scandinavia, not merely in Germany, but in the countries themselves. His personal worth to The Centre was therefore high, and they were glad to pay him £400 a month.

Rössler himself concentrated on political and military intelligence, while Schnieper, who specialised in technical material, acted as his secretary and typed his reports. As The Centre began to develop the use of microdots (q.v.), Schnieper trained himself to be an expert in microphotography, and arranged for the onward transmission of reports in this form.

The channel of communication with The Centre was the concealment of the microfilms in food parcels which were sent to a "letter-box" in Düsseldorf. This was a practically fool-proof method at the time, for the Swiss were generous in sending food parcels to their German friends in their hundreds daily. Nevertheless it was this which brought the activities of the cell to an untimely end.

After working for five years — from 1947 to December 1952 — just before Christmas in 1952 they sent a food parcel to a mythical Heinrich Schwartz in Düsseldorf. For some reason or other, "Schwarts" did not claim the parcel, which was returned to Switzerland in January 1953. As there was no sender's address on it, it was opened and the microfilms were discovered hidden in jars of figs and honey. They contained reports on British airfields in West Germany, on the recent American army manoeuvres and on the US Air Force in Britain.

The Swiss BUPO had little doubt about the source of this exceptionally high-grade material, and Rössler and Schnieper were watched for a time, and then arrested. They had no hesitation in revealing their recent activities, and as they had not been engaged in espionage against Switzerland they received the light sentences of a year for Rössler and nine months for Schnieper. The Swiss could have deported both of them, but they pleaded that if they were sent back to Germany they would be liable for prosecution there for espionage; and they were not eager to go behind the Iron Curtain, either.

So, "in view of their great services to Swiss Intelligence during the war, and because they are stateless persons," they were imprisoned for the few months mentioned above.

Rössler died in 1962, still denying that he had ever engaged in espionage; and without divulging who his German contacts had been, or giving any hint as to their identity.

BIBLIOGRAPHY :

The Lucy Ring — Pierre Accoce and Pierre Quet London, 1967).

RSHA (Rechssicherheitshauptamt).

The RSHA was founded on September 27th, 1939 by order of Himmler who was himself Reichsführer SS and Head of the German police. It was a body set up to coordinate the work of:

Gestapo —
Geheime Staatspolizei (or secret police).

SD —
Sicherheitsdienst (espionage group in SS).

Kripo —
Kriminalpolizei (ordinary criminal police).

The RSHA offices were in Berlin behind the Potsdamer Platz.

There were originally six, but later seven, sub-divisions, each having further sub-divisions:

Office 1. Personnel Questions.

Office 2. Administrative matters.

Office 3. SD internal affairs.

Office 4. Operational Sections of the Gestapo.

Office 5. Operational Sections of Kripo.

Office 6. SD external affairs. Foreign. Political Intelligence.

Office 7. Ideological research.

There were 7,000 members of the RSHA at Head Office.

From 1939 to June 1942 the Head of the RSHA was Heydrich, from 1942 to 1943 it was Himmler, and from 1943 to the end of the war it was Kaltenbrunner.

Well-known officials in the RSHA included:

Ohlendorf — head of office 3.

Nebe — head of office 5.

Schellenberg — head of office 6.

Ohlendorf and Nebe commanded the Einsatzgruppen (action commandos). Nebe is now dead, Ohlendorf was executed in 1951, and Schellenberg, after some time in jail, was released and died in 1952.

In Germany itself the Gestapo and SD kept separate identities and merely reported to respective sections of RSH A on their duties. The Gestapo and SD offices throughout Germany were supervised by some thirty HSS u PF, (Höhere SS und Polizeiführer) each immediately under Himmler. In territories occupied by Germany in Eastern Europe — Poland and Russia — special groups called Einsatzgruppen (action commandos) were employed in the task of exterminating Jews. These groups were under orders from the RSHA and they sent back to the RSHA office regular reports of their activities against Jews and partisans in Russia. These Einsatzgruppen were roughly 400 to 500 strong and were composed of Waffen SS and Ordnungspolizei and officered by volunteers from the Gestapo, Kripo and SD. They were under army command for some duties but took other orders, e.g. extermination, — from the RSHA as a rule. In sub-division B4 of Office 4 the director was Eichmann whose particular responsibility was 'Jewish Affairs'.

541

The RSHA was the nerve centre of all secret police activities and the directing centre for the extermination of Jews.

At the end of the war the RSHA burnt all its documents and only very recently have these been reconstructed from other sources. As a result of these laborious researches some fifty SD officials of RSHA were likely to be charged in 1968, with mass murder. Nine were actually already under arrest.

In fact in May 1969 doubt arose whether they would ever be prosecuted. In the previous autumn the penal code was altered in such a way that the maximum penalty for abetting in murder was reduced to 15 years, provided the accused did not act 'out of base motives'. The West Berlin Prosecutor's Office asked that Court proceedings against seven of them be stopped on grounds that 'base motives' could not be proved.

BIBLIOGRAPHY :

History of Germany 1815-1945 — W. Carr (London, 1963).

RUSSIAN INTELLIGENCE ORGANISATION.

The machine for the administration of government invented by Soviet Russia is a vast one, and it has its counterpart in the system of espionage which they have adopted. The Russians, like the Japanese, also appear to have a predilection for large numbers, under the illusion that the more spies you have, the more intelligence you will collect.

With the establishment of the Soviet regime in Russia, a secret service was set up comprising a number of inter-related organisations, the most important of which — and the largest — were and still are the Directorates of Intelligence and Counter-Intelligence of the Ministry of the Interior. Besides these Directorates, the Ministry of Defence and the General Staff have their own intelligence organisations, which are chiefly concerned with strategical intelligence, while the Ministry of Foreign Affairs, through its agents attached to Russian diplomatic missions abroad, and the Ministry of External Trade, through its agents working with Soviet trade delegations abroad, maintaining their own espionage organisations.

It is, however, the Ministry of the Interior, briefly known as the MVD, and the Ministry of State Security, the KGB — since the death of Stalin there has been an ostensible reorganisation and the adoption of other names — which play the largest and most important roles on the Russian espionage stage. The MVD — which was dissolved in 1962 and replaced by the Ministry of Law and Order, though this did not noticeably change its functions, which is true of all other name-changes of the various departments of the security forces — combined, with functions similar to those of the British department MI6 (since the establishment of the Ministry of Defence, D16) and the US Central Intelligence Agency, other functions which are carried out by the Special Branch (q.v.) in England and the FBI (q.v.) in America. The KGB carries on extensive espionage activities against foreign governments and their agents.

The headquarters of the Soviet organisation are in Moscow. They consist of the First and Second Directorates, which deal with external intelligence.

The first Directorate, owing to the difference in interpretation of terminology by the Russians, is known as the Directorate of Counter-espionage, though it collects strategic and general intelligence. It employs agents abroad, and though it claims that its function is counter-espionage — it purports to **protect** Russia's military secrets and political and economic information — its work is actually akin to what is commonly defined elsewhere as espionage.

The Directorate is divided into twelve main divisions all coming under one main authority known as The Centre (q.v.) and there are various agencies which co-ordinate its work with the intelligence departments of the Ministries of Defence, Foreign Affairs and External Trade. Of the twelve divisions, six are of the highest importance, and the chief is undoubtedly the Foreign Division, for it combines intelligence research, intelligence collection and intelligence dissemination. It controls the activities of all secret agents, selects their missions, and receives and collates the reports of agents.

The Operative Division, as its name denotes, controls the actual operations of networks, appoints the chiefs of the networks, who are known as Resident Directors (q.v.), chooses agents to be sent abroad, and looks after communications. It has special agents attached to all Russian diplomatic and consular missions and trade delegations.

The Information Division collects other information of every kind which may have even a remote interest to intelligence. With the exception of military and strategic information, it collects material dealing with every aspect of political, economic, social and cultural life in foreign countries.

The Secret Division provides the false papers, cover stories, codes, "letter-boxes" (q.v.), maps, and all the other paraphernalia which agents may require.

The Communications Division maintains communications, from radio to and from networks, to special routes for "escaping" agents and others.

The Recruiting and Training Division has a role in the Russian organisation rarely, if at all, found in the espionage system of any country except, perhaps, Japan and Nazi Germany. In the countries of the West, the small hard core of permanent agents has been drawn nearly always from the military, and for the rest, selected men and women from all walks of life have been drawn into the ranks, combining their espionage duties with the ordinary business of earning a living, though in times of emergency they have been recruited on a full-time basis and given a brief training. It may seem a haphazard arrangement, but in the British experience, at all events, it has produced the really brilliant results.

Such haphazard measures are not in keeping with the cut-and-dried bureaucracy-tainted ideas of the Russians. They select their recruits carefully and then submit them to a long and rigid course of training. While this system has the advantage of instilling absolute loyalty, the rigidity of training has produced defects in performance not unlike those experienced by the Germans, whose agents can only deal with situations for which they have been trained. Some recruits are Russians, living in Russia, and are eventually sent to operate as members of embassy and consular staffs; but the bulk of recruits are Communist nationals of the country in which they are to operate. In the latter case, the standard of loyalty is not quite so high as that achieved by the Russian recruits, though the care with which they are selected is no less than that exercised in the case of Russians.

The normal procedure for recruiting a non-Russian agent is for the recruiting officer — generally a specially trained embassy official — to acquire every scrap of background information about a potential candidate that he possibly can. If this background makes him a suitable candidate he is then recommended to headquarters before any move is made to inform him that he has been selected or to sound him out.

These non-Russian agents are drawn from the ranks of scientists, civil servants, or anyone with contacts who may be useful sources of restricted information. They fall roughly into two categories: those who are ideologically sound Communists and who are prepared to betray their country for ideological reasons; and those who can be blackmailed or corrupted. Those who can be blackmailed are usually sexual perverts or have committed criminal acts undetected by the authorities, while those who can be corrupted are normally in serious financial straits.

The Russians' faith in large numbers leads them to recruit vast armies of spies. The exact number is naturally unknown, but it is estimated by experts who have access to reliable sources of information that the non-Russian agents run to between three-quarters of a million and a million. The backbone of Soviet espionage is, however, the 12,000 Russian nationals.

In every country in the world, it may safely be said, Russian espionage has its network of spies. In some countries there may be more than one network.

The bureaucratic method of administration which distinguishes Russian espionage at headquarters level is maintained at network level. The

Russian passion for analysing and recording inundates the network headquarters with rivers of dangerous paper, discovery of which — as in the Arcos case in London in 1927 (q.v.) — has led to the break-up of many a network. There is, however, another reason for this paper work — Resident Directors are changed from time to time, and the Russians argue that a detailed record of the network's activities is essential for a smooth take-over.

The First Directorate's functions correspond to those performed by Western espionage organisations. The diagram given here illustrates clearly how the various departments inter-relate.

The Second Directorate is an entirely Russian conception and has no counterpart in any Western country. Its full name is the Second Directorate of Positive State Security, and its main divisions number four. First is the Propaganda Division, which controls subversive activities in foreign countries by propaganda means. It maintains contact with Communist Parties abroad, its agents are limited in their intelligence-gathering activities purely to political intelligence, and one of its main objects is to create and maintain Fifth Columns.

Second is the Special Division, the most infamous of which is the Ninth Section for Terror and Diversion, called, even by the Russians themselves, SMERSH (see under **Khokhlov, Capt Nicolai).** This was the instrument of Stalin's power, by which he removed opponents at home and organised the assassinations or kidnappings of anti-Communist organisation chiefs abroad.

Third, the Individual Division, keeps an eye on all Soviet citizens at home and abroad and on those residing officially abroad. Its function is to discover the degree of reliability of all who are state servants and this includes all but the lowliest workers and peasants. Upon the reports of its agents a man or woman is promoted or liquidated.

Finally, there are the Allied Divisions. These are responsible for the satellite and Communist countries.

This very brief description of the Soviet espionage organisation while it deliberately

546

omits very many of the lesser ramifications of the system, clearly shows how far-reaching the influences of the Russian secret service are. For- tunately for the Free World it has many defects which prevent it from being one hundred per cent effective.

RUSSIAN RECRUITING TECHNIQUES see under **Gouzenko, Igor.**

SADOVNIKOV, V. see under **Petrov, Vladimir.**

SAFETY-PIN MEN see under **McKenna, Marthe.**

SALICH, Hafis see under **Gorin, Mikhail.**

SANSOM, Mrs Odette (Allied agent, World War II).

Born of French parents in 1912, at the age of nineteen she married an Englishman, Roy Sansom, by whom she had three children, who were still very young at the beginning of World War II. When the British evacuated Dunkirk, the War Office put out a request to the public for photographs of the French Channel coast. Mrs Sansom replied that she had a few snapshots of the Boulogne area, which she knew very well. As a result she was interviewed by SOE who asked her if she would be willing to work with the Resistance in France as a radio operator. Despite the fact that her children were still so young, she agreed. She landed
548

in the south of France on 30th October, 1942, and became the radio operator of Peter Churchill (q.v.).

The trapping of Churchill and Mrs Sansom is recounted under Churchill's entry. The tremendous courage with which she faced her captors has taken on the quality of a legend. She managed to deflect Gestapo attention from Churchill by insisting that she was the leader of the network, not he. During fourteen terrible interrogations, in the course of which she was branded on the base of the spine with a red-hot iron and had some of her toe-nails removed, she adamantly refused to talk.

Eventually she was sent to Ravensbrück concentration camp, where she was alternately treated with kindness and cruelty by the women guards. She escaped the fate of other women agents in the camp with her, who were executed towards the end of the war on orders from Berlin.

She was awarded the MBE and, at the end of the war, the George Cross.

BIBLIOGRAPHY:
Odette — Jerrard Tickell (London, 1949).

SAVARY, General (Director of French intelligence, under Napoleon).

When Napoleon dismissed Joseph Fouché from the Ministry of Police and the Directorship of Intelligence Services, he replaced him with General Savary.

Fouché (q.v.) to be revenged on Napoleon, removed all the files from the Ministry of Police, including those containing the names of all his agents, before he left his office. He told Napoleon that he had destroyed them, but in fact he had merely transferred them to a secret hiding place. His motive for this action seems to have been a belief that Napoleon, deprived of his knowledge and the records of his ministry, would be shorn of much of his power, and would be compelled to reinstate him. He had, however, counted without Savary.

Savary was a plodding, uninspired man, but at the same time, extremely painstaking and methodical. Fouché, in his spring-cleaning operation, had overlooked one register of names and addresses of subordinate, third-rank agents. Taking this as a basis, Savary was able to reconstruct most of Fouché's service. It was a feat of which any man might be proud, but the achievement was not sufficient to restore the police to their former power.

Savary's reputation rests solely upon one fact — that he discovered Karl Schulmeister, one of the most brilliant spymasters in the history of espionage (q.v.).

SCHELIHA, Josef (Soviet agent, World War II) see under **Red Orchestra, The.**

SCHILDBACH, Gertrude see under **Reiss, Ignace.**

SCHIRMER, Hans see under **Hoffmann, Lothar.**

SCHNIEPER, Xaver (Soviet agent, during and after World War II) see under **Rossler, Rudolf.**

SCHOOLS see under **Schragmuller, Dr Elsbeth.**

SCHRAGMÜLLER, Dr Elsbeth (Abwehr agent World War I).

In August 1914, there was studying at Freiburg university

a young post-graduate research worker, studious and thorough, clever, though by no means a genius, of good Westphalian stock, fluent in French, Italian and English, who, a year before, had obtained a degree of Doctor of Philosophy for a thesis on **Die Bruderschaft der Borer und Balierer von Freiburg und Waldkerch** — the ancient guilds of Freiburg and Waldkerch. From this young doctor Colonel Walter Nicolai, head of the Abwehr, (q.v.) soon after the outbreak of World War I, began to receive letters asking him to use his influence to obtain for the writer a post at the front. Nicolai ignored the first few letters, but, probably to rid himself of the boredom of this kind of importuning, arranged for the applicant a post in the civil censorship bureau in occupied Brussels.

Within a fortnight, Lieutenant Schragmüller, by a keen application to the somewhat monotonous duties of the censorship office and by the exercise of a keen intelligence, had come to the notice of the intelligence officers of the occupation army. Not only did the lieutenant deal with twice as much work as any other member of the censorship bureau, but by an apparently natural flair and understanding of military strategy and tactics, had been able to supply many items of important military interest.

Some of the information had, in fact, been so valuable that it had been forwarded direct to General von Beseler, commanding the army corps investing Antwerp, and before long the general was so impressed with the reliability of the intelligence that he grew curious to know the sender. So he gave orders for Lieutenant Schragmüller to report to his headquarters.

Next day he was in his office with one of his intelligence officers, Captain Refer, when Schragmüller's arrival from Brussels was announced, and as soon as the lieutenant stepped through the door, both the general and the captain were so overcome with surprise that their reception of the visitor was almost discourteous. For instead of the bright young subaltern they had been expecting, they found themselves confronted by a young, slim blonde in whose steel-blue eyes was an intensity indicating a singleness of purpose rarely met with in a young woman in her middle twenties, and who, despite a certain wistfulness of expression, by her complete lack of embarrassment, betrayed in her whole bearing a quick and sharp intelligence.

When the men had recovered from their surprise, and had asked a few questions to reassure themselves that there had been no mistake, their subsequent interrogation of Fräulein Dr Lieutenant Elsbeth Schragmüller revealed that they had before them a most extraordinary young woman. That the information she had culled from the letters which went to her for censorship was not based on a happy chance but on a real understanding of military affairs became more and more evident with every searching question she answered. Before the interview had lasted half an hour, Beseler was convinced that here was spy material of high calibre, which, despite the fact of unusual sex, must be used. So, telling her to return to the censorship bureau for the time being, he informed the delighted though surprised lieutenant that he would arrange for her appointment to the Special Intelligence Corps with all possible speed.

The Nachrichtendienst (as the Abwehr was then called) though not yet properly geared for the great expansion which a state of war imposes on intelligence services, had already three training schools for agents in operation, one of which, at Baden-Baden, (where ironically until a short time ago SMERSH, the Russian assassination department of intelligence, also had a school) was in the charge of Major Joseph Salonek, whose object was to co-ordinate the training and methods of the German and Austro-Hungarian military secret services. It was to this school that Dr Schragmüller was posted within three weeks of her interview with General von Beseler.

The Baden-Baden curriculum imposed a rigorous regimen on its pupils. They ceased to exist as persons and became numbers; they were subjected, women as well as men, to the strictest military discipline; they lived in obscure lodgings and were allotted a small sum of pocket money each week. Classes began at 8 in the morning, and finished in the late afternoon. Tests in secret inks, the reading and drawing of maps and plans, unit designations and badges of rank, the uniforms of the armies on both sides, and in security, were the order of the day.

Security was high on the list — though few of the agents who graduated from the German schools were ever really proficient in it in practice — and the lengths to which it was taken in the school in Baden-Baden were hilariously excessive. It is common practice in espionage training circles that all pupils live at the schools under code names, and it is strictly forbidden for them to disclose their antecedents, or, if they are already known, the missions selected for them. All the Baden-Baden pupils lived in private lodgings, as has been said, and were forbidden to meet and circulate socially in off-duty hours, which meant, in fact, that they were cut off from all social life. But most extraordinary of all were the masks covering the upper part of the face which all had to wear while on the school premises. At the end of the day's instruction they left the school at three-minute intervals, so that none should know in which part of the town others lived, or should be tempted to strike up an ac-

quaintance. A small army of detectives was employed to keep watch on all out-of-school activities of each individual embryo agent.

Dr Schragmüller graduated from Baden-Baden, as she had from Freiburg university, *cum laude*. If she had expected to be given an assignment behind the enemy lines, she was to be disappointed. When she had completed the course Major Salonek told her that she had been used as a guinea-pig, to discover how the trained mind would react to espionage schooling. She had proved that the highly educated person of penetrating intellect could be transformed into a highly qualified spy.

Agents as qualified as she was, however, were far too valuable to be squandered on any except the most vital missions, and as there was no mission of this calibre at present in view, she was being posted to a new school which was being set up in Antwerp, with the sole purpose of training really expert agents who would be required to penetrate England and the French Channel ports, and to keep a check on the highly developed espionage system which the

Allies were establishing in Neutral Holland. She was being promoted in rank and would join the teaching staff of the Antwerp school forthwith.

The house in which the Antwerp school had been established was one on the corner of the rue de la Pepiniere and the rue de l'Harmonie. It had entrances in both streets. In command was a veteran intelligence expert, Major Groos, and he was supported by the finest staff of instructors that the ND could muster.

Never before had the Germans employed a woman as an instructor in espionage, and there is no trace that they have ever done so since. This is not to be wondered at; the reputation of Elsbeth Schragmüller is still remembered with a shudder by all male German intelligence teachers. With the singleness of purpose which she had displayed in her abstruse academic researches, she applied herself to her new work with an ardour unmatched — became of its quite different quality — by even the most outstanding of her male colleagues. She established a distinct advantage over her fellow teachers by witholding herself from all petty cliques and jealousies and by refusing to become involved in the internal military politics of the school. Within a short time she was dominating both the school and the staff, and it was not long before she was rapidly gaining notoriety in foreign espionage circles, where she was known as Tiger Eyes, the Beautiful Blonde of Antwerp, and the Terrible Doctor Elsbeth.

She gave herself without stint to her work, on which she is reputed to have spent twenty hours a day. She subjected herself to the most rigid discipline and exacted it of those who came to the school for instruction. She would never allow herself to be photographed, and after the war steadfastly refused to write her memoirs. As a result many pretty women spies were tempted to claim that they were the Blonde of Antwerp, such was her reputation by the end of the war. But during the war, Elsbeth Schragmüller's real identity was never discovered, even by the British who made several attempts to do so, putting some of their best agents on the job.

Dr Schragmüller has been credited with at least one innovation in espionage practice — The Sacrifice, an agent whose life is deliberately sacrificed in order to distract attention from agents carrying out particularly difficult missions. A man or woman is chosen who is not good agent material, so that he betrays himself, or herself, by his own incompetence; or a spy whose activities have become an embarrassment — Mata Hari is said to have become such a one — or whose loyalty has become suspect is used. Even in a profession where deceit plays a major role in the *modus operandi*, The Sacrifice is regarded with distaste. There is no doubt at all that Elsbeth Schragmüller was patriotic in the extreme, and certain of her activities display the presence in her make-up of a high degree of sadism. Whether she was betrayed into her sadistic acts by her patriotism it is not possible to say now, but she must be absolved from the charge of inventing The Sacrifice. The Russian secret police, the Ochrana (see under **Russian Intelligence Organisation**) had used it often during the thirty years preceding World War I, and so had the brilliant and treacherous Austrian spy-master, Colonel Alfred Redl (q.v.).

The course at the Antwerp school lasted fifteen weeks, and into it was crammed a curriculum which must have daunted many a good potential spy. Unlike the embryo agents of Baden-Baden, those of Antwerp lived at 10 rue de la Pepinière. The house was built round a small courtyard, and though the bedrooms of the pupils were comfortably furnished, all windows overlooking the rue de l'Harmonie were shuttered and barred, light and ventilation coming only from those giving on to the courtyard.

Dr Schragmüller had come to the conclusion that the masks used by other schools were quite valueless as a means of preventing recognition, and they were abandoned by the Antwerp school. Instead, far more rigorous precautions were taken. For the first three weeks of his being at the school, that is, until he had proved his potentialities, the agent was locked in his room. His meals were served in his room, and instructors visited him there to give him his introduction to espionage techniques. When he had proved himself, he was permitted access to other clearly defined parts of the house and to exercise in the courtyard.

The Fräulein Doktor spent much time with each agent. She may have taught some subject, but her main pre-occupation was to stir the man's or woman's patriotic sentiments to such a pitch that spying for and dying for the Fatherland were the most desirable crowns for all good Germans. And while she was imbuing her pupils with such powerful sentiments, she also dinned into them a number of rules of behaviour, drawn up by her and designed to make operation as rewarding as possible.

Some of these precepts are worth stating, for they demonstrate the role that common sense plays in espionage, and especially in that most important aspect of it — security.

"When you are bargaining directly with an informant, always do so on your own ground. Make him travel away from his home as far as possible, preferably by night, by a tedious round-about route. A tired informer is less cautious and suspicious, less disposed to lie or to bargain shrewdly. You will make sure that you, on the other hand, are fresh and alert.

"Never develop an *idée fixe* about some item of intelligence you think you can or must obtain. This will lead you into making yourself conspicuous by your inquiries. Collect every bit of information you can, but without showing interest in any of it.

"Always record the information you collect if you cannot absolutely trust your memory, but record it in terms of absolute innocence. Figures and dimensions you have to report may best be remembered as items of personal expenditure. You have seen, on a visit to Chatham, **ten** heavy naval guns on lorries, ready for mounting. You remember, however, the excellent fish dinner you had there which cost you **ten** shillings.

"If you burn a letter, do not believe you have made it unreadable and do nothing more about it. Microscopic examination can reveal writing or printing on ash. Pound the ashes to fine powder and scatter it to the winds. Merely tearing up paper into small scraps is as dangerous as leaving it whole. Even putting small scraps down the lavatory is no real safeguard.

"Avoid any temptation to be too clever or too original about methods of communication and so on, unless you are quite sure that your invention is really new. Rely rather on proven techniques.

"Never talk or behave mysteriously. There is only one circumstance in which you may do so: a person who has something really important to communicate and is half-ready to do so, can often be fully persuaded by being told something — preferably wholly fictitious — in a confiding way, with a slightly mysterious air, for he will be flattered by it.

"Conceal whatever linguistic gifts you have, to encourage others to talk more freely in your hearing."

Dr Schragmüller remained at the Antwerp school until the liberation of Belgium. As the war progressed, so her ruthlessness became more pronounced and her singleness of purpose more frantic. Many of her spies achieved remarkable successes; others failed her, and toward the end she did not hesitate to liquidate those who did fail but who escaped the vengeance of the Allies. Espionage circles throughout the Allied world were weighted down by the terrible reputation of the unidentified Blonde of

Antwerp, for this reputation added a special psychological obstacle to all the other normal and abnormal obstacles encountered by agents, which must be overcome if success is to be achieved.

Gradually, however, the tide turned, and the Germans had to retreat from Belgium. With them went Dr Schragmüller, not only back to Germany but to an obscurity so complete that all attempts to find and identify her failed.

In the early 1930s a woman was admitted to a Swiss sanatorium for the treatment of drug addiction, and it became known that she was an ex-German Agent. Actuated no doubt by wishful thinking, certain reporters suggested that the woman was Elsbeth Schragmüller, who had taken to drugs to compensate for the loss of the power she had wielded in the four years of war. The newspapers of the world took up the story, and this proved too much for the Doktor, whose self-pride would not allow this besmirching of her reputation to pass unrefuted. So she revealed that since the end of the war she had been a lecturer at Munich university, living a life, outside her academic activities, completely cut off from all contacts, her mother being her only companion. She died in the early part of World War II.

All espionage agencies maintain schools in which they train their agents. The Abwehr of Nazi Germany had a famous school at the Klapstock Pension in Hamburg; today the Russian KGB have schools at Karlshorst, in East Germany, while their main training establishment is at Kuchino, on the outskirts of Moscow; pre-World War I Japan had a very famous school at Vladivostock, on Russian territory, disguised as a juijitsu school and an even more famous one at Hankow; and the Chinese People's Republic have a school in Nanking for teaching revolutionary techniques, to which pro-Communist Africans are sent for training. During World War II, the British organisation SOE maintained more than a score of schools scattered throughout the British Isles.

BIBLIOGRAPHY:

Die Weltskriegsspionage — Lieutenant-General Paul von Lettow et al (Munich, 1932).

Memoirs of a Spy — Nicholas Snowden (Miklós Soltész) (New York, 1933).

SCHREIEDER, Josef (Chief of Gestapo counter-intelligence, Holland, World War II) see under Giskes, Col H. J.

SCHULMEISTER, Karl (Director of espionage for Napoleon).

Karl Schulmeister was the son of an Alsatian Lutheran pastor. He grew up, however, firmly convinced that the pastor's wife had allowed herself to be seduced by a Hungarian nobleman of ancient lineage and that he was the offspring of this illicit union. Nothing was farther from the truth, and it must be accepted that it was nothing more than a folie de grandeur, from which Schulmeister continued to suffer during the greater part of his espionage career, and which manifested itself in various forms.

During the early part of his life he nursed his folie in secret, informing only a very few of his closest friends, and since he saw no alternative for the time being, he accepted the modest middle-class conditions in which he was raised. He married a local girl and made

557

his living from a strange combination of trades—he set himself up as a grocer-cum-ironmonger.

By his middle twenties, however, his **folie** had taken a firmer hold on him. It was unworthy of him, he believed, to be content to suffocate his noble birth, and he decided to make for himself a glittering social position. His dream was to be able to wear one day the insignia of the Legion of Honour.

But to be society's cynosure required resources far in excess of the modest though adequate income provided by the grocery-ironmongery, and so he turned to a business then thriving among Alsatians of the frontier — smuggling — for which he soon found he had a particular flair. With money in his purse, he set about acquiring the social accomplishments that one of his noble birth must have. Elegant clothes, dancing lessons from a marquis, a natural gay wit, and an extraordinarily nimble blade soon brought him the recognition he felt he deserved.

In his new role he made the acquaintance in 1799 of Colonel Anne-Jean-Marie-René Savary (q.v.), an officer on Napoleon's staff, who was promoted from colonel to general and appointed Minister of Police when the former Minister, Joseph Fouché (q.v.), fell foul of his master's anger. Savary's rise was meteoric but not, in the circumstances, strange, for very early in his career he won the confidence of Napoleon, and became one of his most trusted lieutenants. What was strange was that, though normally not very perceptive of outstanding qualities in others, he should recognise, under Schulmeister's veneer of social grace, the genius that was to make him, in time, one of the most brilliant directors of espionage in the history of spying. Having occasion for the services of a confidential agent not long after their first meeting, Savary proposed to Schulmeister that he should help him. Schulmeister's complete success cemented the relationship between him and the colonel who called increasingly upon his services, for which he was wise enough to pay well.

It was the treacherous deceit with which the young duc d'Enghien was lured onto French soil, seized, and summarily executed by Napoleon, which brought Schulmeister to the emperor's notice, for it was he who had forged the letter purporting to come from the duc's mistress, which had provided the fatal bait. And since Napoleon himself at that time, possibly more than at any other, needed the services of an outstanding agent, Schulmeister's future was assured from that first meeting.

Continuing his campaign of European conquest, by the end of 1804 Napoleon was turning his attention to Austria and Russia. Brilliant though he was as a strategist and tactician, Napoleon's successes were not based solely on these qualities. He made it a point of first importance in planning a campaign to discover all he could of the personal characteristics of the generals who would be opposing him.

At the head of the Austrian armed forces was Marshal Mack. Mack was by no means a great soldier, but he came of one of the oldest of Austrian families, and on that account wielded great influence. The Austrian emperor and the Austrian people looked to him to perform the impossible.

Napoleon, wishing to have a more accurate evaluation of Mack's character than the

marshal's popularity at home projected, asked Schulmeister to go to Vienna to find out what he could. Napoleon could not know, for it is doubtful whether Schulmeister had any suspicions of it himself, that this mission to the Austro-Hungarian capital was to become so outstanding in its achievements that had it been the last mission Schulmeister undertook it would have assured his inclusion high in the ranks of the world's master spies for all times.

Schulmeister arrived in Vienna using his role of Hungarian nobleman of mysterious parentage as his cover. Viennese society warmed to the handsome, elegant young man who had been deported from France for suspected espionage for Austria, and soon he was meeting the Marshal himself. Though Austrian intelligence records showed that Schulmeister had never been in its service, he obviously knew a great deal about civil and military conditions in France, and Mack was impressed. He took the young man under his wing, introduced him to all the most exclusive military clubs in Vienna, bestowed on him a commission, and appointed him to his personal staff.

It has happened before and since that a spy has been able to place himself in an exceptionally strategic position for the performance of his mission, but very rarely has it happened that he has risen to be director of intelligence for the country upon whom he is spying. But this was the position that Schulmeister attained.

The results scarcely need enumerating. The most secret of all Austrian plans were communicated to Napoleon. Equally important was the deception he was able to practice on the marshal which inspired in him that quality fatal to all generals — overconfidence. The way in which this was done was brilliant.

At Schulmeister's request, newspapers full of false information concerning conditions in France were printed secretly and smuggled to him. Letters purporting to come from malcontents in Napoleon's armies arrived almost daily, reporting gossip and "eye-witnesses'" reports of military disaffection, civil disturbances, and other difficulties facing the French ruler, which had they been true, would have made it quite impossible for Napoleon to embark on a campaign while they continued to exist. And Mack believed them to be true. As he saw the situation, France was on the verge of insurrection.

In the circumstances, therefore, it seemed quite natural when Napoleon began, apparently, to withdraw his frontline troops from the Rhine back into France. Mack who was occupying the strategic city of Ulm with thirty thousand men, could not resist setting out in pursuit, and received the shock of his life when he caught up with the French troops of Marshal Ney much sooner than he expected, and found that the reason for his doing so was that instead of retreating Ney was advancing.

Not only was Ney advancing, but he was ready to fight; and what was more, his fellow generals, Soult, Dupont, Marmont and Lannes, were not long in appearing to support his flanks. With the arrival of Murat, the French ring around Mack's army was closed, and within three days he could do nothing but surrender.

Meanwhile, Schulmeister had managed to "escape" through

the French lines and return to Vienna, where he found the Austrian and Russian emperors in urgent council of war. Provided by Napoleon with cunningly forged documents to support his arguments as to the best strategy to follow, he ended by convincing the emperors that their only hope of retrieving the situation was to adopt his suggestions.

There were among high Austrian officials, however, a number who had had their doubts about Schulmeister for some time. Soon discrediting rumours began to circulate, and taking advantage of the situation thus engendered, they obtained permission to arrest him. Had he been brought to trial, there can be no doubt that he would have been condemned and executed, but before the case against him could be prepared, Murat advanced upon Vienna, and within a few days accepted its surrender. Within a few weeks more, the battle of Austerlitz put an end to Austrian resistance.

Napoleon rewarded Schulmeister with a large sum of money, which, added to the ex gratia payments Mack and the Austrian emperor had heaped upon him, provided him with sufficient means to meet his by now extravagant personal tastes. But he had also tasted the excitement and the success of espionage and found them sweet, so he continued working for General Savary, soon to be ennobled as duc de Rovigo, carrying out missions for him which took him as far afield as England and Ireland.

For a time Napoleon made him censor and French Commissary of Police in Vienna, but in 1809 he was appointed Commissary-General of the Imperial Armies in the field. As such he was responsible for supplying all the French troops under arms outside France, and he found it a highly satisfactory post from the financial point of view. The commissions which contractors were willing to pay him soon provided him with an extensive private fortune, with part of which he purchased two splendid estates which together would be valued in excess of £500,000 today.

But money was not enough. He still had not achieved his chief ambition — to receive from the emperor the Legion of Honour. Again and again he was able to persuade

561

influential friends to solicit Napoleon on his behalf, but each time Napoleon refused saying, "Gold is the only suitable reward for spies."

In 1810 Schulmeister suffered a reverse of fortunes which would have persuaded any normal man to put an end to his espionage activities. In this year Napoleon married the Austrian Archduchess Marie Louise, who naturally harboured a just resentment against the man who had played such a prominent part in her father's defeat, and she and her retinue began a powerful series of intrigues against him which he was powerless to resist. This was largely due to Napoleon's attitude toward his spies and spy-masters. He believed, and said so on more than one occasion, that the spy is only one small remove from the traitor. At the same time, he was more than willing to profit from their dangerous activities, which played a large part in his military successes.

Napoleon succumbed to his Austrian wife's demands — some say to obtain relief from her shrill tongue — and Schulmeister was dismissed. Unlike many in higher places, he did not go over to the other side on his banishment, but retired to his estates. Nor did he harbour any resentment against Napoleon; in fact, it was his continuing loyalty to his master which was responsible for his ultimate disgrace.

For his support of Napoleon during the Hundred Days, after Waterloo he was arrested and only saved his head by paying a large ransom equal to three-quarters of his entire fortune. In attempts to recoup his losses, he dabbled on the Bourse, in which activity he proved much less successful than in deceiving respected marshals and emperors. Within a very short time he had lost every sou.

Poorer than he had ever been before, he lived another forty years, dying in 1853. And he would have been poorer than he actually was, had not the government granted him a concession to open a tobacco kiosk in Strasbourg.

BIBLIOGRAPHY:

Schulmeister — L. Diffenbach (London, undated).

Spy and Counter-Spy — R. W. Rowan (New York, 1928).

SCHULZE-BOYSEN, Harro see under **Red Orchestra, The.**

SEBES (Dutch agent, World War II) see under **Giskes, Col H. J.**

SECRET INKS.

Writing in liquids which are not visible to the naked eye until treated in some way, is a practice almost as ancient as espionage itself. Two simple materials which produce invisible writing are lemon-juice and onion-juice, which can be made visible by the simple process of heating them.

In more recent times secret ink has become much more sophisticated, a variety of chemicals being used, some of which are so advanced that they require a process as complicated as the photographic developing process to make them visible. This has been necessitated by the fact that censors and counter-espionage organisations have produced tests for the presence of messages written in secret inks, antidotes as it were, easy to apply to any suspected piece of "letter-paper".

In World War II the Germans produced a secret ink that could only be revealed by a complicated photographic developing process, but which, at the same time, was extremely simple for the agent to use. It consisted of a tablet about the size of and having the appearance of an aspirin which was dropped into ordinary ink. The message was written in this doctored ink, which when exposed to the air, within a few minutes became invisible, until developed. This particular ink had many advantages. The tablets could be kept in an aspirin bottle; if the agent were in danger of being caught, he could swallow them without any serious effects; since the ink was initially visible, it was very easy to use. But its most remarkable property was that it could be used on newsprint, which is notoriously bad as an agent for a secret ink.

The Russians had a similar ink in use after World War II. It was dissolved in ordinary water. Its chief drawback was that it could not be seen except for a fleeting moment while it was still wet on the page.

A much more sophisticated Russian secret ink in use until a few years ago consisted of an impregnated page in an ordinary book. Its chief drawback was that it required a sheet of glass which was placed under the paper receiving the message, which is not an easily disguised article to include in an agent's equipment.

Nowadays, though secret inks still have their uses, they are rapidly being replaced by the microdot (q.v.).

SECURITY.

Security, or rather the spy's observance of security, is his Staff of Life. What is really meant by security is doing nothing that will give the slightest clue about the spy's true role.

During World War II, Norwegian Resistance issued a table of rules which were designed to protect Resistance workers from compromising themselves. The list ran as follows:

Don't gossip in public places.

Don't commit secret information to paper unless absolutely necessary.

Don't call on an associate one has not seen for some time without first telephoning him to make sure that the Gestapo is not in control of his home and he himself under arrest.

Don't use your own telephone to contact an associate, always use a public call-box.

Be prepared for the Gestapo to come and inquire for you at your work during the day, or at home at night; but remember they can come on some innocent mission. If you can escape them, do so. If you are arrested, accept it with dignified silence or haughty indignation. Don't defy them. Take warm clothing with you.

All these points seem, on the face of them, to be simple commonsense, and that is really what they are. Indeed, security is ninety-five per cent commonsense.

One of the agents who practiced security *par excellence* was Jules Silber (q.v.), the German agent who operated in the British postal censorship department from 1914 to 1922 without being caught. He never bought photographic material twice at the same shop. To explain his absences from his rooms in the evenings, he let it be known that he was an addict of the theatre. (Actually in these absences he was at his photographic studio photographing documents.) To lend colour to this cover-story, he bought theatre tickets, and left the stubs lying about his sitting-room.

When in Paris during his mission in World War II, the British agent Ronald Seth (q.v.) excused his absences by saying that he was working in the Bibliotheque Nationale on a translation of Ovid's **Art of Love.** Had he been challenged, he could have produced several pages of translation which he had prepared beforehand. After the war, he completed his translation and published it.)

Noor Inayat Khan (q.v.) was a bad security risk because she had not been taught to observe the customs of the country in little matters like putting milk in a cup before the tea (the English style) instead of the milk into the tea (the French style). Worse, she did not destroy her "plain" language versions nor her encoded versions of any of the messages she transmitted. Consequently, when she was arrested the Gestapo found all the information she had transmitted during her period of operating.

The German spy Werner Wälti, who landed in Scotland during World War II, betrayed himself by answering with the German **Ja** instead of the English **Yes** when buying a railway ticket.

Security means that not only must the spy be able to support his cover by actual or circumstantial evidence, but that he must do nothing that will arouse suspicion, or even a hint of suspicion.

SECURITY CHECKS.

A security check is a secret sign inserted in a radio message by the encoding agent or radio-operator which conveys to the receiver that the message is genuine and not being sent under duress. Security checks take many different forms. They can be the mutilation of a letter at set intervals; the changing of the sixteenth and thirty-second letters by X, for example; or they can be much more elaborate, such as that used by the British agent Ronald Seth during World War II.

Seth's security check consisted of one complete group of letters, which he reached by adding the date, to his birthdate, plus the date of the battle of Waterloo. Thus:

Date: 14th October
    1968 14108
His birth date:
    5th June 1911   .. 05061
Waterloo date:
    18th June 1815   .. 18065
                   ―――――
                   37234

The 37234 was then converted into letters by means of a comparative table, e.g. EGIEN, which was then incorporated into the message, put twice through double transposition, and so completely lost until the message was decoded. Any message sent by Seth not containing this check should have been suspected immediately.

When the Germans discovered that SOE were using security checks SOE countered by giving their agents false security checks, which captured agents were told they might give to the Germans. Any message containing the false check, ought to have been immediately suspect.

For a devastating example of the failure to adhere to the security check principle **see under Giskes,** Colonel H. J.

SEDLACEK, Colonel (Russian Resident Director) see under **Rossler, Rudolf.**

SEMICHASTNY, Vladimir.

Director of Russian intelligence, appointed to succeed Alexander Shelepin in 1961, when the latter was promoted to the Secretariat of the Central Committee. He was about 40 in 1958. He is by birth a Ukrainian, a colourless individual, scarcely known even

566

inside Russia. His one outstanding public performance was his condemnation of Boris Pasternak, when the latter was awarded the Nobel Prize, and he startled the world and most of his fellow-countrymen by likening Pasternak to a pig.

Before his appointment as chief of the KGB he was First Secretary of Komsomol (the Communist League of Youth). An active anti-Stalinist, when appointed First Secretary of the Party in Azerbaijan, he carried out a ruthless Stalinist purge in that republic.

There is little doubt that he might not have received his present eminence had he not been a close friend of Shelepin, and also had not Nikita Krushchev wanted a dull individual in that particular post when he appointed Semichastny.

SEROV, General Ivan A.

Appointed Chief of the Russian Secret Police and Chairman of the Committee of State Security (the KGB i.e. Russian intelligence) in succession to Sergei Kruglov, in 1954.

Known throughout the Soviet Union and the satellite countries as The Butcher or Ivan the Terrible, Serov was more akin to the infamous Beria in character and achievement than any other head of Russian intelligence since Beria's removal.

He was an eminent Stalinist. Before and during World War II he had been responsible for the organisation of espionage in Germany. In 1941 he ordered and organised the deportation of one and a half million Poles, for which he received from Stalin the Order of Lenin. He is believed to have organised also the Katyn Forest massacre of almost the whole of the Polish officer corps, though the Russians insist that the Nazis were responsible. He oversaw the mass deportations of whole ethnic groups within the Soviet Union between 1943 and 1945, as Deputy Commissar for State Security.

When the NKVD (People's Commissariat for Internal Affairs) was split, in 1941, into two ministries, the MVD (Ministry of the Interior) and MGB (Ministry of State Security) he became deputy chief of SMERSH (q.v.), and after Stalin's death he was appointed chairman of the newly formed KGB (Board of State Security). In 1956 he succeeded Sergei Kruglov (q.v.) as Minister of Internal Affairs, while retaining control of the security services, which included espionage and counter-espionage.

In March 1956, Serov visited London to discuss with the Special Branch (q.v.) the security arrangements for the visit of Marshal Bulganin and Mr Krushchev. He received an almost violent reception from the British public and did not return with the two politicians, as he should have done.

During the Hungarian uprising, he arranged the kidnapping of the Hungarian prime minister Nagy. Two years later he was sacked by Krushchev on the grounds that he had not detected the alleged conspiracy of Malenkov, Molotov and Kaganovitch for the overthrow of Krushchev. But he was a powerful man, and by late 1959 had come to the fore again as chief of the GRU (Military intelligence), and a little later still of SMERSH in its new guise of GUKR, the Army's internal security department.

In 1962, however, his opponents were strong enough to put an end to his infamous career. In March of that year he was deprived of his seat on the Supreme Soviet, and was stripped of all the medals and honours awarded him by Stalin.

567

In 1963 he disappeared from sight when his last appointment, a minor post on the General Staff of the Army was taken from him.

SETH, Ronald (British agent, World War II).

Ronald Seth was born in 1911. On leaving Cambridge university, he went to Tallinn, Estonia, where he held the posts of English teacher in Anna Torvand-Tellmann's English College, and Lecturer (later Professor) of English Language and Literature, in the university of Tallinn.

At the outbreak of World War II, he returned to England, and in October 1939, after broadcasting commentaries on the Finno-Russian war, he joined the staff of the BBC Digest of Foreign Broadcasts as sub-editor. When the BBC Monitoring Intelligence Bureau was set up, Seth was one of the four original founder-members. After the fall of France, when the department was evacuated to the country, he was appointed Chief Intelligence Supervisor.

He left the BBC in March 1941, and joined the ranks of the RAF. After passing out he was commissioned as an Intelligence Officer in Bomber Command. While in this post, after Hitler launched his attack on Russia, and the Wehrmacht overran the Baltic States he put up a plan for sabotaging the oil-shale mines in eastern Estonia. This plan met with the approval of the authorities, and he was asked to make it effective.

In January 1942, he was seconded to Special Operations Executive (SOE) (q.v.), and was trained by them in every branch of espionage and sabotage. He was parachuted, "blind", on to the Kolga peninsula, on the northern coast of Estonia, at midnight on 24th October, 1942.

His parachute lines became entangled in telegraph wires and a tree, and he found himself surrounded by a party of German soldiers. He had missed falling on their field-post by yards. Owing to the closing down of the weather, he was able to escape immediate capture, but he lost all his equipment, including his radio transmitter and his sabotage materials.

While trying to contact former friends, he wandered about the peninsula by night, and lay up by day. On 5th

November he made contact with a friend, and while he was negotiating the purchase of a fishing boat in which he hoped to reach Sweden, he was denounced to the Germans by his friend's niece.

Having failed to kill himself — he had lost his cyanide tablet and his pistol jammed — he gave himself up. After 180 hours of interrogation by the Secret Field Police and torture by the Gestapo in an attempt to make him reveal his radio wave-lengths, which the Germans required in order to be able to work his transmitter back to England, on 24th December, 1942, he was taken out for public execution in the square in front of the Baltic Station, the main station of Tallinn. As the lever was pulled, the trap failed to drop. (It was discovered after the war that a number of his former university students had tampered with the scaffold during the night, having first distracted the attention of the German guards.) The failure of the contraption drew from the watching crowd a somewhat hostile reaction, and the young officer in charge of the execution ordered his return to prison.

An intended second attempt by the Tallinn commander to hang him on New Year's Eve was frustrated by the arrival of orders from the commander-in-chief of the Baltic area that Seth should be taken to Riga for further interrogation.

Early in February 1943, Seth was transferred to Frankfurt-am-Main, where he was questioned — and tortured again — by Luftwaffe intelligence, who then handed him over to the Gestapo. A further 120 hours of interrogation by the Gestapo failed to evoke any response from him, and he was put into solitary confinement in the Frankfurt **Untersuchungsgefängnis** (Remand Prison) to await orders for his disposal from Berlin.

Colonel Walter Schmidt of the Waffen SS was put in charge of the case. Schmidt in civilian life, was a costume jeweller of Pforzheim, and before the war he had spent several months each year in England. He was sympathetic towards Seth, who was also befriended by Criminal Commissar Bütt of the Gestapo, who was in charge of the cases of agents of SOE captured in western Europe.

After a brief trial by a secret

People's Court, Seth was sentenced to beheading. For some reason his execution was delayed, and early in December 1943 Bütt and Schmidt took him to Paris where it was suggested he should agree to return to England to transmit meteorological information to the Luftwaffe in France. He was given his liberty, the rank of Sonderführer in the Luftwaffe, and trained by Luftwaffe intelligence in German transmitting procedures, codes and secret inks.

Three days after D-Day, on the eve of his being landed in England, he was re-arrested on the orders of the Gestapo, and put into solitary confinement in the Cherche Midi prison in Paris. There he was tortured once more as he was suspected of having made contact with French Resistance.

In mid-August his Luftwaffe chief brought to him a high-ranking officer of the SS Political Intelligence Department, who suggested that Seth could again save his neck by carrying out political espionage in an officer prisoner of war camp near Brunswick.

During his stay in prison, Seth had developed a serious attack of scabies, which covered

him from head to foot. The SS officer put him in the SS hospital in the square Bois de Boulogne for treatment while he returned to Berlin for instructions.

While in this hospital, Seth was able to write a 30,000 word report of his mission to date, and to include in it the names and addresses of German agents who were to be left in France when the Germans retreated, details of the codes being used by the Luftwaffe intelligence agents, and samples of his secret inks. With the help of a French woman orderly, he smuggled this report out of the hospital into the hands of the Director of Recording at Radiodiffusion Française, whose acquaintance he had made and to whom he had confided his story orally. The director handed this report to a British officer on the day after Paris was liberated. The effectiveness of the report was vitiated, however, by a series of blunders. First, it was sent to the wrong organisation, who kept it for several weeks wondering what to do about it; second, it was forwarded to Air Ministry Intelligence, though clearly marked SOE; third, it remained in an In-tray for several weeks, and its significance was not appreciated until February 1945, by which time it was virtually useless.

A few hours before the arrival of the Americans on the outskirts of Paris, the SS officer returned, and with him Seth fled back into Germany. He entered Oflag 79, near Brunswick, from where he supplied falsified political intelligence to the SS. While attempting to draw the attention of the Senior British Officer to the fact that one of his officers was in the service of the Germans, Seth brought suspicion on himself, and unable to reveal his real identity, he was placed by the British in "protective custody". A plan to seize him by British officers and throw him out of a top-storey window was frustrated by the Senior British Officer.

Though never left for a moment to himself, Seth was able to get word to the SS of what had happened. He was rescued from the camp early in March by the SS officer, and taken by him to his apartment in Berlin.

Towards the end of March, it was suggested to Seth that he should carry to London a peace feeler from Himmler, whom he met briefly on 1st April. To this he agreed, and on 12th/13th April he was put across the frontier into Lichtenstein.

His return to England was bureaucratically delayed by the British embassy in Berne. When he did eventually reach England on 22nd April, he was refused access to Churchill, and given to understand that no one believed his story of the peace offer.

Exactly a week later Count Bernadotte arrived in London with his peace offer from Himmler, which was set out practically word for word as Seth had delivered his.

While in the Frankfurt prison, Seth had been set to making paper-bags. He concludes his account of his experiences with, "If my children ask me, 'What did you do in the war, Daddy?' I shall reply, 'I made 57,000 paper-bags for Germany.'" He still feels that this is the best description of his wartime efforts.

On demobilisation, "though I didn't know one end of a brick from another," he was appointed Regional Building Industries Officer, Southern Region, Ministry of Works. It

571

was an appointment not without a touch of irony, for part of his duties included the manning of the Bedfordshire brick works with German prisoners of war.

In 1948 he returned to teaching, which he forsook in 1952 for full-time writing.

Seth has one great regret. After the war, Commissar Bütt and Colonel Schmidt were arrested by the Allies and tried as war criminals. They appealed to Seth to give evidence on their behalf. When as a still serving officer, Seth applied for permission to do so, his application was not granted. The two men received sentences of fifteen and ten years. Walter Schmidt killed himself in his cell a few days after being sentenced.

I.W.H.

BIBLIOGRAPHY:

"A Spy Has No Friends" — Ronald Seth (London, 1952).

SHELEPIN, Alexander (Director of Russian intelligence).

Alexander Shelepin was appointed director of Russian intelligence on Christmas Day 1958. His appointment coincided with a decree of the Supreme Soviet which drew the teeth of the security services with regard to the action they had been used to taking against their victims under the rule of Beria and Serov: that is, trials by the security police were no longer legal, all criminal offences must be submitted to the processes of the Supreme Court.

Shelepin was forty when he was appointed. Up to this time he had been a Party official, and chairman of Komsomol, the Communist youth organisation.

The Supreme Soviet's new ruling automatically called for the reorganisation of the KGB, and here Shelepin's experience stood him in good stead, for he had done much to make Komsomol an up-to-date organisation. Taking the opportunity of purging the Beria-nominees still holding posts in the security services, he eventually produced a security organisation of great efficiency. In doing so, he cut the KGB staff drastically, brought in a number of younger Komsomol and Party members and did much to remove the gruesome reputation which the KGB had always had among Soviet citizens since the days of Beria's predecessors.

This in no way implied,

however, that he was a liberal. His plump, amiable appearance hid a ruthlessness which was to be feared by those who crossed him as much as Beria's or Serov's had been.

While carrying out these reforms in the security forces, he also waged war on the bribery and corruption that, even under the Soviets, still permeated the whole of Russian society. It is to his credit that he stamped it out, even if only temporarily.

In 1961 he was elected to the Secretariat of the Party, and in December 1962 he became First Deputy Prime Minister. In 1964 he was elected a full member of the Praesidium.

When Krushchev was removed, Shelepin retained his post of First Deputy Prime Minister under Kosygin; and it is believed by the Kremlinologists that he is bound to be Prime Minister in the not too distant future.

SHUGAR, David see under **Soviet Canadian Network.**

SIDOVORICH, Ann see under **Soviet American Network.**

SILBER, Jules (German agent, World War I).

The cover work which the spy adopts is as important to him as his cover story. Ideally it will bring him into direct contact with the source of the information he is seeking; but if this is not possible, then it must provide him with time and opportunities for making indirect contacts. A classical example of the former was the cover work adopted by the German spy Jules Silber in World War I.

Silber had left Germany about thirty years before the outbreak of World War I. He had worked for the British in the South African War, and for his services had received a certificate of recommendation.

He was in America when World War I broke out, but though he had been absent for so long from his fatherland, he had not lost his love for it, and decided that he must do something to help. His choice fell upon espionage, though he had no experience of it and did not even know how a spy operated. He had, however, a fund of solid common sense, and how he turned himself into a spy of the first class by his own unaided efforts emphasises how much of espionage practice is plain common sense

573

and not the occupational mumbo jumbo which many writers of fiction would have us believe it is.

His first step was to attempt to reach England, where, he correctly assumed, the most frequent opportunities for acquiring the best espionage information would present themselves. Believing that his certificate from the British would not be a good enough document for gaining entry to the United Kingdom — those were the days before passports — he decided to go to Canada, where he might find such requirements less restrictive and where he might be able to obtain a newer set of papers which would be acceptable to the British authorities. So it turned out, and when he arrived in London in October 1914 in possession of Canadian identity papers, the Home Office was prepared to classify him as a Commonwealth citizen. They were also helpful when it came to selecting a job, for on account of his ability to speak a number of European languages he was offered a post in the Postal Censorship Department.

When he began to work there, he had only a vague idea that he might be able to pick up snippets of information that might be useful to Germany from the letters he would be required to read. He had no notion how to contact German intelligence, nor how he could maintain communications with them if he did. But he had not been long in the Censorship Department before he discovered that the method of working provided him not only with a means of communication, but one which if he preserved the most elementary security precautions, would be undetectable.

It will be recalled that, in World War I, Holland was not involved. As in the Second World War, Switzerland, Sweden and Portugal were used by both sides as what might be termed as "clearing houses" for espionage. Holland filled a similar role in World War I. Both the Germans and the western Allies maintained branch headquarters there, through which agents operating in enemy territory could pass information by means of codes and secret inks in letters to so-called "safe addresses".

The work of the Censorship Department was organised on a regional basis. Separate groups of censors were responsible for all mail going out of England and coming into England from each neutral country. Once a censor was allocated his region, it was very rare for him to be moved from it to another.

Silber was appointed to the Dutch section, and his particular area was southern Holland, taking in Rotterdam, Breda, Tilburg and Eindhoven, where the espionage organisations of both sides were especially active.

In the Censorship Department one of the most important aids was the Suspect List. This was a list of known and suspected German "safe addresses". All mail going to and coming from these addresses was given extra special attention by the British censors.

In addition, some British "safe addresses" forwarded their intelligence direct to their headquarters in England instead of going through the branch headquarters in Holland. The censors were able to recognise these letters from various indications made on their envelopes, and were supposed to forward them to intelligence headquarters without opening them.

The third point which aided an enemy agent in the Censorship Department was that the individual censor, having opened, read and passed the letters — with or without deletions — resealed the envelope, stamped it **Passed By the Censor,** and sent it on its way without any second person seeing it.

Silber had not been very long in the Censorship Department before the significance of all this became very apparent to him. Guided by his inbred Teutonic thoroughness, he waited some months before taking his first step, which was to contact German intelligence by a letter to a "safe address", which he got from the Suspect List. In this first letter he told the German authorities who he was and the method by which he could communicate to them valuable information which he was able to glean from letters written by un-security-minded British citizens to friends living in Holland. He stipulated that should German intelligence accept his offer of aid, they should leave him to work entirely on his own, making no attempt to contact him through agents in England or by letter, though the latter method might be used in an emergency. The German authorities agreed at first on the grounds that they had nothing to lose, and later found that the flow of Silber's information proved him to be one of those extremely rare people, a man with a natural aptitude for espionage work, possessed of a special kind of shrewdness which made it possible for him to recognise the intelligence value of apparently uninteresting material without previous training.

Having received the formal acceptance of his offer by means of a letter sent via a "safe address", Silber began to supply his material, The method he used was simple and effective. He used the type of envelope known as the "window" envelope, with which the name and address of the recipient is written on the letter itself — not on the envelope — and the letter is so folded that the address shows through the transparent "window".

By choosing any address within his own region of Holland, he would write a simple, innocent letter and mail it in London, knowing that it would eventually arrive on his desk complete with the London postmark. It required

no great skill in sleight of hand for him to slit open the envelope, extract and pocket the innocent letter, replace it with a letter containing intelligence which he had prepared beforehand and addressed to one of the German "safe addresses", stamp it **Passed By the Censor,** and remail it.

Not only did Silber send intelligence to Germany in this way, but he was able to procure in the course of his official duties, secret documents which he would photograph. These he would pocket as he left the office in the evening, photograph them, and return them to their files next morning before anyone had missed them.

One thing he refused to do — he would not tell the German authorities which of their safe addresses the British knew. He argued that if he did so, and the Germans replaced them, the British would not be long in suspecting that someone in the Censorship Department was betraying this information. Though the German authorities tried to persuade him to do this from time to time, he remained adamant.

As a result of this, and other

precautions he took, he remained undetected in the Censorship Department until the Armistice, with not even a breath of suspicion falling on him. On the disbanding of the department, he returned to Germany, where he wrote a full account of his activities, which was published in 1932, to the great embarrassment of British counter-espionage, for the book was the first it knew of a German spy called Jules Silber, who had operated for four years from a government department.

Undoubtedly the most important of Silber's coups was his discovery of the British use of Q-ships. The U-boat was as great a menace in World War I as it was in World War II, and it is indicative of the straits to which the British had been pushed that they were driven to adopt as an anti-U-boat weapon a device not at all in accord with their normal code of sportsmanship. Old merchant ships already allocated to the scrap-yards were reprieved, made as seaworthy as possible, armed with powerful guns camouflaged under deck structure and manned with Royal Navy crews. They then went to sea masquerading as

independently sailed merchantmen.

U-boat tactics up to this time had followed a set pattern. On meeting an independently sailed merchantman, that is, a merchant vessel not sailing in convoy, the U-boat would surface, order the crew to take to the boats, and then sink the ship with gunfire. When a Q-ship, as the British decoy merchantman was called, was accosted in this way, half the crew, with exaggerated alarm, did as the U-boat ordered them. Once the boats were away, the U-boat closed range in order to make sure of sinking her. As soon as the U-boat was at point-blank range and before the guns were fired, the camouflage was suddenly lowered and the decrepit old ship's deck was seen to be bristling with guns, and before the U-boat had recovered from the shock it was already sinking.

The mysterious failure of several U-boats to return to base had been puzzling the Germans for some time, when one day Jules Silber read a letter from a young woman to a friend in south Holland. The address at the top of the letter was in a small town not far from the naval dockyards at

Devonport, and in her chatty way, the writer told her friend, "At the moment we are happy to have my brother Philip living with us. While he is at sea we are always extremely worried for his safety, but he has been put on a shore job at Devonport and is likely to remain there for some months. It's something to do with refitting old ships. He doesn't say very much, but as you know, he is a gunnery officer. He has permission to live at home, as we are so near Devonport."

This was exactly the kind of careless talk that it was the function of the Censorship Department to frustrate. As a censor, Silber recognised this immediately, but his instinct as a spy told him that here was information of the greatest importance, if only it could be expanded.

Normally, Silber's security was of the highest order, but he was so convinced of the importance of this item, that he put aside his usual caution. He asked for permission to have the afternoon off, on a plea of feeling unwell, and he then took a train and called upon the young woman. He presented himself to her as a high

official of the Censorship Department and produced her letter. Did she realise that in writing what she had, she had not only been acting very dangerously but was even committing a crime? Did she realise that her brother, even by hinting at what he was doing, was also committing an offence under the Official Secrets Act, for which he could be court-martialled, dismissed from the Service and imprisoned?

He spoke sternly, and because the young woman had behaved in all innocence, he scared her considerably, and she pleaded with him, if he could not overlook her own offence, at least to keep her brother out of it. He said he was not certain whether he could. What exactly had her brother told the family?

For a quarter of an hour he questioned her, relaxing his sternness and coaxing her; and as he did so, his spirits rose, for though the brother had not been specific, by reading between the lines Silber now knew that the British were refitting ancient merchantmen, installing guns, and sending them to sea with naval crews. He closed the interview by telling her that if she would promise never to be so careless again in her letter writing, he was prepared to overlook this offence. But she must never tell anyone about his visit to her, because that would mean trouble for him, since by taking no action he was not fulfilling his duty. Greatly relieved, naturally the young woman gave her most solemn promise.

Within a few days, the German authorities received the information and now it was the turn of the British to be mystified. In every action undertaken by a Q-ship so far, the U-boat had been sunk, so there could be no possibility of the Q-ship being compromised by that source. But after a few weeks the U-boats no longer surfaced and ordered the crews of lone merchantmen to take to the boats; instead unrestricted U-boat warfare was ordered, and all merchantmen independently sailed were sunk without warning.

BIBLIOGRAPHY:

Invisible Weapons — Jules Silber (London, 1932).

The Spy Who Wasn't Caught — Ronald Seth (London, 1966).

SINON (Greek agent, 1215 (?) BC).

For ten years the Greek armies had laid siege to Troy, and were no nearer to capturing it than when they had first appeared before its walls demanding that Paris should return to Menelaus the wife whom he had abducted. Yet none of the Greek leaders was prepared to withdraw, and it occurred to Ulysses that what arms had failed to accomplish, wile might.

After some thought he worked out a plan. The Greeks should appear to have departed. They would in fact be hiding behind a small group of islands not far from the Trojan coast. When they left they would leave behind a huge wooden horse, in the hollow belly of which Greek warriors would be hidden. The Trojans would have to be persuaded to drag the horse inside the city, and while they slept the warriors inside the horse would come out of their hiding-place and open the gates of the city to admit the Greek armies, who would have returned under cover of darkness.

All that was required was some means of making certain that the Trojans would take the horse into their city, and this, Ulysses suggested, could be done if an **agent provocateur** were left behind who would relate a story that would make the Trojans anxious to preserve the wooden horse. After much thought, such a story was concocted, and Sinon, an intimate friend of Ulysses, volunteered to act as the agent.

So, for several days, from the walls of their city the Trojans watched the Greeks building their gigantic horse of wood, puzzled to know what's its object could be. The day after the horse was finished, the first light of dawn revealed the plain before the city empty of Greek tents, Greek horses and Greek troops. All that remained among the smouldering camp-fires was the giant horse.

Beside themselves with delight, the Trojans threw open their city's gates and poured out to where the wooden horse stood. As they gazed upon it, they found themselves no nearer to finding its meaning than they had been when they had theorised during its building.

Presently their attention was distracted from the horse by a commotion in the distance, and as they watched they saw a

small party of their own men approaching, dragging between them a prisoner. He was a young man, bound with handcuffs and chains, and bleeding from wounds.

They brought him to Priam, their aged king, and he stood cowering, and muttering to himself, "O god, where shall I go? What shall I do? The Greeks have abandoned me, and now the Trojans will kill me."

Priam was touched by the young man's appearance, and in a kindly voice, asked him who he was and what he was doing there. Why had he not left with his companions?

Encouraged by the old man's kindness, the young man replied that his name was Sinon. He had been sent to Troy as a squire to the hero Palamedes, who had been stoned to death, because he had continued the war. Now the Greeks were sorry for what they had done, and believed that the stoning of Palamedes was bringing them bad luck. This had been confirmed when ambassadors they had sent to consult the Delphic oracle had returned with the message that if they wished to return home in safety they must appease the gods with a human sacrifice.

"The choice fell upon me," Sinon declared, "because I had once been Palamedes' squire. They prepared me for the sacrifice, but during the night, I broke away from the guards and hid myself in the reeds and mud of the lake. Who their victim was who replaced me, I do not know."

"But what is the meaning of this great horse?" Priam asked.

"The seer Calchas told them that besides offering a human sacrifice they must build this great horse to atone for stealing the image of the goddess of war, Pallas Athene, from its shrine within your city."

(Ulysses had entered the city one night with his friend Diomedes and had stolen the sacred image in the hope that deprived of it the Trojans would surrender.)

"When they set up the image in the camp its eyes glared, sweat broke out all over it, and three times it fell from its pedestal. Calchas said that this meant that the Greeks must go home, since they would never defeat the Trojans until they had appeased the gods in the temples of Athens. But they would not have fair weather for the voyage home, unless they made this horse as an offering to the goddess. At the same time, however, he said they must build the horse so big so that you would not be able to take it into your city and so come under its protection, for once you did get the horse inside the city then nothing could stand in the way of your waging war right up to the Greek strongholds."

Unfortunately, Priam and his people fell for Sinon's skilfully told tale, as Ulysses had hoped they would. They dragged the horse into the city, pulling down part of the wall in order to achieve their object.

Then they gave themselves up to a day of feasting which, as night began to fall, gave way to orgies and the orgies to drunken sleep. When the city was quiet, the warriors came out of the belly of the horse, opened the city gates and Ulysses and his men fell upon the stupified citizens and killed them and burned their city.

BIBLIOGRAPHY:
The Illiad of Homer.

SKINNARLAND, Einar see under **Haukelid, Knut.**

SLEEPER.

This is espionage jargon for

an agent who is put into the field some time before he is required to operate. Kim Philby (q.v.) is a classic example of a sleeper. He was engaged and trained by the KGB several years before he entered the British secret service and the Foreign Office. It was not until he was in a position to transmit information of any importance that he became an active agent. Usually, however, sleepers are employed as go-betweens.

SMERSH.

SMERSH is not an invention of Ian Fleming, but a very real and terrible department of Russian intelligence whose function is to assassinate, kidnap or otherwise remove all the enemies of the Russian state (in effect, the leaders) who live outside the boundaries of Russia. Its official title is the Ninth Division for Terror and Diversion. The name SMERSH is derived from its motto — **Smert Shpionen**, Death to Spies.

It plans its operations with great patience and thoroughness. It maintains laboratories and experimental workshops where drugs are tried out and special weapons are invented,

all with the object of making their killings appear to be the result of natural causes, or to facilitate the assassin's escape.

The existence of SMERSH had only been surmised up to the time of the defection of one of its star operatives, Captain Khokhlov (q.v.) who not only gave full details of the Division, but brought with him some of the strange weapons with which he had been provided to assassinate the Ukrainian leader, Igor Ckolovich.

Since Khokhlov's defection several other SMERSH agents have come over to the West, in particular Pyotr Deriabin (q.v.) and Bogdan Stashynsky (q.v.).

Its most famous victim was Lev Trotsky.

The post-Kruschev leaders of Russia have fostered the idea that SMERSH has itself been liquidated. In fact, it has merely been renamed CUKR, disguised as the internal security department of the Army.

BIBLIOGRAPHY:
The Executioners — Ronald Seth (London, 1967).

SMIT, Hendroka see under **Wenzel, Johann.**

SMITH, Durnford see under **Soviet Canadian Network.**

SOKOLOV, Major see under **Soviet Canadian Network.**

SORGE, Richard (Soviet agent in Japan, before and during World War II).

Number 30 Nagasakimachi, Azabu-ku, Tokyo, was a disgrace to the neighbourhood. It was a two-storied house built of wood and bamboo, but it was so dilapidated that every time the respectable inhabitants of the neighbourhood passed it, they shuddered for they were proud of their own neat, more carefully preserved homes.

The tenant of 30 Nagasakimachi was, in the eyes of his neighbours as disreputable as his house. He was a German named Richard Sorge, a journalist, correspondent in Tokyo of a number of leading European newspapers.

In 1938, Sorge had been the tenant of 30 Nagasakimachi for close on four years, and when, one evening in the autumn of that year he gave a party which developed into a minor orgy, his neighbours shuddered, but were not surprised. Such parties were a periodic feature of Sorge's existence.

Sorge, at this particular party, had been indulging in a favourite pastime — challenging his Japanese officer guests to a drinking competition. It would appear that, as always, Sorge was the winner, for as he watched his guests being carried to their cars, bowing slightly to each departing figure, though he swayed slightly, he still knew what he was about.

But not all his guests were drunk, and when he suddenly announced that he was going to a geisha house, four of them said they would go with him. A young German diplomat, himself the soberest of them all, watched the five men pile themselves into a car, and drive off. Then he, too, went to his own car and drove home. But if he had waited ten minutes or so, he would have seen the first car return to the house, and the five men disembark and go inside.

These special guests were a Japanese called Ozaki Hozumi; Branko de Voukelich, a former Yugoslav army officer; Max Klausen, a German businessman; and a second Japanese, Miyagi Yotoku. Ozaki was the

583

political correspondent of the leading Japanese newspaper Asah Shimbun, and had friends and contacts among the highest Japanese official circles. He was also a great expert on Chinese-Japanese relations, and had written five "classic" books on the subject. Voukelich, like his host, was a newspaper correspondent, contributing to the French review **La Vue,** and the Yugoslav daily paper **Politicia.** Klausen was in the import-export trade, really a superior commercial traveller. Miyagi, who came of an old and greatly respected Japanese family, was an artist. He had spent many years abroad, but had returned to his mother-country about 1934 and had since made his living by his painting.

The five men sat down among the debris of the party, Sorge began to talk, and continued for some time without interruption from the others. Anyone looking on would have assumed, and rightly, that he was the leader of the quintet. Had they heard what he was saying they would have discovered that they had interests other than those described in the paragraph above, interests not at all so harmless as their ostensible occupations.

For the word which came again and again to Sorge's tongue was **security.** Security, he repeated, must guide them in every single action during the coming months. The slightest security risk was to be sufficient to cause them to cancel anything they proposed to do. The most important phase of their operations was fast approaching, and if anything happened to prevent them from being in a position to be at their most effective then, it would be nothing short of a tragedy.

To give support to his exhortation he explained the background of events. Munich had recently marked a temporary victory for Germany. As he saw it, Hitler would be encouraged to launch an attack on France during the summer of next year. If France became involved in war, Britain must also engage on the side of France. Hitler understood this, and in order to achieve an equipoise was attempting to persuade Japan to join the Axis Powers, and as a bait was offering to sign a secret pact with Russia which would remove any threat by Russian to Japan, while the latter continued her military activities in China.

The Soviet Union, Sorge went on, was chiefly interested in what Japan intended to do in Manchuria, the boundaries of which marched with Asiatic Russia. If Russia could be assured that Japan was planning to keep the direction of her activities southwards, she would not be so disturbed by Japan's adherence to the Axis Pact. This had been the burden of a recent report by Sorge to his superiors, the longest report he had ever submitted.

His audience were impressed by the arguments and adjurations of their leader, and presently the meeting broke up; and in the months and years which were to follow, they were to carry out Sorge's orders, until Sorge himself forgot all about Security, with dire results.

But this was not to happen before the five men in the ramshackle bamboo house had achieved some of the most remarkable exploits in the history of world espionage.

Richard Sorge was born in 1895, the second son of a German oil-driller who had emigrated to the Baku oil-fields, where the pay was good.

By the time he was of school age, the family had returned to Berlin, and before very long his serious German masters were commenting on the young Sorge's high level of intelligence.

When World War I broke out he joined the army, and within a short time had been wounded in the leg. In 1916 he returned to the front line, where he found that much of the confidence with which his companions had marched against the enemy had been replaced by fear. Again, his career as a combatant was cut short by a second and much more serious wound.

Sorge's paternal grandfather had for several years been private secretary to Karl Marx. While waiting for his wounds to heal, Richard began to study Marx's writings and found the ideas which the author of **Das Kapital** expounded, attractively exciting.

When he had joined the army, Sorge had been studying political economy and history, and when he was demobilised he enrolled in the universities of Kiel and Hamburg, graduating from the latter in the spring of 1920 as a Doctor of Political Science. The same day

585

that he graduated he joined the German Communist Party.

For a time he taught history in a Hamburg school, but was dismissed when the headmaster discovered that he was not only teaching Communism to his pupils, but recruiting members to the Party in school time. He then became a coal-miner, and continued his evangelising at the coal-face with such effect that production was slowed down and he was again dismissed.

These events and the fact that his grandfather had been Marx's secretary marked Sorge out for special attention from the GPC, and presently it was suggested to him that he should go to Moscow for special training. Three weeks later he was in Moscow. But before he went he had had it made plain to him by the German police that they had marked him down as a Communist. Indeed, he almost came to grief before he had begun, and all because, merely to relieve the boredom of waiting with nothing to do, he had contrived to become the lover of a woman who was a police informer.

The day following his arrival in Moscow, Sorge was seen by

Dimitri Manuilsky, then head of the foreign intelligence division of the Comintern. Like Alexander Foote (q.v.) Sorge had had no idea of what the Party were going to do with him. When he left Manuilsky, however, he knew that he was going to be a spy.

The next five years Sorge spent under training. He had a remarkable facility for languages and by 1928 he was as fluent in Russian, English and French as he was in his native German. In 1928 he was sent to Los Angeles for a year to find out all he could about the American film industry, whose propaganda value the Russians fully appreciated, after which he returned to Moscow.

In 1929 Sorge was sent to London, with what object is not clear. On all his travels he had never once met anyone who remembered him from his agitating days in Kiel and Hamburg. Now, however, he was visited by Special Branch officers — he had forgotten to register as an alien — who, in the course of questioning him, asked him if he had ever lived in Hamburg.

Sorge was very much impressed, and reported to Moscow, "England knows more about spying than any other nation." He also realised that the officers had not been convinced by his denials, and that he would never be able to work in England.

In the following year he was transferred to the GRU — Army intelligence. Almost at once, such was the reputation he had gained among his chiefs, that he was sent to the Far East as Resident Director with headquarters in Shanghai. His instructions were almost a **carte blanche.** All that was specifically demanded was information about Chiang Kaishek's growing Nationalist army. For the rest, whatever he thought might be useful he could submit. He was also allowed to choose his agents— something unheard of in Russian intelligence before or since — and within a short time he had recruited the four men who had attended his party in the Tokyo suburb that evening in 1938.

When Japan began to emerge as a potent force in the Far East, The Centre promoted its Director, Colonel Beldin to General, and relieving him of all other duties, instructed him to organise a special Far East intelligence section with the Japanese government and its secrets as the magnet of its activities. Beldin recalled Sorge to Moscow, and for several months they consulted and discussed and eventually decided. Sorge was to move his base from Shanghai to Tokyo, and take with him whoever he wished to have. He chose his faithful four.

Before returning to the Far East, Sorge made a protracted visit to Germany. It says little for the efficiency of the Abwehr and the Gestapo that they had no inkling of his former activities. By the use of his considerable charm, he had quickly obtained posts as correspondent in Tokyo for a number of leading newspapers. Not only that, he also impressed leading Nazis, and on the eve of his departure for Tokyo, the Press Association gave a reception in his honour which was attended by Josef Goebbels, Minister of Propaganda and Public Enlightenment. In fact, he was an outstanding political commentator, and his reports were always given close attention.

Of the five men who formed the Unit, Sorge and Ozaki were without doubt the most successful. There was little to

587

choose between their respective brilliance, though it derived, in each case, from different qualities. While Sorge was capable of assessing the value of his information with such penetration that he sent nothing to Moscow that was useless, he missed nothing that was of use.

Ozaki, on the other hand, besides being an expert interpreter of political trends throughout the Orient in general, and China in particular, had contacts which brought him into the highest Japanese political circles. It was the combination of the two which was the basis of his success, for without his flair for evaluation, the documents and other information which came his way would have been valueless.

His most useful contact was Prince Konoye, whom he knew intimately. When Konoye became Prime Minister this connection increased in value a hundredfold.

Towards the end of 1935, the Japanese Foreign Minister placed before the Cabinet for consideration, a draft of proposed diplomatic and economic aims for the coming year. This document was an extremely important one, for it revealed in advance all the diplomatic moves Japan was contemplating, and because of this, was classified Most Secret.

It was a complex document, too, and the secretary to the Cabinet, breaking all professional etiquette, mentioned the draft to Ozaki, and went so far as to let him see a copy, suggesting that if the Prime Minister agreed, Ozaki, the China expert, should submit his comments on those sections relating to China. Ozaki replied that if he were to do this, he would need time to study the document carefully, a point which was fully appreciated.

Prince Konoye was only too pleased to have the benefit of Ozaki's experience in Chinese affairs, and agreed that he should have all the time he needed. As the document was Most Secret, however, it could not be allowed to go beyond official precincts, so Ozaki was provided with a private room in the Cabinet offices, and there, undisturbed, he photographed the draft page by page.

When Ozaki told Sorge what he had achieved, the latter could not believe him, until Voukelitch developed the film and he could see for himself. Then quickly recovering from his astonishment, he extracted the vital points, encoded them and had Klausen transmit them within a few hours of receiving the first sight of them.

If Sorge had been surprised by Ozaki's coup, Moscow was even more taken aback by the implications of the plan. If the document were genuine, then it was quite clear that Japan was intending no threat to Russia. On the contrary, so that she might be secure on her northern frontier while she attacked southwards in China, Japan was proposing a treaty of friendship with the Soviet Union. This was the main point which emerged — Japan was definitely not planning any attack on Russia in the foreseeable future.

Moscow was not long in urging Sorge to try to confirm, by any means whatsoever, that the document was not a red herring, concocted for the very purpose of misleading the Kremlin. The only sure way in which Sorge could do this was to sound — in his guise of political commentator — the German ambassador, Herbert von Dirksen. This he did, and by skilful questioning received the confirmation he was after. Miyagi brought further confirmation. He learned from a

staff officer that large scale models of South China were being built to assist in planning strategy and tactics. Both Dirksen's information and Miyagi's news could mean only one thing — that Japan was contemplating attacking China, and would, therefore, have no time to attack Russia for some time to come.

This was enough for Sorge. Making a full report of his interview with Dirksen and of Miyagi's information, he sent it with the micro-film of the Japanese draft to Moscow, and had the satisfaction of receiving from General Beldin the laconic compliment, "Your report valid and accepted."

This extraordinary coup had many far-reaching effects not only on Soviet policy, which was now switched to strengthening Russia's defences in the west, but also on Sorge and his unit. It revealed, for example, that experts like Ozaki could obtain access to the highest official information with comparative ease, while remaining entirely unsuspected. Ozaki was encouraged by his success, and from this time operated with what can only be described as scintillating brilliance. The document helped

589

other members of the cell as well, particularly Voukelitch, to entrench themselves even more deeply in the confidence of their respective contacts. Besides dealing with China and Russia, the draft also dealt with Japan's policy towards the west. By planting skilful hints among his British, French and American acquaintances, he was able to forecast that Japan's attitude towards their countries would become tougher, and when this did happen, he came to be regarded as a valuable and trustworthy contact. In return he received much useful information.

Sorge used the same tactics at the German embassy. There he greatly impressed the military attaché, Colonel Eugene Ott, who soon began to look upon him as a close friend. This contact was to prove even more valuable later when Ott succeeded Dirksen, on the latter's appointment to London.

Besides all this, the coup set the standard for future achievements. After a beginning such as this, neither Sorge nor his men would have been human had they not been encouraged to reach out for even greater heights. And they achieved them!

590

From now — 1935 — until the launching of the German attack on Russia in 1941, the unit knotched up the following major coups:

1. A clause-by-clause draft of what was to become known as the Anti-Comintern Pact between Germany, Italy and Japan six weeks before the Pact was laid before the Japanese Parliament.

2. Five weeks advance information of Japan's attack on China.

3. Japanese plans to attack America in the Pacific; though he could not specifically state that it would be at Pearl Harbour, Sorge did forecast it would be in the south, and he thought Pearl Harbour the place.

These alone were brilliant achievements, but in between a steady and quite voluminuos flow of high-grade intelligence was put in train for Moscow. With the exception of Rudolf Rössler's achievements in Switzerland, no known network in modern espionage history has been so successful.

Not everything went smoothly all the time, however. There were a number of alarms, when it looked as though the Unit might be compromised.

But Sorge was generally able to straighten things out before the climax came.

As the years went by, naturally pressure from the Kempei tai, Japanese counter-espionage, began to mount. Colonel Osaki, chief of the Kempei tai, had become aware that there was a clandestine organisation in Japan's midst by the discovery of an illicit radio transmitter operating to he knew not where. At this time, the Kempei tai were comparatively backward in detection by radio direction-finding. The D/F equipment it had had a range of only two miles, which in a city the size of Tokyo was useless, and Sorge made Osaki's task more difficult by changing the wavelength after every 250 groups sent, and by changing his code after every transmission. This was security par excellence.

Though he did not progress very far with the passage of years, Osaki was a determined and utterly persistent man. By one process after another he eliminated possibilities until he came to Sorge, Voukelitch, Ozaki and Klausen. For some reason he eliminated Miyagi. He decided to concentrate on Sorge, and arranged to meet

him socially.

The meeting took place in the Fuji Club, one of Sorge's favourite haunts. Sorge found Osaki to be a typical Japanese with a taste for **sake** — hot rice brandy, the Japanese national drink — and for women. During their discussions on the latter subject, Osaki said that one of the most beautiful girls in Tokyo was a new dancer in the club. At first Sorge was not interested, which was extraordinary, for he was a highly-sexed man who had scandalised the staider members of the German colony and the Japanese community by his many violent and blatant love-affairs. 'However, the colonel praised the girl's qualities so insistently and extravagantly that at last Sorge's interest was roused.

Presently the cabaret was announced and the dancer Kiyomi performed the Rice Dance. She wore a traditional mask so that the beauty of her features could not be judged, but the rest of her body was sufficiently striking to impress itself favourably on Sorge.

For the next week or two, Sorge visited the Fuji Club every evening. Each evening he sent Kiyomi flowers and notes begging her to meet him. Each evening Kiyomi tore up the notes and returned the flowers.

Then one evening Sorge's table was unoccupied. Frightened that she had gone too far, after her dance she hurried to her dressing room to telephone Osaki and ask what she was to do now. But when she came into her dressing-room, she saw Sorge sitting there, waiting for her. Within a few moments she had capitulated.

Kiyomi was still Sorge's mistress when he was able to forewarn Stalin of the imminent Japanese attack on Pearl Harbor. He had made up his mind, in the days before he obtained definite information, that this was to be his last task. When he had sent the message to Moscow, the Unit would disband and its members scatter.

The Unit had been working without a break for eight years, and the strain was beginning to tell. The Kempei tai were showing signs of getting too close. He had no idea how close they were. Colonel Osaki was waiting only for Kiyomi to produce for him absolutely irrefutable evidence of Sorge's illegal activities.

One evening, while he was waiting for the date of the Japanese attack on Pearl Harbor to be confirmed, he was at his usual table watching Kiyomi dance the Rice Dance. But his thoughts were far away. He was worried. Miyagi had not put in an appearance for a week. Voukelitch was in a very nervous state, and reluctant to move very far from the extra-territoriality of the French embassy. The Yugoslav knew nothing in particular, but had a strong sensation of standing on the edge of a volcano.

During the dance, a waiter approached Sorge's table, and unobtrusively dropped on to it a little ball of rice paper. Sorge smoothed out the paper and saw that it was a message from Miyagi. It was a disquieting message. Miyagi was being watched twenty-four hours a day by the Kempei tai.

Behind her ornate mask, the sharp eyes of Kiyomi had seen the waiter drop the paper ball, had watched Sorge smooth it out, read it, put it into his pocket, pay his bill and leave. As soon as she had finished her dance, she hurried to her dressing-room and telephoned Colonel Osaki.

A check on the waiter

revealed that he frequently visited the office of Ozaki, and had also been seen in the company of Miyagi. The Colonel already knew that Sorge and Ozaki were friends.

No one meeting Sorge next day would have known that he was now more desperately worried than he had ever been. He breakfasted as usual with Ambassador Ott. He lunched with Klausen and told him to be on board the boat, from which they transmitted their messages, that evening. He tried to get in touch with Voukelitch and Ozaki and failed.

In the evening, he was at his usual table at the Fuji Club. As Kiyomi danced in the half-darkness, several people came into the restaurant. But Sorge's table was at the edge of the dancing floor and came into the bright ring of the spot-light. Again a paper ball fell on to Sorge's table. Again Kiyomi saw. Again Sorge read the note and put it into his pocket. But this time he did not leave.

Kiyomi had arranged to go with Sorge that night as soon as her dance was over. He followed her to her dressing-room at once, and she knew that he could not have had time to destroy the note. She made up her mind to get it, so, overcoming her native modesty, she allowed Sorge to watch her change.

As they got into his motor-car, Sorge told Kiyomi that instead of going to No 30 Nagasakimachi, they were going to the villa which he rented on the Izu Peninsular, where they would cook dinner and stay the night. This proposal took Kiyomi by surprise, as she did not know that he had the villa, but she was so anxious to get the paper from him that she did not demur.

After they had left the city, Sorge suddenly stopped the car by the roadside and began to make love to her. Presently, momentarily satisfied, he drew away from her and took from his pocket two cigarettes, his lighter and the piece of paper. As she watched him flick the lighter, Kiyomi's heart sank. She was certain that when he had lit the cigarettes, he would burn the paper. But the lighter refused to work, and though Kiyomi searched for hers, she could not find it.

With a sharp gesture of annoyance, Sorge threw the cigarettes out of the car window, and tearing the paper to

593

small pieces, threw the scraps after the cigarettes. Then he drove on.

Now, though untrained in counter-espionage, Kiyomi was an intelligent girl. At the next telephone call-box they came to, she asked Sorge to stop while she telephoned her parents to tell them that she was staying the night with a girl-friend. Sorge sat in the car while she called Colonel Osaki and quickly explained to him what had happened and where he would find the scraps of paper.

Arrived at the villa, Sorge told Kiyomi to prepare the food while he attended to some private business. He went to the beach and rowed in a dinghy out to the boat where Max Klausen was waiting for him.

There he gave Max two messages to send to Moscow.

The first read: "Japanese carrier force attacking United States Navy at Pearl Harbor probably dawn 6th November."

The second told The Centre that the Unit had been compromised and that he had disbanded it, and had instructed its members to save themselves as best they could.

He and Max shook hands,

hoped they might meet again some day, and went their ways. At the villa Sorge ate what Kiyomi had prepared, and immediately took her to bed. It seemed that Sorge had a presentiment that he would never make love again, and Kiyomi said afterwards that he had so many orgasms she lost count before he seemed finally satiated and fell asleep at dawn.

And while they loved and slept, Colonel Osaki moved.

Agents were already waiting for Klausen when he arrived back at his house in Tokyo. Voukelitch was dragged from the embraces of Samusaki, once his mistress, now his wife. Miyagi, who, though watched for twenty-four hours a day, had managed to pass Sorge the last vital message, tried to stab himself to death as the agents broke down his door. He was rushed to hospital and treated, and eventually recovered. Ozaki, dressed in his finest robes, was awaiting the agents with oriental fatalism.

Sorge did not sleep long. The new day, 15th October, 1941, was only a few hours old, when he got up from beside the sleeping Kiyomi and went to the lounge, where he poured himself a stiff drink. As he raised the glass to his lips, there were knocks on the door. When he opened it, Colonel Osaki and two assistants bowed themselves in.

The Colonel said nothing. He merely handed Sorge a piece of paper on which the scraps of Miyagi's message, left by the roadside, had been pasted together.

Without a glance at Kiyomi, who, he realised suddenly, had betrayed him, he swallowed his drink, and went out with the Colonel.

Miyagi broke down first under the torture inflicted on him by the Kempei tai. Klausen gave way not long after. But while Miyagi betrayed only his own, so to speak, private ring, Klausen implicated Sorge, Voukelitch and Ozaki. Voukelitch behaved with all the courage and loyalty of a former officer, and no torture or brutality could make him talk. Sorge and Ozaki were not tortured, but when they were shown Miyagi's and Klausen's confessions, they realised they had no hope, and set down their own full confessions.

Eventually, the cases against them were completed. Miyagi was too ill to face trial, and

was kept indefinitely in the prison hospital. Voukelitch refused to answer all questions put to him except to acknowledge his name and address, and his profession. He was sentenced to life imprisonment. Max Klausen proved co-operative and was recommended to mercy. He, too, received a life-sentence, while his wife Anna, who had acted as courier for Sorge on several occasions was given three years.

Ozaki and Sorge were sentenced to death. They were allowed to appeal but their appeals were dismissed.

It is customary in Japan for death sentences to be carried out within six months of pronouncement. Strangely, and for no reason that has yet come to light, the executions of the two men were delayed for two years.

On 9th October, 1944, Sorge and Ozaki died on the same gallows within half an hour of one another.

One evening three years later, the guests at the Seven Delights Club in Shanghai were listening entranced to a new Japanese cabaret singer, when suddenly they heard her falter, and then stop altogether. As they watched bewildered,

595

she screamed and rushed from the floor.

In her dressing-room she seized her coat and handbag and hurried out of the rear entrance of the club. Members of the club staff ran after her. They saw her turn the corner of the street, and stopped dead in their tracks as revolver shots rang out.

In the following silence they hurried on, and came upon her lying in the gutter.

Kiyomi was dead. SMERSH had avenged their brilliant agent.

BIBLIOGRAPHY:

Sorge — Master Spy — Major-General C. Willoughby (London, 1950).

The Man With Three Faces — Hans-Otto Meissner (London, 1955).

SOBELL, Morton see under Soviet American Network.

SOVIET AMERICAN NETWORK (Atomic espionage, 1941-1953).

Klaus Fuchs (q.v.) the traitor who gave atomic secrets to Russia, had not long been back in London from his assignment in America, when he made contact with Semion Kremer, the secretary to the Russian military attaché in London. The two men had first met in May or June 1942, and during the eighteen months until Fuchs was sent to work in the United States, he had handed Kremer copies of his monthly reports. He was, therefore, already deeply involved in atomic espionage when he arrived in the United States, and it was a naturally corollary that he should soon become a member of the Soviet network in America concentrating on the discovery of the West's atomic secrets.

In charge of this network was Anatoli Yakovlev, who arrived in America early in 1944 ostensibly as vice-consul in New York. He took over from the man who had shown tremendous vigour and judgement in organising the American network, Semion Semionov, to whose work the success of the Atomic Division of The Centre (q.v.) owed a very great deal.

Yakovlev's network included four outstanding American Communist spies — Harry Gold, David Greenglass and the husband-and-wife team of Julius and Ethel Rosenberg. This quartet were Communists and agents of long standing, and it was probably as much due to their experience as to their situations which placed them strategetically for their work, that they were assigned to Yakovlev.

Harry Gold had been born in Berne, Switzerland, to Russian parents. His family emigrated to America while he was still a child, and the family name was changed from Golodnotzky to Gold. Harry received a good university and technical education in the US, developed left-wing tendencies, and in 1935 was approached by the Soviet espionage agency in America, and agreed to work for them. During his heyday his speciality was the theft of industrial chemical secrets. He was chosen by Yakovlev to act as go-between with Ruchs.

David Greenglass had been a member of the Young Communist League of America in his youth, a point which seemed to have eluded the FBI, for when America entered the war in December 1941 he was called up, given technical training and in July 1944 posted to the Manhattan District Project at Oak Ridge, Tennessee. His sister was Ethel Rosenberg, under whose in-

fluence he readily undertook to divulge the secrets of his work.

Julius Rosenberg had been a Communist, and an extremely ardent one, from the early days of Communism in America. He was also one of the espionage pioneers in that country, and had already achieved great successes in obtaining radar secrets before he was ordered to go underground, after his brother-in-law's posting to Oak Ridge, in order to concentrate on atomic espionage. It was he who had converted Ethel Greenglass to Communism and then married her; and she was to prove invaluable in persuading her much younger brother to pass on his vital secrets.

Attached to the Rosenberg ring were also Abraham Borthman, Miriam Moskowitz and Morton Sobell. But this ring was only one of three rings in the American network.

At the University of California's Radiation Laboratory, Vasili Zubilin of the Soviet embassy in Washington had organised a ring of Communist Party groups and secret Communists, which he placed under the direction of two officials of the San Francisco consulate —

Grigori Kheifets and Peter Ivanov Among their outstanding agents was Steve Nelson, who led the ring at the Radiation Laboratory. He even tried to enlist the services of Dr J. Robert Oppenheimer, who was to be the future director of Los Alamos, the most important of all the American atomic plants. Oppenheimer refused categorically, and informed the director of the Manhattan District Project of the approach, with the result that the FBI began to watch Nelson, though no move was made for a considerable time.

The third ring was concentrated on Chicago, where atomic research was also in progress. In the absence of a consulate here, the Russians put in a professional agent as leader, Arthur Adams, a man who was a spy of very long experience, but in 1942 he was approaching his sixties, and was severely handicapped by rheumatism. His chief source was Clarence Hiskey, a chemist working in the Metallurgical Laboratories on the large-scale production of plutonium for atomic bombs.

In 1944 Hiskey's espionage activities came to the notice

of the FBI. It seems incredible, but all that happened to the chemist was that he was called up for active service in the army, and sent to Alaska. Before he went, he managed to persuade John Chapin, another chemist to take over his spying duties for him. In his turn, Chapin was compromised, and this led to Adams's activities being revealed. But in those days, the US Administration did not prosecute known Soviet spies, and he was allowed to leave America.

Now, although there had been close collaboration between the American network and the Canadian network (q.v.) Igor Gouzenko's (q.v.) disclosures in 1945 gave no indication of the existence of the American set-up. This was almost entirely due to Yakovlev's absolute insistence on the observance of security procedures at all times. Yet ironically it was the very first failure to observe security which brought about the end of the American network.

Harry Gold had already attracted the attention of the FBI in 1947, and they had even interviewed him at his home in Philadelphia. But he had been able to assure them that they were mistaken and they were prepared to take his word for it. It was not until Fuchs was arrested in London and talked that Gold again came into the picture; and this would not have been possible but for a security slip which Yakovlev had made some years earlier.

A few days before the explosion of the first atomic bomb in 1945, David Greenglass, at the Los Alamos plant, had prepared a highly important report, which Yakovlev desperately wished to forward to Moscow. A courier, Ann Sidorovich, was detailed by Yakovlev to collect this report from Greenglass, but for some reason or other she was prevented from carrying out instructions. Instead of waiting until she could, and apparently having no other courier available, he instructed Gold, who was the courier for Fuchs, to undertake the assignment.

When Fuchs was eventually arrested, he named Gold as his go-between. Gold was arrested, and because of this one trip to Los Alamos, was able to name Greenglass. Greenglass also talked and named Julius and Ethel Rosenberg.

The FBI now swooped. With the Rosenbergs they also arrested most of the lesser members of the network. When the trials were finished, the Rosenbergs had been sentenced to death and were executed in 1953; Gold and Sobell were sentenced to thirty years imprisonment; Greenglass to fifteen years; Borthman to seven and Miriam Moskowitz to two.

As soon as Gold was arrested, Yakovlev fled. True, he was indicted with Gold, but this was a pure formality.

BIBLIOGRAPHY:
The Atom Spies — Oliver Pilat (London, 1954).

SOVIET CANADIAN NETWORK (Atomic espionage, 1941-1945).

(This should be read in conjunction with the preceding article on Soviet atomic spying in America.)

When The Centre (q.v.) decided to embark on atomic espionage in Canada, the existing network was employed. The only change was an intensification of its activities.

The director of military espionage in Canada at the outset of the atomic espionage

599

programme in the Dominion was Sergei Koudrivtzev, whose cover was the post of First Secretary of the Legation, and it was he who passed The Centre's orders to the network's leader, Major Sokolov. In 1943 Koudrivtzev was replaced by Colonel Zabotin, (see under **Gouzenko,** Igor) and this corresponded with the arrival of the British scientists in Canada. It was Zabotin who was to emerge as the real villain of the Canadian piece.

With the extension of the network's role, two agents of long standing, Sam Carr and Fred Rose, came into their own at last. Both men had been prominent in the Canadian Communist Party from its inception. Carr, a Ukrainian whose real name was Schmil Kogan, had emigrated to Canada as an agricultural worker in 1924, and almost at once became a member of the Young Communist League. In 1929 he had been summoned to Moscow and put through a course at the Lenin Institute. From that date until 1942 his activities were more concerned with political agitation than espionage.

Fred Rose was a Pole by birth — his real name was

Rosenberg — and had emigrated to Canada in the 1920s. From the first moment he had been in the pay of Soviet military espionage (GRU). At the time that he came under Zabotin's orders he was a Member of the Canadian Parliament. It was he who brought to Zabotin's notice David Lunan, editor of **Canadian Affairs,** a journal devoted to military topics, and Lunan was to prove invaluable in suggesting recruits for the network. In a very short time through the efforts of Lunan aided by Rose, a cell of scientists had been formed, among whom was the greatest expert on explosives on the American continent, Professor Raymond Boyer, of McGill University.

It was Boyer who reported to Moscow that a new plant was being built at Grand Mere in Quebec — actually the location of the plant was at Chalk River — for the production of uranium. The engineers for the plant were to be recruited from McGill, and experiments had already shown that uranium could be used "for filling bombs".

It was to Chalk River that Nunn May, Fuchs and Pontecorvo eventually came.

With the assistance of Major Rogov, a member of his staff, by 1944, Zabotin had organised a small compact ring consisting of four Canadian government officials. Leader of the ring was Durnford Smith, a research engineer in the National Research Council; Ned Mazerall, a member of the same body; Isador Halperin, an artillery expert who had access to secret information from the Canadian Army Research and Development Establishment; and David Lunan already mentioned. Lunan collected the information provided by the other three, and passed it to Rogov, who passed it to Zabotin.

Among the contacts of these four were Professor Boyer, who was considered the star of the ring by his superiors; James Benning, who was employed in the Department of Munitions with the task of preparing the quarterly forecast of war production; and Benning's brother-in-law, Harold Gerson, who worked with a Crown company engaged in the production of chemicals and explosives. In addition there was Eric Adams, who filled a confidential post in the Bank of Canada investigating industrial plans for finance purposes; Matthias Nightingale, who could supply information about all Canadian air bases; David Shugar, an expert in radar; and in the lower echelons, Agatha Capman, an employee of the Bank of Canada, who acted as go-between.

With the exception of Agatha Capman, all those mentioned above were not members of the ring as such, but extremely valuable sources from whom all the important information was derived.

It is one of the many mysteries of the whole strange affair, that the activities of none of these people became known to the counter-espionage agencies, and might never have done so but for the defection of Igor Gouzenko. They worked with unremitting devotion to their task and completely undisturbed, and by the time the atom bomb was detonated over Hiroshima they had passed to Moscow every scrap of significant information on the composition of the bomb with one or two possible exceptions.

After Gouzenko's defection, Zabotin went on working in

601

Canada for some time. Not until the arrests began did The Centre close down Zabotin's headquarters staff of fifteen, and recall them all to Russia with their chief. The reason for this delay was that Zabotin did not know how many documents Gouzenko had taken with him, since so many had been marked up in the register as officially burned, nor how compromising they would be. For their part the Canadian authorities were hampered in taking quick action, because in all the documents the agents were referred to only by their operational-names (q.v.) and these took many months to identify.

BIBLIOGRAPHY:

The Atomic Spies — Oliver Pilat (London, 1954).

SPECIAL BRANCH (Department of the London Metropolitan Police).

Among its other activities, such as organising the security arrangements for guarding important official visitors to London, the Special Branch of the Metropolitan Police co-operates with the British counter-espionage organisation better known as MI5, but now designated DI5. The agents 602

of MI5 have no powers of arrest. When they have tracked down a foreign spy operating anywhere in the country and have gathered sufficient evidence to satisfy a court, MI5 hands the case over to the Special Branch. The Special Branch makes the arrests and the charges, and prepares the case for the Crown. In this way, only on very rare occasions, are MI5's agents required to appear in court to give evidence, which protects the identity of the organisation's agents.

SPECIAL OPERATIONS EXECUTIVE (SOE).

Special Operations Executive was a British secret organisation formed during World War II to carry out sabotage, to equip and train underground Resistance armies, and incidentally to gather intelligence, in the German Occupied countries of Europe. The American Office of Strategic Services (OSS) (q.v.) was modelled on it and the two organisations, in the latter part of the war, collaborated with great effect.

The SOE was organised on what was known as the Country basis, that is, there was a section for each country, which recruited, trained and maintained its own agents. The training was carried out in schools attached to each section, and in specialist schools centrally controlled by headquarters SOE.

The commander of SOE during its most effective period of operations was Major-General Sir Colin Gubbins KCMG. Parliamentary responsibility was maintained through the Minister of Economic Warfare.

Though it was guilty of many errors, and was the victim of a good deal of Abwehr cunning, it is true to say that had it not existed and operated with the skill that it did, the underground armies of Europe would not have been able to play the decisive role they did in the liberation of Europe.

BIBLIOGRAPHY:

Inside SOE — E. H. Cookridge (London, 1967).
SOE in France — M. R. Foot (official history) (London, 1966).

SPENCER, Victor see under **Munsinger Affair, The.**

STAHL, Lydia (Russian agent, between the wars).

Lydia Stahl was an American citizen, but a Russian by birth. Her birth-name was Chkalov. She had emigrated to America during the Revolution, become naturalised, and when her only son died in 1919, returned to Europe, where she settled in Paris.

In the French capital she came into contact with Communists, and was converted. Noting her high intelligence, The Centre quickly involved her in espionage, and assigned her to the United States, at the same time, however, ear-marking her for France in due time.

In 1928, her really professional network was joined by Robert Switz, the son of a wealthy American family, who had been attracted to Communism, skilfully indoctrinated, and then invited to become a Russian agent in America.

In 1931 he married a nineteen-year-old girl who agreed to work for the network, and in a very short time became one of its prominent members. She and her husband were trained in photography.

The Switzes, and particularly the wife were specially groomed to replace Lydia Stahl, whom The Centre wished to transfer to Paris, where Russian espionage, in 1933, was in the doldrums. They took over from her on her departure.

However, the seizure of power by Hitler necessitated a reorganisation of the German networks, and this affected the other networks operating elsewhere in Europe, and in July 1933 the Switzes were assigned to Paris to help Lydia Stahl.

Stahl's operations in France were destined to be short-lived, however. One of her close friends, Ingrid Bostrom, was arrested in Finland and talked. The Finns passed on her information to the French counter-espionage, and began an investigation of Lydia Stahl's background, during which they discovered the existence of her network. Because Switz had contacted her shortly after his arrival in France, he was also put under surveillance, and his meeting with Markovich, Resident Director of the French networks, was observed.

Markovich escaped when the network was rounded up. Though most of the agents had been found in possession of compromising material, the French authorities did not

believe they had enough evidence to satisfy the courts. For the next three months they continued their investigations but without result. Then one day two parcels of film were left at the French consulate in Geneva by an unknown person, and Switz's finger-prints were found on the film.

Confronted with this, Switz talked. Five others followed his example, with the result that twenty-nine agents were arrested and the French networks completely smashed. Because of the help they had given to the authorities the Switzes were given suspended sentences; even Lydia Stahl, on account of political necessity, received only some months.

BIBLIOGRAPHY:
Soviet Espionage — D. J. Dallin (New York, 1955).

STANDEN, Antony see under Walsingham, Sir Francis.

STASHYNSKY, Bogdan (Soviet agent, 1950s).
Bogdan Stashynsky was born in the west Ukrainian village of Borshtshevice, near Lvov, on 4th November, 1931. In the summer of 1950, a young student, he was caught travel-

ling on a train without a ticket. He was not prosecuted on condition that he supplied the security police with information about Ukrainian anti-Bolshevik revolutionaries. This he agreed to do, and pleased his employers so well that within a short time he had been selected to become a secret agent for the KGB. After an intensive period of training he carried out several assignments in West Germany, until, in 1957, he was ordered to liquidate Lev Rebet, a leader of the Ukrainian exiles, who lived in Munich.

Stashynsky, using the cover-name (q.v.) of Siegfried Dräger, arrived in Munich in April 1957 to watch Rebet's movements, and plan the killing. He waited outside Rebet's office at 8 Karlplatz, and when Rebet left, followed him in the tram as far as the Münchener Freiheit stop, and in this way discovered where he lived. He then returned to Moscow and reported.

In May and July, he made two more reconnaissance trips. On each trip he took a room at the Hotel Grünwald, from the window of which he was able to keep a watch on 9 Dachauerstrasse, the offices of the Ukrainian exile newspaper, where Rebet worked before he went to his own office in the Karlsplatz. Then early in September, Stashynsky was sent to the SMERSH training school in Karlshorst, East Berlin, and there was visited by a senior SMERSH technician, who demonstrated the use of the weapon which was to be used to kill Rebet. This weapon was a metal tube, about as thick as a finger and seven inches long, divided into three sections which screwed together. In the lower section there was a firing pin which was fixed and could be released by pressing a spring. On being released, the pin detonated a small percussion cap, which caused a metal lever in the middle section to move and crush a glass ampoule in the upper section. This ampoule contained a poison resembling water in appearance, but which issued from the mouth of the tube in the form of vapour when the ampoule was crushed. (It was, in fact, prussic acid.) If this vapour were fired into a man's face from a distance of about one and a half feet, he would drop dead immediately on inhaling the vapour, which left no trace in the body. Thus it was not possible to prove that the victim had met a violent death. The operator was protected from the harmful effects of the vapour by swallowing an antidote-tablet of sodium thio-sulphate a short time before firing, and by inhaling the vapour from another ampoule containing amyl-nitrate immediately after firing.

On 8th October he received orders to go to Munich forthwith and carry out his assignment. He flew to Munich on the following day and took a room at the Stachus hotel. On the 10th and 11th October he saw no sign of Rebet, but on the 12th he caught his victim on the stairway of the Karlsplatz office building, fired the spray-gun in his face and fled.

Rebet was found on the stairs where he had fallen. The inquest verdict was death from natural causes.

Well pleased with Stashynsky's performance, in 1959 the KGB sent him once more to Munich to track down another prominent Ukrainian exile leader, Stefan Bandera, and found that he was living at 7 Kreittmayerstrasse under the name of Stefan Popel. On 15th October he attacked Bandera with a mark 2 model of the

606

spray gun at the door of the apartment. Unfortunately for SMERSH, the inquest on Bandera was carried out within a very short time of his death, and the cause of death was discovered.

Stashynsky subsequently claimed that these two killings weighed heavily on his conscience. Shortly before his second assignment he had met and married an East German girl, Inge Pohl. After the Bandera assassination, he told Inge what his job was, and she urged him to defect to the West. But this was more easily said than done, for they were living in Moscow and had no opportunity of escaping.

By the autumn of 1960 Inge was pregnant, and there were complications. At Christmas, after much pleading, the KGB allowed her to return to her parents home in East Berlin. Her son was born in March 1961, but the KGB refused to allow Stashynsky to leave Moscow to visit the mother and baby. On 9th August the child died, and at last the KGB relented and allowed Stashynsky to travel to Berlin for the funeral, though under heavy escort.

Barely an hour before the

funeral was to take place, Stashynsky and his wife, together with Inge's sixteen-year-old brother, evaded the KGB guards and were able to reach Falkensee, a few miles from Berlin. From there they took a taxi to East Berlin, and then crossed into West Berlin, where they surrendered to the American authorities.

One day later, and they would not have been able to escape by this route. During the night of the 13th/14th August, 1961, the Berlin Wall was built.

Stashynsky was subsequently brought to trial by the West German authorities on a double-murder charge. The prosecution had taken great pains to check Stashynsky's story in so far as this was possible, and found that he had told the truth in his statements. The sentence, therefore, was a light one of eight years' penal servitude.

BIBLIOGRAPHY:

The Executioners — Ronald Seth (London 1965, New York, 1966).

STEINHAUER, Gustav see under **Ernst, Karl.**

STEPHENSON, Sir William (British director of intelligence in the United States, World War II).

In World War I, Sir William Stephenson was a fighter pilot in the Royal Flying Corps, the fore-runner of the RAF. Before he was himself shot down and taken prisoner by the Germans he accounted for twenty-six enemy aircraft.

He was a Canadian by birth, but after the war he settled in England. He won the King's Cup Air Race in 1934.

He had always had an interest in radio, and foresaw the development of commercial radio and television, and after demobilisation he obtained a financial participation in a number of radio companies. He was also an inventor, and while still a very young man he patented a system of transmitting pictures by wireless, with the result that he was a millionaire before he was thirty.

His commercial interests became very extensive, and he travelled a good deal all over the world. Arising out of his business activities in Germany in the 1930s, he was able to supply Winston Churchill with information about Hitler's secret rearmament programme.

Early in the war he carried out a dangerous intelligence mission to Finland on behalf of the British government, and it was as a result of his great success on this assignment that Churchill, on becoming Prime Minister, asked him to become the director of British intelligence in the Western Hemisphere.

Stephenson set up his headquarters in New York, calling his organisation the office of British Security Co-ordination (BSC). He quickly and completely won the confidence of the American authorities, and developed close friendships with J. Edgar Hoover of the FBI, and General "Wild Bill" Donovan, chief of the OSS. The outcome was a close and amicable co-operation between the British and American secret services in the Western Hemisphere.

The cover for the BSC was the protection of British shipping in American ports, and of war materials supplied by America under Lend-Lease. In fact, BSC grew into a considerable organisation, which operated in practically every field of clandestine operations from the training of agents and saboteurs, espionage and counter-espionage, and subversive activities of all kinds.

For his services, Stephenson was knighted in 1945, and President Truman gave him America's highest civilian honour, the Presidential Medal for Merit.

Dr Hugh Dalton, under whose responsibility BSC had been placed when he had been Minister for Economic Warfare, wrote to Stephenson a letter of congratulations on this last honour, a passage from which read:

"I should further like to place on record the fact that you did all this of your own goodwill, and received no remuneration of any kind."

BIBLIOGRAPHY:

The Quiet Canadian — H. Montgomery Hyde (London, 1962).

STIEBER, Wilhelm (Director of Prussian intelligence).

Wilhelm Stieber was born on 3rd May, 1818, in Marsburg, Saxony, where his father was a minor official in the civil service. Wilhelm had not yet reached his teens when Herr Stieber was transferred to Berlin, where he educated his son with a view to ultimate ordination in the Lutheran ministry.

Before he completed his education, however, Stieber had decided that he had no vocation for the ministry and turned his attention to the study of law. In Law he found at last the best use for his intellectual powers, qualified without difficulty, and within a short time had become one of the most sought-after criminal lawyers in Berlin.

His clients were the riff-raff of the criminal world, little maladjusted men who took to crime as the only mode of expression they had — so far as they could see — of kicking against authority. Stieber's personality was such that he was able to get inside the minds of these petty criminals, and they were prepared to accept him as their champion. They did not know, and for many years were never to discover, that he was one of the most ardent of monarchists.

Stieber always acted for the defence, and his success in this role was phenomenal. Between 1845 and 1850 he successfully defended 3000 clients.

His success was not based on his brilliance as a lawyer, however. Almost as soon as he had begun to practice at the Bar, he had accepted employment by the police as an **agent provocateur** to smell out proscribed radicals, the enemies of the monarchy and the monarchists. He was also the editor of the **Police Journal,** and thus had constant dealings with the police. From these contacts he was able to gain information in advance regarding the evidence which the police intended to bring against his clients. So he went into court fully prepared to meet with rebuttal and legal arguments the facts and arguments put forward by the prosecutors. And, surprisingly, it never seemed to occur to the police that they were supplying the material for his success.

His championship of the underdogs, as he called them, was by no means altruistic. The contacts he made with the underworld he used to obtain information about the radicals, and as an **agent provocateur** he was as successful as he was a defender of petty criminals.

But Stieber was an ambitious man. It was not his intention always to be an **agent provocateur** and defender of petty criminals. He had his attention fixed on high places, and one or more of those high places he intended to fill.

His brilliant, quick-moving intellect also made him an opportunist but even he must have been somewhat overwhelmed by the prospects which suddenly opened up before him one day in 1848. On this day, King Frederick William of Prussia found himself alone and unaccountably involved in one of those disturbances which were beginning to become far too frequent occurrences in Berlin. Someone had recognised the king and called out an insult. This had attracted the attention of others, and soon the credulous, timorous Frederick found himself faced by an hostile crowd. It seemed for a moment that he might receive physical harm. He looked about him but could see no way of escape.

Like many timorous men, the king had a certain courage. He could not escape, he would not try to argue with these ill-mannered subjects; he would stand and wait for the blows which he was sure would come. At that moment a man detached himself from the crowd, which stood a little way off, and walked towards him, shouting out as he came "Death to the tyrant!" But when he came up to the king, instead of striking him he whispered, "Don't be afraid, your Majesty. I'm a police agent. My men are in the crowd. They will see that nothing happens to you."

Then shouting another insult, the man seized the king's arm and began to hustle him along the pavement. As they came level with a door a few yards down, the man made a sudden movement toward it, opened it, pushed the king through, and bolted it on the inside.

Breathing heavily with his own excitement, the man then asked the king's indulgence, explaining that he was not a police agent, but that he had had to say something so that Frederick's courage should not fail at the last moment.

"You certainly saved my life," the king said. "What is your name?"

"Wilhelm Stieber, sire."

"I shall not forget it!" the king promised him.

And Frederick William did not forget. Until he went quite mad in 1857, he heaped reward upon reward on Stieber. In 1850 the lawyer was made Commissioner of Police. In the following year he visited England, ostensibly to inspect the Great Exhibition, but really to check up on the activities of Karl Marx and other Prussian radical exiles living in England. In 1852 he went to Paris, where, posing as a liberal and in his old role of **agent provocateur** he obtained a list of the radicals still living underground in Germany. His return was marked by the wholesale arrests of these men and women.

During the years which followed he became such an ardent supporter of autocracy that he almost outrivaled the autocrat himself. This ardour he translated into action against the radicals, thereby strengthening his own position with the king.

But in the course of these activities he made many enemies, and when the king was put away, he was dismissed from his post and was fortunate not to be the object of worse revenge. Believing it would be wiser to travel for a time, he went to St Petersburg, where, between 1858 and 1863, he assisted in reorganising the Russian secret service.

There is one aspect of this phase of Stieber's career which, at first sight, appears extraordinary, though when we come to know him better we find that it fits snugly into the jigsaw of the man's genius. While in disgrace and helping the Russians, he collected all the military information he could lay hands on and sent it to Berlin, where it was found to be of great value.

Always the optimist, he believed that his disgrace would not last for ever, and in 1863 he proved himself right. He persuaded the proprietor of the **Norddeutsche Allegemeine Zeitung** to inform Bismarck that he wished to return home and that he could be of some service to the Chancellor, who had reached that stage in his plans for the aggrandisement of Prussia at which he had decided on the elimination of Austria.

He proposed to Stieber that he should organise an espionage network for a reconnaissance of Austria's defences. Stieber agreed, but told Bismarck that he would undertake the mission in person. So he set off and two years later he had supplied the Prussian military authorities with intelligence so complete and perfect concerning Austrian defences that when the attack was launched, Austria was defeated in seven days.

His **modus operandi** was ingenious. He supplied himself with a cart on which he loaded religious statuettes "blessed by the Pope". Thus equipped he wandered about the Austrian countryside selling his wares to the simple peasantry. In the taverns he produced a different "line" intended for his male drinking companions — a series of pornographic drawings which not only sold like hot cakes but made him hail-fellow-well-met. No one suspected the motives of a vendor of filthy postcards when he asked searching questions about the forces stationed in such and such an area, or the strength of a fortification here, a fortification there.

Between his return from his mission and the launching of the attack, Stieber organised an entirely new section of the secret police and went into the field as its commander. We recognise this force as the forerunner of the Intelligence Corps. Though primarily intended to protect the persons of the king, his ministers and generals, Stieber's secret police were also to prevent foreign spies from obtaining Prussian

military secrets. It was, in fact, counter-espionage and counter-espionage in those days was a new concept. This was the first of Stieber's contributions to modern spycraft.

It was not the only innovation he made to espionage practice. He introduced military censorship, which he tied with another new idea — false propaganda aimed at keeping up morale at home and at misleading the enemy.

As a result of his success in the Seven Days' War, Stieber was restored fully to favour, and appointed a Privy Councillor. From this time he went from strength to strength, for Bismarck had need of him. With Austria reduced to a quiet, harmless nation, no longer a European power, Bismarck was turning his eye towards France. Once more he personally made a reconnaissance and then organised a network so vast that nothing like it had been heard of before in espionage history.

In the invasion zones his agents listed the stock of every single farm, so that when Prussian billeting officers and messing officers went about their tasks, they would know exactly how many cattle, how many sheep, how many chickens, and how many eggs Farmer Lebrun could supply for their needs. Other agents ferreted out the exact amount of the savings of the leaders of urban and rural communities. The state and dimensions of roads and byroads, the size and capacity of bridges, the sites of stores of arms and ammunition dumps, and the numbers and types of transport — all were listed. Nothing escaped him.

Stieber's personal qualities were a blend of tireless application to the task in hand, cunning, subtlety, and utter, even ferocious, ruthlessness. He demanded similar qualities in every single one of his agents. He insisted that everyone who was even suspected of having a knowledge of Prussian military strength should be liquidated. He decreed that when a company of Prussian soldiers passed through a village they should be preceded by outriders who were to warn all the inhabitants to get indoors and close their shutters. Any peasant who peeped from behind his shutters while the company passed was to be seized, tortured and hanged.

But while he demanded such excessive security, Stieber did not complain if his agents were caught, tortured and hanged. It served them right for being careless.

Stieber was in the closest contact with and deep in the confidence of Bismarck. The Junkers, however, hated him, and lost no opportunity for snubbing him. But no insult seemed to affect him. With infinite patience he collected every scrap of discreditable information against all those who hated him so, and though they might snub him, they never dared to do more.

After the successful conclusion of the Franco-Prussian War, in which Stieber played no less a role than he had in the Austro-Prussian War, he set about organising a system of permanent resident spies abroad on a scale never before conceived. Waiters in foreign hotels, workers in factories, hair-dressers, itinerant German bands, prostitutes of particular skills which made them attractive to the jaded sexual palates of high-ranking naval and military personnel and civil servants, all had their place in his organisation. Money was poured into the project on a scale comparable with the vast

613

sums now being spent by the American government on their Space Programme. All Europe was aware of the existence of Stieber's secret army, was impressed and frightened by it, and for the most part, did little to counteract it.

Within Prussia itself Stieber's secret police were almost as numerous and certainly as ubiquitous. There were many citizens who were discontented with the doctrine known as the Prussian Idea, which aimed at suppressing completely the liberty of the individual. Many victims of the Idea could visualise only one way of restoring individual freedom — the removal of its chief exponents, the Emperor, and his Chancellor. In his later years, as Minister of Police, Stieber was constantly being called upon to protect his masters from assassination. It was to deal with this situation that Stieber introduced the Green House, another innovation.

The Green House, situated in Berlin, was an establishment where every type of sexual perversion could be practiced. Whenever he wished to coerce a prominent man in government or some other importan

walk of life into becoming the tool of his intelligence, Stieber gave him the run of The Green House, until he was completely compromised and then used blackmailing threats of exposure unless he did exactly all that Stieber demanded. If the man were not a pervert before, in very cunning ways he was introduced to perversions, generally with the aid of drugs, with similar results. By this means he uncovered many an assassination plot before it was fully developed.

The Green House was the last of Stieber's innovations, however. He outlived William I and remained in office after Bismarck had been dismissed. Sometime before he retired and settled down to write his reminiscences, after fifty years' service as a spy, he received in 1876 a visit from some strange little men who had come from the other side of the world to seek his advice on organising an espionage service of their own. By complying with their request he insured that the mark of his brilliant touch was left on espionage practice and in espionage history long after his influence on the service he had built up in his own country had waned.

He died a wealthy and much decorated man in 1892, his last years made painful by a crippling arthritis.

BIBLIOGRAPHY:

Denkwurdigkeiten des Geheimen Regierungsrathes Dr Stieber aus seinen Hinterlassen Papieren bearbeitet — J. Auerbach (Munich, 1882).

STEINER, Renata see under **Reiss, Ignace.**

STRINGER.

Espionage jargon for a part-time agent, who nearly always hires himself out for set rewards. He is, for this reason, seldom used in any more important role than that of a cut-out or a decoy. Some authorities believe that Mata Hari was a stringer, who was sacrificed by German intelligence to put Allied counter-intelligence off the scent of more important agents.

STURME, Carl (Abwehr agent, World War I) see under **McKenna, Marthe.**

SUKULOV, Victor (Russian agent, World War II) see under **Red Orchestra, The.**

SWITZ, Robert and Marjorie Russian agents, 1930s) see under **Stahl, Lydia.**

TACONIS (Dutch agent, World War II) see under **Giskes, Col H. J.**

TACHIBAKA, Commander Itaru see under **Kono, Torchichi.**

TALLMADGE NETWORK, The (American War of Independence).

After the capture and execution of Nathan Hale (q.v.) by the British in New York, Washington realised that isolated agents ran the risk of stultifying their achievements by reason of working on their own. Their intelligence died with them if they had not passed it on before being captured. The best way of removing the risk was by establishing a network.

Washington chose Major Benjamin Tallmadge to organise and control this network and Tallmadge selected as his agents Robert Townsend of New York and Oyster Bay, Long Island; Abraham Woodhull, Austin Roe, Enoch Hale

(Nathan's brother) and Caleb Brewster. Tallmadge, Robert Townsend and Enoch Hale had all been members of the class of 1773 at Yale. It may be that Washington's choice fell upon Tallmadge, and Tallmadge's upon Townsend and Enoch Hale, on account of this relationship, in the belief that personal friends of the dead spy ,Nathan Hale, would be emotionally moved to avenge his death.

Having no training or experience to help them, these leaders had to devise their own methods of operating, and their success indicates that all possessed a natural flair for espionage and in particular a keen appreciation of the value of security. They all adopted cover names which hid their identities so perfectly that not one of their friends or fellow officers, except the commander-in-chief, was aware of their espionage roles. Tallmadge was known as Mr John Bottom, Woodhull as Samuel Culper senior, and Townsend as Samuel Culper Junior. Townsend was to prove himself by far the most ingenious member of the network.

Townsend carried on a mercantile business in New York,

bringing food products into the city from the Long Island farms. Like the village store of today, Townsend's place of business was the meeting place not only of American but of British gossips. No "Careless Talk" warning posters were displayed in the store, and the acutely attuned ears of the proprietor received all the unguarded chatter of his customers, especially of the British soldiers and their wives, and transmitted it to his commander.

Woodhull had always lived at Setauket, Long Island. Having accepted the role of agent, he remained there, living as quietly as possible in order not to attract attention.

Roe lived in New York City itself. His role was that of courier, for which he had perfect cover; he operated Robert Townsend's pack trains, which maintained quite a regular service between the north shore of Long Island and New York. Thus without arousing comment from his neighbours or suspicion from the enemy, Roe could frequent Townsend's store and if he rode from the city to Setauket, where Woodhull lived, no one thought it strange.

When Woodhull at Setauket received Townsend's dispatches from Roe, he would hurry to the shore and at a certain place look out for a black petticoat and a number of handkerchiefs hung on a washline in a certain way. This would indicate that it was safe to approach Brewster, the second courier.

Brewster was a boatman, who plied regularly in Long Island Sound and had done so for so many years that he aroused no suspicions either. He received the reports from Woodhull and sailed them across Long Island Sound to the mainland coast of Connecticut, where he handed them to Enoch Hale or Tallmadge himself, who carried them direct to General Washington.

The agents believed that security would best be served if they used a code, but they had no knowledge of cipher work, and so invented a code of their own, which was so complicated that it required a small "pocket dictionary" for both encoding and decoding. Certain letters represented specific words, names of places or of individuals.

Thus a message from one of the "Culpers" reads "Dqpeu

617

Beyocpu agreeable to 28 met 723 not far from 727 & received a 356", which decoded read, "Jonas Hawkins agreeable to appointment met Robert Townsend not far from New York and received a report." In the code 15 represented advice, 286 ink, 592 ships, 711 General Washington, 712 General Clinton, the British commander, 728 Long Island, 745 England. Despite its complexities, however, it was effective; no message was ever compromised.

General Washington gave strict orders that there should never be any delay in forwarding the "Culper" dispatches, and only once did Tallmadge take it upon himself to disobey this order, with results that may be said to have launched sistematic military counterespionage in North America.

British troops had occupied Oyster Bay, and British soldiers among them a Colonel Simcoe, were quartered in Robert Townsend's house there, looked after by Townsend's sister, Sarah. One evening late in August 1780, Colonel Simcoe was entertaining a fellow officer named Major André (q.v.).

Sarah Townsend, who was aware of her brother's espionage activities, was supervising the serving of dinner and at the same time listening to the conversation of the two officers in the hope of picking up information that might be useful to her brother. During dinner a letter arrived addressed to John Anderson. She asked Simcoe if he knew anyone of that name, and André said he did, and pocketed the letter. Later she saw André open the letter and read it, and as she was serving the coffee became interested in the conversation which turned upon the American stronghold and main supply base at West Point.

Sarah, rightly believing that her brother would be interested in what she had seen and heard, next morning induced a susceptible young British captain, Daniel Young, to send a messenger to her brother's store in New York to ask him to send her supplies. She gave the batman, detailed by Young for the errand, a sealed note, which, she said, was a list of the things she needed. Within an hour of Robert Townsend's receiving the message, it was on its way to Tallmadge via Roe, Woodhull and Brewster.

There now occurred one of those real-life coincidences

which, if encountered in fiction, would be dismissed with scepticism. Half an hour before Townsend's dispatch arrived, Tallmadge had received a note from General Arnold saying that a friend of his called John Anderson was likely to be passing his way, and as he did not know the region, requested that an escort of dragoons might conduct him to West Point.

For some reason or other, which he was never afterwards able to explain, Tallmadge, who usually forwarded Townsend's dispatches direct to General Washington unread, opened this letter and deciphered it, and to his surprise, came again upon the name "John Anderson", with the additional information that his true identity was likely to be the British Adjutant General, Major John André.

The unanswered question which sprang at once to Tallmadge's mind was "Why should this influential British officer be going to visit an American general under an assumed name?" Tallmadge decided that he must discover the answer and gave orders for John Anderson to be traced and held for questioning.

Immediately subsequent events have been related under Major André's entry. Briefly he was on his way to Arnold to negotiate the latter's betrayal of West Point to the British. He met Arnold, and while making his way back to the British lines in civilian clothes, was captured and held as a spy.

It was Tallmadge who, on 26th September, 1780, took André to Washington's headquarters. Washington refused to see him. The following day he was court-martialled, sentenced to death and on 2nd October, hanged.

The capture and death of André had a direct effect on Tallmadge's New York network. Robert Townsend seems to have feared some sort of betrayal as a retaliation for the execution of the British officer. In a letter he wrote to Tallmadge eighteen days after the execution he clearly reveals this. In it he says he is happy to know that Arnold does not know his name. He was not greatly surprised by Arnold's conduct, for it was no more than he expected of him. He goes on:

"I never felt more sensibly for the death of a person whom

I knew only by sight, and had heard converse, than I did for Major André. He was a most amiable character . . . I believe General Washington felt sincerely for him, and would have saved him if it could have been done with propriety.

"The long time I have been out of town prevents my giving you any information of consequence . . . I hope and expect that all my letters are destroyed after they are perused."

As soon as the news of André's arrest reached him, Townsend shut his store in New York and left the city for some weeks. He returned, however, when it seemed that his fears were groundless, and continued to operate until the end of hostilities.

Washington spent 17,617 dollars on his espionage organisation, so his carefully kept ledgers reveal. Probably no other commander has been so ably served by his secret agents for so small a cost.

All the men in the Tallmadge network survived the outbreak of the War of Independence by fifty years or more. As President, Washington paid them frequent visits. He appreciated the risks they had run to supply him with intelligence,

620

and was determined that no harm should come to them. Documents relating to espionage were sealed, and more than a century passed before these agents were identified.

BIBLIOGRAPHY:

History of America — J. Winser (New York, 1887) Parts 6 and 7.

American Archives (Washington, 1837-1853).

TANIA (real name Tamara Bunke) (Soviet agent with Che Guevara).

Tania was sent by the KGB to join Che Guevara, the Cuban guerrilla leader, when he was in Bolivia organising guerrilla warfare in that country.

Her father was Erich Bunke, a professor of languages in Buenos Aires, where Tania was born on 19th November, 1937. In the early 1950s the Bunkes returned to East Germany for a short time, where Tania entered Humboldt university to study political sciences. Since the Bunkes were communists, Tania obtained a post in the East German Ministry of State Security, and before long she was carrying out minor missions in the espionage field. In

1961 she was taken over by the KGB.

Becoming disturbed by the anti-Russian manifestations of the Cuban radical revolutionary leadership, the KGB decided to send an agent to find out what was really happening, and Tania was chosen to go to Havana. She went under the cover-name of Laura Guterrez.

Her instructions were to concentrate on Che Guevara, who was considered the most anti-Russian of the Cuban military leaders. This she did very successfully, and became his mistress. When Che moved to Bolivia she accompanied him and shared all the hardships encountered by Che and his band of guerrillas.

When the Bolivian forces eventually tracked down Che and his forces, Tania was killed in an ambush. She was four months pregnant.

It is clear from his diaries that until he died Che Guevara had no idea of Tania's real role.

BIBLIOGRAPHY:

Secrets of the Guevara Diaries — Andrew St George (*Sunday Telegraph* 21st July, 1968).

TCHEKA or Cheka.

The first designation of the Russian intelligence organisation. It was established in 1917, and gets its name from the initials of the Russian title Vserossiyskaya **Tch**rezvychaynaya **K**osmisiya Po Borbe s Kontr-revolutsyey i Sabotazhem pri Soviete Narodnikh Komisarov — i.e. Tch K, pronounced in Russian **Tcheka.** The English translation of this cumbersome title is All-Russian Extraordinary Commission for the Combat of Counter-Revolution and Sabotage attached to the Council of People's Commissars.

The chairman of the first Commission, and ipso facto director of Russian intelligence was Felix Dzershinsky.

The appellation of the Russian intelligence organisation has been changed at intervals throughout Soviet history, but though its name may have changed, and at some periods its place within the administration varied, under whatever name the organisation has remained the Tcheka.

TERWINDT, Beatrix (Dutch agent, World War II) see under **Giskes, Col H. J.**

THOMPSON, Harry Thomas (American traitor, spied for

Japanese in mid-30s).

One day in 1934 a young man accosted another in a Los Angeles street and asked for a light.

"I don't even have a drag," he said, shaking his head.

The first man — he might have been three or four years older — looked at him intently. Then he asked another passer-by for a light, and when he had lit his cigarette offered a packet of **Camels,** saying, "Down on your luck?"

The first young man took a cigarette and lit it from the glowing end held up to him. He took a deep pull, and the unaccustomed bite of the smoke in his lungs made his head reel. He swayed, a hand to his eyes.

The more experienced older man read the signs.

"When did you eat last?" he asked.

"The day before yesterday — I've got one solitary nickel in the world!"

"Jesus! You'd better come home with me!"

He hailed a taxi, and the young man made no protest as he was half-pushed into it. At the apartment, as the food began to take effect and the colour came creeping back into

the young man's cheeks, the older man introduced himself.

"I'm Harry Thompson."

"I'm Willard Turntine from St Louis."

Under questioning he revealed that he was living on the beach while he looked for work. He was eighteen years old.

"You seem a nice enough kid," Thompson commented. "You'd better stay here with me until we get something worked out."

Turntine accepted gratefully.

Harry Thomas Thompson was in his early twenties. He had been a yeoman in the US Navy, but now, like Turntine, he was unemployed. Unlike Turntine, however, he was not short of money.

There has never been any proof, nor even a suggestion, that Thompson had any motive other than kindness for a penniless boy when he invited Turntine to stay with him. Turntine never at any time subsequently hinted that the older man made any physical approach to him.

Turntine liked Thompson more as he came to know him better, but after a time his curiosity began to be roused by the fact that although

Thompson had no job he always had plenty of money, some of which he was pleased to give to the younger man.

Plucking up courage one day, Turntine asked Thompson where his money came from, and was given the vague but even more tantalising answer that he would know some day — perhaps. For it seems that now that he really knew him Thompson had developed ideas about Turntine.

Though no longer in the navy, Thompson seemed to hanker after his former life aboard the **Colorado,** the **Mississippi** and the **Texas,** the battleships in which he had served. For whenever these vessels, and the radio-controlled ship **Utah,** in which some of his naval friends now served put into San Diego and San Petro, he always went to meet his old associates and have a drink with them.

Thompson took Turntine with him on some of these trips, and the boy was surprised to hear his friend asking very searching questions about ship movements, developments in equipment and changes in orders.

There is no doubt that of the two Thompson was the dominant character. On the other hand, Turntine was no fool, and he was observant. He also had courage.

He asked Thompson why, since he had left the Service because he did not like it, he made these visits to naval vessels, and received the reply, "I just like to keep in touch with what's going on." But Turntine was not satisfied. He kept his suspicions to himself, but as every day passed he read more and more sinister implications into his friend's behaviour, and watched him more and more closely. And so he discovered Thompson's association with a Japanese.

Choosing his time, he asked Thompson who the Japanese was, and what the relationship was between them. As a result of what Thompson said he knew then that his friend was deep in treachery. Indeed, Thompson made no attempt to deny it.

"The world owes me a living. O.K.?" he said. "If my country won't give me a living, some other country will."

Now that Turntine knew the truth Thompson realised that for his own safety the boy must also be compromised. He spoke to his Japanese contact and he agreed to see Turntine. The name of the Japanese was Tanni, and a meeting was arranged in Los Angeles. Tanni, however, could not make up his mind.

His secret no longer a secret, Thompson became careless about concealing communications which he received from Tanni from time to time. By Christmas 1934, Turntine's conscience had become so uneasy that he decided that he must go to the authorities. A suitable opportunity did not occur, however, until the end of January 1935, when Thompson announced that he was going away for a few days. Turntine knew that the flagship USS **Pennsylvania** was anchored at San Diego. He went to San Diego, and by sheer persistence was at last taken before Admiral Joseph M. Reeves. He told Admiral Reeves his story, and Reeves was impressed. He told the boy to go back to Long Beach and carry on as usual, taking great care not to let Thompson know what he had done.

The admiral immediately passed Turntine's story to the Office of Naval Intelligence. ONI agents, moving quickly, went to Long Beach and closely interrogated Turntine. They had already checked on him and found that he had a clean record.

They were as impressed as the admiral had been, especially when they saw one of the letters from Tanni, which Turntine had been able to extract from the garbage tin into which Thompson had carelessly thrown it. Giving him the same instructions to carry on as before, they told him that he might hear from them later. They then went away to try to discover Tanni's identity.

Tanni presented a problem, but eventually he was traced to Palo Alto. This suggested that he might be a language student at Stanford University — and so it turned out to be. By comparing the handwriting of the Tanni letter with the handwriting of the one or two Japanese studying at Stanford, they discovered that Tanni's real name was Toshio Miyazaki.

Miyazaki had entered the United States on 24th August 1933, and almost immediately had enrolled at Stanford. Though only thirty, he was already a lieutenant-commander in the Japanese Navy.

Miyazaki was now permanently shadowed by the ONI, who, a day or two after he had been identified, followed him to San Francisco. There he dined well, and spent an hour or two in a brothel, leaving just in time to catch the train to Los Angeles, where he took a taxi to $117\frac{1}{2}$ Weller Street (see under Furusawa, Dr). He was Dr Furusawa's guest until the following evening, when he took a taxi to Long Beach, and visited Thompson, now returned from his trip, at his apartment on Linden Street.

Thompson was aware of the impending visit. Earlier in the evening he had tossed Turntine a five-dollar bill, saying "Go out and lose yourself for an hour or so, will you? I've got a doll coming."

ONI agents had installed themselves in the building opposite the apartment building and were able to see into Thompson's room. As soon as Miyazaki arrived he handed Thompson a wad of dollar bills, and then took from his brief-case a large sheet of paper. The two men bent low over the paper for a quarter of an hour or so, and then

Thompson went into the bedroom, returning with a sheaf of papers, which he handed to Miyazaki one at a time. Each paper was fully discussed, it seemed.

It was after ten o'clock when the Japanese eventually left, taking Thompson's notes with him. He drove straight back to Los Angeles in a taxi, which took him to the Red Mill brothel. He was in the brothel for three-quarters of an hour, and then he caught the night-train for San Francisco. On the following morning he was attending his lectures at Stanford.

The agents next discovered that Miyazaki banked at the Yokohama Specie Bank in San Francisco. His account revealed that he had been paying Thompson two hundred dollars a month. He was meticulous in meeting his financial commitments with Thompson.

The day following Miyazaki's visit to his apartment Thompson told Turntine that he was rejoining the Navy, and bought himself a petty officer's uniform. Turntine, who was now co-operating fully with the ONI asked Thompson bluntly whether he too was going to be given a chance of working for the Japanese. Thompson told him that Tanni could not find work for him at the moment, and for the first time uttered a threat.

"If you ever tell anyone about what's going on, or that you met Tanni, you won't live long!"

Dressed in his uniform, Thompson went to San Pedro, where he spent most of his time in the bars, buying drinks for sailors and skilfully questioning them about the Fleet's future activities.

The ONI were now convinced that Thompson was a dangerous menace. They approached the State Department with the request that both he and Miyazaki should be arrested. But the State Department was falling over itself at this time not to antagonise the Japanese in any way, and refused point-blank to authorise Miyazaki's apprehension. All the ONI could do was to warn sailors not to talk to Thompson.

Thompson masqueraded in his petty officer's uniform for several months. During this time he met Miyazaki frequently, either at his own apartment in Linden Street or at the St Francis Hotel in San Francisco.

When the sailors would no longer talk to him Thompson had to confess to Miyazaki that he believed there had been a leak and that he suspected Turntine. Miyazaki did not directly order Thompson to remove Turntine permanently, but suggested that this would be the best solution. To protect Turntine, the ONI secured work for him in San Francisco, so that he need no longer live with Thompson.

When Turntine told Thompson that he had got a job as a salesman in a San Francisco department store Thompson was at once more suspicious than ever. But when Turntine was able to produce letters on headed stationery Thompson appeared satisfied.

After Turntine left Thompson began to crack up. He took to drinking heavily, his bouts sometimes lasting for several days at a time. His behaviour perturbed Miyazaki, who visited him at Linden Street. ONI agents watching from the building opposite surmised from Thompson's demeanour and Miyazaki's gestures that the Japanese was sternly rebuking his agent.

When Miyazaki left, Thompson sat down at his table and spent an hour or two trying to compose a letter. It gave him great difficulty. He made several false starts, screwing up the sheets and tossing them into the waste-paper basket. The ONI could not legally enter Thompson's apartment, but they arranged for the contents of the wastepaper basket to be handed to them. Among the screwed up sheets was found a rough copy of the final draft of the letter he had at last managed. It was addressed to Tanni (Miyazaki) and thanked him. It was, in fact, his resignation from the Japanese espionage service.

Miyazaki, realising that Thompson's usefulness was at an end, accepted the resignation. His superiors, anxious lest he might be compromised by the demoralised American, ordered his return to Japan.

The evidence against Thompson was so conclusive that, now the Japanese had flown, there could be no excuse for postponing his arrest. A brief announcement was made to the public in the press on 5th March 1936. At his subsequent trial Turntine was the prosecution's star witness, but others showed that Thompson had been in the service of the Japanese since 1933. In July 1936 he was sentenced to fifteen years in the federal penitentiary on McNeil Island.

BIBLIOGRAPHY:

Betrayal From the East — Alan Hynd (New York, 1943).

THOMSON, Sir Basil.

Basil Thomson was a son of Archbishop William Thomson of York. Born in 1861, and educated at Eton and Oxford, he was called to the Bar. He joined the Colonial Service and served in Fiji and Tonga, of which, for a time, he was prime minister.

In 1896 he entered the prison service and became governor of Dartmoor and Wormwood Scrubs prisons. In 1913 he was appointed Assistant Commissioner of the Metropolitan Police and director of the Criminal Investigation Department.

He was knighted in 1918, and in the following year he became director of intelligence. He retired in 1921. He died in March, 1939.

Thomson, as director of the CID during World War I, and responsible for the Special Branch (q.v.) worked in close collaboration with MI5 and with Admiral Sir Reginald Hall, director of Naval Intelligence. These activities brought him into contact with most of the spies caught in Britain during World War I, in particular Captain Fritz von Rintelen (q.v.). He also interviewed Mata Hari (q.v.) as she passed through London on her way to Spain shortly before she was arrested in France.

BIBLIOGRAPHY:

Queer People and **The Story of Scotland Yard** — Basil Thomson (London, 1922 and 1935 respectively).

THURLOE, John (Oliver Cromwell's director of intelligence).

Lord Protector Cromwell's chief danger sprang from cruelly curbed Royalists at home and the Court of James Stuart abroad. Cromwell was a dictator, and was no different from any other tyrant who has attempted to subdue a people by depriving it of liberty. But his opponents within the realm were of a different mettle from those who sat complacently under the terrorism of Hitler, Mussolini and Stalin. The Royalists of England were men of spirit and courage, and since they were circumscribed by oppressive measures which prevented overt activity, they resorted to plots.

To combat the ever constant threats, Cromwell was prepared to devote to his intelligence service, the sum of £70,000, the modern equivalent of £1,500,000. By means of a large number of agents he not only knew what was happening within his Protectorate, but was aware of every counsel taken behind closed and barred doors abroad.

His director of intelligence was John Thurloe. Born in an Essex parsonage in 1616, Thurloe was educated for the law, and became a member of Lincoln's Inn in 1647. In 1651 he was secretary of an English mission to the Netherlands, and on his return in 1652 he was appointed secretary to the Council of State (Cabinet) with a residence in Whitehall. Not long after this, Cromwell, impressed by his qualities, put him in charge of the intelligence department.

Thurloe's chief assistant was an Oxford don, Dr John Wallis. Wallis was the natural successor of Walsingham's (q.v.) cipher expert Phelippes (q.v.). It is claimed that there was not a single code known at the time that the doctor could not break.

Thurloe was served by every type of agent — renegade, Royalists, driven by penury to treachery, scholars, scoundrels, exiled heads of families and young rakes in need of his sovereigns to pay their mistresses. He even used the technique which later became general; he reprieved potentially useful criminals from the gallows on the sole condition that they would spy for him.

Among his successes was the eventual disbandment of the Sealed Knot, a Royalist secret society. For years under Oliver Cromwell, Thurloe had pitted his wits and a large number of his agents in running this organisation to earth, without success. After Oliver's death, when Richard his son had succeeded him as Protector, Thurloe managed to bribe Sir Richard Willis, a leading member of the Sealed Knot, to betray his fellow members. The society had to dissolve itself but the outcome for which Thurloe had most hoped eluded him; he did not apprehend Charles Stuart.

Charles was able to escape because Thurloe was compromised by one of his own agents, Sir George Downing, the British Resident in Holland. Downing already recognised the stirrings in favour of the Restoration of the monarchy, and warned Charles Stuart of Willis's defection. This enabled Charles to remove himself from Thurloe's area of activity.

Although not officially employed by Charles II, Thurloe was often consulted by him until he died on 21st February, 1668.

Charles II suffered from a chronic impecuniosity, which affected even his secret services. On 14th February, 1668, a week before Thurloe died, his successor, Mr Secretary Morrice, complained most bitterly in the House of Commons that he was allowed only £700 a year for intelligence. Three days later this princely sum was increased by £50 a year. Only one inference can be drawn from this fact — that neither Charles nor his advisers were interested in intelligence; for there was no Francis Walsingham among his courtiers willing to employ his private fortune on the State's behalf, or the Sovereign's.

On the other hand, Sir George Downing, who was still British Resident in The Hague, was continuing some of his spying activities in which he had engaged under Thurloe. He told Samuel Pepys on 27th December, 1668, that "he had so good spies, he hath had the keys taken out of De Witt's pocket when he was a-bed, and his closet opened, and papers brought to him, and left in his hands for an hour, and carried back, and laid in the place again, and the keys put into his pocket again. He says that he hath always had their most private debates, that have been but between two or three of the chief of them, brought to him an hour after, and an hour after that hath sent word thereof to the King, **but nobody here regarded them.**"

This was tantamount to breaking into the bedroom of the President of the United States, taking the keys of his safe from his trousers pocket, opening his safe, and so on . . . for John De Witt was the Grand Pensionary of Holland, the head of state.

TIEBEL, Erwin see under **Felfe, Heinz.**

630

TIMMERMANN, Alphonse (German agent, World War II).

The uncertainty of parachute and submarine landings of agents in Great Britain prompted Admiral Canaris, director of the Abwehr, (q.v.) to look round for another means of effecting entry into the Islands, and found two to hand that seemed ready made. These were the "refugee" from the Continent via the North Sea in a small boat; and the "refugee" escape route via Spain.

The first to arrive by the former route were four Belgians who had been picked up from a small motor-boat by a naval vessel which had gone to the assistance of a bomber in difficulties. Only one of the four, Alphonse Timmermann, could speak English at all well, and he explained how they came to be where they were.

They had been members of the Belgian Resistance and had been warned that their arrest by the Gestapo were imminent. This was a likely story for many genuine Resistance workers had made their escape by any number of means when the Gestapo had got hot on their trail. So, disguised as fishermen and forging a fishing permit, Timmermann said, they had stolen a boat and set out for England. They had been turned back at the first attempt by a German patrol vessel, and on two subsequent occasions had found the patrols too much for them.

Almost in despair of ever escaping, they had eventually procured a small but ancient trawler. They then ran into difficulties with the elements, and had given up hope when they were picked up.

This story and the credentials of the four men were checked by Belgian government officials in London and by Counter-espionage officers, and Timmermann was given a post in the Belgian exiled government's colonial division, while the others were allowed to join the Free Belgian Forces.

It was the custom of British counter-espionage, however, to keep all such cases under review for some time, and presently one of their agents who had previously worked in Belgium, visited the Belgian club one evening when Timmermann was there. The agent was sure that he recognised in Timmermann the interpreter at the Belgian Gestapo headquarters in the rue aux Laines, Brussels.

Timmermann was at once put under surveillance and his lodgings searched. There the officers discovered a radio transmitter, ingredients for making invisible ink, copies of documents he had made from the files with which he worked, and pound and dollar notes to the value of £280.

Confronted with this evidence, Timmermann broke down, and confessed that his escape had been arranged by the Gestapo. He was executed in Wandsworth prison, London, in 1942.

TORII, Lieutenant-Commander see under **Furusawa, Dr Takashi.**

TOWNSEND, Robert see under **Tallmadge Network, The.**

TREBITSCH LINCOLN, Isaac (Professional spy, pre-World War I).

Isaac Trebitsch Lincoln was born in the Hungarian town of Paks, not far from Budapest. The exact year of his birth is not known. One source, the French journal **Vu**, gives it as 1872; but an account written about his early life by an

American called Blood-Ryan, gives it as 1879.

His parents were Jews. About his father's source of livelihood there is again some uncertainty. Some say that Trebitsch senior owned a small but thriving boat-building business, while others contended that he was a corn-merchant.

Isaac was a younger son, and his parents intended that he should become a rabbi. For this reason, at great personal sacrifice, they sent him to a good school in Budapest. During his childhood and youth he was very religious and very proud of his race. As he approached manhood, however, he became temporarily diverted from his rabinnical preparations by finding that he had a predilection for unorthodox adventures, which, for the most part, involved the inmates of brothels. Believing that the calling of rabbi might restrict his enjoyment of these tendencies, he decided to become an actor. His father, however, was bitterly opposed to the idea, and the first serious rift appeared between them on account of it. This rift was not entirely healed though Lincoln did not pursue his project.

Throughout the extraordinary career of this man, the brilliance of his strange mind and his intellectual powers are always in evidence. He displayed the beginnings of these qualities as a student, especially in the facility with which he acquired a fluency in foreign languages. By the time he was seventeen, he was proficient in German and English, as well as being outstanding in his command of his native Hungarian.

In 1896, when he was seventeen, he left Hungary for the first time. It would seem that this visit abroad was inspired by police interest in his activities.

He came to England, where he arrived with very little money in his pocket, and was found in a common-lodging-house in the Jewish quarter of London, Whitechapel, by a Reverend Mr Epstein, a missioner of a society for promoting Christianity among the Jews. This society, the London Jews Society, offered to help him when he expressed a desire to be converted to Christianity, and he was sent to the Wanderer's Home at Park Place, Bristol. But his behaviour at the Home proved unsatisfactory, and he was returned to London.

Somewhat perturbed by this turn of events, and fearing that the Society might wash its hands of him, he approached the missioner of the Barbican Mission, the Reverend C. T. Lipshytz, and pleaded to be given another chance. At the end of six months, Lipshytz was still not satisfied with his progress and refused to allow him to be baptised.

Shortly after this, Lipshytz had to be absent from home for a few days, and during his absence Lincoln got into his rooms and stole his wife's watch and chain and various other articles of value. He had already stolen a passport belonging to a Jew called Neumann. With this passport he travelled on the Continent, where he committed various crimes before returning to England.

The police now became interested in him again, and he moved to Hamburg, where he studied theology and was baptised into the Methodist Church. Two years later he returned to London, and had the affrontery to approach Lipshytz and after telling him that he was a reformed character and had been baptised, asked for his forgiveness, clearly in the hope that Lipshytz would not inform the police of his return to England.

Lincoln now joined a Lutheran seminary, where he so impressed his teachers that they urged him to go to Canada as a missionary himself. Before this happened, however, there was a slight contretemps. It was discovered that he had seduced a sea-captain's daughter. When called before the principal of the seminary he did not deny it, but claimed that they were to be married. When this was conveyed to the girl's father, he took steps to see that Lincoln kept his word.

After their marriage, he was ordained into the Lutheran ministry, and with his wife set out for Canada. In Canada he had considerable success as a missionary, particularly in the timber mining camps. His addresses during the Halifax International Missionary Exhibition won him great fame, and he afterwards boasted, "I was the only foreign missioner invited by the Lieutenant-Governor to dine."

He now forsook the Lutheran Church and joined the

633

Anglican, and on Christmas Day 1902 he was ordained into the Anglican ministry by the Archbishop of Montreal. Three months later he was pleading strain of overwork. He resigned his living in Canada, and returned to England. After a brief visit to Hamburg, he applied to the Archbishop of Canterbury for a licence to officiate in England. This was granted him, and he was sent to a temporary curacy at the little Kentish village of Appledore. He did not stay there long. As one of the Appledore churchwardens put it, "Mr Trebitsch was too ambitious for Appledore. He was so clever and his mind so full of ideas, that this quiet little village irked him. He was all for being in Parliament and a Minister. I believe he had visions of being Prime Minister. He was clever enough, I'm sure."

In 1905 he resigned his curacy with the fixed intention of entering Parliament. From Kent he went to York, and became a teacher in a Quaker school there. Through this connection he made the acquaintance of Mr Seebohm Rowntree, of the cocoa family, a prominent Quaker and an equally prominent Liberal. Rowntree appointed him his private secretary and a special investigator for his sociological project.

He left Rowntree in August 1909, having announced that he was going to stand for Parliament at the next General Election. He had already been chosen, in the previous April, as prospective Radical candidate for Darlington, but how this came about is not clear. It would seem, however, that he had used money entrusted to him by Rowntree for the purpose.

In the autumn of 1909, he applied for naturalisation as a British subject, which was granted him. It was now that he added Lincoln to his name, and became known as Trebitsch-Lincoln, or simply Lincoln.

Perhaps to everyone's surprise but his own, Lincoln was successful, and returned to Parliament with a majority of 29. He made his maiden speech in the House of Commons on 23rd February, 1910.

Unfortunately for him, the 1910 Parliament was short-lived. Eleven months after entering the House, Lincoln found he was no longer a member. He was asked to stand again, but refused. Members of Parliament were unpaid in 1910, and though the following Parliament was to reintroduce payment for members, this had not been announced. It was on purely financial grounds that Lincoln surrendered his ambition of becoming Prime Minister.

Realising that only money can make money successfully, he borrowed from Rowntree, the London Joint Stock Bank and others, and plunged into European oil. Before long he was in dire financial straits, and he was adjudged a bankrupt.

It is asserted that it was at this time of his money troubles that he thought of becoming a spy. It was the time of the Balkan Wars of 1912 and 1913 and he offered his services as an agent to the Bulgarians. But seeing that he could increase his income by having more than one master, he also became an agent for the Turks, the enemies of the Balkan League.

He did not survive long in this role of double-agent, however, for Bulgarian intelligence quickly discovered what he was doing and arrested him and condemned him to prison. From this predicament his escape was engineered by Colonel Walter Nicolai, chief of the German Abwehr.

If this story is true, it puts a new complexion on his later activities. It is quite certain that Nicolai did not perform this service for him gratuitously. The price must have been Lincoln's agreement to become a German agent; and if he became a German agent, he was clearly acting in this capacity when he returned to England in August 1914, and offered his services to British intelligence.

The British refused his offer, and this seems to have been responsible for the beginning of his almost pathological hatred of the British, which he developed in later years. They did, however, offer him a job in the Hungarian Section of the Postal Censorship Department.

Colour is lent to the theory that Lincoln was, in fact, a German agent, by his next proposal. Shortly after he joined the Censorship he again proposed that he should become a British agent. To impress his application on the authorities, he sent with it a fantastic plan for luring part of the German fleet out into the North Sea, where it could be destroyed by the Royal Navy. The plan if accepted, would, however, have meant revealing to him the exact whereabouts of almost every unit of the British North Seas Fleet. So once again his offer was declined.

Mrs Lincoln, who was German, with their four sons, had come with him to England, and Lincoln was to insist later that it was her unhappiness caused by her ignorance of the fate of her mother, who was living in Hamburg, that eventually persuaded him to go to Rotterdam to try to find out from the German Consul there how his mother-in-law was faring. It was believed, however, that his real intention was to persuade his German masters to give him information which would convince the British of his usefulness as a spy. On 29th December, 1914, he had an interview at The Hague with Lieutenant-General von Ostertag, who had formerly been military attaché in London, and was now chief of the Abwehr in Holland.

On his return to London,

he again approached British intelligence, proudly announcing that while visiting the Germans in Holland, he had been able to acquire details of the code used by all German agents. Some say that he invented the code himself; others that it was a bogus code supplied by Ostertag.

Admiral Hall, director of Naval Intelligence, was so suspicious of Lincoln that he decided that the danger he constituted must be removed. It had recently been discovered that while in Rowntree's employ, he had forged Rowntree's signature to a draft. Rowntree was unwilling to take legal proceedings, but Admiral Hall had heard about the matter and called Lincoln to the Admiralty for an interview, during which he hinted that if Lincoln remained in London, he might find himself in the dock at the Central Criminal Court.

Lincoln took the hint. He left forty-eight hours later in a ship bound for the United States.

On his arrival in America, Lincoln had no doubt whatever that the newspapers would open their arms and their columns to a new journalist of his capabilities. The best way of attracting attention, he believed, was to produce a series of sensational articles. This he did, and in them released all his hatred of Britain in an attempt to prove that Germany was entirely innocent of all responsibility for the war. These articles were published, and brought him to the notice, not only of the general public, but to the enemies of the Entente Powers in America.

In fact, he was having such an affect on public opinion that the British began to regret that they had not kept him in England, under their surveillance. Since America was neutral, they could not apply for his extradition, even when British intelligence discovered that he was sending information to the Abwehr. But they were able to persuade Rowntree to press forgery charges against him.

Lincoln was arrested and an extradition order was made, but before he could be deported, he escaped from prison, and was at large for some weeks. Authority, however, caught up with him, and he was re-arrested. He was brought to England in 1916, tried at the Old Bailey for forgery and sentenced to three years' imprisonment.

By the time he had served his sentence, the war was over. On his release he left England, and all sight of him was lost. It was discovered later that after several adventures on the Continent he went to China. He had grand ideas of helping the Chinese to transform themselves into a first class military and naval power. The Chinese were not impressed, and Lincoln next turned up in Ceylon, using the name of Dr Leo Tandler, and apparently deeply interested in Buddhism.

While he was there, in 1926 one of his sons was sentenced to death in England for murder. Lincoln applied for permission to see his son before he was hanged. This was granted, but Lincoln arrived after the execution through running short of money in France.

He returned to the Far East, where he settled in Shanghai. Gathering about him three Buddhist monks and six Bhikshunis, or begging women, he declared himself to be Abbot Chao-kung.

The last to be heard of him was an announcement made

over the Japanese radio. It said that Abbot Chao-kung had died in Shanghai on 7th October, 1943, after an unsuccessful operation.

TREMBLAY, Father Joseph de see under **Richelieu, Cardinal.**

TREPPER, Leopold (Chief of Soviet network in Belgium, World War II).

Leopold Trepper was a Polish Jew of outstanding espionage experience when he was appointed Resident Director of the Soviet network in Belgium during World War II. He had a talent for making swift and correct judgments, was extremely daring, and prepared to act on his own initiative. He had escaped the Purge of 1937 by convincing Stalin of his loyalty, and the fact that he escaped the second Purge of intelligence agents in 1938, automatically ear-marked him for high rank later.

His second-in-command was Victor Sukulov, a Latvian by birth and a former Red Army officer, who sometimes assumed the cover-name of Edward Kent. Sukulov had originally been selected to organise a network in Denmark, but

while he was on his way to Copenhagen, war had broken out, and he was instructed instead to assist Trepper in Belgium.

The Belgian network was much more extensive in organisation and scope of operations than the Dutch. It worked from a villa in the Etterbeck suburb of Brussels, which was also inhabited, in part, by an elderly Belgian widow, who had no suspicion of her tenants' true role.

The Centre (q.v.) had intended to use the Belgian network only if war broke out between Russia and Germany, and except that it was ordered to infiltrate German agencies, like the Organisation Todt, it kept to this plan. When Hitler launched Barbarossa, the network swung immediately into action. By this time Trepper had so highly organised his network that in the first few days of the fighting on the Eastern Front it sent no fewer than five hundred messages to Moscow. The transmitting techniques of its operators were so good that German direction-finding equipment could not locate its posts. In addition, the codes used, defied all expert German codeographers' attempts to break them. Unfortunately for the network, their Russian masters demanded so much from them, that they were soon transmitting for five hours at a stretch. Consequently, German counter-espionage was able to find them.

On the night of 13th December, 1941, German troops, under the direction of the Abwehr, raided the villa. They found the transmitters, a number of false documents, supplies of invisible ink, and Mikhail Makarov, Sophie Pozanska and Rita Arnould.

During the raid Trepper arrived at the villa, but was able to convince the Germans that he was an itinerant rabbit-seller, and they let him go. Sukulov also escaped by being elsewhere.

Pozanska was able to take her cyanide tablet before the Germans realised what she was doing. Makarov died under torture without having betrayed anything. Rita Arnould, however, not only told all she knew, but voluntarily gave the Germans a photograph of Trepper. When her usefulness was ended, she was beheaded.

Trepper, known as the Grand Chef, and Sukulov, known as the Petit Chef, escaped to Unoccupied France, from where, with the help of Johann Wenzel (q.v.) as their operator, they continued to work. A little later Trepper was appointed Resident Director for France, where two or three networks were operating independently of each other, each in direct contact with The Centre. He welded them into a single organisation, and of all the Russian networks operating in Western Europe, with the possible exception of The Red Orchestra (q.v.) the French organisation was the most outstanding.

The greatest threat to the French network came from the members of the Belgian network who had decided to co-operate. In October 1942 the Abwehr officers who had been responsible for catching the Brussels agents arrived in Paris, bringing with them some of these collaborators. Within a short time of their arrival, a couple of score of Soviet agents had been seized.

Their chief objective was naturally Trepper, but they did not know where he was living. Several attempts to draw him out failed, but finally one of his agents betrayed his cover-organisation, the trading company Simex. Trepper was able to go underground, however, but he eventually fell into German hands through his own carelessness.

In a diary which he had left on his desk in his Simex office, the Germans found an entry noting an appointment with his dentist, and he was arrested in the dentist's chair on 16th November, 1942. At first he refused to talk, but when he learned that if he did not he would be handed over to the Gestapo to undergo their particular methods of persuasion, he co-operated one hundred per cent. As a result most of the networks were destroyed.

The Petit Chef, Victor Sukulov, however, established a network in Marseilles, which worked successfully for a couple of months, until it, too, was discovered.

Trepper collaborated with the Germans in the "radio game" for several months, and as a result of his activities, the French Communist Resistance one of the most powerful and active groups in France, was rendered largely ineffectual.

Permitted to live in a private house, Trepper managed to

escape from his guards in June 1943, and was never seen again by the Germans. Recalled to Moscow at the end of the war, obediently he went, though he must have known that his fate would be death.

The Petit Chef, Victor Sukulov, was arrested some time after Trepper. On being arrested he flatly refused to say a word. No threats nor tortures would move him. He asked to be executed. Then one day he was confronted with a friend, Margarete Barcza. On seeing her he seemed to go quite mad. He rushed to her and embraced her, then, turning to the Gestapo officer with them, said that he would tell all if Barcza were set free.

Within a few weeks both were back in Marseilles, playing the radio game for the Germans. He even offered to try to make contact with Alexander Foote's network (q.v.) operating in Switzerland. He failed because the Englishman was too wary for him.

Foote reported what had happened to The Centre, and that was the end of Sukulov's usefulness to the Germans. He was fortunate, however; they did not liquidate him, and when France was liberated, he retreated into Germany with the Werhmacht, while Barcza set up home in Brussels. There he visited her secretly from time to time, living underground to escape both Russian and Allied attentions. Shortly after the war he went to the Balkans, and there disappeared. SMERSH had caught up with him at last.

BIBLIOGRAPHY:

Forty Years of Soviet Spying — Ronald Seth (London, 1965).

Unmasked — Ronald Seth (New York, 1965).

TRIANGULATION.

Triangulation is a technique used to pinpoint secret radio transmitters. A rough description is as follows: Three radio receivers situated in different areas so that they represent the angles of a triangle have revolving antennae which enable them to take bearings on a radio signal transmitted within their triangle. The courses of the bearings are plotted on a map, and where they intersect indicates the general area of the secret radio. A special van equipped with sensitive instruments is sent to the area, and drives around the streets until it receives its loudest signal from the transmitter. This can be so accurate that the house in which the secret transmitter is operating can be indicated.

The Germans developed the technique during World War II in their efforts to discover the secret radio transmitters of the various Resistance movements in their occupied territories. The Russians are now believed to have developed the technique to its ultimate refinement.

TRUTH DRUGS.

The term 'truth drug' seems to be a layman's term for something not recognised by doctors. It is likely that certain anaesthetics used in a controlled way could be used to reduce resistance, but it is difficult to define this further. We have found three 'truth' drugs listed as 'truth sera' used in psychological investigation of a therapeutic or criminological nature. The doctors with whom we discussed this were of the opinion that a drug is only able to make a subject confess what he **wants** to confess. It would be unlikely to overcome a **determination** not to reveal certain facts. It is known history that the views of these doctors have at times been proved wrong.

Scopolamine (hyoscine)

This is one of the Belladonna alkaloids and can be obtained from Deadly Nightshade, Henbane and Jimson Weed. It is the most active of these alkaloids because of its greater solubility. It has a depressant action on parasympathetic nerves and in larger doses on autonomic ganglia; that is to say, it not only affects the central nervous system, but also those nerves which normally act independently and keep essential functions such as the heart, bowel and bladder actions going. For this reason it is a very risky drug to use except in very controlled circumstances as well as being highly toxic. When combined with morphine, it produces 'twilight sleep' in which the patient remains more or less conscious but is usually unable to recall the unpleasant circumstances of the event. It became popular for use during childbirth.

Sodium Thiopental (Pentathal).

A short-acting barbiturate used mainly in anaesthesia. It is administered intravenously, and must be given in very carefully controlled doses. It

is very difficult to obtain the level of consciousness where a patient becomes susceptible to interrogation as when it is administered intravenously it usually knocks one out straight away.

Amobarbital

Another barbiturate with slightly longer lasting effects.

Another technique is narco-analysis. This is a method of psychological investigation conducted by a trained interrogator, in which the conscious or unconscious unwillingness of a subject to confess memories or feelings is diminished by the use of a drug that induces a semi-somnolent state.

During World War II the German Abwehr (q.v.) counter-espionage units made wide use of scopolomine. The Communist counter-espionage organisations are also believed to be making extensive use of both truth-drugs and narco-analysis. If this is so, then it may be assumed that the democratic counter-espionage organisations are using them also.

TSUBOTA, Dr (Japanese agent, Dutch East Indies, mid-30s).

When the Japanese were

preparing their assault on the Pacific and Asia, they launched a massive espionage operation throughout the Far East in 1936. In the Dutch East Indies they introduced some innovations in the field of espionage, which made their efforts there not only entirely successful, but noteworthy in spying history.

One of these innovations was the use of trained medical men as spies. These men were specially prepared officers of the Japanese Army Medical Corps. Working as labourers, waiters and clerks, both in their work, and particularly in their leisure, they set themselves to study the sanitation and general health conditions of the islands, so that when the Japanese armies arrived they would know exactly what must be done to prevent the outbreak of epidemics.

The moving force in this operation was a certain Dr Tsubota. It was he who invented another innovation — what he proudly called his "male Mata Haris".

As the time drew near for the invasion of the Indies it became more and more imperative for the Japanese to know the Dutch military plans.

But when the Japanese, after the start of the China war, in their great need for raw materials began to demand them arrogantly from the Indies, the Dutch unaccountably stiffened in their resistance to bullying. Security was tgihtened, and a new awareness of what was happening produced a serious threat to Japanese espionage.

Dutch officers and men no longer patronised the Japanese hotels. Even the prostitute-spies in the ordinary brothels suddenly found their clients to be extremely ignorant all of a sudden.

It was at this time that Dr Tsubota conceived his novel idea. .

Large numbers of the clerks in the employment of the Dutch Military Administration were Javanese. Always intelligent, often high-born, a high proportion of them were homosexuals. In those days there was a far greater distinction between the East and the West's views on homosexuality. Regarded with repugnance in the West, it was quite acceptable in the East.

These Javanese clerks, in whom the Dutch had great confidence, by the very nature of their work were clearly in possession of many of those secrets the Japanese wished to learn. Dr Tsubota, therefore imported and trained a number of the most handsome homosexuals he could find and set them to seduce the Javanese clerks.

Though Tsubota's scheme might seem far-fetched to occidental minds, judging by the bulk of the intelligence which the Japanese possessed when they landed in the East Indies, it was an undoubted success.

TSOU Ta-peng (Chinese Communist intelligence chief).

An intelligence agent of long-standing, Tsou Ta-peng is certainly the most powerful man in Chinese intelligence after K'ang Sheng (q.v.). During the Sino-Japanese War he served in the Department of Social Affairs under K'ang Sheng. Later, after carrying out several intelligence assign-

ments, he became Director of the Information Administration Bureau and also of the Liaison Department of the People's Revolutionary Military Council.

In March 1958 he was appointed vice-chairman of the newly formed Commission for Cultural Relations with Foreign Countries — in reality an espionage organisation, and in 1961, he became vice-chairman of the People's Association for Cultural Relations with Foreign Countries, an allegedly non-official organisation. From these points of vantage he controlled the executive of all the intelligence agencies, his responsibility being that of seeing that the espionage plans of the government, Party and People's organisations were carried out.

TURNTINE, Willard James see under **Thompson, Harry Thomas.**

UBBINK (Dutch agent, World War II) see under **Giskes, Col H. J.**

VANDENBURG AFB.

The headquarters of NSA (q.v.) headquarters on the west coast, from where SAMOS spy satellites are launched to be put into orbit over the USSR.

VANDERWYNCKT (French agent, World War II) see under **Khan, Noor Inayat.**

VAN HEMERT see under **Giskes, Col H. J.**

VANHOUTTE, Marie-Louise (Allied agent, World War I) see under **Dubois, Alice.**

VASSALL, John (British traitor, post-world War II).

John Vassall was the son of a Church of England clergyman. After leaving school at the age of sixteen, he spent a short time in a bank, but finding this occupation wearisome, he applied to the Civil Service, and was accepted as a temporary Grade III clerk in the Admiralty. He returned to the Admiralty after having served in the Royal Air Force as a photographer from 1943

until he was demobilised late in 1946. At the beginning of 1948 he was taken on to the permanent establishment as a clerical officer.

He was not an outstanding clerical officer, and, in fact, he missed promotion again and again throughout his career. It is a curious revelation that a man of such junior rank could have access to some of the most important State secrets, yet this is what happened to him when, in 1953, he was posted to the British embassy in Moscow as a Writer in the office of the naval attaché.

Vassall had one characteristic which should have precluded him from being sent to Moscow at all. He was a homosexual, and though a man may not go about advertising the fact that he is a deviate from the sexual norm, Vassall was the type of homosexual whom experienced men of the world could and ought to have recognised.

Because of this difference, Vassall found life in Moscow lonely, and because he was lonely and a homosexual, he was just the sort of man Soviet espionage was always looking for. When they found him, they played upon his loneliness, invited him to parties, encouraged him in the practice of his deviation, and then took photographs of him in compromising sexual embraces. With these photographs they blackmailed him, by threats of exposure, into spying for them.

That is his story, and there is no reason to disbelieve it, for it is a classic Soviet espionage manoeuvre. Nevertheless, The Centre had judged him perfectly, for they were sure they took no risk in behaving as they did, since they were certain that he was not the type who would expose their blackmailing attempts. They had known about his homosexuality before he arrived in Moscow, even if the British security service did not, and they also knew that he was a weak, vain man, who tried to compensate for what he lacked in life by trying to move in superior social circles. His efforts in this direction cost much more than his weekly £15 a week salary, and The Centre promised him good financial rewards provided he produced the right information.

By September 1955 he had begun to operate. He removed secret documents from the naval attache's office, slipped out of the embassy, handed them to a Soviet contact, who photographed them immediately and returned them to Vassall who put them back in the files before they were missed.

This went on for ten months, until he was posted back to London in July 1956. This move might have put an end to his usefulness to The Centre had he not been posted to the Naval Intelligence Division in the Admiralty, which gave him access to even more important information than he had been able to obtain hitherto.

His job with NID lasted a year, and was followed by a period when he was not so useful. But once more The Centre's luck was in, for he was put in the private office of the Civil Lord, where he was required to act as a kind of wet-nurse to his chief.

The Centre had kept their promise as far as rewards went, and the £15-a-week clerk was able to live in Dolphin Square, one of the most exclusive and expensive areas in London. There he furnished his small apartment with expensive antiques.

British Security was extremely lax throughout the

whole of the time that Vassall worked for the Admiralty. It apparently had not known that he was a homosexual when they had passed him; now they did not discover the comparative opulence in which he lived. Some of his colleagues knew about the apartment and the kind of genteel grace with which he conducted his life, but knowing his background, his hints that he had received one or two small legacies from dear old ladies they regarded as a satisfactory explanation.

After two and a half years of tending to the Civil Lord's creature comforts, in October 1959 Vassall was moved again, and this time to a department which made him much more valuable than he had ever been. As a clerk in the secretariat of the Naval Staff there passed through his hands information concerning radar, torpedo and anti-submarine and gunnery trials, Allied tactical and exercise publications, communications, Fleet operational orders and tactical instructions and so on.

With the exception that he now photographed the documents himself, for which he had been equipped by the

RAF, he carried out the espionage procedures which had been explained to him in Moscow, and his observance of security was so good that, except for a year when he ceased his activities after the Portland Case (q.v.) on The Centre's instructions, he was still carrying out the routine when he was arrested in September 1962.

For more than six years he had been successfully passing secrets to Moscow before suspicion began to light on him. And it might not have lighten on him then had not the Blake case called for the setting up of yet another Committee of investigation, the Radcliffe Committee, to inquire into the organisation and working of all the security departments. As a result of the Radcliffe findings and the suggestions made for the better working of the security departments, the staff of Admiralty security did review its personnel, Vassall's background was noted, he was placed under surveillance and discovered.

There was no point in his attempting to deny what he had been doing, for in his apartment, when it was searched were found seventeen Admiralty documents, and his photographic equipment. He talked about all he knew. At his trial at the Old Bailey he was sentenced to eighteen years imprisonment.

BIBLIOGRAPHY:

The Vassall Affair — Dame Rebecca West (London, 1963).

VENGLER, Joseph (Luxembourg Resistance leader, World War II).

Joseph Vengler was a young scoutmaster, who, with two artisans, founded the **Corps Front Luxembourgeois,** the second Resistance organisation to be set up in the Grand Duchy. Untrained in any kind of clandestine activity, the CFL was soon put out of action by the Germans. Claud and Siedler were beheaded, but on account of his youth, Vengler was sentenced to perpetual imprisonment.

He was sent to Sieburg prison, where, with other prisoners, he was set to work making shells. A natural leader, it was not long before he had organised in the prison a group to which he gave the name of **Kodak,** whose members, he estimated, made no

less than 125,000 dud shells every month.

Later Vengler persuaded the prison commandant to make him his secretary. In this position he was able to falsify the ration accounts, order more food, and improve the meagre diet of his fellow-prisoners. He also had access to the card-index of prisoners, and by destroying some of the cards and altering others, he was able to save many — the figure is put at 200 — from the more notorius concentration camps and from death in the gas chambers.

In February 1945, he organised the escape of twenty-one prisoners, including two German officers who had been arrested after the 20th July Plot. They hid up in the woods near the prison, and every day Vengler risked his life to take them food until the Allies arrived the following month.

He survived the war, and is remembered as one of the heroes of Luxembourg Resistance.

VfK (Military Intelligence).

Apart from the Ministry of State Security which has to guarantee security within its own sphere of control and, together with Chief Administration Reconnaissance mainly collect information about leading political and military offices in Western Europe the DDR (German Democratic Republic) has a Military Intelligence Service at its disposal. This is part of the Administration for Co-ordination. Through Agents operating in West Germany and Western Europe, this Administration's task is mainly to secure information concerning military matters in general, military policy and armaments.

Since 1st September, 1957, the head of this organisation has been Colonel Willi Sagebrecht. His Predecessor was the former Major-General Karl Linke who was dismissed from his post at the end of July 1957.

The Administration for Co-ordination is organised in three main departments — 'A', 'C', and 'T', covering evaluation, technical matters and administration respectively. Some 400 officers, NCO's and men belonging to the VfK form the main directing staff.

The VfK works closely with the 'Independent Department' of the 'Political Administration' of the 'National People's Army'.

The Soviets have seconded numerous liaison officers (up to 1959 these were called 'advisors') to both the Soviet Zone's Secret Services, through whom they are able to exercise a dominating influence over their activities.

BIBLIOGRAPHY:

East Berlin Main Centre of Agitation and Sedition (West German Embassy, London, 1962).

VOGELER, Wilhelm see under **Wenzel, Johann.**

VOLF, Colonel (Czech agent post World War II) see under **Rössler, Rudolf.**

VOUKELEVITCH, Branko de (Russian agent, pre-World War II) see under **Sorge, Richard.**

WALLIS, Dr John (English agent, 17th century) see under **Thurloe, John.**

WALSINGHAM, Sir Francis (Director of intelligence to Elizabeth I).

Francis Walsingham came of a strongly Protestant family. He studied law, intending to make it his career, but because of his Protestant background, when Mary Tudor came to the throne, for safety's sake he moved to the Continent, and remained there until the danger was past. He was slim, dark and handsome to the point where he might have been taken for an Italian, and there is reason to believe that he used his good looks and charm during his voluntary exile to make useful contacts in France and Italy, from whom he learned the art of intrigue.

On Elizabeth I's accession, he returned home, and because of his experience of foreign parts he came to the notice of Lord Burghley, the Secretary of State, who engaged him to return to Europe as a secret agent to discover what the French king might be plotting, with the help of the Jesuits, against the queen. Burghley had already established the nucleus of a secret service to keep track of Catholic plots at home, and when Walsingham proved himself a most competent agent in his foreign missions, Burghley recalled him and made him chief of this secret service.

This was in 1569. He was not to remain in this post long. However, for in 1570 the activities of the French king were such that Burghley decided that he must have in Paris a man well versed in secret affairs, and dispatched Walsingham to be ambassador at the French Court, where he assumed direct control of all British agents working in France. He remained ambassador in France until 1573, when he was appointed to succeed Burghley as Secretary of State, on the latter's promotion to Lord High Treasurer. As Secretary of State Walsingham resumed active control of the secret service.

Walsingham's measures to thwart the Catholic plotters at home and abroad have been described elsewhere **(see under**

Marlowe, Christopher), and there is no doubt that it was entirely due to his secret vigilance that no plot to assassinate Elizabeth ever came to fruition. Had his reputation rested on this alone he would have held his place as one of the outstanding British directors of intelligence. That place, however, was doubly assured by his espionage work in connection with the Spanish Armada in 1588.

In the mid-sixteenth century Philip II of Spain believed that he had been given the divine mission of restoring all erring Protestants to the Roman Catholic fold, and he was of the opinion that if he could achieve this with England, he would find it easier to subdue the rest of Protestant Europe. He tried, first of all, to gain control of England by suggesting marriage to his late wife's sister, Elizabeth I, but when she returned him an unequivocal refusal, he said that he would have to resort to military conquest, and put preparations in hand to this end.

It was not long before the news of the Spanish intentions reached England, and Walsingham decided that he must have a network of agents to keep

652

him informed of Philip's progress in his preparations. He already had in his employ two young men and one of these named Antony Standen, he sent into the field with **carte blanche** to discover what Philip was doing. How Standen was to operate was entirely up to him, but he must produce results.

Throughout the intervening centuries, Standen's genius had not been diminished by the brilliance of later agents. Instead of making for Spain, he set out for Tuscany, using the cover name of Pompeo Pellegrini. This was not his first visit to Tuscany; he had made a stay of some years there before entering Walsingham's service. He was on good terms with the most important members of the Tuscan government, and particularly with Giuseppe Figliazzi, the Tuscan ambassador designate to Spain.

Elizabeth Tudor had inherited all the parsimonious traits of her grandfather, Henry VII, and, in addition, seemed incapable of appreciating the value of secret service. That is the kind interpretation. Another, and much more likely explanation, was her penchant for letting other people pay, if they could be persuaded to do so. At all events, she refused to allocate sufficient funds to Walsingham to support his organisation. The Secretary of State, however, had made good use of his office and had quickly amassed a huge private fortune. Despite all her less likable traits, Walsingham had a genuine love for the Queen, and she had no more loyal a subject. Add to this Walsingham's hatred of the Roman Catholic Church, and you have the true motive for his action in financing English secret service out of his private purse. This idiosyncracy was to ruin him ultimately; when he died in 1590, he had not only spent his vast fortune, but was many thousands of pounds in debt.

Walsingham paid his agents the generous sum of £100 a year, roughly the equivalent of £3,000. Standen's expenses were so heavy however, that when he wished to engage a Fleming to undertake work in Spain, he had to borrow a hundred crowns in order to pay the man.

This Fleming, whose name is not recorded, was a real discovery. One of his brothers was working for no less a person than the Marquis of Santa Cruz, whom Philip had appointed Grand Admiral of the Armada that was to conquer England. The hundred crowns proved an excellent investment, for late in 1586 the Fleming sent to Standen exact copies of the Grand Admiral's progress reports to his kind, giving the numbers of vessels he could then command, their crews and armed forces, their stores, ammunition and armour.

Communications in those days were as hazardous as they were slow. But Standen had dispatched the Fleming to Spain in the train of embassador Figliazzi. On the journey the Fleming made friends with the officer responsible for seeing that the diplomatic bag from Madrid to Florence arrived safely at its destination, and with judicious financial encouragement, the Fleming persuaded the officer to include a private letter to Signor Pompeo Pellegrini in the official mailbag.

Though the Fleming was Standen's chief agent, he was not the only informant Standen had in Spain. Wherever preparations for the Armada were under way, he planted an agent. On the basis of the report from the Fleming and these agents, and from information which he had acquired on the Rialto and in Genoa, where Philip was trying to raise loans, and other centres of Spanish activity, Standen was able to inform Walsingham that in his opinion the Armada could not sail in 1587. Acting on disclosures of where various units of the Spanish fleet were stationed, Sir Francis Drake sailed to "singe the King of Spain's beard".

These forays of Drake's and other difficulties into which the Armada planners ran could not, in the face of Philip's grim determination to conquer England, delay his expedition indefinitely. Standen appreciated this, and against the day when the Spanish galleons would sail, he organised along the French Atlantic coast a network of agents whose task, was to keep track of the Armada's progress towards England, once it was on its way. As soon as an agent sighted the Spanish fleet, he rode posthaste for the nearest Channel port, crossed to England, and presented the information to Walsingham. This

was made possible by the fact that the Spanish galleons were slow and unwieldy ships in any case, and contrary winds on this journey necessitated their having to tack a good deal, which added to the slowness of their progress, and allowed them to be outstripped by fast horsemen. Thus, from within a day or two of the Armada's setting sail, the English commanders were provided with thoroughly reliable information of the Duke of Medina Sidonia's progress towards England. (The Duke had succeeded Santa Cruz on the latter's death in 1587.)

The lookouts on Plymouth Hoe were not there in the hope of catching sight of the Armada, but were acting on the certainty that they would, for so successful had been Standen's organisation that the Armada hove in sight almost to the minute he had estimated it would.

When Drake and Frobisher, Hawkins and Grand Admiral Lord Howard of Effingham sailed out of the south coast ports to harry the galleons of Spain, they knew the exact potential of their giant adversaries. They had worked out beforehand the tactics they would employ, and they knew exactly how close in to the galleons they must sail, both to put themselves out of range of the Spanish guns — with whose poor angle of depression Standen had acquainted them — and to make their own fire, under these conditions, most effective.

"God blew with His winds and they were scattered" was the motto on the comemorative medal which Elizabeth ordered to be struck. While it is true that violent storms administered the **coup de gràce** to Medina Sidonia, it is equally true that it was the efforts of the English fleet which prevented the Spanish Armada from reaching the Thames, and Lord Howard's success sprang directly from Standen's intelligence.

Walsingham had a penchant for engaging men of letters and kindred professions as agents. Besides Marlowe, who as a dramatist, some say, would have rivalled Shakespeare had he lived, there was the Scots poet William Fowler, the playwright and actor Anthony Munday, the author Matthew Royston, and possibly though there is no definite proof, Ben Jonson.

Walsingham is among a very small band of directors of intelligence who did not use his secret service to further his own private ends.

BIBLIOGRAPHY:

Mr Secretary Walsingham and the Policy of Queen Elizabeth — Conyers Read (London, 1925).

WALTERS, Anne-Marie (British agent, World War II).

When war broke out in September 1939, Anne-Marie Walters was a school-girl of fifteen. Before the Germans had surrendered in May, 1945, she had taken a short-cut to womanhood by serving as a courier with the French Resistance in Guyenne and Gascony for almost a year.

Anne-Marie's father was English, her mother French. She had been educated and brought up on the Continent, and though completely fluent in both English and French, she belonged more to her mother's people than to her father's.

In the summer of 1943 she came into contact with the French Section of SOE (q.v.). The French Section was unsatiable; it swallowed up its agents at an incredible rate and in incredible numbers; it could never, it seemed, get enough. That was one of the reasons why it recruited women and young girls. That was why, after giving her a brief language test and extracting from her an assurance that she was willing to "leave England," it recruited Anne-Marie despite the fact that she was only just nineteen.

Throughout the summer months of 1943, Anne-Marie trained. By the end of October her training was finished and she was scheduled to drop into France during the November moon-period. She was not to drop alone, but was to be accompanied by a young medical student of twenty, called Jean-Claude Arnault. Both of them were to operate with groups directed by Lieutenant-Colonel George Starr, known as the Patron, whose personal courier and liaison officer Anne-Marie was to be. Their "Field" was to be that part of southwestern France composed roughly of the Departments of the Dordogne, Lot-et-Garonne, Gers, Haute-Garonne and Haute-Pyrénées.

Because of the weather throughout the whole of the November moon-period it was

impossible for the two agents to be dropped. Not until 16th December were they told at last to stand by. Even on this occasion fog prevented their operation from being completed, and on the return to England their aircraft had to crash land, killing four of the crew.

The two young people asked to be sent the following night, thinking that their nerve might crack if they had to wait much longer; but they were so bruised and shaken that the doctors said they must rest. But at last, on 3rd January, 1944, they were eventually dropped into Gascony.

She began her courier duties immediately, and successfully performed them until the network with which she was working was compromised, and in August 1944 she made her escape into Spain over the Pyrenees. She had many narrow escapes, but exhibited a tremendous quickness of reaction which extracted her from many a tight corner. Such contretemps were not of her making but reading of them one is impressed by the fact that not only is the courier's task an exacting one, but dangerous to a degree, one calling for the highest courage.

The account of her experiences, **Moondrop to Gascony,** written with a quiet calm and complete absence of sensationalistic highlights, reveals as no other work of the **genre** does, the intricacies of the "courier's art".

For her services, Anne-Marie was awarded the MBE.

BIBLIOGRAPHY:

Moondrop to Gascony — Anne-Marie Walters (London, 1946).

SOE in France — M. R. Foot (London, 1966).

WANG Wei-chen (Chinese agent in Brazil).

Under cover of correspondent of the New China News Agency in Brazil, Wang Wei-chen operated as an espionage agent. When President João Goulart was overthrown by a military junta in 1964, the junta arrested Wang and eight other Chinese, and accused them of espionage and subversion. All were sentenced to ten years' imprisonment by a court-martial, but were deported in 1965.

WASSMUSS, Consul (Espionage activities in Persia, World War I).

When World War I broke out in August 1914, the situation in Persia was already somewhat confused, for a struggle had commenced between the Germans and the British for the glittering prize of Persian oil concessions. In this struggle the German Consul in Persia, Wassmuss, was playing an important role, and when other German officials accepted their passports on the opening of hostilities, and made for home, he decided to stay behind.

He had a genius akin to that of Colonel T. E. Lawrence. He spoke several Arabic dialects, and he understood the Arab mentality in all its tortuous circumvolutions. He had also selected for his chief weapon one which the Middle Eastern mind appreciated — gold. On the Kaiser's personal instructions, his supplies of this commodity were almost limitless.

Previously, by international agreement, Persia had been protected by a neutral force. This force was composed entirely of Swedes, and the British were not long in discovering that with his gold Wassmuss had contrived to get them all in his pocket. Without any sententious moralising — for Great Britain was a first-class power in those days — the British at once sent an expeditionary force to take over. It was this force that Wassmuss now had to elude.

This he managed to do, taking with him a fortune amounting to 140,000 gold marks. In the safety of the hills, where his previous dispensations had made him powerful friends among the local chieftains, he cast off the role of fugitive and began to work to achieve his ambition, which was to control all German political propaganda along the Persian Gulf, keep southern Persia subservient to German influences, hamper the British oil transactions, and keep the hill tribes in such a state of ferment that every move the British forces made would be met everywhere with armed Persian hostility, thus tying down valuable troops which might have been used more profitably in Europe.

The bulk of this he achieved with gold. But he proved his genius, if proof were needed —

for very soon the British were marking him down as being worth two army corps — by marrying the daughter of one of the most powerful chiefs, a gesture which, he proclaimed, symbolised the alliance of Germany and Persia.

The ceremony was the most splendid that could be arranged, and many years later it was still referred to with awe in those parts. Wassmuss's secret service funds defrayed all expenses. Everyone of note in southern Persia was invited, and besides, a vast throng of farmers and fishermen, shepherds and peasants. The money was well spent, for the subsequent dividends were enormous. In addition, to a large army of spies recruited that day, the impression made on rich and poor alike was deep — a man who could affort to spend so much money on his wedding feast must belong to a rich and powerful nation, on whose side it would be wise to be.

Thereafter, whatever Wassmuss wanted he got, and he was generous. The tribes found it worth their while to harry the British with increasing energy. His influence stretched as far afield as Afghanistan, where he vigorously promoted a native uprising. The British were so perturbed by his success that they offered a £3,000 reward for his capture, dead or alive, which they subsequently raised to two lakhs of rupees, £14,000.

Presently, he was stretched to the limit, and because of Allied activities, fresh funds could not reach him, and he had to retrench. But he kept the Persians still on his side by a campaign of propaganda, skilfully handled, and the most fantastic lies.

The battle of the Somme caused public opinion in Persia to waver; he held it firm by announcing that German armies had invaded England and that King George V had been publicly executed. But though such lies might succeed for the time being, eventually the truth had to become known, and unfortunately it did become known at the moment that America entered the war.

Angry at being deceived, his former gold-digging friends turned on him. Soon he was being besieged by furious "creditors", all demanding that he should honour forthwith the paper promises he had made to them when his gold had run out. Somehow he managed to hold them off, and to protect himself. Not until the Armistice was signed did he slip secretly away.

BIBLIOGRAPHY:

The **Crater of Mars** — F. Tuohy (London, undated).

WEBSTER, Timothy (Northern agent, American Civil War).

(For Webster's role in the Baltimore conspiracy, see under **Pinkerton, Allan**).

After Lincoln's Inauguration, the simmering embers of the Civil War burst into flames. The capital was cut off, as some had believed it would be, by the cutting of rail and telegraph communications; and everywhere Southern spies swarmed about, because the North had no counter-espionage organisation to deal with them.

Pinkerton's agent, Timothy Webster, was the first to break the blockade. He arrived in Washington with letters from the President's friends sewn into his waistcoat by Mrs Warne of Chicago. These he delivered with such promptness together with a quantity of information about secessionist activities which he had gathered on the way, that Lincoln sent him back to Chicago with an invitation to his chief to visit the Federal capital.

Pinkerton accepted the invitation, and on arrival discussed the intelligence arrangements which he held to be essential if the South was to be prevented from knowing beforehand what the North's military intentions were. Three months later a certain Major Allen reported to the staff of General McClellan. Nothing was known about him and his duties seemed vague to his fellow officers.

The early victories of the Southern armies were due almost entirely to espionage information which their agents ran no risk in gathering. At least, they had run no risk until the arrival of Major Allen at McClellan's headquarters.

Major Allen, who was, of course, Pinkerton, made his headquarters in a house on 1st Street, Washington, and from there he organised his espionage as well as Counter-espionage activities. Unfortunately he had not enough trained agents to meet all the demands made upon his organisation and had

to rely on untrained, inexperienced men who at the outset were more of a liability than an asset. There is a great deal of difference between the ordinary work of a detective and the work of a spy. Superb investigator though he was, Pinkerton was not himself equipped with the necessary knowledge and experience for a spy-master. So there were days of fumbling and failure, of groping and experiment.

Pinkerton's star was undoubtedly Timothy Webster. This detective under the new conditions imposed by the nature of his new work, was soon shown to be a natural agent, brilliant in the execution of military intelligence requirements. There are some who hold, that in the light of what happened to Webster, Pinkerton was at fault in thrusting so much on such an outstanding spy.

Webster now went into Maryland and Virginia, and it was not long before he was deeply in the confidence of the secessionists of those States. Whatever information he gathered he reported to Pinkerton in person, a risk which neither he nor his chief should have accepted or countenanced.

On one such visit to Pinkerton, Webster was indeed arrested by another Northern agent in Baltimore. Pinkerton went to question him, and arranged for him to escape from his guards while being taken to Fort McHenry for internment as a suspected Southern agent.

Though this incident was fortuitous, it greatly enhanced Webster's reputation with his Southern contacts, and when he returned to Richmond, Virginia, the Southern capital, he was received everywhere and in a very short time was cognisant with the plans of the Southern blockade runners, which he passed to Washington.

Webster's outstanding achievement was the safe conduct he acquired from the Southern Secretary of War which permitted him to make a tour with a government contractor with whom he visited an extensive part of Southern territory, noting all the warlike activities which he saw on the way. But his own unceasing activities were now beginning to take their toll of him physically.

About this time General McClellan was preparing for his attack on the Yorktown peninsula, the object of which was to capture Richmond, with the hope of putting the end to the war. So Richmond was now the focus of Pinkerton's attention.

Webster was sent there with another agent, a Mrs Lawton, to find out exactly as possible the strength of the garrison and reserves held there. He had not been there long when suddenly all communications from him stopped.

Not knowing what to do, Pinkerton was persuaded to send two agents called Lewis and Scully to find out what had happened. They found Webster in a Richmond hotel completely incapacitated by rheumatism, and unable to move from his bed. But Southern agents had already marked down the two men, and before they could make any attempt to escape, they were arrested. Finally when it came to a choice of talking or hanging, they broke down and confessed, and in so doing betrayed Webster.

Webster was arrested, brought to trial and on the evidence of the two agents condemned to death. Attempts were made to secure his reprieve, but these were so ineffective that no stay of execution was granted. So the North lost one of its outstanding sources of intelligence, and Pinkerton lost an agent whom he might have preserved had he realised the burden which he had loaded on to the man, and attempted to mitigate it.

BIBLIOGRAPHY:

The Spy of the Rebellion — Allan Pinkerton (New York, 1877).

WEIGELS, Otto (German agent, World War I) see under Ernst, Karl.

WEINBERG, Joseph see under Soviet American Network.

WEISENBORN, Gunther (German agent, World War II) see under Red Orchestra, The.

WENNERSTROM, Colonel Stig (Swedish traitor, spied for Russia 1948 to 1963).

Stig Wennerström was born in 1906, the son of an army captain. At the age of twenty he decided on a career as a military flier. In 1929 he entered the Swedish Navy as a cadet, and in 1930 applied for flying training. His appli-

cation was approved, and pending his transfer he was posted to the naval base at Karlskrona.

During the waiting months, having a fair amount of free time on his hands, Wennerström enrolled in various language courses. He already spoke German with a certain fluency, which he now worked to improve, but he concentrated on Russian, at which he was very successful.

In 1931 he went to the flying school, and when he had completed the course, he served for three years as a pilot in the Air Force, though he was still a naval officer. Towards the end of 1933 he applied for a scholarship offered by the Swedish Ministry of Defence for language study abroad. On being awarded it, he went to Riga and there lived with a Russian family, while attached to the Swedish legation there.

On his return from Latvia (very proficient in Russian) he was formally transferred from the navy to the air force, and when the Second World War broke out he had attained the rank of captain. In 1940 the Swedish government decided to assign an air attaché to the Moscow embassy for the first time, and because of his language qualification, Wennerström was selected for the post.

It was now that he began to dabble in mild forms of espionage.

As he had grown up he had developed into a somewhat strange individual. He was not an out-giving person, which made it difficult for one to get to know him, and his approach to his work was pedantic in the extreme. He certainly overestimated his abilities.

In his post as attaché, he naturally came into contact with his opposite numbers at the various embassies, and since he represented a neutral power, among these contacts were both the German and Allied attachés. There is always a certain amount of exchange of information between various missions, and when Wennerström was approached by the Germans for help — this was before the outbreak of the Russian-German war — he complied in so far as he could.

In March 1941, Wennerström was recalled to Sweden and assigned to the Defence Staff as an air intelligence officer, though he continued to be accredited to the Soviet government, a fact which resulted in his name being included in the diplomatic invitation list. He retained his contact with the Germans, but now made closer contact with the Russians, becoming well acquainted with the Soviet air attaché in Stockholm, Colonel Nikolai Nikitushev.

In the autumn of 1943, he was transferred to southern Sweden on flying duty, and there, in Satenäs, he met Americans, for Satenäs was the assembly point for American bombers which made forced landings in Swedish territory after raiding Germany.

Promoted major, in 1945 he was reassigned to Stockholm, to find his friends of the German embassy no longer there. He quickly re-established himself in the diplomatic life of the capital, becoming a frequent guest at the Russian and American embassies.

According to his later story, shortly before leaving for Moscow to attend a Soviet air display of the first Russian jets, Wennerström was approached by American intelligence, who asked him to post a parcel as he passed through Leningrad on his way to

Moscow, which he agreed to do.

Early in 1948 he was posted to Moscow once more, again as air attaché but with the rank of colonel. Almost from the moment of his arrival he began turning over to the Russians practically all the intelligence information that came his way in the course of his official duties, his chief contact being Nikitushev, the former air attaché in Stockholm. There can be no doubt that by this means the Russians had a great deal of secret information concerning NATO air plans made available to them. He pleased the Russians so much, that they secretly awarded him the rank of major-general.

When in 1952, Wennerström was assigned to Washington, he was even better placed to supply the Russians with vital material. According to his own admission he was in constant contact with Soviet officials for this purpose, until his recall to Stockholm in 1957.

His new post was an important one in the Command Office. He had access to documents relating to secret airfields, underground submarine and destroyer pens, the entire radar defences as well as the latest and most secret equipment which made up Sweden's highly costly and highly complex defence system, all of which he made available to the very people against whom they were directed — the Russians.

Presently it began to dawn on the Swedes that there had been a leak of secret information. Suspicion fell on Wennerström, but he was so highly regarded that the authorities refused to entertain the idea that he could be a traitor, and nothing was done. The counter-espionage agency, however, began to suspect him more and more as the months passed, and eventually their suspicions gained support from a report volunteered to the police by the maid at the Wennerström house, to the effect that she believed the Colonel might be engaged in some illicit business. The grounds for her suspicions were that though he claimed to know nothing about photography, there was a room in the house, usually kept locked, in which there was highly complicated photographic machinery.

Swedish counter-espionage now intensified their surveillance of the Colonel, and when the maid handed to them several packets containing films of secret documents which she had found concealed in a flower urn in the Wennerström house, on 20th June, 1963, they arrested him. In February 1964, Wennerström was sentenced to life imprisonment. The damage he had done to his country was so great as to be unassessable.

BIBLIOGRAPHY:

An Agent In Place — Thomas Whiteside (London, 1967).

WENZEL, Johann (Soviet agent in Holland, World War II).

Johann Wenzel, German by birth, was a veteran member of the German Communist Party. He organised a Soviet network in Holland in the Second World War, appointing the Dutch Communist, Anton Winterink, as his second-in-command.

The network had its own radio, which was operated by Wilhelm Vogeler and a woman called Hendrika Smit. Though independent of it, the network worked closely with the Belgian network under Leopold Trepper (q.v.), by means of

three couriers — Maurice Peper, and Jacob and Hendrika Hilboling.

From 1939 to 1940 the network, on The Centre's instructions, remained inactive. But when the German invasion of Holland took place, they reported on German troop movements in the country.

When the Belgium network was uncovered by the Abwehr (q.v.) in December 1941, and most of its members were liquidated, its two leaders, who had escaped, made their way to Unoccupied France, from where they continued to operate. Johann Wenzel was sent from Holland to be their radio link, but this was a most unfortunate move, for Wenzel had been betrayed by one of the arrested Belgian agents. However, he continued to operate successfully for six months, until in June 1942 his transmitter was located and he was arrested.

The Germans offered to spare Wenzel's life if he would co-operate with them in sending false information to the Russians. Wenzel at first refused, but eventually, under pressure, agreed. When his usefulness to the Germans was finished, they executed him.

BIBLIOGRAPHY:
Forty Years of Soviet Spying —
Ronald Seth (London, 1965).

WILLIS, Sir Richard see under
Thurloe, John.

WINTERINK, Anton see under
Wenzel, Johann.

WOODHULL, Abraham see
under **Tallmadge Network,
The.**

WOLLWEBER, Ernst(Russian
agent, between Wars).

An outstanding member of
the German Communist Party,
highly regarded by Moscow
for his skill and cunning as an
"underground" leader in the
Nazi period. Under cover of
membership of the West European Bureau of the Comintern,
based in Copenhagen, Den-
mark, he was assigned the task
of organising a Russian network on the advent of the
Nazis, whose members were to
be recruited mainly from the
Seamen's Unions.

He chose between thirty and
forty men, mostly of Scandinavian nationality, though a few
German Communists were included. Their assignments were
not so much espionage as
sabotage, the targets being

ships and any plant in any
country outside Germany
which was helping the Nazis
to re-arm, for example, the
power-stations which operated
in the Swedish iron-ore fields.

Wollweber's network sur-
vived, despite several defeats
by Counter-espionage, until
1941, when Wollweber and his
Swedish branch were arrested,
and he received three years'
imprisonment. After the War,
Wollweber was appointed East
German Minister for State
Security i.e. director of espionage.

Once more, however, Woll-
weber's activities in this role
have been more concerned
with sabotage than with
espionage. It is widely held
that the mysterious explosions
and fires that have occurred
in naval vessels and civilian
liners — e.g. the fires in the
Queen Elizabeth, the **Queen
Mary** and the **Empress of
Canada** in 1953, and the
explosion in HM aircraft
carrier **Indomitable** — in the
last twenty years have been
carried out under the direction
of this master saboteur. In
these operations he has used
specially trained mobile units
who receive their instruction
in the Maritime School at

666

Wustrow. His operations on land have chiefly included the smuggling of strategic material from the west.

The East German agency has nevertheless carried out a few espionage assignments, all of which have been of an extremely serious nature — e.g. the securing from West Berlin police the West's plans for preventing the numerous kidnappings of West Germans, and reports on the organisation of the West German police forces.

BIBLIOGRAPHY:
Soviet Spy Net — E. H. Cookridge (London, undated).

WYNNE, Greville (British agent, 1960s).

Greville Wynne was a British businessman, the managing director of Mobile Exhibitions Ltd, a travelling trade show, with which he toured eastern Europe. In 1962 he was forty-three, he was married with one son, and lived in Chelsea, a fashionable quarter of London.

In December 1960 he met, while on a visit to Moscow, Colonel Oleg Penkovsky, a member of Soviet military intelligence (GRU), who conveyed to him that he, Penkovsky, wished to make con-

tact with the West. Wynne agreed to help him. When he returned from another visit to Moscow in April 1961, Wynne took with him a letter from Penkovsky, to British intelligence, and over the next eighteen months he acted as courier between the colonel and London. During this time Penkovsky came to London twice on official visits, and on each occasion he was interrogated both by British intelligence officers and the American CIA.

On 2nd November, 1962, Wynne was arrested in Budapest, where he was with his travelling exhibition, by the Hungarian secret police at the request of the KGB, and taken to Russia. Shortly before Wynne was being seized in Budapest, Penkovsky was arrested in Moscow.

Both men were brought to trial in Moscow on 7th May, 1963. After hearings held in public and amid considerable publicity, on 11th May Wynne was sentenced to eight years' imprisonment and Penkovsky was sentenced to death for treason.

Penkovsky confessed at his trial that he had handed over to the British and Americans five thousand frames of film, and on his visits to London had verbally given MI6 and the CIA practically every Russian intelligence secret of which he had knowledge. On 16th May, the Soviet news agency Tass announced, "The spy Oleg Penkovsky has been executed."

After serving eleven months of his sentence, Wynne was exchanged for the Russian agent held by the British, Gordon Lonsdale (see under **Portland Spy Case, The**) at Checkpoint Heerstrasse in Berlin, at dawn on 22nd April, 1964.

BIBLIOGRAPHY:

The Man from Moscow — Greville Wynne (London, 1967).

The Penkovsky Papers — Ed. Piotyr Deriabin (London, 1965).

YAGODA, Genrikh Gregorevich (Director of Russian Intelligence).

Yagoda was the son of a Latvian peasant. He first came into prominence as assistant chief of the Special Division of the OGPU of which the Ninth Section was SMERSH, to which post he was appointed by Vyacheslav Menzhinsky, when the latter succeeded Dzerzhinsky when the first OGPU's chief suddenly died in 1926. There is no doubt that he received this important post because Stalin thought highly of him, for when Menzhinsky introduced him to the other departmental chiefs he told them that "the young man enjoys the full confidence of Stalin".

Though he had had no formal education and his appearance was coarse and his accent impossible, Yagoda quickly showed that he was a man of ruthless energy. Within a few months he was promoted to be Menzhinsky's deputy.

Yagoda owes his subsequent rise to the post of director of the OGPU, which he did when his chief died in May 1934, to the fact that Menzhinsky had no interest whatsoever in foreign espionage and was content to leave such matters entirely to his deputy. This made Yagoda the most influential man in the OGPU, and in fact he was its effective chief throughout Menzhinsky's period of office. There came a time, however, when real power alone was not enough for him; he wanted the kudos of the formal position, too, so in 1934 he poisoned Menzhinsky.

As soon as he was appointed Yagoda reorganised the OGPU yet again. The changes he made were far-reaching, and the OGPU emerged as a fully-fledged People's Commissariat for Internal Affairs (NKVD). The basic organisation of the Russian intelligence system today still rests on Yagoda's plan.

Despite his heavy responsibilities he still found time to take a close interest in the activities of the section of his organisation which interested him most — SMERSH. He introduced the concept of "the executioners", calling them the Mobile Squads for Special

Tasks. He also proposed more subtle ways for killing SMERSH's victims, especially poisoning. He had been interested in poisons since a brief period in his youth when he had studied pharmacy, and it was on his orders that the nowworld-notoriousSMERSH laboratory was set up. Whenever he could find a spare moment he would carry out his own experiments with poisons in the laboratory at the side of the toxicologists he employed.

In 1936, Stalin obviously thought he was becoming too powerful for he ordered Yagoda's arrest. At his trial Yagoda confessed that he had poisoned Valerian Kuibyshev, a former Commissar for Heavy Industry; his chief Menzhinsky; Maxim Gorky, the famous Soviet author; and Gorky's son, Maxim Peshkov.

Yagoda was shot in the cellars of his own prison, the Lubyanka.

BIBLIOGRAPHY:

Soviet Spy Net — E. H. Cookridge (London, undated).

YAKOVLEV, Anatoli (Russian Resident Director in America) see under **Soviet American Network.**

YAMAKI, Commander Akira see under **Farnsworth, John S.**

YARDLEY, H. O. (American cryptologist).

Herbert Osborne Yardley was born in Worthington, Indiana, in April 1889. He had wished to become a criminal lawyer, but at the age of 23 he entered the State Department as a coding clerk. Nothing could have been more felicitous than this fortuitous event, for before long Yardley discovered that he had almost magical powers as a cryptologist. He describes in his book **The American Black Chamber,** how one night, not long after he joined the State Department, he took a coded message from Colonel House to President Wilson and, much to his own surprise, had solved it within a few hours. After this he became so immersed in cryptology that, "It was the first thing I thought of when I awakened, the last when I fell asleep."

His powers in this field were recognised by US government authorities, and shortly after the outbreak of World War I, at the age of 27, he was made chief of the newly established cryptology section of MI8. Under his leadership MI8 expanded rapidly. Among its many successes, the chief, perhaps, was the solution of a message that led to the conviction of Lothar Witzke, the only German spy condemned to death in America in World War I.

In August 1918 Yardley came to Europe to learn all he could about his subject from the Allies. He studied British methods in London, and French methods in Paris.

After the Armistice he led the cryptographic bureau of the American delegation to the Peace Conference. When this job came to an end, in an effort not to have to return to the State Department code room, he submitted to the Chief of Staff a plan for a permanent organisation "for code and cipher investigation and attack".

His plan was approved by the State Department and the Chief of Staff, and in October 1919 he inaugurated the organisation which has since become famous all over the world as the American Black Chamber to assist both the SD and Military Intelligence. Because for legal reasons the State Department's contribution to the organisation could not be spent in Washington, Yardley moved to New York, to a four-storey brownstone at 141 East 37th Street, just to east of Lexington Avenue where he set up shop with a staff of twenty, prominent among whom were Dr Charles Mendelsohn from MI8, Victor Weiskopf a former MI8 agent, and F. Livesey, who became Yardley's chief assistant.

One of the Black Chamber's first assignments was to break the Japanese codes. After many days and nights of feverish work and failure, these very intricate codes were eventually solved. The success was of outstanding use to Washington during the naval disarmament conference of 1921.

The Black Chamber's activities must have upset a number of foreign governments, and one, at all events, seems to have made it the object of espionage activities, for on one occasion the brownstone was broken into and the offices ransacked. After this, the organisation moved to 52 Vanderbilt Avenue, where it set up under the feeble cover of The Code Compiling Company.

In 1924, the funds for the upkeep of the Black Chamber were drastically reduced, and half the staff had to be dismissed. Only Yardley's total commitment to his work made him go on.

Then suddenly in 1929 the organisation was disbanded. Yardley had been obtaining copies of foreign telegrams through the co-operation of the presidents of the Western Union and the Postal Telegraph Company. Now these organisations were beginning to make difficulties, using as their argument the secrecy of the telegraph services. The new Secretary of State, Stimson, now heard of the Black Chamber's existence for the first time, and thoroughly disapproved of it. He withdrew the State Department's contribution, without which Yardley could not carry on.

Yardley now fell on bad times, for not only was he without employment, but the Depression ate up his private financial resources. Eventually, he had the idea of writing a book about the Black Chamber in order to raise money. On 1st June, 1931, after part-

serialisation in the **Saturday Evening Post,** the book was published by the Bobbs-Merrill Co. of Indianapolis, and had an instant success with the public. It gave serious offence to other American cryptologists, however, who saw it as casting a slur on all other American cryptographic efforts, and a storm broke, caused chiefly by W. F. Friedman, head of the Department of Ciphers, and an even greater cryptologist than Yardley. The upshot of the incident was the passing of a bill by Congress "For the Protection of Government Records", which put a stop to further sales of Yardley's book.

Yardley remained unperturbed by all the commotion, and concentrated on the production of a secret ink which he hoped would restore his fortunes. It did not.

He then returned to writing, and branched out into adventure novels based on cryptology in one form or another. One, **The Blonde Countess,** was bought by MGM and turned into a film called **Rendezvous.**

In 1938 Chiang Kai-shek engaged Yardley to solve the codes of the Japanese armies then invading China. He remained in China until 1940, and after a brief spell as a restaurant proprietor in Washington, he went to Canada to set up a code-breaking bureau, but pressure from one source or another compelled the Canadians to dispense with his services. Until the end of World War II he served in the Office of Price Administration.

He died of a stroke on 7th August, 1958, and was buried in Arlington National Cemetry with military honours.

BIBLIOGRAPHY:

The American Black Chamber — H. O. Yardley (Indianapolis, 1951).

The Codebreakers — David Kahn (London, 1966).

YEO-THOMAS, Wing-Commander F. F. E. (British agent, World War II).

The intelligence organisation connected with General de Gaulle's Free French Forces in London were for the most part at loggerheads with SOE throughout the greater part of the war. The differences sprang for the most part from French jealousy, which was partly justified by SOE's rather highhanded behaviour in not consulting or informing de Gaulle of their activities either actual or projected. The situation had become so tense by 1943 that both SOE and the BCRA (the Free French intelligence organisation) decided that something must be done, and it was arranged that representatives of both organisations should go to France and try to sort things out on the spot. Yeo-Thomas was selected to go as SOE's representative.

In this connection Yeo-Thomas made three journeys to Paris, and it was on the last of these that he was betrayed by his courier, who had been arrested by the Gestapo. The object of this last mission was to rescue from prison the BCRA officer, Major Pierre Brosselet, who had been caught by the Germans and was in Rennes prison. On the morning of the day before that planned for the rescue, he arranged to meet his courier at the Passy métro station in Paris, to receive from the young man final reports from the agents who were to carry out the operation. As he turned to leave the station he was pounced on by Gestapo agents.

He had not been expecting it, so there was no time for him to swallow his cyanide tablet. Even in the motorcar which carried him to Gestapo headquarters, he was viciously beaten and his tortures began as soon as he arrived there. Beaten into semi-consciousness, he was stripped naked, and with his hands handcuffed behind him, he was made to stand on a telephone directory. He was then attacked by two men with fists and boots. When he still refused to talk he was again struck with fists, boots and an oxgut whip with a flexible steel rod inside it.

Still maintaining silence, and still handcuffed and his feet chained, he was thrown into a bath of ice-cold water and held under until he lost consciousness, while an audience of uniformed German girls laughed and mocked at him. Each time he lost consciousness, he was pulled out of the bath, revived, questioned and then thrown back into the bath. This happened several times, and when all failed to make him talk, he was beaten with rubber coshes about the head and testicles. In twelve hours, all these tortures were repeated several times.

He resisted all efforts to make him talk. He knew that if he could hold out for twenty-four hours all his group would be able to disappear, and this he did.

After many months in prison, he was sent to Buchenwald concentration camp, where he escaped death by a hair's-breadth. As the American troops advanced towards Buchenwald, he managed to escape, but was recaptured before he got far. A second attempt was successful, and he made contact with the American army.

Yeo-Thomas was awarded the George Cross for his services.

After the war, he returned to Paris where he managed a dress-designing business. The terrible tortures which the Gestapo had inflicted on him, however, permanently damaged his health, and he died, still in middle age, in 1964.

BIBLIOGRAPHY:

The White Rabbit — Bruce Marshall (London, 1952).

SOE in France — M. R. Foot (London, 1966).

YEZHOV, Nicolai (Russian director of espionage).

Yagoda was succeeded by Nicolai Yezhov, secretary of the Central Committee of the Communist Party, as chief of the NKVD. It was he who organised the mass arrests and ordered the mass killings during the Great Purges. The executions during his short reign — he was arrested and executed in 1938 — were on a scale unprecedented in Soviet history, and were so outstanding, in fact, that they were given a special name — **Yezhovschina.**

YOSHIKAWA, Takeo (Japanese agent in Honolulu at time of Pearl Harbor).

Takeo Yoshikawa was a young ensign of the Imperial Japanese navy, aged only 25 but possessing an amazing theoretical knowledge of the US Navy.

He arrived in Honolulu on 27th March, 1941, under the cover-name of Tadasi Morimura, ostensibly assigned to the Japanese consulate general as a secretary. It is apparent from his behaviour on arriving in Hawaii that he had received very little, if any, training in espionage techniques, for from the moment of his arrival he made himself objectionable to the other members of the consulate staff by his frequent late arrival at the office, his bouts cf drunkenness and openly having women staying in his quarters over night. On one occasion he went so far as to insult the consul general, Nagao Kita — with impunity.

However, during the next nine months he toured all the islands of the group, and within a week or two of his arrival was sending valuable information about the dispositions of units of the American fleet in the area, concentrating chiefly on Pearl Harbor, the great naval base. He had no code of his own, and his messages were sent to Tokyo in the consulate's diplomatic code, and signed by Kita.

American codeographers in Honolulu were aware of what was happening, but were unable to discover precisely the information Yoshikawa was sending by the refusal of the cable authorities to break their rule of secrecy. One small crack was made in this defence when the US 14th Naval District's intelligence officer, Captain Irving S. Mayfield, was able to persuade the president of the Radio Corporation of America (RCA), David Sarnoff, to let intelligence see all the Japanese cables sent via the RCA. The Japanese, however, used all the cable companies in Honolulu in turn, and RCA's next turn did not come until 1st December.

On 2nd December, the Office of Naval Intelligence (ONI) issued a memorandum which placed the Japanese Carrier Divisions 1 and 2 and other important units in home waters. This appeared to explain why the Honolulu cryptologists had not intercepted any traffic from the carrier divisions for some days. Actually, six of the carriers were, at that moment, steaming eastwards, and late in the afternoon of 2nd December they received a coded message from Tokyo indicating that war with America had been decided upon, and they were to proceed to the attack.

On 2nd December, also, the Japanese consulate general in Honolulu received instructions from Tokyo to destroy all high level codes. Thereafter, Yoshikawa's messages would be transmitted in the lower level code known as PA-K2.

Now, although the American cryptanalysts were able to break the high level intelligence codes, they were not familiar with the diplomatic codes of which PA-K2 was one. Though

they worked on it feverishly, its secrets eluded them, right up to the evening of 6th December, when at 6.00 p.m. the transmitting clerk tapped out Yoshikawa's last message in it. This message read, "On evening of the 5th, the battleship **Wyoming** and one sweeper entered port. Ships at anchor on 6th were: 9 battleships, 3 minesweepers, 3 light cruisers, 17 destroyers. Ships in dock were: 4 light cruisers, 2 destroyers. Heavy cruisers and carriers have all left. It appears that no air reconnaissance is being carried out by the fleet air arm."

As with so many of his previous messages, this one contained several errors. The battleship was the **Utah,** not the **Wyoming;** there were 6 light and 2 heavy cruisers in harbour, not 3 light and no heavy cruisers; there were 29 destroyers, not 17; 4 minesweepers instead of 3; and 8 minelayers and 3 seaplane tenders which he did not mention at all.

However, the error was in favour of the Japanese, for when they struck at **Pearl Harbour** twelve hours later, their bag of American warships was so much the greater.

BIBLIOGRAPHY:
The Codebreakers — David
   Kahn (London, 1966).

Z

ZABOTIN, Colonel (Russian Resident Director, World War II) see under **Gouzenko, Igor.**

ZIEVERT, Karl (German spy in Russia, World War I).

Karl Zievert was a German by birth, who before the outbreak of World War I had lived in Russia for forty years. Shortly before the outbreak of the war he was appointed chief of the Russian postal censorship office in Kiev, having joined the censorship service some years earlier.

The Russian postal censorship was designed to strengthen the autocracy of the Tsar. The letters of most leading Russian citizens, as well as of the masses, was therefore inspected, and anything which might threaten the safety or position of the Tsar was reported to the secret police.

In his capacity as chief censor in Kiev, Zievert had access to the correspondence of a long list of eminent people, including the Chief of the General Staff, General

Michael Alexeiev, Mme Brussilov, wife of General Brussilov, and Count Bobrinsky, who after the outbreak of the war, became Russian governor of the occupied Austrian territories. Like Jules Silber (q.v.) long exile from his home-land had not quenched his patriotism, and in 1914 he offered his services both to the German and Russian intelligence services.

After the Revolution, Zievert and his colleagues were arrested and charged with treason. They were found guilty and deported to Siberia.

ZILBERT, Mark (Russian agent in America between wars).

Mark Zilbert was appointed Resident Director of the American networks in 1931 in succession to the first Resident Director, a Russian named Tschatzky, who had been a member of the Amtorg staff. Zilbert was required to concentrate on the gathering of naval information, and his contact in this work was a Communist, Solomon Kantor, who had formerly been engaged on secret orders for the US Navy as a draftsman for the Arma Engineering Corporation.

Though no longer in a position personally to acquire the information Zilbert required, Kantor nevertheless had a contact who was still working for Arma, a man called William Disch. For six months Disch and Zilbert met regularly every week, and at each meeting Disch handed over the secret documents Zilbert wanted, and in return received between one and two hundred dollars.

However, unknown to Zilbert, after the first meeting Disch had told his employers what was happening, and they had passed him on to the Office of Naval Intelligence. The ONI instructed Disch to keep up his contact with Zilbert and detailed the documents he should hand over. Whenever he went to his rendezvous with Zilbert, Disch was followed, but the ONI could not discover for whom Zilbert was working.

After some weeks, because of a Japanese attempt to penetrate the naval base at San Diego, the ONI, who were short-staffed, turned over the Disch-Zilbert case to the FBI. The FBI devised a scheme for finding out who Zilbert's superiors were. They told Disch that the next time he handed documents to Zilbert he must insist that they were returned to him within a couple of hours. Agents then followed Zilbert and saw him enter the Amtorg offices, from which they opined that he was a Soviet agent.

Instead of arresting him at once, the FBI decided to watch him for a time. Unfortunately, soon after the Russians discovered the spuriousness of Disch's documents, and Zilbert broke off all contact with him. Even then the FBI did not arrest Zilbert, who left the country within a week or two.

BIBLIOGRAPHY:
Soviet Espionage — David J. Dallin (New York, 1955).

ZIMMERMANN TELE-GRAM, The (World War I).

At the beginning of World War I, the British Admiralty set up a small department whose duty it would be to break the secret messages sent in code by England's enemies. The department rapidly grew, and by 1915 had moved into still somewhat crowded quarters, which had a designation that was to become famous in the world annals of espionage

— Room 40 OB (OB standing for Old Buildings of the Admiralty).

It was in Room 40 that at 10.30 a.m. on 17th January, 1917, the Rev William Montgomery, an outstanding authority on the Fathers of the Early Church, turned cryptanalyst, and his colleague Nigel de Grey, working on a German encoded message, came upon one of the most extraordinary incidents in the history of cryptography.

The message, which comprised a thousand numerical code-groups was dated Berlin, 16th January, and was addressed to Count John von Bernstorff, the Kaiser's ambassador in Washington. Though the crypt-analysts were able to read only part of the message, there were phrases in their so far imperfect deciphered version which indicated that the secret cable was of the very first importance.

By the beginning of 1917 there was no prospect of ending the war, which everyone had expected would last only a few weeks, but was now dragging into its third year. On land the Allies had suffered gigantic losses, the Hindenburg Line was unbreached and

Russia was virtually on her knees.

Things were as bad for the Central Powers. Their troops were locked in ineffectual trench-warfare, civilians were living almost exclusively on potatoes and fifteen-year-olds were being conscripted for the armed services. No hope of peace was in sight.

In three days time, Woodrow Wilson would be inaugurated for his second term as president of the United States, having won the election of December 1916 with the slogan, "He kept us out of the war."

There was, however, a military faction in Germany which believed that if Germany unleashed unrestricted U-boat warfare England would soon be "gasping in the reeds like a fish". For several months the generals had been hammering away at the politicians to introduce this most unethical act of war. Alone among the politicians the foreign minister, Zimmermann, saw the point of the military's pleading. On the other hand, he was quite convinced that the sinkings of American merchantmen would bring the United States into the war, and he concocted a plan which he hoped would off-set this danger to a considerab!e degree.

His plan was to propose a military alliance with Mexico. To persuade them to accept it, he offered a number of inducements.

At this time the Mexican ambassador was in Switzerland and unable to wait until his Excellency's return, Zimmermann sent his proposal to the German minister in Mexico, von Eckardt. As there were no direct transmitting facilities between Germany and Mexico, he routed his telegram via Washington. To make sure he sent it by two ways — to Colonel House, President Wilson's special adviser, who had arranged with Wilson to have coded reports from embassies cabled directly to him, thus by-passing the State Department; and via Sweden to Washington, the pro-German Swedish government having agreed to send German messages as its own, through Buenos Aires to Washington. Room 40 monitored both routes, and thus it was that the Zimmermann telegram came into their hands.

It took Montgomery and de Grey several days to break the German code, but when they succeeded, the telegram read thus:

We intend to begin on the first of February unrestricted submarine warfare. We shall endeavour in spite of this to keep the United States of America neutral. In the event of this not succeeding, we make Mexico a proposal of alliance on the following basis:

Make war together, make peace together, generous financial support, and an understanding on our part that Mexico is to reconquer the lost territory in Texas, New Mexico and Arizona. The settlement in detail is left to you.

You will inform the President (of Mexico) of the above most secretly, as soon as the outbreak of war with the United States of America is certain, and add the suggestion that he should on his initiative, invite Japan to immediate adherence and act the mediate between Japan and ourselves.

Please call to the President's attention the fact that the ruthless employment of our submarines now offers the prospect of compelling

681

England in a few months to make peace.

Zimmermann,

On 22nd February, 1917, Sir Reginald Hall, Director of Naval Intelligence, with the approval of the British Foreign Office, showed the Zimmermann telegram to Edward Bell, a secretary of the American embassy in London. Bell's initial reaction was disbelief but Hall was able to convince him of its authenticity.

Together they went to Grosvenor Square, and there with Ambassador Page and First Secretary Irwin Laughlin, they spent many hours trying to decide how to present the telegram to the American Government in such a way that its authenticity was accepted and the maximum impact that this German perfidy would make.

It was decided that the British government should hand the telegram officially to Page, and this was done on 23rd February, by Foreign Secretary Balfour. At 1 p.m. on 24th February, Page forwarded the telegram to Washington with a carefully worded explanation of how the British came to have the telegram and at the same time protect the British method of acquiring it.

When Wilson was shown the telegram later in the evening he showed "much indignation". After consultation with Secretary of State Lausing, the President decided to publish it in the press. This was done on 1st March.

All America was stunned. The House of Representatives immediately passed a bill for arming American merchant ships, but the Senate was more cautious, wondering if it were not a crude British plot. Eventually however, the Senate was persuaded as to its genuineness.

The Germans, who had no idea that the British monitored their diplomatic cables, were puzzled. To everyone's surprise Zimmermann publicly admitted that he had sent the telegram.

On 2nd April, Wilson, who those months before had declared that it would be a "crime against civilization", to lead America into war, went to Congress and asked for a declaration of war against Germany.

Probably no other exploit of cryptographers anywhere has had more far-reaching consequences than the deciphering

of the Zimmermann telegram
by Room 40.

BIBLIOGRAPHY:
The Zimmermann Telegram —
Barbara W. Tuchman (London, 1959).

ZUBILIN, Vasili see under
Soviet American Network.

Dourlein, Pieter. *See under* Giskes, Colonel H. J.

Downing, George (alias Harry Rawlings). *See under* Carranza, Lieutenant Ramon

Downing, Sir George. *See under* Thurloe, John

Dräger, Siegfried (cover-name). *See* Stashynsky, Bogdan

Drake, Sir Francis, 654

Drugs, use in espionage of. *See* Truth drugs, espionage activity and use of

DST (Direction de la Securité du Territoire), 160, 161

Du Barry, Comtesse, 56-57

Dubendorfer, Rahel. *See under* Rössler, Rudolf

Dubois, Alice (cover-name of Louise de Bettignies), 61, 404

Ducimetière, Rose, 176-77

Dukes, Sir Paul, 177-79

Dulles, Allen, 391, 479, 482, 483. *See also under* CIA (US Central Intelligence Agency)

Dunlap, Jack, 419-20

Durieux, Tilla, 322

Dutch Resistance, World War II, 242-66

Dzershinsky, Felix E., 59, 179-80, 669

Eastland, James, 94

Eckardt, von. *See under* Zimmerman Telegram, the

Edward VII, King of England, 184

Edwards (cover-name). *See* Eisler, Gerhard

Efron, Serge. *See under* Reiss, Ignace

Eichmann, Adolf, 306, 541

Einsatzgruppen (action commandos), 541

Eisenhower, Dwight D., 120, 121, 125, 377, 418, 479-80, 481, 482, 483, 489, 496

Eisler, Gerhard, 181-82

Eitner, Horst, 71-72

El-Hafez. *See* Hafez, General Amin el-

Elizabeth (Russian empress), 154, 155

Elizabeth I, Queen of England, 146, 373, 374, 401, 431, 435, 652-53, 655

Elliott, George, 364, 365

Elser. *See under* Best, Captain S. P.

Empress of Canada (liner), 666

Enghien, Duc d', 558-59

Englandspiel. *See under* Giskes, Colonel H. J.

Erdberg, Alexander. *See under* Red Orchestra, the

Erickson, Eric, 183

Ernst, Karl, 184-87

Espionage (espionage organisation, techniques): cells, 141; control agents, 262; couriers, 141-42; cover-names, 142, 275; cover work, 573; cut-outs (go-betweens), 142; intercepted messages, 304; legal residents and, 357; letter-boxes and, 357-58; microdots (microphotography), 403-4; monitors, 405; networks and chiefs, 141, 416; operational names, 142; radio and radio operators, 498-500, 641; schools for intelligence (*see under* Schragmüller, Dr. Elsbeth); secret inks, 563-64; security, 564-65; security checks, 565-66; sleepers, 581-

WITHDRAWAL